THE NEW CAMBRIDGE SHAKESPEARE

GENERAL EDITOR
Brian Gibbons

ASSOCIATE GENERAL EDITOR
A. R. Braunmuller, *University of California, Los Angeles*

From the publication of the first volumes in 1984 the General Editor of the New Cambridge Shakespeare was Philip Brockbank and the Associate General Editors were Brian Gibbons and Robin Hood. From 1990 to 1994 the General Editor was Brian Gibbons and the Associate General Editors were A. R. Braunmuller and Robin Hood.

MACBETH

This is the most extensively annotated edition of *Macbeth* currently available, offering a thorough reconsideration of one of Shakespeare's most popular plays. A full and accessible updated introduction studies the immediate theatrical and political contexts of *Macbeth's* composition, especially the Gunpowder Plot and the contemporary account of an early performance at the Globe. It treats such issues as whether the Witches compel Macbeth to murder; whether Lady Macbeth is herself in some sense a witch; whether Banquo is Macbeth's accomplice in crime; and what criticism is levelled against Macduff. Several possible new sources are suggested, and the presence of Thomas Middleton's writing in the play is proposed. An extensive, well-illustrated account of the play in performance examines several cinematic versions, such as those by Kurosawa and Roman Polanski, and a brand-new introductory section on recent performances and adaptations brings the edition completely up to date.

THE NEW CAMBRIDGE SHAKESPEARE

All's Well That Ends Well, edited by Russell Fraser
Antony and Cleopatra, edited by David Bevington
As You Like It, edited by Michael Hattaway
The Comedy of Errors, edited by T. S. Dorsch
Coriolanus, edited by Lee Bliss
Cymbeline, edited by Martin Butler
Hamlet, edited by Philip Edwards
Julius Caesar, edited by Marvin Spevack
King Edward III, edited by Giorgio Melchiori
The First Part of King Henry IV, edited by Herbert Weil and Judith Weil
The Second Part of King Henry IV, edited by Giorgio Melchiori
King Henry V, edited by Andrew Gurr
The First Part of King Henry VI, edited by Michael Hattaway
The Second Part of King Henry VI, edited by Michael Hattaway
The Third Part of King Henry VI, edited by Michael Hattaway
King Henry VIII, edited by John Margeson
King John, edited by L. A. Beaurline
The Tragedy of King Lear, edited by Jay L. Halio
King Richard II, edited by Andrew Gurr
King Richard III, edited by Janis Lull
Love's Labour's Lost, edited by William C. Carroll
Macbeth, edited by A. R. Braunmuller
Measure for Measure, edited by Brian Gibbons
The Merchant of Venice, edited by M. M. Mahood
The Merry Wives of Windsor, edited by David Crane
A Midsummer Night's Dream, edited by R. A. Foakes
Much Ado About Nothing, edited by F. H. Mares
Othello, edited by Norman Sanders
Pericles, edited by Doreen DelVecchio and Antony Hammond
The Poems, edited by John Roe
Romeo and Juliet, edited by G. Blakemore Evans
The Sonnets, edited by G. Blakemore Evans
The Taming of the Shrew, edited by Ann Thompson
The Tempest, edited by David Lindley
Timon of Athens, edited by Karl Klein
Titus Andronicus, edited by Alan Hughes
Troilus and Cressida, edited by Anthony B. Dawson
Twelfth Night, edited by Elizabeth Story Donno
The Two Gentlemen of Verona, edited by Kurt Schlueter
The Two Noble Kinsmen, edited by Robert Kean Turner and Patricia Tatspaugh
The Winter's Tale, edited by Susan Snyder and Deborah T. Curren-Aquino

THE EARLY QUARTOS
The First Quarto of Hamlet, edited by Kathleen O. Irace
The First Quarto of King Henry V, edited by Andrew Gurr
The First Quarto of King Lear, edited by Jay L. Halio
The First Quarto of King Richard III, edited by Peter Davison
The First Quarto of Othello, edited by Scott McMillin
The First Quarto of Romeo and Juliet, edited by Lukas Erne
The Taming of a Shrew: The 1594 Quarto, edited by Stephen Roy Miller

MACBETH

Updated edition

Edited by

A. R. BRAUNMULLER

University of California, Los Angeles

CAMBRIDGE
UNIVERSITY PRESS

CAMBRIDGE
UNIVERSITY PRESS

University Printing House, Cambridge CB2 8BS, United Kingdom

Cambridge University Press is part of the University of Cambridge.

It furthers the University's mission by disseminating knowledge in the pursuit of education, learning and research at the highest international levels of excellence.

www.cambridge.org
Information on this title: www.cambridge.org/9780521680981

© Cambridge University Press 1997, 2008

First published 1997
Updated edition 2008
16th printing 2021

Printed in Singapore by Markono Print Media Pte Ltd.

A catalogue record for this publication is available from the British Library

Library of Congress Cataloguing in Publication data
Shakespeare, William, 1564–1616.
Macbeth / edited by A. R. Braunmuller. – Updated ed.
    p.   cm. – (New Cambridge Shakespeare)
Previous ed.: 1997.
Includes bibliographical references.
ISBN 978-0-521-86240-0 (hardback) – ISBN 978-0-521-68098-1 (pbk.)
1. Macbeth, King of Scotland, 11th cent. – Drama.   2. Kings and rulers – Succession – Drama.
3. Regicides – Drama.   4. Scotland – Drama.   I. Braunmuller, A. R., 1945–   II. Title.   III. Series.
PR2823.A2B73   2008
822.3/3 – dc22   2008015484

ISBN-13-978-0-521-86240-0 Hardback
ISBN-13-978-0-521-68098-1 Paperback

CONTENTS

ILLUSTRATIONS

Illustrations 1, 3, 5, and 12 are reproduced by courtesy of the Henry E. Huntington Library; illustrations 2 and 13 by courtesy of the Kunsthaus, Zürich; illustration 4 by courtesy of the Folger Shakespeare Library, Washington, D.C.; illustration 6 by courtesy of the National Maritime Museum, Greenwich, London; illustration 7 by courtesy of the Biblioteca reale, Turin; and illustrations 16 and 17 by courtesy of the Shakespeare Centre Library, Stratford-upon-Avon.

ACKNOWLEDGEMENTS

'If I have done well, and as fitting the story, it is that which I desired: but if slenderly and meanly, it is that which I could attain unto.'[1] Most of what I say about *Macbeth* must already have been said in the voluminous writings about the play, and anyone who reads Thomas Wheeler's excellent '*Macbeth*': *An Annotated Bibliography*, 1990, will understand how little there is that has not been said about this compelling play. I acknowledge debts I recall and apologise for failing to acknowledge those I do not.

A children's rhyme assures us that big fleas have little fleas to bite'em; editors have editors, and even associate general editors have a general editor. For me, the editor's editor is Brian Gibbons, and his light touch and gentle bite made me always wish for the most succinct and clearest phrase, note, and collation. Paul Chipchase, Sue Gibbons, Judith Harte, and Sarah Stanton did more to improve this effort than they will ever say, or I will ever know.

Now I essay the impossible task of parsing my further indebtedness. Those creditors include R. A. Foakes, whose edition of *A Midsummer Night's Dream* helped me shape the Introduction here, students in the courses named English 247 and 142C (at the University of California, Los Angeles), and my research assistants – several of whom were supported by my university's Center for Medieval and Renaissance Studies under the direction of, first, Michael J. B. Allen and, latterly, Patrick Geary, and others of whom were supported, just as generously, by the Research Committee of my university's Academic Senate, who also supported my own work – (chronologically, as memory serves) Kari Schoening, Owen Staley, Margaret Sullivan, Jerome Arkenberg, Karl Hagen, and Billy Phelan, who helped over several years. These individuals' compulsiveness, argumentativeness, and learning often equalled my own, and I thank them, as I also thank the institution, UCLA, that supported them and me.

Michael Cohen, David Stuart Rodes, and I worked long and valuably on an electronic, multi-media version of *Macbeth*, now published as a CD-Rom ('The Voyager *Macbeth*, 1994), and I learned much from our joint venture. A fragment of Michael Cohen's effort appears here in Appendix 1; David Rodes's beneficent influence has pervaded not just this edition and our electronic version, but all my university service. Our joint effort also allowed me to be instructed (but not convinced) by Lisa Harrow. Many colleagues at UCLA – Charles A. Berst, Robert W. Dent, Claire McEachern, Donka Minkova, Alan Roper, Norman J. W. Thrower, Robert N. Watson – taught me things (from maps to philology, Shaw to annotation to Davenant) I needed to know and did not. The Sheriff's Department of Los Angeles County retrieved my stolen automobile and the edition it contained with remarkable dispatch, and I thank those public servants.

---

[1] 2 Maccabees 15.38, cited by Gordon Crosse, *Shakespearean Playgoing 1890–1952*, 1953, p. 159.

My debts extend, geographically, far beyond Los Angeles to: Lee Bliss (Santa Barbara, California), Constance Jordan (Claremont, California), Stephen Orgel (Stanford, California), F. J. Levy (Washington), Thomas L. Berger (Canton, N.Y., and London), Leonard Tennenhouse (Providence, Rhode Island), for a remark he has probably now forgotten, Barbara Mowat (Washington, D.C.), Alan Dessen (North Carolina), John Astington (Ontario), Randall McLeod (or any passing cloud), Alan Somerset and his extraordinary computer program, 'Feste', and Paul Werstine (also Ontario), Pauline Croft, J. P. Ferris, G. R. Proudfoot, the Tivoli Research Group, Joanna Udall (all in London), Robert Baldwin (Greenwich), Peter Holland (Cambridge), Jenny Wormald and the generous folk of the Oxford Text Archive (Oxford), Mary White Foakes and Sylvia Morris of the Shakespeare Centre Library (Stratford-upon-Avon), Niky Rathbone and the Birmingham Public Library's Shakespeare Library's staff and their unfailing good humour (Birmingham), Gareth Roberts for help with matters alchemical (Exeter), Akiko Kusunoki (Tokyo).

To heap one Pelion on another and also to repeat, I should say I am especially grateful to Thomas L. Berger, Pauline Croft, Brian Gibbons, Victoria Hayne, Gail Kern Paster, Linda Levy Peck, Billy Phelan, G. R. Proudfoot, Sarah Stanton. And, again, my work has been generously assisted by the following organisations: the Research Committee, Academic Senate, University of California, Los Angeles; the National Endowment for the Humanities; the Folger Shakespeare Library, Washington, D.C.

All were generous, and, even more important, all were patient.

A. R. B.

For the 2008 edition my colleagues Yogita Goyal, Jack Kolb, Donka Minkova, Joseph Nagy, and Stephanie Jamieson offered generous help. Stephen Orgel and Frank Kermode both pointed out the same (egregious) error, now corrected. I thank Alison Tara Walker for her thoughtful help in gathering and commenting on materials for this section and Nick Moschovakis for sharing several drafts of his contribution to *'Macbeth': New Critical Essays*. Melissa Vineyard made this second edition better.

Los Angeles, Washington, Stratford, London

ABBREVIATIONS AND CONVENTIONS

1. Shakespeare's plays

Shakespeare's plays, when cited in this edition, are abbreviated in a style slightly modified from that used in the *Harvard Concordance to Shakespeare*. Other editions of Shakespeare are abbreviated under the editor's surname (Furness, Hudson) unless they are the work of more than one editor. In such cases, an abbreviated series title is used (Cam., Oxford). When more than one edition by the same editor is cited, later editions are discriminated with a raised figure (Theobald²). All quotations from Shakespeare, except those from *Macbeth*, use the lineation of *The Riverside Shakespeare*, under the general editorship of G. Blakemore Evans.

Ado	*Much Ado About Nothing*
Ant.	*Antony and Cleopatra*
AWW	*All's Well That Ends Well*
AYLI	*As You Like It*
Cor.	*Coriolanus*
Cym.	*Cymbeline*
Err.	*The Comedy of Errors*
Ham.	*Hamlet*
1H4	*The First Part of King Henry the Fourth*
2H4	*The Second Part of King Henry the Fourth*
H5	*King Henry the Fifth*
1H6	*The First Part of King Henry the Sixth*
2H6	*The Second Part of King Henry the Sixth*
3H6	*The Third Part of King Henry the Sixth*
H8	*King Henry the Eighth*
JC	*Julius Caesar*
John	*King John*
LLL	*Love's Labour's Lost*
Lear	*King Lear*
Mac.	*Macbeth*
MM	*Measure for Measure*
MND	*A Midsummer Night's Dream*
MV	*The Merchant of Venice*
Oth.	*Othello*
Per.	*Pericles*
R2	*King Richard the Second*
R3	*King Richard the Third*
Rom.	*Romeo and Juliet*
Shr.	*The Taming of the Shrew*
STM	*Sir Thomas More*
Temp.	*The Tempest*
TGV	*The Two Gentlemen of Verona*
Tim.	*Timon of Athens*

Tit.	*Titus Andronicus*
TN	*Twelfth Night*
TNK	*The Two Noble Kinsmen*
Tro.	*Troilus and Cressida*
Wiv.	*The Merry Wives of Windsor*
WT	*The Winter's Tale*

2. Editions, adaptations, other works of reference, and periodicals

Works mentioned once in the Commentary appear there with full bibliographical information; all others are cited by the shortened titles listed below.

Abbott	E. A. Abbott, *A Shakespearian Grammar*, 3rd edn, 1870; references are to numbered sections
Adams	J. Q. Adams (ed.), *Chief Pre-Shakespearean Dramas*, 1924
Adelman	Janet Adelman, *Suffocating Mothers: Fantasies of Maternal Origin in Shakespeare's Plays*, '*Hamlet*' to '*The Tempest*' 1992
AEB	*Analytical and Enumerative Bibliography*
Agate	James Agate, *Brief Chronicles*, 1943
Allen	Michael J. B. Allen, 'Macbeth's genial porter', *ELR* 4 (1974), 326–36
Armstrong	William A. Armstrong, 'Torch, cauldron and taper: light and darkness in *Macbeth*', in Antony Coleman and Antony Hammond (eds.), *Poetry and Drama 1570–1700*, 1981, pp. 47–59
AV	The Holy Bible, 1611 (Authorised Version)
Barlow	Frank Barlow, 'The King's Evil', *EHR* 95 (1980), 3–27
Barrough	Philip Barrough, *The Methode of Phisicke*, 1583
Bartholomeusz	Dennis Bartholomeusz, '*Macbeth*' and the Players, 1969
Bate	Philip Bate, *The Oboe: An Outline of its History*, 3rd edn, 1975
BBC	British Broadcasting Corporation
Belman	Thomas Dekker, *The Belman of London* (1608), in Oliphant Smeaton (ed.), '*The Guls Hornbook*' and '*The Belman of London*', 1904
Bevington	David Bevington, *Action is Eloquence: Shakespeare's Language of Gesture*, 1984
Biggs	Murray Biggs *et al.* (eds.), *The Arts of Performance in Elizabethan and Early Stuart Drama*, 1991
Blackfriars	*Macbeth*, ed. R. W. Dent, 1969 (Blackfriars Shakespeare)
Bloch	Marc Bloch, *The Royal Touch* (1923), trans. J. E. Anderson, 1973
Blurt	Thomas Dekker (?), *Blurt, Master Constable* (1602), ed. Thomas L. Berger, 1979
Booth	Stephen Booth, '*King Lear*', '*Macbeth*', *Indefinition, and Tragedy*, 1983
Bradley	A. C. Bradley, *Shakespearean Tragedy* (1904), rpt. 1955
Braunmuller, *Letter-Book*	A. R. Braunmuller (ed.), *A Seventeenth-Century Letter-Book*, 1983
Brennan	Anthony Brennan, *Onstage and Offstage Worlds in Shakespeare's Plays*, 1989

Brooke	*The Tragedy of Macbeth*, ed. Nicholas Brooke, 1990 (Oxford Shakespeare)
Brooks	Cleanth Brooks, *The Well Wrought Urn*, 1947
Bullough	Geoffrey Bullough (ed.), *Narrative and Dramatic Sources of Shakespeare*, 8 vols., 1957–75
Burnim	Kalman A. Burnim, *David Garrick, Director*, 1961
Byrne	Muriel St Clare Byrne, 'Fifty years of Shakespearian production: 1898–1948', *S.Sur.* 2 (1949), 1–20
c.	*circa* ('about', used for an uncertain date or dates)
Cam.	*Macbeth* in *The Works of William Shakespeare*, ed. W. G. Clark and W. A. Wright, '2nd edn', 9 vols., 1891–93, VII (1892) (Cambridge Shakespeare)
Camden	William Camden, *Remains Concerning Britain* (1605), ed. R. D. Dunn, 1984
Campbell, *Life*	Thomas Campbell, *Life of Mrs Siddons*, 2 vols., 1834
Capell	*Macbeth* in *Mr William Shakespeare, his Comedies, Histories, and Tragedies*, ed. Edward Capell, 10 vols., 1767–8, IV
Capell, *Notes*	Edward Capell, *Notes and Various Readings to Shakespeare*, 3 vols., 1779–80; references are to vol. II (1780), first pagination-sequence, unless otherwise noted
Caretti	Laura Caretti (ed.), *Il Teatro del personaggio: Shakespeare sulla scena italiana dell'800*, 1979
Carlisle	Carol Jones Carlisle, *Shakespeare from the Greenroom*, 1969
Carlson	Marvin Carlson, *The Italian Shakespearians*, 1985
Carter	Thomas Carter, *Shakespeare and Holy Scripture*, 1905
Cercignani	Fausto Cercignani, *Shakespeare's Works and Elizabethan Pronunciation*, 1981
Chambers	*Macbeth*, ed. E. K. Chambers, 1893 (Warwick Shakespeare)
Changeling	Thomas Middleton and William Rowley, *The Changeling* (1622), ed. George W. Williams, 1966 (Regents Renaissance Drama)
Chapman	*The Plays of George Chapman: The Tragedies*, gen. ed. Allan Holaday, 1987
Clarendon	William Shakespeare, *Select Plays: Macbeth*, ed. W. G. Clark and W. Aldis Wright, 1869 (Clarendon Press Series)
Clark	Arthur Melville Clark, *Murder Under Trust, or, The Topical 'Macbeth'*, 1981
Clark, 'Inversion'	Stuart Clark, 'Inversion, misrule and the meaning of witchcraft', *P&P* 87 (May 1980), 98–127
Clarkson and Warren	P. S. Clarkson and C. T. Warren, *The Law of Property in Shakespeare and the Elizabethan Drama*, 1942
Coleridge	Samuel Taylor Coleridge, *Coleridge's Criticism of Shakespeare*, ed. R. A. Foakes, 1989
Collier	*Macbeth* in *The Works of William Shakespeare*, ed. J. Payne Collier, 8 vols., 1842–4, VII (1843)
Collier ²	*Macbeth* in *The Plays of William Shakespeare*, ed. J. Payne Collier, 1853
conj.	conjecture, conjectured by
corr.	corrected

Cotgrave	Randle Cotgrave, *A Dictionarie of the French and English Tongues*, 1611
Crosse	Gordon Crosse, *Shakespearan Playgoing 1890–1952*, 1953
Daemonologie	James VI and I, *Daemonologie* (1598), ed. G. B. Harrison, Bodley Head Quartos, 1924
Damned Art	*The Damned Art: Essays in the Literature of Witchcraft*, ed. Sydney Anglo, 1977
Davenant	*Macbeth, a Tragedy* [adapted by William Davenant] With all the alterations . . . and New Songs. As it's now acted at the Dukes [*sic*] Theatre, 1674
Davies, *Life*	Thomas Davies, *Memoirs of the Life of David Garrick*, 2 vols., 1780
Davies, *Micellanies*	Thomas Davies, *Dramatic Micellanies* [*sic*], 3 vols., 1783–4
De Quincey	Thomas De Quincey, 'On the knocking at the gate in *Macbeth*' (1823), in *The Collected Writings of Thomas De Quincey*, ed. David Masson, 14 vols., 1889–90, x, 389–95
Dekker	*The Dramatic Works of Thomas Dekker*, ed. Fredson Bowers, 4 vols., 1953–61
Dent	Robert W. Dent, *Shakespeare's Proverbial Language: An Index*, 1981; reference is to proverbs by letter and number
Dent, *PLED*	Robert W. Dent, *Proverbial Language in English Drama Exclusive of Shakespeare*, 1984; reference is to proverbs by letter and number
Dessen	Alan Dessen, *Elizabethan Stage Conventions and Modern Interpreters*, 1984
Dessen, 'Problems'	Alan Dessen, ' "Taint not thy mind . . .": problems and pitfalls in staging plays at the New Globe', in Franklin J. Hildy (ed.), *New Issues in the Reconstruction of Shakespeare's Theatre*, 1990, pp. 135–57
Dolan	Frances E. Dolan, *Dangerous Familiars: Representations of Domestic Crime in England 1550–1700*, 1994
Donohue, *Dramatic Character*	Joseph W. Donohue, Jr, *Dramatic Character in the English Romantic Age*, 1970
Donohue, 'Mrs Siddons'	Joseph W. Donohue, Jr, 'Kemble and Mrs Siddons in *Macbeth:* the Romantic approach to tragic character', *ThN* 22 (1967–8), 65–86
Doran	Madeleine Doran, 'The *Macbeth* music', *S.St.* 16 (1983), 153–73
Downer	Alan S. Downer, *The Eminent Tragedian: William Charles Macready*, 1966
Dutch Courtesan	John Marston, *The Dutch Courtesan* (1605), ed. M. L. Wine, 1965 (Regents Renaissance Drama)
Dyce	*Macbeth* in *The Works of William Shakespeare*, ed. Alexander Dyce, 6 vols., 1857, v
Dyce ²	*Macbeth* in *The Works of William Shakespeare*, ed. Alexander Dyce, 9 vols., 1864–7, vii (1866)
ed., eds.	editor(s), edited by
Edelman	Charles Edelman, *Brawl Ridiculous: Swordfighting in Shakespeare's Plays*, 1992

Edmonton	Thomas Dekker *et al.*, *The Witch of Edmonton* (1621) in Peter Corbin and Douglas Sedge (eds.), *Three Jacobean Witchcraft Plays*, 1986 (Revels Plays)
edn	edition
Edward III	*Edward III*, ed. Giorgio Melchiori, NCS, 1998
EHR	*English Historical Review*
ELH	*ELH: A Journal of English Literary History*
ELN	*English Language Notes*
ELR	*English Literary Renaissance*
Everett	Barbara Everett, *Young Hamlet: Essays on Shakespeare's Tragedies*, 1989
F	*Mr. William Shakespeares Comedies, Histories, and Tragedies*, 1623 (First Folio)
F2	*Mr. William Shakespeares Comedies, Histories, and Tragedies*, 1632 (Second Folio)
F3	*Mr. William Shakespear's Comedies, Histories, and Tragedies*, 1663–4 (Third Folio)
F4	*Mr. William Shakespear's Comedies, Histories, and Tragedies*, 1685 (Fourth Folio)
Farnham	Willard Farnham, *Shakespeare's Tragic Frontier* (1950), rpt. 1963
Fidele and Fortunio	Luigi Pasqualigo, *Il Fedele*, trans. Anthony Munday (?), *Fidele and Fortunio* (1585), ed. Percy Simpson, MSR, 1909
Foakes	*The Tragedy of Macbeth*, ed. R. A. Foakes, 1968 (Bobbs-Merrill Shakespeare)
Focus	John Russell Brown (ed.), *Focus on 'Macbeth'*, 1982
Folger	*The Tragedy of Macbeth*, ed. Barbara A. Mowat and Paul Werstine, 1992 (New Folger Library Shakespeare)
Forman	Simon Forman, *Booke of Plaies* (Bodleian Library MS. Ashmole 208, folios 207r-v), in E. K. Chambers, *William Shakespeare: A Study of Facts and Problems*, 2 vols., 1930, 11, 337–8
Furness	*Macbeth*, rev. edn, ed. H. H. Furness, Jr, 1903 (New Variorum)
Gardner	Helen Gardner, 'Milton's "Satan" and the theme of damnation in Elizabethan tragedy', in F. P. Wilson (ed.), *English Studies 1948*, 1948, pp. 46–66
Garner	Bryan A. Garner, 'Shakespeare's Latinate neologisms', *S.St.* 15 (1982), 149–70
Geneva	The Holy Bible, 1560 (Geneva translation)
Gerard	John Gerard, *The Herball, or Generall Historie of Plantes*, 2 vols. [continuously paginated], 1597
Globe	*The Works of William Shakespeare*, ed. W. G. Clark and W. Aldis Wright, 1865 (Globe Edition)
Golden Age	Thomas Heywood, *The Golden Age*, 1611
Greg	W. W. Greg, *The Shakespeare First Folio*, 1955
Grey	Zachary Grey, *Critical, Historical, and Explanatory Notes on Shakespeare*, 2 vols., 1754
Halio	*Macbeth*, ed. Jay L. Halio, 1972 (Fountainwell Drama)

Halliwell	*Macbeth* in *The Works of William Shakespeare*, ed. James O. Halliwell, 16 vols., 1865, XIV
Hanmer	*Macbeth* in *The Works of Mr William Shakespear*, ed. Thomas Hanmer, 6 vols., 1743–4, V (1744)
Harbage	Alfred Harbage, *Theatre for Shakespeare*, 1955
Harcourt	John B. Harcourt, '"I pray you, remember the porter"', *SQ* 12 (1961), 393–402
Heal	Felicity Heal, *Hospitality in Early Modern England*, 1990
Heath	Benjamin Heath, *A Revisal of Shakespear's Text*, 1765
Henslowe	*Henslowe's Diary*, ed. R. A. Foakes and R. T. Rickert, 1961
Hierarchie	Thomas Heywood, *The Hierarchie of the Blessed Angells*, 1635
Hinman	Charlton Hinman, *The Printing and Proof-Reading of the First Folio of Shakespeare*, 2 vols., 1963
HLQ	*Huntington Library Quarterly*
Honest Mans	*The Honest Mans Fortune*, ed. J. Gerritsen, 1952
Houlbrooke	Ralph A. Houlbrooke, *The English Family 1450–1700*, 1984
Hudson	*Macbeth* in *The Works of Shakespeare*, ed. H. N. Hudson, 11 vols., 1851–59, IV (1852)
Hughes	Alan Hughes, 'Lady Macbeth: a fiend indeed?', *Southern Review* (Adelaide) 11 (1978), 107–12
Hughes, *Irving*	Alan Hughes, *Henry Irving, Shakespearean*, 1981
Hunter	*Macbeth*, ed. G. K. Hunter, 1967 (New Penguin Shakespeare)
Hunter, *New*	Joseph Hunter, *New Illustrations of the Life, Studies, and Writings of Shakespeare*, 2 vols., 1845
Jackson	Zachariah Jackson, *Shakespeare's Genius Justified*, 1819
Jaech	Sharon L. Jansen Jaech, 'Political prophecy and Macbeth's "sweet bodements"', *SQ* 34 (1983), 290–7
Jenkin	H. C. Fleeming Jenkin, 'Mrs Siddons as Lady Macbeth. From contemporary notes by George Joseph Bell', *The Nineteenth Century* 3 (1878), 296–313, as rpt. in Fleeming Jenkin, *Papers on Acting*, III (1915), 25–68
JHI	*Journal of the History of Ideas*
Johnson	*The Plays of William Shakespeare*, ed. Samuel Johnson, 8 vols., 1765, VI
Jones, *Origins*	Emrys Jones, *The Origins of Shakespeare*, 1977
Jones, *Scenic*	Emrys Jones, *Scenic Form in Shakespeare*, 1971
Jonson	Ben Jonson, *The Complete Plays of Ben Jonson*, ed. G. A. Wilkes, 4 vols., 1981–2
Keightley	*Macbeth* in *The Plays of William Shakespeare*, ed. Thomas Keightley, 6 vols., 1864, VI
Knight	*Macbeth* in *The Pictorial Edition of the Works of Shakespeare*, ed. Charles Knight, 6 vols., *Tragedies*, II, 1841
Knight, *Imperial*	G. W. Knight, *The Imperial Theme* (1931), 3rd edn, corr. rpt., 1954
Knights	L. C. Knights, 'How many children had Lady Macbeth?' (1933), rpt. in Knights, *Explorations*, 1946, pp. 1–39
Knowles	[Anonymous,] *Sheridan Knowles' Conception and Mr Irving's Performance of Macbeth*, 1876
Lancashire	Thomas Heywood and Richard Brome, *The Late Lancashire Witches*, 1634

Langham	Robert Langham (or Lanham), *A Letter* (1575), ed. R. J. P. Kuin, 1983
Larner	Christina Larner, *Witchcraft and Religion*, 1984
Leiter	Samuel L. Leiter *et al.* (comp.), *Shakespeare Around the Globe: A Guide to Notable Postwar Revivals*, 1986
Lexicon	Alexander Schmidt, *Shakespeare Lexicon*, 3rd edn rev. Gregor Sarrazin, 1901; reissued, 1968; references are adapted to the forms used by *OED*
Linthicum	M. C. Linthicum, *Costume in the Drama of Shakespeare and his Contemporaries*, 1936
Long	John H. Long, *Shakespeare's Use of Music: The Histories and Tragedies*, 1971
Macbeth Onstage	Michael Mullin (ed.), *'Macbeth' Onstage: An Annotated Facsimile of Glen Byam Shaw's 1955 Promptbook*, 1976
Mackinnon	Lachlan Mackinnon, *Shakespeare the Aesthete*, 1988
Macready, *Diaries*	*The Diaries of W. C. Macready, 1833–1851*, ed. William Toynbee, 2 vols., 1912
Mahood	M. M. Mahood, *Shakespeare's Wordplay*, 1957
Maid's Tragedy	Francis Beaumont and John Fletcher, *The Maid's Tragedy*, ed. Howard B. Norland, 1968 (Regents Renaissance Drama)
Malone	*Macbeth* in *The Plays and Poems of William Shakespeare*, ed. Edmond Malone, 10 vols., 1790, IV
Marlowe	Christopher Marlowe, *The Complete Works of Christopher Marlowe*, ed. Fredson Bowers, 2nd edn, 2 vols., 1981, except *Tamburlaine* (see below)
Mason	John Monck Mason, *Comments on the Last Edition of Shakespeare's Plays*, 1785
Massinger	Philip Massinger, *The Plays and Poems of Philip Massinger*, ed. Philip Edwards and Colin Gibson, 5 vols., 1976
MED	*Middle English Dictionary*; references are adapted to the forms used by *OED*
Milton	*Poetical Works of John Milton*, ed. Helen Darbishire, 2 vols., 1952–5
Mirror	J. C. Gray (ed.), *Mirror up to Shakespeare: Essays in Honour of G. R. Hibbard*, 1984
MLN	*Modern Language Notes*
MLR	*Modern Language Review*
Morley	Henry Morley, *The Journal of a London Playgoer, from 1851 to 1866*, 1866
MSC	*Malone Society Collections*
MSR	Malone Society Reprints
Muir	*Macbeth*, ed. Kenneth Muir (1951), rev. ed, 1984 (Arden Shakespeare)
Mullin	Michael Mullin, 'Strange images of death: Sir Herbert Beerbohm Tree's *Macbeth*, 1911', *Theatre Survey* 17 (1976), 125–42
Mulryne	Ronnie Mulryne, 'From text to foreign stage: Yukio Ninagawa's cultural translation of *Macbeth*', in *Shakespeare from Text to Stage*, ed. Patricia Kennan and Mariangela Tempera, 1992, pp. 131–43

n., nn.	note, notes
N & Q	*Notes and Queries*
Nashe	Thomas Nashe, *The Works of Thomas Nashe*, ed. R. B. McKerrow, rev. edn, F. P. Wilson, 5 vols., 1958
Newes	*Newes from Scotland* (?1591) in *Daemonologie*
Norbrook	David Norbrook, '*Macbeth* and the politics of historiography' in Kevin Sharpe and Steven N. Zwicker (eds.), *Politics of Discourse*, 1987, pp. 78–116
Nosworthy	J. M. Nosworthy, *Shakespeare's Occasional Plays: Their Origin and Transmission*, 1965
NS	*Macbeth*, ed. J. D. Wilson, rev. edn, 1950 (New Shakespeare)
OED	*Oxford English Dictionary*, 2nd edn
Oxford	*William Shakespeare: The Complete Works*, gen. eds. Stanley Wells and Gary Taylor, 1986; collations and apparatus for this edition appear in *Textual Companion*
P&P	*Past and Present*
Padua	Promptbook of F (University of Padua Library) prepared *c.* 1625–35, in G. Blakemore Evans, *Shakespearean Prompt-Books of the Seventeenth Century*, 7 vols., 1960–89, I, i, and I, ii
Patten	William Patten, *The Expedicion into Scotlande of . . . Edward, Duke of Soomerset*, 1548
Paul	Henry N. Paul, *The Royal Play of Macbeth*, 1950
Peele	*The Life and Works of George Peele*, gen. ed. C. T. Prouty, 3 vols., 1952–70
Pepys	*The Diary of Samuel Pepys*, ed. Robert Latham and William Matthews, 11 vols., 1970–83
PMLA	*Publications of the Modern Language Association* (of America)
Pope	*Macbeth* in *The Works of Mr William Shakespear*, ed. Alexander Pope, 6 vols., 1723–5, v (1723)
Pope [2]	*Macbeth* in *The Works of Mr William Shakespeare*, ed. Alexander Pope, 10 vols., 1728, VII
PQ	*Philological Quarterly*
Prolusions	Edward Capell, *Prolusions; or, Select Pieces of Antient Poetry*, 1760
Prophesie	*The Whole Prophesie of Scotland, England, and some part of France*, 1603
Q	quarto
Q1673	*Macbeth: a Tragedy.* Acted at the Dukes-Theatre, 1673 (a quarto)
Queens	*The Masque of Queens* in *Ben Jonson: Complete Masques*, ed. Stephen Orgel, 1969
r	recto (the right-hand page when a manuscript or book is opened)
Reader	Vivian Salmon and Edwina Burness (ed.), *A Reader in the Language of Shakespearean Drama*, 1987
RenD	*Renaissance Drama*
RSC	Royal Shakespeare Company
RES	*Review of English Studies*

rev.	revised, revised by
Ritson	Joseph Ritson, *Remarks, Critical and Illustrative*, 1783
Riverside	*The Riverside Shakespeare*, text ed. G. B. Evans, 1974
Robbins	Rossell Hope Robbins, *Encyclopedia of Witchcraft and Demonology*, 1957
Rosen	Barbara Rosen, *Witchcraft in England, 1558–1618*, 1969
Rosen and Porter	David Rosen and Andrew Porter (eds.), *Verdi's 'Macbeth': A Sourcebook*, 1984
Rosenberg	Marvin Rosenberg, *The Mask of 'Macbeth'*, 1978
Rothwell and Melzer	Kenneth S. Rothwell and Annabelle Henkin Melzer, *Shakespeare on Screen: An International Filmography and Videography*, 1990
Rowe	*Macbeth* in *The Works of Mr William Shakespear*, ed. Nicholas Rowe, 6 vols., 1709, v
Rowe [2]	*Macbeth* in *The Works of Mr William Shakespear*, ed. Nicholas Rowe, 6 vols., *c.* 1710, v
Rowe [3]	*Macbeth* in *The Works of Mr William Shakespear*, ed. Nicholas Rowe, 9 vols., 1714, vi
rpt.	reprint, reprinted
SB	*Studies in Bibliography*
Schäfer	Jürgen Schäfer, *Shakespeares Stil: Germanisches und Romanisches Vokabular*, 1973; unpaginated citations refer to Appendix 3
Schanzer	Ernest Schanzer, 'Four Notes on "Macbeth"', *MLR* 52 (1957), 223–7
Scot	Reginald Scot, *The Discoverie of Witchcraft* (1584), ed. Brinsley Nicholson, 1886; reference is by book and chapter
Scotland	'Historie of Scotland' in Raphael Holinshed *et al.*, *The . . . Second Volume of Chronicles*, 1587; reference is by page number and column (a = left-hand column, b = right)
Scouten	Arthur H. Scouten, 'The premiere of Davenant's adaptation of "*Macbeth*"', in *Shakespeare and Dramatic Tradition*, ed. W. R. Elton and William B. Long, 1989, pp. 286–93
SD	stage direction
SH	speech heading
Shaheen	Naseeb Shaheen, *Biblical References in Shakespeare's Tragedies*, 1987
SHR	*Scottish Historical Review*
sig., sigs.	signature, signatures (printers' indications of the ordering of pages in early modern books, often more accurate than page numbers)
Singer	*Macbeth* in *The Dramatic Works of William Shakespeare*, ed. Samuel Weller Singer, 10 vols., 1826, iv
Singer [2]	*Macbeth* in *The Dramatic Works of William Shakespeare*, ed. Samuel Weller Singer, 2nd edn, 10 vols., 1856, ix
Sisson	C. J. Sisson, *New Readings in Shakespeare*, 2 vols., 1956
Slater	Ann Pasternak Slater, *Shakespeare the Director*, 1982
SP	*Studies in Philology*
Spenser	*The Poetical Works of Edmund Spenser*, ed. J. C. Smith and E. De Selincourt, 1912

Sprague	Arthur Colby Sprague, *Shakespeare and the Actors: The Stage Business in his Plays 1660–1905*, 1944
SQ	*Shakespeare Quarterly*
S.St.	*Shakespeare Studies*
S.Sur.	*Shakespeare Survey*
Staunton	*Macbeth* in *Routledge's Shakespeare*, ed. Howard Staunton, 50 parts in 3 vols., 1857–60, parts 42–3 (September-October 1859)
Steevens	*Macbeth* in *The Plays of William Shakespeare*, ed. Samuel Johnson and George Steevens, 10 vols., 1773, IV
Steevens [2]	*Macbeth* in *The Plays of William Shakespeare*, ed. Samuel Johnson and George Steevens, 10 vols., 1778, IV
Steevens [3]	*Macbeth* in *The Plays of William Shakespeare*, ed. George Steevens and Isaac Reed, 15 vols., 1793, VII
Stone	George Winchester Stone, Jr, 'Garrick's handling of *Macbeth*', *SP* 38 (1941), 609–28
Stratford	Shakespeare Memorial Theatre, later the Royal Shakespeare Theatre, Stratford-upon-Avon, England
subst.	substantively
Sugden	E. H. Sugden, *A Topographical Dictionary to the Works of Shakespeare and his Fellow Dramatists*, 1925
Swander	Homer Swander, 'No exit for a dead body: what to do with a scripted corpse?', *Journal of Dramatic Theory and Criticism* 5 (1991), 139–52
Tamburlaine	Christopher Marlowe, *Tamburlaine the Great (Part 1 and 2)*, ed. J. S. Cunningham, 1981 (Revels Plays)
Textual Companion	Stanley Wells *et al.*, *William Shakespeare: A Textual Companion*, 1987
Theobald	*Macbeth* in *The Works of Shakespeare*, ed. Lewis Theobald, 7 vols., 1733, V
Theobald [2]	*Macbeth* in *The Works of Shakespeare*, ed. Lewis Theobald, 8 vols., 1740, VI
ThN	*Theatre Notebook*
Thomas	Keith Thomas, *Religion and the Decline of Magic*, 1971
Tieck	Dorothea Tieck (trans.), *Macbeth* in *Shakespeare's dramatische Werke*, IX, 1833
TLN	Through Line Number(s) in *The First Folio of Shakespeare*, ed. Charlton Hinman, 1968; each line within each play in numbered
TLS	*The Times Literary Supplement*
Topsell	Edward Topsell, *The Historie of Foure-Footed Beasts*, 1607
TQ	*Theatre Quarterly*
Travers	*The Tragedy of Macbeth*, ed. Charles Travers [i.e. Tweedie?], 1844
True Lawe	*The True Lawe of Free Monarchies* (1598) in *Minor Prose Works of King James VI and I*, ed. James Craigie, 1982
uncorr.	uncorrected
Upton	John Upton, *Critical Observations on Shakespeare*, 1746
Utopia	*Utopia* in *The Complete Works of St Thomas More*, IV, ed. Edward Surtz, S.J., and J. H. Hexter, 1965

v	verso (the left-hand page when a manuscript or book is opened)
Waith	Eugene M. Waith, 'Manhood and valor in two Shakespearean tragedies', *ELH* 17 (1950), 262–73
Warburton	*Macbeth* in *The Works of Shakespear*, ed. William Warburton, 8 vols., 1747, VI
Warning	*A Warning for Faire Women*, 1599
Watson	Robert N. Watson, *Shakespeare and the Hazards of Ambition*, 1984
Webster	John Webster, *The Duchess of Malfi* (*c.* 1613–14), ed. J. R. Brown, 1964 (Revels Plays), and *The White Devil* (*c.* 1612), ed. J. R. Brown, 2nd edn, 1966 (Revels Plays)
Werstine	Paul Werstine, 'Line division in Shakespeare's dramatic verse: an editorial problem', *AEB* 8 (1984), 73–125
Whately	Thomas Whately, *Remarks on Some of the Characters of Shakespeare*, 1785
White	*Macbeth* in *The Works of William Shakespeare*, ed. R. G. White, 12 vols., 1857–66, x (1861)
White [2]	*Macbeth* in *Mr William Shakespeare's Comedies Histories Tragedies and Poems*, ed. R. G. White, 3 vols., 1883, III
Wickham, 'Castle'	Glynne Wickham, 'Hell-castle and its door-keeper', in *Aspects of 'Macbeth'*, ed. Kenneth Muir and Philip Edwards, 1977, pp. 39–45
Wickham, 'Fly'	Glynne Wickham, 'To fly or not to fly? The problem of Hecate in Shakespeare's *Macbeth*', in *Essays on Drama and Theatre: Liber Amicorum Benjamin Hunningher*, 1973, pp. 171–82
Widow's Tears	George Chapman, *The Widow's Tears* (*c.* 1605), ed. Akihiro Yamada, 1975 (Revels Plays)
Williams	Gordon Williams, *A Dictionary of Sexual Language and Imagery in Shakespearean and Stuart Literature*, 3 vols., 1994
Williams, 'Play'	George Walton Williams, '*Macbeth:* King James's play', *South Atlantic Review* 47.2 (1982), 12–21
Winter	William Winter, *Shakespeare on the Stage*, series 1 (1911)
Witch	Thomas Middleton, *The Witch* (*c.* 1613–15?), ed. W. W. Greg, MSR, 1950
Woodstock	*Woodstock: A Moral History* (*c.* 1591–4), ed. A. P. Rossiter, 1946

Unless otherwise noted, quotations from the Bible are taken from Bishops' Bible (1568).

INTRODUCTION

Violent in action and memorably written, difficult to perform and yet extraordinarily popular on stage, granted by actors and audiences its own special 'curse',[1] William Shakespeare's *Macbeth* strongly resists critical and theatrical exposition. Despite these manifest contradictions, an early-twentieth-century critic asserts that the play 'is distinguished by its simplicity . . . Its plot is quite plain. It has very little intermixture of humour. It has little pathos except of the sternest kind. The style [of the play's language] . . . has not much variety . . .'[2] Like many speeches in *Macbeth*, each of these apparently straightforward claims is paradoxical: each is true and at the same time misleading. Further, these claims are both true and false to the play's life in the theatres of early Jacobean London and in the theatres of many times and many places since. Moreover, these claims are often false to the play's complex relation with the social and political circumstances in which it was first written and first performed. As I understand my introductory task, it is to give an account of a magnificent early-seventeenth-century English play as it was originally conceived and as it might have been first played in a faraway and impossible-to-retrieve moment or series of moments in Jacobean London. It is also my task to present its afterlife in times and places very distant from the historical William Shakespeare, from his extraordinary acting company, and from their once living, now irretrievably lost, social, commercial, political, theatrical world.

To that end, I consider here: the play in its Jacobean, early-seventeenth-century moments – especially its possible political meanings – and its likely relation to documentary sources; the play's treatment of time and of time's varied evocations (family, succession, birth and death); the many ways in which the play allows or withholds knowledge and belief for the characters and the audience; the ways the play affects the audience through language; the ways the play has been performed in early and later times and in other places and media.

---

[1] See Iona Opie and Moira Tatem (eds.), *A Dictionary of Superstitions*, 1989, p. 396, and Richard Huggett, *The Curse of 'Macbeth' and Other Theatrical Superstitions*, 1981. The nature of the play's 'curse' (which derives at least partly from its representation of the demonic and, practically, from its many sword-fights and the consequent physical danger to the actors) and the remedies for that curse, especially for quoting it outside the theatre, are elaborate. My favourite version is that of the distinguished actor Patrick Stewart, who taught me this remedy when I made the mistake of quoting one of the sisters' lines in the play: to remove the curse of quoting *Macbeth* outside the theatre, one must immediately speak an equal number of lines from Shakespeare's *A Midsummer Night's Dream*. Other recorded remedies include walking around the theatre building three times.

[2] A. C. Bradley, *Shakespearean Tragedy*, 1904, rpt. 1955, p. 309. Later critics have, sometimes justly, derided Bradley's version of *Macbeth*, but the issues he identified – history, identity, violence, sovereignty, for example – have not gone away. See, among many, Francis Barker, *The Culture of Violence: Tragedy and History*, 1993, pp. 51–92; Sheldon P. Zitner, 'Macbeth and the moral scale of tragedy', *Journal of General Education* 16 (1964), 20–8; and Robert B. Heilman, 'The criminal as tragic hero: dramatic methods' (1966), rpt. in Kenneth Muir and Philip Edwards (eds.), *Aspects of 'Macbeth'*, 1977, pp. 26–38.

Macbeth in legend, *Macbeth* in history

James Stewart or Stuart (1566–1625), the sixth king of that name to rule Scotland, believed, or claimed to believe, that he descended from one Banquo, Thane of Lochaber in the eleventh century when Scotland's king was Macbeth (see illustration 1). In late March 1603, the same King James VI became the first of that name to rule England. Barely two years later, Samuel Calvert commented on political drama, public response to it, and official failure to react:

> The Plays [i.e. the players?] do not forbear to present upon their Stage the whole Course of this present Time, not sparing either King, State or Religion, in so great Absurdity, and with such Liberty, that any would be afraid to hear them.[1]

Calvert assumes that audiences would be 'afraid' to hear or see plays representing a living monarch, secrets of state, and controversial religious matters ('King, State or Religion'), and that such plays should be treated specially and usually censored.

Samuel Calvert was probably right, or at least conventional for his time. Queen Elizabeth I's first proclamation seeking to control the subject and content of drama (16 May 1559) used words that were regularly repeated and echoed in official and unofficial documents: 'her majestie doth . . . charge [her officers] . . . that they permyt none [i.e. no 'common Interludes'] to be played wherin either matters of religion or of the governaunce of the estate of the common weale shalbe handled or treated . . .', and thirty years later the Privy Council sought closer theatrical control because the companies had 'handle[d] in their plaies certen matters of Divinytie and of State unfitt to be suffred'.[2] To offer the public a play representing living monarchs almost always drew official attention and usually censorship. Less than eighteen months after James's accession, his newly patented London acting company, the King's Men, twice performed a now-lost play, 'the tragedie of Gowrie'. *The Tragedy of Gowrie* presumably dealt with the alleged attempt by the Earl of Gowrie and others to assassinate James on 5 August 1600, when he was still King of Scotland only.[3] *The Tragedy of Gowrie*

---

[1] Samuel Calvert to Ralph Winwood, 28 March 1605, in Winwood, *Memorials of Affairs of State*, 3 vols., 1725, II, 54. Calvert may refer specifically to the controversy *Eastward Ho* caused; see p. 12 below. The Comte de Beaumont, the French ambassador, an observer admittedly grinding a diplomatic and political axe, vividly noted: 'what must be the state and condition of a prince [King James], whom the preachers publicly from the pulpit assail, whom the comedians of the metropolis bring upon the stage, whose wife attends these representations in order to enjoy the laugh against her husband' (letter, 14 June 1604, quoted from E. K. Chambers, *The Elizabethan Stage*, 4 vols., 1923, I, 325), and Henry Crosse, a fairly temperate critic of the theatre, complains that 'there is no passion wherewith the king, the soveraigne majestie of the Realme was possest, but is amplified, and openly sported with, and made a May-game to all the beholders, abusing the state royall' (*Vertues Commonwealth* (1603), sig. p3).

[2] Quoted from Chambers, *The Elizabethan Stage*, IV, 263 and 306, respectively. Matters of religion and state were the most frequently censored dramatic subjects throughout the Tudor and Stuart period.

[3] See W. F. Arbuckle, 'The "Gowrie Conspiracy"' [in two parts], *SHR* 36 (1957), 1–24 and 89–110. Scottish public opinion immediately doubted official claims about the events (Arbuckle, pp. 13–14), and an Edinburgh pamphlet, *Gowries Conspiracie* (1600), supporting James's version, appeared less than a month later, soon enough for George Nicolson, the English agent in Scotland, to send a copy south on 3 September (Arbuckle, p. 18). Valentine Simmes's London edition of this text, *The earle of Gowries conspiracie*, was entered in the Stationers' Register on 11 September 1600 and published, possibly soon after, with the date '1600'. Such speedy printing and reprinting may indicate a propaganda war and/or contemporary anxieties about attacks on monarchs.

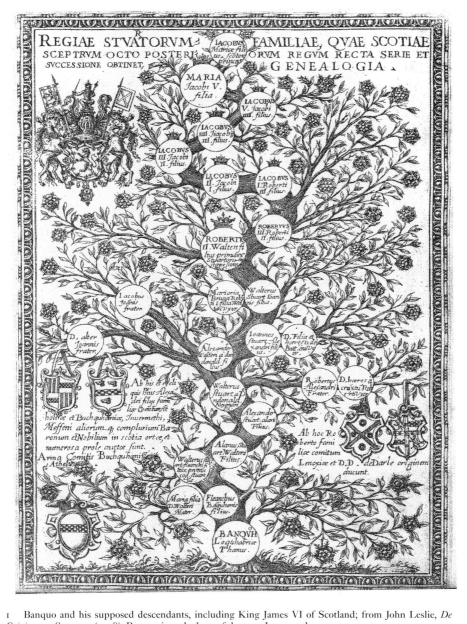

1   Banquo and his supposed descendants, including King James VI of Scotland; from John Leslie, *De Origine . . . Scotorum* (1578). Banquo is at the base of the tree, James at the crown

was quickly suppressed,[1] and its fate suggests how politically and practically difficult it was to write and perform plays concerning the Stuart monarchy and its well-known vicissitudes in Scotland and in England. Many years later, the British monarchy, now Hanoverian, faced an effort to restore the Stuarts, and after the Battle of Falkirk (1746), when Scottish troops, supported by the French, won a temporary advantage, 'The king was advised to go to the theatre and to command the tragedy of Macbeth', and the play was performed.[2] In the anxious times of a largely Scottish insurrection against the British (or English) central government in 1746, *Macbeth* was considered a pro-English, pro-monarchical, anti-rebel, and (curiously) anti-Stuart play.

Given even this brief context, it is a nice understatement to say that 'Shakespeare's task in writing *Macbeth* was . . . extremely problematic.'[3] From a very different perspective, another critic agrees: '*Macbeth is* a play about Scotland, seized at a crucial moment of transition in its history . . .'[4] However distant these early-seventeenth-century debates and problems may seem, they were living difficulties for the King's Men, for William Shakespeare as playwright, and for their audiences at the Globe theatre and elsewhere. Those difficulties entailed not only who might have rightfully ruled Scotland in the eleventh century, but who might justly rule Scotland and, more controversially, England, in the seventeenth.

Looking back to early Jacobean London, we recognise that these early-seventeenth-century debates affect our understanding of *Macbeth*'s origins. Reversing the telescope of time, we must suppose that those debates shaped the play's creation. The problems of situating the composition and earliest performances of *Macbeth*, and of determining its sources in written documents, contemporary events, and early Jacobean culture, are interdependent matters, often with no certain answers. One place to start is with the often-remarked 'connection' between the play and the accession of the Scottish King James VI as England's King James I, whose family provided England's and Scotland's native monarchs until the death of Queen Anne in 1714. Arguments linking *Macbeth* with King James or with specific events in the early seventeenth century divide into the 'topical' *Macbeth* and the 'occasional' *Macbeth*. First, the play may be studied as a 'topical' or general repository of references to events, ideas, or persons in the years immediately after James's accession,[5] second, as a more specific response to the unprecedented 'occasion' of a Scottish king becoming England's king, third, as a response to an even more precise 'occasion', when James's brother-in-law, the Danish King Christian IV, first visited England.

---

[1] For these performances and their suppression, see John Chamberlain to Ralph Winwood, letter, 18 December 1604, in N. E. McClure (ed.), *The Letters of John Chamberlain*, 2 vols., 1939, 1, 199.

[2] See Thomas Davies, *Memoirs of the Life of David Garrick*, 2 vols., 1780, 11, 136.

[3] David Norbrook, '*Macbeth*, and the politics of historiography', in Kevin Sharpe and Steven N. Zwicker (eds.). *Politics of Discourse: The Literature and History of Seventeenth-Century England*, 1987, p. 93.

[4] John Turner, '*Macbeth*', in Graham Holderness *et al.* (eds.), *Shakespeare: The Play of History*, 1988, p. 120. Just before this remark, Turner says: 'two rival Scottish traditions of interpreting relations with England, the unionist and the nationalist . . . have been brought together . . . in *Macbeth* . . . to problematise our understanding of historical progress by the theatrical experience of tragedy'.

[5] For extensive, sometimes persuasive, arguments about the play's topicality, see Arthur Melville Clark, *Murder Under Trust: The Topical 'Macbeth'*, 1981.

TOPICAL *MACBETH*

Claims for a topical *Macbeth* cannot be substantiated and may be circular. There are some striking pieces of what may be 'evidence'. Consider the Porter in *Macbeth*:

> Here's a farmer that hanged himself on th'expectation of plenty. Come in time – have napkins enough about you, here you'll sweat for't. (*Knock*) Knock, knock. Who's there in th'other devil's name? Faith, here's an equivocator that could swear in both the scales against either scale, who committed treason enough for God's sake, yet could not equivocate to heaven. O, come in, equivocator.
>
> (2.3.3–10)[1]

Critics have linked the Porter's words with the notorious imprisonment, trial, and execution (1606) of the Gunpowder plotters, who had sought to blow up Parliament, along with the king and his family, and many aristocrats and judges on 5 November 1605. Among those executed was the Superior of the English Jesuits, Father Henry Garnet, who espoused the doctrine of 'equivocation' ('here's an equivocator that could swear in both the scales . . .') and used the alias 'Farmer' ('Here's a farmer that hanged himself . . .').[2]

Among other topical evidence, there is Matthew Gwinne's brief Latin pageant, 'Tres Sibyllae' (Three Sibyls), welcoming King James to St John's College, Oxford, on 27 August 1605, apparently drawing upon chronicle accounts of Macbeth and Banquo meeting the three witches, and pandering to James's belief that he was descended from Banquo.[3] Gwinne's pageant, recited by 'tres quasi Sibyllae' (three persons like sibyls), is quite conventional. Although the repeated uses of 'Salve' (Hail) in addressing king, queen, and royal prince seem close to the witches' words in *Macbeth* Act 1, Scene 3, they do in fact duplicate a sibyl's prophetic greeting that Queen Elizabeth had heard thirty years earlier, when one 'Sibylla' intercepted her as she rode through the Earl of Leicester's park at Kenilworth Castle with the words, 'All hayle, all hayle, thrice happy prince, / I am *Sibilla* she / Of future chaunce, and after happ, / foreshewing what shalbe.'[4] Gwinne's seemingly significant language may 'prove' only that he could read Raphael Holinshed's *Chronicles* (see pp. 13–15 below) as well as any other author eager to please the new king.[5] Most of the proposed links between *Macbeth*,

---

[1] For the contemporary socio-economic resonances of 'plenty', see Richard Wilson, *Will Power: Essays on Shakespearean Authority*, 1993, chapter 4, esp. pp. 83 ff., and the authorities there cited.

[2] See also 5.5.42–3. Prosecutors repeatedly emphasised the various names ('false appellations' in Sir Edward Coke's words) used by the Gunpowder Plot conspirators and the doctrine of equivocation at Garnet's trial, 28 March 1606; see T. B. Howell (comp.), *A Complete Collection of State Trials*, 33 vols., 1809–26, II, columns 225 (multiple names), 234 (Garnet as 'Farmer'), 234–5, 238–9 (equivocation).

[3] See Geoffrey Bullough (ed.), *Narrative and Dramatic Sources of Shakespeare*, 8 vols., 1957–75, VII, 470–2, for the Latin text (published with Gwinne's *Vertumnus sive Annus recurrens* in 1607) and an English translation. On equivocation in the play, see Frank L. Huntley, '*Macbeth* and the background of Jesuitical equivocation', *PMLA* 79 (1964), 390–400, and, more generally, Lowell Gallagher, *Medusa's Gaze: Casuistry and Conscience in the Renaissance*, 1991, pp. 1–120. Another possible topical reference would place at least some of the play's composition after mid 1606: see 1.3.6 n.; see also p. 15 below.

[4] 'The princely pleasures at Kenelworth Castle', in *The Whole woorkes of George Gascoigne* (1587), sig. A1r, following p. 352.

[5] Anthony Nixon's account of James's visit to Oxford, *Oxfords Triumph* (1605), mentions (sig. B1r) 'three little Boyes comming foorth of a Castle, made all of Ivie, drest like three Nimphes'; Nixon thus 'echoes' Macbeth's history in Raphael Holinshed's *Chronicles* (1587) and anticipates Simon Forman's eyewitness account of a Jacobean performance of *Macbeth*. See pp. 13–15 and 57–8 below.

the Gunpowder Plot, and Gwinne's pageant prove to be vague, circumstantial, or undatable.[1]

If *Macbeth* contains allusions to the Gunpowder Plot, some of its text must have been composed after 5 November 1605; if the play alludes to the conspirators' trials, convictions, and executions, some of its text must have been composed about the first quarter of 1606. If the First Witch's mention of a sailor who is 'master o'th'Tiger' (1.3.6) refers to one specific historical ship, as her eerily precise reference to that historical ship's tumultuous voyage might suggest, then her lines could not have been written before that particular *Tiger* returned to England (27 June 1606) and the ship's travails became known.[2] If William Warner's additions to *Albions England*, published at an unknown date in 1606 (see p. 10 below), echo, rather than anticipate, *Macbeth*, the play must have been publicly performed or its subject-matter and perhaps its text have become publicly known before Warner composed his text.

Verbal similarities between *Macbeth* and *Antony and Cleopatra* suggest that the two plays may have been written at about the same time. Macbeth, awaiting the murderers, compares himself and Banquo with Mark Antony and Octavian (Shakespeare's Octavius), the man who became Augustus Caesar, the first Roman emperor:

> There is none but he [Banquo],
> Whose being I do fear; and under him
> My genius is rebuked, as it is said
> Mark Antony's was by Caesar.   (3.1.55–8)

Yet these verbal similarities say nothing certain about priority or proximity of composition.[3] *Macbeth*, although its general style is very different, has many linguistic and imaginative links with Shakespeare's *The Rape of Lucrece*, published in 1594, many years before *Macbeth* seems to have been written and performed.[4] Around the same supposed time of *Macbeth*'s original composition, Volumnia in *Coriolanus* powerfully compares mother's milk and blood, two of *Macbeth*'s most evocative liquids:

> The breasts of Hecuba,
> When she did suckle Hector, looked not lovelier
> Than Hector's forehead when it spit forth blood
> At Grecian sword, contemning –   (*Coriolanus* 1.3.40–3)

---

[1] See J. Leeds Barroll, *Politics, Plague, and Shakespeare's Theater*, 1991, pp. 133–52.

[2] See 1.3.6 n. It is impossible to know how widespread the knowledge of the *Tiger*'s voyage might have been.

[3] *Antony and Cleopatra* and *Macbeth* are also dramaturgically similar; see p. 24 below and p. 28 n. 1. The plays also have similar 'arming scenes' (*Macbeth* 5.3 and *Antony* 4.4), where love, or memories of love, interrupt preparations for war. More generally, the Shakespearean tragedies that probably preceded and succeeded *Macbeth* – *King Lear* and *Antony and Cleopatra*, respectively – follow what may be a psychologically or authorially explicable treatment of time. In *King Lear*, time is memorably expressed as ageing, or the coming-into-being of a past; in *Antony and Cleopatra*, time is treated as a present past, as nostalgia (see e.g. Michael Neill (ed.), *Ant.*, 1994, pp. 94–8); in *Macbeth*, time is treated as a future-in-the-present (see 1.5.54–6 and pp. 20–3 below) or as the future made a changeless present.

[4] See e.g. 2.1.55 n. For the many links between *The Rape of Lucrece* and *Macbeth*, see G. W. Knight, *The Imperial Theme*, 1931, 3rd edn, corr. rpt., 1954, p. 133, and Kenneth Muir (ed.), *Mac.*, 9th edn, 1962, Appendix D.

These lines are part of Volumnia's reply to Virgilia's anxious worry – 'O Jupiter, no blood!' – for her husband's safe return from war. They also rewrite in Shakespearean 'Roman' terms Lady Macbeth's willingness to dash out the brains of the child she suckled (1.7.54–9; see p. 36 below). Blood for milk, in Shakespeare's Rome and Shakespeare's Scotland.[1] The plot of *Coriolanus* also puts ambiguous 'heroes', Coriolanus and Aufidius, into conflict, as does the plot of *Macbeth*: Macbeth *versus* Banquo, who acknowledges 'cursèd thoughts' (2.1.8) which might be thoughts of usurpation; later, Macbeth *versus* Macduff, who disastrously abandons his family and becomes at least technically a regicide; still later, Macbeth *versus* Malcolm, who also flees and whose royal claim rests on Duncan's nomination (1.4.37–9) and remains at best arguable.[2] By joining an attractive hero–villain with ambiguously moral or ambiguously 'good' opponents, *Macbeth* resembles *Richard III* among Shakespeare's earlier plays.[3]

Further, Shakespeare's Roman plays and English history plays emphasise *shame* as a motive for royal and aristocratic acts. Macduff cannily manoeuvres Macbeth, who supposes himself invincible ('I bear a charmèd life which must not yield' (5.8.12)), into battle by threatening public humiliation:

> Then yield thee coward,
> And live to be the show and gaze o'th'time.
> We'll have thee, as our rarer monsters are,
> Painted upon a pole and underwrit,
> 'Here may you see the tyrant.'
>   (5.8.23–7)

Social and political humiliation and near-raucous comedy are closely joined here, as they are in *Antony and Cleopatra* (see p. 28 n. 1 below); earlier in *Macbeth* (Act 2, Scene 3), the Porter insistently if unself-consciously combines 'high' political events with 'low' bodily functions. Before choosing suicide, Cleopatra imagines public humiliation were she to submit to Roman power (*Antony and Cleopatra* 4.12.33–9, 5.2.108–24); Richard III uses his physical deformity as ambition's spur (*Richard III* 1.1.14–51); and Aufidius cleverly names Coriolanus a 'boy of tears' (*Coriolanus* 5.6.100) when the political, deadly moment is right.

Although traditional chronologies place *Macbeth* after *King Lear* and before *Antony and Cleopatra* and *Coriolanus*, those chronologies are uncertain.[4] Amidst these

---

[1] R. B. Parker (ed.), *Cor.*, 1994, p. 52, compares Volumnia's behaviour in general and Lady Macbeth's ' "unsexing" herself (with a comparable distortion of breast-feeding to child-murder) . . .' Dying, Cleopatra links death and suckling when she compares the fatal asp to a child: 'Dost thou not see my baby at my breast, / That sucks the nurse asleep?' (*Ant.* 5.2.309–10).

[2] Critical suspicion of Banquo begins with Bradley, pp. 304 and 306–8; for the play's ambivalent treatment of Macduff and Malcolm, see pp. 88–93 below.

[3] Emrys Jones, *Scenic Form in Shakespeare*, 1971, pp. 199–224, discusses *Macbeth*'s structural (and some verbal) links with Shakespeare's earlier plays, especially *Richard III* and (more surprisingly) *Henry VI, Parts 2* and *3*. For *Richard III*'s relation with *Macbeth*, see also p. 71 below and n. 5.

[4] For the traditional argument, see E. K. Chambers, *William Shakespeare: A Study of Facts and Problems*, 2 vols., 1930, I, 249–50 and 271, and for *Macbeth*, ibid., 1, 471–6, but Chambers admits (1, 251) that *Lear*, *Macbeth*, and *Antony and Cleopatra* come 'in no certain order'. A counter-claim appears in Barroll, *passim*, but esp. chapters 5–6. Barroll speculates that *Macbeth* was written 'by the end of 1606' (p. 177) and may have been first performed 'at court, December–February 1606–7' (p. 153); Barroll's argument for both composition and performance partly depends upon the frequent theatre-closures for the plague

uncertainties, there is one highly probable claim. When Scotland's King James became England's King James in March 1603, his accession made a Shakespearean Scottish play commercially viable and creatively attractive. King James and his Scottishness created an occasion, and at some point Shakespeare and the King's Men apparently seized the popular, commercial moment, as they had less successfully done in performing *The Tragedy of Gowrie*.

OCCASIONAL *MACBETH*

Macbeth has been called an 'occasional' play in two senses: first, the argument runs, Shakespeare would not have composed a play on a Scottish subject had not a Scottish king come to the English throne. This claim seems very probable. Second and more specific, some scholars believe Shakespeare composed the play as a 'compliment' to King James, perhaps even as an entertainment when King Christian IV of Denmark, James's brother-in-law, visited his fellow monarch from 17 July to 11 August 1606.[1] James's interest in witchcraft and the King's Evil (compare 4.3.141–61),[2] and his belief that he was descended from Banquo, have been claimed, plausibly, as links between the new king and Shakespeare's play, but the more specific claim that *Macbeth* was written to honour the Danish king's visit, or that the play was performed before James and Christian – who did not speak English[3] – lacks any proof. The royal visit included many dramatic performances – three unnamed plays by the King's Men, another by the company that had recently been punished for anti-Scottish satire in *Eastward Ho*, another by the Children of Paul's – as well as bear-baitings and demonstrations of fencing and wrestling.[4] Yet John Heminge of Shakespeare's company received the customary £ 10 per play,[5] and the records mention no extraordinary costs, as we might have expected if *Macbeth* had been performed, since in a full-blown royal performance it would probably have required some unusual costumes, props, and machinery. Unlike masques and other courtly entertainments, few public theatre plays (such as *Macbeth*) were premièred at court and/or written for a specific royal occasion. In 1606, plague

(see p. 9 below, n. 1), and it is weakened by the unargued assumption (pp. 17 and 19) that in the Jacobean period Shakespeare did not continue to write plays when London performances were forbidden. Equally uncertain is *Macbeth*'s chronological relation with *Pericles* (1609), a play deeply interested in birth, death, and parenthood.

1 See e.g. C. C. Stopes, *Shakespeare's Industry*, 1916, pp. 95–109; J. W. Draper, '"Macbeth" as a compliment to James I', *Englische Studien* 72 (1937–8), 207–20; Henry N. Paul, *The Royal Play of Macbeth*, 1950; J. M. Nosworthy, *Shakespeare's Occasional Plays, Their Origin and Transmission*, 1965, chapter 1; Clark, esp. chapters 5 and 7.

2 On James's interest in witchcraft, see *Newes from Scotland* and *Daemonologie*, in James VI and I, *Daemonologie*, ed. G. B. Harrison, 1924; for the topicality of James's ambivalent attitude toward healing the King's Evil, see F. David Hoeniger, *Medicine and Shakespeare in the English Renaissance*, 1992, chapter 16, esp. pp. 276 and 281–2.

3 See Michael Hawkins, 'History, politics and *Macbeth*', in John Russell Brown (ed.), *Focus on 'Macbeth'*, 1982, pp. 155–88; p. 186. Hawkins's entire article is essential for the study of *Macbeth*, and Hawkins's Appendix, pp. 185–8, powerfully refutes the claims of Henry N. Paul.

4 See David Cook and F. P. Wilson, 'Dramatic records in the declared accounts of the Treasurer of the Chamber, 1558–1642', *MSC* 6 (1962 for 1961), 44–6, and W. R. Streitberger, 'Jacobean and Caroline Revels accounts, 1603–1642', *MSC* 13 (1986), 15.

5 Cook and Wilson, 'Dramatic records', p. 44.

had closed the theatres for many months. Economic necessity, therefore, as well as the commercial value of performing at court, might have led the King's Men to present *Macbeth* there first.[1]

Nothing stronger than hypothesis and circumstantial evidence joins *Macbeth* with either James's accession or Christian's visit, yet no English tragedy (as opposed to comedies and histories) on Scottish subjects earlier than *Macbeth* has survived. Four Scottish tragedies are known to have been written; they are for us only titles: 'a Tragedie of the Kinge of Scottes' (1567–8), 'Robart the second Kinge of scottes tragedie' or 'the scottes tragedi' (September 1599), 'malcolm Kynge of scottes' (April 1602), and 'the tragedie of Gowrie' (already mentioned).[2] A satiric remark in Will Kemp's *Nine Daies Wonder* (1600) implies that Macbeth and what Kemp calls 'Prophetesses' (possibly the beings who later became the 'sisters' of *Macbeth*) had already appeared in a ballad.[3] Kemp had been the principal comic actor in the Lord Chamberlain's Men (the earlier name of the King's Men), and he might therefore have known a now-lost Macbeth-play.[4]

Before *Macbeth*, English dramatists and their audiences generally understood Scotsmen as a comical, alien, dangerous, and uncivilised people – as Frenchmen who spoke a form of English, perhaps.[5] The historic Franco-Scottish alliance, the 'auld alliance',

[1] Among likely plays and entertainments, George Peele's *Arraignment of Paris* requires Queen Elizabeth as a participant and was advertised as having been performed at court; one version of Ben Jonson's *Every Man Out of His Humour* ends with an address to Elizabeth and was apparently performed at court, perhaps before it appeared at the Globe. Jonson's *Sejanus* may also have been performed first at court; see Philip Ayres (ed.), *Sejanus*, 1990, p. 9, citing E. K. Chambers. A few other plays may have been designed for royal performance before appearing in public theatres: see e.g. Glynne Wickham, '*The Two Noble Kinsmen* or *A Midsummer Night's Dream, Part II* ?', in G. R. Hibbard (ed.), *Elizabethan Theatre VII*, 1980, pp. 167–96. Generally, however, plays were performed publicly and then performed (sometimes adapted) at court. For the effort and expenses required by dramatic productions at court, see Glynne Wickham, *Early English Stages*, 3 vols., II, pt. 1 (1963), chap. 8. For a different view about *Macbeth*, see Barroll, p. 153; he notes (p. 144): 'Beginning in June 1606, there would be no public presentations of plays in London for seven or eight months' because of the plague 'and thus no performance of *Macbeth* at the Globe'; such a long closure might make original performance at court more likely. Parker (ed.), *Coriolanus*, pp. 86–7, argues that *Coriolanus* may have been written and rehearsed, perhaps before paying audiences, under similarly difficult conditions. If Parker's guess is accurate, both writing and rehearsal of *Coriolanus* contradict Barroll's assumptions about *Macbeth* (see p. 7 above, n. 4).

[2] For the first and second, see Clark, pp. 11–12; on the second, see Henslowe, p. 124, and James Shapiro, '*The Scot's Tragedy* and the politics of popular drama', *ELR* 23 (1993), 428–49; on the third, see Henslowe, pp. 199–200.

[3] Bullough, VII, 429.

[4] David Wiles, *Shakespeare's Clown: Actor and Text in the Elizabethan Playhouse*, 1987, p. 34. Dover Wilson (NS, pp. xli–xlii) thought a Macbeth-play existed in Elizabeth's reign, and G. B. Evans (private communication, 30 May 1994) has noted many verbal similarities between F *Macbeth* and *A Warning for Faire Women* (printed 1599), a Lord Chamberlain's Men's play.

[5] Typically, Scots and Scotland were material for comedies (such as Robert Greene's *James IV*, which includes an English invasion to rectify Scottish royal abuses, or the anonymous *Pinner of Wakefield*), or for history plays concerning the long medieval wars against Scotland (e.g. Peele's *Edward I*, Marlowe's *Edward II*, and the anonymous *Edward III*, in which Shakespeare probably had a hand and which includes a 'treacherous' Scottish invasion of northern England, repulsed by Edward III in person and involving the capture of David, King of Scots), or for national stereotypes and comic effects, as in *Henry V* and the quarto versions (1600, 1619) of Portia's ridiculed suitors in *The Merchant of Venice*. In the last instance, the Folio discreetly changes a satiric reference to a 'Scottish lord' to 'other lord'; perhaps similarly, Shakespeare transferred the Hero–Claudio plot in *Much Ado* from the Scottish setting of his source (Ariosto) to Italy (see Bullough, 11, 62). *Edward III* in particular, and very unlike *Macbeth*, draws attention to Scottish

made these two countries seem especially likely to take advantage of any English internal dissension: 'if Lincolnshire seke to distroye Englande, what wonder is hit if Fraunce and Scotlande sometime have fought [i.e. sought?] to offende me?', one English propagandist wrote.[1] And the possibly Shakespearean *Edward III* (?1593) dramatises an earlier period, the fourteenth century, when English ambitions in France coincided with the designs of the Scots (England's 'everlasting foe'[2]) and the French on England. In *Edward III*, David, King of Scots, promises the French ambassador, 'That we with England will not enter parley, / . . . nor take truce' (*Edward III* 1.2.22–3). The text of *Henry V* alludes to this episode, where Westmoreland succinctly gives the English view:

> But there's a saying, very old and true,
> *'If that you will France win*
> *Then with Scotland first begin.'*
> For once the eagle England being in prey,
> To her unguarded nest the weasel Scot
> Comes sneaking, and so sucks her princely eggs,
> Playing the mouse in absence of the cat
> To 'tame and havoc more than she can eat.[3]

Unmentioned in *Henry V* are England's frequent attacks upon and invasions of Scotland. Queen Elizabeth engaged in very few independent foreign military adventures, but her first (1560) was against Scotland, when she intervened in Scottish factional struggles, hoping to install a puppet-régime or even to conquer the country.[4]

Lamenting Queen Elizabeth's death and praising King James as the first monarch to unite '*Britaine*', William Warner's *A Continuance of Albions England* (1606) adds to a work first published in 1586 and often republished and enlarged; Warner's 1606 additions include a chapter (94) 'Of *Makbeth* the Tyrant . . .', perhaps alluding to Shakespeare's *Macbeth*, another (95) on the Gunpowder Plot, and one (90) 'Of the long continued League and Confedracie betweene the *French* and *Scots* against the *English* . . .'[5] Although Andrew Boorde practised medicine in Glasgow, his *Fyrst Boke of the Introduction of Knowledge* (?1547) is a compendium of the stereotypes that English popular and political writing kept alive for Shakespeare's audience:

> I Am a Scotyshe man, and trew I am to Fraunce;
> In every countrey, myselfe I do avaunce;
> I wyll boost myselfe, I wyll crake and face;

speech, using such conventional stage-Scots as 'whinyards' (thought to be an especially Scottish weapon; see Supplementary Note 4.3.162, pp. 259–60 below), 'Jemmy' (for 'Jimmy'), and 'bonny' (see Giorgio Melchiori (ed.), *Edward III* (1998), 1.2.33 and 57, respectively; subsequent quotations cite this edition). Later, King Edward specifically compliments the Countess of Salisbury for her ability to imitate King David's speech: ' "Even thus", quoth she, "he spake" – and then spoke broad, / With epithets and accents of the Scot, / But somewhat better than the Scot could speak' (2.1.29–31).
[1] Richard Morrison, quoted in Anthony Fletcher, *Tudor Rebellions*, 3rd edn, 1983, p. 5.
[2] *Edward III* 1.2.15.
[3] Andrew Gurr (ed.), *H5*, 1992, 1.2.166–73; Westmoreland's 'saying' has been found as early as 1548.
[4] For a wry, knowledgeable account, see C. G. Cruickshank, *Elizabeth's Army*, 2nd edn, 1966, pp. 207–36; for English fears of French intervention, see esp. p. 211.
[5] William Warner, *A Continuance of Albions England* (1606), sig. b2r.

> I love to be exalted, here and in every place.
> an Englyshe man I cannot naturally love,
> Wherefore I offend them, and my lorde above . . .
> I am a Scotyshe man, and have dissymbled muche,
> and in my promyse I have not kept touche.
> Great morder and theft in tymes past I have used . . .[1]

We cannot completely reimagine sixteenth- or early-seventeenth-century English attitudes toward Scotland and its people, or even contemporary English knowledge of them, but surviving documents tell an ominous tale.

English fear and prejudice had deep roots. Raphael Holinshed's *Chronicles* (see pp. 13–15 below) begin with William Harrison's 'Description of Britaine' where chapter 4 comments on the Scots:

How and when the Scots, a people mixed of the Scithian and Spanish blood, should arrive here out of Ireland, & when the Picts should come unto us out of *Sarmatia*, or from further toward the north & the Scithian Hyperboreans, as yet it is uncerteine . . . the Scots did often adventure hither [i.e. into the British Isles] to rob and steale out of Ireland, and were finallie called by them Meats or Picts (as the Romans named them, because they painted their bodies) to helpe them against the Britains, after the which they so planted themselves in these parts, that unto our time that portion of the land cannot be cleansed of them. I find also that as these Scots were reputed for the most Scithian-like and barbarous nation, and longest without letters . . . For both Diodorus *lib. 6.* and Strabo *lib. 4.* doo seeme to speake of a parcell of the Irish nation that should inhabit Britiane in their time, which were given to the eating of mans flesh, and therefore called Anthropophagi . . . it appeareth that those Irish, of whom *Strabo* and *Diodorus* doo speake, are none other than those Scots of whom *Jerome* speaketh *Adversus Jovinianum, lib. 2* who used to feed on the buttocks of boies and womens paps, as delicate dishes.[2]

Cannibalistic, violent, unlettered – these are qualities English audiences associated with the Celts whom their supposed ancestors and Roman armies had forced to the margins of the British Isles; similar fear and prejudice appear elsewhere in plays and other documents, public and private.[3] For instance, Henry Percy, Earl of Northumberland, wrote to James VI about Anglo-Scottish hostility shortly before his accession as England's king: 'the name of scotts is harche in the earres of the wulgar . . . [but] the memoriss of the ancient woundis betuene england and scotland will soune be cancelled when conscience in there harts sall proclame your ryght'.[4] James I himself and his royal

---

[1] Andrew Boorde, *Fyrst Boke*, ed. F. J. Furnivall, Early English Text Society, extra series 10 (1870), pp. 135–6.

[2] Raphael Holinshed *et al., The First . . . Volumes of Chronicles*, 1587, pp. 5b–6a. The claim that the peoples of Ireland and Scotland were related seems historically correct: migration and invasion from the Continent forced peoples from the north of Britain across the Irish Sea, and close connections (both friendly and unfriendly) between Ireland and Scotland persisted into Jacobean times.

[3] See, e.g., A. R. Braunmuller, *George Peele*, 1983, chapter 6 (on *Edward I*), and Phyllis Rackin, *Stages of History*, 1990, pp. 170–5.

[4] John Bruce (ed.), *Correspondence of King James VI. of Scotland*, Camden Society 78 (1861), 56. Both the English and the Lowland Scots considered Highlanders, denizens of the parts of Scotland where *Macbeth* is imagined to take place, especially savage and uncivilised: see John Major (Mair), *A History of Greater Britain*, ed. and trans. Archibald Constable, 1892, pp. 48–9. For early modern perceptions of the Highlander, see T. C. Smout, *A History of the Scottish People 1560–1830*, 1969, pp. 42–6.

predecessors and successors found Highlanders a difficult, recalcitrant, independent people.[1]

James was enthusiastically welcomed on his accession, not least because he had a male heir, but the king and his Scottish entourage quickly became objects of courtly envy and theatrical derision,[2] as they did, for instance, in *Eastward Ho* by George Chapman, Ben Jonson, and John Marston. Chapman and Jonson went to prison and Marston into hiding for various offences including a passage where one of their slightly criminal characters described life in the new Virginian colony as free of the usual impediments to larceny except for the criminal competition of

a few industrious Scots, perhaps, who, indeed, are dispersed over the face of the whole earth. But as for them, there are no greater friends to Englishmen and England, when they are out on't, in the world, than they are. And for my part, I would a hundred thousand of 'em were there [Virginia], for we are all one countrymen now, ye know; and we should find ten times more comfort of them there than we do here [in London] . . .[3]

In short, better 100,000 Scots in Virginia than any Scot in London.

Shakespeare's audiences probably had a crude and garish image of Highlanders, but English readers might have known a more generous view of the Scots as fighting men. Before the Battle of Pinkie (or Musselburgh), an English writer noted:

Thoughe they [Scottish warriors] me[a]nt but small humanit[i]e, yet shewed thei . . . much civilit[i]e, both of fayre play . . . & of formall order to chyde [the English force] ear [ere] they fought.[4]

In the 1550s, an English listing of national stereotypes ambivalently named 'the Scots for boldness', but several decades later William Camden recalled the Scottish alliance with France and less ambiguously notes:

with manlike courage and warlike prowesse, they [the Scots] have . . . maintained [their kingdom] at home, [and] . . . also hath purchased great honour abroad. For the French cannot but

[1] In *Basilikon Doron* (1598), James VI, who five years later became James I of England, repeated Mair's views (see preceding note) when he cautioned his infant son, Prince Henry, about the Highlands and advised him on how he should deal sternly with the Highlanders when he became king; see C. H. McIlwain (ed.), *The Political Works of James I*, 1918, p. 22. *Basilikon Doron* was reprinted in London (1603), along with many other of James's writings, when he ascended the English throne. For James's Highland policy, see Maurice Lee, *Great Britain's Solomon*, 1990, pp. 196–203, and for the availability of *Basilikon Doron* in the theatrical community, see p. 15 below, n. 1. Prince Henry died young, in November 1612. Just before the prince's death, Henry Peacham envisaged Highlanders (or 'redshanks') among the national enemies that the future king of a united Scotland and England might face: 'whether TURKE, SPAINE, FRAUNCE, or ITALIE, / The REDSHANKE, or the IRISH Rebell bold, / Shall rouze thee up, thy Trophees may be more, / Than all the HENRIES ever liv'd before' (Henry Peacham, *Minerva Britanna*, 1612, p. 17; I have slightly modernised the spelling).
[2] For courtly resistance to James and his Scottish followers, see e.g. Neil Cuddy, 'Anglo-Scottish union and the court of James I, 1603–1625', *Transactions of the Royal Historical Society*, 5th series, 39 (1989), esp. pp. 110–15; for public theatrical responses, see George Chapman, Ben Jonson, and John Marston, *Eastward Ho*, ed. R. W. Van Fossen, 1979, pp. 4–7, and A. R. Braunmuller (ed.), *A Seventeenth-Century Letter-Book*, 1983, pp. 370–89 and 452–6.
[3] *Eastward Ho* 3.3.44–52. The play contains other anti-Scot satire, and the actors may have been even more satirical (e.g. accents, costumes) in performance. For the playwrights' fates, see Braunmuller, *Letter-Book*, pp. 452–3.
[4] William Patten, *The Expedicion into Scotlande of . . . Edward, Duke of Soomerset*, 1548, sig. Hir.

acknowledge they have seldome atchieved any honourable acts without Scottish hands, who therefore are deservedly to participate [share] the glorie with them.[1]

Camden's remark may be as much anti-French as pro-Scot, yet his preference is a telling one.

Camden shows an admirable judiciousness, but popular – or at least recorded – hostility to James and his Scottish entourage spread from court gossip and the theatre, where topicality then as now sold places, to the floor of Parliament. In February 1607, Sir Christopher Piggott astonished the House of Commons when he interrupted a debate on the union of Scotland and England, a union James dearly sought; this outburst sent Piggott to the Tower:

let us not join murderers, thieves, and the roguish Scots with the well-deserving Scots. As much difference between them as between a judge and a thief... They ['the roguish Scots', presumably] have not suffered above two kings to die in their beds, these 200 years.[2]

Piggott only slightly exaggerated the violence of Scottish history and all too accurately recalled the political weakness of her kings. That weakness included most recently James VI, who had often found himself the announced or virtual captive of various aristocratic factions. The violence and the weakness both appear in *Macbeth*.

DOCUMENTS

Although Shakespeare's own writings were one of his main sources – he 'copied from himself'[3] – the principal printed source for the plot of *Macbeth* also served as a source for Shakespeare's English history plays: the massive *Chronicles* (first published in 1577 and later expanded (1587) into the version Shakespeare read) compiled by Raphael Holinshed and others. The text of this work is divided into three 'volumes' (though published as two separately bound books); the histories of Scotland and Ireland in 'volume' II serve to separate the histories of pre- and post-Conquest England in 'volumes' I and III, respectively. The 'Historie of Scotland' contains two accounts Shakespeare unquestionably appropriated, one of the reign and murder of King Duff, the other of Macbeth's rise and reign.[4]

---

[1] See Thomas Wilson, *Arte of Rhetorique* (1553) as quoted in A. J. Hoenselaars, *Images of Englishmen and Foreigners in the Drama of Shakespeare and His Contemporaries*, 1992, p. 20, and William Camden, *Remains Concerning Britain* (1605), ed. R. D. Dunn, 1984, pp. 15–16.

[2] For the incident and its aftermath, see *Journals of the House of Commons*, 95 vols., 1803–57, I, 333, 335–6, and 344; for Piggott's alleged words, see William Cobbett, *Parliamentary History of England*, 36 vols., 1806–20, I, column 1097. Of the historical period *Macbeth* deals with, John Dover Wilson notes, 'Out of the nine kings who reigned betwen 943 and 1040 all but two were killed, either in feud or directly by their successors' (NS, p. viii).

[3] G. K. Hunter, 'Shakespeare's reading', in Kenneth Muir and S. Schoenbaum (eds.), *A New Companion to Shakespeare Studies*, 1971, p. 59; see p. 6 above, n. 3 and p. 7 n. 1. On internal borrowings in *Macbeth*, see Jonathan Goldberg, 'Speculations: *Macbeth* and source', in Jean E. Howard and Marion F. O'Connor (eds.), *Shakespeare Reproduced: The Text in History and Ideology*, 1987, pp. 242–64. More generally, see Jones, *Scenic*, chapter 7.

[4] Holinshed and his collaborators consulted numerous sources; the main ones for Macbeth's reign seem to have been Hector Boece, *Scotorum historiae* (1526, 1575), and John Bellenden's Scots translation of it (?1540). For other sources of Scottish history available to Holinshed (and therefore possibly to Shakespeare), see Norbrook, and Supplementary Note 1.3.30, pp. 255–6 below. R. A. Law, 'The composition of *Macbeth* with reference to Holinshed', *Texas Studies in English* 31 (1952), 35–41, provides tabular summaries of where *Macbeth* parallels and deviates from Holinshed.

In the first narrative, the wife of 'Donwald', a hitherto loyal nobleman in whom Duff placed 'a speciall trust', urges her husband 'to make . . . awaie' King Duff 'and shewed him the meanes wherby he might soonest accomplish it'; 'kindled in wrath by the words of his wife',[1] Donwald secretly murders the king, smuggles the body out of the castle, and buries the corpse in a river bed. During Duncan's 'fained treatie' with the invading Sueno, drugged drinks stunned the Danish soldiers, and the army fell 'into a fast dead sleepe, that in manner it was unpossible to awake them'.[2] Similarly, Lady Macbeth promises to make Duncan's 'two chamberlains', his most intimate guards, 'spongy [drunken] officers' (1.7.63, 71). Holinshed stresses that Duff trusted Donwald, that the king had frequent difficulties with witches, and that louring darkness and bizarre events (including equine cannibalism and strange contests between birds of unequal ferocity)[3] pestered Scotland until Duff's body was found and properly buried.

In Holinshed's account, Macbeth's career is influenced by his ambitious spouse: his wife 'lay sore upon him to attempt' regicide 'as she that was verie ambitious, burning in unquenchable desire to beare the name of a queene'.[4] According to Holinshed, Banquo is a fully committed co-conspirator; he is murdered after the passage of some time because Macbeth fears 'he should be served of the same cup, as he had minstred to his predecessor',[5] but Banquo's ghost does not interrupt a royal banquet, and Lady Macbeth does not walk in her sleep. Holinshed elaborately details Macbeth's ten-year-long reign as a good and responsible ruler, his trust in witches and wizards, the 'testing' of Macduff by Malcolm, and the coming of Birnam Wood to Dunsinane, and includes many other events and even phrases that were transmuted into *Macbeth*. At one point, Holinshed interrupts his narrative to give a detailed genealogy of 'the originall line of those kings, which have descended from . . . Banquho',[6] and the list, ending with the then King James VI of Scotland, would have made the 'show of kings' in Act 4, Scene 1, easier to invent.

One of the kings who reigned between Duff and Duncan was Kenneth, a good king who none the less secretly poisoned Duff's son in order to ensure his own son's succession. Conscience, however, 'pricked' Kenneth:

And (as the fame [rumour, tale] goeth) it chanced that a voice was heard as he was in bed in the night time to take his rest, uttering unto him . . . 'Thinke not Kenneth that the wicked slaughter of Malcome Duffe by thee contrived, is kept secret from the knowledge of the eternall God: thou art he that didst conspire the innocents death . . . even at this present that there in hand secret practises to dispatch both thee and thy issue out of the waie . . .' The king with this voice being striken into great dread and terror, passed that night without anie sleepe comming in his eies.[7]

King Kenneth's torment, so similar to Macbeth's imaginings (Act 2, Scene 2), is elaborated still further in a volume Shakespeare may have known, and which his theatrical colleague, the actor Edward Alleyn, possessed, *Rerum Scoticarum historia* (1582). Its

---

[1] *Scotland*, p. 150a; the whole narrative appears on pp. 149a–152.   [2] *Ibid.*, p. 170a.
[3] *Ibid.*, p. 152a: 'horsses in Louthian, being of singular beautie and swiftnesse, did eate their owne flesh . . . There was a sparhawke also strangled by an owle.' Compare 2.4.10–20.
[4] *Ibid.*, p. 171a.   [5] *Ibid.*, p. 172b; compare 1.7.10–12.
[6] *Ibid.*, pp. 172b–174a.   [7] *Ibid.*, p. 158a.

author was the distinguished scholar and neo-Latin dramatist George Buchanan, who tutored the young King James.[1] For at least one incident – the death of Siward's son and his father's reaction to it – Shakespeare could have consulted two known sources: the very end of Holinshed's 'volume' I, concerning the period just before the Norman invasion, and William Camden's *Remains Concerning Britain* (1605).[2]

Aside from Holinshed's *Chronicles* and the dramatist's possibly direct use of Holinshed's own sources, such as Hector Boece's *Scotorum historiae* (1526, 1575) and Buchanan's *Rerum Scoticarum historia*, many other texts may have contributed to the language of *Macbeth* – Seneca's Latin tragedies, for instance, and Samuel Daniel's *Arcadia Reformed* (performed during the royal visit to Oxford in 1605 and published as *The Queenes Arcadia* the next year).[3] Yet 'when all is said, Shakespeare's main source was Holinshed'.[4] 'What he [Shakespeare] did not find in Holinshed was any indication how to shape this narrative material for the stage',[5] and that shaping must be our main concern.

Macbeth in the mind

SUCCESSION, TIME, AND FAMILIES

The historical era of Macbeth's reign was as controversial in Scottish political debate and historiography as the reigns of John or of Henry IV were in England.[6] In both

---

[1] See Bullough, VII, 509–17, and Norbrook, who seems confident (pp. 87–8) that Shakespeare knew Buchanan's history. King James and Buchanan held deeply divergent views of monarchical authority; see e.g. Pauline Croft, 'Sir John Doddridge, King James I, and the antiquity of Parliament', *Parliaments, Estates and Representation* 12 (1992), 103. For Edward Alleyn's ownership of Buchanan's *Rerum Scoticarum historia*, see J. R. Piggott, 'Edward Alleyn's books', in Aileen Reed and Robert Maniura (eds.), *Edward Alleyn: Elizabethan Actor, Jacobean Gentleman*, 1994, pp. 63–5. Buchanan's book, printed in Edinburgh and later on the Continent but not in London (see I. D. McFarlane, *Buchanan*, 1981, pp. 512–14, and John Durkan, *Bibliography of George Buchanan*, Glasgow University Library Studies, 1994, pp. 218 ff.), had been recalled for censorship in Scotland and prohibited in England (see McFarlane, pp. 414–15, 437, and 437 n. 55). The book was, however, well known in the Sidney circle and approvingly mentioned in Spenser's *A View of the Present State of Ireland* (written *c.* 1598); see James E. Phillips, 'George Buchanan and the Sidney circle', *Huntington Library Quarterly* 12 (1947–8), 23–55, esp. pp. 49–55. Given Alleyn's interest, Buchanan's *Rerum Scoticarum historia* might have been a common theatrical source like Holinshed's *Chronicles*. Alleyn also owned King James's *Basilikon Doron* and *Daemonologie*, both potentially relevant to *Macbeth*'s composition, and many of James's published speeches.

[2] 'The Historie of England' in Holinshed, *The First . . . Volumes of Chronicles*, p. 192a. A nearby page (p. 195a) gives an account of King Edward's ability to prophesy and to cure the King's Evil (see *Macbeth* 4.3.148–61). Lee Bliss suggested to me that Shakespeare drew this incident from Camden, and it has not been noted before; see Camden, p. 216 (sig. 2B2v in the 1605 edn). Camden's *Remains* are probable sources for *King Lear* (see Bullough, VII, 274, 288, 322) and *Coriolanus* (see Parker (ed.), *Coriolanus*, p. 3).

[3] See Bullough and, for other sources and possible influences, Kenneth Muir, *The Sources of Shakespeare's Plays*, 1977, chapter 29. In addition to the possible source mentioned in the previous note, the present edition suggests new sources and analogues to the play's language, or elaborates upon earlier suggestions, in 2.3.75 n., 5.1.64 n., and the Supplementary Note to 3.1.91–107, pp. 257–8 below.

[4] Muir, *Sources*, p. 215.   [5] Jones, *Scenic*, p. 199.

[6] See R. J. Adam, 'The real Macbeth: King of Scots, 1040–1054', *History Today* 7 (1957), 381–7; R. James Goldstein, *The Matter of Scotland: Historical Narrative in Medieval Scotland*, 1993, chap. 4; and Norbrook. All three emphasise how later Scottish and English political developments may have distorted the historical accounts on which Shakespeare's own documentary sources drew. Norbrook concentrates on sixteenth-century issues, Adam and Goldstein discuss earlier ones.

countries, the past and its most notably disputed successions fostered, if censorship did not intervene, discussion of legitimate sovereignty, tyranny, usurpation, and deposition. Entering this simultaneously 'historical' and contemporary debate, *Macbeth* was indeed 'extremely problematic'.

Holinshed makes clear enough that the Duncan-Macbeth-Malcolm period saw Scotland begin to move from its traditional system of royal succession – tanistry – to primogeniture, the system which later became common and which was by Shakespeare's day long-established.[1] Under tanistry, a ruler's successor was elected from a parallel family line, so that, for example, nephew (and not necessarily eldest nephew) succeeded uncle.[2] When Duncan nominates (1.4.35–9) his eldest son, Malcolm, as his successor, he abruptly introduces a system half-way between tanistry and primogeniture. In this instance, Duncan wishes eldest son to succeed father, excluding any younger brothers (e.g. Donaldbain) or cousins, but the very nomination indicates that eldest son succeeding father (primogeniture) is not established practice.[3] Henry VIII's controversial attempts to settle the royal succession made such questions vivid for an English audience, as did the recent, much-debated succession of James himself.[4] The system in early Scotland has been described as 'circulation with elimination' where 'Tension between incumbent and successor is relieved at the expense of increased conflict between the potential successors themselves',[5] as indeed we see in *Macbeth*.

Primogeniture, tanistry, and Duncan's intermediate proposal all attempt to assure a monarchy's and therefore a family's continuity, its triumph over time, but primogeniture and Duncan's *ad hoc* proposal both value father-to-eldest-son successions exclusively and thus strongly imply the age-old metaphor of the king as 'father' to his subjects (*pater patriae*), making a complex association linking royal progenitor, royal authority, and royal succession.

Here, experiences and words in which all people share to some degree – parenthood and birth, adolescence, maturation and death – metaphorically legitimate a particular

---

[1] Primogeniture became settled English law in the 'last years of Henry II' (Frederick Pollock and F. W. Maitland, *The History of English Law before the Time of Edward I*, 2nd edn with new introduction by S. F. C. Milsom, 2 vols. (1898; 1968), II, 274). For tanistry's implications in Scottish historiography and Jacobean political thought and debate, see Norbrook, pp. 86–8. Hawkins, 'History, politics and *Macbeth*', in *Focus*, p. 175, citing an earlier scholarly debate, rightly says 'Shakespeare refers [in the play] neither to the law of tanistry nor to Duncan's own unlawful tenure of the throne', but the dialogue's silence says nothing about what knowledge shaped the play and nothing about what the audience might know of arcane (and therefore interesting?) Scottish practice.

[2] I have simplified tanistry and its possible permutations. For its operation and anthropological functions in Ireland, Scotland, and elsewhere, see the Introduction to Jack Goody (ed.), *Succession to High Office*, 1966, and J. H. Stevenson, 'The law of the throne – tanistry and the introduction of the law of primogeniture', *SHR* 25 (1927–8), 1–12; for tanistry and primogeniture in sixteenth-century Scottish political debate and Shakespeare's and Holinshed's sources, see Norbrook.

[3] On this important point, see Michael Hawkins, 'History, politics and *Macbeth*', in *Focus*, p. 175. Hawkins goes on, unhappily, to imagine what happens off-stage to produce Macbeth's selection as king after Duncan's death, but notes that the unseen, unspoken, events are 'the nearest the play comes to tanistry'.

[4] Hawkins, 'History, politics and *Macbeth*', p. 175, and A. R. Braunmuller (ed.), *John*, 1989, pp. 56–60.

[5] Goody, *Succession to High Office*, pp. 33 and 45.

political structure. Shakespeare makes these metaphors, extended to include 'servants'
as 'children' of the father–king, pervasive in the play. They explain Macbeth's succinct
avowal, 'our duties / Are to your [Duncan's] throne and state, children and servants'
(1.4.24–5), and his later self-accusing lines on why he should not murder Duncan.
Duncan's status as kinsman, ruler, and guest all argue 'against the deed':

> First, as I am his kinsman and his subject,
> Strong both against the deed; then, as his host,
> Who should against his murderer shut the door,
> Not bear the knife myself.

(1.7.13–16)

So also, to take two rather disparate examples, Macbeth agonises over the 'unlineal
hand' (3.1.64) which will deny his (possibly imaginary)[1] son the crown, and his wife
says she cannot kill King Duncan because he resembles her father (2.2.12–13) – as the
metaphorical argument of royal authority insists he must.

The sisters (or 'witches') attack this tight, mystifying association of parents and
children with rulers and subjects when they predict that one adult male, Macbeth,
will become king while another adult male, Banquo, will not be king but a begetter
of kings. What they represent as paradoxical, that Banquo is 'lesser' and 'greater'
than Macbeth and 'Not so happy, yet much happier' (1.3.63–4), is a paradox only
under the assumptions of both primogeniture and an unfailing succession of male
heirs, generation upon generation. So construed, Macbeth's kingship – or his hope
of it – is itself deeply paradoxical, since he is not son to a king, and Banquo's line
will reign in Scotland only if Macbeth's line, as well as Duncan's, fails or is deposed.
Succession entails mortality. As Macbeth casually says, 'By Finel's death, I know I
am Thane of Glamis' (1.3.69): by the death of my (or the) father I (the son) am who
I am.[2]

The crisis of succession in *Macbeth* is expressed as a crisis of metaphor. When
Macbeth first speaks of regicide explicitly rather than figuratively, he treats father–son
succession, the quasi-primogeniture of Duncan's naming Malcolm Prince of Cumberland, as the obstacle: 'that is a step / On which I must fall down, or else o'erleap, /
For in my way it lies' (1.4.48–50). Duncan the metaphorical father–king has created
a metaphorical son–successor – has combined fatherhood with political succession.
If primogeniture and metaphor combined lead Macbeth to contemplate regicide, the
same union of patrilineal succession and thinking-through-metaphor leads him to kill
Lady Macduff and her children:

---

[1] Whether Lord and Lady Macbeth have (or have had) children in the play's fictional world is a long-lasting
theatrical and critical question, much debated as a practical and thematic issue and much ridiculed as a
non-existent one. See e.g. Knights, 'How many children had Lady Macbeth', and Marvin Rosenberg, *The
Masks of 'Macbeth'*, 1978, Appendix, 'Lady Macbeth's indispensable child', pp. 671–6, calling for a cradle
and the sound of a child in 1.5 and the cradle's return in 5.1. This demand has to my knowledge only once
been even partly met: Bengt Ekerod's 1955 Stockholm production included 'a cradle next to which the
Lady read her husband's letter [in 1.5]. There was no other sign of the baby . . .' (Ann Fridén, '*Macbeth*'
in the Swedish Theatre 1838–1986, 1986, p. 235).
[2] Compare Katharine Eisaman Maus, 'Transfer of title in *Love's Labor's Lost*: language, individualism,
gender', in Ivo Kamps (ed.), *Shakespeare Left and Right*, 1991, pp. 210–11.

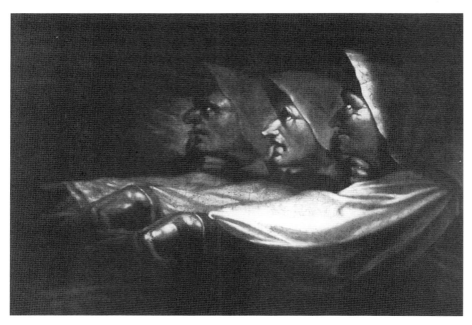

2   *The Witches of 'Macbeth'*: Henry Fuseli's eighteenth-century interpretation of the sisters in Act 1, Scene 3

> From this moment,
> The very firstlings of my heart shall be
> The firstlings of my hand. And even now
> To crown my thoughts with acts, be it thought and done.
> The castle of Macduff I will surprise;
> Seize upon Fife; give to th'edge o'th'sword
> His wife, his babes, and all unfortunate souls
> That trace him in his line.   (4.1.145–52)

While 'firstlings' most plainly conveys 'first things' – here, Macbeth's immediate impulses or thoughts – an archaic meaning of 'firstlings' is children, 'firstborn'. Macbeth's reflection moves from one meaning to the other, from the sudden joining of heart and hand, the unreflective joining of thoughts and acts, to generational murder, to giving 'to th'edge o'th'sword' Macduff's 'wife, his babes, and all unfortunate souls / That trace him in his line'. The same metaphorical extensions and 'arguments' that pertained when he earlier vowed loyalty to Duncan's 'throne and state, children and servants' now lead Macbeth to murder Macduff's family and retainers. Loyalty and tyranny each follow 'naturally' from the play's controlling familial–political metaphors.

As Macbeth understands the sisters' words, deceptive words 'That palter with us in a double sense' (5.8.20), they suggest he will gain the throne through interrupting generation, through stopping human continuation in time, though he rarely reflects upon the corollary that he himself would or might thus lack a lineal successor.

Consequently, he first envisages, and then undertakes to create, a world in which acts have no consequences, no duration beyond the moment of their enactment, no reach in time and beyond time into eternity:

> If it were done when 'tis done, then 'twere well
> It were done quickly. If th'assassination
> Could trammel up the consequence and catch
> With his surcease, success, that but this blow
> Might be the be-all and the end-all – here,
> But here, upon this bank and shoal of time,
> We'd jump the life to come.   (1.7.1–7)

For a moment, these hypothetical thoughts dissuade him:

>   But in these cases,
> We still have judgement here that we but teach
> Bloody instructions, which being taught, return
> To plague th'inventor. This even-handed justice
> Commends th'ingredience of our poisoned chalice
> To our own lips.   (1.7.7–12)

Lady Macbeth soon ridicules (1.7.35ff.) her husband's anxiety about the consequences of his actions and persuades him to 'screw' his 'courage to the sticking-place' (1.7.60) because she has already accepted (in Act 1, Scene 5) that regicide is necessarily an attack on time's progression and duration.

'Rapt' by witch-inspired (or witch-encouraged) royal visions, Macbeth writes an account of his meeting that similarly inspires his wife.[1] He serves her as the witches served him, and she responds as he did:

> Thy letters have transported me beyond
> This ignorant present, and I feel now
> The future in the instant.   (1.5.54–6)

This extraordinary remark, anachronistically condensing the future into the present, hints how time and human experience in time will be compressed and squeezed later in the play, so squeezed and compressed that the be-all *will* be the end-all, and time itself a syllable:

> Tomorrow, and tomorrow, and tomorrow
> Creeps in this petty pace from day to day
> To the last syllable of recorded time . . .   (5.5.18–20)

For Macbeth, repeated syllables ('Tomorrow, and tomorrow, and tomorrow') represent time's slowing and, at 'the last syllable', time's end. For Lady Macbeth, repeated acts – 'It is an accustomed action with her, to seem thus washing her hands; I have

---

[1] See Barbara Everett, *Young Hamlet*, 1989, p. 104: 'One of the play's most touching and subtle moments is that which brings Lady Macbeth before us for the first time, and she is reading Macbeth's letter: he exists for her when he isn't there. He exists too much for her when he isn't there, she plans and thinks ahead too much for him, she too much connives, putting her image of Macbeth's future where her conscience should be . . .'

known her continue in this a quarter of an hour' (5.1.24–6)[1] – and repeated words – 'Out, damned spot! Out, I say! . . . No more o'that, my lord, no more o'that' (5.1.30, 37–8) – represent the same collapse of change (and of hope and ambition) into a repetition where automatic words and acts eerily imitate life:

> DOCTOR You see her eyes are open.
> GENTLEWOMAN Ay, but their sense are shut.   (5.1.21–2)

Many actors and many critics have taken Lady Macbeth's behaviour here as a lightly rationalised version of demonic possession; for them, Act 5, Scene 1, is the final result of her invocation of the 'spirits / That tend on mortal thoughts' (1.5.38–9). The effect of Macbeth's letter upon Lady Macbeth, so similar to the effect upon him of the sisters' even more ambiguous words, suggests that he is (or becomes) a witch, just as a confusion of ends with means, 'trifles' with 'deepest' consequences, transforms Lady Macbeth into a witch in Act 5, Scene 1 (see pp. 33–5 below).

If, in *Macbeth*, kings are fathers of son–successors and of children–subjects and if, 'In *Macbeth* . . . usurpation is imagined as an attack on the order of time itself',[2] it follows that the play must consider the impossible possibility of unparented children because through procreation, through becoming parents, humanity ordinarily takes its revenge on time's passing and on the inevitability of any generation's death and every generation's replacement by another generation also destined for death and replacement. If 'the order of time itself' is to be attacked, so must the order of procreation also become vulnerable and put in question. Macbeth's need to make the moment the be-all and end-all, to condense future and hence duration into the instant, means human procreation must cease – in fact, cannot exist. Lady Macbeth's ambitious hope (1.5.54–6) compresses the future into the instant. Her husband's acts compress past, present, and future into one timeless, unchanging moment. Lady Macbeth's hope and Macbeth's acts are secular and, for the Christian audience, sacrilegious versions of the world's end:

> Awake, awake!
> Ring the alarum bell! Murder and treason!
> Banquo and Donaldbain! Malcolm, awake,
> Shake off this downy sleep, death's counterfeit,
> And look on death itself. Up, up, and see
> The great doom's image. Malcolm, Banquo,
> As from your graves rise up and walk like sprites
> To countenance this horror.   (2.3.67–74)[3]

In a moment, Donaldbain asks, 'What is amiss?' (2.3.90), and Macbeth describes the familial and the dynastic stalemate his regicide has created:

---

[1] The Gentlewoman's 'a quarter of an hour' insists upon the ordinary world's time-keeping, a systematic regularity destroyed by and denied to the Macbeths, who have adopted and promulgated a very different 'accustomed action'.

[2] Michael Neill, 'Remembrance and revenge: *Hamlet, Macbeth* and *The Tempest*', in Ian Donaldson (ed.), *Jonson and Shakespeare*, 1983, p. 41.

[3] For the biblical elements here, see 2.3.72 n. and 2.3.75 n. below.

3   The bleeding Captain at 1.2.22 describes how Macbeth 'unseamed' an enemy 'from the nave to th'chaps': 'nave' might be either the umbilicus or (as in this image) the crotch. The engraving is from the title page of Robert Fludd's *Utriusque cosmi historia* (1617–19). See G. L. Hersey, *Pythagorean Palaces: Magic and Architecture in the Italian Renaissance*, 1976, p. 99, on the difference between images of man-in-circle found in editions of Vitruvius, where the umbilicus is the centre of the circle, and man-in-circle-and-square by Leonardo da Vinci, where the umbilicus is the centre of the circle, but the base of the penis is the centre of the square

> You are, and do not know't.
> The spring, the head, the fountain of your blood
> Is stopped, the very source of it is stopped.   (2.3.90–2)

The sons' bloodline, the royal line, is 'stopped' and does not flow into the future through successive sons who become kings. Considering the possibility that Malcolm and Donaldbain have themselves killed their father, Ross sees a form of filial cannibalism and equates it with the sons' self-thwarting desire to become king: 'Thriftless ambition that will ravin up / Thine own life's means' (2.4.28–9).

Macduff and his family illustrate what Macbeth's attack on time and procreation might mean at the level of the person. Macduff himself fulfils the Second Apparition's seemingly impossible condition – 'none of woman born / Shall harm Macbeth' (4.1.79–80) – because Macduff was 'Untimely ripped' (5.8.16) from his dead or dying mother's womb. Macduff was born not of a 'woman' but of a near corpse.[1] Once Macduff flees to England, Lady Macduff continues the play's profound linking of family and state when she translates political act into familial terms. She describes her husband's son, now abandoned by Macduff, as 'Fathered he is, and yet he's fatherless' (4.2.27), asserting the paternal paradox (fathered/fatherless) that matches her husband's paradoxical birth (mothered/motherless). Moments later, Macbeth's dynastically inspired murders sweep away mother and son, 'Those precious motives, those strong knots of love' (4.3.27), whose abandonment later leads Malcolm to suspect Macduff, a man not of woman born.

These episodes and paradoxes express some of the play's most obsessive interests, if not exactly its 'values': the way political and dynastic succession-in-time depends upon a cycle (birth, death, birth); the importance of motherhood and fathering, and the unanticipated ways (Caesarean birth, 'unlineal' usurpation) each may become unpredictable; the echoing statements and restatements among the sisters or witches, Lady Macbeth, and Lady Macduff. Lady Macduff, ostensibly the play's single 'good' female character, speaks to Ross – albeit anxiously and domestically – much the same fatally equivocal language as the sisters offer Banquo and Macbeth in Act 1, Scene 3, and Macbeth alone in Act 4, Scene 1. Her human uncertainty here soon reappears when Malcolm and Macduff spar, circularly and inconclusively, in Act 4, Scene 3.

Macduff is as isolated in time as Macbeth. Macduff's paradoxical birth meets the Second Apparition's strange condition for one who might harm Macbeth, and Macduff does quell tyranny and restore, violently, Duncan's interrupted (but also dubiously legitimate) succession. Yet that same birth and the actions it entails place Macduff so far outside traditional genealogical or familial narrative that his wife denies him as husband, as father of their son, as, indeed, a wise, a loyal, or even a natural man (see 4.2.1–27,

---

[1] Thus, the shade of Posthumus's mother describes his birth as having taken place after her death: 'Lucina lent me not her aid, / But took me in my throes, / That from me was Posthumus ript' (*Cymbeline* 5.4.43–5); compare the First Gravedigger's ingenuity on when suicide is not suicide (*Hamlet* 5.1.9–20), and Richard, Duke of Gloucester, who was a breech (or 'Agrippan') birth, whose mother 'coulde not bee delivered of hym uncutte', according to Thomas More (*The History of King Richard III*, ed. Richard S. Sylvester, in *Complete Works of St Thomas More*, II (1963), 7 and 167), and who was 'sent before [his] time / Into this breathing world, scarce half made up' (*R3* 1.1.20–1).

discussed above). Macbeth initially claims a secure, explicable place in genealogy and succession: 'By Finel's death, I know I am Thane of Glamis' (1.3.69). From this moment forward, however, that security melts away, dissolved by a complex acid of ambition, miscalculation, and murder, until – in a strange echo of Macduff – Macbeth ends outside lineal successions, stripped of family ties, helplessly wading in blood, finally treading-in-place without advance or retreat or change. The 'good' (2.4.20), but flawed revenger Macduff and the criminal hero mirror each other and confound empathy and interpretation. According to Ross, Macbeth's rule melds birth and family with tyranny – under him, Scotland 'cannot / Be called our mother, but our grave' (4.3.167–8) – but of course Macduff's mother's body is also a place of birth and death, a place 'untimely'. Macduff is thus 'untimely' in every possible way. He entered life, as his mother left it, in a temporally abnormal way; he enters Macbeth's final moments in a time-destroying and fatally time-anticipating way; he installs Malcolm as king and thus makes Macbeth's supposed line 'untimely'.

MASTER OF HIS TIME: 'DOUBLY REDOUBLED STROKES'
As Macbeth's concern for the 'be-all and end-all' and Macduff's unusual mothered/motherless condition demonstrate, *Macbeth* is deeply interested in the nature of time – time as experienced by the person (our individual progress from life to death), time as experienced by the family (an individual person's perpetuation through child-bearing), time as experienced by the state (the succession of one monarch by another), and finally and most largely, time as we experience the play's performance.

Dismissing his lords and ladies until evening comes and it is time for the banquet celebrating and validating his kingship, Macbeth orders:

> Let every man be master of his time
> Till seven at night; to make society
> The sweeter welcome, we will keep ourself
> Till supper-time alone.   (3.1.42–5)

Characteristically and disastrously, he does not acknowledge that 'A man is master of his liberty; / Time is their master' (*Comedy of Errors* 2.1.7–8): time masters human beings (we die), but time also masters our disposition of our 'free' time, our liberty, our freedom of choice. Also characteristically, Macbeth now keeps and will keep himself 'alone', as he is now and will be: 'why do you keep alone, / Of sorriest fancies your companions making' (3.2.8–9), and 'honour, love, obedience, troops of friends, / I must not look to have' (5.3.25–6).

'Style' in *Macbeth* has been called 'vehement to violence, compressed to congestion',[1] but so also is the play's very ordering as an audience experiences it. Verbal style and narrative arrangement are indistinguishable. The play's more technical or dramaturgical handling of time makes the reader's or spectator's temporal experience unlike that in any other Shakespearean tragedy. *Macbeth* (about 2,108 lines long) is the third shortest

---

[1] Frederick J. Harries, *Shakespeare and the Scots*, 1932, p. 117. Harries's chapter 10 collects nineteenth-century literary views of the play's language and plot.

of the plays included in the First Folio; only *The Comedy of Errors* (approximately 1,777 lines) and *The Tempest* (approximately 2,062 lines) are shorter, and *Julius Caesar* (approximately 2,477 lines) is the only other tragedy with fewer than 3,000 lines. Brief as a play, *Macbeth* also has many brief scenes. Traditional division produces scenes which average about 75 lines: 'This multiplicity of scenes must be a deliberate dramatic device to give an impression of rapid and bustling action, as in *Antony and Cleopatra*', where scenes average 'no more than 73 lines'. The 'shortest scenes in *Macbeth* have 12 and 10 lines: *Antony and Cleopatra* has two scenes of 4 lines only'.[1]

How powerfully this brevity and rapidity may affect an audience appears in Maurice Morgann's eighteenth-century comment on Shakespeare's practice:

The Understanding must, in the first place, be subdued; and lo! how the rooted prejudices of the child spring up to confound the man! The Weird sisters rise, and order is extinguished. The laws of nature give way, and leave nothing in our minds but wildness and horror. No pause is allowed us for reflection: . . . daggers, murder, ghosts, and inchantment, shake and possess us wholly . . . we, the fools of amazement, are insensible to the shifting of place and the lapse of time, and till the curtain drops, never once wake to the truth of things, or recognise the laws of existence.[2]

Event and image – 'daggers, murder, ghosts, and inchantment' – crowd one another and subdue Enlightenment rationality. '[R]ooted prejudices', here associated with the pre-rational child, domineer over adult understanding, which recognises 'the laws of existence', and make spectators 'the fools of amazement'.

Since Shakespeare explores humanity-in-time through narratives of royal succession, birth and death in time, or since Shakespeare dramatises narratives of royal succession and thereby explores the paradoxes of humanity-in-time, the way Shakespeare orders those narratives has special importance, and the ordering of *Macbeth* proves rather strange. George Walton Williams claims that King James's intellectual and dynastic interests influenced Shakespeare 'in so commanding a manner as severely to strain the coherence of the play'.[3] Williams sees two conflicting narratives ('two parallel fables') and two conflicting political interests in *Macbeth*. One narrative is the kinging and unkinging of Macbeth; the other narrative is the attack on Banquo's line and that line's eventual accession and supposed Jacobean survival through Malcolm's successful counter-attack on Macbeth.[4] The former narrative places our first view of King Macbeth at the play's centre and in the middle of the audience's temporal experience, the banquet scene (Act 3, Scene 4); untypically for Shakespeare's dramaturgy, the regicide occurs quite early in *Macbeth* (Act 2, Scene 3), a subordinate dramatic position rather than in the 'middle' or at the 'end' of the play (as in *Julius*

[1] Greg, *First Folio*, p. 389 and nn. 1 and 3; line counts and comparisons here are Greg's. Knight, *Imperial*, pp. 327–42, extensively compares *Macbeth* and *Antony*.
[2] Maurice Morgann, *An Essay on the Dramatic Character of Sir John Falstaff*, 1777, sig. F3r.
[3] George Walton Williams, '*Macbeth*: King James's play', *South Atlantic Review* 47.2 (1982), 12–21; quotation from p. 13.
[4] *Ibid.*, p. 14.

Caesar and *Richard II* respectively) – both more 'important' locations for Shakespeare's dramaturgy.[1]

The second narrative emphasises Malcolm's revenging of Duncan's death, a revenging which (according to Holinshed's narrative and James's legendary descent from Banquo's son, Fleance) eventually led from Malcolm's kingship to a descendant of Fleance becoming the father of King Robert II, 'the first of the Stuart kings',[2] and therefore to James's ancestor. The new King James I of England, insecure as King of Scotland throughout his reign there, could hardly have enjoyed a narrative of eleventh-century Scottish king-killing, but he might have welcomed a competing narrative of his own supposed ancestry, leading to the 'show of kings', where Banquo's and Fleance's and James's line stretches out, as Macbeth fears, 'to th'crack of doom' (4.1.116) and culminates in Malcolm's final triumph and thus in James's dynastic claims and present rule. Though I doubt that Shakespeare very much tailored *Macbeth* to James's special interests – the play contains too many subversive possibilities for that – Williams identifies a central structural problem in *Macbeth*. There *are* two competing narratives. One subordinates Duncan's death to Macbeth's becoming king; the other, contradictorily, elevates (in the apparitions and kingly show of Act 4, Scene 1) the future greatness of Banquo and therefore of his descendants, the Stuarts.[3]

Williams's proposals are literary and historical, readerly and source-influenced. Emrys Jones's study of *Macbeth* stresses theatrical 'rhythms' (the prosodic or musical metaphor is at once appropriate and distracting) and finds a 'three-part division' in the play:

Part One ('Duncan') occupies Acts One and Two, Part Two ('Banquo') Act Three, and Part Three ('Macduff') Acts Four and Five. The first and second of these three parts are followed by a marked pause . . . Act Three forms a fairly short unit in itself . . . the opening of Act Four has an inevitable recapitulatory effect, taking us back to the beginning of the play with its similar witchcraft concerns . . .[4]

Jones here mixes structural or rhythmical insights with unprovable suggestions about intermissions or 'intervals' in Jacobean performances (that is, moments when the play

---

[1] *Ibid.*, p. 16. The earliest theatrical scripts of *Richard II, Julius Caesar,* and *Macbeth* almost certainly were not divided into 'Acts', but rather (at most) 'Scenes'; the later, printed, act and scene divisions, however, merely number a spatial and temporal sequence: however artificial '*Macbeth* Act 3, Scene 4' is as a reference, the text it delimits is still about the 'middle' of a knowledgeable audience's temporal experience of the play, just as '*Julius Caesar* Act 2, Scene 3' is earlier than the 'middle' of an audience's experience of the entire play. Here and elsewhere I assume an audience, presumably Shakespeare's own earliest audience, long accustomed to the rhythms of early modern London theatre.

[2] Williams, 'Play', p. 18.

[3] *Ibid.*, p. 19: 'By inserting the legend of Banquho into the middle of the legend of Mackbeth, Shakespeare has strained the traditional structure of this sort of play. He has transferred the murder of the king from its accustomed position in the middle of the play to a location of secondary significance, and he has inserted the murder of Banquo in the king's rightful and central place.'

[4] Jones, *Scenic*, pp. 195–6; Jones's chapter 7 contributes essentially to the study of *Macbeth*. Mark Rose, *Shakespearean Design*, 1972, pp. 160–2, claims that the banquet scene (3.4) divides the play into two 'movements' and 'each movement has its own centerpiece, the murder scene [which Rose, pp. 39–43, regards as an undivided 2.1–2.3] coming just in the center of the first and the England scene [4.3] in the second' (p. 161).

ceases and non-dramatic or more everyday events – having a drink, eating an orange or some nuts, going to the toilet, hearing a musical interlude – can occur). Nevertheless, Jones's insights do identify a tripartite theatrical structure or rhythm that valuably counterpoints Williams's equally persuasive bipartite narrative structure. And the play's language seems to endorse both views through its constant counterpoint of doubleness and triplicity. When Macbeth reminds himself that Duncan is his guest in 'double trust', he cites three, not two, relations of trust:

> He's here in double trust:
> First, as I am his kinsman and his subject,
> Strong both against the deed; then, as his host,
> Who should against his murderer shut the door,
> Not bear the knife myself.   (1.7.12–16)

And then he immediately says, 'Besides, this Duncan / Hath borne his faculties so meek . . .' Having made 'double' into three reasons, he now adds a fourth.

Multiples – doubles, triples, quadruples – are deeply characteristic of the play's language, most famously in the sisters' 'Double, double toil and trouble' (4.1.10), but multiplying verbal play with singles and doubles also appears in a highly polite, emotionally charged moment when Lady Macbeth turns an excessively arithmetical compliment to the man and king she has already prepared to kill:

> All our service,
> In every point twice done and then done double,
> Were poor and single business . . .   (1.6.15–17)

'Twoness' – multiples of 'two' (here, 'twice done', 'done double') – appears often in *Macbeth*; James Nosworthy also identifies triadic elements – the three sisters themselves, for instance, and their 'Thrice to thine . . .' (1.3.33–4) or their three threes in 'nine times nine' (1.3.21) – 'in contexts that are evil, and usually satanic'.[1] In an early, apparently straightforward narrative moment, we hear a 'report' confounding easy mathematics where 'double' becomes 'doubly redoubled' and more:

> If I say sooth, I must report they were
> As cannons over-charged with double cracks;
> So they doubly redoubled strokes upon the foe.   (1.2.36–8)

Are the cannons 'over-charged' twice, or four times, or eight times, or sixteen times, ('double', 'doubly', 'redoubled')? These numberings are faint echoes of the sisters' doublings and of the equivocal double meanings of

> these juggling fiends . . .
> That palter with us in a double sense,
> That keep the word of promise to our ear
> And break it to our hope.   (5.8.19–22)

---

[1] J. M. Nosworthy, '*Macbeth, Doctor Faustus*, and the juggling fiends', in *Mirror*, p. 221. See also e.g. 1.2.37–8 n., 1.6.16 n. and 4.1.2 n. below.

Numbers and numbering recur throughout *Macbeth*. How many times does a bell ring for Macbeth or Lady Macbeth, how many kings stretch out before Macbeth in Act 4, Scene 1, how many gashes are enough to kill a man, how often will the dead rise up in Act 3, Scene 4, and after? Each of these timings and each of these numberings finally reduces to a character's (especially Macbeth's) linguistic attempt to make time numerable. Were time or timing (an actor's and a dramatic character's special need) so submissive to number, they might also submit to a human ordering or even to human control. Time, however, can be neither numbered nor controlled, as *Macbeth* manifests.

Like literary critics, theatrical critics have puzzled over the structure of *Macbeth* and its special challenges for actors. Without the language of rhythm or of bipartite or tripartite structure, James Agate shouldered the journalist's burden of instant criticism and identified a capital problem:

> I have to admit that for the first time in my experience Macbeth [here, John Gielgud] retained his hold upon this play till the end. There is a technical reason for the difficulty, the fact that Macbeth is given hardly anything to grip the play with. With the banqueting scene [Act 3, Scene 4], which is only half-way, the part is almost over. After that we have the apparition scene [Act 4, Scene 1], in which Macbeth is virtually a spectator. Then comes the murder of Lady Macduff [Act 4, Scene 2], the long business about Malcolm, the revelation to Macduff [i.e. Act 4, Scene 3], and the sleep-walking scene. Macbeth's next appearance is with Seyton, and whether the play is to stand or fall depends upon the power of the actor to suggest the ravages of mind, soul, and even body endured since we saw him last.[1]

From an actor's point of view, Michael Redgrave echoed Agate's worries,[2] but critics have found Act 5 'a carefully thought out and superbly rhythmical solution to a large structural problem'. This 'solution' is 'a ritualistic unfolding: everything is taken in its due time', a structure 'which gives this final phase a movement suggestive of preordained ceremony'.[3] The *Macbeth* here rhythmically and structurally described is also a play deeply committed to order, the order of refined dramatic structure and the order of political and historically endorsed orthodoxy.

Most unusually for a Shakespearean tragedy, *Macbeth* contains little overt comedy (principally the Porter in Act 2, Scene 3) and little bawdy (principally the Porter, again, and the sisters in Act 1, Scene 3, and in Act 4, Scene 1, where the lines may not be Shakespeare's at all).[4] The absence of comedy may result from the absence of a subplot.

---

[1] James Agate, review of *Macbeth*, directed by Harcourt Williams, 19 March 1930, Old Vic (London), rpt. in Agate, *Brief Chronicles*, 1943, p. 227. Agate goes on to praise Gielgud's Macbeth in Act 5. To some degree, Agate here complains about a fact of early Stuart drama: Antony is absent from the final act of *Antony and Cleopatra* and the Duchess is missing from the last act of Webster's *The Duchess of Malfi*; Coriolanus has relatively few lines in the last act of *Coriolanus*.

[2] See pp. 55–7 below.   [3] Jones, *Scenic*, pp. 223–4.

[4] On theatrical attempts to introduce comedy, see p. 68 below, and for the original Porter, see Appendix 1, p. 280. Very rarely, Macbeth himself is a successful comic. In Adrian Noble's RSC production (with Sinead Cusack as Lady Macbeth), a 'Freudian study in childlessness' (Michael Billington, *The Guardian*, 27 September 1995), for instance, one critic found Jonathan Pryce (Macbeth) 'a bogeyman, a joker, a card, a childless husband who delights in the company of children. In the banquet scene [3.4], flailing his hands and shaking his head like a dog coming out of water, he clowns his way out of a real fit into a false one so plausibly that though we know the jest will be shattered on the third [*sic*] appearance of Banquo's ghost, the foaming fury of Macbeth's reaction prickles the scalp when it comes' (*The Observer*, 16 September

While it is true, and consonant with Renaissance learned theory, that Shakespeare's tragedies often contain but do not develop stunted or stifled gestures toward sub-plots, and while *Macbeth* is also arguably Shakespeare's most history-play-like tragedy, his 'true' histories spawn additional plots great and small. Here are no tavern roisterers (Falstaff, Poins, Bardolph, and their ilk), hardly any common, non-aristocratic characters, no sybaritic hangers-on, no bastards, few talkative, satirical soldiers, no brawlers of whatever social status, no social or cultural outsiders.

Except for the three sisters, the reporting soldier of Act 1, Scene 2, the Porter (briefly), and the Old Man of Act 2, Scene 4 (also briefly), *Macbeth* largely lacks the commonsensical, humorous, salacious, scatological, 'foreign' or non-naturalised voices that typically diminish and thereby evaluate the speech, values, and behaviour of high-status, 'heroic' characters in Shakespeare's other tragedies and histories.[1] When Macduff threatens to make dead or captured Macbeth 'the show and gaze o'th'time', a 'rarer monster . . . / Painted upon a pole' (5.8.24–6),[2] he offers a humiliation Cleopatra fears (see p. 7 above), but not a 'popular' re-evaluation of Macbeth's deeds. Macduff's imagined carnivalesque display diminishes Macbeth without judging and therefore without valuing his acts: the victim (Macbeth) is diminished, the audience amused but unenlightened.

'Except for the three sisters'. The sisters – only once named 'witch' (1.3.5) in the dialogue, though always *Witch* and *Witches* in speech headings and stage directions – provide the ironic and satiric, the unconventional or demystifying, views otherwise almost absent from *Macbeth*, barring the highly personal, psychological modes of Lady Macbeth's somniloquy (Act 5, Scene 1) and her husband's increasingly grim reflections on what he has done and has to do.[3] Terry Eagleton declares 'that positive value in *Macbeth* lies with the three witches' and that 'The witches are the heroines of the piece', because they 'expose a reverence for hierarchical social order for what it is' and inhabit 'their own sisterly community' on that social order's 'shadowy borderlands', though he does not explain what 'positive value' or the sisters' status as 'heroines' might mean.[4] These imagined 'sisters', with their communal and antimilitaristic values, may be contrasted with the comic (or perhaps anxiously dismissive) treatment of witches

1986). For a general view of this production, see Roger Warren, 'Shakespeare in England, 1986–87', *SQ* 38 (1987), 363.
[1] Among Shakespeare's other tragedies, Cleopatra's conversation (*Ant.* 5.2.242–79) with the countryman–clown who provides the asp that poisons her most nearly approaches the dramatic effect – high seriousness clashing with humdrum concerns laconically expressed – of the Porter's monologue with himself. That the Porter's speeches are monologue rather than dialogue, however, forces the audience to join disparate verbal and emotional registers and, as so often in *Macbeth*, denies the audience even minimal guidance from the dramatist; see Appendix 1, p. 280 below. In the handling of comic viewpoints that both deflate high seriousness and evaluate it, *Macbeth* and *Antony and Cleopatra* represent one range of dramaturgical choices, *Lear* (with the Fool) and *Coriolanus* (with the Citizens and tribunes) another.
[2] On this speech, see 5.8.25–7 n.; see also Halio and p. 7 above.
[3] Lady Macbeth's actions have been found a 'sub-plot': 'In *Macbeth* there is a great deal of focus devoted to the actions of the tyrant to the exclusion of any sub-plot activity, but we are concerned also with the power of Lady Macbeth in urging on her husband and then with the decline of her influence and its consequences as he isolates himself from her' (Anthony Brennan, *Onstage and Offstage Worlds in Shakespeare's Plays*, 1989, p. 308).
[4] Terry Eagleton, *William Shakespeare*, 1986, p. 2. Frances E. Dolan, *Dangerous Familiars: Representations of Domestic Crime in England 1550–1700*, 1994, pp. 224–5, agrees that 'the drama frequently locates witches in a space apart, a female-dominated world placed both outside of the household and at the margins of

and witchcraft in other early modern English plays and with Samuel Johnson's view of the comic, 'ridiculed' witches that prevailed in the eighteenth-century theatre Johnson knew.[1] One way of dealing with a real or perceived fear of witchcraft is to make witches not fearsome but silly, comic, and ridiculous; the eighteenth-century English theatre typically took this course, perhaps unthinkingly, perhaps out of the practical need to provide work for the company's comic actors. In nineteenth-century productions, the witches eventually achieved both respectful and terrific treatment.

PROSPECT OF BELIEF: WITCHES, WOMEN, AND MEDIATED KNOWLEDGE
For most audiences of *Macbeth*, the ideas of witchcraft, more particularly the violent and sometimes socially pervasive persecutions of the 'witch' those ideas sponsored (and that prevailed in Europe and North America from the fifteenth to the eighteenth century), are incomprehensible, repellent, temporally 'foreign' and even alien. And yet rural and/or unlettered people and the most intellectually sophisticated European élites accepted the existence of witches and witchcraft and proceeded, more often legally than illegally, to impose their beliefs, with fatal results. Stuart Clark eloquently rebukes the unthinking modern view:

> The idea of witchcraft was not then a bizarre incongruity in an otherwise normal world; like all manifestations of misrule it *was* that world mirrored in reverse, and the practices of the alleged witches were no less (and no more) meaningful than those of ordinary men and women.[2]

Persecution of the witch and of witchcraft made 'meaningful' the ordinary, seemingly natural, daily practice of the great mass of individuals – learned or not, poor or rich, influential or powerless, or somewhere among these classifications – who defined themselves as not-witch, not practising witchcraft, not politically and socially aberrant or, in Clark's terms, not 'inverted'.

In early modern England, witches and witchcraft were political matters as well as personal, familial, and communal ones. Biblical precedent identified witchcraft with treason: 'For rebellion is as the sinne of witchcraft' (1 Sam. 15.23). Following that precedent as well as their own self-interested desire for public order, Tudor and Stuart governments sought to regulate and, if possible, extirpate various practices labelled 'witchcraft' by common folk, local magistrates, the legal apparatus, and learned authorities.[3] Ordinary people, scholars, courtiers, and royalty all considered witches or other figures associated with a hard-to-define 'magic' or supernatural – 'cunning' or 'wise' women and men, magicians, sorcerers, etc. – to be sometimes useful, but often

---

dramatic representation' but argues that 'in *Macbeth*, unlike [Thomas Middleton's] *The Witch* or [John Marston's] *Sophonisba*, the boundary between the world of the witches and the world of the other characters is indistinct.'

[1] See Dolan, pp. 217 and 220–3, and headnote to 1.1 below.
[2] See Stuart Clark, 'Inversion, misrule and the meaning of witchcraft', *P&P* 87 (1980), 98–127; quotation from p. 127.
[3] See Stuart Clark, 'King James's *Daemonologie*: witchcraft and kingship', in Sydney Anglo (ed.), *The Damned Art: Essays in the Literature of Witchcraft*, 1977, pp. 156–81, esp. p. 176, where Clark quotes a passage from William Perkins's *Discourse of the Damned Art of Witchcraft* comprehensively identifying enmity to the state with the witch's acceptance of the devil. Clark, 'Inversion', esp. pp. 117–19, elaborates this view.

threatening, to a variety of familial, social, and political structures, assumptions, and values.[1]

Historians find it difficult to decide whether the witch-persecutions of the late six-teenth century in England and Scotland were driven by popular or élite anxieties and purposes, varied as those anxieties and purposes were, and shifting, perhaps impon-derable, as such designations as 'popular' and 'élite' prove to be.[2] What seems unde-batable, however, is that post-Reformation Scottish beliefs about and attitudes toward witches, and conceptions of their supposed practices, were quite different from English ones, especially during the 1590s, a period when witch-prosecutions increased in both Scotland and England and a period that must have influenced Shakespeare and the audiences of the first performances of *Macbeth*. The main difference between Scotland and England in these matters 'was not in the content, but in the relative significance of diabolism in the two countries and in the relative ferocity of the punishments for convicted witches'.[3]

English 'witches' were typically old women without familial or communal support; their supposed 'crimes' were practical and often economically destructive – causing a cow to stop giving milk or some other domestic beast to die, causing butter not to churn properly, crops to fail – or highly personal – causing a family member to die inexplicably, or a man to become sexually incapable, or a woman to be infertile. According to both popular belief and legal claims, accused witches contracted their souls to the devil in return for a 'familiar', usually a common animal such as a toad, cat, fly, or dog, which assisted her (only rarely 'his') demonic designs.

In 1590, King James VI visited Denmark to meet and marry King Christian IV's daughter, Anna. During that visit James may have learned and certainly debated con-tinental European witch-theories, which were much more virulent and lurid than con-temporary English ones. He apparently took these ideas back to Scotland and there introduced them to public circulation.[4] These beliefs included not merely the witch's contracting her or his soul to the devil, but a demonic 'pact' that involved sexual inter-course with Satan ('the witches' Sabbath'), the 'black Mass' and other inverted religious practices, and numerous activities such as stealing and eating children, exhuming bod-ies, parodying baptism using cats and other animals, flying through the air, and sailing the sea in sieves.[5]

How the play's 'sisters' are to be portrayed and understood has proved a continuing problem for both producers and readers of *Macbeth*. Indeed, critics and producers

[1] The Introduction in Barbara Rosen, *Witchcraft in England, 1558–1618*, 1969, and Dolan, *Dangerous Famil-iars*, pp. 171–210, provide helpful guides to, and summaries of, contemporary, especially English, witch-beliefs and practices and details of witch-persecutions. For the more general ambivalence towards magical thought and practices, see Keith Thomas, *Religion and the Decline of Magic*, 1971, *passim*.
[2] See e.g. Dolan, pp. 178–80, for an inconclusive summary and citations of the debate.
[3] Christina Larner, *Witchcraft and Religion*, 1984, p. 77; on increased prosecutions, see *ibid.*, p. 18.
[4] Clark, 'King James's *Daemonologie*', p. 157, and Larner, p. 10. See also Jenny Wormald, 'James VI and I: two kings or one?', *History* 68 (1983), 187–209.
[5] On how the relatively benign, or at least less socially threatening, English 'pact' differed from that in continental witch-belief, see Rosen, pp. 15–17. Clark, 'Inversion', offers an elegant study of witchcraft and the discourses of inversion; for 'political' inversion, especially relevant to *Macbeth*, see *ibid.*, pp. 111–17.

4   The exhibiting of an enemy's severed head is an ignominious punishment that figures twice in *Macbeth*:
see 1.2.23 and 5.9.20 SD. This engraving from J. C. Visscher, *Londinium Florentiss[i]ma Britanniae Urbs*
(1616), shows the heads of traitors displayed on London Bridge. A Swiss visitor who saw the bridge counted
'more than thirty skulls', boiled and tarred for preservation, 'of noble men who had been executed and
beheaded for treason and other reasons' (*Thomas Platter's Travels in England, 1599*, trans. Clare Williams,
1937, p. 155)

have puzzled over precisely why the sisters appear in the play. For much of the play's
performance history, they have been comic figures, wearing 'blue-checked aprons' and
'high crowned black hats' even early in the twentieth century, and providing spectacle
(they gave the performance song, dance, and occasions for ever more elaborate demonstrations of 'flying' and other forms of 'vanishing').[1] Gradually, however, the theatre's
witches grew more fearsome and demonic and consequently harder to integrate into

[1] Kalman A. Burnim, *David Garrick, Director*, 1961, p. 109.

conceptions of 'heroic' behaviour and tragic responsibility. By the mid nineteenth century, they had achieved psychological status, at least for critics.[1]

Later critics unfamiliar with the theatre and without, seemingly, much interest in theatrical history have also puzzled over the witches. Willard Farnham's learned account finds them 'demons of the fairy order . . . fiends in the shape of old women who do evil wherever and however they can', though they do not 'resemble human witches' (i.e. the supposed 'witches' of Elizabethan and Jacobean prosecutions),[2] and W. C. Curry, equally learned, imagines – from an arm-chair, not a place in the theatre – a stage-spectacle where beings he calls the 'Weird Sisters' (who have 'a dark grandeur, and a terror-inspiring aspect') 'surmise with comparative accuracy' Macbeth's 'inmost thoughts' 'from observation of facial expression and other bodily manifestations'.[3] For G. L. Kittredge, 'The Weird Sisters . . . are the Norns of Scandinavian mythology. The Norns were goddesses who shaped beforehand the life of every man . . . for their office was not to prophesy only, but to determine.'[4]

Notoriously, Tyrone Guthrie cut the play's first (Folio) scene from his 1934 Old Vic production on the joint grounds that the scene was not by Shakespeare (an improbable claim) and that 'by making the three Weird Sisters open the play, one cannot avoid the implication that they are a governing influence of the tragedy . . . Surely the grandeur of the tragedy lies in the fact that Macbeth and Lady Macbeth are ruined by precisely those qualities which make them great . . . All this is undermined by any suggestion that the Weird Sisters are in control of events',[5] and directors no less than critics[6] have struggled with the sisters' part in the dramatic architecture as well as in the moral and tragic meanings of the play. Are the sisters, for instance, subordinate to other, still more powerful, demonic forces? Hecate, who clearly arrives to rebuke them as their superior in Act 3, Scene 5, may not have been part of the play's original conception, but what of 'our masters' (4.1.62), perhaps the Apparitions or perhaps some force or forces sending the Apparitions? Glen Byam Shaw (Stratford, 1955) and Peter Hall (Stratford, 1967) sternly rejected the sisters and Lady Macbeth as determining forces. In Hall's words,

It has been said that he [Macbeth] wouldn't have done it if he hadn't met the witches; but the witches are not the three Fates saying go and do it, they see into the seeds of time, they know what can happen and what Macbeth wants to happen, but they certainly don't make him do it.[7]

[1] See William Wetmore Story, cited at p. 71 below. Hazlitt had earlier recognised how important a 'serious' treatment of the witches was: 'The Witches . . . are indeed ridiculous on the modern stage, and we doubt if the Furies of Aeschylus would be more respected' (William Hazlitt, *The Characters of Shakespear's Plays* (1817), ed. A. W. Pollard, 1903, p. 19).

[2] Willard Farnham, *Shakespeare's Tragic Frontier*, 1950, rpt. 1963, p. 99; Farnham's discussion of the play's possible sources (pp. 79–91) is valuable.

[3] Walter Clyde Curry, *Shakespeare's Philosophical Patterns*, 2nd edn, 1959, pp. 77–8.

[4] George Lyman Kittredge (ed.), *Macbeth*, 1939, p. xviii.

[5] Programme note quoted in James Agate's *Sunday Times* review, 8 April 1934, rpt. in *Brief Chronicles*, 1943, p. 229; Agate comments acidly 'that the play is not a tract by Samuel Smiles but a tragedy by William Shakespeare'.

[6] Farnham, *Shakespeare's Tragic Frontier*, p. 81: 'The witches . . . never, even by suggestion, bind him [Macbeth] to evil-doing . . . they tempt him to commit crimes for which he is to assume full moral responsibility . . .'

[7] Peter Hall, rehearsal talk with the company, quoted in the programme, p. 3, of his heavily Christianised 1967 RSC production; see also Samuel L. Leiter (ed.), *Shakespeare Around the Globe*, 1986, p. 377. Contradicting

Spectators of *Macbeth* will probably agree, however, that 'he wouldn't have done it' – Macbeth would not have killed Duncan – without Lady Macbeth's urgent sexual taunts and insinuations:

> Was the hope drunk
> Wherein you dressed yourself? Hath it slept since?
> And wakes it now to look so green and pale
> At what it did so freely? From this time,
> Such I account thy love. Art thou afeard
> To be the same in thine own act and valour,
> As thou art in desire? Wouldst thou have that
> Which thou esteem'st the ornament of life,
> And live a coward in thine own esteem,
> Letting I dare not wait upon I would,
> Like the poor cat i'th'adage? . . .
>   What beast was't then
> That made you break this enterprise to me?
> When you durst do it, then you were a man.
> And to be more than what you were, you would
> Be so much more the man.   (1.7.35–45, 1.7.47–51)[1]

As motivation, these lines ally Lady Macbeth with the sisters, and early audiences might have understood Lady Macbeth as a witch, or as possessed by the devil, long before her sleepwalking in Act 5, Scene 1. Her extraordinary invocation of the 'spirits/ That tend on mortal thoughts' (1.5.38–9) especially pleads:

>   make thick my blood,
> Stop up th'access and passage to remorse
> That no compunctious visitings of nature
> Shake my fell purpose nor keep peace between
> Th'effect and it. Come to my woman's breasts
> And take my milk for gall, you murd'ring ministers,
> Wherever in your sightless substances
> You wait on nature's mischief.   (1.5.41–8)

Here Lady Macbeth invokes two 'unnatural' conditions: stopping up the circulation (or in Jacobean scientific terms, the ebbing and flowing) of blood that makes her more compassionate ('compunctious') than a male, and ending her menstruation ('visitings of nature'), the shedding of blood that typified a female in contemporary English culture and signified her ability to bear children.[2]

Pierre Le Loyer's French treatise on fantasy, translated into English and published (1605) about the time of *Macbeth*'s composition, discusses the unusual psychological state male doctors supposed a woman underwent when menstruation ceased:

---

centuries of stage practice, Hall continues: 'It has also been said that without Lady Macbeth he wouldn't have done it; but if you take that view you must endorse a weak vacillating Macbeth with a tough virago of a lady booting him from behind. I do not believe that either.' For Byam Shaw's view, see pp. 81–2 below.

[1] Lady Macbeth's reference to 'the poor cat i'th'adage' is proverbial and 'common'; see p. 47 n. 2 below.
[2] See 1.5.41–2 n. and *OED* Visit *sb* 4; Alice Fox, 'Obstetrics and gynaecology in *Macbeth*', *S.St.* 12 (1979), 127–41; Jenijoy La Belle, ' "A strange infirmity": Lady Macbeth's amenorrhea', *SQ* 31 (1980), 381–6.

the blood of their monthly disease [i.e. unease, discomfort] being stopped from his course, through the ordinary passages and by the matrix dooth redound and beate backe again by the heart . . . Then the same blood, not finding any passage, troubleth the braine in such sorte, that . . . it causeth many of them to have idle fancies and fond conceipts, and tormenteth them with diverse imaginations of horrible specters, and fearefull sights . . . with which being so afflicted, some of them doe seeke to throwe and cast themselves into wells or pittes, and others to destroy themselves by hanging, or some such miserable end.[1]

Like Le Loyer's normative amenorrheal woman, Lady Macbeth suffers 'diverse imaginations of horrible specters, and fearefull sights' in Act 5, Scene 1, and the play's most unreliable narrative moment claims that Lady Macbeth destroyed herself 'by hanging, or some such miserable end' (Le Loyer): the 'fiend-like queen', Malcolm says, 'as 'tis thought, by self and violent hands / Took off her life' (5.9.37–8).[2]

This same physical condition, or its absence, also linked women with witches. The valiantly sceptical Reginald Scot records medical scholars' claim that amenorrhea, the absence of menstruation that might mark menopause, also defines female witches, who constitute a sub-category of 'melancholike' persons:

Now, if the fansie of a melancholike person may be occupied in causes which are both false and impossible; why should an old witch be thought free from such fantasies, who (as the learned philosophers and physicians saie) upon the stopping of their monethlie melancholike flux or issue of bloud, in their age must needs increase therein [i.e. in melancholy], as (through their weakenesse both of bodie and braine) the aptest persons to meete with such melancholike imaginations: with whome their imaginations remaine, even when their senses are gone.[3]

King James, sometimes notably rationalist, recognised and was puzzled by the fact modern scholars stress: accused witches were overwhelmingly female and usually old.[4]

Shakespeare's earliest audiences might thus associate Lady Macbeth's invocation in Act 1, Scene 5, with an aberrant desire to be both a fantast (a 'melancholike') and a witch, a woman seeking to deny what her culture understood as a woman's defining 'nature' – her ability to bear children – and a woman seeking to become what established doctrine most feared, a renegade or 'wayward' woman, a witch or uncontrolled wife.[5]

Post-menopausal women – 'some of them beyng a while frutefull, but after widowes, and for that suppressed of naturall course [menstruation]' – were also, according to the

[1] Pierre Le Loyer [Loier], *Treatise of Specters*, trans. Z. Jones, 1605, ff. 110r–v. See Patricia Crawford, 'Attitudes to menstruation in seventeenth-century England', *P&P* 91 (1981), 47–73.
[2] Malcolm's 'as 'tis thought' is an extraordinary qualification, marking the narrative's uncertainty and, perhaps, Malcolm's politically motivated effort to portray the previous régime as insane or despairing.
[3] Reginald Scot, *The Discoverie of Witchcraft* (1584), ed. Brinsley Nicholson, 1886, III, 9. I owe this reference to Billy Phelan. For a sapient analysis of Scot's work, especially in comparison with Johan Weyer's *De Praestigiis Daemonum*, see Sydney Anglo, 'Reginald Scot's *Discoverie of Witchcraft*: scepticism and sadduceeism', in *Damned Art*, pp. 106–39.
[4] *Daemonologie*, pp. 43–4; years later, when James questioned Sir John Harington on the point, Harington could only offer a coarse joke (see N. E. McClure (ed.), *The Letters and Epigrams of Sir John Harington*, 1930, p. 110; letter 35 (?December 1603)). For contemporary views of post-menopausal women as 'witches', see G. R. Quaife, *Godly Zeal and Furious Rage: The Witch in Early Modern Europe*, 1987, p. 163, and, more significantly, Ralph A. Houlbrooke, *The English Family 1450–1700*, 1984, p. 213.
[5] '[T]he play [*Macbeth*] also offers, in the figure of Lady Macbeth, the drama's most vivid manifestation of the witch as a dangerous familiar and her witchcraft as "malice domestic," as an invasion of the household and its daily life' (Dolan, p. 226).

surgeon–anatomist John Banister, supposed to 'have beardes . . . being then [as widows and non-menstruating women] bearded, hearie [hairy], and chaunged in voyce'.[1] The description may only hypothetically suit Lady Macbeth, but its most provocative claim – 'bearded, hearie' – concerning women whose 'naturall course' has been 'suppressed' anticipates Banquo's view of the sisters:

> You seem to understand me,
> By each at once her choppy finger laying
> Upon her skinny lips; you should be women,
> And yet your beards forbid me to interpret
> That you are so.
>
> (1.3.41–5)

According to one popular play, 'the women that / came to us, for disguises must weare beardes, / & thats they saie the token of a witch'.[2] Melancholy, fantasy, amenorrhea, bearded women form what seems a conventional series of cultural assumptions. They suggest that Lady Macbeth seeks to become, or is, what her culture considered a witch. She has also sought, or been associated with, characteristics traditionally 'male' – lack of compunction, a beard, no menstruation.

Macbeth makes some of the associations clear:

> Bring forth men-children only,
> For thy undaunted mettle should compose
> Nothing but males.
>
> (1.7.72–4)

Another Shakespearean character explicitly joins ideas of witchcraft with a woman's 'unfeminine', 'masculine' behaviour when Leontes angrily derides Paulina as 'A mankind witch' (*Winter's Tale* 2.3.67). Leontes' epithet combines humanity ('mankind') with a woman's 'male' ('mankind') aggressiveness and with demonhood ('witch'). Closer in time to Lady Macbeth's creation, the characterisation of Volumnia, Coriolanus's mother, shows a similarly complex – and arguably for Shakespeare and at least the male spectators a similarly disturbing – mixture of stereotypical gendertypes, though the added demonising quality of 'witch' does not appear in *Coriolanus*.[3] Rather surprisingly, given the frequent application of 'witch' to Cleopatra and the word's use elsewhere as opprobrium (see 1.3.5 n.), no speaker calls Volumnia 'witch'. Indeed, 'witch' does not occur in *Coriolanus*; there, the only 'witchcraft' is Coriolanus's own:

> I do not know what witchcraft's in him [Coriolanus], but
> Your [Aufidius's] soldiers use him as the grace fore meat,
> Their talk at table, and their thanks at end,
> And you [Aufidius] are darkened in this action, sir,
> Even by your own . . .
>
> (*Coriolanus* 4.7.2–6)

---

[1] John Banister, *The Historie of Man*, 1578, sig. B2v. Banister is never very original and cites pseudo-Hippocrates (*Epidemics* VI) here. On how hair might discriminate masculine from feminine, see Joan Cadden, *Meanings of Sex Difference in the Middle Ages*, 1993, pp. 181–3. I owe these two references to Billy Phelan.

[2] *The Honest Mans Fortune*, ed. J. Gerritsen, 1952, 2.1.23–5.

[3] For a survey, see Parker (ed.), *Coriolanus*, pp. 48–53, and Janet Adelman, *Suffocating Mothers: Fantasies of Maternal Origin in Shakespeare's Plays, 'Hamlet' to 'The Tempest'*, 1992, pp. 147–9.

For some members of *Macbeth's* earliest audiences, another of Lady Macbeth's claims would have been memorable and unusual, to say the least. Urging Macbeth to kill Duncan, she invokes a terrible analogy:

> I have given suck and know
> How tender 'tis to love the babe that milks me:
> I would, while it was smiling in my face,
> Have plucked my nipple from his boneless gums
> And dashed the brains out, had I so sworn
> As you have done to this. (1.7.54–9)

Special terror here depends upon the nursing mother's closeness to, and tenderness for, the suckling child. While '[c]ontemporary opinion was strongly in favour of a mother feeding her own child',[1] English royal, aristocratic, and 'gentle' women (i.e. members of the gentry) did not typically nurse their own children. Instead, they employed wet-nurses, lactating (usually lower-class) women who nursed the child.[2] Elizabeth Clinton, dowager Countess of Lincoln, described and attacked the snobbery such nursing practices encouraged:

And this unthankfulnesse [not breast-feeding], and unnaturalnesse is oftner the sinne of the *Higher*, and the *richer sort*, then of the meaner, and poorer, except some nice and prowd idle dames, who will imitate their betters, till they make their poore husbands beggars. And this is one hurt which the better ranke doe by their ill example; egge, and imbolden the lower ones to follow them to their losse . . .[3]

We may suppose that the countess's remarks are deeply influenced by her elevated social class and its attendant privileges and contempts, not to mention her regretful admission that she did not breast-feed her own eighteen children.[4] Still and yet, Elizabeth Clinton's concern for babies remains, along with her stiletto dissection of upward mobility.

Upper-class English women did not nurse their children, unlike the majority of mothers. The presumably wide knowledge of this practice – it marked social distinction (as Elizabeth Clinton demonstrates) and therefore must have been emphasised and publicised – supports Coleridge's independent, critical, unhistoricised comment when he disagreed with the then-prevailing view of Lady Macbeth as a monster.[5] A possibly singular bequest may suggest the culture's general attitude. John Greene, a lawyer

---

[1] Patricia Crawford, 'The sucking child: adult attitudes to child care in the first year of life in seventeenth-century England', *Continuity and Change* 1 (1986), 31.

[2] Regular playgoers would have been reminded of this aristocratic practice: see e.g. Giovanni of his mother, Isabella: 'I have often heard her say she gave me suck, / And it should seem by that she dearly loved me, / Since princes seldom do it' (Webster, *White Devil* 3.2.336–8), and Dekker, *Westward Ho* 1.2.117–20, for the supposed damage suckling did to a woman's beauty. In *The White Devil*, Richard Burbage, who may have been the first Macbeth, acted Ferdinand (see Appendix 1, p. 280 below, and Edwin Nungezer, *A Dictionary of Actors*, 1929). See, generally, Valerie Fildes, *Breasts, Bottles and Babies: A History of Infant Feeding*, 1986.

[3] [Elizabeth Clinton], *The Countesse of Lincolnes Nursurie*, 1622, sig. C2r.

[4] See *ibid.*, sigs. DIV and C4r-v.

[5] Lady Macbeth's assertion (1.7.54–9, quoted above), Coleridge said, 'though usually thought to prove a merciless and unwomanly nature, proves the direct opposite; she brings it as the most solemn enforcement to Macbeth of the solemnity of his promise'; she tries 'to *bully* conscience'. See Samuel Taylor Coleridge, *Coleridge's Criticism of Shakespeare*, ed. R. A. Foakes, 1989, pp. 105–6.

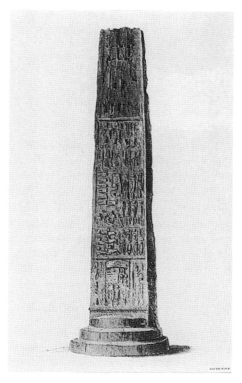

5   Sweno, the 'Norwegian lord' whose invasion of Scotland fails at the beginning of *Macbeth*, is remembered
in the name 'Sueno's Stone', which is given to this pillar (dating from some time between the ninth century
and the eleventh) which still stands near Forres in Scotland. See 1.2.58–63 and the Commentary at 1.2.31–62.
This engraving from *Vetvsta monvmenta* (1747–1835), plate 49, shows the south face of the stone

who eventually became Recorder of London, specified in his will that his daughters
should have £1000 apiece 'except Margaret who was to have a further £100 "because
her mother nursed her"'.[1] Whatever the aristocracy's practice, indeed whatever the
practice of those lower in the social order, a mother's nurturing attachment to her child
affected in this single instance how a father bequeathed his wealth.

   In William Harrison's 'Description of Scotland' we read, as Shakespeare almost
certainly did:

sith it was [in ancient Scotland] a cause of suspicion of the mothers fidel[i]tie toward hir husband,
to seeke a strange nurse for hir children (although hir milke failed) each woman would take
intollerable paines to bring up and nourishe hir owne children . . . nay they feared least [lest]
they should degenerat[e] and grow out of kind, except they gave them sucke themselves . . .[2]

[1] E. M. Symonds, 'The Diary of John Greene (1635–57 [*sic*, for 1659]), Part III', *EHR* 44 (1929), 116.
[2] *Scotland*, p. 21a; for Shakespeare's knowledge of this Harrison text, see 3.1.91–107 n. below. In his dedicatory epistle, Harrison claims (*ibid.*, p. 4) that 'the skilfull are not ignorant' of Hector Boece's *Scotorum
historiae* (1526, 1575), but that Bellenden's Scots translation is known to 'verie few Englishmen . . . bicause
we [English readers] want [lack] the books'.

Here, Harrison translates and distorts John Bellenden's Scots translation of Hector Boece's *Scotorum historiae* (1526, 1575), where Scottish mothers are specifically distinguished from English mothers. Bellenden writes:

Ilk moder wes nurice to hir awin barne [Each mother was nurse to her own child]. It was ane suspition of adultre [adultery] aganis ony woman quhare hir milk failzeit, the wemen thocht yair barnis war not tender nor kyndly to thaym, bot gif thay war nurist als weill with the mylk of thair breist, as thay war nurist afore with the blude of thair wambe. Attoure [Moreover] thay held that thair barnis war degenerat fra thair nature and kynd, gif thay war nurist with uncouth mylk.[1]

Harrison omits Boece's claim that where the mother's milk 'fails' ('quhare hir milk failzeit'), the failure signals the mother's adultery. Further, Boece and Bellenden claim, milk from any woman other than the biological mother made the child so nursed 'degenerate from their nature and kind' – that is, wet-nursing made the child non-natural and from a genealogical or dynastic point of view invalid, a failed heir.

However distortedly information about Scottish maternal practice may have descended to Shakespeare and his audiences, Lady Macbeth's claim was at once terrible and unusual. An aristocratic, a royal, woman had 'given suck' and that nurturance would have been foreign to English aristocratic practice and her rejection of the 'babe' repulsive. Considered within the play's arguments over various lineal successions – 'proper' dynastic orderings – Lady Macbeth's vow and threat (1.7.54–9) violate not only a local, 'strange' Scottish practice, but also invalidate possibly royal succession from her body. Her language and that of Boece and Bellenden return the audience to the succession-crises in Act 1, Scenes 3 and 4, where the political conflicts with the familial and biological.

Words and images of birth enter the play's dialogue often, but nowhere so complicatedly as in the choric Act 2, Scene 4:

> Thou seest the heavens, as troubled with man's act,
> Threatens his bloody stage. By th'clock 'tis day
> And yet dark night strangles the travelling lamp.
> Is't night's predominance, or the day's shame,
> That darkness does the face of earth entomb
> When living light should kiss it? (2.4.5–10)

The heavens' 'bloody stage' is, of course, the theatre where we learn of Duncan's murder and the theatre where the murderous battles of Acts 1 and 5 take place, but it is also the 'bloody' moment of birth: 'travelling lamp' (the sun) puns through the Folio's spelling ('trauailing') on 'travailing' (labouring), a word that includes the 'labour' or 'travail' of giving birth.[2] Here, the 'travelling [or 'trauailing', birthing] lamp', the sun (or son), contends with strangling night. Soon, murderous dark kills the light – 'Who did strike out the light?' (3.3.22) – and the witches later invoke a 'birth-strangled babe', a child strangled in labour ('travail') or just after birth.[3] In Act 3, Scene 3, Macbeth's hired murderers attack Fleance, a son who may grow up to be the 'sun' to darkened Scotland;

[1] John Bellenden, *Hystory and Croniklis of Scotland* (?1540), sig. D1r [first sequence] (headed: 'Ane prudent doctryne maid be [by] the auctoure concernyng baith the new maneris and the auld [old] of Scottis').
[2] See *OED* Travail *v* and Travel *v*.
[3] On the two possibilities, see 4.1.30 n. below.

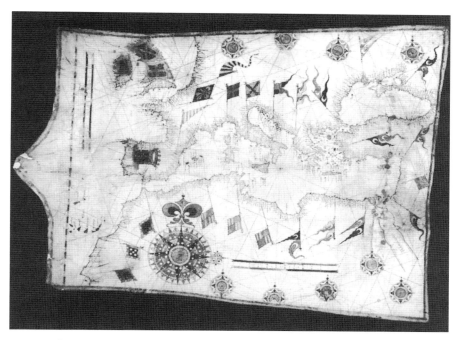

6   A sixteenth-century 'card of the sea' by Sebastão Lopes, c. 1555, showing sea-routes and landmarks for
voyages around the Mediterranean: see the First Witch's mention of 'th'shipman's card' at 1.3.16. Here,
'Aleppo' (1.3.6) is marked, and a castle at the western end of the Mediterranean, indicating the mapmaker's
native land, Portugal

so, too, 'dark night' strangles the moving ('travelling') light of the sun, which is also
the 'travailing' source, the mother-giving-birth, and son/sun of hope for the future.

Prophecy is perhaps the sisters' most significant contribution to the play's intellectual
complexity and at the same time one of the play's most memorable theatrical and
emotional effects. And the prophecies they offer are not only of future kingship ('All
hail Macbeth, that shalt be king hereafter' (1.3.48)), but of secure future kingship:

> Be bloody, bold, and resolute; laugh to scorn
> The power of man, for none of woman born
> Shall harm Macbeth.
>
> (4.1.78–80)[1]

Tragic plots deeply involved with prophecy – the plots of Sophocles' *Oedipus Rex* or
Macbeth, for example – paradoxically confound tragedy and human speculation about
the tragic.[2] Macbeth himself early and late understands prophetic irony:

---

[1]   Discussing similar political prophecies in *2H6*, Jean E. Howard, *The Stage and Social Struggle in Early
Modern England*, 1994, p. 135, appropriately cites Howard Dobin, *Merlin's Disciples: Prophecy, Poetry and
Power in Renaissance England*, 1990; Dobin makes only passing reference to *Macbeth*. For the numerous
and savage Tudor statutes attempting to control political prophecy and specifically prophecies concerning
the monarch's death, see John Bellamy, *The Tudor Law of Treason: An Introduction*, 1979, *passim*.

[2]   For the issue in Sophocles' play and a summary of critics' puzzlement, see Richard A. McCabe, *Incest,
Drama and Nature's Law*, 1993, pp. 71 ff.; for a most un-oracular oracle, one suited to romance rather than
tragedy, see *WT* 3.2.132–6.

> If chance will have me king, why chance may crown me
> Without my stir. (1.3.142–3)

> And be these juggling fiends no more believed
> That palter with us in a double sense,
> That keep the word of promise to our ear
> And break it to our hope . . . (5.8.19–22)

To recognise irony is not to escape either irony or the temptations of prophecy, as Macbeth's response to the sisters' display in Act 4, Scene 1, shows:

> Then live, Macduff, what need I fear of thee?
> But yet I'll make assurance double sure
> And take a bond of fate: thou shalt not live,
> That I may tell pale-hearted fear it lies,
> And sleep in spite of thunder. (4.1.81–5)

Macbeth instantly acts to confirm what he believes needs no confirmation. His planned and accomplished action, the murder of Lady Macduff and her children, makes fatal reality out of his over-confidence and his insecurity. Doubt and deaths are the paradoxical result of prophecy and paltering.

Macbeth's perceptions prove otherwise diminished and diminishing. The destructive actions they justify make Macbeth a destructive fool, or a dupe, or the self-aware automaton who says:

> I am in blood
> Stepped in so far that should I wade no more,
> Returning were as tedious as go o'er. (3.4.136–8)

and

> Tomorrow, and tomorrow, and tomorrow
> Creeps in this petty pace from day to day
> To the last syllable of recorded time;
> And all our yesterdays have lighted fools
> The way to dusty death. (5.5.18–22)

Macbeth's reflections are trapped at the level of human agency. He understands, but understands only, the tactics needed to become king and fulfil what he construes as prophecy. He castigates himself not for seeking the murderous ends he sought but for seeking them in an ineffective way, as he had in lamenting the failure of 'our poor malice' (3.2.14).

Unexpressed in Macbeth's seemingly helpless ironic perceptions is a larger difficulty the prophecies pose – choice, or intended action, and hence responsibility for one's acts. If the prophecies are true before the play begins, or before Macbeth and Banquo hear them, or before Macbeth and Banquo have acted, where is the willed action that allows the audience to discover responsibility and hence to experience guilt? If Macbeth could never act otherwise, could never *not* choose to murder Duncan, and if, putatively,

Banquo could never resist thoughts of usurpation, 'the cursèd thoughts that nature / Gives way to in repose' (2.1.8–9), where is the tragedy, the dire consequence of an ignorant or misunderstood act, of these events? If, alternatively, the prophecies only become true when they are enacted by responsible and hence arguably tragic and guilty human agents, how may they be called 'prophecies' at all?

From a Christian perspective, the likely perspective of both Shakespeare and most of the original audiences, this conundrum represents 'the great debate of the [European] sixteenth and seventeenth centuries on the freedom of the will being turned into drama', as Helen Gardner remarked in a classic essay.[1] According to Gardner, 'It never occurs to us that Macbeth will turn back, or indeed that he can . . . [A]long with this incapacity for change to a better state, or repentance, go two other closely related ideas':

> The initial act [i.e. the murder of Duncan] is an act against nature, it is a primal sin . . . and its author knows that it . . . [is] so. It is not an act committed by mistake; it is not an error of judgment, it is an error of will. The act is unnatural and so are its results; it deforms the nature which performs it. The second idea is the irony of retributive justice. The act is performed for an imagined good . . . but a rigorous necessity reigns and sees to it that . . . the desire is only granted ironically . . . [because] the desire is for something forbidden by the very nature of man.[2]

While we should not unthinkingly assent to Gardner's Christian assertion (or assumption) of 'the very nature of man', it seems unquestionable that Macbeth has not, as Gardner says of Marlowe's Dr Faustus, 'escaped the necessity of choice'.[3]

Questions of the individual's freedom or boundedness in action and questions of the individual's responsibility or submission to some external agent (God, Fate, Necessity) are the basic but not simple questions any prophetic act raises.[4] By incorporating prophecy in what the First Folio termed a 'Tragedie', Shakespeare, like Sophocles, presents but does not solve ageless human anxieties about how freely we may act in time. These anxieties are especially present for a Christian audience. A great deal of the play's emotional power derives from raising these complex anxieties and denying them resolution. Trying to decide whether the effect is 'tragic' or the play a 'tragedy' is beside the point. The point lies in the effort to resolve those questions, the effort to tame into thought and language what remains wild, inexplicable, compellingly disturbing.

---

[1] Helen Gardner, 'Milton's "Satan" and the theme of damnation in Elizabethan tragedy', in F. P. Wilson (ed.), *English Studies 1948*, 1948, pp. 46–66; quotation from p. 50 n. 1.
[2] Gardner, pp. 48–9. King-Kok Cheung, 'Shakespeare and Kierkegaard: "dread" in *Macbeth*', *SQ* 35 (1984), 430–9, considers Macbeth's and Lady Macbeth's fascinated compulsion to perform deeds they know are wrong, citing Kierkegaard's 'dread of sin produces sin' (p. 435). Macbeth's purported inability to turn back is one version of the deadly Christian sin of despair; see Bettie Anne Doebler, *"Rooted Sorrow": Dying in Early Modern England*, 1994, *passim*, but esp. pp. 173–80.
[3] Gardner, 'Milton's "Satan"', p. 53. See Robert N. Watson, *The Rest Is Silence: Death as Annihilation in the English Renaissance*, 1994, chapter 4, esp. pp. 149 and 152.
[4] See Jones, *Scenic*, p. 206, citing Susanne Langer's distinguished *Feeling and Form* (1953): 'in the case of *Macbeth*, at any rate in this first part of the play, the "virtual future" is not only the mode of the dramatic genre to which *Macbeth* belongs: it is also its *subject*. The early scenes of *Macbeth* are "about" the immediate future . . .' Compare G. K. Hunter's excellent discussion of the complex word 'security' (3.5.32) in his edition of the play, pp. 21–3, and the more general issue of whether the sisters act independently or as subordinates to still larger demonic energies.

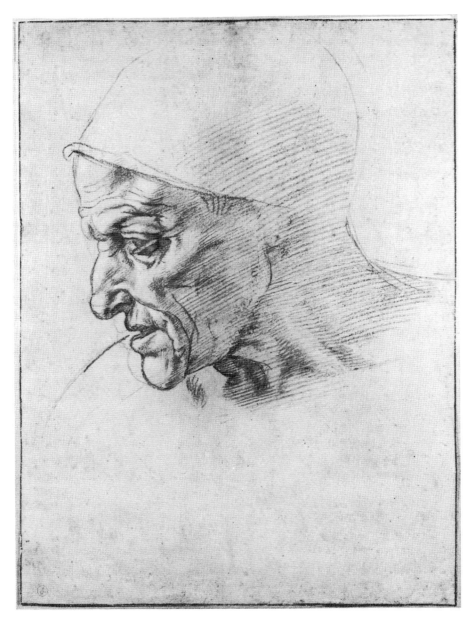

7 Michelangelo's drawing of the 'Head of the Cumaean sibyl', depicting a legendary, aged, prophetic woman, was in fact modelled on an old man (see Michael Hirst, *Michelangelo Draftsman*, 1988, p. 40). Compare Banquo's puzzlement when he meets the bearded, ambiguous sisters at 1.3.43–5

Indeed, the play achieves its effects by *not* solving its questions and by conveying their undecidability through a brutal plot, magnificent language, and above all, the sisters.

'WHAT DO YOU MEAN?': THE LANGUAGES OF *MACBETH*

At least since the Restoration diarist Samuel Pepys recorded attending *Macbeth* – 'a pretty good play, but admirably acted'[1] – on the fifty-ninth anniversary of the Gunpowder Plot, 5 November 1664, and undoubtedly long before that, audiences have enjoyed its theatrical spectacle, its marvels and magic – what Pepys later called 'variety' and 'divertisement'.[2] Shakespeare's play has equal pleasures for the listening imagination.

Despite the play's exciting linguistic variety, hostile comments from the seventeenth and the twentieth century attack its language. On unknown authority, John Dryden cited Ben Jonson, Shakespeare's greatest rival and (at least by the time he wrote a fine commendatory poem for the 1623 First Folio) eloquent admirer: 'In reading some bombast speeches of *Macbeth*, which are not to be understood, he [Jonson] used to say that it was horror; and I am much afraid that this is so.'[3] Dryden himself asserted:

he [Shakespeare] often obscures his meaning by his words, and sometimes makes it unintelligible ... the fury of his fancy often transported him beyond the bounds of judgement, either in coining of new words and phrases, or racking words which were in use into the violence of a catachresis. 'Tis not that I would explode the use of metaphors from passions ... but to use 'em at every word, to say nothing without a metaphor, a simile, an image, or description, is I doubt to smell a little too strongly of the buskin.[4]

A. C. Bradley, a sympathetic late-Victorian reader of *Macbeth*, partly agrees: 'The diction has in places a huge and rugged grandeur, which degenerates here and there into tumidity.'[5] Almost two-and-a-half centuries after Dryden's death, James Thurber imagined himself marooned in a hotel with reading matter as random and ill-assorted as that found in a dentist's waiting-room. One fellow-resident was stuck with *Macbeth*, which she found, Thurber says, 'a Murder Mystery'. She especially notes the moment when Macduff describes finding Duncan's body:

---

[1] Robert Latham and William Matthews (eds.), *The Diary of Samuel Pepys*, 11 vols., 1970–83, v, 314. On this anniversary of the Gunpowder Plot, Pepys almost certainly saw William Davenant's adaptation, quite possibly its première; see Arthur H. Scouten, 'The premiere of Davenant's adaptation of *Macbeth*' in W. R. Elton and William B. Long (eds.), *Shakespeare and Dramatic Tradition*, 1989, pp. 286–93.

[2] Pepys, VII, 423 (28 December 1666), and VIII, 7 (7 January 1667); Pepys describes William Davenant's adapted text which indeed contained, as he said, 'variety of dancing and music' (VIII, 171; 19 April 1667).

[3] John Dryden, 'Defence of the epilogue', in George Watson (ed.), *Of Dramatic Poesy and Other Critical Essays*, 2 vols., 1962, 1, 173. Dryden may be putting words in an elder and deeply respected playwright's mouth here, but 'it was horror' is none the less a peculiar phrase, allowing one to imagine Dryden's 'Jonson' saying that the play's occasional linguistic confusion conveys 'horror' rather than that the play's language is horribly confused.

[4] 'The grounds of criticism in tragedy', prefixed to *Troilus and Cressida* (1679), in Watson (ed.), *Of Dramatic Poesy*, 1, 257. Dryden gives no examples, but *Macbeth* is full of evocative but logically confusing (and therefore neo-classically offensive) figurative language: 'Was the hope drunk / Wherein you dressed yourself? Hath it slept since? / And wakes it now to look so green and pale / At what it did so freely?' (1.7.35–8), for example.

[5] Bradley, p. 265; in a later (p. 310) comparison of *Macbeth* with Seneca, Bradley describes some of the play's language as 'turgid bombast'.

'Macduff discovers it,' she said, slipping into the historical present. 'Then he comes running downstairs and shouts, "Confusion has broke open the Lord's anointed temple" and "Sacrilegious murder has made his masterpiece" and on and on like that.' The good lady tapped me on the knee. 'All that stuff was *rehearsed*,' she said. 'You wouldn't say a lot of stuff like that, offhand, would you – if you had found a body? . . . You wouldn't! Unless you had practiced it in advance. "My God, there's a body in here!" is what an innocent man would say.'[1]

The lady's complaint echoes Dr Johnson on Milton's *Lycidas*: 'Where there is leisure for fiction there is little grief.' Here, Thurber's reader concludes, where there is leisure for personification there is little personal feeling.

Dryden's possibly fictitious Jonson, and Dryden himself, and Bradley, and Thurber's imaginary reader all hear the play's linguistic, especially metaphorical, volatility, a volatility that sometimes reaches near-incomprehensibility in marvellous but unparaphrasable language:

> this Duncan
> Hath borne his faculties so meek, hath been
> So clear in his great office, that his virtues
> Will plead like angels, trumpet-tongued against
> The deep damnation of his taking-off.
> And pity, like a naked newborn babe
> Stiriding the blast, or heaven's cherubin horsed
> Upon the sightless couriers of the air,
> Shall blow the horrid deed in every eye,
> That tears shall drown the wind.   (1.7.16–25)

> Come, seeling night,
> Scarf up the tender eye of pitiful day
> And with thy bloody and invisible hand
> Cancel and tear to pieces that great bond
> Which keeps me pale. Light thickens,
> And the crow makes wing to th'rooky wood;
> Good things of day begin to droop and drowse,
> Whiles night's black agents to their preys do rouse.   (3.2.46–53)

Writers bold enough to comment on these speeches have generally admitted both defeat and admiration. Of the first passage, Dr Johnson said, 'the meaning is not very clear; I have never found the readers of Shakespeare agreeing about it'.[2] The play has language to puzzle not only Johnson, but anyone.

---

[1] James Thurber, *My World – And Welcome To It*, 1942, pp. 35–6. George Bernard Shaw achieves a similar effect in a burlesque of Act 1, Scenes 5 and 7, where Lady Macbeth's lines are mostly intact and Macbeth's are modern and colloquial (e.g. 'What the devil is a limbec?'); see Bernard Dukore (ed.), George Bernard Shaw, 'Macbeth Skit', *Educational Theatre Journal* 19 (1967), 343–8.

[2] On the first speech, see also Cleanth Brooks, *The Well Wrought Urn*, 1947, pp. 21–46. On the second speech, see William Empson, *Seven Types of Ambiguity*, 1930, 3rd edn, 1953, pp. 18–20 and 81–2, and R. A. Foakes, 'Poetic language and dramatic significance in Shakespeare', in Philip Edwards *et al.* (eds.), *Shakespeare's Styles*, 1980, pp. 79–83. On their Hebridean walking tour, Samuel Johnson had to endure James Boswell's numerous quotations of *Macbeth*; see James Boswell, *Journal of a Tour to the Hebrides*, ed. Frederick A. Pottle and Charles H. Bennett, 1961, *passim*, but esp. the entry (29 August 1773) recording their visit to 'Macbeth's Castle'.

Rather than offer yet another interpretation of Macbeth's extraordinary speech on 'pity, like a naked newborn babe', a speech eloquently discussed by Cleanth Brooks and Helen Gardner among many others,[1] I offer a shorter example, equally condensed and equally typical of the play's most complex way with words. When Ross and Angus ceremonially announce that Duncan has granted Macbeth a new title, 'Thane of Cawdor' (1.3.87–105), Macbeth divides into a public man, publicly acknowledging a deliberately public honour – 'Thanks for your pains', 'I thank you, gentlemen' (1.3.116, 128) – and into a musing, reflective mind seeking the links among sudden, new honour and the sisters' earlier predictions:

> Two truths are told,
> As happy prologues to the swelling act
> Of the imperial theme. (1.3.126–8)

This small portion of Macbeth's speech shows the way the play's language, or, more precisely, the way this character's language, shifts from one verbal register or matrix to another. One matrix is the language of the theatre: 'prologues' are familiar introductory or explanatory figures who preface an entire play or an 'act' of one; after the prologue, an audience would expect the stage to fill (or 'swell') with other actors representing the persons and enacting the events the prologic character predicted or promised. Another matrix is the language of rhetoric and of music: 'theme' is a speaker's or thinker's subject or topic, or possibly (the meaning is barely established in the late sixteenth century) a recognisable – 'hearable' – set of repeated or varied notes.[2] 'Two truths', Macbeth says, introduce an extended passage (of thought, argument, music) leading metaphorically to empery or kingship, and the 'imperial theme' turns from static to active, from contemplation to incitement. From mentally debating what it might be like to be king, Macbeth's reflection (or rather the highly compressed language Shakespeare gives the character) now introduces the possibility of acting to achieve kingship.[3] A final linguistic matrix arises from the 'swelling' of a pregnant woman's body. Speaking to Banquo – 'Thou shalt get kings, though thou be none' (1.3.65) – the sisters raise the play's most intractable and profound issue, the questions of generation, children, inheritance, the prolonging of a familial line. Their emphasis is almost but not quite unremarked – 'Do you not hope your children shall be kings, / When those that gave the Thane of Cawdor to me / Promised no less to them?' (1.3.117–19) – but with 'swelling' (of pregnancy or of impregnating penis) this brief passage acknowledges the possibility that the 'imperial' or royal goal might be barren, that the sisters 'Upon my head . . . placed a fruitless crown / And put a barren sceptre in my gripe' (3.1.62–3).

In these passages, the play's language moves rapidly among many images and many linguistic possibilities; this shifting brings together the eloquent, the homely, the

---

[1] See Brooks, pp. 21–46, and Helen Gardner, *The Business of Criticism*, 1959, pp. 52–61.
[2] On the musical meaning of 'theme', dated to 1597, see *OED* Theme 4; the rhetorical meaning (see 1.3.128 n.) is far older.
[3] This shift or glide from a more or less abstract and static mental consideration to an active intention occurs often in the play; see, e.g., 1.5.14–23 and n.

8 'memory . . . Shall be a fume, and the receipt of reason / A limbeck only' (1.7.65–7). The two limbecks shown here illustrate alchemical distillation in *The Works of Geber* (1678), reproducing an image from the Latin edition of 1545. The limbeck on the right is set on a furnace. See Gareth Roberts, *The Mirror of Alchemy*, 1994

proverbial, and the brilliantly theatrical helter-skelter. Among many extraordinary verbal effects in Macbeth's reflection upon killing Duncan (1.7.12 ff.), for example, '*n*aked new*b*or*n* *b*a*b*e' subtly patterns the sounds of *n* and of *b*, making a rhetorical chiasmus of the middle term, 'newborn', where the sounds 'cross' and coexist.[1]

This later passage, when Macbeth has determined to kill Banquo and Fleance, begins with Macbeth's intimate endearment, 'Be innocent of the knowledge, dearest chuck, / Till thou applaud the deed' (3.2.45–6). If a 'noble' hero may be so tender amidst the slaughter past and to come, and so bourgeois as to use 'chuck', a 'citizen' term,[2] then so too the man and child he would kill employ an innocently 'humble' diction:

BANQUO How goes the night, boy?
FLEANCE The moon is down; I have not heard the clock.
BANQUO And she goes down at twelve.
FLEANCE   I take't, 'tis later, sir.   (2.1.1–3)

---

[1] A similar, more extended antimetabole using *d* and *b* appears in 'I will not be afraid of *d*eath and *b*ane / Till *B*irnam Forest come to *D*unsinane' (5.3.60–1). Compare the different but similar auditory experience of 'bear [bare?] the knife myself' (16) and 'borne his faculties' (17).

[2] For the social connotations of endearments, see Supplementary Note 3.2.45, pp. 258–9 below.

And when Banquo dies, a single pentameter unites a passing comment about the weather with the command for his death:

> BANQUO It will be rain tonight.
> FIRST MURDERER   Let it come down.   (3.3.18)

With little help from the dialogue, the actor playing Lady Macbeth must shift the audience's imagination from plot-orientated fact to gnawing moral self-examination:

> LADY MACBETH Is Banquo gone from court?
> SERVANT Ay, madam, but returns again tonight.
> LADY MACBETH Say to the king, I would attend his leisure
>   For a few words.
> SERVANT   Madam, I will.   *Exit*
> LADY MACBETH   Nought's had, all's spent
>   Where our desire is got without content.
>   'Tis safer to be that which we destroy
>   Than by destruction dwell in doubtful joy.   (3.2.1–7)

Almost at once, Lady Macbeth must turn from self-reflection and seek to assuage Macbeth's scorpion-filled mind.

Lady Macbeth's couplets (3.2.4–7) have a quasi-proverbial force, and many well-known lines quote proverbs or have a substratum of proverbial language or thought.[1] One proverb, 'Things done cannot be undone', contributes to three strategically placed moments, at the beginning, the middle, and the end of the play:

> If it were done when 'tis done, then 'twere well
> It were done quickly.   (1.7.1–2)

>   Things without all remedy
> Should be without regard; what's done, is done.   (3.2.11–12)[2]

Come, come, come, come, give me your hand; what's done cannot be undone. To bed, to bed, to bed.   (5.1.57–8)

Sedimented, even ossified, commonplaces of wisdom or observation, proverbs and proverbial language make ordinary the play's events and the speakers' reactions while simultaneously and starkly showing how far beyond the ordinary, the proverbial, the stony, these events and attitudes are: proverbs toll through important moments in Act 3 – 'Men are but men'; 'Fair face foul heart'; 'And there's an end'; 'Blood will have blood.'

The language of *Macbeth* combines sublime magniloquence – which the neo-classical critics Ben Jonson, Dryden, and Dr Johnson found distasteful – with everyday

---

[1] For the first act alone, see the notes to 1.2.67, 1.3.123 and 145, 1.4.11–12, 1.7.44–5.
[2] These lines include another proverb: 'Where there is no remedy it is folly to chide.'

language that also has great theatrical power. After Duncan's murder is discovered, Macbeth has two speeches that certainly 'say nothing without a metaphor, a simile, an image':

> Had I but died an hour before this chance,
> I had lived a blessèd time, for from this instant,
> There's nothing serious in mortality.
> All is but toys; renown and grace is dead,
> The wine of life is drawn, and the mere lees
> Is left this vault to brag of. (2.3.84–9)

And then:

> Who can be wise, amazed, temp'rate, and furious,
> Loyal and neutral, in a moment? No man.
> Th'expedition of my violent love
> Outran the pauser, reason. Here lay Duncan,
> His silver skin laced with his golden blood
> And his gashed stabs looked like a breach in nature,
> For ruin's wasteful entrance. There the murderers,
> Steeped in the colours of their trade; their daggers
> Unmannerly breeched with gore. Who could refrain,
> That had a heart to love and in that heart
> Courage to make's love known? (2.3.101–11)

These speeches mix Macbeth's sorrow, which may be genuine, or partly so, with the lies needed to conceal guilt and win the kingship.

In the brief interval between Duncan's murder and its discovery, Shakespeare faced a different dramatic problem. As in the aftermath of the discovery, Macbeth must conceal and deceive, but here – before Duncan's death is known – the problem is more acute because the moment (the porter with a hangover, the impatient noblemen) has a lower emotional temperature. Plainer, everyday language and rhetoric must convey the deceit. Thus, Macbeth's simple answer to Macduff's 'Is the king stirring, worthy thane?' so perfectly mixes deceit and truth that it deserves the gasp the line sometimes earns: 'Not yet' (2.3.38). 'Not yet' means, of course, both 'Duncan has not awakened until now' and 'Duncan will never again stir.' ('Not yet' = 'not so far' and 'no longer'.) The effect is repeated and intensified when Lennox asks, 'Goes the king hence today?', and Macbeth replies, 'He does – he did appoint so.'[1] Once again, Macbeth deceives and tells the truth as the witches do. He is the serpent but looks like the flower. The nerve-wrenching sequence concludes with Lennox's grand catalogue of portents, to which Macbeth replies truthfully and laconically, ''Twas a rough night' (2.3.53).[2]

---

[1] 'Goes the king hence' is a euphemism for 'Does the king die'; see 1.5.57 n.
[2] Speaking this line, David Garrick 'shew[ed] as much self-condemnation, as much fear of discovery, as much endeavour to conquer inquietude and assume ease, as ever was infused into, or intended for, the character' (Thomas Wilkes, *A General View of the Stage*, 1759, p. 249).

In the following act, similarly complex verbal simplicity greets the murderers: 'Well then, now have you considered of my speeches?' (3.1.77). Those first three words offer the actor an enormous range of possibilities.[1] Are they off-hand conversational filler ('Stand at ease', or 'Please be seated', or 'Listen to me', or 'Thank you for coming'), or the hesitant stutterings of a man ordering death, or the abrupt autocratic directions of a feared tyrant? At Stratford in 1955, Laurence Olivier

stood centre-stage . . . The murderers stood down-stage, left and right respectively. Olivier glanced arrogantly from one to the other, crooked the index finger of each hand in terrible invitation and made 'well' into a question. He paused. The murderers looked at one another. The index fingers swept downwards and pointed straight at the floor on each side of him. He said 'then' as a command. They moved slowly towards him like frightened stoats. Almost humorously, but with an edge of impatience, he said 'now', and an act of hypnosis was completed.[2]

Simple language, particularly euphemistic or indefinite language, continually counterpoints the play's extravagant rhetoric and dense metaphor. Thus, murder appears as 'it' – 'If it were done' (1.7.1), 'so, it will make us mad' (2.2.37), 'Thou canst not say I did it' (3.4.50) – and the grooms' guilt-dispelling drunkenness joins Lady Macbeth's half-manic excitement at committing murder as 'that' – 'That which hath made them drunk, hath made me bold' (2.2.1). Later, death is 'absence' (3.1.135) and 'safe' (3.4.25), and 'sent to peace' (3.2.20), dead.

A related linguistic register makes such indefinition a source of comedy: millions of obscene jokes and hundreds of dramatic scenes turn upon double, triple, or uncertain referents for 'it', or 'that', or equally innocuous words and phrases. While *Macbeth* has few comic moments and its wordplay is more often grim than fanciful, the way language blurs rather than clarifies, confuses rather than makes plain, connects paltering sisters and self-deceiving criminals and jokey Porter. Thus, the Porter's words – 'come in', 'stealing out', 'it' (again), 'lie' (and 'lye'), 'shift' – duplicate, make more intense and trivial and painful, the same linguistic acts when Macbeth and his lady speak them.

Appropriately for a play where prophecy and misunderstanding propel the action, paradox, oxymoron, antithesis, and self-contradiction fill the dialogue:

One of the play's most haunting and pervasive stylistic characteristics is a speech-rhythm that constantly contracts into self-checking half-rhyming half-lines: a device, surely, that realizes the foreshortening, the terrible presentness which Macbeth forces on himself, an existence without breadth and without perspective.[3]

Macbeth echoes the 'paltering' sisters – 'Fair is foul, and foul is fair' (1.1.12) – when he observes that the pathetic fallacy has failed: 'So foul and fair a day I have not seen' (1.3.36). It is a stormy yet victorious day, but victory and storm has each its place,

---

[1] Their punctuation, or editorial repunctuation, is therefore uncertain.

[2] Gareth Lloyd Evans, 'Macbeth in the twentieth century', *TQ* 1, 3 (1971), 39. After Olivier drew the Murderers to him, 'the three figures stood in a black-cloaked huddle, looking as sinister a group as the three Witches of Act 1' (R. A. Foakes (ed.), *Macbeth*, 1968, p. xxiv).

[3] Everett, p. 89. See also Eagleton, *William Shakespeare*, pp. 2–4; Margaret D. Burrell, '*Macbeth*: a study in paradox', *Shakespeare Jahrbuch* 90 (1954), 167–90; Madeleine Doran, 'The *Macbeth* music', *S.St.* 16 (1983), 156. See Textual Analysis, pp. 267–71 below, for the play's half-lines.

its category, and neither can influence or change the other. They coexist, but they do not interpenetrate, and only the musing mind would or could find sunshine and victory appropriate, if unpredictable, companions. By contrast, the words Macbeth unconsciously echoes are not a stable antithesis, a conversational *bon mot* as his remark is, but rather a worrying, endless, finally 'tedious' (3.4.138) and idiot-like (see 5.5.26) alternation: 'Fair is foul, and foul is fair' (1.1.12). For the witches, distinction exists only in its annihilation by or in alternation with its opposite. Categories – fair, foul – exist, but rather than being defined by difference or opposition, each *is* the other.

Macbeth's speech absorbs the 'sickening see-saw rhythm'[1] of witch-language – 'This supernatural soliciting / Cannot be ill, cannot be good' (1.3.129–30) – and he accurately echoes witch-thinking when he claims, 'nothing is, / But what is not' (1.3.140–1), a formulation precisely anticipating the Second Apparition's promise that 'none of woman born / Shall harm Macbeth' (4.1.79–80) and encapsulating at this moment and the later one time, birth, imagination, ambition, and their various defects. The initial paradox (how can one predicate anything of 'nothing'?) is explained by a further paradox (all that is, is not), and both are understood when we recognise that Macbeth speaks of the difference between 'present' conditions and 'imaginings' of the future, though the former are 'fears' and the latter 'horrible'.[2] None the less, his phrase denies reality or existence to both that which is and that which is not, to what he fantasises and what he imagines, to killing the king and being the king. In a play where submitting to or commanding time becomes a dominant issue, rhetorical conflict invades even the act of telling the time: echoing Banquo (2.1.1), Macbeth asks, 'What is the night?', and his wife replies, 'Almost at odds with morning, which is which' (3.4.126–7). Struggling with time and its consequences – birth and death, usurpation and punishment – Lord and Lady Macbeth sense time 'at odds' with itself, time *now* conflicting with time *then* and time *to come*.

Lady Macbeth's 'which is which' echoes the play's varied use of repetition, ranging from alliteration and assonance to repeated words and phrases, and rhyme.[3] Rhymes are the most easily heard and most easily remembered repetitions. They fill the sisters' speeches, which generally use trochaic tetrameter couplets, 'the fairy dialect of English literature', and *Macbeth* has more scenes that end with one or more couplets than any other Shakespearean play – both a higher proportion of such scenes, and the highest absolute number of them.[4] As well as rhyming, witch-language also alliterates – 'nine times nine . . . peak, and pine' (1.3.21–2) – but so does Macbeth's language:

[1] Knights, p. 20.
[2] Much later, Lady Macbeth speaks a similarly self-cancelling phrase, ''Tis safer to be that which we destroy' (3.2.6). Here, the word 'present', as in 'Present fears', has already been used once of death (1.2.64) and once of the honours Duncan bestows on Macbeth (1.3.53) and therefore represents both foul and fair. In *Poets' Grammar*, 1958, pp. 48–57, Francis Berry argues that 'the whole play is Future minded' and that the future indicative, especially associated with Lady Macbeth, 'drives the play', while Macbeth in this speech and elsewhere (e.g. 1.7.1ff.) employs the future subjunctive.
[3] On verbal repetition, see Maynard Mack, Jr, *Killing the King*, 1973, pp. 160–4, 173–4; Doran, pp. 159–60; G. W. Williams, '"Time for such a word": verbal echoing in *Macbeth*', *S.Sur.* 47 (1994), 153–9.
[4] See Edwin Guest, *A History of English Rhythms*, ed. W. W. Skeat, 1882, p. 179, and D. L. Chambers, *The Metre of 'Macbeth'*, 1903, pp. 19–23. On the witches' rhythms, see also 3.5.4 n.

9   This fresco of hell imagined as a castle was formerly in the Chapel of the Holy Cross, Stratford-upon-Avon. It includes various devils, one of them perhaps a devil 'porter of hell-gate' as at 2.3.1–2. See Glynne Wickham, 'Hell-castle and its door-keeper', in Kenneth Muir and Philip Edwards (eds.), *Aspects of 'Macbeth'*, 1977, pp. 39–45

> I had else been perfect;
> Whole as the marble, founded as the rock,
> As broad and general as the casing air:
> But now I am cabined, cribbed, confined, bound in
> To saucy doubts and fears.   (3.4.21–5)

Beside the alliteration on *c* ('casing . . . cabined, cribbed, confined') and the abrupt tremor, *ck*, in 'rock', this passage exemplifies many of the play's more subtle verbal effects: the way 'doubts' echoes the *d*s of the past participles and the vowels of 'bound' and 'founded', for example, or the way the *s*-sound runs from 'else' to 'as' to 'casing' to 'saucy' and 'fears'.[1] The word 'perfect' repeats more largely in the play and weaves solicitation and over-confidence with guilt and death: it begins in Macbeth's 'Stay, you imperfect speakers' (1.3.68), continues in his letter ('the perfectest report' (1.5.2)), reappears in Banquo's death, which will make Macbeth's health 'perfect' (3.1.107) and require 'the perfect spy o'th'time' (3.1.129), and concludes in the Messenger's assurance that he is 'perfect' in Lady Macduff's 'state of honour' (4.2.63).[2] 'Issue' also occurs frequently in the play. Before Act 5, Scene 4, we have heard it five times, each time with the meaning 'progeny' or 'children'; Siward then uses the word to mean 'result, outcome': 'But certain issue strokes must arbitrate. / Towards which, advance the war' (5.4.20–1). At once, varied meanings – children, the future, a dynasty's existence, the outcome of war against a tyrant – coalesce. Macbeth's fear of the 'unlineal hand' (3.1.64) depriving him of a 'fruitless crown' and Banquo's witch-inspired hope of 'children [who] shall be kings' (1.3.84) collide in 'issue', a word that now means not only 'children', but also victory or defeat, the result (the 'issue' and outcome) of an Anglo-Scottish war against Macbeth.

These rhetorical, sonic, and logical devices spin the mind, whirl it into endless oscillation, but the play, brief and with an angrily forceful plot, also imposes a kind of imagistic claustrophobia. A. C. Bradley identified important features of the play's figurative language:

> Darkness . . . even . . . blackness, broods over this tragedy . . . it [gives] . . . the impression of a black night broken by flashes of light and colour, sometimes vivid and even glaring . . . above all, the colour is the colour of blood.[3]

---

[1] Alliteration, here in Macbeth's speech and later (5.1) in his wife's, is the verbal equivalent of a human's inability to change or evolve through time; the recurrence to a letter or a sound voices an inability to escape a singular act – for Macbeth and Lady Macbeth, that act is murder – or move forward in time beyond or after the act. Compare Macbeth's soliloquy, 'Tomorrow, and tomorrow, and tomorrow . . .' (5.5.18–27).

[2] For a discussion of the play's uses of 'clear', see Doran, pp. 163–5. 'Present' is another repeated word; see e.g. 1.2.64, 1.3.53, 1.3.136. Jürgen Schäfer, *Shakespeares Stil: Germanisches und Romanisches Vokabular*, 1973, Appendix 2, details Shakespeare's characteristic pairing of Germanic and romance synonyms in the play. Among many other significantly repeated words in *Macbeth*, consider 'strange', used in *Macbeth* more frequently (sixteen times) than in any other Shakespearean text except *The Tempest* (eighteen times), and note that both *The Tempest* and *Macbeth* are unusually short Shakespearean plays (see pp. 23–4 above) and that the audience might therefore hear the word's repetition with unusual force. Only *Measure for Measure* (fifteen times), *Antony and Cleopatra* (fourteen times), and *Much Ado About Nothing* (eleven times) use 'strange' more frequently than ten times among the First Folio plays.

[3] Bradley, pp. 266–7.

10   'The King' by Hans Holbein the Younger (1538): an image from the 'dance of death', showing Death
as a skeleton pouring wine for a king. Compare King Macbeth and Banquo's Ghost in Act 3, Scene 4, and
see the Commentary at 3.4.37 SD

Yet, like other critics eager to see bipolar oppositions in the play's language and structures, Bradley does not notice how complex the colour-associations are. Macbeth's
famous

> Will all great Neptune's ocean wash this blood
> Clean from my hand? No: this my hand will rather
> The multitudinous seas incarnadine,
> Making the green one red.   (2.2.63–6)

powerfully puns on 'incarnadine', which means 'make red' and 'make flesh' or 'make
flesh-coloured'. For a murderer, his own flesh, or his victim's, might be blood-red, or
bloody, whatever the colour of the skin that covered that flesh. No simple code will
decipher the play's chromatic figures. Black and darkness may often be evil, white and
light good, red bloody, but the white of lily and linen is also cowardly, brightness Satanic,
red the colour of courage and the 'painting' of a drunkard's nose, and dark night the

time of restorative sleep.[1] Shakespeare often uses repeated (or 'iterative') images and 'image clusters',[2] and *Macbeth* brims with images of light and dark, of contraction and expansion (dwarf and giant, for example), of liquids (water, wine, milk, urine, blood), of horses that throw their riders or eat each other, of birds good and bad (owls, ravens, wrens, sparrows, hawks, eagles, martlets), of clothing (robes, seams, linings, sleeves, breeches), of procreation (children, eggs), and of sounds (knells, crickets, owls, clocks, bells, trumpets, knockings).[3]

Verbal and non-verbal sounds are especially prominent as fact and image in Act 2, Scene 2, where Macbeth hallucinates, it seems, a voice murdering sleep and Lady Macbeth hears both the sounds of nature (the owl's shriek, the crickets' cry) and her husband's steps as he returns from killing Duncan. The uncanny and indefinite 'voice' Macbeth hears (2.2.38) echoes the 'voice' of the crown Lady Macbeth hears, or says or thinks she hears, in Act 1, Scene 5. Later, with a gallantry both futile and ironic, Macduff tries to shield Lady Macbeth from knowledge of her crime:

> O gentle lady,
> 'Tis not for you to hear what I can speak.
> The repetition in a woman's ear
> Would murder as it fell. (2.3.76–9)

'Repetition in a woman's ear' murders as it falls again and again in Act 5, Scene 1, when Lady Macbeth repeats the echoing *Knock* of Act 2, Scene 3, and obsessively repeats words and actions:

No more o'that, my lord, no more o'that . . . To bed, to bed; there's knocking at the gate. Come, come, come, come, give me your hand; what's done cannot be undone. To bed, to bed, to bed.
(5.1.37–8, 56–8)

Sound-as-sound and sound-as-image make a brief moment wonderfully evocative. Macbeth reassures his wife:

>   ere the bat hath flown
> His cloistered flight, ere to black Hecate's summons
> The shard-born beetle with his drowsy hums
> Hath rung night's yawning peal, there shall be done
> A deed of dreadful note.
> LADY MACBETH   What's to be done?
> MACBETH Be innocent of the knowledge, dearest chuck,
>   Till thou applaud the deed. (3.2.40–6)

---

[1] Notable productions or adaptations of *Macbeth* in Africa and elsewhere demonstrate the imagery's malleability; consider e.g. Adrian Stanley's so-called 'Zulu' *Macbeth*, Glamis (*sic*!) Stadium, 1961, in what was then Salisbury, Southern Rhodesia (see *Johannesburg Star*, 5 April 1961, and *The Sphere*, 3 June 1961); *The Black Macbeth*, London, March 1972; Natal Theatre Workshop's production of Welcome Msomi's *UMabatha*, Aldwych Theatre, London, April 1972, which was revived at the Civic Theatre, Johannesburg, June 1995 (see Philip Revzin, 'A Zuluized "Macbeth"', *The Wall Street Journal*, 14 June 1995, p. A16). See illustration 19. For U.S. examples, see Ruby Cohn, *Modern Shakespeare Offshoots*, 1976, pp. 60–73, starting with Orson Welles's 'voodoo' *Macbeth* (New York, 14 April 1936).

[2] See Edward Armstrong, *Shakespeare's Imagination*, rev. edn, 1963.

[3] See, generally, Caroline Spurgeon, *Shakespeare's Imagery and What It Tells Us* (1935), Wolfgang Clemen, *The Development of Shakespeare's Imagery* (1951), and M. M. Mahood, *Shakespeare's Wordplay* (1957).

Before Lady Macbeth may applaud, before she claps as a theatre audience might (or so Macbeth hopes), at the deaths of Banquo and Fleance, husband, wife, and audience must hear an insect's sleepy humming as the sound of a church bell ringing the death of a day's labour, or the death of a parishioner. Tolling, the bell's open 'mouth' seems a human yawn, but its sound – its 'note' – marks and invites murder, the dreadful deed, the 'dreadful note', and the notably infamous. Hearing another, not metaphorical, bell, Macbeth went to an earlier crime:

> The bell invites me.
> Hear it not, Duncan, for it is a knell
> That summons thee to heaven or to hell.   (2.1.62–4)

The 'knell' returns twice more, tolling for the dead of Scotland, especially Macduff's family and retainers (4.3.172–3), and then for Siward's son (5.9.17).

With so much else that has become drained of meaning, sound loses its terror for Macbeth when he nears his end. Senses – taste, hearing, vision – marry in death:

> I have almost forgot the taste of fears;
> The time has been, my senses would have cooled
> To hear a night-shriek and my fell of hair
> Would at a dismal treatise rouse and stir
> As life were in't. I have supped full with horrors;
> Direness familiar to my slaughterous thoughts
> Cannot once start me. Wherefore was that cry?
> SEYTON The queen, my lord, is dead.
> MACBETH   She should have died hereafter;
> There would have been a time for such a word.   (5.5.9–17)

Macbeth's last phrase, 'a time for such a word', joins time with language, timing with speech, and directs us to the characters' recurrent failures to synchronise their words with events. There never should have been a 'time' for a word so infective as 'hail' – 'All hail Macbeth, that shalt be king' nor, Macbeth wishes, should there ever have been a time for so profoundly weary a word – 'She should have died' – as 'hereafter'. This moment's 'hereafter' became inevitable once there was a time when Macbeth heard the word first: 'All hail Macbeth, that shalt be king *hereafter*' (1.3.48; my italics).

Macbeth in performance

The history of *Macbeth* performed shows that there are only a few main production decisions. The answers make a performance taxonomy that persists through changes in costume and cast, changes in political and social emphases, changes in ideas of heroism, of the supernatural, and of the relation between women and men, parents and children, humankind and time. Equally, the history of *Macbeth* on stage shows how difficult theatrical interpretation, like dramatic criticism, has found those decisions. How should the sisters be represented? When did the idea of killing Duncan occur to Macbeth or Lady Macbeth? Which of the two is the stronger, the more resourcefully dedicated to death and supremacy? How should an actor perform what Michael Redgrave called the 'notoriously' difficult part of Macbeth? Redgrave specified the apparent contradiction

11   Two witches insert a cock and a snake into a cauldron, invoking thunder and rain: an image from Ulric
Molitor's *De Lamiis et phitonicis mulieribus* (1489). See 4.1.1–34

that Macbeth 'is described as noble and valiant', although 'during the whole play we see him do nothing that is either noble or valiant'.[1] Should the audience witness a palpable Ghost of Banquo in Act 3, Scene 4, or should the actor playing Macbeth in sheer imagination create the ghost as he created the dagger in Act 2, Scene 1? How is

[1] Michael Redgrave, 'Shakespeare and the actors', in John Garrett (ed.), *Talking of Shakespeare*, 1954, p. 138. Compare Bradley, p. 291: 'the first half of *Macbeth* is greater than the second, and in the first half Lady Macbeth not only appears more than in the second but exerts the ultimate deciding influence on the action'.

an actor to perform Macbeth after his long absence between Act 4, Scene 1, and Act 5, Scene 3?[1]

PERFORMANCE AND ADAPTATION BEFORE 1800

Macbeth seems always to have been a popular play on stage and in print. It is one of Shakespeare's most frequently performed plays since 1660 in England and later in other places and has been often revised, reimagined, and adapted to other media (opera, crime and historical novels, popular songs, silent and sound films, television, video, etc.), travestied, burlesqued, used as a starting point for satire, and employed in political cartoons and commercial advertising.[2]

Although no one can know how Jacobean professionals presented *Macbeth* (see Appendix 1, pp. 280–3 below), it is one of the handful of Shakespearean plays for which an early eyewitness account survives. Dr Simon Forman – astrologer, quack, accomplice in the poisoning of Sir Thomas Overbury, adviser to the Privy Council during the investigation of the Gunpowder Plot[3] – claims he witnessed a Globe performance of *Macbeth*, most likely in 1611:

In Mackbeth at the Glob[e], 1610 [i.e. 1611?], the 20 of Aprill . . . [Saturday], ther was to be observed, firste, howe Mackbeth and Bancko, 2 noble men of Scotland, Ridinge thorowe a wod [wood], the[re] stode before them 3 women feiries or Nimphes, And saluted Mackbeth, sayinge, 3 tyms unto him, haille Mackbeth, king of Codon; for thou shalt be a kinge, but shalt beget No kinges, &c. Then said Bancko, What all to Mackbeth And nothing to me. Yes, said the nimphes, haille to thee Bancko, thou shalt beget kinges, yet be no kinge. And so they departed & cam to the Courte of Scotland to Dunkin king of Scotes, and yt was in the dais of Edward the Confessor. And Dunkin bad them both kindly wellcome, And made Mackbeth forth with Prince of Northumberland, and sent him hom to his own castell, and appointed Mackbeth to provid for him, for he would sup with him the next dai at night, & did soe. And Mackebeth contrived to kill Dunkin, & thorowe the persuasion of his wife did that night Murder the kinge in his own Castell, beinge his guest. And ther were many prodigies seen that night & the dai before. And when Mack Beth had murdred the kinge, the blod on his handes could not be washed of[f] by

---

[1] Commenting on productions since 1955, Michael Billington offers this summary view: 'First, the play cannot work without a magnetic central pair: it is much more a star vehicle than a company show. Second, though it needs a consistent imaginative world, no amount of hectic design can compete with Shakespeare's poetic scene painting. Third[,] it is a play of breathless narrative excitement which appears broken-backed once you slice it in half [by introducing an interval]' (*The Guardian*, 27 September 1995).

[2] See, for example, Arthur Colby Sprague, *Shakespeare and the Actors: The Stage Business in His Plays 1660–1905*, 1944, chapter 5; Dennis Bartholomeusz, *'Macbeth' and the Players*, 1969; Rosenberg; Bernice Kliman, *Shakespeare in Performance: 'Macbeth'*, 1992; Cohn, chapter 2. There is no narrative history of *Macbeth*'s uses in song, novel, advertisement, etc., but see Thomas Wheeler, *'Macbeth': An Annotated Bibliography*, 1990, pp. 897–939. Kenneth S. Rothwell and Annabelle Henkin Melzer, *Shakespeare on Screen: An International Filmography and Videography*, 1990, pp. 147–71, lists film and video versions of *Macbeth*, which are second in number only to those of *Hamlet*. For actors' written discussions of the performed play, see Carol Jones Carlisle, *Shakespeare from the Greenroom*, 1969, chapter 5. Among many treatments see such novels (historical and mystery or thriller) as Marvin Kaye, *Bullets for Macbeth* (1976), Nigel Tranter, *MacBeth the King* (1978), Dorothy Dunnett, *King Hereafter* (1982), Ngaio Marsh, *Light Thickens* (1982), Nicolas Freeling, *Lady Macbeth* (1988), and such plays as Gordon Bottomley, *Gruach* (1921), Barbara Garson, *MacBird* (1966), Charles Marowitz, *A Macbeth* (1971), Eugene Ionesco, *Macbett* (1972), Tom Stoppard, *Dogg's Hamlet, Cahoot's Macbeth* (1980).

[3] See Beatrice White, *Cast of Ravens*, 1965, *passim*, and Mark Nicholls, *Investigating Gunpowder Plot*, 1991, p. 13.

Any meanes, nor from his wives handes, which handled the bloddi daggers in hiding them, By which means they became both moch amazed & Affronted. The murder being knowen, Dunkins 2 sonns fled, the on[e] to England, the [other to] Walles, to save them selves, they being fled, they were supposed guilty of the murder of their father, which was nothinge so. Then was Mackbeth crowned kinge, and then he for feare of Banko, his old companion, that he should beget kinges but be no kinge him selfe, he contrived the death of Banko, and caused him to be Murdred on the way as he Rode. The next night, beinge at supper with his noble men whom he had bid to a feaste to the which also Banco should have com, he began to speake of Noble Banco, and to wish that he wer ther. And as he thus did, standing up to drincke a Carouse to him, the ghoste of Banco came and sate down in his cheier behind him. And he turninge About to sit down Again sawe the goste of Banco, which [af]fronted him so, that he fell into a great passion of fear and fury, Utterynge many wordes about his murder, by which, when they h[e]ard that Banco was Murdred they Suspected Mackbet.

Then MackDove fled to England to the kinges sonn, And soe they Raised an Army, And cam into Scotland, and at Dunston Anyse overthrue Mackbet. In the meantyme whille Macdovee was in England, Mackbet slewe Mackdoves wife & children, and after in the battelle Mackdove slewe Mackbet.

Observe Also howe Mackbetes quen did Rise in the night in her slepe, & walke and talked and confessed all, & the docter noted her wordes.[1]

Forman's description deviates from the Folio narrative (e.g. Macbeth as 'Prince of Northumberland' rather than Malcolm as Prince of Cumberland; Macbeth as 'king of Codon' rather than Thane of Cawdor; a scene of bloody handwashing after the murder) and records some questionable details – Raphael Holinshed's account of Macbeth's reign (read or remembered) apparently 'contaminates' Forman's diary-entry – but there can be little doubt that Forman saw *Macbeth*, probably on the day, month, and year (adjusted for an easy error)[2] he says he did.

Aside from Forman's account and the probable early revision of the play by Thomas Middleton (see Textual Analysis, pp. 271–5 below), evidence of the play's history before 1660 is mostly speculative: John Webster echoes *Macbeth* 2.2.57–8, 4.3.221, and 5.1.37 in *The White Devil* (*c.* 1612); ghost-scenes in Thomas Middleton's *The Puritan* (1607) and Francis Beaumont's *The Knight of the Burning Pestle* (*c.* 1608, printed 1613) may record other dramatists' responses to Banquo's Ghost in *Macbeth* Act 3, Scene 4; the anonymous *Thorny Abbey, or The London Maid* (*c.* 1615, first printed in *Gratiae Theatrales*, 1662) uses Holinshed's King Duff narrative, probably because *Macbeth* did; Middleton's *A Game at Chess* (1624) imitates *Macbeth* Act 4, Scene 3; Henry Killigrew's

[1] Simon Forman, *Booke of Plaies* (Bodleian Library MS. Ashmole 208, folios 207r–v), as edited in E. K. Chambers, *William Shakespeare: A Study of Facts and Problems*, 2 vols., 1930, 11, 337–8, slightly modernised. A facsimile of Forman's entry appears in S. Schoenbaum, *William Shakespeare: Records and Images*, 1981, illustration 3.

[2] 20 April was a Saturday in 1611, not 1610 (as Forman's manuscript has it): the error (if it is one) is plausible because Jacobeans dated the new year in two ways, from 1 January, the modern practice, and from 25 March (the legal year); if Forman thought about years in the latter style, '1611' would have been less than a month old on 20 April, and he might have made what is still a common mistake after the 'new' year begins. Forman's probable borrowings from Holinshed are discussed by Leah Scragg, 'Macbeth on horseback', *S.Sur.* 26 (1973), 81–8, and the critical significance of Forman's 'errors' by Stephen Orgel, 'Acting scripts, performing texts', in Randall McLeod (ed.), *Crisis in Editing: Texts of the English Renaissance*, 1994, pp. 268–72.

The Conspiracy (1635) may imitate the use of the Murderers in *Macbeth*.[1] The possible 'echo' in *The Knight of the Burning Pestle* is particularly interesting because Jasper's entrance as a fake ghost may suggest how Richard Burbage, the actor who probably first played Macbeth (see Appendix 1, p. 280 below), or another early actor of the part reacted to Banquo's Ghost, or how an early audience expected an actor to react upon seeing a stage-ghost:

When thou art at thy Table with thy friends
Merry in heart, and fild with swelling wine,
Il'e come in midst of all thy pride and mirth,
Invisible to all men but thy selfe,
And whisper such a sad tale in thine eare,
Shall make thee let the Cuppe fall from thy hand,
And stand as mute and pale as Death it selfe.[2]

About 1639–42, John Milton jotted notes on subjects for plays or poems, including – after a detailed outline of 'Adam unparadiz'd' – 'Scotch [hi]stories or rather brittish of the north parts'. Among his proposed subjects were:

Duffe, & Donwald

a strange story of [*deleted*: revenging] witchcraft, & murder discover'd, & reveng'd. Scotch [hi]story. 149. &c.

. . . . .

Kenneth

who having privily poison'd Malcolm Duffe, that his own son might succeed is slain by Fenela. Scotch hist[ory]. p. 157. 158. &c.

Macbeth

beginning at the arrivall of Malcolm at Mackduffe. The matter of Duncan may be express't by the appearing of his ghost.[3]

Milton's numerals refer to pages in Holinshed's *Chronicles* (1587), and Milton's subjects include the three Holinshed-narratives Shakespeare apparently consulted in writing *Macbeth*. The note on 'Macbeth' envisages a Greek-derived tragedy, like Milton's *Samson Agonistes*, in which the action would begin with *Macbeth* Act 4, Scene 3, and

[1] For the Webster echoes, see the respective Commentary notes; the *Puritan* 'reference' – 'weele ha the ghost ith white sheete sit at upper end a'th Table' (*The Puritan*, 1607, sig. H1v) – has been firmly disputed in R. V. Holdsworth, '*Macbeth* and *The Puritan*', *N & Q* 235 (1990), 204–5, because similar material in other texts by Thomas Middleton seems to 'explain' the incident better than an allusion to *Macbeth*; for *Thorny Abbey*, see William M. Baillie (ed.), *A Choice Ternary of English Plays*, 1984, pp. 26–30 (date), 33–6 (links with *Macbeth*), 270–5 (Holinshed in *Macbeth* and *Thorny Abbey*); for *A Game at Chess*, see R. C. Bald's edn, 1929, p. 16, and Margot Heinemann, *Puritanism and Theatre*, 1980, p. 164; for Killigrew, *The Conspiracy*, see Martin Wiggins, *Journeymen in Murder: The Assassin in English Renaissance Drama*, 1991, p. 202.
[2] *The Knight of the Burning Pestle*, 1613, sig. I3r, slightly modernised.
[3] *John Milton Poems: Reproduced in Facsimile from the Manuscript in Trinity College, Cambridge*, 1972, p. 41. See e.g. 'Milton's "Macbeth"', in John W. Hales, *Folia Litteraria*, 1893, pp. 198–219; E. E. Kellett, 'Macbeth and Satan', *London Quarterly and Holborn Review*, July 1939, pp. 289–99; W. R. Parker, *Milton: A Biography*, 2 vols., 1968, I, 190–1, and II, 843 n. 15.

12   The Great Seal of King James I, from Francis Sandford, *A Genealogical History of the Kings of England* (1677), p. 514: the seal illustrates James I's ceremonial accoutrements: sceptre, ball, mound. See 4.1.120 and Supplementary Note, p. 259 below. Sandford describes the 'Sceptre of the Flower-de-Lize . . . and . . . the Ball or Mound with a Cross on the top thereof' in his *History*, p. 519

use Duncan's ghost as a narrator of prior events.[1] While these notes do not mention Shakespeare's *Macbeth*, Milton could certainly have known the performed and printed play; he wrote a splendid commendatory poem for the Second Folio (1632), and in his *Poems* (1645) famously described 'the well-trod stage' where 'sweetest *Shakespear* fancies childe / Warble[s] his native Wood-notes wilde' ('L'Allegro', lines 131 and 133–4). Milton's knowledge of both Shakespeare performed and the theatre may have been direct: his father (also John Milton) apparently served as a trustee of the King's Men's Blackfriars theatre property for Richard Burbage's widow Winifred and her children after the famous actor's death in 1619.[2]

---

[1] Hales, *Folia Litteraria*, pp. 211–12, infers from Milton's separate notes on 'Duffe & Donwald' that Milton would not have combined that story with Macbeth's as Shakespeare did.
[2] See Herbert Berry, 'The stage and boxes at Blackfriars' (1966), rpt. in Berry, *Shakespeare's Playhouses*, 1987, pp. 70–1.

From the period of Milton, two important promptbooks of *Macbeth* have been identified: the 'Padua' promptbook of *c.* 1625–35 (a copy of the 1623 Folio named for its present custodian, the University of Padua library) and the 'Smock Alley' promptbook of *c.* 1674–82 (a copy of the 1663–4 Folio named for the Dublin theatre in which it was performed).[1] Although the Padua promptbook may not report the earliest public theatre-practices, it fascinatingly records a performance text predating those that the Restoration's very different cultural and professional circumstances created. Remarkably, the Padua promptbook anticipates later acting texts by reducing the Folio's verbal density: the 'hard' language of Macbeth's speeches in Act 1, Scenes 3 and 7 is trimmed; the Porter's part is cut entirely, as is Macbeth's interview with the murderers in Act 3, Scene 1; in Act 4, Scene 2, Ross loses his most impenetrable language (from 'I dare not speak' to 'Each way and none'); Macbeth's powerful soliloquy (Act 5, Scene 3) on 'the sere, the yellow leaf' is cut; *the other three Witches* of Act 4, Scene 1, disappear, though Hecate may remain.

Political or religious concerns may have motivated some of these and other cuts: Macbeth's soliloquy on royal *pathos* ('To be thus is nothing . . .') in Act 3, Scene 1, is harshly treated, and his now celebrated soliloquy, 'I have lived long enough . . .' (5.3.22ff.), implying a desire for death, may have been cut for the same reason; concerns about blasphemy, profanity or simply 'inappropriate' comedy might account for the Porter's disappearance here as they seem to do in later theatrical versions. Padua also makes more obviously practical (and later very popular) cuts: Act 3, Scene 6, is deleted, for instance, and Act 4, Scene 3, loses more than sixty lines, though part of the English Doctor episode remains. The Padua promptbook is also the first known document to specify a 'Cauldrone' in the opening stage direction for Act 4, Scene 1, and interestingly directs Macbeth to enter before the last line of Lady Macbeth's opening speech of Act 2, Scene 2, 'Whether they [the comatose grooms] live or die'.[2] The Smock Alley promptbook has been influenced by William Davenant's Restoration adaptation, possibly as seen in the theatre rather than read in the 1674 text. Like Davenant, the persons who marked the Dublin promptbook reduced the Jacobean text's verbal complexity, cut or combined several of Shakespeare's thanes and messengers, and severely reduced the Porter's rôle, but allowed Lady Macbeth to appear in Act 2, Scene 3, as many later theatre texts did not. The adapters 'Clearly . . . have one aim in mind: entertainment at any cost'.[3]

The quarto *Macbeth* published in 1673 may represent a revised version performed before the theatres were closed in 1642 or just after professional playing legally resumed

---

[1] See G. Blakemore Evans (ed.), *Shakespearean Prompt-Books of the Seventeenth Century*, 7 vols., 1960–89, 1, i (General Introduction, Introduction to Padua *Macbeth*, collations), 1, ii (facsimile of Padua *Macbeth*), and v, i (Introduction and collations to Smock Alley *Macbeth*) and v, ii (facsimile of Smock Alley *Macbeth*). My discussion depends upon Evans's superb work. Evans has also identified a 1694 version of *Macbeth*, based on F2 and probably prepared for amateur performance at an English Roman Catholic foundation in France; see G. Blakemore Evans, 'The Douai Manuscript – six Shakespearean transcripts (1694–95)', *PQ* 41 (1962), 158–72, esp. pp. 171–2.

[2] For a more comprehensive discussion of 'Padua', its cuts, and their significance, see Orgel, 'Acting scripts', pp. 255–8.

[3] Evans, *Shakespearean Prompt-Books*, v, i, p. 19; for further details of the Smock Alley changes, see Evans *passim*.

about 1660. William Davenant's adaptation, published posthumously in 1674, but probably performed in 'December 1666 or . . . [in] November 1664',[1] supplanted the Folio version until 1744, when David Garrick offered London audiences a text closer to the Folio.[2] Thereafter, Davenant's version gave way slowly (Spranger Barry used it at Covent Garden in the 1750s, for example), and some of Davenant's lines and stage business have persisted into twentieth-century productions.[3] Colley Cibber, who knew only Davenant's adaptation on stage, thought that Mrs Betterton, 'tho' far advanc'd in Years', outstripped her younger competitor Mrs Barry – superior in 'Strength, and Melody of Voice' – because Mrs Betterton commanded 'quick and careless Strokes of Terror, from the Disorder of a guilty Mind'.[4] Samuel Pepys, also knowing only Davenant's adapted spectacle, identified a singular oddity: the play 'appears a most excellent play in all respects, but especially in divertisement, though it be a deep tragedy; which is a strange perfection in a tragedy, it being most proper here and suitable'.[5]

An anonymous pamphlet, *An Essay on Acting . . . of a certain fashionable faulty actor . . .* [with] *A short criticism on his acting of Macbeth* (1744), apparently David Garrick's effort to promote his own first appearance in the part (7 January 1744),[6] satirises the acting tradition as Garrick found it. Garrick's contemporary rival was James Quin, and the pamphlet attacks Quin's Macbeth – a 'Man . . . out of his Depth' – in Act 2, Scene 2, by pretending to criticise Garrick's performance:

he [the actor playing Macbeth] should not rivet his Eyes to an *imaginary* Object [the dagger], as if it *really* was there, but should shew an *unsettled Motion* in his Eye, like one not quite awak'd from some disordering Dream; his *Hands* and *Fingers* should not be *immoveable*, but *restless* . . . *Come let me clutch thee*! is not to be done by *one* Motion only, but by several *successive Catches* at it, first with one Hand, and then with the other, preserving the same Motion, at the same Time, with his Feet, like a Man, who out of his Depth, and half drowned in his Struggles, *catches* at *Air* for *Substance*: This would make the Spectator's Blood run cold, and he would almost feel the Agonies of the Murderer himself.[7]

Whatever any spectator felt then, my blood runs as cold as Quin's must have done at this savaging of a style now found over-declamatory and over-acted. Garrick's own performance of the dagger soliloquy – when he 'rivet[ed] his Eyes to an *imaginary*

---

[1] See Scouten, 'The premiere of Davenant's adaptation of *Macbeth*', pp. 290–1, though Q1673 is not quite 'Shakespeare's play' (Scouten, p. 290), since it makes some 'editorial' changes and includes two additional witch song-routines; see Appendix 2, pp. 284–6 below. Some of Davenant's changes are discussed in Appendix 2, but they are too extensive and interesting for easy summary; see, in part, Hazelton Spencer, ''D' Avenant's *Macbeth* and Shakespeare's', *PMLA* 40 (1925), 619–44, esp. pp. 628–41, and Richard Kroll, 'Emblem and empiricism in Davenant's *Macbeth*', *ELH* 57 (1990), 835–64.

[2] By G. W. Stone's counts, Folio *Macbeth* has approximately 2,341 lines, Davenant's version 2,198, Garrick's 2,072; see George Winchester Stone, Jr, 'Garrick's handling of *Macbeth*', *SP* 38 (1941), 609–28, esp. 621. For a slightly different count, see p. 23 above.

[3] Bartholomeusz, p. 94; Burnim, *David Garrick*, p. 110; Rosenberg, pp. 111–12. As late as W. C. Macready's farewell *Macbeth* in 1851, for example, all of Q1673's and Davenant's witch-song and witch-spectacle still appeared; see Alan S. Downer, *The Eminent Tragedian: William Charles Macready*, 1966, pp. 318–38.

[4] Colley Cibber, *An Apology for the Life of Mr Colley Cibber, Comedian*, 1740, p. 96.

[5] Pepys, VIII, 7 (7 January 1667).

[6] For the attribution to Garrick, see Davies, *Life*, I, 163–4.

[7] [David Garrick?] *An Essay on Acting*, 1744, sigs. D1r–v.

Object, as if it *really* was there' – became a kind of hallmark and travelling party-piece which received extravagant praise.[1]

Satire obscures Garrick's complaints, but he apparently attacks a traditional piece of business when he pretends to praise the way Macbeth first toasts the absent Banquo and then recognises the Ghost:

the Glass of Wine in his Hand should not be dash'd upon the Ground, but it should fall *gently* from him, and he should not discover the least Consciousness of having such a Vehicle in his Hand, his Memory being quite lost in the present Guilt and Horror of his Imagination.[2]

This passage seemingly means that Garrick found Quin's nerveless 'Horror' inappropriate and preferred a violent dashing of the glass. Later anecdote records Quin's reactions to his young rival's performance, including surprise at the 'new' (actually Shakespearean and newly restored) imprecation, 'The devil damn thee black, thou cream-faced loon. / Where got'st thou that goose-look?' (5.3.11–12).[3]

Through superb talent, assiduous amateur scholarship, and adroit self-promotion, Garrick made himself a star not only in the theatre but among an Enlightenment constellation – Samuel Johnson, David Hume, Joshua Reynolds – that equalled any in the continental European galaxy. One contemporary is wholly adulatory and, significantly, praises Garrick's performance of the later acts:

Garrick could alone comprehend and execute the complicated passages of Macbeth. From the first scene, in which he was accosted by the witches to the end of the part, he was animated and consistent.[4]

While Garrick's *Macbeth* exploited the best contemporary scholarship (that of Theobald, Johnson, Warburton, and Styan Thirlby),[5] his text also made many of the same cuts as Davenant and included a good deal of Davenant's supposedly unacceptable writing.[6] Davenant had Macbeth die on-stage with a single line, 'Farewell vain World,

---

[1] On Garrick's second Parisian visit in July 1765, 'en chambre, dans son habit ordinaire, sans aucun secours de l'illusion théâtrale', Garrick delivered the speech to a rapt audience; see F. A. Hedgcock, *Un Acteur cosmopolite: David Garrick et ses amis français*, 1911, p. 25. On the same tour, Charles Collé's diary records another semi-private performance of the dagger-scene as 'une espèce de pantomime tragique' (Hedgcock, p. 65). Such recital-demonstrations, including scores of dagger-scenes where Garrick's powers before a non-English-speaking audience were especially praised, became common during his continental visits; see Hedgcock, pp. 115–19, for France, and Thomas Davies, *Dramatic Micellanies* [*sic*], 3 vols., 1783–4, II, 141, for Italy.

[2] *An Essay on Acting*, sig. D3r. The 'business' Garrick attacks may be Jacobean; see the quotation from *Knight of the Burning Pestle*, p. 59 above.

[3] 'And when he [Quin] heard Garrick declaiming: "The devil damn . . . that goose-look?" he asked him where he had found such strange language' (Percy Fitzgerald, *A New History of the English Stage*, 2 vols., 1882, II, 162). Garrick's promptbook omits the oath, though it keeps the 'undignified' goose-reference (Bartholomeusz, p. 74).

[4] Davies, *Micellanies*, II, 133–4; even more fulsome descriptions appear in a work dedicated to Garrick: [Francis Gentleman,] *The Dramatic Censor*, 2 vols., 1770, I, 107–8.

[5] See Stone, pp. 615–17, and Bartholomeusz, p. 46. What most scholars consider Garrick's 'promptbook', a marked copy of *Macbeth* in *Bell's Edition of Shakespeare's Plays*, 9 vols. (1773–4), I (1773), is now in the Folger Shakespeare Library, Washington, D. C. (Burnim, p. 108).

[6] Like Davenant, Garrick omitted the Porter of *Macbeth* 2.3, most of 4.2 (Lady Macduff and her son), most of Malcolm's self-accusation in 4.3, and 5.2; see Stone; Burnim, chap. 6, esp. p. 104; Bartholomeusz,

and what's most vain in it, *Ambition*', which Garrick replaced with his own execrable pastiche – a blend of Dryden and Marlowe:

> 'Tis done! the scene of life will quickly close.
> Ambition's vain, delusive dreams are fled,
> And now I wake to darkness, guilt and horror;
> I cannot bear it! let me shake it off –
> 'Two' not be; my soul is clogg'd with blood –
> I cannot rise! I dare not ask for mercy –
> It is too late, hell drags me down; I sink,
> I sink – Oh! – my soul is lost for ever!
> Oh![1]

David Garrick's performances as Macbeth were supported by those of Hannah Pritchard as Lady Macbeth – he effectively abandoned the rôle after her retirement – and he remains perhaps the only English actor to have conquered the part (see illustration 13). Almost two centuries later, a distinguished critic succinctly praised and faulted Laurence Olivier by comparing him to Garrick: 'Since it would seem that with the exception of Garrick a great Macbeth has never been in the calendar, it is reasonable to expect that the new one should be lacking in perfect adequacy.'[2]

John Philip Kemble, eighteenth-century London's other memorable Macbeth, was, like Garrick, a distinguished actor-manager; like Garrick, Kemble rejoiced in a superb Lady Macbeth (Sarah Siddons, his sister); like Garrick, Kemble cultivated a reputation as a scholarly exponent of the 'true', as opposed to the adapted or revised, Shakespearean text. Contemporary accounts and Kemble's promptbook show that his performances, also like Garrick's, kept much of Davenant's adaptation and even further reduced the material which neo-classical taste found unacceptable. Kemble's performances also increased the spectacle: though Shakespeare's three witches were treated fairly seriously, Kemble deployed a chorus of fifty or more singing, dancing, comic witches from at least 1794 onward.[3] Lady Macduff and her son vanish, and their deaths are reported only; the Porter is omitted. And, continuing long theatrical practice, the dialogue's coruscating metaphor is reduced yet further.[4]

Kemble was 'An actor whose style combined an unswerving, even regularity with occasional outbursts of great emotion'; his manner and physique made him an

---

chap. 4. Garrick also retained many of Davenant's genteelisms – e.g. replacing 'stool' (3.4.68) with 'chair', a change that remained in Macready's text (Downer, p. 332).

[1] *Bell's Edition of Shakespeare's Plays*, 1, *Macbeth* pagination sequence, p. 69.

[2] James Agate, reviewing Michel Saint-Denis's Old Vic production, 26 November 1937; see Agate, *Brief Chronicles*, 1943, p. 241.

[3] See Joseph W. Donohue, Jr, 'Kemble's production of *Macbeth* (1794): some notes on scene painters, scenery, special effects, and costumes', *ThN* 21 (1966–7), 69, and J. C. Trewin, 'Macbeth in the nineteenth century', *TQ* 1, 3 (1971), 28.

[4] Kemble cut 'in 1, 7 five lines developing the metaphor of "pity, like a naked new-born babe"; in 11, 2 five lines around the metaphor of "Sleep that knits up the raveled sleave of care"; in 111, 1 seventeen lines of the comparison of men to dogs; in 1v, 2 nine lines of meteorological violence culminating in "nature's germens tumble all together" . . .' (Charles H. Shattuck (ed.), *John Philip Kemble Promptbooks*, 11 vols., 1974, v, *Macbeth* promptbook, p. ii). Siddons's misquotations in her 'Remarks on the character of Lady Macbeth', in Thomas Campbell, *Life of Mrs Siddons*, 2 vols., 1834, 11, 10–34 – e.g. 'I would scorn' for 'I shame' (2.2.67) – probably reflect the text she performed rather than a poor memory.

13   Henry Fuseli's representation, *c.* 1766, of David Garrick as Macbeth entering to Hannah Pritchard as Lady Macbeth after the murder of King Duncan, Act 2, Scene 2. For a discussion of this watercolour and another contemporary painting of the same performers, see Stephen Leo Carr, 'Verbal–visual relationships: Zoffany's and Füseli's illustrations of *Macbeth'*, *Art History* 3 (1980), 375–85

exceptional Coriolanus but a less exceptional Macbeth. Since, however, he 'specialized in the subjective presentation of excited mental states in characters whose grip on exterior reality was at best tenuous',[1] his Macbeth complemented Sarah Siddons's famous Lady Macbeth:

Macbeth in Kemble's hand is only a co-operating part. I can conceive Garrick to have sunk Lady Macbeth as much as Mrs Siddons does Macbeth, yet when you see Mrs Siddons play this part you scarcely can believe that any acting could make her part subordinate . . . She turns Macbeth to her purpose, makes him her mere instrument, guides, directs, and inspires the whole plot. Like Macbeth's evil genius she hurries him on in the mad career of ambition and cruelty from which his nature would have shrunk.[2]

[1] Joseph Donohue, 'Macbeth in the eighteenth century', in *TQ*, 1, 3 (1971), 23; for an extended analysis of Kemble's performance, see Donohue, 'Kemble and Mrs Siddons in *Macbeth*: the Romantic approach to tragic character', *ThN* 22 (1967–8), 65–86, and Donohue, *Dramatic Character in the English Romantic Age*, 1970, pp. 253–69.
[2] H. C. Fleeming Jenkin, 'Mrs Siddons as Lady Macbeth. From contemporary notes by George Joseph Bell', *The Nineteenth Century* 3 (1878), 296–313, on Siddons's performance in Edinburgh *c.* 1809, as reprinted in Jenkin, *Papers on Acting*, III (1915), 25–68; quotation from pp. 35–6. Decades later, the 'evil genius'

The actor who – quite contrary to Garrick's lunging astonishment – greeted the sisters in Act 1, Scene 3, 'with marked inattention and indifference . . . in a *stately* posture, waving the hand with *studied* dignity', became at the end of Act 1, Scene 5, a much subdued figure, with Siddons's Lady Macbeth 'Leading him out, cajoling him, her hand on his shoulder clapping him'.[1]

Returning with the bloody daggers and uncertain of the Lady's whereabouts, Kemble's Macbeth spoke the lines from 'Didst thou not hear a noise?' (2.2.14) 'like a horrid secret – a whisper in the dark' and at the end of the scene stood 'motionless . . . his eye fixed . . . quite rooted to the spot', and Siddons's Lady Macbeth repeats some of the action from Act 1, Scene 5:

Then alarm steals on her, increasing to agony lest his reason be quite gone and discovery be inevitable. Strikes him on the shoulder, pulls him from his fixed posture, forces him away, he talking as he goes.[2]

Sarah Siddons's Lady Macbeth overshadowed her brother's Macbeth,[3] though the turning-point in the characters' relative 'strength' occurred, in their performances as in so many others, during the banquet scene (Act 3, Scene 4). More than 150 years later, Edith Evans commented on Lady Macbeth's 'usually inexplicable collapse' in Act 3, Scene 4 (or somewhere unseen by the audience between that scene and Act 5, Scene 1), and explained why she had never taken the part: 'there's a page missing' – that is, Shakespeare did not supply the character with a bridge or motivation for the change.[4] Kemble – repeating Garrick's business – violently threw his cup of wine when the Ghost first appears; one commentator sarcastically demanded a return to

interpretation prevailed in a discussion of Henry Irving's Macbeth; see the anonymous pamphlet, *Sheridan Knowles' Conception and Mr Irving's Performance of Macbeth*, 1876, p. 19.

[1] A. B. G. [i.e. Augustus Bozzi Granville?], *Critical Observations on Mr Kemble's Performances at the Theatre Royal Liverpool*, 1811, p. 22, and G. J. Bell in Jenkin, p. 44 n. 19. For Garrick's reaction, see Bartholomeusz, p. 41. Nearly a century later, Ellen Terry repeated the gesture to her Macbeth, Henry Irving; see Alan Hughes, *Henry Irving, Shakespearean*, 1981, p. 100.

[2] G. J. Bell in Jenkin, pp. 56–7 n. 44. Going to replace the daggers in Duncan's chamber, Mrs Siddons 'turn[ed] towards him [Macbeth] stooping, and with the finger pointed to him with malignant energy sa[id] "If he do bleed," etc.' (Bell in Jenkin, p. 55 n. 43). Nearly two centuries later (1955), Vivien Leigh's Lady 'push[ed]' her Lord off-stage here (see Michael Mullin (ed.), *Macbeth Onstage: An Annotated Facsimile of Glen Byam Shaw's 1955 Promptbook*, 1976, p. 91).

[3] Many observers commented on what one called Kemble's 'calm, slow, phlegmatic enunciation, oftentimes carried to affectation' and did not enjoy the way he spoke Macbeth's soliloquy opening Act 1, Scene 7: 'like a *speech* to be recited' and 'the sedate, determined reasoning of a cool logician . . . the serene and calm reflection of a metaphysical speculator'. See, respectively, for the first and third quotations, A. B. G., *Critical Observations*, pp. 21 and 24, and for the second, G. J. Bell in Jenkin, p. 45. The same criticism was made much later of Henry Irving's delivery of this soliloquy as 'calm, cold, over-logical . . . passionless' (*Sheridan Knowles' Conception*, p. 13).

[4] Edith Evans, quoted in Jack Tinker's review of the Dench–McKellen *Macbeth, Daily Mail*, 10 September 1976; Tinker continues: 'Miss Dench . . . lets us read that missing page. First, by exerting a powerful sexual sway over her husband . . . Then, finding her support brusquely rejected once he has come to power, she is a shattered ghost by the time she has to officiate at the otherwise ghostless feast.' The Edith Evans anecdote may well be apocryphal: another 'nice story' attributes her refusal to play Lady Macbeth to 'the lady's "lack of hospitality"' (Janet Suzman in Carole Woddis (ed.), *'Sheer Bloody Magic': Conversations with Actresses*, 1991, p. 105). For other twentieth-century testimony here, see Maxine Audley (Lady Macduff, Stratford, 1955), p. 80 below.

Quin's 'Horror of his Imagination'.[1] On the Ghost's second appearance, Garrick's practice seems to have been undecided, sometimes horrified and immobile, sometimes vigorously forcing the Ghost off-stage.[2]

The moment raises two further questions: does the audience see the Ghost? and how does Lady Macbeth respond to the Ghost? Literary and theatrical critics made the first choice turn on some over-realistic questions: if the Ghost of Act 3, Scene 4, is visible to Macbeth and the audience but not to the guests or to Lady Macbeth, then (critics agree) our awareness associates us with guilty Macbeth. Shakespeare was not so logically scrupulous. Both Banquo and Macbeth see the witches in Act 1, Scene 3, and the Folio text clearly expects the audience to see the witches in Act 3, Scene 5, and Act 4, Scene 1, though in the last case, Lennox has witnessed neither witches nor apparitions. If we believe Simon Forman's Jacobean account, the Ghost seems to have been visible from the earliest performances, but when Kemble reopened Drury Lane on 21 April 1794 with the young Edmund Kean, according to legend, as one of the many goblins, Kemble omitted a visible Ghost of Banquo and thus initiated a long theatrical and critical debate.[3] Kemble 'chid and scolded' the Ghost, imagined or not, 'and rose in vehemence and courage as he went on', but Mrs Siddons, defying contemporary critics – who generally maintained that Lady Macbeth does not here know of Banquo's death and supposes Macbeth is reliving the murder of Duncan – 'imagined that the last appearance of *Banquo's* ghost became no less visible to her [Lady Macbeth's] eyes than it became to those of her husband'.[4] Once the Ghost (invisible to the audience) is driven off and the guests are chaotically dismissed, Mrs Siddons's Lady Macbeth was 'Very sorrowful. Quite exhausted'. Kemble exited strongly, leaving her to follow.[5]

[1] A. B. G., *Critical Observations*, p. 25. Macready simply put his beaker down (Downer, p. 331).
[2] See Bartholomeusz, pp. 67–8.
[3] For the possibility that Kemble was the first producer to omit the visible ghost, and for Kean as 'goblin', see William Winter, *Shakespeare on the Stage*, series 1, 1911, pp. 461 and 466, respectively. For Banquo's Ghost, see Mrs Siddons's account in Cambell, *Life*, II, 185–7. Kemble 'restored it [the Ghost] only some years later' (Donohue, 'Kemble and Mrs Siddons in *Macbeth*', p. 82); the Ghost does not enter in the late Siddons promptbook (Mrs Inchbald's *British Theatre*, 1808, vol. 4, p. 44; compare Bell in Jenkin, p. 35) until about 3.4.88, but the Ghost's two entrances (3.4.37 SD and 3.4.88 SD) had been fully restored by 1811 (Donohue, *Dramatic Character*, p. 265 n. 59). So far as I can find, the experiment of omitting a visible ghost was next tried in a Drury Lane (London) revival, 2 December 1876, when Joseph Knight (*Theatrical Notes*, 1893, p. 162) objected to it, although Irving used some sort of optical illusion in 1875, later replaced with a physical actor (Hughes, *Irving*, p. 107), and still later replaced with another illusion (see p. 78 below).
[4] See, respectively, G. J. Bell in Jenkin, p. 63, and Siddons, 'Remarks', in Campbell, *Life*, II, 30. Siddons prefaces her conclusion: 'it is not possible that she [Lady Macbeth] should hear all these ambiguous hints about *Banquo* [in Act 3, Scene 2] without being too well aware that a sudden, lamentable fate awaits him'. On whose ghost the on-stage audience imagines, see also Robert F. Willson, Jr, 'Macbeth the player king: the banquet scene as frustrated play within the play', *Shakespeare Jahrbuch* (Weimar), 114 (1978), 107–14. At Stratford in 1955, the Ghost exited (at 3.4.71) by walking between Lord and Lady Macbeth, thereby demonstrating that it is invisible to her; see *Macbeth Onstage*, p. 147.
[5] See Bell in Jenkin, p. 65, and Donohue, 'Kemble and Mrs Siddons in *Macbeth*', p. 84. W. C. Macready used the same business (Downer, p. 333).

LATER STAGINGS AND VERSIONS

The theatrical and critical history of *Macbeth* often reflects changing social attitudes towards women and towards the relations between women and men.[1] Even after David Garrick removed from the staged play some of Davenant's crowd-pleasing witch-business – they sang, they danced, they flew – the witches were still (in 1833) treated primarily as comic rather than as threatening, ominous, or indefinably evil:

> It has been always customary, – heaven only knows why, – to make low comedians act the witches, and to dress them like old fishwomen . . . with as due a proportion of petticoats as any woman, letting alone witch, might desire, jocose red faces, peaked hats, and broomsticks.[2]

If theatrical or cultural conceptions or prejudices stipulate witches who do not somehow radiate danger or threaten evil, productions will stress Lady Macbeth as instigator or promoter of regicide and violence. Alternatively, the less comical the witches, the more they appear causative. And the more they seem to be causative agents, the more they will be associated with, or represented as, demonic women.[3] For more than 150 years after the Restoration, performances usually represented Lady Macbeth as a 'bloody-minded virago' or 'female fiend', driving her heroic, noble husband – 'even the dupe of his uxoriousness' – to more and more violent acts.[4] Hannah Pritchard and Sarah Siddons adopted this characterisation, or so those who saw them thought, though in retirement Mrs Siddons described the character quite differently.[5]

The necessarily twinned possibilities that Lady Macbeth might be a tender, companionate wife, eager to advance her husband's career and to please him, and that Macbeth himself is not an heroic dupe and/or a superstitious warrior but the main, controlling

---

[1] On this approach to theatre history, see: 'to recognise the limited and culturally bound character of the evidence is not to despair of theatre history. Rather it serves to rescue it from mere antiquarian accumulation of memorabilia, providing a point of access into cultural history, a means of exploring the dynamic created by the interaction of the culture of the past on the culture of the present' (John Webster, *The Duchess of Malfi*, ed. Kathleen McLuskie and Jennifer Uglow, 1989, p. 3), and for the wider implications of performances in the nineteenth century, see e.g. Nina Auerbach's characterisation of the Victorian woman-mythos: 'victim and queen, domestic angel and demonic outcast' (*Woman and the Demon: The Life of a Victorian Myth*, 1982, p. 9).

[2] Fanny Kemble, *Journal*, 18 February 1833, quoted in Sprague, p. 224. Laughable witches – almost always men – persisted in the theatre partly because *Macbeth* provides few opportunities for a company's comic specialists. Powerful as modern audiences find his contribution, the Porter may have originated as a practical concession to the King's Men's main comic actor (see Appendix 1, p. 280 below). Like the Padua promptbook, many post-Restoration productions cut the Porter (probably for his obscenity), but (as compensation?) Davenant's ludicrous witches continued well into the nineteenth century, though performances as early as that of Powell and Yates on 20 January 1768 and those of Macklin in the next decade presented the witches 'seriously' (Bartholomeusz, pp. 95 and 89).

[3] This latter reflection (not obvious to me), I owe to Christine Krueger; here, theatrical performance substantiates Adelman's critical approach to *Macbeth*.

[4] See, respectively, [Francis Gentleman,] *Dramatic Censor*, 1, 87 and 89, and William Hazlitt, 'Mr [Edmund] Kean's Macbeth', *The Champion*, 13 November 1814, rpt. in Hazlitt, *Dramatic Essays*, ed. William Archer and Robert W. Lowe, 1895, p. 30. Significant portions of Hazlitt's review are reprinted in the *Characters of Shakespear's Plays*, 1817. Notably, the two 'historical' narratives in Holinshed's *Chronicles* that Shakespeare most relies on, the reigns of King Duff and King Duncan, both contain wives who are labelled as ambitious and homicidal.

[5] See her 'Remarks' in Campbell, *Life*, II, 10–34; among others, J. Comyns Carr, *Macbeth and Lady Macbeth*, 1889, notes (p. 11) the discrepancy between Siddons's 'Remarks' and her recorded performances; see also G. J. Bell in Jenkin, *passim*.

criminal, arose in the aftermath of the long-dominant Pritchard–Siddons tradition.[1] By the late 1830s and early 1840s, these ideas entered English-language criticism. William Maginn commented:

> To a mind so disposed, temptation is unnecessary. The thing [the planned regicide] was done [in Act 1, Scene 3]. Duncan was marked out for murder before the letter [of Act 1, Scene 5] was written to Lady Macbeth, and she only followed the thought of her husband. Love for him is in fact her guiding passion . . . Bold was her bearing, reckless and defying her tongue, when her husband was to be served or saved . . .[2]

A few years later, presciently joining textual, critical, and theatrical insight, George Fletcher absolves the witches and Lady Macbeth and arraigns Macbeth, who has 'the purpose, not suggested to him by any one, but gratuitously and deliberately formed within his own breast, of murdering his royal kinsman . . . to usurp his crown'.[3]

Fletcher's essay is far more comprehensive, though less eye-catching, than Maginn's similarly character-centred, moralistic analysis. Fletcher wrote at a major turning-point in conceptions of *Macbeth*, and he advocates controversial propositions that governed criticism and performance well into the twentieth century,[4] judging Macbeth a 'moral coward' given to '*poetical whining*' (pp. 125 and 152). Lady Macbeth is a loving wife who 'covets the crown for her husband even more eagerly than he desires it for himself' and wants to make him 'happier as well as greater' (pp. 119 and 118); she goes mad when she discovers 'that all she had mistaken in Macbeth for "the milk of human kindness" was but mere selfish apprehensiveness' and 'that he is capable of no true affection . . . even towards *her*' (p. 157). The weïrd sisters are neither comedians nor the phantoms of superstition, but 'spirits of darkness' which Shakespeare uses to develop 'the evil tendencies inherent in [Macbeth]' (pp. 143 and 141). Splenetically, Fletcher inveighs against the Davenant–Garrick–Kemble textual tradition: cutting the Porter 'destroys . . . the coherence and probability of the incident' (p. 163); keeping Lady Macbeth off-stage in Act 2, Scene 3, produces 'doubly gross improbability' (p. 164);[5]

---

[1] For an overview of how theatrical versions of the relation between Macbeth and Lady Macbeth changed, see Marvin Rosenberg, 'Macbeth and Lady Macbeth in the eighteenth and nineteenth centuries', in *Focus*, pp. 73–86; on changing theatrical versions of Lady Macbeth, see Rosenberg, pp. 158–205. Donohue, *Dramatic Character*, pp. 257 and 268, sees 'conjugal love' as motivating Mrs Siddons's Lady; I do not.

[2] William Maginn, 'Lady Macbeth', *Bentley's Miscellany* 2 (1837), 550–67, as reprinted in Maginn, *Miscellaneous Writings*, ed. Shelton MacKenzie, 5 vols., 1855–7, III (1856), 171–208; quotations from pp. 194 and 197.

[3] George Fletcher, '*Macbeth*: Shakespearian criticism and acting', *Westminster Review* 41 (1844), 1–72, reprinted and slightly revised as 'Characters in "Macbeth"' in his *Studies of Shakespeare*, 1847, pp. 109–98; quotation from p. 113. Fletcher seems to be the first writer to claim that Macbeth planned usurpation prior to the action dramatised in the play.

[4] Character-analysis dominates Fletcher's essay until its final sections on textual 'corruptions' and the acting tradition. Fletcher's views of the sisters partly arise from moral anxiety: 'we should not mistake him [Shakespeare] as having represented that spirits of darkness are here permitted absolutely and gratuitously to seduce his hero from a state of perfectly innocent intention . . . such an error . . . vitiates and debases the moral to be drawn from the whole piece. Macbeth does not project the murder of Duncan because of his encounter with the weird sisters; the weird sisters encounter him because he has projected the murder . . .' (p. 143). Parenthetical references in this paragraph are to Fletcher's *Studies in Shakespeare*. Fletcher's views reappear at least as recently as Byam Shaw's 1955 production; see p. 82 below.

[5] Eighteenth-century productions, including those with Sarah Siddons, and many nineteenth-century ones cut Lady Macbeth from this scene: see Davies, *Micellanies*, II, 152–3.

suppressing 'the scenes [*sic*] in Macduff's castle' – the murder of Lady Macduff and her son – is 'most injurious of all' (p. 166).

Fletcher admired Helen Faucit as Constance in *King John* and proposed her as a Lady Macbeth potentially greater than Sarah Siddons. London theatregoers could have seen Faucit's Lady Macbeth for one performance with William Charles Macready at Drury Lane on 17 April 1843, but reports from Dublin, Paris, and Edinburgh allowed Fletcher to add a postscript (21 December 1846):

> her possession of that *essentially feminine* person . . . together with that energy of intellect and of will, which this personation equally demands, – have enabled her to interpret the character with a convincing truth of nature and of feeling, more awfully thrilling than the imposing but less natural, and therefore less impressive grandeur of Mrs Siddons's representation. Her performance, in short, would seem to have exhibited . . . not the 'fiend' that Mrs Siddons presented to her most ardent admirers – but the far more interesting picture of a naturally generous woman, depraved by her very self-devotion to the ambitious purpose of a merely selfish man.[1]

Two decades later, Henry Morley confirmed these accounts: Faucit's Lady Macbeth is 'essentially feminine, too exclusively gifted with the art of expressing all that is most graceful and beautiful in womanhood, to succeed in inspiring anything like awe or terror'; at the end of Act 3, Scene 4, she 'collapse[d] into [the] weariness of life-long torture'.[2] This production included the wholly unShakespearean but not entirely Victorian detail of Fleance's silent presence in Act 3, Scene 1, where Faucit's Lady Macbeth played 'her fingers about the head of the child *Fleance* . . . The fingers of the woman who has been a mother, and has murder on her soul, wander sadly and tenderly over the type of her lost innocence.'[3]

Just what this Victorian conception of Lady Macbeth as 'essentially feminine' meant, appears from Henry Morley's admiring description of Faucit's Imogen (in *Cymbeline*), 'the purest and most womanly of Shakespeare's women':

---

[1] Fletcher, *Studies*, p. 198; 'fiend' had been used by Siddons ('Remarks' in Campbell, *Life*, II, 19) and her admirers. Other English-language critics found Faucit's Lady Macbeth revolutionary: see William Carleton to William Stokes, letter, Dublin, 27 November 1846, quoted in Helen Faucit, *On Some of Shakespeare's Female Characters*, enlarged edn, 1891, pp. 401–3, and Theodore Martin, *Helena Faucit*, 2nd edn, 1900, pp. 159–60 (an anecdote not substantiated by 'Christopher North' [i.e. John Wilson], 'Dies Boreales. No. V', *Blackwood's Edinburgh Magazine* 66 (November 1849), 620–54).

[2] Henry Morley, *The Journal of a London Playgoer, from 1851 to 1866*, 1866, pp. 350 and 353, discussing a Faucit–Samuel Phelps Drury Lane performance, 3 December 1864. Carol J. Carlisle, 'Helen Faucit's Lady Macbeth', *S.St.* 16 (1983), 205–33, reprints many contemporary criticisms with a scene-by-scene reconstruction of Faucit's performance; my account is independent of Carlisle's and sometimes disagrees with it.

[3] Morley, pp. 352–3. Faucit apparently adopted the gesture from Macready (see Downer, p. 329). Sprague (pp. 247–8) reports that Kemble brought on Fleance in this scene, as did Herbert Beerbohm Tree (see Gordon Crosse, *Shakespearean Playgoing, 1890–1952*, 1953, p. 39), and Fleance appeared in 3.1 as recently as Byam Shaw's 1955 Stratford production (*Macbeth Onstage*, p. 118) and Roman Polanski's film of *Macbeth* (1971), where Macbeth tweaks Fleance's cheek at this moment. Late in her career, Faucit seems to have been the first English actress since before Garrick's time to appear in Act 2, Scene 3 (Carlisle, 'Helen Faucit's Lady Macbeth', pp. 218–19), and see headnote to Act 2, Scene 3.

all the qualities that blend to form a womanly perfection, – simple piety, wifely devotion, instinc-
tive, unobtrusive modesty, gentle courtesy, moral heroism, with all physical cowardice, – no thin
ideal, but a very woman, who includes among her virtues aptitude for cookery.[1]

Stereotyped and culturally determined as this view of 'womanly perfection' is, Morley
knew it deviated sharply from the Betterton–Barry–Pritchard–Siddons Lady Macbeth:
Faucit offered 'a most harmonious interpretation of the part according to that reading which finds all its womanhood in *Lady Macbeth*'s character'.[2] Fletcher praised
(9 October 1847) Samuel Phelps's then-new Sadler's Wells production for 'dismissing
in toto the operatic insertions, and restoring the suppressed characters, scenes, and
speeches', though Fletcher still grumbled over Banquo's visible ghost and thought
'The "weird sisters," though divested in great part of their former grossness by
Mr Phelps's treatment, still need a little more refining.'[3]

Theatre dotes on old tradition and new fashion. While some audiences, actors,
and critics continued to espouse earlier ideas, theatrical and critical perception of the
witches gradually changed in concert with Faucit's 'new', 'feminine' Lady Macbeth
and the Lady's newly independent, criminal and/or cowardly husband. By the middle
of the nineteenth century, William Wetmore Story's observations had become fairly
conventional: Lady Macbeth, 'having committed one crime, dies of remorse'; Macbeth
'is a thorough hypocrite' and 'a victim of superstitious fears, and a mere coward'; 'The
witches are a projection of his [Macbeth's] own desires and superstitions. They . . .
prophes[y] in response to his own desires' and are therefore neither instigators nor
determinants of his behaviour.[4]

Eighteenth- and nineteenth-century critics often compared Richard III with
Macbeth – the two were the most notable Shakespearean villain–heroes – and
Edmund Kean, the tragic actor whose brief career spanned the end of Kemble's and
the beginning of Macready's, was an unsurpassable Richard III, but a relatively weak
Macbeth, 'deficient in the poetry of the character'.[5] Macready, unremittingly com-
petitive and relentlessly self-critical, probably spoke true when he complained that 'a
newspaper . . . gave me very moderate praise for Macbeth, observing that though good,
it was not so good as Kean's, which was a total failure'.[6]

[1] Morley, p. 355.
[2] Morley, p. 353, commenting on a return visit, 17 December 1864, to the Faucit–Phelps production.
[3] Fletcher, *Studies*, p. 383. Specifically, Phelps 'dropped the music and the interpolated words, restored Lady
Macduff and her son, killed Macbeth off-stage and brought on his head on a pole'; see Muriel St Clare
Byrne, 'Fifty years of Shakespearian production: 1898–1948', *S.Sur.* 2 (1949), 2.
[4] William Wetmore Story, 'Distortions of the English stage as instanced in "Macbeth"', *National Review* 17
(1863), 292–322, as reprinted in his *Excursions in Art and Letters*, 1891, pp. 232–86; quotations from pp.
240, 241, 246, and 264. See the discussion of Henry Irving's performances, pp. 77–8 below.
[5] See Hazlitt, 'Mr Kean's Macbeth', pp. 30–1. For other comparisons of Richard III with Macbeth, see e.g.
William Guthrie, *An Essay upon English Tragedy*, 1757, pp. 12–13; Elizabeth Montagu, *An Essay on the
Writings and Genius of Shakespear*, 1769, p. 178; [Francis Gentleman,] *Dramatic Censor*, 1, 106; Thomas
Whately, *Remarks on Some of the Characters of Shakespeare*, 1785; J. P. Kemble, *Macbeth and King Richard
the Third*, 1786, enlarged edn, 1817; Winter, pp. 467–8; Farnham, *Shakespeare's Tragic Frontier*, pp. 104–
5; Donohue, *Dramatic Character*, chapter 8. The Richard III–Macbeth comparison is so ingrained that
Davies, *Micellanies*, II, 168, attributes *Macbeth* 3.2.55 ('Things bad begun, make strong themselves by ill')
to *Richard III*.
[6] William Toynbee (ed.), *The Diaries of W. C. Macready 1833–1851*, 2 vols., 1912, 1, 112 (11 March 1834).

Macready was one of the few to criticise Helen Faucit, 'whom I do not like; she wants heart';[1] he was also the earliest and finest Macbeth to play opposite her Lady Macbeth, and he generously recognised her new interpretation:

Rehearsed Macbeth; was very much struck with Miss Faucit's rehearsal of Lady Macbeth, which surprised and gratified me very much. Acted [that night] Macbeth as well as my harassed mind and worn-down body would let me. Called for [by the audience] and well received. Would have taken on [stage, for a curtain call] Miss Faucit, but she [had taken off her costume] . . . Spoke . . . afterwards . . . with her about her acting, which was *remarkably* good.[2]

Macready compromised between the 'old' heroic Macbeth and the 'new' weak but criminal Macbeth.[3] One 'judicious and effective innovation' was his 'air of bewildered agitation upon coming on the stage [in Act 1, Scene 5, presumably] after the interview with the weird sisters', and George Bell, an experienced playgoer, describes Macbeth facing Banquo's Ghost on its second appearance:

Macready plays this well. Even Kemble chid and scolded the ghost out! and rose in vehemence and courage as he went on. Macready began in the vehemence of despair, but, overcome by terror as he continued to gaze on the apparition, dropped his voice lower and lower till he became tremulous and inarticulate, and at last uttering a subdued cry of mortal agony and horror, he suddenly cast his mantle over his face, and sank back almost lifeless on his seat.[4]

It is noticeable that Macready, the unnerved and superstitious victim, was quite ready to use his hero's truncheon on other actors or impertinent members of the audience (see illustration 14).[5]

Macready, having played opposite Faucit's 'new' Lady Macbeth, was also partner to one of his era's most violent (or 'most imperial')[6] Lady Macbeths, the American Charlotte Cushman, whose

style of acting, while it lacked imagination, possessed in a remarkable degree the elements of force . . . [s]he was intensely prosaic, definitely practical, and hence her perfect identity

---

[1] *Ibid.*, 1, 322 (1 June 1836).

[2] *Ibid.*, 11, 174 (Dublin, 6 June 1842), on Faucit's first public performance of Lady Macbeth; for other reactions to her performance, see p. 70 above, n. 1. Faucit and Macready had further successes in Edinburgh and Paris. Faucit's later Macbeth, Samuel Phelps, a manager justly honoured for recovering Shakespeare's texts theatrically, was also, Faucit said, a 'very inadequate successor' to Macready, who himself regarded Phelps as an actor who was 'afraid to play the first and averse to take the second characters'. See Faucit, *Shakespeare's Female Characters*, p. 234, and Macready, *Diaries*, 1, 427.

[3] See G. H. Lewes, *On Actors and the Art of Acting*, Leipzig, 1875 (not the '2nd edn' of London, also 1875), pp. 46–7: 'nothing could have been less heroic than his [Macready's] presentation of the great criminal. He [Macready] was fretful and impatient under the taunts and provocations of his wife; he was ignoble under the terrors of remorse; he stole into the sleeping-chamber of Duncan [2.2] like a man going to purloin a purse, not like a warrior going to snatch a crown.'

[4] See, respectively, *Morning Herald*, 10 June 1820 (a review of Macready's first *Macbeth*) quoted in Frederick Pollock (ed.), *Macready's Reminiscences*, 2 vols., 1875, 1, 214, and G. J. Bell in Jenkin, p. 63 n. 58. Downer, pp. 318–38, reconstructs Macready's *Macbeth*, with its 'elaborate scenery and crowds of well-drilled supers' (Crosse, p. 35).

[5] For the truncheon used to strike another actor, see James E. Murdoch, *The Stage, or Recollections of Actors and Acting*, 1880, pp. 104–6; as an implement to threaten riotous audience members, Macready, *Diaries*, 11, 425 (New York, 10 May 1849). At least once, the truncheon disconcertingly broke; see Macready, *Diaries*, 1, 75 (4 November 1833). See also Sprague, pp. 229 and 406 n. 18.

[6] Winter, p. 500.

14   William Charles Macready (with heroic truncheon) as Macbeth

with . . . the materialism of Lady Macbeth . . . [Cushman exhibited] the coarse features and
harsh voice of the heroine of a melodrama . . . This is one of Shakespeare's grandest dramatic
conceptions dragged down to the lowest level of a mere sensational exhibition.[1]

[1] Murdoch, *The Stage*, pp. 240 and 242.

After his first performance with Cushman in Boston, Macready commented: 'Miss Cushman . . . interested me much. She has to learn her art, but she showed mind and sympathy with me; a novelty so refreshing to me on the stage.'¹ Macready grew more critical of Cushman, especially after her first, highly successful visit to England, but she learned from him and seems to have repeated some of his technique, and even in these early performances an English observer could consciously compare the two:

> with this great and cultivated artist she held her own. She had not had his experience, but she had genius. There were times when she more than rivalled him; when in truth she made him play second . . . I have seen her throw such energy, physical and mental, into her performance, as to weaken for the time the impression of Mr Macready's magnificent acting.²

Macready seems to have been proudest of his performance in the fifth act (after Lady Macbeth is finally off the stage!), where he emphasised both 'pathos' and a kind of desperate physical heroism.³

Macbeth is not the only Shakespearean play to have provoked riots, but it has occasioned several, including the most deadly one of all. Chance or commercial shrewdness may explain why Kemble chose *Macbeth* for the first night (18 September 1809) when new prices were demanded for many places in the rebuilt Covent Garden Theatre: the 'O. P.' ('Old Price') disturbances ensued for seventy days. Earlier, in October 1773, Charles Macklin, an actor then in his seventies and famed for comedy and for an innovative Shylock, had played Macbeth at Covent Garden. Macklin's enemies, perhaps a pro-Garrick group, and the partisans of 'Gentleman' Smith (the actor of Macbeth whom Macklin had displaced) objected and hired a *claque* who fomented another destructive but non-fatal riot at a performance of *The Merchant of Venice* (18 November 1773).⁴ If Charlotte Cushman was a throwback to earlier ideas of Lady Macbeth, her countryman Edwin Forrest, who also had a successful career in England, was 'the robust warrior'⁵ Macbeth in the older mould. In New York in 1849, he and Macready (who was appearing at the Astor Place Opera House) offered two directly competing interpretations, and the ensuing public disagreements, fuelled by the actors' well-publicised antagonism and by jingoistic, xenophobic, and dimly 'patriotic' energies, produced the 'Astor Place riot' in which twenty or more people died (10 May 1849).⁶

---

¹ Macready, *Diaries*, II, 230 (Boston, 23 October 1843); in December, the two performed *Macbeth* in New York.

² Letter to a Boston, Massachusetts, newspaper, 1863, quoted without further identification in Emma Stebbins, *Charlotte Cushman: Her Letters and Memories of Her Life*, 1879, p. 32. On Cushman's learning from Macready, see Joseph Leach, *Bright Particular Star: The Life and Times of Charlotte Cushman*, 1970, pp. 120–1.

³ For 'pathos', see the *Morning Herald* review cited at p. 72 above, n. 4; for Act 5, see Macready, *Diaries*, II, 495–6 (26 February 1851, his farewell).

⁴ See William W. Appleton, *Charles Macklin: An Actor's Life*, 1960, pp. 178–86.

⁵ Winter, p. 474. My account slights North American performances *in toto*; for some redress, see Charles H. Shattuck, *Shakespeare on the American Stage*, 2 vols., 1976–87, and the comprehensive list and knowledgeable commentary in Thomas Wheeler, *Macbeth: An Annotated Bibliography*, 1990, pp. 767–812, esp. pp. 807–12.

⁶ See Richard Moody, *The Astor Place Riot*, 1958, and the slightly pro-Macready discussion in Downer, pp. 290–310. Lawrence W. Levine, *Highbrow/Lowbrow: The Emergence of Cultural Hierarchy in America*, 1988, considers the riot 'a struggle for power and cultural authority . . . simultaneously an indication of and

Although Helen Faucit's 'new' Lady Macbeth had been anticipated in Germany,[1] the older conception of the part remained, and remains today, a living theatrical possibility. In 1857, Adelaide Ristori (illustration 15), then Italy's greatest tragedienne and first international star, and later to be mentioned by George Eliot and James Joyce, travelled to London with *Macbetto*, an Italian verse-adaptation by Giulio Carcano which Verdi used as a basis for his opera, *Macbeth*.[2] Ristori gave a traditional, Siddons-like performance, albeit underplayed and nuanced so that critics were struck by her subtle facial and postural acting and the way she ignored traditional actor's 'points':

Madame Ristori conceives *Lady Macbeth* as a woman who pens up her emotions, who is watchful, self-contained, who fights against compunctious visitings of nature without letting a stir be seen . . . [In Act 1, Scene 6,] [t]here is . . . a false expression playing faintly now and then across her face . . . When at the close [of Act 1, Scene 7] he [Macbeth], for the first time, speaks as an accomplice, her face brightens with exultation . . . and . . . she repeats the . . . exit [of Act 1, Scene 5].[3]

Having 'hurried over' Lady Macbeth's admission, 'Had he not resembled / My father as he slept, I had done't' (2.2.12–13), Ristori reacted emotionally to Macbeth's description of Duncan's body (2.3.104–7): 'and then the point is made that ninety-nine actresses in a hundred would assuredly have tried to make before'.[4]

Ristori performed Lady Macbeth in English in London (Drury Lane, 3 July 1882) and, later, in New York and Philadelphia with Edwin Booth, but she made her earliest impression supported 'feebly enough' by a cast speaking Italian before an English audience (who could refer, like some modern opera audiences, to a parallel-text Italian–English libretto).[5] While that libretto by Carcano followed the Folio fairly closely, it was also severely cut: all of Lady Macbeth's scenes are present except Act 3, Scene 1;

a catalyst for the cultural changes that came to characterise the United States at the end of the [nineteenth] century' (p. 68). See also Richard Nelson, *Two Shakespearean Actors*, 1990, a play about the actors' rivalry and this incident.

[1] Rosenberg (pp. 175–8) finds the 'devoted wife' interpretation of Lady Macbeth several decades earlier in performances by Rosalie Nouseul and Frederike Bethmann and in criticism by Franz Horn and Ludwig Tieck in Germany.

[2] On Giulio Carcano and Verdi, see Laura Caretti, 'La regia di Lady Macbeth', in Laura Caretti (ed.), *Il Teatro del personaggio: Shakespeare sulla scena italiana dell'800*, 1979, pp. 167–9. For Ristori's English and Irish tours, see Cristina Giorcelli, 'Adelaide Ristori sulle scene britanniche e irlandesi', *Teatro Archivio* 5 (September, 1981), 81–147, esp. pp. 103–8 and 128–9; pp. 142–5 identify Ristori in Eliot and Joyce. Tommaso Salvini and Ernesto Rossi also achieved considerable success as Macbeth in England and America; see Winter (an eyewitness of Salvini), pp. 486–9; Caretti; Marvin Carlson, *The Italian Shakespearians*, 1985, chapters 7 and 15. According to Henry James, Salvini was particularly effective because he did not rant; he also restored such frequently omitted characters as the Porter and Third Murderer (Carlson, pp. 94 and 96–7). For Rossi and Salvini, see Caretti and Giorcelli *passim*.

[3] Morley, pp. 186–8 (25 July 1857); for the similarity of Ristori's and Siddons's performances, see Adelaide Ristori, *Studies and Memoirs*, 1888, p. 258. Giorcelli, 'Adelaide Ristori', offers a full selection of contemporary accounts.

[4] Morley, p. 189; see 2.3.112 n. below.

[5] See Carlson, p. 35; Adelaide Ristori, *Memoirs and Artistic Studies*, trans. G. Mantellini, 1907, p. 107; Henry Knepler, *The Gilded Stage*, 1968, p. 113; Morley, p. 218. Tommaso Salvini and Ernesto Rossi also performed in bilingual productions in the United States (Carlson, pp. 54–5).

15 Adelaide Ristori as Lady Macbeth

only the first seven lines of Act 3, Scene 2, remain. The libretto ends barely a page after Lady Macbeth's final appearance in Act 5, Scene 1.[1]

In this emphasis upon Lady Macbeth, in its consequent diminution of her husband's part, as well as in many other cuts and shifts of emphasis, the Ristori version echoes the greatest adaptation of *Macbeth* and the only one in which we may today have a sense of the play's nineteenth-century, and perhaps earlier, form and appeal: Giuseppi Verdi's *Macbeth*. '[T]he first Italian opera to make a real attempt to be Shakespearean', Verdi's *Macbeth* is not his finest operatic response to 'a favorite poet of mine, whom I have had in my hands from earliest youth, and whom I read and reread constantly' – Verdi's *Otello* and *Falstaff* are undeniably greater and usually more beautiful – but '[staging] ideas from London, where this tragedy has been produced continually for over 200 years' influenced his first *Macbeth* (1847), and Verdi apparently knew Macready's London performance and, certainly, Ristori's later ones, and they influenced the revised version (Paris, 1865).[2] In Verdi's opera, along with the intensification of Lady Macbeth there went an immediately controversial treatment of the witches and other supernatural or 'grotesque' material, redolent of Victorian non-musical stagings.[3]

After W. C. Macready, only two Victorian–Edwardian English actor-managers, Sir Henry Irving (the first theatre knight) and Sir Herbert Beerbohm Tree (the second), contributed significantly to views of *Macbeth*. As a young actor, Irving had been 'instructed' by Charlotte Cushman,[4] and in 1875 he offered a controversial, anti-Cushman interpretation when Kate Bateman was an undistinguished Lady Macbeth. Though his Lyceum Theatre became 'a national institution', this first *Macbeth* was instantly attacked: 'the irresolution' Macbeth 'displays in the earlier scenes' of the play arises from 'personal fear', and Irving's Macbeth is a 'cowardly, remorseless villain . . . from the very first'.[5] In 1888 Irving played Macbeth again, in a fresh interpretation, with Ellen Terry as Lady Macbeth,[6] and Percy Fitzgerald reviewed the new production more positively: 'The Scotch chieftain and his lady are shown, not simply as mere human, but almost creatures of necessity, subservient to

---

[1] See the Italian–French libretto, trans. Giulio Carcano and P. Raymond-Signouret, *Répertoire de Mme A. Ristori*, 1858; I have not seen the Italian–English 'libretto' Morley (p. 191) mentions, but it is likely to be identical with *Macbeth* (New York: Sanford, Harroun, 1866) 'adapted expressly for Madame Ristori'; the libretto published for the 1876 performances also survives (see William Weaver in David Rosen and Andrew Porter (eds.), *Verdi's 'Macbeth'*, 1984, p. 148 n. 16). For further details, see Carlson, chapter 3, and, for the later New York version, Caretti, p. 169 n. 51 and p. 170.

[2] See, respectively, the following in Rosen and Porter: William Weaver (p. 147); Verdi to Léon Escudier, 28 April 1865 (p. 144); Verdi to Alessandro Lanari, 22 December 1846 (p. 27), and (on later stagings) Verdi to Escudier, 23 January 1865 (p. 90); Weaver (p. 144, on Verdi and Macready); Verdi to Escudier, 11 March 1865 on Ristori (p. 110 and see p. 111).

[3] For early Italian responses, see especially Marcello Conati in Rosen and Porter, pp. 231–3, and, for the *genere fantastico*, see Verdi to Lanari, 17 May 1846 (*ibid.*, p. 4 and n. 1). For the emphasis on Lady Macbeth, see Jonas Barish, 'Madness, hallucination, and sleepwalking', *ibid.*, pp. 149–55.

[4] Leach, *Bright Particular Star*, p. 267.

[5] See Crosse, p. 18, and *Sheridan Knowles' Conception*, p. 7. The anonymous author goes on to complain that Irving's Macbeth 'has no genuine conscientious scruples. He never really hesitates in his purpose, but simply lacks the pluck or the nerve necessary for its execution. Lady Macbeth is the opposite of all this – the man irresolute and weak, the wife strong and determined' (p. 15).

[6] Hughes, *Irving*, p. 92.

the pressure of a weak, nerveless nature in the one case, and of a devoted conjugal affection in the other.'[1] Some critical views changed between 1875 and 1888, and part of the reason must be the change from Kate Bateman to Ellen Terry, who had already established a reputation as 'feminine' and 'gentle' and claims in her diary that 'Those who don't like me in it [*Macbeth*] are those who don't want, and don't like to read it fresh from Shakespeare, and who hold by the "fiend" reading of the character.'[2]

Terry had no doubts about Irving's choices:

His *view* of 'Macbeth,' though attacked and derided and put to shame in many quarters, is as clear to me as the sunlight itself. To me it seems as stupid to quarrel with the conception as to deny the nose on one's face. But the carrying out of the conception was unequal. Henry's imagination was sometimes his worst enemy.[3]

All the old arguments over the relative strengths and relative heroisms of Lord and Lady Macbeth returned. 'The reading of the character [Macbeth] is robbed of one of its most effective dramatic elements in the loss of the contrast between a noble and ignoble side of Macbeth's nature'; Ellen Terry's performance, though beautiful, is 'the whitewashing of Lady Macbeth'.[4] Twenty years after she first played Lady Macbeth, Terry rebutted this view of Irving's Macbeth when she famously recalled him 'in the last act after the battle when he looked like a great famished wolf, weak with the weakness of a giant exhausted, spent as one whose exertions have been ten times as great as those of commoner men of rougher fibre and coarser strength'.[5]

After Macready withdrew from the stage, the nineteenth-century theatre saw increasingly tender, 'feminine', 'wifely' Lady Macbeths and increasingly criminal and violent Macbeths, in no small part because the play's spectacle was shifted from comic and mechanically equipped witches to witches, no less spectacular and no less equipped, but now having supernatural and demonic mystery. Whatever the complaints about Irving's cowardly Macbeth or Terry's too tenderly beautiful Lady Macbeth, critics agreed on the power of the witches in their performances:

they are always enveloped in awe-inspiring gloom . . . or by . . . ruddy glow . . . even the *nil admirari* materialist spectator of today is more inclined to shudder than to sneer.[6]

And Irving found, when he took his *Macbeth* to the United States in 1895, a 'solution' to the problem of Banquo's Ghost – 'a greenish light shining on an empty stool' – that satisfied his audience.[7]

---

[1] Percy Fitzgerald, 'Macbeth', *The Theatre* n.s. 13 (February 1889), 101.

[2] Ellen Terry, *The Story of My Life*, 1908, p. 306.

[3] *Ibid.*, p. 303. For a representative attack on Terry's performance, *see The Stage*, reprinted in *TQ* 1, 3 (1971), 34. Hughes, *Irving*, chapter 3, analyses Irving's *Macbeth* in detail, and I draw upon that discussion extensively and gratefully.

[4] *Illustrated Sporting and Dramatic News*, 5 January 1889.

[5] Terry, *Story*, pp. 303 and 306, respectively. According to William Poel's hostile account (*The Times*, 31 December 1888, quoted in W. Moelwyn Merchant, *Shakespeare and the Artist*, 1959, p. 139), Irving accepted Holinshed's chronology and played Macbeth as an old man in Act 5; the Byam Shaw production (Stratford, 1955) made the same choice (see p. 80 below, n. 3).

[6] *Illustrated Sporting and Dramatic News*, 5 January 1889.

[7] Shattuck, *Shakespeare on the American Stage*, 11, 183; Shattuck's treatment (11, 176–83) of this production repays close attention. Compare Komisarjevsky's 1933 Stratford version of this episode (p. 79 below).

Herbert Beerbohm Tree, 'rising into the second place [after Irving] as a producer of Shakespeare'[1] on the London stage, could have known A. C. Bradley's influential critical account (1904) of *Macbeth*. Tree is usually remembered for his elaborate and highly detailed illusionistic productions, in which he raised 'illustrative' Shakespeare to new and eventually self-defeating heights, taking hints from the text to produce finical, time-consuming, and unscripted *tableaux vivants*.[2] Yet Ellen Terry's son, Edward Gorden Craig, who played Malcolm in Irving's tours in the 1890s and was himself an innovative artist ahead of his time, originally designed (1908) the sets for what became Tree's 1911 *Macbeth*.[3] Those designs never reached the stage, but they deeply influenced the production, helping to make it at least semi-expressionistic and to thrust the audience into an experience of the text as if from Macbeth's point of view: 'Our attempt . . . will be to create . . . that awe-inspiring atmosphere which is suggested by the poet.'[4]

Edward Gordon Craig, one hopes, had little to do with Tree's version of Act 1, Scene 7, where the dialogue 'was performed with the [audible accompaniment] . . . of Duncan and the court at dinner', or with Duncan's and his followers' silent appearance at the end of the scene, 'to give a blessing to his hosts and their house', followed by the cackling re-entrance of the witches.[5] (Off-stage sounds of revelry here have since become commonplace.) Tree's 'Cauldron scene' (Shakespeare's Act 4, Scene 1), however, recalls productions stretching back to Kemble and before; the witches, omnipresent if unShakespearean witnesses throughout the play, now multiply into a demonic, ghostly chorus surrounding this scene.[6] Weak, conventional, or unmemorable as Tree's performance as Macbeth may have been – few contemporary accounts even mention his Lady – his production did anticipate such theatrically important versions as Theodore Komisarjevsky's 1933 Stratford production, where the audience shared Macbeth's mental experience, including an Act 4, Scene 1, in which Macbeth spoke the Apparitions' prophecies during a dream-sequence.[7]

Following Irving's and Tree's, there are no enduringly important English-language stagings of *Macbeth* until Glen Byam Shaw's 1955 production at Stratford and Trevor Nunn's 1976–8 productions at Stratford and in London.[8] Byam Shaw's production,

---

[1] Crosse, pp. 18–19.

[2] For the possibility that Bradley influenced Tree's production, see Michael Mullin, 'Strange images of death: Sir Herbert Beerbohm Tree's *Macbeth*, 1911', *Theatre Survey* 17 (1976), 125–42, pp. 140 and 142 n. 22. Tree's may have been the earliest (1916) largely unadapted cinematic *Macbeth*; Robert Hamilton Ball, *Shakespeare on Silent Film*, 1968, pp. 229–35, amusingly recounts how London's West End met Hollywood.

[3] The fullest treatment of Craig's long interest in *Macbeth* is Paul Sheren, 'Edward Gordon Craig and *Macbeth*', Ph.D. dissertation, Yale, 1974; see Sheren's condensed discussion, *TQ* 1, 3 (1971), 44–7.

[4] See Mullin, pp. 126–7; I rely on this essay's treatment of Tree's production here. Tree cut about one-third of the Folio text; for details, see Mullin, p. 141 n. 8.

[5] See Cary Mazer, *Shakespeare Refashioned: Elizabethan Plays on Edwardian Stages*, 1981, p. 12; Crosse, p. 39.

[6] For a photograph of Tree's scene, see Mullin, figure 2; this production seems to have been the singing witch chorus's 'positively . . . last appearance' (Byrne, p. 2).

[7] See Crosse, pp. 97 and 136, and Michael Mullin, 'Augures and understood relations: Theodore Komisarjevsky's *Macbeth*', *Educational Theatre Journal* 26 (1974), 20–30.

[8] This sentence uncharitably passes over many significant productions. For instance, F. R. Benson's early-twentieth-century performances (see Crosse, p. 31); Barry Jackson's production (London, 1928), the first

explicitly 'starring' Laurence Olivier and Vivien Leigh (illustration 16), was much anticipated and people agreed that, once the 'strangeness' of the 'unfamiliar stresses' that Olivier gave the verse had worn off, it was 'much the best performance of the part in our time', according to J. C. Trewin, who went on to say that it might even be 'the best since William Charles Macready's' (which Trewin could not possibly have seen); Olivier's 'interpretation of Macbeth met with the kind of consensus of approval among critics given in earlier years to players like Garrick and Mrs Siddons'.[1] Leigh's 'frail, porcelain beauty' (much admired) and her 'kind of coldness, even hardness' (much criticised) did not satisfy those who expected Siddons-like domination, though one critic praised her for showing 'that Macbeth and his Lady were lovers before they were criminals'.[2] Leigh's performance of Act 5, Scene 1, when, grey-haired and staring, she alternated 'senile and childish tones', was also effective.[3]

Maxine Audley (Lady Macduff), one of the few actors praised for a supporting performance here,[4] identifies a pattern that recalls many earlier productions:

what I thought was so clever of Olivier was to realize that the part of Macbeth is one long build up to the end . . . It's a long, straight line upwards, ending with the great fight . . . When he comes to his wife [in 1.5], she's up, she goes completely the other way. I always feel very strongly he's at his lowest ebb and she's absolutely at her peak and they completely change over. I think they cross at the end of the Banquet Scene. She's geared herself and steeled herself to get through this terrific ordeal, and by the time . . . [the guests have] all gone, she has already gone. She's finished.

And indeed Byam Shaw directed that Leigh 'sinks down on her knees leaning against Kings [*sic*] throne' before she manages to exit when Olivier, renewed, summoned her,

in modern dress, which also gave 'blasted heath' and 'bloody man' their modern British slang rather than their Jacobean resonances (see, in general, Michael Mullin, '*Macbeth* in modern dress: Royal Court Theatre, 1928', *Theatre Journal* 30 (1978), 176–85); Komisarjevsky's production (Stratford, 1933), discussed above; Donald Wolfit's performances (see e.g. Crosse, p. 147); not to mention Christopher Plummer's widely admired performance (Stratford, Ontario, 1962; see Leiter, p. 375), or Maggie Smith's in the same place, 1978 (see Leiter, p. 385), or the Simone Signoret–Alec Guinness production (directed by William Gaskill, Royal Court, London, 1966), or Glenda Jackson's fascinating and Plummer's lamentable performances (New York and elsewhere in North America, 1988). Richard Eyre's otherwise undistinguished Royal National Theatre, London, production (1993) offered a fine Macduff (James Laurenson). For the remarkable changes in British Shakespearean productions from the mid nineteenth century to the mid twentieth, see Byrne and Crosse, *passim*.
[1] See George Scott, *Truth* 155 (17 June 1955), p. 770; J. C. Trewin, *Birmingham Post*, 15 June 1955 (second notice); *Macbeth Onstage*, p. [249], citing Richard David, 'The tragic curve', *S.Sur.* 9 (1956), 122–31, where the remark does not appear. *Macbeth Onstage*, p. 11 n. 3, lists 48 periodical reviews of the production. Byam Shaw's text closely paralleled Henry Irving's (see Hughes, *Irving*, p. 91).
[2] See, respectively: *Daily Mail*, 8 June 1955; Patrick Gibbs, *Daily Telegraph*, 8 June 1955; Ivor Brown, *Drama*, Autumn 1955, p. 34. Leigh's performance of Lady Macbeth, like Ann Todd's (Old Vic, London, 1954, directed by Michael Benthall; see also David, 'Tragic curve') probably suffered from critics' assumptions or preconceptions based on the actress's cinematic appearances, especially in non-Shakespearean roles; see, generally, Byrne, p. 11.
[3] Patrick Gibbs, *Daily Telegraph*, 8 June 1955. Here Byam Shaw and Leigh duplicated the 1888 Irving–Terry production, where, more or less following Holinshed's account, many years were supposed to have passed between the end of the Folio's Act 3 and the beginning of its Act 5; see Hughes, *Irving*, pp. 109 and 112.
[4] Scott, *Truth*, p. 770.

16   Act 2, Scene 3, in Glen Byam Shaw's 1955 Stratford Memorial Theatre production. Macbeth (Laurence Olivier) attends the fainting Lady Macbeth (Vivien Leigh)

'Come, we'll to sleep . . .'¹ This pattern necessarily meant that Olivier's Macbeth began quietly, with, for example, only a 'slight start' when all-hailed as 'king hereafter'; critics complained about this restraint, which extended until the discovery of Duncan's murder, the first great 'explosion' of this production, followed by two later peaks in the banquet scene and the final duel.² Byam Shaw exploited the actor's great physical presence and gymnastic agility in these later climaxes. When the Ghost reentered Act 3, Scene 4, upstage and between two royal thrones, immediately after Macbeth's 'Would he were here', Olivier initially recoiled, but then, pushing Lady Macbeth and her excuses aside ('Think of this, good peers, / But as a thing of custom'), Olivier jumped upon the banqueting table in a great swirl of robes and desperate bravery.³

Byam Shaw's directorial notes stress how much he sought the audience's admiration for Macbeth and Lady Macbeth:

---

¹ *Macbeth Onstage*, pp. [251] and 153. In the Irving–Terry production Macbeth and Lady Macbeth 'crossed' (i.e. their respective strengths changed) at the beginning of Shakespeare's Act 3 (Hughes, *Irving* p. 105) as they did in the 1996 Stratford production directed by Tim Albery with Bríd Brennan and Roger Allam.

² See, respectively: *Macbeth Onstage*, pp. 43 and [249], and Milton Shulman's famous remark, 'restraint run amok' (*Evening Standard*, 8 June 1955).

³ For the Ghost's and Macbeth's action, see *Macbeth Onstage*, p. 149; most contemporary critics praised Olivier's extraordinary effects here.

After he has committed the crime . . . all that is bad in his character bursts out . . . but the magnificence & courage of his nature remain till the end. He never becomes a brutish villain like Iago [in *Othello*] or Aaron [in *Titus Andronicus*].

Her loyalty to her husband is magnificent. The way she behaves in the banquet scene is beyond praise. In spite of her complete lack of compassion & goodness of heart one cannot but have the greatest admiration for her courage & loyalty.[1]

Byam Shaw's comment on Lady Macbeth has a Victorian flavour, and in performance Vivien Leigh made a relatively weak and certainly a subordinate impression, but Olivier managed to fascinate, rather than repel, the audience, or at least the critics, right through the final, dangerously violent battle with Macduff. This concentration on flawed heroism meant in turn that the witches 'are certainly not the Fates. If we felt that Macbeth was, through them, fated to murder the King it would completely destroy the tragedy of the story'; yet, in keeping with Macbeth's paradoxical 'heroism', the witches 'should be terrible & yet strangely wonderful – because anything evil is, always, fascinating & wonderful in some way . . . They must have tragic stature.'[2] At the first rehearsal, Shaw spoke frequently of hell, damnation, and the devil, and generalised still further, 'this is the most moral play, & is the strongest possible warning against evil & sin'.[3]

Only one other English-language staging since 1945 merits comparison with the 1955 Stratford production, and it could not be more different. Following an unsuccessful Christian–demonic production of *Macbeth* with Helen Mirren (Lady Macbeth) and Nicol Williamson (Macbeth), where 'sex [was] the essence of' the Macbeths' 'tragedy' (Stratford and London, 1974–5),[4] Trevor Nunn directed Judi Dench (Lady Macbeth) and Ian McKellen (Macbeth) in a sternly 'ensemble', not 'star', production (1976–8), first at The Other Place (Stratford), later in Newcastle-upon-Tyne, later at the Royal Shakespeare Company (RSC)'s main house (also Stratford), and still later at the Warehouse, then an RSC London venue. Unlike most English-language productions since 1660, this one deployed a small cast, fourteen persons according to Nunn, but varying slightly from year to year.[5] Nunn's production expressed the demonic freshly and seriously, making witchcraft vital in a way Orson Welles's 'voodoo' *Macbeth* (New York, 1936) did not and replacing Welles's more than faintly racist view with an anthropologically sophisticated version.[6] These witches have true and complete powers. They cannot be distanced or ignored as 'primitive' or 'other'. They are at once psychologically explicable and irrational.

---

[1] *Macbeth Onstage*, pp. 152–3. Commenting on Act 1, Scene 5, Shaw wrote: 'She has . . . an extraordinary intensity of purpose. She adores her husband. Her ambition for him is beyond everything' (*ibid.*, p. 59).

[2] *Macbeth Onstage*, p. 30; compare Peter Hall's view, p. 32 above.

[3] *Macbeth Onstage*, pp. 16–17.

[4] See Leiter, pp. 380–1, quoting Benedict Nightingale, *New York Times*, 23 May 1975.

[5] '14 actors . . . involved in an intense debate . . . touching constantly on the question of whether there is a meaning to being alive' (Trevor Nunn, Royal Shakespeare Company newspaper, August 1976). Robert Cushman, *The Observer*, 12 September 1976, put the cast he saw at sixteen.

[6] Nunn's version here, so different from the generally Christian interpretation he earlier adopted (Stratford, 1974), may owe something to Charles Marowitz's radical adaptation (Wiesbaden, May 1969; see next note).

A strongly marked chalk circle cirumscribed the playing space (barely visible at the top of illustration 17), and the audience saw a rehearsal studio rather than a formal stage: actors not needed for the moment sat or stood cirumferentially, sometimes reacting to the events within the circled 'acting' space, sometimes simply awaiting their moments to perform.[1] Macbeth (McKellen) always traversed the circle anticlockwise or 'widdershins' – a reversal traditionally thought of as Satanic or unlucky – whereas other characters moved in a 'moral' or 'virtuous' clockwise way to their places and eventually their exits.[2] Nunn's production made no attempt at realistic illusion; when theatrical effects were needed, the audience saw how those effects – thunder, lightning – came about. A great 'thunder-sheet' was the stage's backdrop, and when thunder was needed, the audience saw it made. Paradoxically, the sensation was the reverse of artificial. Seeing sounds and lightning made, the audience understood they were not 'natural' but created, created – violently and with an absolute evil – by forces not theatrical but far beyond the theatre or indeed Shakespeare. These effects were not 'effects', but something, some *things*, happening outside human comprehension and beyond human explanation.

In a further paradox, this extraordinary production did not relieve Macbeth and Lady Macbeth of responsibility. They discussed, undertook, consciously chose to perform terrible acts, but while they did so from calculated ambition they were also seen to be environed by forces which no audience could understand and no character resist. They were at once responsible and unknowing, in a powerful and ultimately tragic fashion. And still, the acts were committed. In a way quite beyond the reach of rational explanation, but a way also full of theatrical energy and emotional power, Nunn's production made Macbeth and Lady Macbeth simultaneously guilty agents and victims.

Theatrical tradition is a powerful drug, narcotic or ecstatic. Henry Irving having once hoisted Macbeth's sword onto his shoulder in 1888, John Gielgud would consciously imitate him in 1930,[3] and more than a century after Irving and more than half a century after Gielgud, so would Alan Howard (Royal National Theatre, London, 1993). Less happily, Davenant's spectacle and Davenant's witches, however transmogrified, always trivialising and intrusive, long plagued even the most distinguished performances: Garrick–Pritchard, Kemble–Siddons, Macready–Faucit. Sometimes leading, sometimes following theatrical practice, literary critics have been likewise bemused, likewise puzzled. And always the simplest questions have proved the hardest to answer in both performance and criticism.

FURTHER VARIATIONS: KUROSAWA, POLANSKI, NINAGAWA

There have been two distinguished cinematic versions of *Macbeth*, one a medieval Japanese adaptation, *Kumonosu-ju* (*Throne of Blood* in English, but more accurately

---

[1] Charles Marowitz's *A Macbeth* (1971), with a cast of eleven, including three Macbeths (representing 'the Timorous, the Ambitious, the Nefarious'), probably influenced this and other elements (e.g. the demonism permeating the cast) in Nunn's production. See 'Exercises to A Macbeth [*sic*]' in *The Marowitz Shakespeare*, 1978, pp. 70–9, and 'Introduction', p. 14; the quotation here is from 'Introduction', p. 15.

[2] See 1.3.33 n. and Clark, 'Inversion', pp. 122–5.

[3] See John Gielgud, *Early Stages*, 1939, p. 168, on his performance in the 1930 Harcourt Williams production at the Old Vic (London), and Sprague, p. 230.

17 Act 4, Scene 1, in Trevor Nunn's 1976–8 RSC production. The sisters (Marie Kean, Judith Harte, Susan Dury) present figures of the Apparitions to a drugged, hallucinating Macbeth (Ian McKellen). A strongly marked black circle circumscribes the playing space, and the audience sees a rehearsal studio rather than a formal stage

and revealingly, *The Castle of the Spider's Web*) directed by Akira Kurosawa (1957), the other a film much closer to Shakespeare's text, *Macbeth*, directed by Roman Polanski (1971).[1] The third 'variation' I consider here is Yukio Ninagawa's theatrical production, also placed in a feudal Japanese milieu.

Kurosawa's subtle, learned adaptation of *Macbeth* is far too complex for summary, and I do not mention many of the film's extraordinary effects.[2] To the dismay of many critics, *Throne of Blood* does not use Shakespeare's text, often replacing the most ver-bally complex moments with tiny, silent gestures and absences of movement. The film's visual imagery exploits the play's metaphors (of birds and their cries, for example, of a horse wildly uncontrolled, of darkness and light), but its narrative deletes entirely Shakespeare's Malcolm and related matters, including the 'English Scene' (Act 4, Scene 3) and the Porter (conversing soldiers fill some of the expository gaps). Captain Washizu (the figure equivalent to Macbeth) and Captain Miki (the figure equivalent to Banquo) encounter a single androgynous witch, spinning thread like a Greco-Roman Fate, in the 'Cobweb Forest' near the 'Cobweb Castle' all seek to control, and Washizu much later returns to the witch and her/his environment to hear a prophecy – Washizu will reign until the Cobweb Forest moves – recalling the Third Apparition's prediction in *Macbeth* Act 4, Scene 1. Toshiro Mifune (Washizu) offers a superb performance,

---

[1] In Kurosawa's film, Toshiro Mifune plays Macbeth and Isuzu Yamada, Lady Macbeth; in Polanski's, the rôles were taken by two actors untraditionally young for the parts, Jon Finch and Francesca Annis. Other notable cinematic and television versions include: Orson Welles's *Macbeth* (1948), based on Welles's earlier theatrical production mentioned above; *Joe Macbeth* (1955; directed by Ken Hughes with Paul Douglas as Macbeth and Ruth Roman as Lady Macbeth); the later of two (1954, 1960) Maurice Evans–Judith Anderson Hallmark Hall of Fame television versions (1960, directed by George Schaefer); the Eric Porter–Janet Suzman *Macbeth* (1970, BBC TV, directed by John Gorrie); the Thames Television version (directed by Philip Casson, 1978) of the Judi Dench–Ian McKellen RSC theatrical production discussed above (for staged *versus* televised versions, see Michael Mullin, 'Stage and screen: the Trevor Nunn *Macbeth*', *SQ* 38 (1987), 350–9); the Nicol Williamson–Jane Lapotaire television production in the BBC 'The Shakespeare Plays' series (1982, directed by Jack Gold), *Men of Respect*, 'Written and directed by William Reilly adapted from the "Tragedy of Macbeth" by William Shakespeare' (Columbia Pictures, 1990). For further details of, and a summary of critical reaction and printed responses to, all but the last, see Rothwell and Melzer, pp. 155 ff. Both *Joe Macbeth* and *Men of Respect* transpose Shakespeare's plot and characters into criminal environments roughly contemporary with the making of the two films (compare Kurosawa's similar translation to a period in Japanese history more-or-less analogous to medieval Scotland and Jacobean England, when the Duncan figure is as violently regicidal as the Macbeth figure). In *Men of Respect*, for example, Macbeth becomes 'Mike Battaglia [= Battle]' (John Turturro), Lady Macbeth, 'Ruth' (Katherine Borowitz), and Duncan, 'Charlie D'Amico [= Friend]' (Rod Steiger); here, the conflict lies among an entirely criminal or near-criminal cast, and D'Amico (Duncan) is just another crime-boss to be toppled. Thus, the characters equivalent to Lady Macduff and her son die in a car-bombing while the husband is detained by a chance telephone call; the witches are a palm-reader/fortune-teller/tealeaf-reader and her husband (compare 'Rosie' in *Joe Macbeth* and see Rothwell and Melzer, p. 155); the Lady Macbeth character worries about cleanliness and walks madly around the restaurant the couple manage as a 'front' for their criminal activities, and she later commits suicide. Birnam Wood disappears, and the Shakespearean prophecy is changed to 'until the stars fall', which they do in a fireworks show.
[2] See James Goodwin, *Akira Kurosawa and Intertextual Cinema*, 1994, pp. 169–91, for a basic analysis of the relations between Shakespeare's play and Kurosawa's film. Useful studies of Kurosawa's film (with references to the substantial number of other critical works) are: Anthony Davies, *Filming Shakespeare's Plays*, 1988, pp. 152–66, and Peter S. Donaldson, *Shakespearean Films/Shakespearean Directors*, 1990, pp. 71–91.

combining vocal range with superlative physical acting; he is matched (at least for a western audience) by Isuzu Yamada (Lady Asaji, Washizu's wife and the figure equivalent to Lady Macbeth). She persuades Washizu to murder Tsuzuki (the film's equivalent to Duncan) by voicing the film's emphatic view of human submission to fate and prophecy when she points out that Tsuzuki 'killed his own master to become what he is now'[1] (an observation true to Holinshed's narrative of Scottish history), and she persuades Washizu to persevere in killing Miki/Banquo and Yoshiteru/Fleance by telling him 'I am with child' when Washizu/Macbeth seeks to fulfil the witch's prophecy (and avoid any dire consequences) by appointing Yoshiteru/Fleance his heir. In a creative revision of *Macbeth*, Kurosawa finds the stillborn child of Asaji a source of the couple's political collapse and part of her subsequent madness. Kurosawa's film echoes Shakespeare's ghostly banquet (Act 3, Scene 4), but places the Murderer's announcement of Miki's death and Yoshiteru's survival after (not before, as in *Macbeth*) the gathered nobles have departed. Washizu then kills the Murderer. Just as Kurosawa's later *Ran* (1985) combines Shakespeare's *King Lear* with *Macbeth*, *Throne of Blood* alludes momentarily to *Hamlet* when a Nohlike poet–dancer (in the scene that echoes *Macbeth* Act 3, Scene 4) tells an interrupted tale that anticipates or recalls or reveals Washizu's treasonable acts. Throughout the film, Lady Asaji's stillness of face and body and her almost mechanical movements, all of which recall or duplicate Noh conventions, are terrifying. Nearly silent, almost always inhumanly composed until the very end (though, for example, she dances frenziedly while Washizu kills Tsuzuki/Duncan out of the audience's view), she prompts Washizu to ever more horrific acts.

Critics originally dismissed Roman Polanski's *Macbeth* (1971) as a serious presentation of Shakespeare's play because the participation of Hugh Hefner, the executive producer, and of Playboy Productions, seemed to be sponsoring a vulgarisation of the play – naked witches (in the film's version of Act 4, Scene 1) and a nude Lady Macbeth (in the equivalent of Act 5, Scene 1) do indeed appear – but later reflection shows this film to be the most distinguished cinematic version of the play, as the presence of Kenneth Tynan as co-author of the screenplay (with Polanski) suggests.

Polanski and Tynan produce an illuminatingly creative revision and echo of theatrical performances, especially of the eighteenth and nineteenth centuries, while also adapting the play to film. Thus, as in many earlier theatrical productions, we see enacted, often violently, moments the Folio's text represents only verbally: the execution of Cawdor; the stormy night that accompanies Duncan's arrival at, and death in, Macbeth's castle; the banquet of Act 1, Scene 7; the drugging of the grooms and the murder of Duncan (where Duncan awakes to see his murderer's indecision before the bloody moment); the wakening grooms, looking at their smeared hands and faces before the avenging Macbeth grasps Lennox's sword to kill them; Duncan's funeral cortège (only alluded to, if that, in Act 2, Scene 4, of Shakespeare's text); Macbeth's installation as king at Scone;

---

[1] English quotations from the film's dialogue cite the sub-titles, translated by Donald Richie, of the videocassette (see Goodwin, p. 242 n. 11). For an English translation of the script by Hisae Niki, see Akira Kurosawa, *'Seven Samurai' and Other Screenplays*, 1992.

the extraordinarily violent murders of Lady Macduff, her children, and her retainers. Soliloquies in Shakespeare's text are sometimes represented as spoken, sometimes as 'voice-over' (where the actor does not visibly speak but the audience hears the actor's voice), sometimes as a combination of 'spoken' and 'over-heard' sounds.

The film also reorders the play's scenes and the sequence of events within scenes. First Murderer self-satisfiedly reports his 'success' in killing Banquo (Shakespeare's Act 3, Scene 4) quite privately, for instance, before he and his murderous colleague are led away to incarceration, and, we assume, death, in an *oubliette*; the second appearance of Banquo's Ghost (in the Folio's Act 3, Scene 4) is omitted; Act 3, Scenes 5 and 6, are deleted from the Folio's sequence (the film moves directly from the banquet to Macbeth's last visit to the sisters) and lines from those scenes are inserted later; offering a cinematic, not theatrical, continuity, the film follows its version of Act 5, Scene 1, with Macbeth's medical–political conversation ('How does your patient, doctor?') from Act 5, Scene 3, and, reversing the Folio's order, the film then turns to an elaborate representation of the flight of the 'false thanes' (5.3.7). The film now introduces lines from the Folio's Act 4, Scene 3, including a powerful moment when Malcolm hands his own sword to the newly bereaved Macduff and says, 'Be this the whetstone of your sword' (4.3.231), and a plangent moment in which Lady Macbeth, distraught, reappears (as, of course, she does not in the Folio) to speak the lines from her husband's letter (Act 1, Scene 5) she had not spoken earlier. Almost at once, the film presents Lady Macbeth's corpse, to which Macbeth speaks 'Out, out, brief candle . . .' (5.5.22ff.). The film concludes with a sequence of violent, acrobatic, highly persuasive sword-fights, ending with Macbeth's decapitation and (in Grand Guignol style) the head's presentation on a pole. Macbeth remains resolute and, until his final moments, invulnerable, as the sisters and apparitions had promised.

Polanski's film, or Polanski and Tynan's script, should be noted for several other innovations. It introduces a young central couple (Jon Finch and Francesca Annis), whose sexuality is an important dramatic element. It treats the Thane of Ross (played by John Stride) as a thoroughly self-serving figure, whose political behaviour repeats, emphasises, and contrasts with that of others (Macbeth, Lady Macbeth, Macduff, for instance): in the film, Ross is the Third Murderer of the Folio's Act 3, Scene 3, an accomplice in the deaths of Lady Macduff and her family and retainers, and he is an overt time-server in following Macbeth and then siding with Malcolm and Macduff. The film concludes with Donaldbain turning back to the witches, in evident hope that they will help him gain the throne (and therefore overthrow Malcolm), as they had earlier led Macbeth to the kingship.

Yukio Ninagawa's Japanese adaptation of *Macbeth* came west in 1985 when Miki-jiro Hira portrayed Macbeth and Komaki Kurihara Lady Macbeth at the Edinburgh Festival,[1] and in 1987, when Masane Tsukayama replaced Hira, at the National

---

[1] See Peter Whitebrook, *The Scotsman*, 24 August 1985. The play was translated into Japanese by Yushi Odashima.

Theatre, London.[1] Ninagawa's 'achingly beautiful' production was not well received in Japan – it was regarded as a false version or translation of medieval Japanese culture – but in European theatres the production was greeted rapturously.[2] Ninagawa said, 'It [the play, *Macbeth*] is set within a Buddhist family altar and everything happens within that frame. There is such an altar in all Japanese houses, but that does not mean that it is a religious frame. The altar is where your ancestors dwell, and the Japanese will talk to their ancestors within this setting quite naturally. It is a link between the living and the world of death . . .'[3] This altar – 'a huge Butsudan . . . closed off downstage by a pair of slatted doors across the whole stage-width'[4] – framed and enclosed the play's performance. The Butsudan's doors are moved 'by two aged crones', who sometimes respond to the play's events[5] and who are Ninagawa's version of the sisters and the Porter of Shakespeare's *Macbeth*, but the 'most pervasive visual image' of the production 'is cherry blossom'.[6] These blossoms, beautiful, fragile, transitory, '[combine] regret at human madness and folly with awareness of earthly beauty'[7] and also recall Kurosawa's cinematic emphasis upon fatality and Polanski's upon repetition.

Macbeth in the mind and in performance: Act 4, Scene 3

Macbeth has some curious narrative discontinuities (or irregularities, or illogicalities), especially in the places – at the end of Act 3 and beginning of Act 4 – where material by another author (probably Thomas Middleton) has probably been inserted into a pre-existing and perhaps wholly Shakespearean text (see Textual Analysis, pp. 271–5 below). Such are the ills that any evolving theatrical text inherits as its producers seek to make it new, fashionable, and commercially attractive, but the dramatic rhythm here is also curious: first, a leisurely and cryptic conversation between Malcolm and Macduff, then an abrupt, even discontinuous, passage (the English Doctor and the King's Evil), followed by Ross's obliquely introduced and brutally announced news from Scotland concluded by the patently 'stirring' move to free Scotland from the tyrant's oppression.

Act 4, Scene 3, may have been maladroitly revised to include references to a disease, the King's Evil, and the English monarch's supposed ability to cure it. King James was

---

[1] See *The Guardian*, 18 September 1987. Pictures of this later production appear in Giles Gordon's thoughtful and not entirely complimentary review, *Plays and Players* 410 (November 1987), 18–19. Gordon notes (p. 18) that 'The musical score . . . is, somewhat deviously, derived from European composers . . .'

[2] Michael Billington, *The Guardian*, quoted in Ronnie Mulryne, 'From text to foreign stage: Yukio Ninagawa's cultural translation of *Macbeth*', in Patricia Kennan and Mariangela Tempera (eds.), *Shakespeare from Text to Stage*, 1992, pp. 131–43; quotation from p. 131. Mulryne's essay is the fullest western treatment of Ninagawa's production I have seen. For criticism of the production in Japan, see Tetsuo Kishi, ' "Bless thee! Thou art translated!": Shakespeare in Japan', in Werner Habicht *et al.* (eds.), *Images of Shakespeare*, 1988, pp. 245–50, esp. pp. 245 and 249.

[3] Michael Leech, interview with Yukio Ninagawa, *What's on in London*, 17 September 1987.

[4] Mulryne, p. 133.   [5] *Ibid.*, p. 135.   [6] *Ibid.*, p. 136.

[7] Michael Billington, of Komaki Kurihara's performance as Lady Macbeth, *The Guardian*, 18 September 1987. On the performance of Kurihara – 'Young, beautiful, raven-haired' (*ibid.*), 'Her manner in the early scenes trembles uncontrollably between that of a coquettish sex-kitten and an unsmiling psychopath' (*The Independent*, 19 September 1987) – see Mulryne, pp. 139–40.

interested in this 'magical' power; and it attracted his subjects' attention throughout his reign.[1] Whether or not it was revised, and whether or not it was well revised, *Macbeth* Act 4, Scene 3, poses some extraordinary theatrical, dramatic, and intellectual puzzles for producers, audiences, and critics.

Before this conversation in the English court (Act 4, Scene 3), Malcolm last appeared discussing his father's murder with Donaldbain:

> MALCOLM [*To Donaldbain*] Why do we hold our tongues, that most may claim
>   This argument for ours?
> DONALDBAIN [*To Malcolm*] What should be spoken here,
>   Where our fate hid in an auger hole may rush
>   And seize us? Let's away. Our tears are not yet brewed.
> MALCOLM [*To Donaldbain*] Nor our strong sorrow upon the foot of motion. (2.3.113–17)

After this *sotto voce* conversation – the other characters are busy guessing at the murderer's identity and reacting to Macbeth's announcement that he has killed the grooms – the focus shifts to Lady Macbeth, who may faint here, or pretend to do so (see 2.3.112 n.), and the other characters' decision to put on 'manly readiness'. The stage empties, leaving the two sons to make their decision.

This dialogue of unbrewed tears and unmoved sorrow may be a later interpolation (see Textual Analysis, pp. 276–7 below); whether it is a second thought or not, one of its evident purposes is to explain the sons' passivity, or their cowardice, which 'generally create[s] laughter', according to an eighteenth-century critic.[2] Their only previous contributions to the scene were two brief questions: Donaldbain's maladroit 'What is amiss?' (2.3.90) and Malcolm's grotesquely fatuous response to Macduff's 'Your royal father's murdered' – 'O, by whom?' (2.3.93). Malcolm and Donaldbain are otherwise silent, and some contributor to the Folio text apparently sought to explain that silence. Explanation paradoxically emphasises the passivity it would justify. What needs no excuse gets none; what does, does. True, the sons' pallid lines underscore the baroque imagery of blood, death, and Doomsday the other characters use, and true, they may indeed have awakened not from beds but graves as Macduff says (2.3.72–4), but it is true also that Donaldbain's fear over their 'fate hid in an auger hole' provides an adequate reason for their silence. As Lady Macbeth's sleepy remarks on knowledge and power suggest – 'Who knows it, when none can call our power to account?' (5.1.32–3) – it may be better to remain silent than to draw attention, even if, or especially if, one is Prince of Cumberland and Duncan's heir-designate (1.4.37–9).

With this ambiguous prelude, the royal sons, now alone on stage, share their last exchange:

---

[1] See Supplementary Note 4.3.148, p. 259 below; Textual Analysis, pp. 278–9 below; Hoeniger, *Medicine and Shakespeare*, p. 8 above, n. 2.

[2] See Francis Gentleman in *Bell's Edition of Shakespeare's Plays*, I, *Macbeth* pagination sequence, p. 27: 'they [Malcolm, Donaldbain] generally create laughter, and their pusillanimous resolution of departure . . . deserves no better treatment'. Gentleman wrote in a theatrical era when Lady Macbeth's part (played by Sarah Siddons, no less) was cut from Act 2, Scene 3. Byam Shaw thought Malcolm and Donaldbain 'begin to panic' here (*Macbeth Onstage*, p. 103).

MALCOLM What will you do? Let's not consort with them.
　　To show an unfelt sorrow is an office
　　Which the false man does easy. I'll to England.
DONALDBAIN To Ireland, I. Our separated fortune
　　Shall keep us both the safer. Where we are,
　　There's daggers in men's smiles; the nea'er in blood,
　　The nearer bloody.
MALCOLM 　　　　　　This murderous shaft that's shot
　　Hath not yet lighted, and our safest way
　　Is to avoid the aim. Therefore to horse,
　　And let us not be dainty of leave-taking,
　　But shift away. There's warrant in that theft
　　Which steals itself when there's no mercy left.　　　　　(2.3.128–39)[1]

Here the issue of self-preservation is palpably central, while in the earlier conversation it is only arguably so. Indeed, the first exchange may have been inserted to explain the second and to diminish what looks suspiciously like cowardice or at least political indifference and a rather unusual failure of the Shakespearean child to mourn its parent.[2] Besides his ugly punning on 'theft' and 'warrant', Malcolm makes one particularly Janus-faced remark: 'To show an unfelt sorrow is an office / Which the false man does easy.' Some members of the audience (especially, perhaps, the students at the Inns of Court, ever watchful for fashionable phrases) may have reached for their notebooks to record the speech under 'Hypocrisy', but the sententious remark really challenges all shows of sorrow and indeed all absences of shows of sorrow. Where does its stress lie? On 'unfelt', on 'false', or on 'easy'? Does the non-false man show an unfelt sorrow with great difficulty, but show it none the less? Does a son, like Malcolm, who is not showing sorrow for his father's death therefore qualify as non-false because his unshown sorrow is in fact unfelt?[3]

　　I propose that someone involved in the making of *Macbeth* thought an audience seeing Act 4, Scene 3, for the first time might find both Malcolm and Macduff somehow suspect or unfixed, their traits either vague or unstable.[4] That 'someone' inserted two choric

---

[1]　This passage is not so textually suspect as the sons' earlier conversation; Brooke seems to find this passage textually puzzling (see his notes *ad loc.* and his Appendix A, pp. 220–1), but erroneous line numbers make his views uncertain.

[2]　A telling analogy, if it is one, might be Hal's seizing the crown when he thinks Henry IV is dead; like Duncan's sons, Hal reacts pragmatically first and mourns later. See Giorgio Melchiori (ed.), *2H4*, 1989, 4.2.167–73 and 211–16.

[3]　Note, too, the use of 'office' with its plural significations: 'That which one ought, or has, to do in the way of service; that which is required or expected'; 'A position or place to which certain duties are attached'; 'A ceremonial duty or service' (*OED* Office *sb* 2, 4, 5, respectively). The dutiful and the potentially hypocritical elements in these definitions cut against both the 'false man' and the speaker.

[4]　So Barbara Riebling finds Malcolm at least; see 'Virtue's sacrifice: a machiavellian reading of *Macbeth*', *Studies in English Literature, 1500–1900*, 31 (1991), 277–9. What I have said and will say about Act 4, Scene 3, may seem no more than a footnote to the second section of Stephen Booth's *'King Lear', 'Macbeth', Indefinition, and Tragedy*, 1983; I hope not, but if so, it is an honourable estate. In Booth's view, the audience believes, falsely but for a time comfortingly, 'that the comprehensibility of the container [here, *Macbeth*] is of the nature of the thing ["tragedy"] contained' (p. 89), and he then argues, a little equivocally, 'that *Macbeth* is itself, as a whole, a kind of equivocation between the fact of limitlessness – indefinition, tragedy – and the duty of art to limit and define' (p. 98). I propose that *Macbeth* represents or dramatises this

scenes to stabilise the audience's attitudes: in Act 2, Scene 4, we first hear Macduff characterised as 'good' (line 20), and the scene supports the adjective through his refusal to attend Macbeth's coronation; in Act 3, Scene 6, Lennox and an anonymous Lord testify to Malcolm's and Macduff's goodness and applaud their alliance with England's holy Edward. Unfortunately, this putative effort confuses the play's narrative, and one desperate critic goes so far as to claim that the pertinent lines of Act 3, Scene 6, are ironic and that Lennox tests the Lord as Malcolm will test Macduff.[1]

As with the epithet 'good Macduff', Act 3, Scene 6, proposes that Malcolm and Macduff hold Scotland's future hopes, but Macduff has fled under mysterious, if not morally ambiguous, circumstances, and his flight creates such extreme dramatic problems that William Davenant rewrote this section of the play and inserted a scene elaborately justifying Macduff's abandonment of his family.[2] According to Davenant, regicide is the unacceptable alternative to flight, and his solution to the problem anticipated Nahum Tate's 1681 revision of *King Lear*, where Gloucester's good son (Edgar) and Lear's good daughter (Cordelia) fall in love, partly to give 'Countenance to *Edgar's* Disguise [as Tom o'Bedlam], making that a generous Design that was before [in Shakespeare's play] a poor Shift to save his Life'.[3] Davenant and Tate justify or palliate what they construe as the 'poor Shift[s]' Shakespeare's characters employ 'to save [their lives]' – that is, Davenant and Tate justify or palliate the characters' represented cowardice.

In *Macbeth* Act 4, Scene 3 – 'slow', 'perverse', 'irritating', 'frustrating', and 'unpleasant' as it is[4] – Malcolm elaborately indicts himself of hyperbolic evil:

> there's no bottom, none,
> In my voluptuousness: your wives, your daughters,
> Your matrons, and your maids could not fill up
> The cistern of my lust, and my desire
> All continent impediments would o'erbear
> That did oppose my will . . .
> With this, there grows
> In my most ill-composed affection such

---

equivocation and therefore smudges, however momentarily, the difference that Booth finds between the play and the experience of it, between tragedy represented or dramatic tragedy experienced in retrospect, and tragedy experienced in life – the fire that destroys a family Christmas, the golden wedding anniversary heart-attack. That is, *Macbeth* knows what it is doing and what Stephen Booth is thinking; on the other hand, 'If audiences were led to take conscious notice of the inconsistency in their evaluations . . . they would presumably set about rationalizing . . . in an effort to make their responses consistent' (p. 115), and I may be doing just that.

[1] See Paul, p. 276, where he claims that Lennox is 'ironical' in Act 3, Scene 6, because 'Lennox knows that Macduff has fled to England but is cautiously trying to find out whether the other lord knows this, and what he thinks about it . . .'

[2] Compare Adelman, pp. 143–4; Macduff and his flight are among the few embarrassments to Adelman's persuasive argument.

[3] Quoted from Tate's dedication to Thomas Boteler, Esq., in Christopher Spencer (ed.), *Five Restoration Adaptations of Shakespeare*, 1965, p. 203; I have converted Tate's italic to roman.

[4] Booth, pp. 107–10; John Munro (ed.), *The London Shakespeare*, 6 vols., 1957, VI, 1088, summarises earlier negative reactions. Many critics find the scene satisfactory; see, for example, Knights, pp. 27–9; Lily B. Campbell, 'Political ideas in *Macbeth* IV.iii', *SQ* 2 (1951), 281–6; Irving Ribner, *The English History Play in the Age of Shakespeare*, 1957, pp. 256–9; Richard S. Ide, 'The theatre of the mind: an essay on *Macbeth*', *ELH* 42 (1975), 361 n. 30.

> A stanchless avarice that, were I king,
> I should cut off the nobles for their lands,
> Desire his jewels, and this other's house,
> And my more-having would be as a sauce
> To make me hunger more, that I should forge
> Quarrels unjust against the good and loyal,
> Destroying them for wealth.   (4.3.60–5, 76–84)

Malcolm finally declares he has none of the 'king-becoming graces', but abounds

> In the division of each several crime,
> Acting it many ways. Nay, had I power, I should
> Pour the sweet milk of concord into hell,
> Uproar the universal peace, confound
> All unity on earth.   (4.3.96–100)

Malcolm claims these evils, it seems, because he distrusts Macduff, particularly because Macduff abandoned 'Those precious motives, those strong knots of love' (4.3.27), his wife and children. Having answered Malcolm's earlier suspicions with blunt denial – 'I am not treacherous' (18) – and plaintive resignation – 'I have lost my hopes' (24) – Macduff now foresees a desperate, bloody, and tyrannical future. He prepares to go:

> Fare thee well, lord,
> I would not be the villain that thou think'st
> For the whole space that's in the tyrant's grasp,
> And the rich East to boot.   (4.3.34–7)

Just as Macduff himself had earlier been carefully ambiguous about his attitudes toward the new king when talking with Ross and the Old Man (2.4.21ff.), Malcolm here intersperses placating or exculpating remarks, remarks that will save him should Macduff prove *either* adherent *or* enemy to Macbeth: 'it may be so perchance' (11); 'Let not my jealousies be your dishonours' (29); 'Be not offended' (37).[1] Malcolm's most notable attempt to have it both ways confounds dramatic representation and the audience's credulity:

> That which you are, my thoughts cannot transpose;
> Angels are bright still, though the brightest fell.
> Though all things foul would wear the brows of grace,
> Yet grace must still look so.   (4.3.21–4)

In one powerful sense, the sense the play would have us understand as the only sense, this remark is true: Macduff may be an honourable man whether or not Malcolm thinks he is, just as angels are bright though Lucifer fell. Unfortunately for trust and reason, the brightest did fall, and in life as in *Hamlet*, thinking makes it so. If Malcolm or the audience thinks Macduff dishonourable, an *agent provocateur*, then effectively Macduff is so, and the campaign to depose Macbeth ends before it starts, along with the audience's certitude. For the audience, the paradox of Act 4, Scene 3, is the flip

---

[1] Ian Richardson's brilliant performance in Peter Hall's 1967 Stratford production 'offered an unconventional Malcolm with an inkling of evil deep inside' (Leiter, p. 378).

side to Lady Macbeth's politically and epistemologically abhorrent confidence – 'Who knows it, when none can call our power to account?' (5.1.32–3) – because the audience has now been placed in the situation of those Scots who think they know but cannot speak and cannot therefore act on their knowledge and its implications.

In the end, Act 4, Scene 3 attacks not just the characters' represented capacity to know one another, but the audience's capacity to discriminate ethically and politically among the represented personages. The scene attacks the bases of drama and admits that attack when the unexpected reversal, equivalent to a sonnet's *volta*, finally arrives and Malcolm chooses to believe Macduff's honesty, his exasperated patriotism and his desperate disappointment:

> Macduff, this noble passion,
> Child of integrity, hath from my soul
> Wiped the black scruples, reconciled my thoughts
> To thy good truth and honour.	(4.3.114–17)

Malcolm believes 'this noble passion, / Child of integrity' on evidence no better than, nor different from, the grounds he had for doubting Macduff's earlier asseverations. The better the actors are at deceiving each other, the better they inevitably are at deceiving the audience, and *vice versa*, as some celebrated actors have acknowledged.[1] Suspicion and trust here both arise from a character's *ethos*, and Macduff justly remarks, 'Such welcome and unwelcome things at once / 'Tis hard to reconcile' (138–9). Indeed, 'tis. The scene has made every assertion, every trust, every doubt 'hard to reconcile'. Here, humans palter with each other just as Macbeth claims the 'juggling fiends' did with him, and just so the play palters in performance and on the page.

Recent performances and adaptations

'Seven *Macbeth*s are coming to this month's Edinburgh Festival, including one on stilts . . . and another, on a bouncy castle . . .'[2] With such riches and such foolishness concentrated in a single festival's single month in one year (2007), it is impossible to mention more than a few recent productions – mostly theatrical, some cinematic, some translations–adaptations, most in English.

Several notable English-language mainstream theatrical productions jostle for attention. Gregory Doran's 1999 RSC production in the Swan Theatre, Stratford-upon-Avon, starred Harriet Walter and Anthony Sher and is well documented.[3] The same company, this time (2004) in the main house at Stratford, provided Dominic Cook's production, starring Sian Thomas and Greg Hicks (who tripled in *Hamlet* that season

[1] Trader Faulkner, who played Malcolm in the 1955 Stratford production, recalls arguing with Keith Michell (Macduff), Laurence Olivier (Macbeth), and Byam Shaw (the director): 'They said, "You're too convincing in the two contradictory aspects of the character. You're convincing when you say you're true and you're totally convincing when you say I didn't mean a word of it"' (*Macbeth Onstage*, p. [252]).
[2] Leader, *Guardian*, 4 August 2007.
[3] See: Gregory Doran's account, '[*Macbeth*] as Performed', in William Proctor Williams (ed.), *Macbeth*, The Sourcebooks Shakespeare, 2006, pp. 11–19 (with production photos); Harriet Walter, *Macbeth*, 2002; Antony Sher, 'Leontes in *The Winter's Tale*, and Macbeth', in Robert Smallwood (ed.), *Players of Shakespeare 5*, 2003, pp. 91–112. Further references to these texts are cited parenthetically by the authors' names. Sher also discusses the production in *Beside Myself: An Autobiography*, 2001, pp. 333–49.

as a memorable Old Hamlet and as the Player King and First Gravedigger). Rupert Goold, who directed the 'arctic' *Tempest* in Stratford (2006), returned with Patrick Stewart (Macbeth) and Kate Fleetwood (Lady Macbeth) at the Chichester Festival in 2007.

Suzanne Greenhalgh's hostile account of Gregory Doran's *Macbeth* (RSC, Swan Theatre, Stratford, 1999; televised, Channel 4, London, 2001) finds it 'haunted' by Trevor Nunn's widely celebrated stage production (1976; see above, pp. 82–3 and illustration 17) and its screen version (1978, directed by Philip Casson).[1] Greenhalgh concludes that 'part of the success of Doran's production was the way it updated what was essentially the same universalist reading of *Macbeth* [as Nunn's] for a different stage and a new millennium, one which could be charged with an equally opportunistic use of the imagery of current events.'[2] The 'current [i.e., 1998] events' cited were, according to Sher, 'the war in Kosovo and the earthquakes in Turkey' (p. 108), whose violence and destruction director and actors studied as preparation for their theatrical and, later, televised performances. Greenhalgh conflates director (Doran) and a principal actor (Sher): 'Sher's *Macbeth* is . . . depoliticized. Doran's preferred model of tragic subjectivity is no longer the hero of classic Hollywood narrative but anyone fleetingly captured by the surveillance cameras that police our [British? English?] streets . . .' (p. 108). Here, it seems, anxiety about near-universal surveillance somehow retro-creates a fantasy 'classic Hollywood narrative'.[3]

About the same performance, Harriet Walter stresses 'the unique and deadly chem-istry between two particular individuals [Lord and Lady Macbeth]' (Walter, p. 18) and sees Act 3, Scene 2 – which begins with Lady Macbeth's brief soliloquy ('Nought's had, all's spent / Where our desire is got without content' [3.2.4–5]) – as 'for both of us the most slippery scene in the play':

> The couple use more than usually tender language to one another . . . but it is as a smokescreen or a means of control rather than as an expression of love. Committing a murder together has bound them in an almost erotic intimacy, but a new lack of trust has crept under their dialogue. (Walter, p. 41)[4]

---

[1] Antony Sher's word for his and Gregory Doran's response to Nunn's production is 'daunted', but he asserts both 'resolved to learn what we could from it' (Sher, p. 103).

[2] Suzanne Greenhalgh, "Alas poor country!" Documenting the politics of performance in two British tele-vision *Macbeth*s since the 1980s', in Pascale Aebischer *et al.* (eds.), *Remaking Shakespeare: Performance across Media, Genres, and Cultures*, 2003, pp. 93–114, citation from p. 114. Just what 'current events' were implied by the 1976 Nunn production is not clear. Greenhalgh's title ('since the 1980s') is misleading; only two productions are discussed extensively, Doran's televised one (2001) and Penny Woolcock's televised quasi-documentary, *Macbeth on the Estate* (London, BBC2, 1997).

[3] In 'Local *Macbeth* / global Shakespeare: Scotland's screen destiny', Mark Thornton Burnett offers a cogent attack on the Doran production's treatment of the few Scottish elements, specifically Duncan and his white robes as 'what is older, Catholic and institutional, the implication being that Duncan incarnates an anterior "golden age". See Willy Maley and Andrew Murphy (eds.), *Shakespeare and Scotland*, 2004, pp. 189–206; quotation from p. 201. Thornton Burnett also discusses Jeremy Freestone's 1996 film of *Macbeth* and Michael Bogdanov's televised version of 1997.

[4] See also 'As it [3.2] begins, both characters want to reconnect, but her need is greater than his. She is defined by his need for her, and that has diminished. Because he cannot be totally honest with her, he is starting to go it alone' (Walter, p. 45).

Both director (Gregory Doran, pp. 14–15) and female lead recalled a spontaneous moment in rehearsal that was incorporated into the performance. At the end of 3.4, in Harriet Walter's words:

Exhausted herself, she [Lady Macbeth] suggests: 'You lack the season of all natures, sleep.'

Then, one rehearsal, Tony [Sher] looked at me and I looked at him and the lameness and absurdity of that line and the agony and horror of what we had done and what we had become burst simultaneously out of both of us with a terrible giggling laughter. We managed to recreate that moment every night.

(Walter, p. 53)

About the play's shape after the banquet scene (3.4), Antony Sher commented in a way that recalls Michael Redgrave's bitter remarks (see above, p. 56) concerning Shakespeare's treatment of his hero in Act 5:

Macbeth propels itself like a jet through the first three acts, then pauses for a long stop-over during the England scene [4.3], and then takes flight again with Lady Macbeth's sleep-walking scene [5.1], and in fact reaches its height . . . it's hard to follow onto the stage. . . . Both the play and the title-role become less interesting after it.

(Sher, p. 109)[1]

To answer this perceived difficulty, the production chose to treat Macbeth's scenes in Act 5 as taking place in a 'bunker' and the hero as having become '[h]alf Führer, half-Godot tramp'. Thus, the 'Tomorrow, and tomorrow, and tomorrow . . .' speech was delivered by a Macbeth who 'could simply gaze into the future with terrible nihilistic clarity . . .' (Sher, p. 109). About the central role, Sher concluded, 'I've never played a character who thinks so much . . . He's a man with an existential headache' (Sher, p. 111).

As has become increasingly common at least since the ending of Polanski's film version (1971), when Donaldbain silently visits the witches, apparently seeking their advice on overthrowing his elder brother (see above, p. 87), this production sought to imply a future of regicide and disorder through having Fleance revealed as a silent spectator of Malcolm's concluding distribution of rewards and punishments.[2]

According to Sian Thomas (Lady Macbeth), Dominic Cook's brisk[3] production (RSC, Stratford, 2004) set the play in late Tsarist Russia.[4] Duncan (Richard Cordery)

[1] For the difficulties the actor of Macbeth faces after the sleep-walking scene, see James Agate's review of John Gielgud in the role (quoted above, p. 27).

[2] The earliest production I know where the final scene uses a character to suggest a future cycle of regicide and deposition is Les Kurbás's, 1924 Ukrainian production: 'still wearing his Fool's [= the Porter's] make-up – the mocking, grinning face – [Amvrosii] Buchma came in costumed as a bishop . . . . He then crowned Malcolm . . . Just as he did so, a new pretender approached, killed the kneeling Malcolm, and took the crown. Without pause, the bishop once again intoned the same words, "There is no power, but from God." As the new king was about to arise, a new pretender murdered him, and the ritual was repeated once again.' See Irene Makaryk, 'Performance and ideology: Shakespeare in 1920s Ukraine', in Irena R. Makaryk and Joseph G. Price (eds.), *Shakespeare in the Worlds of Communism and Socialism*, 2006, pp. 15–37; quotation from p. 28. The chapter includes numerous production photographs. In 'Shakespeare right and wrong', *Theatre Journal* 50 (1998), 153–63, Makaryk examines the Kurbás production in great detail.

[3] With no interval, the performance took about two hours.

[4] Sian Thomas, presentation to UCLA summer school, Stratford-upon-Avon, 23 August 2004. For further details, see Sian Thomas, 'Lady Macbeth', in Michael Dobson (ed.), *Performing Shakespeare's Tragedies Today: The Actor's Perspective*, 2004, pp. 94–105; compare, in particular, Thomas's account of the ending of 3.4 with Walter's.

first appeared (1.4) resplendent in full white military uniform with many medals, Macbeth (Greg Hicks) and Banquo (Louis Hilyer) in battlefield khaki. In this scene, Macbeth stepped forward, expecting to be named Duncan's successor only to be disappointed by Malcolm's being named as Prince of Cumberland. Hicks had earlier (1.3) established an introspective hero, confiding to the audience, shrugging at his revelations of weakness or doubt, asking us to sympathise with him in a self-deprecating, stand-up comedian's sort of way.[1]

The witches arose from an underlit grating at the front of the stage and writhed, wrapping ropes about themselves and tying nautical-style knots. From this heavily lit and shadowed grating later (2.3) rose the Porter, suggesting, perhaps, his alliance with the demonic and hellish, about which he speaks so knowledgeably. He prefaced his first words with a disconcertingly long bout of strenuous laughter – was it at something the audience did not know? at the audience itself? at the damned creatures he was about to describe ('Here's a farmer . . . here's an equivocator . . .')? As so often, the Porter (Forbes Masson) ad libbed comments on current political affairs and responded to the audience's shouted remarks much as we suppose Elizabethan and Jacobean comic actors did.[2]

In the banquet scene (3.4), Macbeth appeared in an ill-fitting formal military uniform – sleeves too long, buttons mis-buttoned – precisely, 'borrowed robes' (1.3.107) that he wore 'like a giant's robe / Upon a dwarfish thief' (5.2.21–2). After the first departure of Banquo's Ghost, Macbeth took his – and the Ghost's – empty chair upon speaking 'I have a strange infirmity . . .' only to leap madly upon the banquet-table, scattering dishes and silver, *à la* Olivier in 1955 (see above, p. 81). Just as he had in 3.1, when his remark, 'we will keep ourself / Till supper-time alone' (44–5), was plainly directed to Lady Macbeth, so here Macbeth starts to kiss Lady Macbeth at his exit, but does not. In a break with traditional practice, she remains while he leaves and the stage clears.

An equally striking moment appeared in the 'England scene' (4.3). Malcolm (Pal Aron) was shabbily dressed (a rug or animal skin over his shoulders) and apparently drunk or hungover. At the end of his recital of Malcolm's supposedly hypothetical weaknesses and sins (4.3.60 ff.), Macduff (Clive Wood) slaps him, as if trying to bring him to his senses. This always-difficult scene omitted the entire episode of Edward the Confessor as magic-dealing king, and in the next act, the production cut the fight between Macbeth and Young Siward.

At the end, Macbeth's head did not appear, and Malcolm's final triumphalist (and always debatably conclusive and debatably positive) speech was very downbeat, as was the news that Scottish thanes were now to be English earls. The performance had a limp, dispirited conclusion, and the audience seemed unsure that the play had ended.

---

[1] 'What Greg Hicks brings out superbly is the character's self-awareness and savage humour . . . Hicks shows how Macbeth uses irony to insulate himself from human contact' (Michael Billington, *Guardian*, 17 February 2005).
[2] See, generally, David Wiles, *Shakespeare's Clown: Actor and Text in the Elizabethan Playhouse*, 1987, p. 161; compare the asp-bearing Clown in *Ant.* 5.2.

Rupert Goold's production (2007) in the Chichester Festival's small Minerva Theatre (283 seats arranged stadium-style with a three-quarters thrust stage) received superlative reviews, especially remarking the performance's emotional intensity. Set somewhere and sometime in post–World War II Soviet Russia or its eastern European reaches, this production had numerous cinematic elements – projections on the stage's back wall of public ceremonies, for example;[1] frequent contrasts between bright light and blackouts; an unusually varied and effective soundscape (music and sound designer, Adam Cork) – combined with an iconoclastic approach to both text-speaking and the ordering of events. Some of the latter included beginning the performance with 'Doubtful it stood . . .', the Captain's opening speech of 1.2, which here concluded, after 'And fixed his head upon our battlements', with the attending nurses (or 'sisters') injecting him with an evidently deadly drug, disconnecting life-support equipment, and revealing themselves as not nursing but weïrd sisters, who then spoke the Folio's opening lines.[2] Another character (Ross?) then resumed the narrative of the battle. Act 3, Scene 6, a series of expository speeches that compromise the implied narrative and time-scheme of the play (see headnote to 3.6, below) was here brilliantly rethought as an interrogation of Ross, bound and tortured, under a bright light in a subterranean cell.

The fluid set is generally 'a composite of kitchen [as in 1.6 and 1.7], military hospital [1.2], torture chamber [3.6] and abattoir',[3] though it once appears to be Moscow's Red Square on May Day during Soviet rule and eventually an entertainment hut complete with a tuxedo-dressed singer and pianist performing an Ivor Novello number (4.3). This genteel 'soiree . . . contrasts strongly with the Macbeths' own brutal barn-dance' (at the start of Act 3, Scene 4).[4] The sisters were a consistently effective part of the performance; they appeared, for example, as servants at the banquet (3.4), where Macbeth (Patrick Stewart) peered into the face of one 'servant' as if recognising her from an earlier meeting. The sisters returned as military nurses in 4.1, where the first three apparitions were corpses in body-bags, resuscitated by the sisters' various ministrations in order to speak their prophecies. Here, a dishevelled Macbeth embraced the sisters.

Like most modern productions, this comparatively long one[5] took an interval after the 'banquet scene' (3.4), but unlike most, the interval here interrupted that scene. The preceding scene (3.3) – the murder of Banquo and Fleance's escape – occurred in a train carriage, evidently filled with fearful would-be escapees from Macbeth's Scotland. The passengers rose, swirled, and rearranged themselves and the stage and its props to form the banquet table (aligned diagonally and coinciding with the imagined train

[1] Video and projection were by Lorna Heavey.
[2] Tyrone Guthrie cut 1.1 entirely (see above, p. 32), as did *Macbeth (A Modern Ecstasy)*, 'a miraculous one-man performance' (Mark Swed, *Los Angeles Times*, 11 December 2004) of the play, starring Stephen Dillane, directed by Travis Preston and designed by Christopher Barreca (Redcat, Los Angeles, 24 November – 12 December 2004 and Almeida Theatre, London, 26 October – 5 November 2005).
[3] Paul Taylor, *Independent*, 6 June 2007.   [4] Michael Billington, *Guardian*, 4 June 2007.
[5] With an announced interval of twenty minutes, the running time was a little more than two hours and forty-five minutes on 11 August 2007. Even longer was John Caird's production with Simon Russell Beale (Macbeth) and Emma Fielding (Lady Macbeth) at the Almeida Theatre, London (2005), where the interval followed Lady Macduff's murder. For a sensitive discussion of this production, see Simon Russell Beale, 'Macbeth', in Dobson (ed.), *Performing Shakespeare's Tragedies*, pp. 106–18.

18 Lady Macbeth (Kate Fleetwood) and Macbeth (Patrick Stewart) in the kitchen setting of Act 1, Scene 7 in Rupert Goold's Chichester Festival production (2007)

carriage's central aisle). Macbeth and his lady welcomed the guests, the scene proceeded and Macbeth terrified his guests with various 'joking' exercises of a tyrant's power to humiliate subjects who must laughingly or silently bear their shame. First Murderer reported his success and failure, Macbeth sat (his back to the audience), and Banquo's Ghost leapt onto the table and strode forward; Macbeth jumped up in horror. Blackout; interval. After the interval, the scene resumes and repeats what we have seen, but now the conversation between Macbeth and First Murderer is fascinatingly pantomimed, and the Folio text is repeated, and the scene proceeds to its accustomed conclusion, but in this variant, Banquo's Ghost does not reappear physically but rather becomes a shaft of light falling on empty space.[1]

Unusually, this production did not lose focus or energy in Acts 4 and 5. The audience had seen Lady Macduff (Suzanne Burden) and her children attend the preliminaries to the banquet in 3.4, where, in a reminiscence of Beerbohm Tree's famous gesture of beheading flowers when he meets the doomed Prince Arthur in *King John*, Macbeth tousled the hair of Macduff's son. The 'England scene' (4.3) here cut (as so often) the matter of King Edward and his medical magic, but paid careful, intelligent attention to the argument between Malcolm (Scott Handy) and Macduff (Michael Feast). The upshot was uncertain: Macduff's 'Such welcome and unwelcome things at once, / 'Tis hard to reconcile' (4.3.138–9) was left hanging until Ross arrived from Scotland with news of new deaths 'Due to some single breast'. When Macduff heard that 'Wife, children, servants, all / That could be found' had been slaughtered, the actor stood silent and nearly motionless (a twitch, perhaps, of one hand) an astonishingly long time – many moments longer than a conventional 'theatrical' pause at this moment would demand or consume. Still the silence went on, daringly, until Macduff dedicated himself to the attack on Macbeth.

The principal set was an underground chamber, and many (descending) entrances were from a sinister industrial elevator (up-stage, centre) complete with double sliding gates; most often, it seemed to be a quasi-medical environment – therapeutic, experimental, or for torture – unless transformed, briefly, to a public square for a military parade, or some other space (e.g., the refugee train compartment mentioned above). A fixed element of the set (down-stage, stage right of centre) was a large, deep, porcelain basin with awkward, industrial chrome pipes and taps. Here, Macbeth washed his hands after the murder of Duncan (Paul Shelley), and here, shockingly, the sleepwalking Lady (in 5.1) attempted to wash hers only to discover a stream of red liquid gushing over her unstained hands.

Throughout, the verse-speaking showed both discipline and daring, with hints of an earlier grand tradition that refused to reduce the text to ordinary rhythms, regular patterns. For instance, Stewart delivered Macbeth's difficult 'Tomorrow, and tomorrow, and tomorrow" (5.5.18 ff.) with lengthened and stressed *and*s. Earlier, when Macbeth sees the air-drawn dagger and thinks of murder's sentinel, the wolf, the wolf's 'howl' was indeed a lingering, almost melodic, howling. The Folio's last exchange between Macbeth and Banquo is filled with Banquo's foreboding and Macbeth's incipient malice:

---

[1] See Henry Irving's 1895 American tour mentioned above, p. 78.

MACBETH If you shall cleave to my consent, when 'tis,
    It shall make honour for you.
BANQUO   So I lose none
    In seeking to augment it, but still keep
    My bosom franchised and allegiance clear,
    It shall be counselled.
MACBETH   Good repose the while.
BANQUO Thanks, sir; the like to you.   (2.1.25–30)

Stewart paused strongly after 'Good', made 'repose' an imperative, and thus turned a conventional salutation into an order, and one containing a secret anticipation of the mortal 'repose' Macbeth foresees. At the end of his dramatic life, Macbeth's last word of his last line – 'And damned be him who first cries, "Hold, enough!"' (5.8.34) – came only after the sword-fight was concluded, a dying sigh.[1]

Among staged adaptations of *Macbeth*, a controversial and difficult one is Welcome Msomi's *Umabatha*, sometimes called the Zulu *Macbeth*, written and originally performed in South Africa (University of Natal, 1970);[2] the production moved to Europe as part of Peter Daubeny's World Theatre Season (Aldwych Theatre, London, 1972) and returned to world stages including that of the newly reconstructed Shakespeare's Globe on Bankside, London (1997) with a large cast, striking choreography and a thrilling musical score. Shakespeare's plot is translated into historical conflicts within the royal reaches of the Zulu nation in the nineteenth century. Debatable historical information suggests that the celebrated Zulu warrior-king, Shaka (?1786–1828) united and extended the Zulu kingdom, but was assassinated by his half-brothers Dingane and Mblangana; the brothers then fall out, and Dingane kills his co-conspirator. These events have obvious analogies with Shakespeare's *Macbeth*. Of special note was the calm integration of African versions of witchcraft less plainly demonic than Shakespeare's. *Umabatha*'s witches more resembled what modern scholarship portrays as the early modern 'wise-woman', a rural or village fixture usually less persecuted than frequently resorted to in times of domestic or local difficulty.

MACBETH FILMED

Macbeth continues to be adapted in films made around the world.[3] Perhaps the most 'exotic' film for western eyes is India's *Maqbool* (directed by Vishal Bharadwaj, Kaleidoscope, 2003), where Shakespeare's plot and characters, much reshaped and reordered, are translated to the upper reaches of Mumbai/Bombay's criminal classes and given

---

[1] The division of the F speech also occurred in the Caird–Beale–Fielding production (see above, p. 97 n. 5).

[2] For the global, racial, and economic complexities surrounding this production in its various guises, see Kate McLuskie, '*Macbeth*/*Umabatha*: Global Shakespeare in a post-colonial market', *S.Sur.* 52 (1999) 154–65.

[3] Concerning Kurosawa's distinguished *Throne of Blood* (see above, pp. 83–6), see Anthony Dawson, 'Reading Kurosawa reading Shakespeare', in Diana E. Henderson (ed.), *A Concise Companion to Shakespeare on Screen*, 2006, pp. 155–75. Dawson is eloquent and insightful on both *Throne of Blood* and *Ran* (1985), which mixes *Macbeth* and *King Lear*. In "Stands Scotland where it did?": the location of *Macbeth* on film' (in Robert S. Miola (ed.), *Macbeth*, 2004, pp. 357–80), Peter Holland subtly considers five filmed versions ranging from Kurosawa to *Scotland, PA*.

19   *Umabatha* at Shakespeare's Globe (London, 2001)

full Bollywood-style treatment, including a rich sequence showing the elaborate, sexy celebration of a wedding uniting two criminal families and establishing the Malcolm-figure as heir-apparent.[1] Amusingly, Maqbool (Irfaan Khan) is assigned the protection racket for Bollywood itself, and we briefly see him stared down by a beautiful female star.

   Tabu stars as Nimmi, mistress to the Duncan figure ('Abbaji', played by Pankaj Kapoor). She foresees being replaced by a younger woman and seeks a new benefactor, both threatening and seducing Abbaji's hitherto loyal second-in-command, Minyan-Maqbool, and leading him to shoot Abbaji as he sleeps beside his waking, watching mistress, eventually splattered by blood and brains. Maqbool's reign deteriorates much as Macbeth's does, and the movie contains characters analogous to Banquo, Fleance, Malcolm, and Donaldbain. Responding to the play's insistence upon birth and childhood, the film reveals Nimmi's pregnancy a short time after Abbaji's murder. Maqbool briefly contemplates the possibility that not he, but Abbaji, is the father. We later see

---

[1] *Maqbool* is in fact an independent, non-Bollywood production; the dialogue is largely in Urdu with a sprinkling of English words and phrases (there are also English-language sub-titles). Though the author mentions *Maqbool* and regrets he has not seen the film, Rajiva Verma's 'Shakespeare in Hindi cinema', in Poonam Trivedi and Dennis Bartholomeusz (eds.), *India's Shakespeare: Translation, Interpretation, and Performance*, 2005, pp. 269–90, offers a fascinating context for *Maqbool* and its theatrical and cinematic antecedents; Trivedi especially notes the addition of song and dance to Indian adaptations of Shakespeare and the multiplication of romantic entanglements to his plots. Just so, *Maqbool*. This volume also includes (pp. 193–203) Laxmi Chandrashekar's '"A sea change into something rich and strange": Ekbal Ahmed's *Macbeth* and *Hamlet*', which describes a folk-based, puppet-influenced (*yakshagana*) production of *Macbeth*.

mother and infant (significantly, it is born prematurely) in the hospital, and still later, Maqbool kidnaps Nimmi in order to keep her safe from retribution; once back in the very bedroom where Abbaji died, she begins obsessively cleaning the walls and soon dies. In the film's final sequence, Maqbool escapes from a police pursuit and slips into the hospital where his now-motherless child is under care; as he approaches the infant's room he sees Guddu (Ajay Gehi), the Malcolm-character, and his wife Sameera (Masumi Makhija) cuddling the baby and taking the future away with them.

The performances of Tabu, Irfaan Khan, and Pankaj Kapoor are superb, but their primacy is under constant threat from Pandit (Om Puri) and Purohit (Naseeruddin Shah), two corrupt policemen on Abbaji's (later Maqbool's) payroll who amuse themselves and sometimes others by casting horoscopes and reciting a few tired clichés about the inevitability of the future.[1] They are, of course, the witches, and they are brilliantly comic – wisecracking, violent, cowardly, always looking out for themselves, conniving.

Such a criminal re-visioning goes back at least to *Joe Macbeth* (1955) and continues in Geoffrey Wright's film (2006) which places Shakespeare's plot, less changed than in *Maqbool* and with the Folio text more or less intact (though not often well-spoken and often rearranged), in the sexualised world of Melbourne crime, especially drug-dealing (and -taking). The film, 'a deeply pointless adaptation'[2] by the director of the equally violent *Romper Stomper* (1992), includes Sam Worthington as Macbeth (also 'M'), Victoria Hill as the Lady, and Lachy Hulme as Macduff. Worthington was quoted as saying, 'When else are you going to get the opportunity to play Macbeth as a 29-year-old bloke in Australia, with machine-guns and fast cars . . .?'[3] Reviewers were less enthusiastic. As always with modern adaptations/revisions, some of the viewer's pleasure arose from finding the original directions by indirections out: hence, for example, a drug-fight occurs in a club named 'The Cawdor', the Malcolm-figure inherits an expensive high-rise apartment building named 'The Cumberland', a vehicle carrying lumber passes, advertising 'Birnam Wood', and Lady Macbeth is first seen mourning graveside with a tombstone for her son, but the film was not rich in successful reimaginings. The Porter and King Edward were not present, as they were not in many nineteenth-century productions, and there were the usual updatings – cell phones, video security measures, machine-guns, and so forth.

The Porter is not the only source of humour in the play; it can be played for macabre laughs throughout, as a sometimes feeble American film, *Scotland PA* (directed by Billy Morrissette, Abandon Pictures, 2001) – i.e., the town of Scotland, Pennsylvania, USA – suggests by setting the play in a benighted small-town fast-food eatery. Ordinary worker-folk rebel against the overbearing franchisee (= Duncan) and attempt to conceal the consequences. The violence, particularly the murders and the deaths,

---

[1] Part of the grimmer side of the prognosticating policemen lies in the fact that 'pandit' (cognate with English *pundit*) means 'learned person' or 'teacher' and 'purohit' means a Hindu priest, specifically one who advises the king. Hence the words are abstract and symbolic as personal names.

[2] Peter Bradshaw, *Guardian*, 13 July 2007.

[3] Christine Sams, 'Meet the modern Macbeth', *Sydney Morning Herald*, 14 August 2006 (cited from www.smh.com.au/news/film/meet-the-modern-macbeth/ accessed 19 July 2007).

of Shakespeare's play are here predictably grotesque – bodies in deep-freezes and so forth – but the film is a Porter's-eye-view of the original's high politics and might have appealed to some (a majority?) at the Globe.[1]

Recent criticism and scholarship

MACBETH IN ITS TIME AND JUST AFTER

Here I examine scholarly, critical work that addresses questions of how *Macbeth* might have been understood by its seventeenth-century audiences or how modern readers and audiences might better understand the play through knowing more about the cultural contexts in which the play was originally performed and understood. I arbitrarily divide these materials from those that examine *Macbeth* critically or in performance since roughly 1700; see the preceding discussion of performances since 1997 and the next section, '*Macbeth* since about 1700'.

A signal advance in *Macbeth* scholarship is Sally Mapstone's careful work on the Scottish historiographic sources for the play, specifically the notoriously difficult (at least in the theatre) Act 4, Scene 3, the 'England scene', in which Malcolm and Macduff discuss kingly vices and virtues.[2] Mapstone considers which Scottish sources underpin Holinshed's account, Shakespeare's principal source:

> . . . Holinshed's own main source is Hector Boece's *Scotorum Historia*, first published in 1527 and reprinted with some revision and additional material up to 1488 by Giovanni Ferreri in 1574. It is frequently stated or assumed that this chronicle was mediated to Holinshed through the translation of John Bellenden, originally composed *c.* 1530–1 and published in revised form *c.* 1540. (p. 160)

Mapstone compares not merely Holinshed's, Boece's, and Bellenden's (translated but also adapted and enlarged) versions of 4.3, but then turns to John Fordun's *Chronica Gentis Scotorum* (*c.* 1360s-1385), where '[t]he episode makes its first and . . . most extended appearance' (p. 168).[3] Mapstone eventually finds the scene ambiguous at best, a skilful undermining of the audience's certainties, but nonetheless she concludes that '[i]n its mixed Scottish and English heritage "the dullest scene in the play" is in fact the key to its political importance' (p. 182). Mapstone's work must henceforth be carefully considered both by those studying Shakespeare's creative practice and by those analysing *Macbeth*'s place in early Jacobean culture.

Arthur Kinney's *Lies Like Truth: Shakespeare, 'Macbeth', and the Cultural Moment* (2001), compiles many 'lexias' – strings of facts, contemporary (*c.* 1600–10) rumours,

---

[1] In BBC1's 'Shakespeare Re-told' television series, *Macbeth* (2005, directed by Mark Brozel) transposes the play (with Peter Moffat's text) into a conflict between an élite chef, Duncan Docherty, and his subordinate, Joe Macbeth (James McAvoy).

[2] Sally Mapstone, 'Shakespeare and Scottish kingship: a case history', in Sally Mapstone and Juliette Wood (eds.), *The Rose and the Thistle: Essays on the Culture of Late Medieval and Renaissance Scotland*, 1993, pp. 158–93.

[3] Mapstone also notes '[t]he Malcolm/Macduff scene is actually one of the most popular and repeated episodes in Scottish historical narratives from the end of the fourteenth century until the end of the sixteenth' (p. 168).

events, writings, and so forth – that the early audiences and any subsequent audiences or readers might know and might combine in myriad ways as they sought, or seek, to understand a performance of the play, then or now.[1] Framed by a discussion of hypertext and computer models of associating bits or bytes of information, Kinney's book consists mainly of a long central chapter, made up of a series of short – six- to twenty-page – lexias on such subjects as 'Theatrical lexias', 'Lexias of Justice', 'Military lexias', 'Lexias of Family'. As the chapter's 348 notes testify, Kinney has drawn information from diverse sources, including scholarship far beyond the literary or theatrical; many original materials are cited, correctly, as 'Quoted in . . .'. Kinney assembles commonplaces many of which are no longer commonplace – *loci* or *loci communes*, technically – in good Renaissance fashion, backed by such authorities as Erasmus and Ramus, and his underlying argument is the analogy among, if not the identity of, early modern methods of ordering and the ordering of the computer and of computer-paralleling theories of the mind's neurological functioning. In some ways, this book recalls G. B. Harrison's *Elizabethan and Jacobean Journals*, 5 vols. (1928–58; reprinted, 1999), one volume of which Kinney cites. Harrison organised his information chronologically, Kinney organises his topically.[2] Novice readers of the play will find Kinney's central chapter especially valuable.

Among those topics, inevitably, are demonology and witchcraft, and Laura Shamas explores, sometimes haphazardly, various backgrounds to early modern witchcraft belief; her effort may assist producers and directors of the play.[3] John Cox distinguishes between the uses of stage devils in *Macbeth* and Barnaby Barnes's *The Devil's Charter*, another King's Men play of 1606.[4] Barnes's devils owe much to 'Italianate ideology', i.e., that of Machiavelli and Guicciardini, while Shakespeare's 'conception of demonic reality had been familiar to English playgoers for almost two hundred years before the advent of the London commercial theatre, for the transformation of Lucifer . . . into Satan . . . occurs in the first pageant of the mystery plays' (p. 943). In short, 'Shakespeare's play [*Macbeth*] is more closely attuned to its dramaturgical heritage than Barnes's' (p. 934).

Demonology and its means are among the topics reopened in Mary Floyd-Wilson's 'English epicures and Scottish witches'.[5] Floyd-Wilson surveys the history of various xenophobic charges and counter-charges about the barbarity (or heroic primitivism) of the Scottish and the weakness (or civility) of the English (see above, pp. 9ff.); she stresses the imagined relations of environment and emotion, turning on the 'passibility' of bodily boundaries. She concludes, '[m]y reading emphasizes the possibility that Shakespeare's *Macbeth* represents its protagonists' troubling susceptibility – and the diminished will it can imply – as barbarically Scottish' (p. 146). These propagandistic

---

[1] Kinney thinks the first performance was in 1606 and also knows (p. 214) when Shakespeare was writing the play – early March 1605.

[2] Another book-length study, Jan H. Blits's *The Insufficiency of Virtue: 'Macbeth' and the Natural Order*, 1996, examines the play scene by scene under the general claim (arising from Macduff's actions) that *Macbeth* represents an evil so persuasive as to render virtue insufficient for success or survival.

[3] Laura Shamas, *'We Three': The Mythology of Shakespeare's Weird Sisters*, 2006.

[4] John D. Cox, 'Stage devilry in two King's Men plays of 1606', *MLR* 93 (1998), 934–47.

[5] *SQ*, 57 (2006), 131–61.

and medico-psychological contexts lead to some valuable readings of famous, difficult passages in 1.5 and 1.7 (pp. 151–6).

Frederick Kiefer offers a deeply researched study of *Macbeth*'s witches and Hecate as they might have been represented in early performances.[1] 'Triple' Hecate (Diana, Luna, Hecate–Proserpina) probably did not have three heads in early performances of *Macbeth*, but might have had three faces, as she does in René Boyvin's engraving of a design by Léonard Thiry (Kiefer, p. 106 and his illustration 23). In the Jacobean theatre, the Hecate-actor might have performed wearing a three-faced mask. Equally, Hecate might have been represented with tangled hair 'entwined with short vipers' as she was in Ben Jonson's *Masque of Queens*, nearly contemporary with *Macbeth* (Kiefer, p. 108). 'The other witches [see 4.1.38 SD], appearing in scenes [*sic*] with Hecate may have carried torches, a visual allusion to Hecate's abode in the underworld. . . Finally, the entry of Hecate may have been accompanied by the noise of barking dogs . . .' (p. 109). Kiefer accepts as evidence of the witches' original appearance Banquo's description of them (1.3.37–45),[2] and points out that Holinshed's and Simon Forman's terms for the witches – 'nymphs', 'fairies' – need not be so benign as modern meanings suggest (see above, pp. 57–8).[3] As for the singing and dancing of Hecate and the witches, both in early and later (seventeenth-century through many nineteenth-century) productions, Kiefer warns that these activities need not be frivolous (or as ridiculous as they seem to have been in eighteenth-century productions – see 1.1 headnote): 'European folklore had long imagined that those in league with Satan sang and danced when they met with him' (p. 115). And, of course, they flew. Kiefer concludes with a discussion of John Marston's classical Roman *Sophonisba* (1605–6) and its eponymous central character: '[t]he witches of *Macbeth* must be closer in costume and makeup to the witch of *Sophonisba* than to the unfortunate Elizabeth Sawyer of *The Witch of Edmonton*' [1621] (p. 119) and a discussion of the witches represented in Ben Jonson's *Masque of Queens* (pp. 120–5).

Macbeth's early staging also interests David Farley-Hills, who uses Mariko Ichikawa's study of entrances and exits in Shakespearean texts to argue for the venue of *Macbeth*'s early performance(s) as that venue or venues might be represented by the Folio's stage-directions.[4] Farley-Hills studies numerous Folio entry-directions and argues that the dialogue's acknowledgements of an entering character and that character's first speaking are so close together as to suggest an acting-space where actors could enter the playing-area from the side(s) rather than from far up-stage (as we suppose they usually did at the Globe and similarly constructed public stages): hence, 'the un-Globe-like promptness with which characters come and go on the stage' (p. 52). The 'pattern' is 'more likely to point to a staging in one of the covered halls used for staging plays at the royal palaces

[1] Frederick Kiefer, 'Hecate and the witches in *Macbeth*', in his *Shakespeare's Visual Theatre: Staging the Personified Characters*, 2003, pp. 101–27.
[2] Readers and others may question Banquo's first description of the witches: see 1.3.37–40 n.
[3] In discussing Simon Forman's account of the early Globe *Macbeth*, Kiefer and other critics mention *MND*'s 'fairies' as charming, non-violent creatures, but John Barton's RSC production of the play (1977) presented them as threatening indeed.
[4] See David Farley-Hills, 'The entrances and exits of *Macbeth*', *N&Q* 50 (2003), 50–5 and Mariko Ichikawa, *Shakespearean Entrances*, 2002.

than at the Globe' (p. 54), and Farley-Hills tentatively endorses Henry N. Paul's belief (in *The Royal Play of Macbeth*, 1950) 'that Shakespeare wrote the play for performance at the Great Hall of Hampton Court' (p. 55). Likewise speculative is Henri Suhamy's 'The authenticity of the Hecate scenes in *Macbeth*: arguments and counter-arguments'; his meticulous and imaginative argument leads him to claim that the Hecate passages (in 3.5 and 4.1) – now usually thought not to be Shakespearean and possibly by Thomas Middleton – are indeed authentically Shakespearean.[1]

The sound or sounds of *Macbeth* as spoken in the earliest performances are a starting point for Christopher Highley's chapter on 'The place of Scots in the Scottish play'.[2] Highley expands his focus from the linguistic to many other aspects of Scotland (Highland and Lowland) and Scottishness – and thus English and Englishness. He justly observes, 'While Malcolm and his new regime are insistently Anglicized and hence legitimized, Macbeth's isolation and descent into tyranny is presented as a process of Gaelicization' (p. 61).

From scenes and speeches to lines: Thomas LaBorie Burns sensitively contrasts Malcolm's advice to the distraught Macduff, 'Dispute it like a man', with Macduff's reply, 'But I must also feel it as a man' (4.3.222, 224): 'note the change from *like* to *as*, indicating a natural way of behavior [*as*], not an imposed performance [*like*]'.[3] Colin Wilcockson argues that the Porter's 'th'other devil's name' (2.3.6) is Satan and that the 'structural pattern' of Act 2, Scenes 3–4 echoes the crucifixion, harrowing of Hell, and Doomsday sequence of Christian belief.[4]

MACBETH SINCE ABOUT 1700

Charles Macklin's Shylock (1741) was epochal in treating the Jewish financier as a dignified, violent, even possibly tragic, figure rather than the comic and buffoonish character that had apparently long held the English stage. Macklin's *Macbeth* at Covent Garden (1773) is usually remembered for the riot instigated, it seems, by a bitter rival for the rôle, William 'Gentleman' Smith and his adherents (see p. 74 above). Matthew J. Kinservik has carefully examined Macklin's manuscript notes for the production and offers a detailed account of contemporary responses to Macklin's performance and its innovative response to the dominant Garrick-inspired interpretation.[5] Although Kinservik acknowledges that '[t]he most common criticism of Macklin's acting is that he delivered his lines in a harsh monotone without varying his emotions' (p. 65), contemporaries nonetheless recognised that Macklin performed 'a Macbeth who was more sinister

[1] Henri Suhamy, 'The authencity of the Hecate scenes in *Macbeth*: arguments and counter-arguments', in Jean-Marie Maguin and Michèle Willems (eds.), *French Essays on Shakespeare and His Contemporaries: 'What Would France with Us?'*, 1995, pp. 271–88. In the same volume, pp. 247–70, Maguin studies *Macbeth*'s light–dark-day–night imagery in 'Rise and fall of the King of darkness'.
[2] In Maley and Murphy (eds.) *Shakespeare and Scotland*, pp. 53–66.
[3] Thomas LaBorie Burns, '*Homo/Vir*: The state of man and nature in *Macbeth*', in Amara da Cunha Resende (ed.), *Foreign Accents: Brazilian Readings of Shakespeare*, 2002, pp. 114–25; citation from p. 122.
[4] Colin Wilcockson, 'The harrowing of Hell motif in Shakespeare's *Macbeth*', *Anglistik* 14.2 (2003), 63–70; pp. 63–4. See 2.3.75 n., where the point is anticipated.
[5] Matthew J. Kinservik, 'A sinister *Macbeth*: the Macklin production of 1773', *Harvard Library Bulletin* 6 (1995), 51–76. On Macklin's production, see also pp. 108–11 in Rebecca Rogers, 'How Scottish was the Scottish play?', in Maley and Murphy (eds.), *Shakespeare and Scotland*, pp. 104–23.

than Garrick had played him' and 'noted the savage tenor of Macklin's performance' (p. 63). Dully delivered as Macklin's Macbeth might have been, Kinservik establishes that 'Macklin's production was considered a direct challenge to Garrick's' (p. 71). As Kinservik observes, Macklin's new interpretation of the role was forward-looking. In the next theatrical generation, Kemble followed the Garrick line (Macbeth sympathetic and/or weak, Lady Macbeth the strong instigator of evil acts), but Macklin's version persisted: '[a] century later, Henry Irving had much greater success with a similar interpretation' (p. 73).

With new stage-business (e.g., a near-fist-fight with Banquo's Ghost in 3.4), Macklin also had new sets and costumes created for his performances: nominally 'Scottish' costumes, at least in Macbeth's appearances in the first and final acts, and for some of his entourage; an outdoor setting for Macbeth's 'Is this a dagger which I see before me'; an up-stage entrance for Macbeth in 1.3 and on-stage army which remained through Macbeth and Banquo's encounter with the witches.

'Arm, arm, and out!' (5.5.45). Without clear evidence in his main sources (see, e.g., Bullough, VII, 505), Shakespeare seems to imagine that Macbeth exits Dunsinane Castle for the final martial struggles, and Siward soon assures Malcolm, 'This way, my lord; the castle's gently rendered. / The tyrant's people on both sides do fight' (5.7.25–6). Charles Ross places these events in a literary tradition, the 'custom of the castle', a feature of medieval romance where a questing knight encounters a castle whose holder imposes some horrid task that must be accomplished in order (for example) to preserve the knight's life or free a prisoner:

Realizing [after Lady Macbeth's death] his future is empty, Macbeth engages in a form of sympathetic magic: he empties his castle to allow its reinscription by others . . . Emptied by Macbeth, Dunsinane welcomes the English as Macbeth fights in the field . . . Shakespeare's direct sources provide nothing like this moment. But the literary roots of a castle that both symbolizes the law and also shelters foul customs stretch back through chivalric romance.[1]

Always a critical issue, the play's language constitutes a 'magical grammar' in Linda Woodbridge's view. It is 'a grammar for causing unpleasant things to disappear: the use of pronouns rather than directly naming nouns, of passive verbs to evade naming who performed the action, of euphemisms to avoid naming actions or agents, of epithets or praise-names rather than proper names, of synonyms and other substitutive devices.'[2] (See above, pp. 43–57, especially pp. 49–51.)

---

[1] Charles Ross, *The Custom of the Castle: From Malory to 'Macbeth'*, 1997, p. 127. In *Shakespearean Tragedy as Chivalric Romance: Rethinking 'Macbeth', 'Hamlet', 'Othello' and 'King Lear'*, 2003, Michael L. Hays proposes a farther-reaching link between tragedy and romance: '*Macbeth* is romance in the delineation of its major characters and the shape of its narrative materials' (p. 98). In particular, Hays defends Act 4, Scene 3, and generally treats Malcolm as a morally, politically, and dramatically significant figure. His chapter on *Macbeth* tendentiously disputes pp. 25–6 and 88–93, above.

[2] Linda Woodbridge, 'Shakespeare and magical grammar', in Allen Mitchie and Eric Buckley (eds.), *Style: Essays in Renaissance and Restoration Literature and Culture in Memory of Harriet Hawkins*, 2005, pp. 84–98; citation from p. 87. Kirilka Stavreva, '"There's magic in thy majesty": queenship and witch-speak in Jacobean Shakespeare', in Carole Levin *et al.* (eds.), *'High and Mighty Queens' of Early Modern England: Realities and Representations*, 2003, pp. 151–68, is conventional.

Common law recognises many categories – 'the corporation, the criminal, the privy council', for instance, as 'legal persons', treated legally as if they were individuals; Elizabeth Fowler proposes the broader category, 'social persons' and lists 'civic roles . . . kinship designations . . . ethnicities . . . literary characters . . . economic persons (individual and collective)' as examples.[1] For *Macbeth*, Fowler claims that 'a fitting investiture of the social person' consists 'overwhelmingly [in] relational acts', specifically the 'three feudal topoi' of 'military service, the [royal] progress, and counsel' (p. 85). Focusing on '[t]he primary figures of *Macbeth* – the monarch [Duncan], the lord, and the wife', Fowler shows in what ways they 'fit', or fail to fit, social bonds; her critical approach best illuminates 'counsel': 'Bad counsel is hauntingly given by Lady Macbeth and by the witches. . . Counsel in the court is evoked powerfully by the failed banquet' (p. 86).

More precise legal matters, specifically Henrician extensions of Edward III's law of treason (which required deeds to be proven) to include treasonous words, interest Rebecca Lemon. Her most striking insight concerns the relation of Macbeth, traitor, and Malcolm, king-to-be. *Macbeth* explores 'the charismatic power of treason' and . . . [i]n the context of the play this infectious representation proves . . . productive for Scotland's future king [Malcolm]'.[2] In the controversial conversation with Macduff (4.3; see above, pp. 88–93), 'Malcolm adopts the villainous characteristics of Macbeth's own reign, employing the deceptive mechanisms alleged of traitors in order to rule his kingdom effectively' (p. 87). Framing her discussion with remarks on convicts' scaffold speeches and suspecting their sincerity, Lemon unnecessarily rests the case on Malcolm's report of Cawdor's execution, specifically Malcolm's use of 'studied': 'He [Cawdor] died / As one that had been studied in his death' (1.4.8–9). Acknowledging the *ars moriendi*, the long tradition of how to achieve a 'good death', Lemon nonetheless sees this use ('studied') as evidence of Malcolm's discovery of 'the duplicitous potential of language' (p. 100) and cites a courtroom witticism by Sir Edward Coke and a contemporary attack on Ambrose Rookwood, one of the Gunpowder Plot convicts: '*Ruckwood*, out of a studied speech would faine have made his bringing uppe and breeding in idolatrie [i.e., Roman Catholicism], to have beene some excuse to his villainie, but a faire talke, would not helpe a fowle deed . . .'[3] Lemon's main argument, one rehabilitating

[1] Elizabeth Fowler, 'The rhetoric of political forms: social persons and the criterion of fit in colonial law, *Macbeth*, and *The Irish Masqve at Covrt*', in Amy Boesky and Mary Thomas Crane (eds.) *Form and Reform in Renaissance England: Essays in Honor of Barbara Kiefer Lewalski*, 2000, pp. 70–103; quotation from p. 71 (subsequent citations of this essay are parenthetical). The *Macbeth* section of this essay is reprinted as '*Macbeth* and the rhetoric of political forms', in Malley and Murphy (eds.), *Shakespeare and Scotland*, pp. 67–86.

[2] Rebecca Lemon, *Treason by Words: Literature, Law, and Rebellion in Shakespeare's England*, 2006, p. 86; subsequent references are cited parenthetically.

[3] T. W., *The Arraignment and execution of the late traytors* (1606), sig. B4v, partly quoted by Lemon, *Treason*, p. 91. (Lemon identifies the author as 'F.W.'; the initials T.W. appear at the end of the epistle dedicatory, 'To All faithfull and obedient Subjects'.) 'Studied' will not bear Lemon's implied meaning of 'deceitful, affected'; *OED*'s first two citations for the participial adjective are Shakespearean: Enobarbus' 'Pardon what I have spoke / For 'tis a studied, not a present thought' and Hermione's 'What studied torments, tyrant, hast for me'. In both, 'studied' means, to quote *OED*, 'Resulting from, or characterized by, deliberate effort or intention; produced or acquired by study; carefully contrived or excogitated; designed, premeditated; deliberate, intentional' with no implication of 'affected, deceitful' (see 1.4.9 n.).

Malcolm and his tactics in 4.3, is among the best of several similar ones in recent criticism.

Farther-reaching is Stephen Orgel's argument about *Macbeth*'s early performance history or histories. He begins by considering the possibility that Hecate's reference to 'this great king' (4.1.130) – Macbeth himself within the fiction – might be an occasionally induced reference to King James, present at a 'version of the play prepared for a single special occasion, rather than the standard public theatre version'.[1] Orgel reconsiders the play's incoherent views of the witches (cheerful here in 4.1, ominous everywhere else) and its stuttering over Malcolm's claim to the throne, Macbeth's legitimate status as king, and Macduff's extraordinarily ambiguous moral and political stature.[2] A tentative proposal emerges: *Macbeth* 'really is an astonishingly male-oriented and misogynistic play, especially at the end, when there are no women left, not even the witches, and the restored commonwealth is a world of heroic soldiers' (p. 150).

Douglas Lanier concludes a wide-ranging survey on '*Macbeth* in Popular Culture' by saying,

> The vitality of *Macbeth*'s adaptation to so many cultural traditions suggests that Shakespeare's tale of dynastic struggles in medieval Scotland has now become a global parable about the temptations and self-destructiveness of ambition and violence, one that continues to find resonance with audiences worldwide.[3]

Lanier's examples range from the Gothic (Edgar Allan Poe's 'The Telltale Heart') to 'a story in the classic horror comic *Adventures into Terror* 27 (1954)' to ' "Banquo's Chair", a much-beloved American radio show first broadcast on *Suspense*, June 1, 1943' (pp. 21–2). Lanier surveys further territory, some familiar, some strikingly not, in sections on the *Macbeth* curse, the 'Infernal Women of *Macbeth*' (not just John Updike's *The Witches of Eastwick*, but Bugs Bunny, too), versions that stress the play's Scottishness and others generalised to samurai or gangster traditions, uses of the play as satire, examples of non-North American–European versions. No such survey could be comprehensive, certainly not in so confined a space, but Lanier's discussion is witty and valuable.[4]

---

[1] Stephen Orgel, 'Macbeth and the antic round', *S.Sur.* 52 (1999), 143–53; quotation from p. 144; subsequent quotations are cited parenthetically. See 4.1.126–31 n.

[2] As Orgel writes, 'historically . . . Macbeth was killed in battle by Malcolm, not Macduff. Shakespeare is following Holinshed here, but why, especially in a play that revises so much else in its source material?' (Macbeth and the antic round', p. 152). See also: 'Although his strange indifference to the safety of his [Macduff's] wife and son disturbs many viewers and readers, it reinforces his status as being outside of succession' (Jonathan Baldo, 'The politics of aloofness in *Macbeth*', *ELR* 36 (1996), 531–60; quotation from p. 543).

[3] Douglas Lanier, '"Hours dreadful and things strange": *Macbeth* in popular culture', in Proctor (ed.), *Macbeth*, pp. 21–33; quotation from p. 33. See further: Douglas Lanier, *Shakespeare and Modern Popular Culture*, 2002.

[4] One addition might be the televised versions of Michael Dobbs's satirical novels: *To Play the King* (1993) and *The Final Cut* (1995), BBC-TV (scripts by Dobbs and Andrew Davies), on the fictional British prime-ministership of Francis Urquhart. The novels and televised adaptations, beginning with *House of Cards*, allude widely to Shakespeare's plays; in the latter two television productions, a continuing character is the security man, one 'Corder' (Cawdor), who protects the prime minister's Lady Macbeth-like wife.

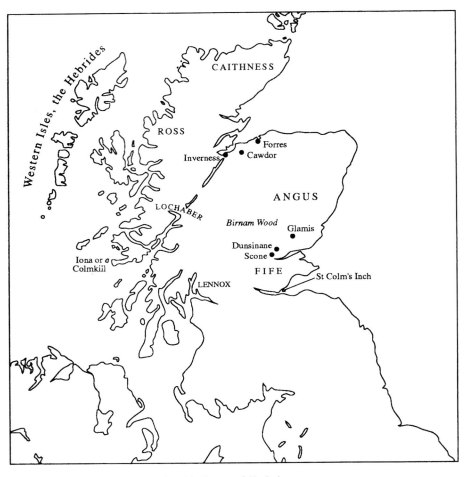

Scotland, showing place names mentioned in the text of *Macbeth*

NOTE ON THE TEXT

The First Folio (F) of Shakespeare's plays (1623) contains the earliest surviving text of *The Tragedie of Macbeth*, where it is sixth among the tragedies, printed between *Julius Caesar* and *Hamlet*; this text is probably derived from a Jacobean playhouse script rather than from a literary or reading text. The theatrical tradition produced two other important seventeenth-century printed texts: a quarto *Macbeth* in 1673 (Q1673) published without Shakespeare's name but generally following F with some additional material and several fascinating 'editorial' readings; and William Davenant's adaptation of *Macbeth*, printed in 1674 and here designated 'Davenant'. Appendix 2, pp. 284–90 below, discusses the relation of Q1673 to F and to Davenant's 1674 version. Q1673, Davenant's play, and Folio *Macbeth* almost certainly include the work of Thomas Middleton, a distinguished younger contemporary of Shakespeare. All modern editions of 'Shakespeare's' play, including this one, should therefore be considered editions of '*Macbeth* by William Shakespeare and adapted by Thomas Middleton', as the 1986 Oxford edition of the *Complete Works* puts it.

The Folio text of *Macbeth* contains many moments where the staging is debatable; this edition pays special attention to such moments. Modern editions differ principally on two matters; first, lineation, particularly in the first half of the play, and second, the treatment of passages almost certainly written by Middleton. Both subjects are discussed in the Textual Analysis, pp. 267–75 below, as are the questions of 'copy' for the Folio, the compositors and printing of F, and the possible revision of F. The Textual Analysis also describes the editorial procedures I have employed and, more important, explains this edition's silent (that is, uncollated) changes to the text as it appears in F.

Shakespeare's plays swoop disconcertingly from language and action that appear unconstrained by time or place to highly precise (and, we must admit, sometimes now unfathomable) references to particular words, customs, ideas, and preoccupations of early modern England. This oscillation especially characterises his tragedies, and *Macbeth* is a supreme example. I have reluctantly offered notes on the play's imaginary locations, which may be in a notional eleventh-century Scotland and England, but were once also on the Globe's stage and were therefore once part of early-seventeenth-century London. Only an Enlightenment editor or reader might guess where the witches are.

This text is a modernised one. For words that are now archaic, the modern equivalent appears if it does not disturb the metre, rhyme, or wordplay; where earlier editions have treated verbal changes as emendations, the collation records the change as a modernisation. Thus, at 1.7.6 this text reads 'shoal' and the collation records F's archaic form, 'Schoole' (which could, of course, at first seem to be the modern word 'school'):

shoal] F (Schoole)

For more complicated changes, the collation begins with the reading accepted into the text followed by the source of that change, then by the Folio reading, and (in chronological order) any other plausible but rejected readings. Thus, a more complicated example (2.2.66) might read:

> green one red] Q1673, F4 (Green one Red); Greene one, Red F; green, One red *Johnson*

which means that this text adopts a (modernised) reading shared by the theatrical quarto of 1673 and F4, the Fourth Folio (1685), that is the equivalent of the First Folio according to modern punctuational conventions, and that Samuel Johnson's edition (1765) repunctuated the phrase and changed its meaning. Another example appears at 2.3.4–5:

> Come in time –] *Brooke*; Come in time, F; Come in, time, Q*1673;* Come in, Time; *Staunton*; come in, time-server; *NS;* Come in farmer, *Blackfriars* (*conj. Anon. in Cam.*)

This collation means: this text adopts Brooke's reading, a modernisation of F's text; Q1673 repunctuated the phrase; Howard Staunton, apparently unaware of Q1673, conjectured the same reading as Q1673 and made 'time' an abstraction; John Dover Wilson (in the New Shakespeare edition) offered an interesting emendation, as did Robert Dent in the Blackfriars edition, following an earlier conjecture. When this text follows F in a phrase longer than one or two words, but other editions have made different choices, the collation records only those places where F differs from the text offered here. Thus the collation for the stage direction at 4.1.131 reads:

> F (*Musicke . . . Dance . . .*); *Globe adds / with Hecate*

indicating that this text differs from F only in the spelling and capitalisation of two words, but that the Globe editors appended a further direction to the original one.

NOTE ON THE COMMENTARY

More frequently than any earlier edition, the Commentary here cites the *Oxford English Dictionary* (*OED*) and other lexical sources, using the *OED*'s terminology for parts of speech (*sb* for 'substantive', a noun; *v* for 'verb', *a* for 'adjective', *ppl a* for 'participial adjective', *vbl sb* for 'verbal substantive', etc.) and the numbered and lettered subdivisions in its entries. Exploiting Jürgen Schäfer's and Bryan A. Garner's work on the *OED* and later texts antedating its citations and adding to these works, the Commentary draws attention to words that may be Shakespearean coinages and notes those places where *Macbeth* is the first text cited for a use or definition. Other editions and earlier students of Shakespeare's language have not always recorded the play's verbal inventiveness; where appropriate, glosses and citations from *OED* and of proverbial language therefore suggest where the play innovates or echoes earlier usage by remarking how frequently a word or phrase occurs, or the date of the first recorded use. This information may be wildly inaccurate, however, since much lexicographical work remains to be done.

When I cite *Macbeth*, references are to lines as numbered here unless otherwise noted; Shakespeare's other plays are cited from the Riverside edition, text ed. G. B. Evans, 1974. Other editors' references to Shakespeare are similarly normalised, as are their references to works where I cite different (and more accurate) editions. (See the List of Abbreviations and Conventions, pp. xi–xxi above, for the works and editions mentioned here, in the Commentary, and in the collation.) Greek and Latin texts are cited from the appropriate Loeb edition with only the translator's name mentioned; unattributed translations are mine. Unless otherwise noted, the Bible is quoted from the so-called Bishops' Bible (1568).

Macbeth

LIST OF CHARACTERS

Speaking characters in order of first appearance:

Three WITCHES

DUNCAN, *King of Scotland*

MALCOLM, *Duncan's elder son, later Prince of Cumberland, later King of Scotland*

CAPTAIN *in the Scottish forces*

LENNOX, *a thane*

ROSS, *a thane*

MACBETH, *Thane of Glamis, later Thane of Cawdor, later King of Scotland*

BANQUO, *a thane*

ANGUS, *a thane*

LADY MACBETH, *Countess of Glamis, later Countess of Cawdor, later Queen of Scotland*

ATTENDANT *in the household of Macbeth*

FLEANCE, *Banquo's son*

PORTER *in Macbeth's household*

MACDUFF, *Thane of Fife*

DONALDBAIN, *Duncan's younger son*

OLD MAN

Two MURDERERS *employed by Macbeth*

SERVANT *in the household of Macbeth*

THIRD MURDERER *employed by Macbeth*

HECATE, *goddess of the moon and of sorcery*

A LORD, *a Scot, opposed to Macbeth*

FIRST APPARITION, *an armed Head*

SECOND APPARITION, *a bloody Child*

THIRD APPARITION, *a Child crowned*

LADY MACDUFF, *Countess of Fife*

SON *to Macduff and Lady Macduff*

MESSENGER, *a Scot*

TWO MURDERERS, *who attack Lady Macduff and her Son*

DOCTOR *at the English court*

DOCTOR OF PHYSIC *at the Scottish court*

WAITING-GENTLEWOMAN *who attends Lady Macbeth*

MENTEITH, *a thane opposed to Macbeth*

CAITHNESS, *a thane opposed to Macbeth*

SERVANT *to Macbeth*

SEYTON, *gentleman loyal to Macbeth*

SIWARD, *general in the Anglo-Scottish forces*

MESSENGER *in Macbeth's service*
YOUNG SIWARD, *Siward's son, in the Anglo-Scottish forces*

Silent characters:
Attendants in Duncan's entourage
Musicians (players of hautboys)
Torch-bearers
Sewer   *in Macbeth's household*
Servants and Attendants
Ghost of Banquo
Three Witches, accompanying Hecate
Eight kings, appearing to Macbeth
Drummers and bearers of colours (flags) in the Anglo-Scottish forces
Soldiers in the Anglo-Scottish forces
Drummers and bearers of colours (flags) in Macbeth's forces
Soldiers in Macbeth's forces

Notes

F does not provide a list. These notes principally concern the semi-legendary and historical individuals dramatised in *Macbeth*, along with information about how proper names might have been pronounced in Shakespeare's theatre.

DUNCAN   Historically, Duncan I (reigned AD 1034–40).

MALCOLM   Historically, Malcolm III (reigned AD 1057–93).

LENNOX   His remark, 'my young remembrance' (2.3.54), may indicate his age.

ROSS   Executed, according to Holinshed (*Scotland*, p. 171b), during the ten-year period of Macbeth's reign as a good king.

MACBETH   Historically, Mormaer of Moray; reigned AD 1040–57. Simon Forman (see pp. 57–8 above) once spells the name 'Mackbet', despite the evidence of the Folio (which rhymes it with 'heath' at 1.1.7–8, and with 'death' at 1.2.64–5 and 3.5.4–5) that the final *th* was sounded; the rhymes with 'death' also strongly imply a short *e* in '*Macbeth*' (Cercignani, pp. 76–7).

BANQUO   Historically, Thane of Lochaber; Simon Forman's spellings (see pp. 57–8 above) – Bancko, Banko, Banco – may indicate Jacobean pronunciation.

LADY MACBETH   Historically, 'Gruoch', a descendant of either King Kenneth II (reigned AD 971–5) or of King Kenneth III (reigned ?AD 997–1005).

MACDUFF   Historically, Thane of Fife; Simon Forman (see pp. 57–8 above) spells this name MackDove and Macdouee (i.e. Macdove), perhaps indicating Jacobean pronunciation; the name rhymes with 'Enough' at 4.1.70–1.

DONALDBAIN   The historical individual's name was also represented as Donald-bane, Donalbane, Donald Bane, or Donald Bán (i.e. 'Donald the Fair'). Reigned as Donald III AD 1093–7.

CAITHNESS   Executed, according to Holinshed (*Scotland*, p. 171b), during the ten-year period of Macbeth's reign as a good king.

SEYTON   For pronunciation of this name, see Supplementary Note on 5.3.19, p. 260 below.

SIWARD   Historically, an Earl of Northumberland who died in AD 1055, two years before Macbeth.

MACBETH

[handwritten: this will be a play of prophecy / fate.]

1.1 *Thunder and lightning. Enter three* WITCHES

FIRST WITCH When shall we three meet again?
    In thunder, lightning, or in rain? *[handwritten: → Disruption of natural order.]*
SECOND WITCH When the hurly-burly's done,
    When the battle's lost, and won.
THIRD WITCH That will be ere the set of sun.   5
FIRST WITCH Where the place?
SECOND WITCH Upon the heath.
THIRD WITCH There to meet with Macbeth.
FIRST WITCH I come, Graymalkin.

Title] *The Tragedie of Macbeth* F (*title page and in running titles throughout*); *The Tragedy of Macbeth* F (*table of contents*)
Act 1, Scene 1 1.1] F (*Actus Primus. Scoena Prima.*) 1 SH FIRST WITCH] F (1.) *throughout* (*sometimes as* 1) 1 again?]
F (againe?); again *Hanmer* 3 SH SECOND WITCH] F (2.) *throughout* (*sometimes as* 2) 5 SH THIRD WITCH] F (3.) *throughout*
(*sometimes as* 3)

Act 1, Scene 1

Perhaps the most striking opening scene in Shakespeare. Coleridge saw a particular contrast with *Hamlet*: 'In the latter the gradual ascent from the simplest forms of conversation to the language of impassioned intellect, yet still the intellect remaining the *seat* of passion; in the *Macbeth*, the invocation is made at once to the imagination, and the emotions connected therewith' (Coleridge, p. 106). This romantic view diverged sharply from that of Johnson, who defended playwright and witches with a relativistic argument, 'however they may now be ridiculed'. The setting is unlocalised, but at least since Komisarjevsky's production (Stratford, 1933) the sisters (or 'witches', see 0 SD n.) have sometimes been imagined as battlefield scavengers.

0 SD *Thunder and lightning* Witches were popularly supposed to 'send raine, haile, tempests, thunder, lightening' (Scot, III, 13); see 1.3.10–13 n.

0 SD WITCHES Only at 1.3.5 does the dialogue use the word *witch*; elsewhere they are named and name themselves 'weïrd sisters', although 'Witches' appears in many SDs. Male actors often play these parts (see C. B. Young in NS, p. lxxii, and e.g. Colin George's production, Sheffield Playhouse, October 1970). In his 1888 souvenir edn, Henry Irving claimed (p. 6), 'this is, I believe, the first time that the weird sisters have been performed by women'; on the eighteenth-century English stage, Ann Pitt

was the only female witch (Carlisle, p. 338). See illustration 2, p. 18 above. For the witches' early costuming, see Supplementary Note, p. 255 below.

1 When The play's first word concerns time, a topic that will become increasingly important and is always more significant than place, 'Where' (6).

3 hurly-burly turmoil, tumult, especially of rebellion or insurrection. Reduplications with suffixed *-y* are common in English (e.g. topsy-turvy, handy-dandy, wishy-washy), but the see-saw childishness is here appropriate to the sisters' obscurely ominous way of speaking and the teetering confusion of opposites to follow.

4 battle conflict F's 'Battaile' could also mean 'body . . . of troops . . . composing an entire army, or one of its main divisions' (*OED* Battle *sb* 8a), a meaning appropriate to the slaughter soon described.

4 lost, and won Possibly proverbial (Dent W408.1); see 1.2.67 n.

7 heath wilderness; uninhabited and uncultivated ground.

9 Graymalkin A cat's name. 'Malkin' is a diminutive of 'Maud' or 'Matilda' (see *OED* Malkin and Mawkin); 'malkin' is also slang for 'slut, lewd woman' (Williams). It was a 'peculiarly English notion' (Thomas, p. 445) that cats and toads (see 10 n.), as well as dogs, rats, and some insects, were likely to be witches'

SECOND WITCH Paddock calls.   10
THIRD WITCH Anon.
ALL Fair is foul, and foul is fair,
　　Hover through the fog and filthy air.

Exeunt

1.2 *Alarum within. Enter King* [DUNCAN,] MALCOLM, DONALDBAIN,
LENNOX, *with Attendants, meeting a bleeding* CAPTAIN

DUNCAN What bloody man is that? He can report,
　　As seemeth by his plight, of the revolt

10–13 SECOND WITCH . . . air.] *Singer*[2] *(conj. Hunter, 'New', II, 165, subst.); All. Padock* calls anon: faire is foule, and foule
is faire, / Houer through the fogge and filthie ayre. F   *Act* 1, *Scene* 2   1.2] F *(Scena Secunda.)*   0 SD.1 *King* DUNCAN,
MALCOLM] *Capell; King Malcome* F   0 SD.1–2 DONALDBAIN] F *(Donalbaine) here and in* SDs *throughout*   0 SD.2 CAPTAIN]
F *(Captaine); Sergeant Cam.*   1 SH DUNCAN] F *(King) here and in* SHs *throughout*

'familiars', non-human agents of their deeds; see
Scot, I, 4; 'Familiar . . . a very quaint invisible devil'
(Webster, *Duchess of Malfi* 1.1.259–60); 'familiars in
the shape of mice, / Rats, ferrets, weasels' (*Edmonton* 2.1.103–4).
　10 Paddock Toad.
　12 Fair is foul, and foul is fair Proverbially,
'Fair without but foul within' (Dent F29); see 1.3.36
and 1.7.81–2 n.
　13 fog An invitation to the audience's imagination, since fog-effects were not possible in early
productions, though smoke (from burning resin)
was.
　13 filthy murky, thick (*OED* Filthy *a* 1b, quoting
this line).
　13 SD Precisely how the witches depart here and
at 1.3.76 (on foot, through a trap-door, or flying?)
is complicated by Hecate's departure in 3.5, which
may stipulate a flying exit but is also probably an
addition by Thomas Middleton (see Textual Analysis, pp. 271–5 below); the sisters' departure in 4.1 –
vanish (4.1.131 SD) – is also probably Middleton's.
Wickham ('Fly', pp. 172–3, 177–8) concludes that
Shakespeare's witches did not fly, but Middleton's
(added) Hecate did. See also Textual Analysis, pp.
272–4. Eighteenth-century editors add SDs – *fly
away* (Rowe), *vanish* (Malone) – recording later and
certainly mechanised stage practice.

Act 1, Scene 2

This scene condenses three conflicts – Macdonald's rebellion, and invasions by Sweno and by
Canute – described in *Scotland*, pp. 168b–170b,
where 'Norwegian' and 'Danish' are indiscrimi-
nately applied to the foreign forces; Shakespeare
(or another author) leaves the third vaguest, perhaps because James VI and I's wife Queen Anne
was Danish. The setting may be imagined as Dun-

can's command post, near a battlefield (as *Alarum*
(0 SD.1) suggests), but distant enough from 'Fife'
(48) to make that a plausible place of origin for Ross
and Angus. Jones, *Scenic*, pp. 208–9, argues that
this scene 'seems modelled on the opening scene of
1 Henry IV', and Mark Rose, *Shakespearean Design*,
1972, pp. 83–8, finds several complex patterns in
the first act; thus, e.g., this scene and the following
two are all 'field' scenes, followed by three 'castle'
scenes.
　0 SD.1 *Alarum* A call to arms; a warning to give
notice of danger (*OED* Alarm *sb* 4a and 5). 'Nor-
mally, the term [a variant spelling of 'alarm'] . . .
signifies a battle . . . and includes clashes of
weapons, drumbeats, trumpet blasts, shouts – anything to make a tumult' (Long, p. 131). 'Every
Souldier shall diligently observe and learne the
sound of Drummes, Fifes, and Trumpets to the
end he may knowe how to answere the same in his
service' (Thomas and Leonard Digges, *An Arithmetical Warlike Treatise named Stratioticos*, rev. edn
(1590), sig. 2C2r); see also Harbage, pp. 52–3.
　0 SD.1 *within* i.e. off-stage. In the Jacobean theatre, *within* indicates the tiring-house which formed
the back wall of the stage. The actors entered from
and exited to this space, where they also changed
their costumes.
　0 SD.2 *meeting* This direction may not be
Shakespeare's; it seems likely to mean that the
wounded speaker is on stage and the king's company enters *to* him. See Supplementary Note,
p. 255 below.
　2 seemeth . . . plight The first of many
inferences (note 'seemeth'), some incorrect, from
appearances visual and verbal; see e.g. 1.2.47 n.
and 1.4.11–12 n.
　2 the revolt Macdonald's rebellion occurred

        The newest state.

MALCOLM   This is the sergeant
        Who like a good and hardy soldier fought
        'Gainst my captivity. Hail, brave friend;   5
        Say to the king the knowledge of the broil
        As thou didst leave it.

CAPTAIN   Doubtful it stood,
        As two spent swimmers that do cling together
        And choke their art. The merciless Macdonald –
        Worthy to be a rebel, for to that   10
        The multiplying villainies of nature
        Do swarm upon him – from the Western Isles
        Of kerns and galloglasses is supplied,
        And Fortune on his damnèd quarrel smiling,

---

7 SH CAPTAIN] F (*Cap.*), *and throughout scene; Ser. / Cam., throughout scene*   9 Macdonald –] *Oxford (after Keightley)*; Macdonwald F; Macdonnell F2–4; Macdonel / *Capell*   13 galloglasses] F (Gallowgrosses); Gallow glasses F2–4   14 quarrel] *Hanmer*; Quarry F

3 **newest state** latest condition.

3 **sergeant** A trisyllable (NS). 'In the 16th c. the title . . . appears . . . to have indicated a much higher rank than in later times' (*OED* Sergeant *sb* 9a), and two knights were 'Sargeaunts' at the Battle of Musselburgh (Patten, sig. H7v; 'captain' (as in 0 SD.2 and SHs throughout this scene) could be used rather vaguely: 'a military leader' (*OED* Captain *sb* 3). Holinshed mentions (*Scotland*, p. 168b) a 'sergeant at armes' killed by the rebels Macdonald commanded.

5 **captivity** capture. (*OED* has no apposite sense.) Holinshed mentions (*Scotland*, p. 169a) another Malcolm, not Duncan's son, whom Macdonald captured and executed in this battle.

5 **Hail** The word the sisters (1.3.46–8) and Lady Macbeth (1.5.53) will use when they greet Macbeth. See 1.3.46 n.

6 **broil** tumult, quarrel (*OED* Broil *sb*¹ 1).

8–9 **two . . . art** i.e. two exhausted ('spent') swimmers grasp each other ('cling together'), hoping to survive, but each thus defeats the other's skill ('choke their art'), and both, paradoxically, drown.

9–13 **The merciless . . . supplied** Editorial repunctuation (including mine) here stipulates what F leaves fruitfully vague: how many clauses explain 'merciless' and whether 'swarm' ends a clause or anticipates one.

9   Macdonald   F2–4   provide   another

in 'Lochquhaber' (*Scotland*, p. 169a), modern Lochaber, the district including Ben Nevis in south Inverness-shire, many miles distant from Fife. See the map, p. 110 above, and headnote to this scene.

10 **Worthy . . . rebel** The combination of worth and rebellion would have been paradoxical to the early audiences; there could be no merit in treason. Compare Satan in Pandemonium: 'by merit raised / To that bad eminence' (Milton, *Paradise Lost* II, 5–6).

10 **for to that** to that end (Abbott 186); 'that' = Macdonald's 'worth' as a 'rebel'.

11 **multiplying villainies of nature** proliferating evils within creation.

12 **swarm** congregate, gather thickly. See *OED* Swarm *v*¹ 1–2, where the word is used concretely of bees and crickets.

12 **Western Isles** The Hebrides. See the map, p. 110 above.

13 **kerns and galloglasses** 'The Galloglass ar pycked and selected men of great and mightie bodies, crewell without compassion . . . the weapon they most use is a batle axe, or halberd . . . The kerne is a kinde of footeman, slightly armed with a sworde, a targett [shield] of woode, or a bow and sheafe of arrows with barbed heades, or els 3 dartes . . .' (John Dymmok, 'A Treatice of Ireland' (*c.* 1600), ed. Richard Butler, in *Tracts Relating to Ireland*, II (1842), 7). Holinshed says the 'Kernes and Galloglasses' joined Macdonald 'in hope of the spoile' (*Scotland*, p. 169a).

14–15 **Fortune . . . whore** Proverbially, 'Fortune is a strumpet' (Dent F603.1).

14 **quarrel** dispute. F's 'quarry' is a variant spelling for many meanings of 'quarrel'; one meaning,

Showed like a rebel's whore. But all's too weak,   15
For brave Macbeth – well he deserves that name –
Disdaining Fortune, with his brandished steel,
Which smoked with bloody execution,
Like Valour's minion carved out his passage
Till he faced the slave,   20
Which ne'er shook hands, nor bade farewell to him,
Till he unseamed him from the nave to th'chaps
And fixed his head upon our battlements.
DUNCAN O valiant cousin, worthy gentleman.
CAPTAIN As whence the sun 'gins his reflection,   25

---

16 Macbeth – well . . . name –] *Keightley; Macbeth* (well . . . name) F   21 ne'er] F (neu'r)   22 chaps] F (Chops)

'a short, heavy, square-headed arrow or bolt . . . used in shooting with the cross-bow' (*OED* Quarrel *sb*¹ 1), may be relevant.

15 rebel's whore i.e. Fortune is sexually promiscuous as her lover, Macdonald, is politically errant. The opprobrium of each term reinforces that of the other, so that the phrase almost becomes an epithet.

15 all's all is; all his.

18 smoked sprayed (blood), perhaps also the effect of 'steaming': see 'reeking' (39) and n.

19 minion dearest friend, favourite child (*OED* Minion *sb*¹ 1b, quoting *1H4* 1.1.81, 83: 'A son who is the theme of honour's tongue . . . Who is sweet Fortune's minion and her pride'). The word was, however, often used opprobriously (= 'paramour, mistress') and could always have some negative connotation; see Williams *sv*.

19 carved out his passage sliced his way. Cutting a route through living flesh adumbrates Macduff's Caesarian birth and his action in the play; see Watson, p. 100.

20 This short line has been much emended; it may be the consequence of deliberate or accidental omission.

20–2 he . . . slave . . . him . . . he . . . him The referents are not clear until Duncan acknowledges Macbeth's victory (24). Then we understand that 'slave' and 'him' (20, 22) = Macdonald, and 'he' (20, 22) = Macbeth. Compositor A (see Textual Analysis, p. 266 below) may have erred, but the passage conveys breathlessly broken grammar and unfixed identities, thus anticipating Macbeth's drift into treason, into being like Macdonald and Cawdor.

21 shook hands Elizabethans customarily shook hands upon meeting as well as parting; see Dent ss6 and e.g. Peele, *David and Bethsabe* line 566 (meeting), and Webster, *Duchess of Malfi* 3.2.131–5 (parting). For civil Scots warriors, see pp. 12–13 above.

22 unseamed him ripped him up. The image is from undoing a garment's seam and represents the body as clothing; the line offers an auditory pun (seem/seam) that may hint that Macbeth's violence defeated deception ('un-seemed').

22 nave navel (umbilicus), probably; this line is the sole support for nave = navel in *OED*. Both 'nave' and 'navel' could also mean 'central part or block of a wheel' (*OED* Nave *sb*¹ 1a); compare *OED* Navel *sb* 3 and Hal's description of Falstaff as 'this nave of a wheel' (*2H4* 2.4.255). Figuratively, then, 'nave' may here refer to the crotch rather than the navel *per se* (see 19 n.). See illustration 3, p. 21 above. For the unusual act of unseaming upward, Steevens³ compared 'Then from the navell to the throat at once, / He [Neoptolemus] ript old *Priam*' (Marlowe, *Dido, Queen of Carthage* 2.1.255–6); as NS, p. xli, notes, Shakespeare apparently remembers this speech in writing the Player King's speech (*see Ham.* 2.2.471 ff.).

22 chaps jaws. F's 'chops' has been superseded.

23 fixed . . . battlements A common practice: Macbeth 'caused the head [of Macdonald] to be cut off, and set upon a poles end . . . The headlesse trunke he commanded to bee hoong up upon an high paire of gallowes' (*Scotland*, p. 169a). See 5.9.20 SD n. Traitors' heads could be seen, weathering, impaled on London Bridge. See illustration 4, p. 31 above.

24 valiant cousin, worthy gentleman Holinshed (*Scotland*, p. 168b) describes Macbeth as a 'valiant gentleman' and explains that Macbeth and Duncan were cousins. See 1.7.16–20 n.

25–8 As . . . swells A complicated and ambiguous passage, but the main meaning is clear: in circumstances that seem positive, a threat unexpectedly appears. Two interpretations have been offered: (1) storms and thunder, like the Scandinavian invasion, come from the east, where

Shipwrecking storms and direful thunders,
So from that spring whence comfort seemed to come,
Discomfort swells. Mark, King of Scotland, mark,
No sooner justice had, with valour armed,
Compelled these skipping kerns to trust their heels,   30
But the Norwegian lord, surveying vantage,
With furbished arms and new supplies of men
Began a fresh assault.
DUNCAN Dismayed not this our captains, Macbeth and Banquo?
CAPTAIN Yes, as sparrows, eagles, or the hare, the lion.   35
If I say sooth, I must report they were
As cannons over-charged with double cracks;
So they doubly redoubled strokes upon the foe.

26 Shipwrecking] F (Shipwracking)   26 thunders,] F (Thunders:); thunders breaking F2–4; thunders break; Pope

the comforting sun also rises (' 'gins his reflection');
(2) when the sun reaches the vernal equinox and
returns ('reflection'), springtime storms (equinoc-
tial gales) occur. The question turns on whether
'spring' = 'source of water' or = 'season of
the year' and whether 'reflection' = 'shining'
or = 'astronomical regression of the sun at the
equinox'. There is no evidence for the last definition (first offered in Singer²), and 'swells' supports
'spring' = 'source of water'.

25 'gins begins (an aphetic form).

25 reflection shining (*Lexicon*); return, regression (*OED* Reflection 4c, citing this line as the first
of only two quotations).

26 Shipwrecking Earliest known use of the participial adjective (Schäfer).

26 direful dreadful, terrible.

26 thunders The verb 'come' is understood
here, though spoken only in 27. Many editors insert
'break'.

28 Mark Heed, pay attention.

28 King of Scotland The dialogue, for the first
time, identifies Duncan as king.

29 valour The word recalls 19 and makes Duncan analogous to personified Justice, Macbeth to
Valour.

30 skipping leaping in fright. See *Wiv.* 2.1.229
and *Lear* 5.3.278.

30 trust their heels run away. 'To trust to one's
heels' was quasi-proverbial (Dent, *PLED* H394.11).

31–62 Historically, the 'Norwegian lord' (31) was
Sweno (Svend Estridsen), who invaded in AD 1041
(Sugden); Sweno's invasion began victoriously in
Fife and extended over a period of time (*Scotland*, pp. 169a–170b). The so-called 'Sueno's Stone'
(dating from some time between the ninth century
and the eleventh), an extraordinary carved pillar

commemorating a battle, probably not this one, still
stands just north-east of Forres. See illustration 5,
p. 37 above.

31 surveying observing, perceiving (*OED* Survey *v* 4c, quoting this line).

31 vantage advantage, benefit (*OED* Vantage *sb*
1a).

32 furbished renovated, revived (*OED* Furbish
v 2); fresh, new.

32 supplies additional troops (*OED* Supply *sb*
5).

35 The sergeant, or captain, speaks ironically:
Banquo and Macbeth were not 'dismayed', but the
subsequent unexpected inversions anticipate the
disorder Macbeth and Lady Macbeth will introduce into Scotland, where all 'natural' orderings
are overturned.

35 sparrows, eagles . . . hare, the lion In each
pair the first is traditionally weak or fearful, the
second, strong and brave; for the second pair, see
Dent H147 and L307.1, respectively.

36 sooth truth.

36 report tell, state. The word is also a pun on
the sound ('report') of the cannons as they fire.

37–8 These lines seem to describe cannon loaded
with four (or eight?) times the usual amount of
powder and (?) shot, conditions that would have
destroyed most Renaissance weapons, but the language echoes the play's insistence on doubling and
doubleness. See pp. 25–7 above.

37 cracks cannon-shots (*OED* Crack *sb* 1b, quoting this line as its earliest post-1400 example).

38 So Thus.

38 doubly redoubled strokes eightfold blows.
Steevens cites 'doubly redoubled' (*R2* 1.3.80).
Compare 'blows, twice two for one' (*3H6* 1.4.50)
and see 1.6.16 n.

Except they meant to bathe in reeking wounds
Or memorise another Golgotha,   40
I cannot tell.
But I am faint, my gashes cry for help.
DUNCAN   So well thy words become thee as thy wounds;
They smack of honour both. Go get him surgeons.

[Exit Captain, attended]

Enter ROSS *and* ANGUS

Who comes here?
MALCOLM   The worthy Thane of Ross.   45
LENNOX   What a haste looks through his eyes! So should he look
That seems to speak things strange.
ROSS   God save the king.
DUNCAN   Whence cam'st thou, worthy thane?
ROSS   From Fife, great king,
Where the Norwegian banners flout the sky
And fan our people cold.   50

---

44 SD.1 *Exit Captain, attended*] Malone (*subst.*); *not in* F   44 SD.2] F; *after* strange (*47*) Dyce   44 SD.2 *and* ANGUS] F;
omitted by Steevens³ *and* SD *follows here* (*45*)

39 Except Unless.

39 reeking steaming or smoking with blood (*OED* Reek v^1 2c, quoting *JC* 3.1.158: the assassins' bloodied 'hands do reek and smoke').

40 memorise another Golgotha commemorate a second Calvary (i.e. create a place like that where Jesus was crucified). See 'And he [Jesus] bare his crosse, & went forth into a place, which is called ye place of dead mens skulles, but in Hebrue Golgotha: Where they crucified hym' (John 19.17–18) and 'The field of Golgotha and dead men's skulls' (*R2* 4.1.144).

42 gashes . . . help Shakespeare and other dramatists often represent wounds as mouths. For Antony, dead Caesar's wounds 'like dumb mouths do ope their ruby lips' (*JC* 3.1.260), a Roman citizen suggests, 'we are to put our tongues into those wounds and speak for them' (*Cor.* 2.3.6–7), and John Beane's many wounds are 'fifteene mouthes' accusing his murderer (*Warning*, sig. H1v). Here, the captain's wounds are speech, as Macbeth's words to his wife (in 1.5) and hers to him (in 1.7) will also be speeches, which are, or lead to, wounds.

44 smack savour, taste (*OED* Smack v^1 2), mixed figuratively with the 'sharp noise' (*OED* Smack v^2 1) the lips make in tasting, hence 'smack' = the sound of the wounds' words.

44 SD.2 For the placing of this SD, see Textual Analysis, pp. 262–3 below. Editors often delete Angus because Malcolm (45) identifies Ross only, and Angus does not speak; Ross and Angus jointly fulfil Duncan's command (64–5) in the next scene ('We are sent' (1.3.98)), however, and enter as a pair in 1.4 and 1.6.

45 Thane Head of a clan; a Scottish rank. A thane owed fealty to the king rather than to another noble, and held lands directly from the king.

46 looks through is visible through (*OED* Look v 20b), appears. Ross, like the bleeding captain (1–2), seems easily interpreted from his appearance. Compare 'Her business looks in her / With an importing visage' (*AWW* 5.3.135–6) and 'There's business in these faces' (*Cym.* 5.5.23).

47 seems appears (*OED* Seem v^2 4b). Ross has the appearance of a person whose looks portend strange matters.

48–58 From Fife . . . fell on us Ross's narrative recommences the battle; see 31–62 n.

48 Fife County on the east coast of Scotland between the Firths of Forth and Tay (Sugden). See the map, p. 110 above, and 2.4.36 n.

49 flout mock, jeer (*OED* Flout v^1, quoting this line). The banners mock through waving, as 'fan' (50) makes clear.

> Norway himself, with terrible numbers,
> Assisted by that most disloyal traitor,
> The Thane of Cawdor, began a dismal conflict,
> Till that Bellona's bridegroom, lapped in proof,
> Confronted him with self-comparisons,   55
> Point against point, rebellious arm 'gainst arm,
> Curbing his lavish spirit. And to conclude,
> The victory fell on us –

DUNCAN   Great happiness! –

ROSS   That now Sweno,
> The Norways' king, craves composition.
> Nor would we deign him burial of his men   60
> Till he disbursèd at Saint Colm's Inch
> Ten thousand dollars to our general use.

DUNCAN No more that Thane of Cawdor shall deceive
> Our bosom interest. Go pronounce his present death
> And with his former title greet Macbeth.   65

ROSS I'll see it done.

---

56 point, rebellious] F; point rebellious, *Theobald*   58 us –] *Keightley* (*subst.*); us. F   58 happiness! –] *This edn*;
happinesse. F   59 Norways'] F (Norwayes)   61 Colm's] F (*Colmes*); Colum's *Oxford*

51 Norway The King of Norway.

52–3 traitor . . . Cawdor Holinshed's account merely notes that Cawdor was 'condemned at Fores of treason against the king' (*Scotland*, p. 171a), but does not involve him in the military rebellion.

54 Bellona Roman goddess of war.

54 bridegroom i.e. Macbeth, who has advanced in marital status from being Valour's minion (19).

54 lapped enfolded, wrapped (Clarendon).

54 proof armour.

55 self-comparisons comparisons with himself (Macbeth, 'Bellona's bridegroom' (54)). Cawdor is forced into an unequal competition ('a dismal conflict' (53)) with Macbeth, but the phrase 'self-comparisons' implies that some common basis exists for comparing the hero and his enemy.

56 Point Sword tip.

56 point, rebellious Editors have changed F's punctuation unnecessarily: one arm or one sword needs to be identified as belonging to the rebel Cawdor; no matter how punctuated, the line will always and ambiguously half-refer to Macbeth as 'rebellious'. Some editors identify 'him' as Norway in order to rationalise 1.3.70–1 (see n.) and 1.3.106, but 'rebellious' better suits the native Cawdor than the invading, and foreign, King of Norway. Compare 20–2 n.

57 Curbing Restraining, controlling. A rider controls a horse through the 'curb', part of the bridle and bit.

57 lavish unrestrained, impetuous (*OED* Lavish *a* 1b, quoting this line).

58 Duncan interrupts Ross's report extrametrically.

59 Norways' Norwegians'. F's form, retained here for the metre, is obsolete (see *OED* Norway²).

59 craves composition i.e. seeks to make peace, surrenders.

60 deign condescend to grant (*OED* Deign *v* 2a, quoting this line as its second instance after one in 1589).

61 Saint Colm's Inch Inchcolm, an island in the Firth of Forth near Edinburgh; see Patten, sigs. MI–IV, and the map, p. 110 above. 'Colm' (named for St Columba) is disyllabic; Oxford prints 'Colum's' to indicate that fact.

62 dollars 'The English name for the German *thaler*, a large silver coin' (*OED* Dollar 1).

64 bosom interest intimate or confidential concern (not quoted at *OED* Bosom *sb* 8d).

64 present instant, immediate.

65 former title i.e. Thane of Cawdor, but Ross has most recently named him 'most disloyal traitor' (52), as Macbeth will soon prove also.

DUNCAN What he hath lost, noble Macbeth hath won.

Exeunt

1.3 *Thunder. Enter the three* WITCHES

FIRST WITCH Where hast thou been, sister?
SECOND WITCH Killing swine.
THIRD WITCH   Sister, where thou?
FIRST WITCH A sailor's wife had chestnuts in her lap
      And munched, and munched, and munched. 'Give me',
            quoth I.
      'Aroint thee, witch', the rump-fed runnion cries.   5

Act 1, Scene 3 1.3] F (*Scena Tertia.*)   4 munched] F (mouncht)   4 'Give me',] *Capell* (*subst.*); Giue me F   5 'Aroint
. . . witch'] *Capell* (*subst.*); Aroynt . . . Witch F   5 runnion] F (Ronyon)

67 lost . . . won Transfer of the title (and the treason) from Cawdor to Macbeth exemplifies how something may be both lost and won, the witches' paradox (1.1.4). The line elegantly varies the proverb 'No man loses but another wins' (Dent M337).

Act 1, Scene 3
   As with all the witch-scenes, the location here is vague (a 'heath' (1.1.7)); Macbeth and Banquo seem to be travelling to 'Forres' (37), perhaps from 'Fife' (1.2.48), many miles distant geographically if not dramatically. For the intersection of human curiosity with prophecy, see *Ant.* 1.2.1–78. Forman (II, 337) apparently says he saw Macbeth and Banquo on horseback, not an impossible stage effect (see *Woodstock* 3.2.132–73), but an unlikely one here (see Leah Scragg, 'Macbeth on horseback', *S.Sur.* 26 (1973), 81–8). See 3.3.11–14 n.
   0 SD *the* F's article (absent in 1.1.0 SD, but present at 3.5.0 SD and 4.1.0 SD) may suggest revision or a theatrical sense of the witches as a dramatic unit or force. Compare 2.1.20 and 4.1.38 SD.
   2 Killing swine English witches were often accused of harming domestic animals.
   4 munched 'A Scottish word signifying to eat with the gums when toothless' (Travers), but 'where shals all munch' (Dekker [and Thomas Middleton], *The Roaring Girl* 2.1.356), a question about where to eat, suggests a more general and English usage.
   5 Aroint The word's meaning is unknown, and Poor Tom's 'aroynt thee Witch, aroynt thee' (*Lear* TLN 1903) is the only other early recorded instance (Schäfer); contextually, it seems to mean 'avaunt! be gone!' Dent W584 cites John Ray, *Collection of*

English Proverbs (1679): 'Aroint thee, witch, quoth Besse Locket to her mother.'
   5 rump-fed A puzzling phrase whose literal meaning is 'fed on rump'. 'Rump' = the hind quarter of both humans and the animals they eat, and the 'rumpe or buttocke peece of meat' (John Florio, *A Worlde of Words* (1598), under Groppone, antedating *OED* Buttock *sb* 2 by twenty-five years) was a desirable cut. Shakespeare elsewhere imagines the 'devil Luxury [Lechery], with his fat rump' (*Tro.* 5.2.55); given the sexual innuendo of the next lines, 'rump-fed' might thus also mean 'fed [i.e. fattened] in the rump, lecherous' (compare Marston's *The Dutch Courtesan* (1605), where the title's courtesan is described as 'a plump-rump'd wench' (*Dutch Courtesan* 4.3.2)), and by the Restoration 'rump' had numerous bawdy meanings (whore, genitals, copulate: see the article 'Rump' in Williams), and scatological vocabulary frequently blurs and exchanges words for fundament and genitals (see e.g. the article 'Arse' in Williams). A link between feeding and lechery has strong biblical precedent: 'when I had fed them to the full, they then committed adulterie, and assembled themselves by troupes in the harlots houses' (Jer. 5.7, AV). Shakespeare's two other uses (*1H4* 2.2.84, *MND* 2.1.45) of phrases compounding a noun with '-fed' are active and support instead the meaning 'fed on rump'; compare 'lust-dieted' (*Lear* 4.1.67). From the witch's point of view, therefore, it may be that the sailor's wife is enviable, selfish, lecherous, and (possibly) sexually satisfied. Perhaps alliteration (rump, runnion) is more important than denotation. See next note.
   5 runnion Abusive term applied to a woman (*OED* Runnion 1, citing only this line and *Wiv.*

> Her husband's to Aleppo gone, master o'th'Tiger:
> But in a sieve I'll thither sail,
> And like a rat without a tail,
> I'll do, I'll do, and I'll do.

SECOND WITCH I'll give thee a wind.   10

FIRST WITCH Thou'rt kind.

THIRD WITCH And I another.

FIRST WITCH I myself have all the other,
> And the very ports they blow,
> All the quarters that they know   15
> I'th'shipman's card.
> I'll drain him dry as hay:
> Sleep shall neither night nor day
> Hang upon his penthouse lid;
> He shall live a man forbid.   20

---

6 Tiger] F (*Tiger*)   11 Thou'rt] *Capell;* Th'art F   15 know] *Capell;* know, F

TLN 2067–8: 'you Witch, you Ragge, you Baggage, you Poulcat, you Runnion'). Williams (under 'Runnion') defines the word as 'penis' and claims the use in *Wiv.* is 'an abusive term . . . comparable to casual use of *prick* today'. The same might be true here. See preceding note.

6 Aleppo Inland trading city in northern Syria, part of the Turkish empire from 1516 to 1918. Its port was Iskanderun (Sugden).

6 master captain, commanding officer.

6 Tiger Common name for a ship. The name also appears in *TN* 5.1.62 and many other contemporary texts. E. A. Loomis, 'Master of the *Tiger*', *SQ* 7 (1956), 457, showed that the calamitous Far Eastern voyage of one *Tiger*, lasting from 5 December 1604 to 27 June 1606, equalled 567 days or 81 weeks (i.e. 7 × 9 × 9, or 'Weary sennights nine times nine' (21)).

7 sieve Sailing in sieves was supposed to be a common witch-practice; it was one of the accusations against the Scottish witches King James personally interrogated in 1590–1 (*Newes*, pp. 13–14).

8 rat . . . tail Steevens observes that witches sometimes turned themselves into rats, but had no body part to match the tail; see also 1.1.9 n.

9 do act; fornicate. 'Many dramatizations of witches as powerful, dangerous agents associate their agency with female sexual desire' (Dolan, p. 212).

10–13 Witches were imagined to control the wind and might sell this power on request; see *Newes*, p. 17 (Scottish witches were accused of interfering with James's return from Denmark with Anne, his bride), and what seems to be Thomas

Nashe's allusion to that event: 'as in *Ireland* [i.e. Scotland?] and in *Denmark* both / Witches for gold will sell a man a wind' (Nashe, III, 272). Muir cites many other references to such witch-practices.

14 Even places of refuge ('ports') cannot escape the winds' ferocity. (*OED* Blow *v*¹ has no apposite meaning.)

15 quarters geographical directions.

16 Although the witches speak a distinctive metre and irregular rhyme, this line is unusually short and another line, rhyming with 'card', may have been omitted.

16 card chart; circular piece of stiff paper (the 'mariner's card' or 'card of the sea' showing the customary 32 points of the compass). *OED* Card *sb*² 3b, 4a admits that the two meanings were not fully distinguished at this date. See illustration 6, p. 39 above.

17 drain him If the first witch intends to be a succubus, her demonic sexual intercourse (see 'do' (9)) will exhaust her sailor-victim.

17 dry as hay A very old simile (Dent H231.1).

18 Sleep . . . day Like the sailor, Macbeth will later (3.2) find sleep difficult, and Lady Macbeth will walk in her sleep (5.1).

19 penthouse lid eyelid. The image derives from analogy between the eyebrow and the projecting second storey ('penthouse') of many Elizabethan buildings. 'Penthouse' could = 'lean-to shed' (Hunter), but Shakespeare's non-figurative uses of the word (*Ado* 3.3.103, *MV* 2.6.1) do not employ that meaning.

20 forbid cursed (*OED* Forbid *v* 2f, quoting only this line and another, using 'forbidden', from 1819).

> Weary sennights nine times nine,
> Shall he dwindle, peak, and pine.
> Though his bark cannot be lost,
> Yet it shall be tempest-tossed.
> Look what I have.
>
> SECOND WITCH   Show me, show me.   25
> FIRST WITCH   Here I have a pilot's thumb,
>   Wrecked as homeward he did come.
>
> *Drum within*
>
> THIRD WITCH   A drum, a drum;
>   Macbeth doth come.
> ALL   The weïrd sisters, hand in hand,   30
>   Posters of the sea and land,
>   Thus do go, about, about,
>   Thrice to thine, and thrice to mine,
>   And thrice again, to make up nine.
>   Peace, the charm's wound up.   35

Enter MACBETH *and* BANQUO

MACBETH   So foul and fair a day I have not seen.
BANQUO   How far is't called to Forres? What are these,

---

21 sennights] F (Seu'nights)   **27** Wrecked] F (Wrackt)   **27** SD] F (*at right margin opposite* come)   **30** weïrd] *Theobald;* weyward F. *See Commentary*   **37** Forres] *Staunton (after Pope);* Soris F

21 sennights weeks. F's 'Seu'nights' (seven nights) shows the etymology.
22 peak, and pine waste away and languish (virtual synonyms with 'dwindle').
23 bark small ship.
27 SD *Drum within* Editors and producers have worried whether the drum indicates an accompanying army; on the contrary, it is a conventional Jacobean way to introduce an important martial character, though Davenant and others added text and business to indicate an off-stage army, or to accommodate a silent one on-stage.
30 weïrd 'claiming the supernatural power of dealing with fate or destiny' (*OED* Weird *a* 1); see also *OED* Weird *sb*, and Supplementary Note, pp. 255–6 below. Theobald's emendation, adopted here, indicates the word's pronunciation as a disyllable.
31 Posters Speedy travellers (*Lexicon*); a Shakespearean coinage (Garner), presumably because 'the fastest way of travel . . . was by post horse' (Foakes).
33 to thine . . . to mine in your direction . . . in my direction (?). The witches here perform some dance, formal movements, or gestures that bind each individual into the group. Jonson's witches

danced 'back to back and hip to hip, their hands joined, and making their circles backward, to the left hand, with strange fantastic motions of their heads and bodies' (*Queens* 330–2; see also Jonson's note, *ibid.*, pp. 541–2, and more generally, Clark, 'Inversion', pp. 122–5).
34 nine An action is repeated three times for each witch.
35 wound up placed in readiness (*OED* Wind *v*[1] 24f, quoting this line). The figurative use probably derives from tightening the strings on a musical instrument, but the witches may have 'wound' themselves 'up' in some stage movement (see 33 n.). The phrase could also mean 'concluded'.
36–107 So . . . robes Hints of how this scene might have been staged and acted appear in Macbeth's letter to his wife (1.5.1 ff.).
36 foul and fair meteorologically unpleasant and militarily successful. Macbeth's words echo the witches' (1.1.12); see p. 51 above.
37 How . . . Forres? How distant is Forres reckoned to be? A Scotticism (Travers).
37 Forres Town east of Inverness and not far from the site of one of the historical battles earlier

So withered and so wild in their attire,
That look not like th'inhabitants o'th'earth,
And yet are on't? – Live you, or are you aught   40
That man may question? You seem to understand me,
By each at once her choppy finger laying
Upon her skinny lips; you should be women,
And yet your beards forbid me to interpret
That you are so.

MACBETH   Speak if you can: what are you?   45
FIRST WITCH   All hail Macbeth, hail to thee, Thane of Glamis.
SECOND WITCH   All hail Macbeth, hail to thee, Thane of Cawdor.
THIRD WITCH   All hail Macbeth, that shalt be king hereafter.
BANQUO   Good sir, why do you start and seem to fear
Things that do sound so fair? – I'th'name of truth   50

(1.2) condensed. Holinshed's account of King Duff's illness describes 'a sort [group] of witches dwelling in . . . Fores' (*Scotland*, p. 149b). See the map, p. 110 above. F's 'Soris' (for 'Foris', i.e. Forres) derives from a misreading of manuscript *f* as *ʃ*. See 69 n.

37–40 What . . . on't Banquo notices the witches; like the king's company in 1.2, he judges appearances, though not so confidently. His speech (38–45) is also the only spoken evidence for the witches' appearance, which may be (and has been in some productions) quite different. Holinshed's 1577 illustration of this scene represents the witches as mortal women, not old, fashionably, even aristocratically, dressed (see Bullough, VII, 494), thus giving the paradox of 'fair is foul' (1.1.12) point. See Supplementary Note to 1.1.0 SD (p. 255 below) and 'I neuer thought so fayre a dame, had been so foule within' (*Fidele and Fortunio* line 703).

42–3 By each . . . lips The witches silence Banquo with eerily synchronised gestures.

42 choppy chapped, cracked by wind and weather. This line is the earliest recorded use under *OED* Choppy; *OED* Chappy *a*¹ shows that spelling as also current.

43 should be look as if you ought to be.

43–4 women . . . beards See illustration 7 and p. 35 above. Compare the insult to Paulina, 'mankind witch' (*WT* 2.3.68).

46–8 Political prophecy, especially on the eve of conflict, has a long history and was dangerous in the Tudor and Stuart period. Shakespeare dramatised such prophecies in *2H6* 1.4 and *John* 4.2.143–57 and 5.1.25–9; Meander thought the rebel Tamburlaine 'misled by dreaming prophecies' (*Tamburlaine, Part 1* 1.1.41). See e.g. Steven Mullaney, *The Place of the Stage*, 1988, chapter 5; Jaech;

Mary C. Williams, 'Merlin and the prince: *The Speeches at Prince Henry's Barriers*', *RenD* n.s. 8 (1977), 221–30; Howard Dobin, *Merlin's Disciples: Prophecy, Poetry and Power in Renaissance England*, 1990. The practice perhaps derived from classical haruspicy, official prophecy based upon the examination of the entrails of animals, etc.

46 All hail Shakespeare elsewhere (*3H6* 5.7.33–4, *R2* 4.1.169–71) associates this phrase with Judas's betrayal of Jesus, as do his contemporaries (see 'the All-haile of a second *Judas*' in *A Letter . . . containing a true Report of a strange Conspiracie* (1599), sig. B2r, and the York and Chester cycles of mystery plays (see M. Hattaway (ed.), *3H6*, 1992, 5.7.34 n.)). See 1.5.53 n.

46 Glamis Metre sometimes requires a disyllable (Gla-miss); elsewhere, modern productions often employ the modern monosyllable, 'Glahms'. The name might have had a particular resonance for Shakespeare and his audience. *Scotland*, p. 320a, reports the trial (1537) of Jane Douglas, Lady Glamis, for attempting to poison James V; she was convicted on false evidence and burned at the stake. Perhaps misled by the manner of execution, subsequent writers recorded her crime as witchcraft. See Robert Pitcairn, *Ancient Criminal Trials in Scotland*, 1, pt 1 (1833), 187–98.

48 king For the audience, only this title is a surprise because we know Duncan has already awarded Cawdor's title to Macbeth (1.2.65); theatrically, the witches' apparent foreknowledge is minimised.

49 start recoil, flinch, make a nervous gesture or movement. For this moment on stage, see p. 81 above.

49–50 fear . . . fair Alliteration ('start', 'seem', 'sound', and 'fear', 'fair') strikes the ear, but the

Are ye fantastical, or that indeed
Which outwardly ye show? My noble partner
You greet with present grace and great prediction
Of noble having and of royal hope
That he seems rapt withal. To me you speak not.   55
If you can look into the seeds of time
And say which grain will grow and which will not,
Speak then to me, who neither beg nor fear
Your favours nor your hate.
FIRST WITCH Hail.   60
SECOND WITCH Hail.
THIRD WITCH Hail.
FIRST WITCH Lesser than Macbeth, and greater.
SECOND WITCH Not so happy, yet much happier.
THIRD WITCH Thou shalt get kings, though thou be none.   65
    So all hail Macbeth and Banquo.
FIRST WITCH Banquo and Macbeth, all hail.
MACBETH Stay, you imperfect speakers. Tell me more.
    By Finel's death, I know I am Thane of Glamis,
    But how of Cawdor? The Thane of Cawdor lives   70
    A prosperous gentleman, and to be king
    Stands not within the prospect of belief,

---

55 rapt] F (wrapt)   69 Finel's] *This edn; Sinells* F. *See Commentary*

---

evocative, morally puzzling wordplay on fear/fair
'is based on antithesis, not identity' (Cercignani,
p. 235) between 'fear' and 'fair'. Compare the contrasts of 'foul' and 'fair' (36 above and 1.1.12), and
of 'fear' and 'foully' (see 3.1.2–3 and n.).

51 fantastical imaginary, products of (our) fantasy.

53 present grace immediate favour. Compare
the last (1.2.64) and next (136) uses of the adjective.

54 noble having . . . royal hope i.e. new title of
honour . . . hoped-for title of king.

54 having possession.

55 rapt entranced. See 141 n. below.

56 seeds of time sources of the future. Compare
Warwick's claim that 'a man may prophesy, / With
a near aim, of the main chance of things / As yet
not come to life, who in their seeds / And weak
beginning lie intreasured' (*2H4* 3.1.82–5), and see
4.1.58 n.

58–9 neither beg . . . nor your hate i.e. Banquo
neither begs your favours nor fears your hate. Alliteration and rhetorical hyperbaton make the line
confusing and ambiguous.

65 get beget, father; perhaps also 'acquire,
obtain'.

69 Finel Historically, Finel (or Finley or Find-
laech) was Macbeth's father (see Bullough, VII, 488
n. 3), and that name should be substituted here just
as 'Forres' is substituted for F's 'Soris' (see 37 n.);
F's '*Sinells*' is an ancient error, the result of a ſ/ſ
error in Holinshed (*Scotland*, p. 168b) and in his
source, the Dundee historian Hector Boece (also
known as Boethius).

70–1 The Thane . . . gentleman This (like
106) is a locally effective objection, but logically
inconsistent for a speaker who confronted 'rebellious' Cawdor 'with self-comparisons' (1.2.55–6)
and could presumably expect him to suffer capital
punishment for treason, as he does (1.4.3 ff.). The
inconsistency is less noticeable because the audience does not yet know Cawdor has died; it may
have arisen through simple oversight or through
1.2 having been written or revised after 1.3.

72 prospect mental looking forward, consideration of something future (*OED* Prospect *sb* 8a,
citing this line as its first example).

No more than to be Cawdor. Say from whence
You owe this strange intelligence, or why
Upon this blasted heath you stop our way   75
With such prophetic greeting? Speak, I charge you.

Witches vanish

BANQUO The earth hath bubbles, as the water has,
And these are of them. Whither are they vanished?

MACBETH Into the air, and what seemed corporal,
Melted, as breath into the wind. Would they had stayed.   80

BANQUO Were such things here as we do speak about?
Or have we eaten on the insane root,
That takes the reason prisoner?

MACBETH Your children shall be kings.

BANQUO   You shall be king.

MACBETH And Thane of Cawdor too: went it not so?   85

BANQUO To th'selfsame tune and words – who's here?

Enter ROSS *and* ANGUS

ROSS The king hath happily received, Macbeth,
The news of thy success, and when he reads
Thy personal venture in the rebels' sight,
His wonders and his praises do contend   90
Which should be thine or his. Silenced with that,
In viewing o'er the rest o'th'selfsame day,
He finds thee in the stout Norwegian ranks,

---

76 SD] F (*in right margin after* you)   89 sight] *This edn;* fight F. *See Supplementary Note, p. 256 below*

---

74 intelligence news, information (*OED* Intelligence *sb* 7a).

75 blasted blighted. Supernatural agency or planetary influence may be implied (so *OED* Blasted *ppl a* 1, quoting this line). 'The heath which is *blasted* in a double sense – both barren and accursed – affords the right setting for the asexual witches . . .' (Mahood, p. 134).

76 charge command, order.

76 SD vanish See 1.1.13 SD n.

79 corporal material, physical, having a body (*OED* Corporal *a* 2).

82 on of (Abbott 181).

82 insane causing insanity (*OED* Insane *a* 3, quoting only this line). Discussing a European writer on witchcraft, Scot (III, 3) mentions witches' requirements for 'powders and roots to intoxicate withall'; compare 'Mens sences, sudden altering out of reason, / Doe bode ill lucke, or doe fore-shew some treason' (Thomas Andrewe, *The Unmasking of a feminine Machiavell* (1604), sig. E1v).

86 selfsame tune identical meaning. Whately (p. 48) thinks 'tune' ridicules the witches' prophecy, but compare 4.3.238 n.

88 reads understands, discerns. *OED* has no strictly apposite meaning, but unless we assume some written report of Macbeth's deeds, the usage must be even more figurative than in Feste's remark about Malvolio's letter: 'to read his right wits is to read thus' (*TN* 5.1.298–9).

89 sight See Supplementary Note, p. 256 below.

90–1 Duncan, at once admiring Macbeth's actions and praising them, finds himself suspended between silence and speech, awe and the impulse to reward.

92 selfsame identical, same. The echo of 86 suggests that Macbeth's honourable martial success and his plan to kill Duncan are themselves 'selfsame'.

93 stout valiant, brave (*OED* Stout *adj* and *adv* 3a).

Nothing afeard of what thyself didst make,
Strange images of death. As thick as tale   95
Came post with post, and every one did bear
Thy praises in his kingdom's great defence,
And poured them down before him.
ANGUS   We are sent
To give thee from our royal master thanks;
Only to herald thee into his sight,   100
Not pay thee.
ROSS   And for an earnest of a greater honour,
He bade me, from him, call thee Thane of Cawdor:
In which addition, hail most worthy thane,
For it is thine.
BANQUO   What, can the devil speak true?   105
MACBETH   The Thane of Cawdor lives. Why do you dress me
In borrowed robes?
ANGUS   Who was the thane, lives yet,
But under heavy judgement bears that life
Which he deserves to lose.
Whether he was combined with those of Norway,   110
Or did line the rebel with hidden help
And vantage, or that with both he laboured
In his country's wrack, I know not,
But treasons capital, confessed and proved,

---

95 death. As] *Pope;* death, as F   95 tale] F (Tale)*;* hail *Rowe*   96 Came] *Rowe;* Can F   100 herald] F (harrold)

---

94 Nothing afeard Not at all afraid.

95–6 As thick . . . with post 'The posts [messengers] came thronging, with tales thronging, to every tale a post, post after post, and tale after tale' (Sisson, II, 193); compare 'every tongue brings in a several tale' (*R3* 5.3.194). 'As thick as hail' (Dent H11) is an old simile, and many have accepted Rowe's emendation ('hail' for 'tale'), but the two words would be hard to confuse in manuscript, and Compositor A probably saw (and therefore set) an unusual word rather than a more familiar, proverbial one.

102 earnest foretaste, pledge (*OED* Earnest *sb²* 1 *fig.*). Ross vaguely suggests some further 'honour', but Macbeth and the audience may suppose the kingship or status as heir apparent to be the 'greater honour'; see 1.4.48–53.

104 addition title.

106–7 Hunter, *New*, II, 153, suggested 'that in fact the ceremony of investiture should take place upon the stage'.

107 Who He who.

109 The line is metrically truncated, but no satisfactory relineation has been proposed.

110 Whether Whichever of the two (*OED* Whether *pron, adj, conj* 3, also noting that the word is sometimes 'used loosely of more than two' as it is here).

111 line reinforce, fortify. Compare 'To line and new repair our towns of war / With men of courage' (*H5* 2.4.7–8) and Hotspur who 'lined himself with hope' (*2H4* 1.3.27) before the Battle of Shrewsbury. There may be figurative overtones of 'lining' a piece of clothing (the 'robes' of 107).

112 vantage additional amount (e.g. of soldiers, weapons, money). See *OED* Vantage *sb* 2b and compare 1.2.31 n.

112 both i.e. the Norwegian invaders and secret, native help.

113 wrack ruin, overthrow.

114 capital mortal. Cawdor's proven treason merits death.

Have overthrown him.

MACBETH [*Aside*]   Glamis, and Thane of Cawdor: 115
The greatest is behind. – Thanks for your pains. –
[*To Banquo*] Do you not hope your children shall be kings,
When those that gave the Thane of Cawdor to me
Promised no less to them?

BANQUO   That trusted home,
Might yet enkindle you unto the crown,   120
Besides the Thane of Cawdor. But 'tis strange,
And oftentimes, to win us to our harm,
The instruments of darkness tell us truths;
Win us with honest trifles, to betray's
In deepest consequence. –   125
Cousins, a word, I pray you.

MACBETH [*Aside*]   Two truths are told,
As happy prologues to the swelling act
Of the imperial theme. – I thank you, gentlemen. –

---

116 behind. – Thanks . . . pains. –] *Capell* (*subst.*); behinde. Thankes . . . paines. F   119 them?] *Rowe;* them. F   125 consequence. –] *Capell* (*subst.*); consequence. F   128 theme. – I . . . gentlemen. –] *Capell* (*subst.*); Theame. I . . . Gentlemen: F

116 **behind** 'in the past' (*OED* Behind *adv* 1c); 'still to come' (*OED* Behind *adv* 4). In the former sense, Macbeth regards as 'greatest' the first two titles (Glamis, Cawdor) the sisters used (46–7); in the latter possible sense, the kingship ('king hereafter' (48)) is 'greatest'.

118 **those that gave** Macbeth understands the sisters, not Duncan, to be the source of his new title.

119 **home** completely, fully (?). Compare *OED* Home *adv* 4a, 'to its ultimate position', a nonfigurative usage; 'All my services / You have paid home' (*WT* 5.3.3–4); 'they have their answer home' ('The Quip', line 24 in *The English Poems of George Herbert*, ed. C. A. Patrides, 1974).

120 **enkindle** inflame with desire (*OED* Enkindle *v* 2b). Compare 'When I burned in desire'(1.5.3).

123 **The instruments . . . truths** 'The Devil sometimes speaks the truth' (Dent D266); compare 'The devil can cite Scripture for his purpose' (*MV* 1.3.98) and 4.3.22 and n.

124 **betray's** betray us.

125 **deepest consequence** gravest (or weightiest) outcome (so *OED* Deep *a* 7b, citing this line). Banquo contrasts a sequence of 'trifles' to an unexpectedly grim conclusion.

126–8 **Two truths . . . theme** For this passage's stylistic complexities, see pp. 45–6 above.

127 **prologues** preliminary events (*OED* Prologue *sb* 1b, quoting 'my death . . . is made the prologue to their play' (*2H6* 3.1.148, 151) as its first example). Theatrically, 'prologues' are actors (like the sisters, or Ross and Angus) who speak before a play (or an 'act' of one) begins.

127 **swelling** expanding, growing. With 'act', 'swelling' might refer to the number of actors who enter after a prologue has spoken or to the number of people who attend upon a king as opposed to a thane (see next note). Compare 'A kingdom for a stage, princes to act, / And monarchs to behold the swelling scene!' (*H5*, Prologue, 3–4). Given the play's concentration on child-bearing and childlessness, it seems likely that 'swelling' has at least a distant connotation of pregnancy; compare 3.1.60–5 and see pp. 45–6 above.

128 **the imperial theme** the subject or topic of empery (= becoming not 'emperor', but king); 'theme' could also have the more active meaning of 'a subject that causes action' (see *OED* Theme 1a and b), so 'imperial theme' might refer not only to the topic of becoming king, but to the actions required of one who would be king.

128 **I thank you, gentlemen** Macbeth again (see 116) interrupts himself, acknowledging Ross and Angus, perhaps in order to conceal his self-communing.

This supernatural soliciting
Cannot be ill, cannot be good. If ill,   130
Why hath it given me earnest of success,
Commencing in a truth? I am Thane of Cawdor.
If good, why do I yield to that suggestion,
Whose horrid image doth unfix my hair
And make my seated heart knock at my ribs   135
Against the use of nature? Present fears
Are less than horrible imaginings.
My thought, whose murder yet is but fantastical,
Shakes so my single state of man that function
Is smothered in surmise, and nothing is,   140
But what is not.

BANQUO   Look how our partner's rapt.

MACBETH If chance will have me king, why chance may crown me
    Without my stir.

BANQUO   New honours come upon him
    Like our strange garments, cleave not to their mould,
    But with the aid of use.

MACBETH   Come what come may,   145

---

130 ill,] *Q1673;* ill? F   133 good,] *Q1673;* good? F   134 hair] F (Heire)

129 soliciting incitement (Johnson).

133–4 suggestion...image The witches' words ('suggestion') have helped create a terrifying mental picture ('image').

134 unfix my hair make my hair stand on end (in fear). Compare 5.5.10–15.

135 seated fixed in position (*OED* Seated *ppl a* 1, quoting this line as the first example); firm-set (*Lexicon* Seat *v* 2).

136 use ordinary course, usual condition or state.

136 Present See 1.2.64 n. and 53 n. above.

138 My thought, whose murder The distorted grammar personifies Macbeth's 'thought' as a being who is murdered by the self, but also suggests Macbeth's intended human victim, Duncan. This short phrase anticipates others: see 2.2.76 and n., and 3.4.142–3 and n.

138 fantastical See 51 n.

139 single state 'unitary condition', 'singular existence', but also perhaps 'weak condition' (Steevens). 'State' probably evokes analogies with the human body, the body politic, and the macrocosm; Brutus says that 'Between the acting of a dreadful thing / And the first motion [suggestion] ... the state of a man, / Like to a little kingdom, suffers then / The nature of an insurrection' (*JC* 2.1.63–4, 67–9).

139–41 function...is not 'All powers of action are oppressed and crushed by one overwhelming image in the mind, and nothing is present to me, but that which is really future' (Johnson).

139 function activity, physical movement.

140–1 nothing . . . not Compare Isabella's confused speech, 'There is a vice . . . For which I would not plead, but that I must; / For which I must not plead, but that I am / At war 'twixt will and will not' (*MM* 2.2.29, 31–3).

141 rapt enraptured, entranced (see 55). Mahood (p. 165) notes that 'the secondary meaning of "wrapped"' appears in Banquo's following images of clothing (143–5).

143 stir movement; agitation (*OED* Stir *sb¹* 1).

144 strange unfamiliar (to us).

144 cleave cling, adhere.

144 mould body (so *OED* Mould *sb³* 4b, quoting only this line and a 1639 translation of French *moule*). The word hints at human mortality, as in 'that womb, / That mettle, that self mould, that fashioned thee' (*R2* 1.2.22–3) and 'men of mould' (*H5* 3.2.22) where 'mould' = earth (*OED* Mould *sb¹* 4b–c).

145 Come what come may Let what happens, happen; a proverb (Dent c529).

> Time and the hour runs through the roughest day.
> BANQUO Worthy Macbeth, we stay upon your leisure.
> MACBETH Give me your favour. My dull brain was wrought
>   With things forgotten. Kind gentlemen, your pains
>   Are registered where every day I turn   150
>   The leaf to read them. Let us toward the king.
>   [*To Banquo*] Think upon what hath chanced and at more
>   time,
>   The interim having weighed it, let us speak
>   Our free hearts each to other.
> BANQUO   Very gladly.
> MACBETH Till then, enough. – Come, friends.   155
>
>   *Exeunt*

1.4 *Flourish. Enter King* [DUNCAN], LENNOX, MALCOLM,
DONALDBAIN, *and Attendants*

DUNCAN Is execution done on Cawdor, or not

---

155 enough. –] *Capell* (*subst.*); enough: F   **Act 1, Scene 4**   **1.4**] F (*Scena Quarta.*)   **1** or] F (*Or*); Are F2

146 Time . . . roughest day Proverbially, 'The longest day has an end' (Dent D90). 'Time' and 'hour' may be the sort of redundancy common in proverbs and proverb-like speech, but Macklin paused before 'hour', making it = 'opportunity' (*Morning Chronicle*, 30 October 1773, quoted by Bartholomeusz, p. 85), a reading proposed in Elizabeth Montagu, *An Essay on the Writings and Genius of Shakespear* (1769), p. 186.

146 roughest stormiest, most tempestuous. Compare 2.3.53.

147 stay upon your leisure await your time, wait until you are unoccupied (*OED* Leisure 3c); the latter meaning emphasises Macbeth's inattention. For the following action (Macbeth courteously directs his companions off-stage), see Bevington, pp. 155–6.

148 favour indulgence. Macbeth excuses his preoccupation.

148 wrought agitated, stirred, worked up (first citation for *OED* Work *v* 14b).

150–1 registered . . . leaf The image is of a notebook ('leaf' = a page) in which Macbeth has written ('registered') a reminder of what he owes Ross and Angus.

152–4 Macbeth makes a nearly identical invitation to Banquo at 2.1.22–4.

152 SD F does not specify that Macbeth speaks to Banquo, and the lines might be public rather than private.

152 chanced happened, occurred (*OED* Chance *v* 1).

152 at more time The phrase is puzzling; it may mean 'at a later time' (partly supported by *OED* At 29a–b) or 'when we have more time'.

153 The . . . it i.e. when we have considered it thoroughly ('weighed') in the meantime ('interim'). The abstract phrasing also gives time itself the capacity to judge and hence recalls Macbeth's thought that chance may crown him (142–3).

154 free frank, plain-spoken (*OED* Free *a* 25a). The adjective is transferred from being an adverb modifying 'speak' (153); compare 1.6.3 n.

Act 1, Scene 4
The setting is presumably Duncan's royal camp, to which Macbeth and Banquo have been summoned.

0 SD.1 *Flourish* A 'trumpet signal indicating the "presence" of authority' (Long, p. 14); 'the royal flourish sounds only for Duncan [in 1.4] and Malcolm [in Act 5] . . . At no point . . . is Macbeth accorded a flourish' (Long, p. 183).

0 SD.1 Oddly, Lennox, a thane, appears before Malcolm, the king's elder son; F usually lists characters in order of rank.

1 Is . . . Cawdor Has Cawdor's execution been carried out. See *OED* Execution 5, citing the phrase 'to do execution'.

1 or not or are not. 'Are' or 'is' is understood.

Those in commission yet returned?

MALCOLM   My liege,
They are not yet come back. But I have spoke
With one that saw him die, who did report
That very frankly he confessed his treasons,   5
Implored your highness' pardon, and set forth
A deep repentance. Nothing in his life
Became him like the leaving it. He died
As one that had been studied in his death,
To throw away the dearest thing he owed   10
As 'twere a careless trifle.

DUNCAN   There's no art
To find the mind's construction in the face.
He was a gentleman on whom I built
An absolute trust.

Enter MACBETH, BANQUO, ROSS, *and* ANGUS

O worthiest cousin,

---

2 liege i.e. liege lord (the feudal superior to whom a vassal owes allegiance). In Shakespeare's day, the title no longer carried legal obligations and was mostly one of great respect.

3–4 A notable example of the play's insistence on mediated knowledge, on information travelling through reports and unofficial channels.

3 spoke spoken (Abbott 343).

5–7 In the early modern period, no matter how recalcitrant convicted criminals had been, they typically did confess, repent, and beg forgiveness as they prepared to face divine judgement; see L. B. Smith, 'English treason trials and confessions in the sixteenth century', *JHI* 15 (1954), 471–98, especially pp. 476–80, and J. A. Sharpe, '"Last dying speeches": religion, ideology and public execution in seventeenth-century England', *P&P* 107 (May 1985), 144–67.

8 Became Graced, befitted (*OED* Become *v* 7).

9 studied skilled, practised. There is no overtone of the modern connotation 'affected', but perhaps an acknowledgement of traditional religious practice (see Beach Langston, 'Essex and the art of dying', *HLQ* 13 (1949–50), 109–29, and Nancy Lee Beaty, *The Craft of Dying*, 1970). 'To owe God a death' is proverbial (Dent G237), and versions appear elsewhere in Shakespeare (e.g. *R3* 2.2.91–5).

10 owed owned. Elizabethan spelling did not distinguish between 'owe' and 'own'; Malcolm may therefore also allude to the idea that every Christian owes God a soul. See 5.9.5 and n.

11 As As if. See Abbott 107, noting that the subjunctive 'were' implies 'if'.

11 careless uncared for (*OED* Careless 4a, quoting this line), unregarded. Cawdor threw away his soul as if it were a trifle he cared nothing about.

11–12 There's no art . . . face A proverbial truism – 'The face is no index to the heart' (Dent F1.1, citing Juvenal, *Satire* 2: 'Frontis nulla fides') – that Duncan has apparently just discovered. Foakes notes the lines' ironic applicability to Macbeth, 'who enters just after they are spoken, or, as some actors have played the part, in time to overhear them'. Immediately before his arrest and execution, the pathetically imperceptient Hastings fails to read the mind in Richard of Gloucester's face: 'never a man in Christendom / Can lesser hide his love or hate than he, / For by his face straight shall you know his heart' (*R3* 3.4.51–3); Vincentio, himself in disguise, uses the truism to flatter and gain his way: 'There is written in your brow, Provost, honesty and constancy; if I read it not truly, my ancient skill beguiles me' (*MM* 4.2.153–5). Compare 'You are well-favoured and your looks foreshow / You have a gentle heart' (*Per.* 4.1.85–6). Duncan's remark might have been prompted by Holinshed's observation (*Scotland*, p. 150a) that King Duff, murdered in one 'Donwald's' castle at Forres, was uncautious because he had 'a speciall trust in Donwald, as a man whom he never suspected'. Compare 1.5.60–4.

12 construction interpretation (*Lexicon*).

The sin of my ingratitude even now   15
Was heavy on me. Thou art so far before,
That swiftest wing of recompense is slow
To overtake thee. Would thou hadst less deserved,
That the proportion both of thanks and payment
Might have been mine. Only I have left to say,   20
More is thy due than more than all can pay.

MACBETH   The service and the loyalty I owe,
    In doing it, pays itself. Your highness' part
    Is to receive our duties, and our duties
    Are to your throne and state, children and servants,   25
    Which do but what they should by doing everything
    Safe toward your love and honour.

DUNCAN   Welcome hither.
    I have begun to plant thee and will labour
    To make thee full of growing. Noble Banquo,
    That hast no less deserved, nor must be known   30
    No less to have done so, let me enfold thee
    And hold thee to my heart.

BANQUO   There if I grow,
    The harvest is your own.

DUNCAN   My plenteous joys,
    Wanton in fullness, seek to hide themselves
    In drops of sorrow. Sons, kinsmen, thanes,   35

---

21   More . . . pay.] F; 'More . . . pay'. *Oxford*

18–20 Would . . . mine i.e. I wish you had
merited lesser rewards so that I might have been
able to pay you adequately; 'proportion' (19) =
an act of proportioning (*OED* Proportion *sb* 6, citing this line): this act Duncan cannot satisfactorily perform because Macbeth's merit outstrips the
available 'thanks and payment'.

20–1 Only . . . pay Shakespearean nobles often
humble themselves in this way; compare 'outward
courtesies would fain proclaim / Favours that keep
within' (*MM* 5.1.15–16).

21 all i.e. all my 'thanks and payment' (19).

22–7 'Macbeth has nothing but the commonplaces of loyalty, in which he hides himself in the
"our"' (Coleridge, p. 108).

23 pays itself i.e. service and loyalty (22) are
their own rewards. See 'Virtue is its own reward'
(Dent v81, first recorded in 1596).

27 Safe toward With sure regard to your love
and honour (Clarendon). 'An expression undoubtedly strained and obscure on purpose' (*Lexicon* Safe
adj and *adv* 4).

28–9 I have begun . . . growing Shaheen compares 'Thou hast planted them . . . they growe, and
bring forth fruit' (Jer. 12.2 (Geneva)).

30–1 nor . . . / No less i.e. and must be no less
known. F's phrase is a double negative.

31 enfold embrace (an implicit direction to the
actor).

32–3 There . . . own Banquo continues Duncan's
metaphor of growth-into-reward and may allude to
the legal principle that the land's owner possesses
the crops thereon no matter who sowed and tended
them (see Clarkson and Warren, pp. 165–6 and 166
n. 11); for the related principle in animal husbandry
see *John* 1.1.123–4.

34 Wanton Luxuriant, profuse (*OED* Wanton *a*
7a).

35 drops of sorrow Duncan weeps for joy.

35–43 Sons . . . you The political import of this
speech is repeated at 5.9.27–40. Duncan's proposal
of his successor (37) might hint that Macbeth or
Banquo, not Malcolm, as it happens, is to be nom-
inated.

And you whose places are the nearest, know:
We will establish our estate upon
Our eldest, Malcolm, whom we name hereafter
The Prince of Cumberland, which honour must
Not unaccompanied invest him only,   40
But signs of nobleness like stars shall shine
On all deservers. [*To Macbeth*] From hence to Inverness
And bind us further to you.
MACBETH   The rest is labour which is not used for you;
I'll be myself the harbinger and make joyful   45
The hearing of my wife with your approach.
So humbly take my leave.
DUNCAN   My worthy Cawdor.
MACBETH   [*Aside*] The Prince of Cumberland: that is a step
On which I must fall down, or else o'erleap,
For in my way it lies. Stars, hide your fires,   50
Let not light see my black and deep desires,
The eye wink at the hand. Yet let that be,
Which the eye fears when it is done to see.   [*Exit.*]

45 harbinger] F (Herbenger)

36 nearest most closely, or intimately, associated (with Duncan).

37 establish settle.

39 Prince of Cumberland Title of the Scottish heir apparent; compare 'Prince of Wales' in England.

40 Not unaccompanied Not alone. Making Malcolm Prince of Cumberland requires that Duncan also honour others, as Malcolm does at the play's end and James I did upon his accession.

40 invest clothe, adorn (*OED* Invest *v* 1b). This meaning shades into more figurative ones, e.g. 'endue with attributes' (*OED* Invest *v* 3a), but the word links the abstract conferring of honour with the imagery of clothing (see 2.4.32 and n.).

41 signs of nobleness tokens of merit (i.e. titles of honour).

42 SD Keightley is apparently the first editor to have realised that 'you' (43) stipulated a change of those addressed.

42 Inverness Town at the head of the Moray Firth, 155 miles north-west of Edinburgh (Sugden) and supposed location of Macbeth's castle. See the map, p. 110 above.

44 rest ... you Macbeth uses courtly and hyperbolic antithesis: (1) anything ('the rest') not done for you is work ('labour'); (2) resting ('the rest') is fatiguing unless done on your behalf; (3) rest is labour when I refrain from serving you. This invo-

luted language conveys polite deference rather than any easily paraphrasable sense: Macbeth stresses that 'you' (Duncan, his importance and his favour to Macbeth) give meaning to whatever 'we' (Macbeth, Lady Macbeth, and presumably their retainers) do, however others may judge our actions.

45 harbinger An officer of the royal household, who preceded the king on his journeys and procured lodgings (NS). Compare 1.6.23 n.

45–6 make ... hearing i.e. make (Lady Macbeth) rejoice at hearing.

50 Stars ... fires Duncan has just said that 'signs of nobleness [= honours] like stars' shall shine on all deserving people (41–2); recently honoured, Macbeth now seeks to escape starlight and betray his desert. The words are entirely metaphorical: 'There is nothing to indicate this scene took place at night' (Clarendon).

52 wink at disregard, overlook; connive at (*OED* Wink *v*¹ 6a–b). The implication of connivance is slight and made more doubtful by the next line.

52–3 Yet let that be ... to see See Johnson's comment on a similiar moment of anxious self-deception in *John* 4.2.231–6: 'bad men use all the arts of fallacy upon themselves ... and hide themselves from their own detection', and Jones, *Scenic*, pp. 204 and 212, where affinities between the 'conspiracy stage' in *JC* and *Mac.* are identified.

DUNCAN   True, worthy Banquo, he is full so valiant,
And in his commendations I am fed;   55
It is a banquet to me. Let's after him,
Whose care is gone before to bid us welcome:
It is a peerless kinsman.
                                        Flourish
                                                                Exeunt

1.5 *Enter* [LADY MACBETH] *alone, with a letter*

LADY MACBETH   [*Reads*] 'They met me in the day of success, and
I have learned by the perfectest report they have more in
them than mortal knowledge. When I burned in desire to
question them further, they made themselves air, into which
they vanished. Whiles I stood rapt in the wonder of it, came   5
missives from the king who all-hailed me Thane of Cawdor, by
which title before these weïrd sisters saluted me and referred

---

58 SD. 1–2] F (*as one line at right margin*)   **Act 1, Scene 5**   **1.5**] F (*Scena Quinta.*)   **0** SD LADY MACBETH] F (*Macbeths Wife*)   **1** SD] *This edn; not in* F   **1–12** 'They . . . farewell.'] F (*They . . . farewell.*)   **2** perfectest] F (perfect'st)   **6** Thane of Cawdor] F (Thane *of Cawdor*); "Thane of Cawdor" *Collier*   **7** weïrd] *Theobald;* weyward F

54–5 Duncan agrees with Banquo's (unheard) remark: Macbeth is just as brave ('full so valiant') as Banquo has said; praising Macbeth gives Duncan pleasure. Macbeth's aside has apparently 'covered' Banquo's comment to Duncan.

56 banquet Wordplay on 'Banquo' (54).

58 peerless without equal. This word 'prepares us for Macbeth's refusal to remain a thane among thanes; only a monarch is literally peerless' (Mahood, p. 44).

Act 1, Scene 5

Lady Macbeth reads her husband's letter and later meets him in some private room of their castle at Inverness, to which Duncan has said he and his court will travel (1.4.42).

1–12 This letter is another example (see 1.2.2, 46, and 1.3.37–40) of mediated and interpreted knowledge; it amplifies (and distorts) an episode we have witnessed (1.3). Concerning such letters, Jonas Barish (in Biggs, p. 36) makes a general point: 'Shakespeare is not concerned about meticulous quotation; he is quite ready to rewrite a passage to include information missing from the "original" version . . .'; Mark Taylor, 'Letters and readers in *Macbeth, King Lear*, and *Twelfth Night*', *PQ* 69 (1990), 31–53, claims (pp. 36–7) that Macbeth's

'letter is a covert directive . . . to push him toward regicide'.

2 perfectest report most reliable testimony. The words may refer to Macbeth's learning of his new title (Cawdor) from Ross and Angus, but he also called the witches 'imperfect speakers' (1.3.68). For F's 'perfect'st', see 5.1.61 n.

5 vanished Another hint of the witches' stage business.

5 Whiles While. The spelling is not archaic, according to *OED*.

5 rapt Compare 1.3.141, where Macbeth is 'rapt' after learning of his new title rather than after the witches' address.

6 missives messengers (*OED* Missive *sb* 3; this line is the earliest citation, and the last is from 1649).

6 all-hailed saluted with 'All hail'. Macbeth's letter transfers the 'all-hail' from the witches to Ross and Angus.

6 Thane of Cawdor Many editors mark this phrase as quoted speech, and F may seek to do the same through printing 'Thane' in roman type with the remainder of the letter in italic, but F does not distinguish the obviously quoted words 'haile King that shalt be' (TLN 356).

me to the coming on of time, with "Hail, king that shalt be."
This have I thought good to deliver thee, my dearest partner of
greatness, that thou mightst not lose the dues of rejoicing by   10
being ignorant of what greatness is promised thee. Lay it to thy
heart and farewell.'

>   Glamis thou art, and Cawdor, and shalt be
>   What thou art promised; yet do I fear thy nature,
>   It is too full o'th'milk of human kindness   15
>   To catch the nearest way. Thou wouldst be great,
>   Art not without ambition, but without
>   The illness should attend it. What thou wouldst highly,
>   That wouldst thou holily; wouldst not play false,
>   And yet wouldst wrongly win. Thou'dst have, great
>   Glamis,   20
>   That which cries, 'Thus thou must do' if thou have it;
>   And that which rather thou dost fear to do,
>   Than wishest should be undone. Hie thee hither,

---

8 "Hail . . . be."] *Pope (subst.); haile . . . be.* F   8 be.] F; be hereafter. *conj. Upton, p. 201*   20 Thou'dst] F
(Thould'st)   21 'Thus . . . do'] NS (*conj. Hunter, 'New', 11, 172*); Thus . . . doe, F. *See Commentary*   21 thou have]
F; thou'dst have *Keightley*

---

9 **deliver** report. Compare 'Sure you have some
hideous matter to deliver, when the courtesy of it
is so fearful' (*TN* 1.5.206–7).

11–12 **Lay . . . heart** Consider it seriously (*OED*
Heart *sb* 42).

14–23 **yet . . . undone** A speech that appears to
be a static description of Macbeth's 'nature' and
inherent moral values ('thy nature . . . is too full
o'th'milk of human kindness' (14–15)) is in fact
Lady Macbeth's progressive meditation on how she
may influence both nature and values (16–20) and
therefore move her husband to action. See p. 33
above.

15 **milk of human kindness** i.e. compassion
characteristic of humane persons (*OED* Milk *sb¹*
2c). F reads 'humane', and 'humane' (= gentle,
compassionate) was not distinguished orthograph-
ically from 'human' before 1700 or later (see also
3.4.76); 'kindness' principally means 'kinship', but
also connotes 'category' ('kind' = classification,
group) and 'naturalness' ('kind' = nature). Later
uses of the phrase 'milk of human kindness' apparently derive from this line. Compare Goneril's
rejection of her husband's 'milky gentleness' (*Lear*
1.4.341) and see 1.7.54–8 and 4.3.98.

16 **catch** snatch (*OED* Catch *v* 21 and 13).

16 **nearest way** most direct route, short-cut. For
the moral overtones, compare the proverbial 'The
shortest way is commonly the foulest, the fairer
way not much about' (Dent W142.1).

18 **illness** wickedness, depravity.

18 **highly** intensely, greatly (*OED* Highly *adv*
3a), but another meaning, 'in or to a high rank'
(*OED* Highly *adv* 2a), hints that 'highly' might
mean 'nobly, in a manner suiting an individual of
high rank'.

19 **holily** with sanctity and devoutness (*OED*
Holily 1, quoting this line, but omitting the implicit
sense, 'guiltlessly').

19–20 **wouldst not . . . win** While this phrase
seems to repeat the preceding one, it makes Macbeth criminally ambitious (he would 'wrongly win')
and self-deceiving (he would 'play false' = cheat)
where the other stressed his high, but holy, ambition.

21 **That which cries** A voice that says (e.g. Lady
Macbeth's own voice, or the crown).

21 **'Thus thou must do'** F does not indicate
what 'That' says. Pope introduced quotation marks
for 'Thus thou . . . should be undone' (21–3), and
most editors follow him or Hanmer, who treated
'Thus thou . . . have it' as the quoted matter. Any
choice would be difficult to convey in the theatre.

21 **if thou have it** i.e. if you would gain greatness (or the crown); 'would' is understood from its
previous uses.

22 **that** A reference to 'Thus thou must do' (21)
– kill Duncan – rather than to 'That which cries'
– the urging or desire to kill Duncan.

23 **Hie** Hurry.

That I may pour my spirits in thine ear
And chastise with the valour of my tongue   25
All that impedes thee from the golden round,
Which fate and metaphysical aid doth seem
To have thee crowned withal.

Enter [ATTENDANT]

                                                  What is your tidings?

ATTENDANT   The king comes here tonight.

LADY MACBETH   Thou'rt mad to say it.
Is not thy master with him? Who, were't so,   30
Would have informed for preparation.

ATTENDANT   So please you, it is true: our thane is coming.
One of my fellows had the speed of him;
Who almost dead for breath, had scarcely more

---

26 impedes] F (impeides)   28 SD ATTENDANT] *Capell; Messenger* F   29 SH, 32 SH ATTENDANT] *Capell* (*subst.*); *Mess.* F   30 were't] F (wert)

24 pour . . . ear The 'spirits' are soon defined as those 'that tend on mortal [murderous] thoughts' (39); Lady Macbeth's words to Macbeth will be metaphorical equivalents of the 'leprous distillment' Claudius pours into King Hamlet's ears (*Ham.* 1.5.63–4).

25 chastise rebuke. Stress on first syllable (Cercignani, p. 36).

25 valour . . . tongue Misogynistically, Elizabethan culture considered men valorous, women talkative; thus Beatrice, 'my lady Tongue', accuses Benedick of unmanliness: 'But manhood is melted into cur'sies, valour into compliment, and men are only turned into tongue' (*Ado* 2.1.275 and 4.1.319–20). This patriarchal belief did grant women the power to encourage men: 'Methinks a woman of this valiant spirit / Should, if a coward heard her speak these words, / Infuse his breast with magnanimity, / And make him, naked, foil a man at arms' (Prince Edward of Queen Margaret, *3H6* 5.4.39–42).

26 impedes hinders, obstructs. This line is *OED*'s earliest citation for 'impede' (Schäfer).

26 golden round i.e. the crown (as at 4.1.87). 'Mrs. Siddons used to elevate her stature, to smile with a lofty and uncontrollable expectation, and, with an arm raised beautifully in the air, *to draw the very circle she was speaking of*, in the *air about her head*, as if she ran her finger round the gold' (Leigh Hunt, *Tatler*, 15 March 1831, quoted in Sprague, p. 232; this action became 'a common

piece of traditional business', according to Michael Mullin, 'Stage and screen: the Trevor Nunn *Macbeth*', *SQ* 38 (1987), 351).

27 metaphysical more than physical, supernatural (White).

27 doth Singular verb in *-th* with plural subject (Abbott 334).

28 SD ATTENDANT The dialogue makes clear that this speaker is a member of the household, an 'attendant', not a 'messenger' (as in F). Costume and perhaps props would have distinguished messenger from attendant in Jacobean productions.

29 Lady Macbeth reacts either because she momentarily thinks the servant refers (treasonably) to Macbeth as 'The king' or because Duncan's unexpected arrival seems too pat, an instant example of 'fate and metaphysical aid' (27).

31 informed reported; given information (an intransitive use; see *OED* Inform *v* 7a, quoting this line as the first example).

31 preparation Pronounced as five syllables.

32–5 As in the report of Cawdor's execution (1.4.2–11), unofficial messengers travel faster than official ones, and Shakespeare stresses the details of speed and exhaustion.

33 had the speed of him outdistanced him (*OED* Speed *sb* 10b, citing only this line and another example from 1646).

34 for breath as a consequence of ('for') lacking air to breathe (?). The meaning is clear but hard to substantiate (see e.g. *OED* For 22).

Than would make up his message.

LADY MACBETH   Give him tending,   35
He brings great news.

Exit [Attendant]

The raven himself is hoarse
That croaks the fatal entrance of Duncan
Under my battlements. Come, you spirits
That tend on mortal thoughts, unsex me here
And fill me from the crown to the toe topfull   40
Of direst cruelty; make thick my blood,
Stop up th'access and passage to remorse
That no compunctious visitings of nature
Shake my fell purpose nor keep peace between
Th'effect and it. Come to my woman's breasts   45

---

36 SD *Attendant] Capell: Messenger* F   45 it] F (hit)

36 raven Traditionally a bird of evil omen (because it was a carrion-eater seen on the battlefield). Compare 'the fatall Raven, that in his voice / Carries the dreadful summons of our deaths' (Peele, *David and Bethsabe* 555–6) and 'the sad presaging Raven that tolls / The sicke mans passeport in her hollow beake' (Marlowe, *Jew of Malta* 2.1.1–2).

36 himself is hoarse i.e. like the gasping messenger.

39 tend on attend, administer to.

39 mortal fatal, murderous; human.

39 unsex me deprive me of my gender (?); compare *OED* Unsex *v*, 'deprive or divest of sex', for which this line is the earliest citation. The verb may mean 'make me not a woman' or, less likely, 'make me not human'.

39 here Actresses have sometimes made 'here' breast (see Sprague, pp. 232–3) or groin; producers must decide whether Lady Macbeth's invocation is figurative or acted out.

40 crown . . . toe Proverbial: 'From the crown of the head to the sole of the foot' (Dent C864.1).

41 direst most dreadful, most terrible.

41–2 thick . . . passage Classical and early modern medical theory held that health and illness, emotions and other psychological states, were the consequence of 'humours' or 'spirit' that passed through the blood to various organs and bodily structures. If the 'thin and wholesome blood' (*Ham.* 1.5.70) became 'thick' or the 'passage' was stopped, no emotional or psychological changes could take

place, although there might be other consequences: 'there be feavers . . . which are ingendered of thickening and stopping of the conduites and passages' (Barrough, p. 168). NS cites 'Thoughts that would thick my blood' (*WT* 1.2.171) and 'if that surly spirit, melancholy, / Had baked thy blood and made it heavy, thick' (*John* 3.3.42–3); compare 'that Italian [i.e. Machiavellian] air, that hath . . . dried up in you all sap of generous disposition' (Chapman, *Widow's Tears* 1.1.131–3). See pp. 33–4 above.

42 access Stress on second syllable (Cercignani, p. 37).

42 remorse pity, compassion; not (as in modern English) bitter repentance for a wrong committed.

43 compunctious remorseful. This line is *OED*'s earliest recorded use (Schäfer).

43 visitings of nature menstruation (?) and, more generally, natural feelings of compassion. The specific meaning (for 'visit') is attested from 1640; see *OED* Visit *sb* 4, and p. 33 above.

44 fell fierce, ruthless. Compare Iago: 'More fell than anguish, hunger, or the sea!' (*Oth.* 5.2.362).

44 keep preserve, maintain. The modern equivalent of 'keep peace' is 'keep the peace'.

45 Th'effect and it The consequence (*OED* Effect *sb* 1a) and 'my fell purpose' (44): an example of hysteron proteron where cause follows effect. Halio defends F's 'hit' (a form as old as 'it' and common into the nineteenth century: see *OED* It *pron* A) as 'success, fulfilment', but without support from *OED*.

And take my milk for gall, you murd'ring ministers,
Wherever in your sightless substances
You wait on nature's mischief. Come, thick night,
And pall thee in the dunnest smoke of hell,
That my keen knife see not the wound it makes,   50
Nor heaven peep through the blanket of the dark,
To cry, 'Hold, hold.'

Enter MACBETH

                         Great Glamis, worthy Cawdor,
Greater than both by the all-hail hereafter,
Thy letters have transported me beyond
This ignorant present, and I feel now   55
The future in the instant.

MACBETH   My dearest love,
Duncan comes here tonight.

LADY MACBETH   And when goes hence?

---

52 'Hold, hold.'] *Capell (subst.); hold, hold. F*

46 take . . . gall Either 'make my milk gall [= bile; bitter liquid]' or 'treat my milk as gall'. Early medical theory held that a mother's blood (see 41–2) was converted into milk (see Patricia Crawford, 'The sucking child: adult attitudes to child care in the first year of life in seventeenth-century England', *Continuity and Change* 1 (1986), 30); here blood becomes gall. Capell (*Notes*, p. 7) says the spirits 'are summon'd magnificently to suck encrease of malignity from the "*gall*" of her breasts'. 'But perhaps Lady Macbeth is asking the spirits to take her milk *as* gall, to nurse from her breast and find in her milk their sustaining poison' (Adelman, p. 135).

46 ministers attendants, executants.

47 sightless invisible; blind.

48–52 Johnson found the language here embarrassingly humble, but D. S. Bland (*Reader*, p. 241) justifies the 'simplicity of vocabulary'.

48 wait on nature's mischief lie in wait for disturbances of nature (Brooke).

48 thick dense, profound. The word appears three times in this act and only once (4.1.33) again.

49 pall cover or drape as with cloth. The verb evokes the noun 'pall' (cloth, altar-cloth, covering for a hearse or coffin, robe, garment) and joins Lady Macbeth's wish with Macbeth's earlier anxieties about 'borrowed robes' (1.3.107). *Barn-*

hart Dictionary of Etymology, 1988, defines *pall* as 'shroud', the wrapping of a corpse. See 1.7.3 n.

49 dunnest murkiest, gloomiest (*OED* Dun *a* 2).

52–3 Great . . . both Lady Macbeth greets her husband with (almost) the sisters' words (1.3.46–8).

52 Rowe added *Embracing him* after 'Cawdor', which presumably reflects a Restoration stage-practice that certainly appeared in mid-eighteenth-century Pritchard–Garrick performances and has since become a defining moment for the actors' relationship.

53 all-hail i.e. associated with the salutation, 'all hail!' The phrase 'all-hail' is treated as an adjective, 'hereafter' as a noun: Macbeth will be 'Greater . . . hereafter' on the authority of ('by') the sisters' 'all hail'. See 1.3.46 n.

54 letters The audience knows only the letter read at the scene's start; these 'letters' prefigure the characters of Macbeth's face, 'a book' (60).

55 ignorant unknowing (Johnson).

56 The future in the instant That which is to come in the present moment, the here-and-now. See p. 19 above.

57 goes hence departs; dies. See 'before I go hence, and be no more (seene)' (Ps. 39.13; '. . . be no more' (AV)), and 'Men must endure / Their going hence even as their coming hither' (*Lear* 5.2.9–10).

MACBETH Tomorrow, as he purposes.
LADY MACBETH   O never
          Shall sun that morrow see.
          Your face, my thane, is as a book where men   60
          May read strange matters. To beguile the time,
          Look like the time, bear welcome in your eye,
          Your hand, your tongue; look like th'innocent flower,
          But be the serpent under't. He that's coming
          Must be provided for, and you shall put   65
          This night's great business into my dispatch,
          Which shall to all our nights and days to come
          Give solely sovereign sway and masterdom.
MACBETH We will speak further –
LADY MACBETH   Only look up clear;
          To alter favour ever is to fear.   70
          Leave all the rest to me.

                                            Exeunt

---

61 matters. To . . . time,] *Theobald;* matters, to . . . time. F   69 further –] *This edn;* further, F; further. F2

58 purposes plans, intends.
58 O never Sarah Siddons (see G. J. Bell in Jenkin, pp. 43–4) repeated 'never', as have many later Lady Macbeths.
59 sun Given the importance of male heirs in the play, a pun on 'son' is not impossible here.
59 that morrow i.e. a new day in which Duncan 'goes hence' alive.
60–1 The analogy of 'face' with 'a book' is proverbial (Dent B531.1); compare 1.4.11–12.
61 beguile deceive, mislead. Theobald's repunctuation changes the line's effect: in F, 'men . . . read' Macbeth's face to pass the time; here, Lady Macbeth urges her husband to deceive 'men' by wearing a deceitful face.
63–4 look like . . . serpent under't The advice is based on the proverbial 'Snake in the grass' (Dent S585), with a Virgilian ancestor (*Eclogues* 3.93) noted in NS. Brooke suggests that the line alludes to Satan in Eden.
64 under't under it.
65 provided for prepared for (*OED* Provide *v* 2a). The verb hovers ambiguously between hospitable and homicidal preparations for Duncan's arrival. Compare the Dauphin's reaction to an

unexpected English attack: 'we will presently provide for them' (*1H6* 5.2.15).
66 dispatch conduct, management (*OED* Dispatch *sb* 5b, citing this line only). Other meanings – death by violence, or execution (*OED* Dispatch *sb* 4 and 5a) – may have influenced the diction here, since Macbeth will later sense that he has 'killed' sleep (2.2.45).
67–8 all . . . masterdom Night and day later prove not testimonies to the Macbeths' 'masterdom', their sovereign power, but rather to their weakness. See e.g. 3.2.16–22 and 5.1.
68 solely exclusively (*OED* Solely *adv* 2).
69 The punctuation adopted here, indicating that Lady Macbeth interrupts Macbeth, suggests his continuing irresolution and her insistent certainty. The punctuation in F and in F2 makes Macbeth more certainly doubtful, Lady Macbeth still more insistent.
69 clear serenely, cheerfully. Adverbial use of *OED* Clear *adj* 2d; compare 1.7.18.
70 Fear always ('ever') changes one's facial expression ('favour'); the construction is inverted to make a significant rhyme.

1.6 *Hautboys, and Torches. Enter King* [DUNCAN], MALCOLM,
DONALDBAIN, BANQUO, LENNOX, MACDUFF, ROSS, ANGUS,
and Attendants

DUNCAN   This castle hath a pleasant seat; the air
          Nimbly and sweetly recommends itself
          Unto our gentle senses.
BANQUO   This guest of summer,
          The temple-haunting martlet, does approve
          By his loved mansionry that the heaven's breath   5

Act 1, Scene 6   1.6] F (*Scena Sexta.*)   0 SD *Hautboys, and Torches.*] F (*Hoboyes*); *Hautboys.* / NS   **4** martlet] *Rowe*:
Barlet F   **5** mansionry] *Theobald;* Mansonry F; masonry *Pope²*   **5** heaven's] F (Heauens)

Act 1, Scene 6

The audience is to imagine the setting as an approach to Macbeth's castle. NS regards the scene as a daylight one, but F and (in a celebrated stage setting) Henry Irving treat it as nocturnal (see Hughes, *Irving*, p. 100). For contemporary ceremonies used in greeting important visitors, see Heal, *passim*, especially pp. 32–3; the guest's rank governed the ceremony; it determined by whom, by how many, and where the guest was met upon arriving at an aristocratic residence.

0 SD *Hautboys, and Torches* Players of hautboys, and torch-bearers. Tudor and early Stuart hautboys (also called 'bombards') were treble members of the shawm family, loud-sounding instruments much favoured in courts and by the military (Bate, pp. 30–3); Langham (p. 41) describes an outdoor welcome for Queen Elizabeth at Kenilworth Castle in 1575: 'This Pageant waz clozd up with a delectabl harmony of Hautboiz, Shalmz, Cornets, and such oother looud Muzik.' The modern oboe, with which editors and critics sometimes confuse the hautboy, was not introduced into England until *c.* 1674–6 (Bate, pp. 40–1; compare Greg, p. 394 n. 18). NS deletes F's *Torches* because they are inappropriate to a daylight scene, which this one may, but need not, be.

1–10 Both Duncan and, more surprisingly, Banquo here accept a superficial appearance and misread a 'face' (note 'temple' and 'breath' (4–5)), the castle's aspect; compare Duncan's reaction to Cawdor's treason (1.4.11–14) and Banquo's to the sisters' appearance and speech (1.3.37–45, 50–2, 81–3, 122–5). Duncan and Banquo misread as 'gentle' (3) and 'procreant' (8) a castle whose 'battlements' will prove 'fatal' to both (1.5.37–8).

1–2 Rowe's relineation (see Appendix 3, p. 292 below), followed here, scans regularly with a trochaic substitution ('Nimbly') at the start of the second pentameter.

1 seat situation, site (*OED* Seat *sb* 18, quoting this line). 3–10 make another transferred meaning – 'place of habitation or settlement (of birds)' (*OED* Seat *sb* 16a) – likely, although *OED*'s evidence is thin.

3 gentle i.e. the sweet air makes our sense gentle. An example of rhetorical prolepsis, where effect is placed before cause (*Lexicon*, Appendix 1.8). Foakes compares 3.4.76.

4 temple-haunting i.e. associated with houses of worship. Compare 'Yea, the sparowe hath founde her an house, and the swallowe a nest for her, where she maie lay her yong: *even* by thine altars, o Lord of hostes, my King, *and* my God' (Ps. 84.3, Geneva). At Duncan's death, 'temple' will mean both 'cranium' and 'house of worship' (see 2.3.60–1 and 2.3.61 n.)

4 martlet A swift, but used also of the swallow or house-martin (birds which build nests (8) attached to the walls of buildings). Peter M. Daly, 'Of Macbeth, martlets, and other "fowles of heauen"', *Mosaic* 12, 1 (1978), 32–8, shows that martlets and related species were common emblems of 'prudent trust' and 'harmony in the realm'. F's 'Barlet' may be an unusual error for 'marlet', which *OED* Martlet² 2 lists as a variant of 'martlet'; elsewhere, F prints 'the Martlet' which 'Builds . . . on the outward wall' (*MV* TLN 1140–1).

4 approve confirm; attest; commend (as at *Ant.* 5.2.149).

5 mansionry 'mansions collectively' (*OED* Mansionry, citing only this (emended) line and an allusion from 1876, but plausibly suggesting an error for 'masonry'). Schäfer treats 'mansionry' as Shakespeare's neologism.

Smells wooingly here. No jutty, frieze,
Buttress, nor coign of vantage but this bird
Hath made his pendent bed and procreant cradle;
Where they most breed and haunt, I have observed
The air is delicate.   10

Enter LADY [MACBETH]

DUNCAN   See, see, our honoured hostess. – The love
That follows us sometime is our trouble,
Which still we thank as love. Herein I teach you
How you shall bid God yield us for your pains
And thank us for your trouble.
LADY MACBETH   All our service,   15
In every point twice done and then done double,
Were poor and single business to contend

6 jutty,] *Malone (in Steevens³)*; Iutty F   9 most] *Rowe;* must F   10 SD LADY MACBETH] F (*Lady*), *and in* SDs *hereafter except 3.2.0* SD   11 hostess.–] *Collier;* Hostesse: F   14 God yield] F (God-eyld)

6 jutty Projecting part of a wall or building.
6 frieze Carved or painted decorative band beneath a building's cornice.
7 Buttress External support for a wall or building.
7 coign of vantage Projecting corner ('coign') of a building 'affording facility for observation or action' (*OED* Coign 1, citing this line as the first example). This phrase keeps 'coign' a living word; 'quoin' has replaced it in other usages.
8 pendent hanging, suspended.
8 bed . . . cradle nest.
9 most F's 'must' repeats the idea of the birds' procreation; Rowe's emendation moves the observation from the birds' fertility (which gives them their symbolic value) to their number (which validates the castle's 'pleasant' and 'heavenly' aspects). Regarding 'most' as 'relatively trite', Brooke retains 'must', interpreted as 'are resolved to' and 'are obliged to'.
9 haunt usually remain, habitually resort.
10 delicate charming, pleasant (*OED* Delicate *adj* 1a).
11–13 The love . . . love Duncan begins a tortuously polite exchange by remarking how he sometimes finds troublesome others' well-meaning

respect and affection, over which they have taken so much 'trouble'.
13–15 Herein . . . trouble Duncan turns a self-deprecating compliment: Lady Macbeth should learn from the king's example to ask God to reward Duncan for the effort she makes and to thank Duncan for providing the onerous occasion. Shakespeare's nobles make such comments often; see *Ado* 1.1.96–103 and *WT* 5.3.3–8.
14 yield reward, recompense.
16–17 In . . . single For the mathematical language here, see p. 26 above.
16 twice...double Lady Macbeth continues the language of duplication and multiplication begun by the Captain (1.2.37–8), continued by the sisters (1.3.33–4, 4.1.10), and soon to be used by Macbeth (1.7.12).
17 single weak, simple, undemanding. The word continues the text's playing with singleness (unity, integrity?) and doubleness (show, not substance?); for Lady Macbeth, or for the play, doubleness may be more valid or effective than singleness.
17 business exertion. In Elizabethan English, the noun still retained its etymological content of 'busy-ness'; compare 1.5.66.
17 contend compete, vie (*OED* Contend 4).

Against those honours deep and broad wherewith
Your majesty loads our house. For those of old,
And the late dignities heaped up to them,   20
We rest your hermits.
DUNCAN   Where's the Thane of Cawdor?
We coursed him at the heels and had a purpose
To be his purveyor, but he rides well,
And his great love, sharp as his spur, hath holp him
To his home before us. Fair and noble hostess,   25
We are your guest tonight.
LADY MACBETH   Your servants ever
Have theirs, themselves, and what is theirs in count
To make their audit at your highness' pleasure,
Still to return your own.
DUNCAN   Give me your hand;
Conduct me to mine host: we love him highly   30
And shall continue our graces towards him.
By your leave, hostess.
                                                            Exeunt

27 in count] F (in compt); to count Q1673   30 host:] *Collier;* Host F

18–21 The syncopation of 'majesty' to a disyllable makes Pope's relineation (see Appendix 3, p. 291 below), accepted here, a series of regular pentameters with a linked final line, although the common early trisyllabic pronunciation 'her*e*mits' would make F's final line regular. These lines end a column, a page, and Compositor A's current stint in F; he may have been running out of space and therefore crowded the speech into roughly equal line-units.
20 **late** recent.
21 **hermits** beadsmen (*OED* Hermit *sb* 2c), persons bound by vow or fee to pray for an individual's spiritual welfare.
22 **coursed** chased, pursued (*OED* Course *v* 2). Figurative meanings of the word arise from a hunter's pursuit of quarry with a pack of hounds; compare 5.7.2.

23 **purveyor** The person who arranges provisions (food, transport, lodging, etc.) for a superior; an official title in the royal household. Accent on first syllable (Cercignani, p. 40).
24 **holp** helped.
25 **To his** Probably elided ('T'his' or 'To's'); see Cercignani, pp. 288–9.
27 **count** account, statement of moneys received and expended (*OED* Count *sb*¹ 3, quoting this line). F's 'compt' is archaic.
30 **host** The word and social duty will be examined ironically (see 1.7.14 and n., 3.4.5).
32 **By your leave** With your permission. Duncan may leave Lady Macbeth behind after greeting her at the castle's imaginary entrance or invite her to lead the way off-stage.
32 **hostess** See 30 n.

1.7 *Hautboys. Torches. Enter a Sewer, and divers Servants with dishes and*
service over the stage. Then enter MACBETH

MACBETH   If it were done when 'tis done, then 'twere well
It were done quickly. If th'assassination
Could trammel up the consequence and catch
With his surcease, success, that but this blow
Might be the be-all and the end-all – here,   5
But here, upon this bank and shoal of time,

Act 1, Scene 7   1.7] F (*Scena Septima.*)   **5** be-all] *Pope;* be all F   **5** end-all – here] *Sisson II, 194 (Rowe subst.);* end
all. Heere F   **6** shoal] F (Schoole)

Act 1, Scene 7

The opening SD makes this a nocturnal, interior scene at Macbeth's castle; Macbeth has withdrawn from the off-stage ceremonial dinner (see 29)
to some more private place. Compare 3.4, where
the audience sees another state dinner. For modern productions and their sound effects, see p. 79
above. Lady Macbeth's arguments encouraging her
husband to murder are similar to Beatrice's incitement of Benedick to kill Claudio (*Ado* 4.1.255–336)
and to Dionyza's arguments justifying a murder she
ordered (*Per.* 4.3).

0 SD.1 *Hautboys. Torches* An abrupt, theatrical
direction for musicians and light-bearers; see 1.6.0
SD n.

0 SD.1 *Sewer* 'The Sewer . . . must from the
[side]boord convay all manner of potages, meats,
and sauces . . . see ye [the sewer] have officers ready
to convay, and servants for to beare your dishes'
(*The Booke of Carving and Sewing [Serving]*, sig.
A6v, appended to Thomas Dawson, *The Second Part
of the good Hus-wives Jewell* (1597)). Armstrong (p.
50) sees a parallel between the 'hierarchical relationships' of sewer and servants, Duncan and subjects.

0 SD.2 *service* something served as food; course
of a meal (*OED* Service *sb* 27b–c). The audience
would see dishes and other utensils. Compare *A
banquet brought in, with the limbes of a Man in the
service* (*Golden Age*, sig. D1r).

0 SD.2 *over the stage* i.e. crossing silently from
one side to the other.

1–4 These tongue-twisting lines (compare
1.5.16–23) force the actor either to gabble or to
speak very slowly.

1–2 'So, while Duncan is . . . eating his "last sup-
per", Macbeth plays Judas, for to Judas Jesus at the
Last Supper said: "That thou doest, do quickly"
(John 13:27)' (Jones, *Origins*, p. 83).

1 If . . . 'tis done The phrase recalls two
proverbs: 'The thing done has an end' (Dent T149)
and 'Things done cannot be undone' (Dent T200).

See 3.2.12 and 5.1.57–8.

2 assassination murder (for political reasons).
This line is *OED*'s first citation for the word
(Schäfer).

3 trammel use nets (to catch fish or fowl); hob-
ble (a horse); bind up or wrap (a corpse). A richly
suggestive word; *OED* Trammel *v* 4 is a figurative
meaning, 'to entangle or fasten up', supported first
by this line and next by a line (probably an allusion
to this one) from Keats.

4 his surcease Duncan's death.

4 success prosperous achievement (*OED* Success *sb* 3); succession of heirs (*OED* Success *sb*
5). This is the play's fourth use of the word and
recalls the others, beginning to make them ironic
(see 1.3.88, 131; 1.5.1); see the fine discussion of
the word in Everett, pp. 96–7.

4–5 that . . . end-all i.e. if the murder of Duncan were an act and event complete and completed
in itself.

4 that but if only.

5 be-all and the end-all the whole being and
that which ends all. According to *OED* Be-all,
Shakespeare invented the phrase and all subsequent
uses are quotations; 'end-all' (*OED* End-all: 'the
finishing stroke') seems to have a dialect existence
independent of this play.

6 bank and shoal sand-bank (or river bank) and
shallow. F's 'Banke and Schoole' could also be modernised as 'bench and school'; *OED* defines 'bank'
(= bench) as referring to the seat of justice, the
mountebank's stage, or the rower's bench (*OED*
Bank *sb²* 1–3), but does not define 'bank' as 'school
bench'. 'Schoole' is a well-attested form of 'shoal'
in the period. Although Macbeth soon mentions
'instructions' and 'justice' (which might be anticipated in 'school' and 'bench'), the phrase seems
more likely to be a characteristic Shakespearean
near-redundancy, treating time as a river: Macbeth momentarily halts time's flow by standing on
a shoal or by grasping the bank. See Mahood, p.
24.

We'd jump the life to come. But in these cases,
We still have judgement here that we but teach
Bloody instructions, which being taught, return
To plague th'inventor. This even-handed justice   10
Commends th'ingredience of our poisoned chalice
To our own lips. He's here in double trust:
First, as I am his kinsman and his subject,
Strong both against the deed; then, as his host,
Who should against his murderer shut the door,   15
Not bear the knife myself. Besides, this Duncan
Hath borne his faculties so meek, hath been
So clear in his great office, that his virtues
Will plead like angels, trumpet-tongued against
The deep damnation of his taking-off.   20
And pity, like a naked newborn babe

---

13 First, as I] F; First, I *Q1673*   20 taking-off] *Capell;* taking off F

7 jump hazard (*OED* Jump *v* 11, citing only this line and *Cym.* 5.4.182, neither especially clear in signification); pass or leap over (?). For the latter, see Booth, p. 170.

8 We always ('still') are punished here because we only ('but') teach others (how to commit our own crimes against ourselves).

10–11 NS compares 'auctorem scelus / repetit suoque premitur exemplo nocens' ('upon its author the crime comes back, and the guilty soul is crushed by its own form of guilt' (Seneca, *Hercules Furens* 735–6, trans. F. J. Miller)). Howard Jacobson, *SQ* 35 (1984), 321–2, also cites 'saepe in magistrum scelera redierunt sua' ('often upon the teacher have his bad teachings turned' (Seneca, *Thyestes* 311, trans. F. J. Miller)).

10 even-handed impartial.

11 ingredience 'ingredients' considered collectively (*OED* Ingredience 1a). Shakespeare's word is obsolete, but modern 'ingredients' is inadequate; 'ingredience' appears in Shakespeare only here, at 4.1.34, and in *Oth.* Q (1622), sig. F3r (where Folio *Oth.* reads 'ingredients').

12 double Macbeth now cites three relations of trust. For two-ness and three-ness, see 1.6.16n., and pp. 26–7 above.

14 as his host For social perceptions of a host's duties, see Heal, chapters 2 and 3.

16–20 'Duncane was so soft and gentle of nature, that the people wished the inclinations and manners of these two cousins [Macbeth and Duncan] to have beene . . . interchangeablie bestowed betwixt them' (*Scotland*, p. 168b). 'The real Duncan was a weak and worthless youth, who was put out of the

way because that was the best that could be done with him' (White[2]).

16 this Duncan this king, who is Duncan (?). While 'this' seems to particularise ('this Duncan rather than another Duncan'), the word also implies that the specific King Duncan who is Macbeth's guest, kinsman, and king belongs to some larger category (of men named Duncan or of kings). The odd formula ('this Duncan') is a form of evasion (compare Lady Macbeth's 'He that's coming' (1.5.64)); it curiously lessens both Duncan's individuality and Macbeth's responsibility and therefore makes killing Duncan less terrible to contemplate.

17 faculties powers, privileges (*OED* Faculty *sb* 11a, quoting this line); 'authority delegated to him' (Heath, p. 385).

18 clear innocent (*OED* Clear *adj* 15a, quoting this line).

19 trumpet-tongued 'Duncan's virtues speak with a trumpet-tongue on this matter of his murder' (Sisson, II, 194); the phrase modifies 'angels'.

21–5 See Brooks (pp. 21–46) for a classic defence 'of the relation of Shakespeare's imagery' here to 'larger symbols' and 'total structures' (p. 30) in the play, and see p. 45 above.

21–2 newborn babe . . . heaven's cherubin The alternative offered here between an image of vulnerability ('babe') and one of heavenly power ('heaven's cherubin') at first seems confused, but the compressed images join together Macbeth's future opponents: Banquo's children, who will succeed to Scotland's throne (see 1.3.65), and the near-divinely endorsed forces (see 4.3.240–2) that will

Striding the blast, or heaven's cherubin horsed
Upon the sightless couriers of the air,
Shall blow the horrid deed in every eye,
That tears shall drown the wind. I have no spur   25
To prick the sides of my intent, but only
Vaulting ambition which o'erleaps itself
And falls on th'other –

Enter LADY [MACBETH]

How now? What news?
LADY MACBETH   He has almost supped. Why have you left the chamber?

---

22 cherubin] F (Cherubin); cherubim *Q1673;* Cherubins *Muir*   28 th'other –] *Rowe;* th'other. F

drive Macbeth from that throne. Brooks (p. 45) comments: 'is Pity like the human and helpless babe, or powerful as the angel that rides the winds? It is both; and it is strong because of its very weakness. The paradox is inherent in the situation itself; and it is the paradox that will destroy the overbrittle rationalism on which Macbeth founds his career.' For a contrary view, see Helen Gardner, *The Business of Criticism,* 1959, pp. 52–61.

22 blast gale; wind of the trumpet-tongued angels.

22 cherubin cherub (second in the traditional nine-fold order of angels). Cherubim commanded the air – '*Seraph* reignes o're Fire; / *Cherub* the Aire' (*Hierarchie*, p. 216) – and were associated with the winds (see Milton, *Paradise Lost* II, 516–18). Renaissance maps often represent the principal winds as cherubs with puffed cheeks. F's 'Cherubin' is a contemporary singular (compare Phrynia's 'cherubin look', *Tim.* 4.3.64); the contemporary plural was 'cherubins' (as at *MV* 5.1.62); modern English follows Hebrew: 'cherub' (singular), 'cherubim' (plural). Some editors choose a plural form ('cherubins' or 'cherubim') because 'couriers' (23) need plural riders, but the condensed metaphorical context makes those choices overliteral, and one cherub might easily be imagined to have charge of four winds.

23 sightless couriers invisible messengers; invisible means of transport, i.e. the winds which invisibly move the air from place to place. The echo of 'sightless substances' (1.5.47) makes plain the contrast of murder and pity, sin and dissuasion from sin. Following Malone and others, Shaheen cites 'He rode upon the Cherubims and dyd flee [fly]: he came fleeyng [flying] upon the wynges of the wynde' (Ps. 18.10, Geneva).

24 blow sound; propel.

24 every eye every organ of sight; every person. The second meaning is a synecdoche.

25 tears i.e. drops of compassion and the 'watering' caused by a foreign object ('the deed') lodged in 'every eye'. Proverbially, 'Little rain lays great winds' (Dent R16), and the line gains its power from hyperbole: 'tears' become rain so powerful as to 'drown' the insubstantial and omnipresent wind.

25–8 I . . . th'other Two interpretations of Macbeth's images have been offered: (1) continuing the equine images of 22–3, Macbeth distinguishes his intent to murder, which he imagines as an unspurred horse, from his ambition to be king, which he imagines as an eager rider who overdoes his vault ('o'erleaps') and thus fails to land in the saddle; (2) horse and rider together fall when the pair fails to over-leap an obstacle. Catherine Belsey, 'Shakespeare's 'vaulting ambition'', *ELN* 10 (1972), 198–201, supports (2) and associates this passage with medieval and later depictions of Pride as a vaulting figure. In either case, the imagery echoes Macbeth's response to the naming of Malcolm as Prince of Cumberland (1.4.48–50). More generally, see R. N. Watson, 'Horsemanship in Shakespeare's second tetralogy', *ELR* 13 (1983), 274–300. Lady Macbeth's entrance interrupts the speech, but the audience may supply 'side' (of the imaginary horse or obstacle) as Macbeth's next (unspoken) word.

29 supped finished dining.

29 Why . . . chamber For the host to leave the table before the chief guest had finished his meal violated protocol; see 'how does your rising up before all the table shew? and flinging from my friends so uncivily' (Dekker [and Thomas Middleton], *The Roaring Girl* 3.2.6–7).

MACBETH Hath he asked for me?

LADY MACBETH   Know you not, he has?   30

MACBETH We will proceed no further in this business.

    He hath honoured me of late, and I have bought

    Golden opinions from all sorts of people,

    Which would be worn now in their newest gloss,

    Not cast aside so soon.

LADY MACBETH   Was the hope drunk   35

    Wherein you dressed yourself? Hath it slept since?

    And wakes it now to look so green and pale

    At what it did so freely? From this time,

    Such I account thy love. Art thou afeard

    To be the same in thine own act and valour,   40

    As thou art in desire? Wouldst thou have that

    Which thou esteem'st the ornament of life,

    And live a coward in thine own esteem,

    Letting I dare not wait upon I would,

    Like the poor cat i'th'adage?

MACBETH   Prithee, peace.   45

    I dare do all that may become a man;

---

39 afeard] F (affear'd)   43 esteem,] *Collier;* Esteeme? F; esteem; *Capell*   45 adage?] *Capell;* Addage. F

---

30 Hath . . . me Macbeth guiltily supposes Duncan has repeated his earlier praise, or wishes to honour him further.

30 Know . . . has Lady Macbeth assumes Macbeth has deliberately withdrawn to avoid Duncan's attention. Capell (*Notes*, p. 10) conjectured 'Know you not? he has.', and his punctuation is more easily spoken. The staging exploits the audience's fluid imagination: 'the precise location is less important than the juxtaposition of Macbeth's isolation with the conviviality taking place in the adjoining room' (Bevington, p. 130).

33 sorts kinds; (social) ranks.

34 worn Opinions (33) are now treated as garments. Compare 'you in the ruff of your opinions clothed' (V. Gabrieli and G. Melchiori (eds.), *STM*, 1990, 2.3.85).

34 gloss superficial lustre (*OED* Gloss *sb²* 1a), shininess. Figuratively, gloss = 'highest value' (because newest); compare 'all his [Achilles'] virtues, / Not virtuously on his own part beheld, / Do in our eyes begin to lose their gloss' (*Tro.* 2.3.117–19).

35 cast aside When dirtied, the richest Renaissance garments were discarded or given away because they could not be cleaned.

35–8 Was . . . freely Lady Macbeth represents

'hope' as a person – first drunkenly hopeful, then comatose, then hungover – who initially dressed himself in a garment (also = 'hope'), but then sleeps himself into a cowardly sobriety. Compare 2.3.20–30.

37 green and pale Popularly imagined consequences of drunkenness, then as now.

39 Such i.e. you are like the fearful, hungover drunkard, bold only when inebriated.

39 account consider.

39–41 Art . . . desire Are you (now sober, unlustful, and detumescent) afraid to be and do what you were and desired to be when you were drunk. For this verbal possibility, see the immediate sexualised language of 'be' (40), 'do' and 'become a man' (46), 'do' (47).

39 afeard afraid.

44–5 Letting . . . adage The adage is 'The cat would eat fish but she will not wet her feet' (Dent C144). Macbeth wants the kingship, but will risk nothing; later, he will find his feet wet with blood (3.4.136–7). Unlike Lady Macbeth, contemporaries used the proverb positively to exhort 'the idle to action' or to note 'that luxury carries penalties' (Martin Orkin in *Reader*, p. 494).

45 Prithee, peace i.e. I pray thee, be quiet.

Who dares do more is none.

LADY MACBETH   What beast was't then
That made you break this enterprise to me?
When you durst do it, then you were a man.
And to be more than what you were, you would   50
Be so much more the man. Nor time, nor place
Did then adhere, and yet you would make both.
They have made themselves and that their fitness now
Does unmake you. I have given suck and know
How tender 'tis to love the babe that milks me: 55
I would, while it was smiling in my face,
Have plucked my nipple from his boneless gums
And dashed the brains out, had I so sworn
As you have done to this.

MACBETH   If we should fail?

LADY MACBETH   We fail?
But screw your courage to the sticking-place,   60
And we'll not fail. When Duncan is asleep,
Whereto the rather shall his day's hard journey

---

47 do] *Rowe;* no F   55 me:] *Capell;* me, F; me – *Rowe*   59 We fail?] F (We faile?); We fail! *Rowe*   60 sticking-place]
Steevens³; sticking place F

47 none i.e. no man. For Macbeth at this moment, daring to kill the king would move him beyond humanity. See next n.

47–51 What ... man Lady Macbeth seems here either to give her version of 1.5 or to be reporting speeches we have not heard: to achieve the kingship ('more than what you were'), Macbeth would necessarily become more intensely masculine ('so much more the man') rather than (as he claims) become no man. See Waith and 4.3.222–6 n.

47 beast Lady Macbeth immediately understands Macbeth's 'none' to mean an animal.

48 break disclose, divulge (*OED* Break *v* 22).

48 enterprise bold, arduous, or momentous undertaking (*OED* Enterprise *sb* 1).

49 durst dared (an obsolete past tense).

52 adhere agree.

52 make both According to his wife, Macbeth seeks to make both occasion and place, seeks to control time and topography. See 1.1.1 n.

53 that their fitness now i.e. now they have become appropriate ('fit').

54–9 See pp. 36–8 above.

55 milks obtains milk by sucking (sole citation for *OED* Milk *v* 1d). Compare Cleopatra's description of the deadly asp: 'Dost thou not see my baby at my breast, / That sucks the nurse asleep?' (*Ant.*

5.2.309–10).

57 his The ungendered 'babe' (55) becomes male.

58–9 sworn ... to this bound myself by oath . . . to this course of action.

59 We fail? F's question mark (which stood for both modern '?' and '!') can represent either interrogation (sincere or scornful) or exclamation (surprised, scornful, or resigned).

60 But Only.

60 screw . . . sticking-place tighten, make taut, your courage to the limit. The underlying metaphor may be from tightening the tuning pegs of a stringed instrument or from winding up the cord on a crossbow. See 79 below, 1.3.35, and 2.2.36; and compare 'wind up invention / Unto his highest bent' (John Marston, *Antonio's Revenge*, ed. Reavley Gair, 1978, 4.3.192–3) and 'Wind up your souls to their full height' (Cyril Tourneur (? but more likely Thomas Middleton), *The Revenger's Tragedy*, ed. R. A. Foakes, 1966, 5.2.7). The 'sticking-place' may also be the place at which a moral individual hesitates or the place beyond which a moral individual refuses to go or a stab-wound (see *OED* Stick *v*¹ 1a and 3.1.51 n., and *OED* Sticking-place 3).

62 the rather the more readily, all the sooner.

Soundly invite him, his two chamberlains
Will I with wine and wassail so convince
That memory, the warder of the brain,   65
Shall be a fume, and the receipt of reason
A limbeck only. When in swinish sleep
Their drenchèd natures lies as in a death,
What cannot you and I perform upon
Th'unguarded Duncan? What not put upon   70
His spongy officers, who shall bear the guilt
Of our great quell?
MACBETH   Bring forth men-children only,
For thy undaunted mettle should compose
Nothing but males. Will it not be received,
When we have marked with blood those sleepy two   75

---

65 warder] F; warden *conj. Schanzer, p. 224*

63 Soundly A transferred adverb: Duncan will sleep 'soundly'; there is perhaps the added irony of a 'sound' (= robust, healthy) sleep that is death.

63 chamberlains Attendants in the royal bed-chamber (*OED* Chamberlain 1a). See 75–6 n.

64 wassail liquor (in which toasts were drunk).

64 convince overcome, conquer.

65–7 memory . . . only Memory, a guard ('warder') of the brain against irrational thoughts or impulses, will become vapour ('a fume') and reason's chamber ('receipt') will merely receive the condensation of a distilling apparatus ('limbeck') – an elaborate, metaphorical description of drunkenness: 'hote wynes, and strong drinckes . . . fill the braine with vapours' (Barrough, p. 11). See illustration 8, p. 46 above. Arnold Davenport (cited in Schanzer, p. 224) over-rationalises the metaphors: 'the receptacle which should collect only the pure drops of reason . . . will be turned into the retort in which . . . undistilled liquids bubble and fume'. In July 1606 (see p. 8 above), James VI and I and his brother-in-law Christian IV of Denmark witnessed a masque of Hope, Faith, and Charity, when 'wine did so occupy' the actors' 'upper chambers' that 'most of the presenters went backward, or fell down' (*Letters and Epigrams of Sir John Harington*, ed. N. E. McClure, 1930, pp. 119–20).

65 warder Soldier or other person set to guard an entrance; watchman (*OED* Warder *sb*[1] 1, quoting 4.1.55). Schanzer's conjecture ('warden' for 'warder') apparently assumes that Compositor A misread a terminal suspension (in 'wardere'?) and ignores the classical, medieval, and early modern understanding of memory's importance to moral judgement and prudence (see Mary Carruthers, *The Book of Memory: A Study of Memory in Medieval Culture*, 1990, pp. 68–71).

66 fume vapour.

66 receipt receptacle (this line is the latest citation for *OED* Receipt *sb* 12a).

67 limbeck alembic (aphetic form), an apparatus used in distilling. The 'beak' of the alembic 'conveyed the vaporous products to a *receiver* [see 'receipt' (66)], in which they were condensed' (*OED* Alembic 1). See illustration 8, p. 46 above.

67 swinish i.e. drunken. Compare 'As drunk as a swine' (Dent S1042).

68 lies Singular verb in *-s* with plural subject (Abbott 333), assisted here by the figurative link between 'sleep' (67) and 'death' (68); see 'sleep, death's counterfeit' (2.3.70).

70 put upon impose; saddle with (*OED* Put *v*[1] 23a, c). Responsibility for the murder will be laid upon the 'chamberlains' (63).

71 spongy absorbent (*OED* Spongy 3b; this line and *Tro.* 2.2.12 are the earliest citations). The men will soak up liquor like sponges.

71 officers office-holders, persons who perform certain duties; not 'military personnel'.

72 quell slaughter, murder.

72–4 Bring forth . . . but males Compare 'if woman do breed man / She ought to teach him manhood' (Webster, *White Devil* 5.6.242–3).

73 mettle spirit, courage. Early modern orthography did not distinguish 'mettle' and 'metal', making possible a pun on male children as metallic warriors armoured in mail (see Adelman, pp. 139–40, and the mail/male pun at Dekker [and Thomas Middleton], *The Roaring Girl* 3.3.18–20).

74 males There may be a pun on 'mail' (= armour). See 73 n.

74 received understood, believed (by others).

75–6 two . . . chamber i.e. two members of the king's bedchamber. In the Jacobean court,

Of his own chamber, and used their very daggers,
That they have done't?
LADY MACBETH   Who dares receive it other,
As we shall make our griefs and clamour roar
Upon his death?
MACBETH   I am settled and bend up
Each corporal agent to this terrible feat.   80
Away, and mock the time with fairest show,
False face must hide what the false heart doth know.

Exeunt

2.1 *Enter* BANQUO, *and* FLEANCE, *with a Torch[-bearer] before him*

BANQUO How goes the night, boy?
FLEANCE The moon is down; I have not heard the clock.
BANQUO And she goes down at twelve.
FLEANCE   I take't, 'tis later, sir.
BANQUO Hold, take my sword. – There's husbandry in heaven,
Their candles are all out. – Take thee that too.   5

---

77 done't] F (don't)   **Act 2, Scene 1**   2.1] F (*Actus Secundus. Scena Prima.*) 0 SD *Torch-bearer*] F (*Torch*)
4 sword. –] *Collier (after Capell)*; Sword: F   5 out. – Take] *Theobald*; out: take F

appointed members of the bedchamber attended
the king's personal needs. See Neil Cuddy, 'The
revival of the entourage: the bedchamber of James
I, 1603–1625', in *The English Court: From the Wars
of the Roses to the Civil War*, ed. David Starkey,
1987, pp. 173–225.
  76 very own.
  77 other otherwise.
  78 As When (*Lexicon*); 'Equivalent to *seeing that*'
(Clarendon).
  79 settled unchanging, undeviating (*OED* Settled *ppl a* 1).
  79 bend up brace, tighten, prepare to act; see
60 n.
  80 corporal corporeal, bodily. See 1.3.79 n.
  80 agent physical resource; muscle (Hunter).
  81–2 'Fair face foul heart' (Dent F3). Macbeth
now repeats his wife's advice (1.5.61–4); see 3.2.32–
4 and n.
  81 mock deceive.

Act 2, Scene 1
  The scene takes place in Macbeth's castle (fic-
tionally, at Inverness). It is liminal: sufficiently out
of doors for stars and moon to be looked for (1–
2), sufficiently indoors for Banquo to get ready for
'sleep' (7).

  0 SD *Torch-bearer* F's SD might mean that Fleance
holds a torch and precedes Banquo (*him*), but F's
punctuation apparently stipulates a torch-bearer
(often referred to as *Torch*), making three actors
in all. Compare 3.3.14 SD.
  1 How goes the night How much of the night
has passed? See *OED* Go *v* 11, quoting 'How goes
the time' (John Marston, *Antonio and Mellida* (*c.*
1600), ed. Reavley Gair, 1991, 3.1.102). Macbeth
virtually repeats the question, 'What is the night?'
(3.4.126).
  4–5 There's . . . out Usually understood as:
'There's thrift ("husbandry") in heaven, they have
extinguished (put "out") their stars ("candles").'
Steevens[3] compares 'Night's candles are burnt out,
and jocund day / Stands tiptoe' (*Rom.* 3.5.9–10);
see also: 'those golden candles fixed in heaven's air'
(Sonnet 21.12) and 'these blessèd candles of the
night' (*MV* 5.1.220). David-Everett Blythe, 'Banquo's candles', *ELH* 58 (1991), 773–8, unconvinc-
ingly proposes the paraphrase 'There's concern (=
"husbandry") for humankind in heaven, they have
displayed (put "out") their candles/stars.'
  5 Take . . . too Banquo, preparing for rest, dis-
arms himself (4) and now removes some other
accoutrement (his dagger or cloak, perhaps, or

A heavy summons lies like lead upon me,
And yet I would not sleep; merciful powers,
Restrain in me the cursèd thoughts that nature
Gives way to in repose.

Enter MACBETH, *and a Servant with a torch*

                 Give me my sword –
Who's there?   10
MACBETH   A friend.
BANQUO   What, sir, not yet at rest? The king's abed.
He hath been in unusual pleasure
And sent forth great largess to your offices.
This diamond he greets your wife withal,   15
          [Gives Macbeth a diamond]
By the name of most kind hostess, and shut up
In measureless content.
MACBETH   Being unprepared,
Our will became the servant to defect,

---

9 SD] F (*subst.*); *after* sword (9) *Capell*   13 hath . . . pleasure] F (hath beene in vnusuall Pleasure); has been to night
in an unusual pleasure *Davenant*   15 SD] *Folger* (*subst.*); *not in* F; *Capell marks as 'a thing deliver'd'* ('*Prolusions*', *p. vi*)
16 shut] F; shut it F2–4

some ceremonial item associated with the state dinner he has just attended) or (as in some productions) hands Fleance 'This diamond' (15).

7–9 Sleep is not inevitably restorative (2.2.40–3);
like drink (2.3.21–2), it can provoke.

8 cursèd thoughts ambitious dreams (prompted
by the sisters' prophecies and Macbeth's recent
success); nightmares (about Macbeth's possible
crimes). Macbeth enters before Banquo chooses
between these alternatives. See 20 and 50–1;
'unstained thoughts do seldom dream on evil' (*The
Rape of Lucrece* 87); and Imogen's bedtime prayer,
'gods, / From fairies and the tempters of the
night / Guard me' (*Cym.* 2.2.8–10).

9 SD *Enter . . . torch* F's placing of the SD
may indicate the moment when the actors enter;
Capell's repositioning makes Banquo anticipate the
entrance. F's *Torch* might indicate a torch-bearer,
but theatrical economy and F's punctuation suggest one servant holding one torch. Compare o SD
and n.

10–11 Challenge and response: Banquo is tense;
Macbeth appears as either a 'merciful power' (7) or
a 'cursèd thought' (8).

14 largess . . . offices gifts to the castle func-
tionaries (Brooke).

15–16 'This diamond' may be a ring or pen-
dant. Banquo, companion to Duncan in 1.6, conveys a royal gift one might expect the king to
deliver personally; compare 2.3.39 n., and Textual
Analysis, pp. 276–7 below. The gift-giving emphasises Duncan's false sense of security and affirms
the social code Macbeth is about to break.

15 greets . . . withal salutes your wife with. The
verb and its complement control both 'diamond'
and 'name' (16).

16 shut up went to bed (in a curtained bed (see
51) within a chamber). The phrase could mean
'concluded' (i.e. ended his speech); the grammar
is stretched to report what Duncan said ('greets')
and then what he has done ('shut up'). Later Folios
make 'shut up' refer to an imaginary case for the
diamond.

17 unprepared unready, unwarned. This easy
social remark (the castle was not prepared to receive
a king) anticipates the ways Macbeth and others do
not foresee what is to come (see, especially, 2.3.119–
27), but also momentarily suggests that Duncan is
'unprepared' for his murder.

18 Our An anticipatory royal plural; compare 22
and 5.6.4.

18 defect deficiency (*Lexicon*).

Which else should free have wrought.

BANQUO   All's well.
I dreamed last night of the three weïrd sisters;   20
To you they have showed some truth.

MACBETH   I think not of them;
Yet when we can entreat an hour to serve,
We would spend it in some words upon that business,
If you would grant the time.

BANQUO   At your kind'st leisure.

MACBETH   If you shall cleave to my consent, when 'tis,   25
It shall make honour for you.

BANQUO   So I lose none
In seeking to augment it, but still keep
My bosom franchised and allegiance clear,
I shall be counselled.

MACBETH   Good repose the while.

BANQUO   Thanks, sir; the like to you.   30

[Exeunt] Banquo[, Fleance, and Torch-bearer]

MACBETH   *[To Servant]* Go bid thy mistress, when my drink is ready,
She strike upon the bell. Get thee to bed.

Exit [Servant]

Is this a dagger which I see before me,
The handle toward my hand? Come, let me clutch thee:

---

20 weïrd] *Theobald;* weyward F   23 it in] F; it *Rowe; omitted by Rowe²*   30 SD] *Capell (subst.); Exit Banquo* F   32 SD
Exit Servant] Rowe; Exit F

19 **free ... wrought** liberally have worked.
19 **All's well** All is not well, as Banquo's next words testify.
22–4 Macbeth's courtly politeness and the apparent royal 'we' intimate his sense of changed (or soon to be changed) status; his desire to talk about the witches contradicts 'I think not of them' (21).
24 **If you would grant the time** Granting or gaining time will become an important issue; Banquo's descendants overreach Macbeth in time.
24 **leisure** See 1.3.147n.
25 **cleave to my consent** agree (or adhere) to my feeling (or opinion); see *OED* Consent *sb* 6.
25 **when 'tis** when it ('the time' (24)) is.
28 **franchised** free. Banquo apparently wishes to remain free of obligation to Macbeth or of implication in his schemes.
29 **the while** in the meantime.
30 **sir** The respectful title introduces a note of subordination (perhaps prompted by 22–4) not present in 1.3.

30 SD See 0 SD n.
31 **drink** An imaginary nightcap. As a code-word for murder, 'drink' is appropriate to the drunken grooms (1.7.63–8, 2.2.53), the drunken-hopeful Macbeth (1.7.35–8), and the speeches of the hungover Porter (2.3.1 ff).
32 **bell** A clapperless bell like a ship's bell, or a gong (see 'strike upon'); this bell is for routine internal communication (compare 'alarum bell' (2.3.68)). See W. J. Lawrence, 'Bells on the Elizabethan stage', *Fortnightly Review* 122 (July 1924), 59–70.
34 **handle ... hand** This detail identifies the dagger as a weapon for, rather than a threat to, Macbeth and makes plain the fact that the dagger is invisible to the audience. As a 'visual metonym' (see Michael Hattaway, *Elizabethan Popular Theatre*, 1982, p. 65), the dagger might have reminded audiences of other literary and dramatic occasions when the secular or demonic realms offer weapons as temptations to despair and suicide – for example, the moment when Tamburlaine's henchmen

I have thee not, and yet I see thee still.   35
Art thou not, fatal vision, sensible
To feeling as to sight? Or art thou but
A dagger of the mind, a false creation,
Proceeding from the heat-oppressèd brain?
I see thee yet, in form as palpable   40
As this which now I draw.
Thou marshall'st me the way that I was going,
And such an instrument I was to use.
Mine eyes are made the fools o'th'other senses,
Or else worth all the rest. I see thee still,   45
And on thy blade and dudgeon gouts of blood,
Which was not so before. There's no such thing:
It is the bloody business which informs
Thus to mine eyes. Now o'er the one half-world
Nature seems dead, and wicked dreams abuse   50
The curtained sleep. Witchcraft celebrates
Pale Hecate's off'rings, and withered murder,

49 half-world] *Clarendon;* halfe World F

display a dagger to Agydas and he understands he must either commit suicide or be killed; see *Tamburlaine, Part 1* 3.2.88–106. Compare 64.

36 fatal deadly, mortal. The adjective is both active and passive: the vision is of mortality (Duncan's death); the dagger is deadly to vision (Macbeth's own). See 38n.

36 sensible perceptible.

37 as to sight The question depends upon an optical theory that vision was the product of beams radiated by the eye and reflected to it.

38 of the mind imaginary. The phrase also yields an image of a dagger *in* the mind, a keen knife that makes a moral and psychological wound (see 1.3.138 and 1.5.50). Encountering Caesar's ghost, Brutus supposes 'it is the weakness of mine eyes / That shapes this monstrous apparition' (*JC* 4.3.276–7).

39 heat-oppressèd subdued, afflicted by heat (considered a quality of the human body and its 'humours'). Macbeth responds to the vision analytically; his explanation is physiological, and the 'heat' might arise from 'anger, or furiousness . . . perturbations of the minde' (Barrough, pp. 2–3).

40 yet still.

40 palpable tangible; perceptible (*OED* Palpable *a* 1–2).

42 Thou marshall'st You guide, usher. Compare 'Our conquering swords shall marshal us the way' (*Tamburlaine, Part 1* 3.3.148).

46 dudgeon hilt, handle. This line is the sole

citation under *OED* Dudgeon *sb*[1] 2, and the word may have Scottish associations, since Cotgrave defines *Dague à roëlles* as 'A Scottish dagger; or Dudgeon haft dagger' (Capell, 'Glossary' in *Notes*, 1, 21). The blood Macbeth now sees covers not merely the blade, but the handle (where it will stain his hand). See 2.3.109 n.

46 gouts spots, splashes. The word derives from French *goutte* (drop) 'and, according to [nineteenth-century or earlier?] stage-tradition, [is] so pronounced' (Clarendon).

47 thing i.e. a dagger. Macbeth corrects his 'eyes', the 'fools' or deceivers of his other senses (44), and says the dagger is imaginary, 'no such thing' (47).

49–64 'He that peruses Shakespeare [in these lines], looks round alarmed, and starts to find himself alone' (Johnson).

49 half-world i.e. the hemisphere in darkness.

50 seems dead i.e. because nature is asleep. Compare 1.7.68 and 2.3.70.

50 wicked dreams Compare Banquo's fears (8–9).

51 curtained See 16n.

51 celebrates performs the rites; honours.

52 Hecate's off'rings Offerings to Hecate, classical goddess of the moon and of sorcery. In Shakespeare's plays, 'Hecate' is always disyllabic and stressed on the first syllable except at *1H6* 3.2.64; F's syncopation of 'off'rings' is not metrically necessary, and some editors print 'offerings'. See 3.2.41 n.

Alarumed by his sentinel, the wolf,
Whose howl's his watch, thus with his stealthy pace,
With Tarquin's ravishing strides, towards his design   55
Moves like a ghost. Thou sure and firm-set earth,
Hear not my steps, which way they walk, for fear
Thy very stones prate of my whereabout,
And take the present horror from the time,
Which now suits with it. Whiles I threat, he lives;   60
Words to the heat of deeds too cold breath gives.

A bell rings

I go, and it is done. The bell invites me.
Hear it not, Duncan, for it is a knell
That summons thee to heaven or to hell.   *Exit*

55 strides] *Pope;* sides F   56 sure] F (sowre)   57 way they] *Rowe;* they may F   61 SD] F (*Bell*), *at right margin*

53 **Alarumed** Warned, prompted to action; compare 1.2.0 SD n.

54 **howl's** howl is.

54 **his watch** Murder's time-piece; the wolf's night-duty. On the second possibility, see 'the Wolfe shal be watchman and keepe many wayes' (*Prophesie*, sig. A3r).

54 **stealthy** This line is *OED*'s earliest citation for the word (Schäfer).

55 **Tarquin** Sextus Tarquinius, the Etruscan prince who raped Lucretia, wife of Lucius Tarquinius Collatinus. She committed suicide, and her relatives and friends led a rebellion (*c.* 509 BC) that overthrew the monarchy and established the Roman republic. See *The Rape of Lucrece* and Iachimo's memory of 'Our Tarquin' when he prepares his mock-rape of Imogen (*Cym.* 2.2.12–14). The analogy here sexualises regicide and was available to contemporaries: addressing Shakespeare, Henry Chettle wrote, 'Sheapheard remember our *Elizabeth*, / And sing her Rape, done by that *Tarquin*, Death' (*Englands Mourning Garment* (1603), sig. D3r).

55 **strides** long steps. Compare 'turn two mincing steps / Into a manly stride' (*MV* 3.4.67–8). F's 'sides' has not been satisfactorily interpreted; it is also hard to explain as the copyist's or compositor's misreading of 'strides', but 'Whoever hath experienced walking in the dark must have observed, that a man . . . always feels out his way by strides, by advancing one foot, as far as he finds it safe, before the other' (Heath, p. 387). Elsewhere, 'stalks' (*The Rape of Lucrece* 365) and 'slunk' (*Tit.* 4.1.63) describe the way Tarquin approached Lucrece's bed.

56 **sure** reliable, steady. *OED* Sure *a* and *adv* records 'sowr' (F: 'sowre'; Q1673: 'sowr') as a form of 'sure'. NS and Shaheen compare 'He hath made the rounde world so sure: that it can not be moved'

(Ps. 93.2, Psalter version).

56 **firm-set** solidly positioned, stable.

58 **prate** blab, tell tales. Compare 'the land bids me tread no more upon't, / It is ashamed to bear me' (*Ant.* 3.11.1–2). Speaking stones are uncommon; Grey (11, 144) thought Luke 19.40 an analogue, but the context (telling the good word) is far from this one. Dent s895.1 ('The stones would speak') cites Gascoigne (1573): 'When men crye mumme and keepe such silence long, / Then stones must speake, els dead men shall have wrong', and Malone cites 'yet will the very stones / That lie within the streetes cry out for vengeance' (*Warning*, sig. G1r). See 3.4.123, where stones move and trees speak.

58 **whereabout** location, position (*OED* Whereabout 4, where this line is the earliest instance given of this interrogative word used as a noun).

59 **take** remove, withhold.

59 **the present horror** i.e. the silence that would be broken by speaking stones.

59 **time** time of night (compare *OED* Time *sb* 13); not, probably, the more general 'circumstances, the times' (*OED* Time *sb* 3d).

60 **threat** threaten. Macbeth accuses himself of bluster.

62 **it** Either (1) Lady Macbeth's preparatory drugging of Duncan's retainers, or (2) the regicide itself.

63–4 The bell has also summoned Macbeth to damnation.

63 **knell** Church bell rung to announce a death. Macbeth imagines he has already committed the murder. See 4.3.172–3 and n, and 5.9.17.

64 SD Henry Irving made an actor's 'point' of this exit when he hesitated an unusually long time before leaving the stage very slowly; see Sprague, p. 241.

2.2 *Enter* LADY [MACBETH]

LADY MACBETH   That which hath made them drunk, hath made me
          bold;
    What hath quenched them, hath given me fire.
              [*An owl shrieks*]
                                                    Hark, peace!
    It was the owl that shrieked, the fatal bellman
    Which gives the stern'st good-night. He is about it.
    The doors are open, and the surfeited grooms   5
    Do mock their charge with snores. I have drugged their
          possets,
    That death and nature do contend about them,
    Whether they live, or die.

          Enter MACBETH [*with two bloody daggers*]

MACBETH   Who's there? What ho?

Act 2, Scene 2   2.2] F (*Scena Secunda.*); *scene continues*, Rowe   2 SD *An owl shrieks*] *This edn; not in* F   8 SD] *This edn; Enter Macbeth* F; *Mac.* [*within*] / Steevens³, *inserting* / *Enter Macbeth* / *after* My husband? (*13*). *See Supplementary Note, p. 256 below*

Act 2, Scene 2
   The setting is somewhere in Macbeth's castle that is private and that has imaginary access to other parts of the castle. By keeping Duncan's murder invisible, Shakespeare increases the audience's complicity and excitement; compare the murdered Duke Humphrey (*2H6* 3.2), carefully described and possibly seen, and Jones, *Scenic*, p. 212.
   1 That The indefinition (what is *That?*) is powerful; even after the audience realises Lady Macbeth refers both to the grooms' drugged drinks and to her own inebriated excitement at what is to come, the doubt over 'That' lingers, and frightens.
   2 quenched extinguished (as water would fire); cooled (as in tempering forged metal). As in 1, Lady Macbeth sees paradoxically antithetical consequences of a single cause – a miniature instance of a common event in the play (compare, for instance, Banquo's and Macbeth's different reactions to the sisters' prophecies in 1.3).
   3–4 W. J. Lawrence, *Shakespeare's Workshop*, 1928, pp. 35–6, compares 'And when the Lambe bleating, doth bid Godnight / Unto the closing day, then teares begin / To keep quicke time unto the Owle, whose voice / Shreikes, like the Bell-man, in the Lovers eares' (*Blurt* 3.1.101–4).
   3 owl Like the raven (1.5.36), the owl was a bird of ill-omen. See 'The screeching owl bodes death' (Dent R33); NS compares 'owls' . . . death-boding cries' (*The Rape of Lucrece* 165).
   3 bellman night watchman. Dekker describes 'The Bell-man of London' as 'a man with a lan-thorne and . . . a long staffe . . . The *Ringing* of

his *Bell*, was not . . . to fright the inhabitants, but rather it was musick to charme them faster with sleepe'; Dekker's narrator admits, 'The sound of his *Voice* at the first put me in mind of the day of *Judgement*' (*Belman*, pp. 109–110).
   4 stern'st good-night i.e. the last good-night, death.
   4 He Macbeth, but the most recently mentioned agents are the 'fatal bellman' and the 'owl' (3), making Macbeth impersonal and allegorical.
   5 surfeited fed or filled to excess (*OED* Surfeited *ppl a* 1, where this line is the earliest citation); hence, sickened by over-indulgence.
   6 This line probably requires contraction ('I've' for 'I have') for the metre.
   6 mock defy, set at nought (*OED* Mock *v* 1C, quoting 'fill our bowls once more; / Let's mock the midnight bell' (*Ant.* 3.13.183–4)).
   6 drugged poisoned. This line is the earliest citation under *OED* drug *v²* 1 (Schäfer).
   6 possets Drinks made of hot milk, liquor, and spices (a delicacy).
   7–8 Lady Macbeth imagines a contest, or an allegorical play, in which abstract figures (Death and Nature) fight over the grooms' lives and consciousnesses.
   7 That So that.
   8 SD For the daggers, see 51. Füssli (Fuseli) recorded Pritchard and Garrick at this moment; see illustration 13, p. 65 above. See Supplementary Note, p. 256 below, for the staging adopted here.
   8 Who's there? Banquo asks the same question of Macbeth at 2.1.10.

LADY MACBETH Alack, I am afraid they have awaked,	
And 'tis not done; th'attempt and not the deed	10
Confounds us. Hark! I laid their daggers ready,	
He could not miss 'em. Had he not resembled	
My father as he slept, I had done't. My husband?	
MACBETH I have done the deed. Didst thou not hear a noise?	
LADY MACBETH I heard the owl scream and the crickets cry.	15
Did not you speak?	
MACBETH When?	
LADY MACBETH Now.	
MACBETH As I descended?	
LADY MACBETH Ay.	20
MACBETH Hark, who lies i'th'second chamber?	
LADY MACBETH Donaldbain.	
MACBETH This is a sorry sight.	
LADY MACBETH A foolish thought, to say a sorry sight.	
MACBETH There's one did laugh in's sleep, and one cried,	
'Murder!', –	25
That they did wake each other; I stood, and heard them,	

10 attempt and . . . deed] *Globe (conj. Hunter, 'New', 11, 182–3); attempt, and . . . deed,* F   11 us. Hark!] *Globe;*
vs: hearke: F   13 done't] F (don't)   22 Donaldbain] F (*Donalbaine*), *throughout act*   25 'Murder!',] *Hanmer* (*subst.*);
Murther, F

9–10 Lady Macbeth's assumption that Macbeth
has failed may reflect her own irresolution (12–13)
or may indicate that she has mistaken Macbeth's
voice for that of one of the grooms (see her question (13)).

10–11 th'attempt . . . Confounds us i.e. murder attempted but not accomplished defeats us.
F's punctuation says that the attempt to kill Duncan, rather than the killing itself, will defeat the
Macbeths' aims; Globe changed the punctuation
to show that Lady Macbeth fears being known as
having attempted regicide without accomplishing
it.

11 Hark Listen, pay attention. Lady Macbeth
interrupts herself, starting at some real or imaginary sound, perhaps of crickets (15), perhaps her
husband's footsteps.

12–13 Had . . . done't Compare Lady Macbeth's assertion about infanticide (1.7.54–8 and n.).
With other monarchical theorists, James VI and I
stressed the identity of king and father (see e.g.
True Lawe, pp. 62 and 74); Duncan's murder violates multiple bonds, many taboos.

13 My father . . . husband Spoken, the line
makes father and husband, king and king-killer,
one.

13 done't done it.

15 crickets Some editors treat this word as a
possessive ('cricket's'), but the earlier 'owl scream'

(rather than 'owl's scream') suggests that F's reading is correct.

16–19 Did . . . descended These exchanges are
set out as they are in F, but editors have tried to
create a single pentameter. See Textual Analysis,
pp. 268–9 below.

23 This . . . sight Pope and later editors add
an SD making this line refer to Macbeth's hands,
or his hands and the daggers, but F's indefiniteness
suggests how the murder has affected Macbeth's
imagination; compare 62, where his hands 'pluck
out' his eyes.

23 sorry painful, grievous; wretched, worthless.

24 Does Lady Macbeth refer to Macbeth's
bloody hands, the bloody daggers, his hands and
the daggers, or does she merely dismiss her husband's fear? Dessen ('Problems', pp. 155–6) suggests that she does not realise Macbeth has mistak-
enly returned with the daggers until 51 and links
this 'not-seeing' with her earlier failure to recognise
Macbeth (13), but it seems more likely she is taking
her hurdles one at a time, first her husband's debil-
itating fear, then the problem of replacing incrim-
inating evidence.

25 one . . . one Apparently Malcolm and Donaldbain, not the two grooms, but the uncertainty
adds to the terror of the moment.

25 in's in his.

26 stood i.e. stood still, stood without moving.

> But they did say their prayers and addressed them
> Again to sleep.
>
> LADY MACBETH   There are two lodged together.
>
> MACBETH One cried 'God bless us!' and 'Amen' the other,
>   As they had seen me with these hangman's hands.   30
>   List'ning their fear, I could not say 'Amen'
>   When they did say 'God bless us.'
>
> LADY MACBETH Consider it not so deeply.
>
> MACBETH But wherefore could not I pronounce 'Amen'?
>   I had most need of blessing and 'Amen'   35
>   Stuck in my throat.
>
> LADY MACBETH   These deeds must not be thought
>   After these ways; so, it will make us mad.
>
> MACBETH Methought I heard a voice cry, 'Sleep no more:
>   Macbeth does murder sleep', the innocent sleep,
>   Sleep that knits up the ravelled sleeve of care,   40
>   The death of each day's life, sore labour's bath,

---

29 'God . . . us!' . . . 'Amen'] *Hanmer* (*subst.*); God . . . vs . . . Amen F   31–2 'Amen' . . . 'God . . . us.'] *Hanmer* (*subst.*); Amen . . . God . . . vs. F   34–5 'Amen'? . . . 'Amen'] *Hanmer* (*subst.*); Amen? . . . Amen F   36 thought] F; thought on *Hanmer*   38–9 'Sleep . . . sleep'] *Johnson*; sleep . . . sleepe F   40 knits] F; rips Q1673

---

27 **addressed** prepared (*OED* Address *v* 10). There may be a hint of 'directed spoken words' (*OED* Address *v* 8a), since Macbeth will soon himself 'address' Sleep (38–43).

28 **lodged** housed, bedded down.

30–1 Capell (*Notes*, pp. 11–12) argues that 'List'ning their fear' should end a sentence rather than begin one, but F's punctuation, a colon before 'Listning' and a comma after 'feare', tends against Capell, and his choice produces a weak following sentence, 'I could not say "Amen" / When they did say "God bless us".'

30 **As** As if (Abbott 107); see 1.4.11 n.

30 **hangman's hands** An executioner's hands would be bloodied when he disembowelled the body of a traitor he had first hanged.

31 **List'ning** Hearing, listening to.

31 **I could not say 'Amen'** Macbeth cannot speak the formulaic word that would free him spiritually so that he could join in the grooms' prayers. Claudius, also a regicide, in *Ham.* 3.3.38–72 meditates on his need for contrition, strives to pray, but gives up despairingly: 'My words fly up, my thoughts remain below' (*Ham.* 3.3.97). Compare Vittoria's horrific dream: 'I trembled, and yet for all this terror / I could not pray' (Webster, *White Devil* 1.2.248–9).

34 **wherefore** why.

36 **thought** meditated, pondered. This line is the last citation under *OED* Think *v²* 2a.

38–43 There is no way of telling how much of this passage (or of 44–6) is quoted speech, and an audience is unlikely to hear fine discriminations; altogether, 38–43 is 'a formal apostrophe to Sleep' (Brooke) in the manner of *The Rape of Lucrece* (e.g. 764 ff. on 'comfort-killing Night'). Clarendon compares Seneca, *Hercules Furens* 1065–81, an apostrophe to sleep that includes the phrases 'vanquisher of woes, rest of the soul, the better part of human life . . . peace after wanderings, haven of life, day's respite' (trans. F. J. Miller).

38 **Methought** It seemed to me.

40 **ravelled** frayed (synonymous with 'unravelled'); untwisted (see next n.).

40 **sleeve** Part of a garment covering the arm (*OED* Sleeve *sb* 1); filament of silk obtained by untwisting a thicker thread (*OED* Sleave *sb* 1, quoting this line as its first figurative use). An audience cannot hear the difference between 'sleave' and 'sleeve', and the play's clothing imagery prompts us to understand 'sleave'.

41 **death of each day's life** i.e. sleep ends each day just as death ends life. Thus, sleep is to death as day is to life, and sleep is to day as death is to life.

41 **bath** therapeutic liquid. *OED* Bath *sb¹* 10

Balm of hurt minds, great nature's second course,
Chief nourisher in life's feast.
LADY MACBETH   What do you mean?
MACBETH Still it cried, 'Sleep no more' to all the house;
'Glamis hath murdered sleep', and therefore Cawdor   45
Shall sleep no more: Macbeth shall sleep no more.
LADY MACBETH Who was it, that thus cried? Why, worthy thane,
You do unbend your noble strength to think
So brain-sickly of things. Go get some water
And wash this filthy witness from your hand.   50
Why did you bring these daggers from the place?
They must lie there. Go carry them and smear
The sleepy grooms with blood.
MACBETH   I'll go no more.
I am afraid to think what I have done;
Look on't again, I dare not.
LADY MACBETH   Infirm of purpose!   55
Give me the daggers. The sleeping and the dead
Are but as pictures; 'tis the eye of childhood
That fears a painted devil. If he do bleed,

---

43 feast.] F (Feast.); feast, – *Cam. (after Theobald)*   44 'Sleep . . . more'] *Johnson;* Sleepe . . . more F   45 'Glamis . . . sleep'] *Johnson;* Glamis . . . Sleepe F

quotes this line as figurative, citing also Chaucer's 'bath of bliss'. Early modern English allows the pronunciation 'bait' (for 'bath') and hence a pun on 'bate', which can mean both 'strife, discord' and 'diminution' (*OED* Bate *sb*[1] 1 and *sb*[2] 2, respectively). This latter ironic possibility is attractive, but unavailable in modern English pronunciation.

42 second course main or principal dishes, hence something that comes after and satisfies more, as sleep does after exertion.

43 Capell (*Notes*, p. 12) compares Southwell's 'St Peters Complaint' (1595), lines 721 ff.: 'Sleepe, deathes allye: oblivion of teares: / Silence of passions: balme of angry sore: / Suspence of loves' (*Poems of Robert Southwell*, ed. James McDonald and Nancy Pollard Brown, 1967).

43 Chief nourisher Compare 'gentle sleep! / Nature's soft nurse' (*2H4* 3.1.5–6).

44–6 Sleep no more . . . sleep no more See 38–43 n. and 'I'll beat the drum / Till it cry sleep to death' (*Lear* 2.4.118–19).

48 unbend The word continues the metaphors of 1.3.35, 1.7.60 and 79.

50 filthy witness morally polluted token (*OED* Witness *sb* 7). Compare 1.1.13 n.

53 sleepy The word is literally accurate: the drugged grooms live, intended to be scapegoats for Duncan's murder.

57 as pictures i.e. because, dead, they do not move. See 1.3.95 and 2.3.70.

57–8 'tis . . . devil 'Bugbears to scare babes' is proverbial (Dent B703); a 'bugbear' (or 'bogey man') was an imaginary figure used to scare children into obedience. Steevens[2] notes Webster's echo: 'Terrify babes, my lord, with painted devils' (*White Devil* 3.2.147).

58 painted pictured, represented graphically; perhaps also 'made up' (compare 'smear' (52), and 2.3.105, 3.4.12).

58 If he do bleed Literally, 'if Duncan's wounds are still fresh enough to be shedding liquid blood' (i.e. the blood has not coagulated). Early audiences might have recalled, however, the then-current superstition that a murdered body, such as Duncan's, bled afresh in the presence of the murderer (see *R3* 1.2.55–61); Lady Macbeth is not, technically, Duncan's murderer, but she is an accomplice and therefore equally guilty in contemporary criminal law. Here, therefore, she may be assuming and accepting her responsibility and her

I'll gild the faces of the grooms withal,
For it must seem their guilt.   *Exit*

Knock within

MACBETH   Whence is that knocking?   60
How is't with me, when every noise appals me?
What hands are here? Ha: they pluck out mine eyes.
Will all great Neptune's ocean wash this blood
Clean from my hand? No: this my hand will rather
The multitudinous seas incarnadine,   65
Making the green one red.

Enter LADY [MACBETH]

LADY MACBETH My hands are of your colour, but I shame

---

65 incarnadine] *Rowe;* incarnardine F   66 green one red] *Q1673*, F4 (Green one Red)*;* Greene one, Red F*;* green, One red *Johnson*

---

guilt, even as she works to incriminate the grooms (59–60).

59 gild paint with gold-colour or gold-leaf. Lady Macbeth immediately speaks (unconsciously? compulsively?) the hackneyed 'gild' / 'gilt' / 'guilt' pun (60), which associates gold with red, painting with deception, royalty with murder. For red–gold substitutions, see 'golden blood' (2.3.105) and 'My red dominical, my golden letter' (*LLL* 5.2.44).

60 SD.2 *within* See 1.2.0 SD. 1 n.

60 Rowe's SD, *Starting*, follows 'knocking' and reflects Restoration stage-practice.

61 appals dismays, terrifies (*OED* Appal *v* 8, quoting 3.4.60). The etymologically accurate 'apales' ('becomes pale': see *OED* Appale) is probably also present (see 68 n.).

62–6 These lines have numerous classical parallels (Sophocles, Catullus, Seneca) and perhaps some sources; see Muir 2.2.59–62 n. Steevens notes earlier English uses of the metaphors: 'And made the greene sea red with Pagan blood' (Anthony Munday, *The Downfall of Robert, Earl of Huntingdon*, ed. John Meagher, MSR, 1965, line 1880) and 'The multitudes of seas died [dyed] red with blood' (Munday and Henry Chettle, *The Death of Robert, Earl of Huntingdon*, ed. John Meagher, MSR, 1967, line 1391). See also 'Thou mighty one [Mars], that with thy power hast turned / Green Neptune into purple' (*TNK* 5.1.49–50).

63–4 Will . . . hand Macbeth's worry has ample precedent. See e.g. Jasper Heywood's translation of Seneca, *Hercules Furens* 1323–9: 'What Tanais, or what Nilus els, or with his Persyan wave / What Tygris violent of streame, or what fierce Rhenus

flood, / Or Tagus troublesome . . . May my ryght hand [n]ow wash from gylt? although . . . The w[a]ves of all the Northern sea on me shed out now wolde, / And al the water therof shoulde now pas by my two handes, / Yet wil the mischiefe deepe remayne' (*Seneca His Tenne Tragedies* (1581), sig. D4r); 'All the water in the sea cannot wash out this stain' (Dent w85, citing *Ado* 4.1.140 f.); 'What if this cursed hand / Were thicker than itself with brother's blood, / Is there not rain enough in the sweet heavens / To wash it white as snow' (*Ham.* 3.3.43–6, Q2 and F, cited by Slater, p. 5).

63 Neptune Classical god of the seas.

65 multitudinous seas numerous oceans ('all the world's seas'); many-waved oceans. This line is *OED*'s earliest citation for 'multitudinous', which Shakespeare uses elsewhere (Schäfer).

65 incarnadine stain red; 'literally make flesh-coloured' (Blackfriars). The earliest citation under *OED* Incarnadine *v* (Schäfer).

66 F's punctuation makes 'the green one' = 'Neptune's ocean'; Johnson's anachronistic reading makes 'one red' = 'uniformly scarlet'. Q1673 and F4 leave the line unpunctuated, and my choice is the modern version of F's reading (see Sisson, 11, 197).

67–8 Traditionally, post-Restoration actresses (Pritchard, Siddons) taunt Macbeth here, but in 1889 Lillie Langtry made Lady Macbeth seek to excuse her own weakness (Sprague, p. 244: 'Lady Macbeth as an heroic character was passing').

67 I shame I am (or, would be) ashamed. See *OED* Shame *v* 1c.

To wear a heart so white.
                    Knock [*within*]
                                        I hear a knocking
At the south entry. Retire we to our chamber;
A little water clears us of this deed.   70
How easy is it then! Your constancy
Hath left you unattended.
                    Knock [*within*]
                                        Hark, more knocking.
Get on your night-gown, lest occasion call us
And show us to be watchers. Be not lost
So poorly in your thoughts.   75
MACBETH   To know my deed, 'twere best not know my self.
                    Knock [*within*]
Wake Duncan with thy knocking: I would thou couldst.

                                        Exeunt

---

76 SD *Knock within*] Steevens (*subst.*); *Knocke* F (*after* deed)

68 white pale with fear (*OED* White *a* 5a, quoting this line). Compare 'blanched with fear' (3.4.116), 5.3.11 and 14–16.

68 SD Knock '[W]hen the deed is done . . . the knocking at the gate is heard, and it makes known audibly that the reaction has commenced; the human has made its reflux upon the fiendish; the pulses of life are beginning to beat again' (De Quincey, x, 393). J. W. Spargo argues 'the Jacobean audience recognized in *Macbeth* [2.2] a crescendo of three ominous portents of death: (1) the wolf's howl; (2) the owl's screech; (3) the knocking at the gate' ('The knocking at the gate in *Macbeth*, an essay in interpretation', in *Adams Memorial Studies*, ed. James McManaway *et al.*, 1948, pp. 269–77; quotation from p. 277. Spargo associates the knocking with the sounds of those who searched houses for victims of the great plague of 1603; see 4.3.167–75 n.

69 south entry southern entrance (to the castle or, later, 'palace' – 3.1.48, 3.3.13). The south was often holy and the north devilish in folklore, but Shakespeare elsewhere associates the south with disease and sickness; see *2H4* 2.4.363, *Tro.* 5.1.18, *Cor.* 1.4.30, *Rom.* 1.4.103, *Cym.* 4.2.349.

71–2 constancy . . . unattended firmness of purpose has left you unsupported. NS paraphrases, 'you have lost your nerve'.

73 night-gown informal clothing, dressing-gown. Most Elizabethans slept naked, and 'night-gowns' were worn outdoors and on such occasions as church services and executions (Linthicum, pp. 184–5). Shakespeare, however, associates 'night-gown' with semi-privacy and the bedchamber. Compare: 5.1.4; *JC* 2.2.0 SD; *Ado* 3.4.18–19, where 'night-gown' is a contemptuous description of a very grand garment; *Oth.* 4.3.16 and 34, where Desdemona's 'nightly wearing' and 'night-gown' seem to be the same; King Henry's early-morning meditations and meeting with his advisers '*in his night-gown*' (*2H4* 3.1.0 SD); *Enter the ghost in his night gowne* (*Ham.* Q1 (1603), sig. G2v).

73 occasion circumstances; chance.

74 watchers persons who stay awake at night, night-watchers (*OED* Watcher c, quoting this line as its second example).

76 To know . . . my self i.e. consciousness of murder could best be borne if I lost my identity (a quibble, perhaps, on Dent K175, 'Know thyself'). Upton (p. 177) paraphrases: 'To know my deed! No, rather than so, 'twere best not know myself.' The implicit claim is that Macbeth as he was and murder are psychologically incoherent; awareness of murder will require a new 'self'. DeFlores asserts that Beatrice-Joanna, having ordered a murder, is recreated by her action: 'Y'are the deed's creature' (*Changeling* 3.4.137).

2.3 *Enter a* PORTER. *Knocking within*

PORTER   Here's a knocking indeed: if a man were porter of hell-
gate, he should have old turning the key. (*Knock*) Knock, knock,
knock. Who's there i'th'name of Beelzebub? Here's a farmer
that hanged himself on th'expectation of plenty. Come in time
– have napkins enough about you, here you'll sweat for't.   5
(*Knock*) Knock, knock. Who's there in th'other devil's name?
Faith, here's an equivocator that could swear in both the scales
against either scale, who committed treason enough for God's
sake, yet could not equivocate to heaven. O, come in, equivocator. (*Knock*) Knock, knock, knock. Who's there? Faith,   10

Act 2, Scene 3   2.3] F (*Scena Tertia.*)*; scene continues,* Rowe   1–2 hell-gate] *Rowe;* Hell Gate F   4–5 Come in
time –] *Brooke;* Come in time, F*;* Come in, time, Q*1673;* Come in, Time*; Staunton;* come in, time-server*; NS;* Come
in farmer, *Blackfriars* (*conj. Anon. in Cam.*)   10 Faith] F ('Faith)

Act 2, Scene 3
    For the scene division here, see Textual Analysis,
p. 265 below. The scene begins at the castle's gate,
moves to some public, probably exterior, space from
which Macduff is led to the 'door' (42) of Duncan's
apartments, but eventually it is necessary to move
to the 'hall' (127), although the 'parley' (75) would
most naturally be held at the gate or from the castle's battlements. The action here permits the actor
playing Macbeth to wash the blood from his hands
and to change costume. The Porter's speeches were
omitted by Davenant, Garrick, Kemble and others.
Capell praised the part (*Notes*, p. 13) as 'masterly
in it's way, and open to no objections but such
as lye against all comic mixture with things serious', and Coleridge (p. 103) condemned it as non-
Shakespearean. The Porter's part is now considered a fine stroke of realistic allegory and dramatic
pacing (Harcourt). Bradley (p. 314) sees a similarity with the asp-bearing clown of *Ant.* 5.2. Lady
Macbeth's part has often been cut from this scene;
see p. 61 above.
    1–2 **porter of hell-gate** doorman at the entrance
to hell (imagined as a castle). Wickham, 'Castle',
discusses medieval and native elements, and Allen
discusses classical elements in the Porter's character, speech, and function. See Supplementary Note,
p. 257 below, and illustration 9, p. 51 above.
    2 **old** frequent, too much.
    3–13 In ancient comic fashion (compare
Launcelot Gobbo, *MV* 2.2.1–32), the Porter speaks
both parts in a series of imaginary dialogues with
'some of all professions' (15) as they arrive in hell
(13–14), but stops when cold (14) and consciousness sober him. Bradley (p. 437 n. 2) noted that
the pattern of the Porter's comic review of near-

allegorical, imaginary persons is virtually the same
as Pompey's listing of prisoners he has met ('Master Rash', 'Master Caper', *et al.*) in *MM* 4.3.1–19.
    3 **i'th'name of Beelzebub** 'We should surely
expect him to say "in the name of my master"
or possibly "in the name of Macbeth"; but, since
Macbeth has just murdered Duncan, "in the name
of Belzebub" or "in the devil's name" is just as
appropriate' (Wickham, 'Castle', p. 42).
    3 **Beelzebub** A popular devil-name, one of the
few found in the Bible (Brooke).
    4 **Come in time** This is a good time for
you to arrive. NS's emendation is 'brilliant'
(Muir), but unnecessary. Q1673's reading, which
Staunton unwittingly accepted and Harcourt (p.
394) guessed, is almost as clever, making the farmer,
a person whose livelihood depends upon the seasons (= 'time'), grammatically parallel with the
equivocator (9–10) and the tailor (12), but the
rhetorical pattern (addresses to new arrivals in hell)
has not yet been established.
    5 **napkins** handkerchiefs (to wipe the 'sweat'
caused by hellfire and perhaps the result of the
'sweating tub', a supposed cure for venereal disease).
    6 **th'other devil** The Porter cannot remember
the name of another devil (Muir).
    7 **Faith** By my faith (a mild oath).
    7 **scales** pans (of a weighing device; here the
'scales' of justice).
    8–9 **for God's sake** A common oath, but the
phrase may refer specifically to Jesuit priests'
equivocal oaths to preserve their lives from political reprisal while also maintaining their faith ('for
God's sake'); see 26 n.

here's an English tailor come hither for stealing out of a French
hose. Come in, tailor, here you may roast your goose. (*Knock*)
Knock, knock. Never at quiet: what are you? But this place is
too cold for hell. I'll devil-porter it no further: I had thought to
have let in some of all professions that go the primrose way   15
to th'everlasting bonfire. (*Knock*) Anon, anon. I pray you,
remember the porter. [*Opens door*]

Enter MACDUFF *and* LENNOX

MACDUFF Was it so late, friend, ere you went to bed,
    That you do lie so late?
PORTER Faith, sir, we were carousing till the second cock, and   20
    drink, sir, is a great provoker of three things.
MACDUFF What three things does drink especially provoke?
PORTER Marry, sir, nose-painting, sleep, and urine. Lechery, sir, it
    provokes, and unprovokes: it provokes the desire, but it takes

17 SD.I] *Brooke; not in* F; *Opens / Capell*

11–12 stealing out of a French hose Possibly
a joke about tailors' skimping on fabric in men's
garments ('hose'), but fashions changed quickly,
and 'French hose' were both loose and tight at
various times in the early modern period, making theft difficult or easy to detect, as the case
might be (Brooke); for analogous details of changing fashions in breeches, see Dekker (and Middleton), *The Roaring Girl* 2.2.71–82. The phrase may
also be sexual innuendo: 'tail' (of 'tailor') = vagina;
'hose' = codpiece = penis. Precisely what (the
theft, the penis) was 'stealing out of' (escaping,
becoming visible) is equivocal. Blackfriars suggests a pun, stealing/'staling' (= urinating), which
would anticipate the Porter's other major interest.

12 roast your goose heat your iron (in the flames
of hell). 'Goose' was a tailor's long-handled iron
and also a slang word for 'prostitute', a source of
venereal disease, the 'French pox' for which a suf-
ferer roasted literally (see 5 n.) and spiritually (in
hell). See also 11–12 n. above.

15–16 primrose . . . bonfire Shakespeare
appears to have invented the phrase 'primrose
path' as a contrast between the easy and attractive pleasures of sin and the consequences of sin,
'th'everlasting bonfire' of hell. Compare 'the primrose path of dalliance' (*Ham.* 1.3.50) and 'the
flow'ry way that leads to the broad gate and the
great fire' (*AWW* 4.5.54–5). Compare 'roast your
goose' (12 and n.).

15 primrose 'abounding in primroses' (*OED*
Primrose *sb* (*a*) 7), a pale-yellow wild and cultivated
flower, 'first-born child of Ver, / Merry springtime's harbinger' (*TNK* 1.1.7–8).

16 bonfire Etymologically, the word derives
from 'bone-fire', a pyre in which human or animal bones were consumed.

17 remember the porter give me a tip (for
opening the gate).

17 SD.I The Porter here performs some action
fulfilling his function as gate-keeper.

20–1 The Porter's lines are apparently prose, but
like other prose passages in the play they have an
iambic rhythm.

20 carousing celebrating, revelling, drinking.

20 second cock second crowing of a rooster (i.e.
a measurement of time before watches and clocks
were common). Compare 'the second cock hath
crowed, / . . . 'tis three a 'clock' (*Rom.* 4.4.3–4), a
comment that does not necessarily mean that 'the
second cock' = 'three o'clock', and 5.1.31.

21 great provoker of three things The Shakespearean clown's typical invitation, a half-riddle
that will, he hopes, catch the interest of a wealthy
interlocutor. *TN* 1.5.1–9, 3.1.16–25, and *AWW*
1.3.39–50 are other instances.

22 With this question, Macduff accepts his rôle
as straight man.

23 Marry A mild oath (in full: 'By the Lady
Mary', 'By the Virgin Mary').

23 nose-painting i.e. the reddening of the sot's
nose. Lady Macbeth angrily dismissed the painted
face and its effects (2.2.57–60).

24 unprovokes calms, depresses, allays (see
OED Un² *prefix* and Provoke *v* 6); this line is
OED's only citation for Unprovoke *v* (Schäfer).

24–5 provokes the desire . . . performance
stimulates sexual interest but inhibits sexual

away the performance. Therefore much drink may be said to be   25
an equivocator with lechery: it makes him, and it mars him; it
sets him on, and it takes him off; it persuades him and dis-
heartens him, makes him stand to and not stand to. In conclusion, equivocates him in a sleep, and giving him the lie,
leaves him.   30

MACDUFF I believe drink gave thee the lie last night.

PORTER That it did, sir, i'the very throat on me, but I requited him
for his lie, and, I think, being too strong for him, though he
took up my legs sometime, yet I made a shift to cast him.

Enter MACBETH

MACDUFF Is thy master stirring?   35
     Our knocking has awaked him: here he comes.
                                                    [*Exit Porter*]

---

34 SD] F; *after 35, Collier*   36 SD *Exit Porter*] *Oxford; not in* F

functioning. For contemporary beliefs about witches and their power to inhibit a male's sexual performance, see Dolan, p. 216. Provoking (or tempting) and unprovoking (or warning) also describe the sisters' words to Macbeth and Banquo in 1.3 since those words provoke Macbeth to regicide but also seem to promise that he will become king 'without . . . stir' (1.3.143); those words promise much to Banquo, who is not 'provoked' to regicide.

26 equivocator Someone who uses ambiguous words; a prevaricator. *OED*'s first citation is from a text composed in 1599, Edwin Sandys's *A Relation of the State of Religion* (first printed 1605 and later reprinted as *Europae Speculum*), where the word is applied to Jesuits and their doctrine of mental reservation. That doctrine permitted one to express virtual falsehoods in a verbally true form to satisfy the speaker's conscience (Sandys, sig. K2v). See p. 5 above. Scot (XIII, 15) uses 'equivocation' to describe banal confidence games, perhaps through analogy with rhetorical 'equivoque', the pun, as in 'strange equivocation' (Webster, *White Devil* 4.2.34).

26–30 it makes . . . leaves him These lines mingle bawdy (developing 23–5) with other meanings.

26 makes . . . mars A proverbial expression (Dent M48).

27 sets . . . on . . . takes . . . off advances . . . withdraws. Besides the bawdy description of a failed erection, the verbs could describe urging dogs to attack and retreat (compare 5.7.2 and n.).

28 stand to set to work (with a pun on the erect penis).

29 equivocates him in a sleep fulfils his lechery only in a dream (Hunter).

29 giving him the lie '(1) deceives him (because he cannot perform sexually as he promised); (2) floors him (as in wrestling); (3) makes him urinate (lie = lye)' (Hunter); (4) makes him lose his erection; (5) accuses him of lying (as Lady Macbeth did Macbeth, 1.7.47–51).

31–3 I believe . . . his lie Macduff, the comic feed here, reignites the multiple jokes of 29 when he asserts that 'drink gave thee the lie last night' (31), but the Porter's reply, 'it did . . . i'the very throat on [= of] me' and 'I requited him for his lie' (32, 33), stresses the single meaning of deliberate deception, the meaning most pertinent to what the Macbeths have done and are about to do. The proverbial 'To lie in one's teeth' (Dent T268) meant 'deep, deliberate lying' (Folger).

34 took up my legs made me unable to stand (because drunk); 'dropped' me (as a wrestler does). Compare 29 n.

34 shift stratagem, ruse (*OED* Shift *sb* 4).

34 cast throw to the ground; vomit (NS subst.).

34 SD Editors have moved Macbeth's entrance to follow Macduff's question, but see Textual Analysis, pp. 262–3 below.

36 SD Oxford added this SD, remarking 'He might leave later', but the Porter and his humour work best by contrast rather than by coincidence.

LENNOX Good morrow, noble sir.

MACBETH   Good morrow, both.

MACDUFF Is the king stirring, worthy thane?

MACBETH   Not yet.

MACDUFF He did command me to call timely on him;
          I have almost slipped the hour.

MACBETH   I'll bring you to him.   40

MACDUFF I know this is a joyful trouble to you, but yet 'tis one.

MACBETH The labour we delight in physics pain. This is the door.

MACDUFF I'll make so bold to call, for 'tis my limited service. *Exit*

LENNOX Goes the king hence today?

MACBETH He does – he did appoint so.   45

LENNOX The night has been unruly: where we lay,
          Our chimneys were blown down, and, as they say,
          Lamentings heard i'th'air, strange screams of death
          And prophesying with accents terrible
          Of dire combustion and confused events,   50

---

43 SD] F (*Exit Macduffe.*)

38 stirring The repetition of 35 sounds awkward unless (or until) it activates the metaphoric identity of sleep (from which Macbeth is supposedly awakened) and death (from which Duncan will never stir). Compare 70.

38 Not yet This phrase 'implies that he [Duncan] will [stir] by and by, and is a kind of guard against any suspicion' (Whately, p. 34). Macbeth might have answered 'No', and 'Not yet' also means 'No longer'; see p. 48 above.

39 timely early. For the dramatic use of Macduff here, see Textual Analysis, pp. 276–7 below.

40 slipped failed in keeping (the appointed time). See *OED* Slip v^1 20c, quoting only this line and another from 1707.

41–3 Unlike F, editors often arrange these exchanges as verse; like other episodes involving short exchanges and action, this one contains stretches of iambic rhythms (e.g. 42), but even a loose iambic pentameter does not extend through the passage.

41 joyful trouble The oxymoron recalls 1.6.11–12.

42 The labour . . . pain Effort we enjoy alleviates suffering. The same idea appears in *Cym.* 3.2.34, *Temp.* 3.1.1–2, and 'What we do willingly is easy' (Dent D407).

43 limited appointed (Muir).

44 Goes . . . hence See 1.5.57 n.

45 He does . . . appoint so For the same equivocation, see 'as he purposes' (1.5.58).

45 appoint order; purpose.

48–9 Lamentings . . . screams . . . accents These sounds are not articulate speech, but inchoate, ominous sounds (like the 'obscure bird's' clamour) that people interpret ('they say') as 'prophesying' (47, 49), just as Macbeth (mis)interpreted the sisters' words in 1.3.

48 screams shrill, piercing cries. This line is the earliest citation for this meaning under *OED* Scream *sb* a (the next citation is from 1708), so the earliest audiences may have understood the sounds more specifically as the 'cries of certain birds and beasts' (*OED* Scream *sb* b, where the earliest citation is from 1513). See Textual Analysis, p. 264 below.

49 prophesying uttering strange things; announcing solemnly (White subst., citing 'And he saide unto me, Prophecie thou upon these bones, & speake unto them: Ye drye bones, heare the worde of the Lorde' (Ezek. 37.4)). The word only equivocally means 'foretelling' since the 'combustions' and 'events' are already 'hatched'.

50 dire combustion dreadful commotion; terrifying disorder.

50 events outcomes, consequences (*OED* Event 3a). Certain causes are 'New hatched' (51) and will mature into 'events' in on-rushing 'time'. The metaphor of hatching (a bird's birth) anticipates 51–2, but the birth of events-in-time recalls Macbeth's soliloquy (1.7.4–5).

New hatched to th'woeful time. The obscure bird
Clamoured the livelong night. Some say, the earth
Was feverous and did shake.
MACBETH   'Twas a rough night.
LENNOX My young remembrance cannot parallel
A fellow to it.   55

Enter MACDUFF

MACDUFF O horror, horror, horror,
Tongue nor heart cannot conceive, nor name thee.
MACBETH *and* LENNOX What's the matter?
MACDUFF Confusion now hath made his masterpiece:
Most sacrilegious murder hath broke ope   60
The Lord's anointed temple and stole thence
The life o'th'building.
MACBETH What is't you say, the life?
LENNOX Mean you his majesty?
MACDUFF Approach the chamber and destroy your sight   65
With a new Gorgon. Do not bid me speak:
See and then speak yourselves.

                                                    Exeunt Macbeth and Lennox
                                        Awake, awake!
            Ring the alarum bell! Murder and treason!

51 time.] F; time: *Theobald*   67 SD *Exeunt . . . Lennox*] *Staunton* (*subst.*); *after* awake! F

51 obscure bird The owl (which is 'obscure' because rarely seen and usually heard only at night).

52 livelong very long.

53 feverous feverish, shaking with fever (a personification). The earth was not 'sure and firm-set' (2.1.56).

53 rough stormy. Macbeth is laconic.

57 The tongue names and the heart conceives, but the rhetorical figure (antimetabole) reorders the grammar: tongue–heart–conceives–names.

59 masterpiece greatest achievement (earliest citation at *OED* Masterpiece 1b).

60 sacrilegious violating sacred things (*Lexicon*); profaning. Sacrilege is specifically the crime of stealing from the church (see 61–2).

60 ope open. The archaic form is needed for the metre.

61 Lord's anointed temple house of worship; Duncan's cranium ('temple') or body (see 'building' (62 and n.)). The Christian New Testament treats all believers as the 'temple' (sanctuary, church, synagogue) of God (1 Cor. 3.16), and bibli-

cal kings, like English ones, were 'anointed' at their coronations; see e.g. David to Saul: 'I had compassion on thee, and sayd: I will not lay myne handes on my maister, for he is the Lordes annoynted' (1 Sam. 24.10). Compare Banquo's proleptic remark on the 'temple-haunting martlet' (1.6.4).

62–4 Macbeth's line (63) might be linked metrically with the one before (Cam.), or Lennox and Macbeth might speak simultaneously (Muir).

62 life o'th'building 'The ark of the covenant in the Holy of Holies can be aptly described as "the life o'th'building"' (Shaheen, p. 164).

62 building body (compare: 'the bloody house of life' (*John* 4.2.210) and 'this mortal house I'll ruin' (*Ant.* 5.2.51)); house of worship (= 'temple' (61)).

66 Gorgon Mythical female being with snakes for hair and the power to turn whoever looked upon her to stone. For 'Duncan's androgyny', perhaps evoked here, see Adelman, pp. 131–3.

68 Ring the alarum bell This bell echoes the bell (or 'knell') summoning Macbeth and Duncan to heaven or to hell (2.1.63–4).

Banquo and Donaldbain! Malcolm, awake,
Shake off this downy sleep, death's counterfeit,   70
And look on death itself. Up, up, and see
The great doom's image. Malcolm, Banquo,
As from your graves rise up and walk like sprites
To countenance this horror.

Bell rings. Enter LADY [MACBETH]

LADY MACBETH   What's the business
That such a hideous trumpet calls to parley   75
The sleepers of the house? Speak, speak.
MACDUFF   O gentle lady,
'Tis not for you to hear what I can speak.
The repetition in a woman's ear
Would murder as it fell. –

Enter BANQUO

O Banquo, Banquo,

---

73 sprites] F (Sprights)   74 horror.] *This edn* (*Theobald subst.*) horror. Ring the Bell. F. *See Supplementary Note, p. 257 below*   74 business] F (Businesse?)   79 fell. –] *Theobald;* fell. F

70 downy soft (a transferred adjective). The best pillows were stuffed with 'down', the fine under-plumage of a bird.

70 sleep, death's counterfeit The similarity of sleep to death was commonplace. See Cicero, *De Senectute* 80: 'Nihil morti tam simile quam somnus' (Nothing is more like death than sleep), cited by Grey (II, 145) in reference to 2.2.41; 'O sleep, thou ape of death' (*Cym.* 2.2.31); Samuel Daniel's superb poem beginning, 'Care-charmer sleepe, sonne of the Sable night, / Brother to death, in silent dark-nes borne' (Sonnet 45 in *Delia* (1592), sig. G3r); 'Sleep is the image of death' (Dent S527).

72 great doom's image simulacrum ('image') of the Last ('great') Judgement ('doom'). See next note. Duncan's death reminds Macduff of the Christian version of the end of time and of the world; indeed, this moment seems metaphor-ically the end of a world, just as Kent ('Is this the promised end?') and Edgar ('Or image of that horror?') wonder at Lear's lamentation over Cordelia (*Lear* 5.3.264–5). See p. 20 above.

73 from your graves rise up As the dead will do at the Christian Last Judgement: 'I knowe that he shall ryse agayne in the resurrection at the last day' (John 11.24).

73 sprites spirits, ghosts. F's archaic word is needed for the metre.

74 To . . . horror See Supplementary Note, p. 257 below.

74 countenance be in keeping with (*OED* Countenance *v* 6, for which this line is the only evidence). The word also means 'give tacit consent to'. 'By a time-serving assent to Macbeth's elec-tion, Banquo puts himself in a position of danger' (Mahood, p. 131).

75 trumpet Presumably, 'trumpet' is a figure of speech for 'alarum bell' (68), but the word jarringly recalls 1.7.18–19 and probably recalls St Paul's description of the time when 'sleepers' (76), the dead (see 70), will 'rise up' from their 'graves' (73) at the Last Judgement (see 72 and n.): 'Beholde, I shewe you a mistere. We shall not all slepe: but we shall all be chaunged. In a moment, in the twynklyng of an eye, at the last trumpe. For the trumpe shall blowe, and the dead shall ryse incor-ruptible, and we shalbe chaunged' (1 Cor. 15.51–2).

75 parley conference under truce. This military term suggests that some of 'The sleepers of the house' (76) are or will be at war, with themselves and/or with those (Macduff, Lennox) who have entered from outside the castle.

76–9 Macduff's anxiety is repeated by the Mes-senger who warns Lady Macduff (4.2.67–8).

79 fell was spoken; issued (from the speaker's mouth). See *OED* Fall *v* 6.

Our royal master's murdered.

LADY MACBETH   Woe, alas.   80

What, in our house?

BANQUO   Too cruel, anywhere.

Dear Duff, I prithee contradict thyself

And say it is not so.

Enter MACBETH *and* LENNOX

MACBETH Had I but died an hour before this chance,

I had lived a blessèd time, for from this instant,   85

There's nothing serious in mortality.

All is but toys; renown and grace is dead,

The wine of life is drawn, and the mere lees

Is left this vault to brag of.

Enter MALCOLM *and* DONALDBAIN

DONALDBAIN What is amiss?

MACBETH   You are, and do not know't.   90

The spring, the head, the fountain of your blood

Is stopped, the very source of it is stopped.

MACDUFF Your royal father's murdered.

MALCOLM   O, by whom?

LENNOX Those of his chamber, as it seemed, had done't.

Their hands and faces were all badged with blood,   95

So were their daggers which, unwiped, we found

---

83 SD] *Davenant; Enter Macbeth, Lenox, and Rosse* F   90 SH, 114 SH DONALDBAIN] F (*Donal.*)

---

83 SD For the change in F's SD, see Supplementary Note, pp. 257 below.

84–9 A speech 'so much in the language of his soliloquies' (Brooke) that it creates numerous theatrical possibilities: it may be spoken aside, 'covered' in the audience's imagination by simultaneous unheard speeches (compare the situations at 1.3.126–41 and 1.4.47–58); it may be spoken publicly and without deceit; it may be spoken to deceive the hearers on stage, but understood with varying degrees of irony by the audience.

84 chance occurrence, mishap (*OED* Chance *sb* 2). 'Chance' usually connotes an accidental, unforeseen event (see 4.3.136 and n.); Macbeth evades his own responsibility for Duncan's death. Compare 'chanced' (1.3.152).

86 mortality life, human existence.

87 toys trifles, rubbish (*OED* Toy *sb* 5, quoting this line). Compare 'Or sells eternity to get a toy' (*The Rape of Lucrece* 214).

88 drawn drained (from a cask).

88 lees dregs.

89 vault earth (with the sky as 'roof'); cellar (where a wine cask would be stored).

89 brag boast.

91 spring Thomas More provides the traditional metaphorical context: 'From the monarch, as from a never-failing spring, flows a stream of all that is good or evil over the whole nation' (*Utopia*, p. 57).

91 head source (of a stream or river); senior male family member.

91 blood family, kindred.

92 stopped blocked, stopped up. Compare Lady Macbeth's prayer (1.5.41–5).

95 badged marked, identified. Liveried servants wore heraldic emblems (badges): these retainers have a new badge, blood, to mark them as Duncan's men. See the clothing images – 'laced', 'steeped', 'breeched' – of 105–9.

Upon their pillows. They stared and were distracted;
No man's life was to be trusted with them.

MACBETH O, yet I do repent me of my fury
That I did kill them.

MACDUFF   Wherefore did you so?   100

MACBETH Who can be wise, amazed, temp'rate, and furious,
Loyal and neutral, in a moment? No man.
Th'expedition of my violent love
Outran the pauser, reason. Here lay Duncan,
His silver skin laced with his golden blood   105
And his gashed stabs looked like a breach in nature,
For ruin's wasteful entrance. There the murderers,
Steeped in the colours of their trade; their daggers
Unmannerly breeched with gore. Who could refrain,
That had a heart to love and in that heart   110
Courage to make's love known?

LADY MACBETH   Help me hence, ho.

---

100 them.] F; them – *Rowe*   104 Outran] F (Out-run)   109 Unmannerly] F (Vnmannerly); Unmanly *Travers*

97 distracted mentally confused.

99–100 A delayed and shocking announcement, since Macbeth has been on stage for almost twenty lines. Rowe's punctuation indicates that Macduff interrupts Macbeth's speech.

100 Wherefore Why.

101 temp'rate temperate, restrained. This contraction and others (e.g. 'amaz'd') are needed for the metre.

102 Loyal and neutral Maintaining allegiance (to Duncan) and disinterested (toward the grooms' apparent guilt).

102 No man No one. The language recalls 1.7.46–7.

103 expedition haste, speed. Compare 'the speed of his rage' (*Lear* 1.2.167).

103 violent love A self-contradictory phrase; compare 42 n., 1.2.10 n., 1.6.11–13.

104 Outran Contrary to many editors' claims, F's 'Out-run' is an archaic past tense; see *OED* Run v A. 14 for the form.

104 pauser one who hesitates (here, for rational reflection). This line is *OED*'s only citation for the word (Schäfer).

105 silver white. See next note.

105 golden red (see 2.2.59 n.). Imagery of rich metals (silver and gold) transforms Duncan's body into a decorated 'temple' (61), or a garment 'laced' with golden threads and streams of blood.

106–7 breach . . . entrance The underlying image is of an opening or break ('breach') in a shore or dike, letting in ruinous (sea)water, or of attacking troops breaking into a castle or walled city: some injurious force overcomes cultivation's or civilisation's boundaries. This complex image represents Duncan's body as a devastated landscape, as Macbeth's violated castle, and as the violated bonds of loyalty and hospitality. Compare Banquo's wounds (3.4.27–8).

106 breach opening, gap. The word's sound anticipates 'breeched' (109).

108 Steeped Dyed. See 'Thence comes it that my name receives a brand, / And almost thence my nature is subdued / To what it works in, like the dyer's hand' (Sonnet 111.5–7).

108 colours of their trade identifying marks of their occupation.

109 Unmannerly breeched Indecently clothed (NS). The image makes the daggers humans wearing impolite or antisocial breeches (trousers) of blood, but also puns on 'unmanly': to dress these daggers in Duncan's blood is to act inhumanly, to act as a man 'Who . . . is none' (1.7.47). Compare 'breach in nature' (106). A single suspended mark of abbreviation differentiated 'Unmannerly' and 'Unmanly' in contemporary handwriting, and they are easily confused.

111 make's make his.

MACDUFF Look to the lady.

                              [*Exit Lady Macbeth, helped*]

MALCOLM [*To Donaldbain*] Why do we hold our tongues, that most
         may claim
      This argument for ours?

DONALDBAIN [*To Malcolm*]   What should be spoken here,
      Where our fate hid in an auger hole may rush   115
      And seize us? Let's away. Our tears are not yet brewed.

MALCOLM [*To Donaldbain*] Nor our strong sorrow upon the foot of
         motion.

BANQUO Look to the lady,
      And when we have our naked frailties hid
      That suffer in exposure, let us meet   120
      And question this most bloody piece of work
      To know it further. Fears and scruples shake us:
      In the great hand of God I stand and thence
      Against the undivulged pretence I fight
      Of treasonous malice.

MACDUFF   And so do I.

ALL   So all.   125

MACBETH Let's briefly put on manly readiness

112 SD *Exit . . . helped*] Brooke (*after 118*); not in F; *Lady Macbeth is carried out* / Rowe (*after 118*)   113 SD,
114 SD,   117 SD] Brooke (*subst.*); not in F

112 Traditionally, Lady Macbeth faints here, and critics have long debated (see Bradley, Note DD, pp. 394–5) whether her collapse is real or feigned (Rowe's SD is *Seeming to faint*). A feigned faint would be hard to convey, though Adelaide Ristori apparently did so 'after what must have been an extraordinary piece of silent acting' (Sprague, p. 247), and obvious deceit risks inappropriate laughter. Citing contemporary exorcism-lore, Hughes (p. 110) suggests that Lady Macbeth is here dispossessed of the demonic powers she invoked in 1.5. Whatever her action, she fails to perform the part she promised (1.7.78–9).
112 SD Should Lady Macbeth exit here or, more traditionally, at 118? I suppose that the Malcolm–Donaldbain conversation, spoken aside, 'covers' the action of helping Lady Macbeth off-stage (see preceding note and Textual Analysis, p. 275 below, n. 4).
113–17 **Why do we . . . foot of motion** These lines probably include a revision of an earlier version of this scene; see Textual Analysis, pp. 275–7 below.
113–14 Why do we remain silent when we may most claim this subject (= 'argument' = Duncan's death) as our own. The question draws attention both to the brothers' silence and to the grandiloquence of what *is* being said.

115 **hid in an auger hole** i.e. concealed in a (figurative) space no larger than a hole or 'auger's bore' (*Cor.* 4.6.87) made by a drill ('auger'). Without knowing the source of danger, Donaldbain fears that he and his brother will attract the attention of their father's murderer. Scot (1, 4) notes the popular belief that witches 'can go in and out at auger holes'.
116 **brewed** brought to readiness. The metaphor anticipates the witches' cookery (4.1.4–38).
117 **upon the foot of motion** ready to move; ready to be revealed.
119 **naked frailties** physical weaknesses (e.g. their near-undress); exposed psychological weaknesses. See 126 and n.
121 **question** debate; investigate.
122 **scruples** doubts.
123 **hand of God** power of God (Upton, pp. 221–2, citing 'Let us deliver / Our puissance into the hand of God' (*H5* 2.2.189–90)).
124 **undivulged pretence** unrevealed purpose (or intention); unexpressed claim (to the crown). The latter meaning would be appropriate to Malcolm, Prince of Cumberland (1.4.38–9) and declared heir to the Scottish throne.
126 **briefly** quickly.
126 **put on manly readiness** get into our usual

	And meet i'th'hall together.
ALL	Well contented.

Exeunt [all but Malcolm and Donaldbain]

MALCOLM What will you do? Let's not consort with them.
To show an unfelt sorrow is an office
Which the false man does easy. I'll to England.   130
DONALDBAIN To Ireland, I. Our separated fortune
Shall keep us both the safer. Where we are,
There's daggers in men's smiles; the nea'er in blood,
The nearer bloody.
MALCOLM   This murderous shaft that's shot
Hath not yet lighted, and our safest way   135
Is to avoid the aim. Therefore to horse,
And let us not be dainty of leave-taking,
But shift away. There's warrant in that theft
Which steals itself when there's no mercy left.

Exeunt

2.4 *Enter* ROSS, *with an* OLD MAN

OLD MAN Threescore and ten I can remember well;

127 SD] *Hanmer (subst.); Exeunt.* F   **133–4** nea'er . . . nearer] F (neere . . . neerer)   **Act 2, Scene 4   2.4**] F (*Scena Quarta.*); Scene II. *Rowe*

or customary garments. Macbeth draws attention to his pretended unpreparedness (see 2.2.73–4). The phrase suggests that the observers have been unmanned, weakened, by Duncan's death and recalls the chamberlains' daggers 'Unmannerly breeched with gore' (109).

128 'Malcolm and Donaldbain suspect everyone' (Foakes).

128 consort keep company, associate. The verb is a late-sixteenth-century development from the noun, one of whose prominent meanings was 'spouse'; hence there may be an underlying link to marriage, procreation, and the sons, not his, who will succeed Macbeth.

129–30 The sentiment fits Macbeth (see 101–11) and, perhaps, Duncan's sons themselves.

130 easy easily. See Abbott 467, arguing that metre explains the substitution.

133–4 The more closely one is related to Duncan, the more likely one is to be killed. Compare 90–2.

134–5 This . . . lighted The murderous design that killed Duncan is not yet finished.

135 lighted landed.

137 dainty particular, scrupulous about (*OED* Dainty *a* 5b).

138–9 A weak couplet, sapped further by the quibble on 'steals'; NS compares the same word-

play on 'theft'/'steal' at *AWW* 2.1.33–4.

138 shift get away unobserved, evade (*OED* Shift *v* 22a). Compare 34 n.

138 warrant sanction, authorisation (*OED* Warrant *sb*[1] 7a). The word is a further pun: a warrant was also a legal document authorising the arrest of a wrong–doer (e.g. Malcolm and Donaldbain as 'thieves' of themselves); see *OED* Warrant *sb*[1] 10.

139 steals A pun: takes unlawfully; sneaks.

Act 2, Scene 4
This scene occurs some time after 2.3 and is choric commentary (like the gardeners' scene, *R2* 3.4) as well as exposition (Duncan to be buried, Macbeth to be crowned; the Old Man – not further identified – has a powerful allegorical and at the same time commonplace effect, like his namesake in Marlowe's *Faustus* 5.1, lines 1707–38. The scene's location is uncertain; it may be outside a building, or within a public area of Macbeth's castle where Macduff might pass as he departs for Fife (36). Many productions cut this scene; when they do not, it is often combined with a pantomime of Duncan's catafalque or other action indicating burial ceremonies.

1 Threescore and ten Seventy (three times a 'score', twenty, plus ten), the biblical limit of human life (Ps. 90.10).

Within the volume of which time, I have seen
Hours dreadful and things strange, but this sore night
Hath trifled former knowings.

ROSS   Ha, good father,
Thou seest the heavens, as troubled with man's act,   5
Threatens his bloody stage. By th'clock 'tis day
And yet dark night strangles the travelling lamp.
Is't night's predominance, or the day's shame,
That darkness does the face of earth entomb
When living light should kiss it?

OLD MAN   'Tis unnatural,   10
Even like the deed that's done. On Tuesday last,
A falcon tow'ring in her pride of place
Was by a mousing owl hawked at and killed.

ROSS   And Duncan's horses, a thing most strange and certain,
Beauteous and swift, the minions of their race,   15
Turned wild in nature, broke their stalls, flung out,
Contending 'gainst obedience as they would
Make war with mankind.

OLD MAN   'Tis said, they eat each other.

---

4 trifled] F; stifled Q*1673*   7 travelling] F (trauailing)   12 tow'ring] F (towring)

3 sore severe, harsh (*OED* Sore a^1 5b).

4 trifled made trivial (the sole example at *OED* Trifle v^1 6).

4 father Honorific title for an elderly man.

5–10 Ross speaks a cautious allegory, testing the Old Man's political sympathies; the imagery of light and dark (good and evil, justice and murder) recalls 1.4.50–3, 1.5.48–52, and 2.1.49–51, and anticipates images to come.

5 act deed; principal division of a play. Compare 'stage' (6).

6 Threatens Singular verb in *-s* with plural subject (Abbott 333).

7 travelling lamp journeying light (a periphrasis for 'sun'). See pp. 38–9 above.

8 predominance superior influence (probably with an astrological connotation). Compare 'we make guilty of our disasters the . . . stars, as if we were . . . knaves, thieves, and treachers [traitors] by spherical predominance' (*Lear* 1.2.120–4); *OED* quotes 'starres predominance' from 1615.

8 shame i.e. embarrassment at 'man's act' (5), the murder of Duncan.

10–20 For Holinshed's version of these 'unnatural' events, see p. 14 above.

11 deed that's done Duncan's murder. Duncan's name is echoed in 'done'.

12 tow'ring soaring. Syncopation preserves the metre.

12 pride of place 'proud place, place in which he [the falcon] visibly prides himself' (Capell, *Notes*, p. 14).

12 place height (or 'pitch') from which the falcon attacks; perhaps 'the air' (Capell, *Notes*, p. 14).

13 mousing owl owl that preys on mice (hence it ordinarily swoops to the earth rather than fighting another bird in the air). This line is the earliest citation at *OED* Mousing *ppl a* (Schäfer).

13 hawked at attacked on the wing (earliest citation for *OED* Hawk v^1 3).

15 minions darlings, most prized specimens. See 1.2.19n.

15–18 Beauteous . . . mankind The underlying assumption here is that horses are naturally subordinate to 'mankind', and the possibility that horses might abandon 'obedience', their training by humans, images a breakdown in nature's order. This collapse extends even to the horses' own natural order: they attack and eat each other. Compare 28–9n. and the parallel between an unruly horse and disordered human passions at *TNK* 5.4.65–91. For horse and owl (13), see p. 14 above.

17 as as if (Abbott 107; see 1.4.11 n.).

18 eat ate. F's 'eat' is pronounced 'et'.

ROSS They did so, to th'amazement of mine eyes
      That looked upon't.

                    Enter MACDUFF

                    Here comes the good Macduff.   20
            How goes the world, sir, now?
MACDUFF   Why, see you not?
ROSS Is't known who did this more than bloody deed?
MACDUFF Those that Macbeth hath slain.
ROSS   Alas the day,
            What good could they pretend?
MACDUFF   They were suborned.
            Malcolm and Donaldbain, the king's two sons,   25
            Are stol'n away and fled, which puts upon them
            Suspicion of the deed.
ROSS   'Gainst nature still.
            Thriftless ambition that will ravin up
            Thine own life's means. Then 'tis most like
            The sovereignty will fall upon Macbeth.   30
MACDUFF He is already named and gone to Scone
            To be invested.

21 Why,] *Pope;* Why F   28 ravin] F (rauen)   29 life's] F (liues)

19–20 They…upon't Like a traveller confirming strange tales, Ross assures the Old Man he has personally witnessed the bizarre episodes of 14–18.

20 SD For the placing of this SD, see Textual Analysis, pp. 262–3 below. The actor was probably costumed in a way that indicated his intention to travel (see 3.1.0 SD n.).

20 good Macduff The first time Macduff receives a positive moral designation.

21 How goes the world What is the state of affairs. A proverbial phrase (Dent w884.1).

21 Why…not? Pope's persuasive repunctuation makes Macduff's question no reply – a cautious man tests his questioner (see 5–10 n.) – but F's line represents an angry speaker unable to control his dangerous honesty.

24 pretend allege as a reason (*OED* Pretend *v* 6). See 2.3.124 n.

24 suborned bribed; instigated to betray a trust.

26 puts upon See 1.7.70 n.

27 'Gainst nature still i.e. like the self-devouring horses and other unnatural events he has just listed.

28–9 Thriftless…means Ambition, the desire to acquire, is paradoxically spendthrift and self-consuming when it leads sons to kill their father, source of their own lives (a subtle analogy with the self-devouring horses that betray mankind's gift of training – similar to a father's bringing-up of his sons – and revert to savagery). The education of sons and the training of horses are made parallel at *AYLI* 1.1.5–16.

28 Thriftless Prodigal.

28 ravin up consume, eat greedily.

29 means resources.

29–30 Then…Macbeth The common assumption is that Macbeth will be king if Duncan's sons are not available.

29 like likely.

31 named chosen.

31 Scone Ancient, now ruinous, city north of Perth and traditional site of Scottish coronations, though James VI was crowned at Stirling. See the map, p. 110 above, and 5.9.42, where Malcolm repeats Macbeth's action.

32 invested installed ceremonially (as king); clothed with royal insignia (see *OED* Invest *v* 4–5). See 1.4.40 and n., and 3.1, headnote.

ROSS   Where is Duncan's body?
MACDUFF   Carried to Colmkill,
   The sacred storehouse of his predecessors
   And guardian of their bones.
ROSS   Will you to Scone?   35
MACDUFF   No, cousin, I'll to Fife.
ROSS   Well, I will thither.
MACDUFF   Well may you see things well done there. Adieu,
   Lest our old robes sit easier than our new.
ROSS   Farewell, father.
OLD MAN   God's benison go with you, and with those   40
   That would make good of bad, and friends of foes.
                            Exeunt

3.1 *Enter* BANQUO [*dressed for riding*]

BANQUO   Thou hast it now, King, Cawdor, Glamis, all,
   As the weïrd women promised, and I fear
   Thou played'st most foully for't; yet it was said

---

33 Colmkill] F (*Colmekill*)   37 Well] F; Well, *Theobald*   41 SD] F (*Exeunt omnes*)   Act 3, Scene 1   3.1] F (*Actus Tertius. Scena Prima.*)   0 SD *dressed for riding*] *This edn; not in* F   2 weird] *Theobald*; weyard F

33 **Colmkill** The island of Iona, one of the western Hebrides (Sugden). Here the ancient graves of many Scottish kings may still be seen. See the map, p. 110 above.

36 **Fife** Ancestral land of Macduff, Thane of Fife; see the map, p. 110 above, and 1.2.48 n.

36 **I will thither** I will go there.

37 **Well . . . well** Ironical repetition of Ross's 'well' (Muir). Theobald's punctuation makes the line social commonplace rather than ominous foreboding.

37–8 **Adieu . . . new** Farewell (we must part), for fear that ('lest') the future ('new' robes of rank or office) will be less comfortable than the past ('our old robes'). These lines elaborate and recall 1.3.106–7 and 143–5; they anticipate 5.2.21–2. Compare the new King Henry V's remark: 'This new and gorgeous garment, majesty, / Sits not so easy on me as you think' (*2H4* 5.2.44–5).

40–1 Compare 'Make your enemy your friend' (Dent E140.1).

40 **benison** blessing.

Act 3, Scene 1
The setting is a formal chamber of Macbeth's castle, where Banquo awaits permission to leave.

This space allows a royal entry as well as the conspiratorial conversations of Macbeth and the murderers, who are ordered to some yet more private waiting-area (139). Many productions (e.g. Stratford, 1974) add a dumbshow of Macbeth's coronation here.

0 SD **dressed for riding** Macbeth later infers (19) Banquo's plans, apparently from his garb. Boots, spurs, or whips ('riding-rods') were common props indicating that a character had recently ridden or would soon ride a horse; see Dessen, p. 39. In many productions from Kemble's in the eighteenth century at least until Byam Shaw's (Stratford, 1955), Fleance also entered here, for various actorly and sentimental effects; see p. 70 above.

1–10 This ambiguous speech may mean that Banquo, seeing Macbeth's success and the fulfilment of the sisters' prophecies, passively colludes in Duncan's murder and now considers some criminal action. According to *Scotland*, p. 171a, Banquo was 'the chiefest' among Macbeth's 'trustie friends' who aided him in Duncan's murder; critics have found Banquo guilty here (see p. 7 above, n. 2).

2–3 **fear . . . foully** A punning antithesis between 'fair' and 'foully'; see 1.3.49–50 n.

3 **played'st** Compare 1.5.19 n.

It should not stand in thy posterity,
But that myself should be the root and father   5
Of many kings. If there come truth from them –
As upon thee, Macbeth, their speeches shine –
Why by the verities on thee made good,
May they not be my oracles as well
And set me up in hope? But hush, no more.   10

Sennet sounded. Enter MACBETH *as* King, LADY [MACBETH *as* Queen],
        LENNOX, ROSS, *Lords, and Attendants*

MACBETH Here's our chief guest.
LADY MACBETH   If he had been forgotten,
    It had been as a gap in our great feast
    And all thing unbecoming.
MACBETH Tonight we hold a solemn supper, sir,
    And I'll request your presence.
BANQUO   Let your highness   15
    Command upon me, to the which my duties
    Are with a most indissoluble tie
    Forever knit.
MACBETH Ride you this afternoon?
BANQUO Ay, my good lord.   20
MACBETH We should have else desired your good advice
    Which still hath been both grave and prosperous

8 Why] F; Who Q1673   10 hope?] F4; hope. F   10 SD.1–2 LADY MACBETH *as* Queen, LENNOX] *Staunton; Lady Lenox* F; *Lady Macbeth, Lenox / Rowe*

4 stand in thy posterity continue, or remain, in those who descend from you.

5–6 father / Of many kings Banquo's descendants included King James, according to popular legend. See illustration 1, p. 3 above.

7 shine look favourably upon (*OED* Shine *v* 1d).

8 made good rendered fact (i.e. the sisters' prophecies fulfilled); see *OED* Make *v*[1] 48.

10 SD *Sennet* Distinctive set of musical notes played on trumpet or cornet and associated with a specific individual.

10 SD *as King* Macbeth's new status would have been conveyed through costume and perhaps props (crown and sceptre might be useful at 62–3) or a throne (for the actor to indicate at 49–50). A contemporary prop-list (Henslowe, pp. 319–21) includes a variety of royal paraphernalia.

13 all thing wholly, completely (*OED* All *adv* 2b); 'everything' (*OED* Allthing).

14 supper evening meal.

16 Command upon me i.e. I am at your dis-

posal. Compare 'thou that hast / Upon the winds command' (*Per.* 3.1.2–3). Banquo substitutes 'command' for 'request' (15); see next note.

17–18 Banquo emphasises his loyalty, perhaps to remind Macbeth of their shared knowledge (i.e. the speech is subtle blackmail), or to reassure Macbeth he has nothing to fear.

19 Ride you this afternoon? Macbeth makes a conventional assumption; see 0 SD n. Following Macbeth's 'I'll request your presence' (15), this question, no matter how casually phrased, indicates his great interest in Banquo's thoughts and plans.

21–3 As at the beginning of Act 2, Macbeth seeks to talk with Banquo; couched as friendly respect, the attention signals Macbeth's interest in, perhaps suspicion of, the other man who met the sisters. 'We' (21) and 'we'll' (23) may be the royal plural or may = the new king and queen.

22 still always.

22 grave serious, important.

22 prosperous successful, fortunate (*Lexicon*).

In this day's council: but we'll take tomorrow.
Is't far you ride?
BANQUO As far, my lord, as will fill up the time   25
'Twixt this and supper. Go not my horse the better,
I must become a borrower of the night
For a dark hour, or twain.
MACBETH Fail not our feast.
BANQUO My lord, I will not.   30
MACBETH We hear our bloody cousins are bestowed
In England and in Ireland, not confessing
Their cruel parricide, filling their hearers
With strange invention. But of that tomorrow,
When therewithal we shall have cause of state   35
Craving us jointly. Hie you to horse; adieu,
Till you return at night. Goes Fleance with you?
BANQUO Ay, my good lord; our time does call upon's.
MACBETH I wish your horses swift and sure of foot,
And so I do commend you to their backs.   40
Farewell.

Exit Banquo

Let every man be master of his time
Till seven at night; to make society
The sweeter welcome, we will keep ourself
Till supper-time alone. While then, God be with you.   45
Exeunt [all but Macbeth and a Servant]

23 take] F; talk *Malone*   43–4 night; . . . welcome,] *Theobald;* Night, . . . welcome: F   45 SD] *Cam. (subst.); Exeunt
Lords.* F

23 **council** Early audiences would probably understand 'Privy Council', the senior officers of state and aristocrats who advised the monarch and directed the day-to-day business of early Stuart government.
23 **take tomorrow** i.e. command your attendance tomorrow (and delay our business from today). Compare 'avail oneself of' (*OED* Take *v* 24). *Textual Companion* (p. 545) defends Malone's emendation, citing the reverse error ('talk' for 'take') in *Hamlet* Q2 and F and *H5* Q and F.
26 **this** i.e. this time, now.
26 **Go . . . the better** If my horse does not go better (i.e. 'fast enough').
28 **twain** two.
34 **strange invention** improbable or outlandish fiction, i.e. accounts of Duncan's death different from Macbeth's version.

35 **therewithal** with it (*Lexicon*).
35 **cause of state** political affair requiring a decision; see *OED* Cause *sb* 8c.
36 **Craving us jointly** Requiring us both together.
42 **master of his time** responsible for his own activities. See p. 23 above.
43–4 F is repunctuated here because 'it is solitude which gives a zest to society, not being master of one's time' (Clarendon, following Theobald).
44 The slightly unusual word-order emphasises the royal plural.
45 For production decisions here, see Appendix 1, p. 282 below.
45 **While** Until (*OED* While *conj, prep* 3b). 'While then' is a Scotticism (Travers) and current in Yorkshire dialect (B. C. Gibbons, private communication).

Sirrah, a word with you: attend those men
Our pleasure?
SERVANT They are, my lord, without the palace gate.
MACBETH Bring them before us.

Exit Servant

To be thus is nothing,
But to be safely thus. Our fears in Banquo   50
Stick deep, and in his royalty of nature
Reigns that which would be feared. 'Tis much he dares,
And to that dauntless temper of his mind,
He hath a wisdom that doth guide his valour
To act in safety. There is none but he,   55
Whose being I do fear; and under him
My genius is rebuked, as it is said

---

46 Sirrah Slighting form of address by social superior to inferior.

46 those men The casual reference suggests that both Macbeth and the servant are familiar with the 'men' and the secrecy needed in meeting them.

48 palace gate The specificity indicates the physical distance Macbeth wishes to keep between himself and his instruments.

49–50 To be . . . safely thus To be king is nothing unless to be safely one (Staunton). The repeated 'thus' urges the actor to some gesture (e.g. indicating the royal trappings, or the throne if there is one).

50–1 Our . . . deep A complex clause with an intransitive and a transitive meaning: 'fears' of Banquo's quality and prophesied future penetrate and adhere (= 'stick') in Macbeth, but as this speech and the remainder of the scene show, those fears will now, or soon, become active and 'stick' (= penetrate, remain fixed) in Banquo (i.e. the whole clause also means 'Our fears stick deep in Banquo'). See *OED* Stick v^1, 4, and *OED* In *prep* 25.

51 royalty of nature royal nature. The phrase is both emphatic praise and an allusion to Banquo's royal progeny predicted by the sisters in 1.3.

52–5 'Tis . . . safety Macbeth, admiring Banquo's circumspect bravery, anticipates a *coup d'état* (see 1–10 n.); the praise echoes 2.3.101–11, where Macbeth claims he could not combine wisdom and valour, 'reason' and 'violent love' (2.3.103–4).

52 dares Compare 1.7.46–7.

53 to in addition to.

53 dauntless fearless, intrepid (*OED*'s earliest

citation for the word is *3H6* 3.3.17).

53 temper temperament, mental constitution. Compare 'A noble temper dost thou show' (*John* 5.2.40).

54–5 He . . . safety Macbeth fears and envies Banquo's behaviour as an alternative to his own murderous response to the sisters' prediction: has Banquo awaited time's evolution as Macbeth thinks he himself should have? Compare 1.3.142–3.

56 being existence; psychological and physical attributes.

57–8 My . . . Caesar Macbeth compares himself to the Roman general and triumvir Mark Antony, who was defeated in the civil wars that ended the Roman republic and inaugurated the Roman empire, and compares Banquo to the historical Octavian (Shakespeare's Octavius), later called 'Caesar' (58) Augustus, the victor in those wars. Shakespeare devoted *JC* and *Ant.* to these events; in the latter play, a Soothsayer warns Antony: 'Thy daemon, that thy spirit which keeps thee, is / Noble, courageous, high unmatchable, / Where Caesar's [= Octavius's and = Banquo's in Macbeth's speech] is not; but near him, thy angel / Becomes a fear, as being o'erpower'd' (*Ant.* 2.3.20–3).

57 genius tutelary spirit. Classical belief held that every individual had a personal spirit (for good or ill), variously named or translated as 'genius', 'daemon', or 'angel' (see quotation from *Ant.* in 57–8n.). This word reinvokes the Porter's speeches in 2.3; see Allen for the complex Greek and Roman meanings.

Mark Antony's was by Caesar. He chid the sisters
When first they put the name of king upon me
And bade them speak to him. Then prophet-like,   60
They hailed him father to a line of kings.
Upon my head they placed a fruitless crown
And put a barren sceptre in my gripe,
Thence to be wrenched with an unlineal hand,
No son of mine succeeding. If't be so,   65
For Banquo's issue have I filed my mind;
For them, the gracious Duncan have I murdered,
Put rancours in the vessel of my peace
Only for them, and mine eternal jewel
Given to the common enemy of man,   70
To make them kings, the seeds of Banquo kings.

---

58 Antony's] F (*Anthonies*)   58 Caesar] F (*Caesar*); *Cesars* / Q*1673*   66 filed] F (fil'd); fill'd Q*1673*, F3–4   71 seeds]
F (Seedes); seed *Pope*

---

58 Caesar Caesar Augustus, first Roman
emperor. Q1673's '*Cesars*' (= Caesar's), repeated in
Davenant, Hanmer, and Dyce[2], corrects the grammar technically and more closely parallels a passage
in *Ant.* (see 57–8n.).
58 He chid See 1.3.50–9.
59 put . . . upon See 1.7.70 n.
60–1 prophet-like, / They hailed See 1.3.46,
1.5.6, 1.5.53. 'Prophet-like' suggests a biblical allusion, but 'hail' appears only in the Christian New
Testament, addressed four times to Jesus (by Judas
and the mocking soldiers at Calvary), once to Mary
at the Annunciation, and once (by Jesus) to the
disciples; see Matt. 26.49, 27.29, Mark 15.18, John
19.3, Luke 1.28, and Matt. 28.9, respectively. For
Shakespeare's association of 'hail' and 'all hail' with
betrayal, see 1.3.46 n.
62–5 Upon . . . succeeding Schanzer (pp. 224–
5) notices that this prophecy is in *Scotland*, but not
mentioned in 1.3, where it would have negated the
mystery of the sisters' equivocation.
62–3 fruitless crown . . . barren sceptre
Recalling the sisters' predictions (see 58), Macbeth
laments that he has no children to inherit his crown
(it is childless = 'fruitless' (62)) and his 'sceptre',
the ceremonial rod of office and figuratively his
penis (understood as the source of a 'son of mine'
(65)), is 'barren' (63), without an heir. Seeking to
rationalise the play's dialogue, critics have endlessly
worried over whether the Macbeths have (or have
had) children (compare 1.7.54–9 and p. 17 above,
n. 1). What matters here is neither numbers nor
family history but Macbeth's ambition and mental

anguish.
63 gripe grip, grasp.
64 unlineal not in a direct line of descent.
66 issue progeny, descendants.
66 filed tainted, polluted (*OED* File *v*[2] 3),
defiled. Travers regards the word as a Scotticism.
68 rancours malignant hatreds, bitter ill-
feelings (*OED* Rancour *sb* 1); 'acids or sours'
(Capell, *Notes*, p. 15).
68 vessel of my peace Compare 1.7.11–12,
where Macbeth anticipates drinking the 'poisoned
chalice' of murdering Duncan, and 'I have drunk,
and seen the spider' (*WT* 2.1.45). The language
seems biblical, and editors have cited Ps. 11.6,
Isa. 51.17, and Rom. 9.22–3, but none of those
texts seems particularly relevant, though the last
includes 'vessel of wrath' and 'vessel of peace' in a
very different context. Geneva glosses 'cup of his
wrath' (Isa. 51.17) as 'this punishment in the elect
is by measure . . . but in the reprobate it is ye just
vengeance of God to drive them to an insensiblenes
& madnes'.
68 vessel cup; perhaps 'communion chalice'
(Brooke).
69 eternal jewel soul.
70 common enemy enemy to all, enemy of all
(i.e. Satan). Compare 'defy the devil! Consider, he's
an enemy to mankind' (*TN* 3.4.97–8).
71 seeds progeny, offspring. *OED* Seed *sb* does
not include this meaning for the plural, which may
be a common printing error, but compare 1.3.56,
4.1.58 and n.

Rather than so, come Fate into the list,
And champion me to th'utterance. Who's there?

Enter Servant and two MURDERERS

[*To Servant*] Now go to the door and stay there till we call.

Exit Servant

Was it not yesterday we spoke together?   75
MURDERERS It was, so please your highness.
MACBETH Well then, now have you considered of my speeches?
    Know, that it was he in the times past which held you so under
    fortune, which you thought had been our innocent self. This I
    made good to you in our last conference; passed in probation   80
    with you how you were borne in hand, how crossed; the instru-
    ments, who wrought with them, and all things else that might to
    half a soul and to a notion crazed say, 'Thus did Banquo.'
FIRST MURDERER You made it known to us.
MACBETH I did so, and went further, which is now our point of   85
    second meeting. Do you find your patience so predominant in

---

73 SD *Servant*] F (*Seruant,*)   73 SD MURDERERS] F (*Murtherers*); *Murtherer*(s) *appears in* SDs *throughout except at* 3.4.32
SD   76 SH MURDERERS] F (*Murth.*); *Mur.* / *Capell;* I. *Mur.* / *Steevens*[3]   77 speeches?] F2; speeches: F   83 'Thus . . .
Banquo.'] *Johnson* (*subst.*); Thus . . . *Banquo.* F

72 **list** The enclosed space where knights con-
tended in formal tournaments (tilts) or to determine a dispute through trial by combat (*R2* 1.3
dramatises an aborted example of the latter). In
Tudor and Stuart England, tilts were entirely ceremonial and only accidentally fatal; many London-
ers would know the tilts annually commemorating
Queen Elizabeth's accession on 17 November.
73 **champion** challenge to a contest, bid defiance to (so *OED* Champion *v* 1, with one other citation, from 1821). This instance is the word's only
use as a verb in Shakespeare, but its uses as a noun
suggest the verb might mean 'fight for', 'uphold',
support' (*OED* Champion *v* 2 and 3, with earliest
citations from the nineteenth century). Therefore,
as Foakes and common sense suggest, Macbeth
may expect Fate to enter the lists against Banquo's
sons and, following the sisters' assurances, fight for
Macbeth.
73 **utterance** uttermost, extremity (*Lexicon*),
furthest limit (here, death).
73 **Who's there** A common dramatic formula
for summoning attendants; it need not be spoken
in response to any speech or event.
73 SD MURDERERS Sometimes imagined as ex-
soldiers (Clarendon; repeated in Muir, quoting Harley Granville-Barker), a masterless, often
vagrant class much feared in early modern Eng-

land and the subject of punitive legal treatment.
(For instance, Black Will, a murderer-for-hire in
Arden of Faversham, is a former soldier.) Despite
F's designation, 'They are not yet murderers but,
by their own claim, ruined men' (Foakes).
77–90 In these metrically muddled lines prosaic
rhythms occasionally give way to iambic pentameter, e.g. F's version of 82–3: 'And all things else,
that might / To halfe a Soule, and to a Notion
craz'd, / Say, Thus did *Banquo*.'
78 **he** Banquo, but the audience infers this identification only from Macbeth's soliloquy.
80 **made good** rendered persuasive or convincing. The echo of 8 now casts Macbeth as a witch
soliciting the Murderers.
80 **conference** discussion, meeting.
80 **passed in probation** proved, demonstrated.
'Probation' is a Scotticism; see *OED* Probation 4
a-b.
81 **borne in hand** deceived, misled deliberately
(a proverbial expression; see Dent H94).
82–3 Dent compares 'He that has but half an
eye (or wit) may see it' (H47), but 'half a soul' (83)
sounds like the Murderers' own souls.
83 **notion** mind, intellect (*OED* Notion 5a,
quoting this line and *Lear* 1.4.228 as the earliest
examples).

your nature, that you can let this go? Are you so gospelled, to
pray for this good man and for his issue, whose heavy hand
hath bowed you to the grave and beggared yours forever?

FIRST MURDERER   We are men, my liege.   90

MACBETH   Ay, in the catalogue ye go for men,
            As hounds, and greyhounds, mongrels, spaniels, curs,
            Shoughs, water-rugs, and demi-wolves are clept
            All by the name of dogs. The valued file
            Distinguishes the swift, the slow, the subtle,   95
            The housekeeper, the hunter, every one
            According to the gift which bounteous nature
            Hath in him closed, whereby he does receive
            Particular addition from the bill
            That writes them all alike. And so of men.   100
            Now, if you have a station in the file
            Not i'th'worst rank of manhood, say't,
            And I will put that business in your bosoms,

---

93 clept] F (clipt)   102 Not] F, F2–4; Nor *Q1673*; And not *Rowe*   102 say't] F; say it *Rowe*

---

87 gospelled imbued with the principles of the 'gospel' (= the Christian New Testament or, generally, Christian teachings). Grey (11, 146) cites 'But I saye unto you, love your enemies, blesse them that curse you, do good to them that hate you, pray for them which hurt you, and persecute you' (Matt. 5.44).

89 yours your families and dependants. Compare 'His wife, his babes, and all unfortunate souls / That trace him in his line' (4.1.151–2).

90 We are men Evidently, the Murderers mean this answer to affirm their pride, their injured merit, their capacity for revenge; the claim echoes ironically Macbeth's 'I dare do all that may become a man' (1.7.46). Proverbially, 'Men are but men' (Dent M541).

90 liege See 1.4.2 n.

91–107 William Harrison's 'Description of Scotland', prefixed to *Scotland*, lists (p. 14) three canine species 'of marvelous condition . . . which are not seene else-where'. The speech is partly 'a symbol of the order that Macbeth wishes to restore . . . [but] [i]n an attempt to re-create an order based on murder, disorder makes fresh inroads' (Knights, p. 24). For the many self-contradictions here and a possible source, see Supplementary Note, pp. 257–8 below.

91 catalogue Wordplay on 'cat' (and dog) is possible here.

92 spaniels Long-haired dogs popular for hunt-

ing game and as pets.

92 curs Watch-dogs or sheep dogs (*OED* Cur 1); the word had not yet become entirely contemptuous.

93 Shoughs A kind of lap-dog. Capell's spelling, 'shocks', indicates a contemporary pronunciation.

93 water-rugs Shaggy water-dogs (?). This line is the only citation under *OED* Water-rug.

93 demi-wolves animals half-wolf, half-dog (the two species can interbreed: see Supplementary Note to 91–107, pp. 257–8 below). F's 'Demy-Wolues' (normalised to 'demi-wolves') is the only example of the word at *OED* Demi- *sb, a, prefix* 11.

93 clept named, called. F's form and the verb itself are archaic.

94 valued file list or dossier ('file') with values (qualities, prices) attached. The earliest citation under *OED* Valued *ppl a*. See 'rank' (102) and n.

96 housekeeper watch-dog. The earliest citation under *OED* Housekeeper 3b.

98 closed enclosed, incorporated.

99 Particular addition Specific mark of distinction.

99 bill catalogue, inventory (*OED* Bill *sb³* 5a, where this line is the last citation).

102 rank sort, quality; row of individuals abreast (as distinct from a 'file' (see 94), individuals aligned one behind the other).

102 say't say it. Rowe sought to improve the metre, which remains irregular.

Whose execution takes your enemy off,
Grapples you to the heart and love of us   105
Who wear our health but sickly in his life,
Which in his death were perfect.
SECOND MURDERER   I am one, my liege,
Whom the vile blows and buffets of the world
Hath so incensed that I am reckless what I do
To spite the world.
FIRST MURDERER   And I another,   110
So weary with disasters, tugged with fortune,
That I would set my life on any chance
To mend it or be rid on't.
MACBETH   Both of you know
Banquo was your enemy.
MURDERERS   True, my lord.
MACBETH So is he mine, and in such bloody distance   115
That every minute of his being thrusts
Against my near'st of life; and though I could
With barefaced power sweep him from my sight
And bid my will avouch it, yet I must not,
For certain friends that are both his and mine,   120
Whose loves I may not drop, but wail his fall
Who I myself struck down. And thence it is
That I to your assistance do make love,

---

114 SH, 138 SH MURDERERS] *Dyce* (*subst.*); *Murth.* F; *Mur.* / *Capell*

104 execution carrying out; doing (*OED* Execution 1, 3b).
104 takes . . . off kills; removes (not quoted at *OED* Take *v* 85f). Compare Duncan's 'taking off' (1.7.20) and 'Took off her life' (5.9.38).
105 Grapples Attaches firmly. The metaphor is from the use of grappling-irons to hold ships together in battle.
106 wear The clothing metaphors continue.
106 in his life i.e. while he lives.
107 perfect flawless, excellent. Compare 129 and 3.4.21.
109 Hath Singular verb in -*th* with plural subject (Abbott 334).
111 tugged with mauled by.
112 set . . . on gamble my life on.
113 mend . . . on't Compare the proverbial 'Either mend or end' (Dent M874).
113 on't of it.

115 distance discord, dissension (*OED* Distance *sb* 1a, quoting this line). Brooke sees a contrast with 'near'st of life' (117).
116 thrusts stabs (compare 'stick' (51)).
117 near'st of life i.e. those things most necessary to life; literally, the vital organs.
118 barefaced naked, open.
119 bid my will avouch make it just because it is my will. Macbeth claims that his absolutism could banish, or kill, Banquo and explain it as Macbeth's mere will; compare 'yet our power / Shall do a curtsy to our wrath, which men / May blame but not control' (*Lear* 3.7.25–7).
121 but wail but I must wail. This phrase depends upon 'may' in the preceding one.
123 make love pay amorous attention (*OED* Love *sb*[1] 7g). Compare Hamlet on Rosencrantz and Guildenstern as spies: 'Why, man, they did make love to this employment' (*Ham.* 5.2.57).

Masking the business from the common eye
For sundry weighty reasons.

SECOND MURDERER   We shall, my lord,   125
Perform what you command us.

FIRST MURDERER   Though our lives –

MACBETH   Your spirits shine through you. Within this hour at most,
I will advise you where to plant yourselves,
Acquaint you with the perfect spy o'th'time,
The moment on't, for't must be done tonight,   130
And something from the palace: always thought,
That I require a clearness. And with him,
To leave no rubs nor botches in the work,
Fleance, his son that keeps him company,
Whose absence is no less material to me   135
Than is his father's, must embrace the fate
Of that dark hour. Resolve yourselves apart,
I'll come to you anon.

MURDERERS   We are resolved, my lord.

124–5 Masking . . . reasons Macbeth repeats (see 119–21), but broadens, his motive for secrecy, answering (as in 118) an unspoken objection from the Murderers. Compare 1.5.50 and 61–4, 1.7.24, and 3.2.46–50.

126 Though our lives First Murderer is presumably about to volunteer his and his companion's lives to achieve Banquo's death.

127 Macbeth's interruption may indicate eagerness to get his plan under way, or impatience at the Murderers' tedious responses to an offer they could not refuse.

127–38 Your . . . anon F represents these lines as a single sentence, marking off the various stages of Macbeth's increasingly disjointed instructions with colons after 'palace' (131) and 'work' (133), semicolons, and commas; modern repunctuation disguises the tumbling phrases and discontinuous thoughts of F.

128 plant position (here, 'hide').

129 perfect fully informed; best. See 107 and next note.

129 spy o'th'time This phrase has not been satisfactorily explained, especially since the essential information of when and where is conveyed in 128 and 130–1, apparently making this line redundant. Johnson thought 'spy' meant secret watcher, and he identified the figure with Third Murderer (see

3.3.1 and n.). Other interpretations – e.g. "'*Spy*," whose proper sence is – espyer, is used here for – espyal' (Capell, *Notes*, p. 16; compare Ritson, p. 75: 'the very time when you are to look out for him') – associate 'spy' (rarely used as a noun by Shakespeare) with 'espial' (= observation), though *OED* does not list one as a form of the other. *MED* Spy v^1 2a, b defines the word as 'wait for . . . opportunity (to do harm); lie in wait'.

131–2 always . . . clearness always known (or 'remembered') that I must be free of involvement.

131 something i.e. some distance from.

132 with him i.e. with Banquo's death.

133 rubs nor botches impediments or flaws. This line is *OED*'s earliest citation for Botch sb^2 (Schäfer).

135 The contradiction of 'absence' and 'material' is an oxymoron that recalls the paradox of 'nothing is, / But what is not' (1.3.140–1).

135 absence death. The euphemism palliates the demand that the murderers commit infanticide, which Shakespeare elsewhere (e.g. *3H6*, *John*) represents as the most heinous possible crime.

135 material important, consequential.

137 Resolve yourselves apart Decide between yourselves in private, but also 'gather the necessary determination (or courage)'. Macbeth wants to give the men time to accept murdering Fleance.

MACBETH   I'll call upon you straight; abide within.

[Exeunt Murderers]

<blockquote>
It is concluded. Banquo, thy soul's flight,   140
If it find heaven, must find it out tonight.   Exit
</blockquote>

3.2 Enter [LADY MACBETH], and a SERVANT

LADY MACBETH   Is Banquo gone from court?

SERVANT   Ay, madam, but returns again tonight.

LADY MACBETH   Say to the king, I would attend his leisure

<blockquote>For a few words.</blockquote>

SERVANT   Madam, I will.   Exit

LADY MACBETH   Nought's had, all's spent

<blockquote>
Where our desire is got without content.   5
'Tis safer to be that which we destroy
Than by destruction dwell in doubtful joy.
</blockquote>

Enter MACBETH

<blockquote>
How now, my lord, why do you keep alone,
Of sorriest fancies your companions making,
Using those thoughts which should indeed have died   10
With them they think on? Things without all remedy
Should be without regard; what's done, is done.
</blockquote>

MACBETH   We have scorched the snake, not killed it;

---

139 SD] *Theobald; not in* F   141 SD *Exit*] *Theobald; Exeunt.* F   Act 3, Scene 2   3.2] F (*Scena Secunda.*)   0 SD LADY MACBETH] F (*Macbeths Lady*)   13 scorched] F (scorch'd); scotch'd *Theobald*

139 straight at once.

140–1 All the preparations have been made (the Murderers were the last link).

140 soul's flight The soul was traditionally imagined as a bird which could fly to heaven. See 'flie, flie commanding soule, / And on thy wings for this thy bodies breath, / Beare the eternall victory of death' (Chapman, *Tragedy of Charles, Duke of Byron* 5.4.259–61).

Act 3, Scene 2
The location is some private area of Macbeth's castle where intimate conversation (8 ff.) is possible.

0 SD LADY MACBETH The actor may appear with regal props, as in 3.1.

4–7 These hesitant couplets with their contradictory rhymes (spent/content, destroy/joy) starkly summarise what the regicides have won and lost (see 1.1.4 and 1.2.67). Compare 3.1.49–50 and,

dramaturgically, Gertrude's 'To my sick soul, as sin's true nature is, / Each toy seems prologue to some great amiss, / So full of artless jealousy is guilt, / It spills itself in fearing to be spilt' (*Ham.* 4.5.17–20).

8 keep alone See 3.1.44–5.

9 fancies hallucinations, delusive visions.

11–12 Things . . . regard 'Where there is no remedy it is folly to chide' is proverbial (Dent R71.1).

11 all any (Abbott 12).

12 what's done, is done The proverb, 'Things done cannot be undone' (Dent T200), links this moment with 1.7.1 ff and 5.1.47–8.

13 scorched slashed, notched, scored (see *OED* Scorch v^3). F elsewhere uses an evocative rhyming pair: 'scotched [as in 'Scot'] him and notched him' (*Cor.* 4.5.186–7). The snake is 'Duncan; alive enough in his sons, and his other friends, to put

She'll close, and be herself, whilst our poor malice
Remains in danger of her former tooth.   15
But let the frame of things disjoint, both the worlds suffer,
Ere we will eat our meal in fear, and sleep
In the affliction of these terrible dreams
That shake us nightly. Better be with the dead
Whom we, to gain our peace, have sent to peace,   20
Than on the torture of the mind to lie
In restless ecstasy. Duncan is in his grave.
After life's fitful fever, he sleeps well;
Treason has done his worst; nor steel nor poison,
Malice domestic, foreign levy, nothing   25
Can touch him further.
LADY MACBETH   Come on. Gentle my lord,
Sleek o'er your rugged looks, be bright and jovial

20 our peace] F; our place F2–4

his wounder *in danger*' (Capell, *Notes*, p. 16); the important point is that the snake's body is cut, but not severed. See next note.

14–15 Shakespeare attributes gender to snakes, adders, and serpents inconsistently, sometimes making them male (*JC* 2.1.32–4, *Shr.* 4.3.177–8), sometimes female (*Tit.* 2.3.35, *MND* 2.1.255, *AYLI* 4.3.109), sometimes neuter (*2H6* 3.1.230). Here, a snake is imagined as female, although metaphorically it represents only males (Duncan and his sons, Banquo and his).

14 close rejoin, heal up (i.e. the wounded snake will recover).

14 our poor malice Macbeth's (and Lady Macbeth's?) 'malice', the murder of Duncan, is 'poor' because it is insufficiently violent; speaking either as king ('our' = royal plural) or for husband and wife, Macbeth seeks consolation for having failed (as yet) to kill enough people (i.e. Banquo and Fleance (see 36–8), perhaps Malcolm and Donaldbain also).

16 Like 22, this is a metrically long line (both are divided in F).

16 frame of things universal order. Compare 'glorious frame of heaven' (*Tamburlaine, Part 1* 4.2.10) and 'loose the whole hinge of things, / And cause the ends run back into their springs' (*Queens* 136–7); see next note.

16 both the worlds suffer earth and heaven be destroyed. See *OED* Suffer *v* 9b, citing only this line and *Temp.* 2.2.34–7, but 'suffer' = die at *TGV* 4.4.15–16 and *MM* 2.2.105–7, and compare 'Mix hell with heaven' (*Queens* 135).

20 peace . . . peace The later Folios vulgarise

the line to avoid repeating 'peace', but 'place' is a pallid word for a kingship gained through murder. For a similar repetition, see 'Though change of war hath wrought this change of chear' (*Tit.* Q1 (1594), sig. B3r), where later texts read 'chance of war'.

21 on . . . lie The implicit image is of the bed as a means or instrument of torture (*OED* Torture *sb* 1b), e.g. a rack.

22 ecstasy frenzy, stupor.

23 life's fitful fever i.e. life is a disease ('fever') causing paroxysms or recurrent attacks (fits, hence 'fitful'). The phrase better describes Macbeth's nightly shaking (19, 22) than it does anything we know of Duncan's life. Compare 'Life is like an ague' (Dent, *PLED* L252.11). This line is *OED*'s earliest citation for 'fitful' (Schäfer).

23 sleeps well Duncan has been sent to the 'peace' (20), the eternal sleep of death, but Macbeth has 'murdered sleep' (2.2.45) for himself and many others who remain alive. Compare 1.7.61–3 and the ironies of 'Soundly' (1.7.63).

24 Treason . . . worst Proverbially, 'Let him do his worst' (Dent W914) and 'The worst is death' (Dent, *PLED* W918.11).

24 nor . . . nor neither . . . nor.

25 Malice domestic Native (= 'domestic', i.e. Scottish) envy or hatred.

25 levy body of men collected to form an army (this line antedates the earliest citation at *OED* Levy *sb*¹ 2b).

27 Gentle my lord i.e. my gentle lord.

28 Sleek Smooth.

28 rugged furrowed.

Among your guests tonight.
MACBETH   So shall I, love,
And so I pray be you. Let your remembrance   30
Apply to Banquo, present him eminence
Both with eye and tongue; unsafe the while, that we
Must lave our honours in these flattering streams
And make our faces vizards to our hearts,
Disguising what they are.
LADY MACBETH   You must leave this.   35
MACBETH O, full of scorpions is my mind, dear wife!
Thou know'st that Banquo and his Fleance lives.
LADY MACBETH But in them Nature's copy's not eterne.
MACBETH There's comfort yet, they are assailable;
Then be thou jocund: ere the bat hath flown   40
His cloistered flight, ere to black Hecate's summons
The shard-born beetle with his drowsy hums
Hath rung night's yawning peal, there shall be done

38 copy's] F (Coppies)

30–2 Let . . . tongue Since Macbeth has just arranged Banquo's murder, this advice presumably means to misdirect Lady Macbeth (Macbeth is now acting independently; compare 1.5 and 1.7), or (as Brooke suggests) it is an attempt to win Lady Macbeth's complicity by stressing Banquo's dangerousness.

30 remembrance thought, regard (*Lexicon*); *OED* Remembrance *sb* 3a has no apposite meaning.

31 present him eminence offer him homage or respect. This line is the sole citation at *OED* Eminence 6. In Elizabethan pronunciation, there was probably some elision ('em'nence'); see Cercignani, p. 280.

32–4 unsafe . . . hearts For the period ('the while') of our insecurity (see 'unsafe') we must wash ('lave') our titles in streams of flattery and make our faces masks ('vizards') for our hearts. Compare 1.7.81–2 and n.

34–5 And make . . . are The implied contrast of face and heart is proverbial: 'Fair face foul heart' (Dent F3).

35–6 You . . . wife These lines might be spoken (and punctuated) to indicate that Macbeth anxiously interrupts Lady Macbeth.

38 Banquo and Fleance are not immortal.

38 copy reproduction, imitation; pattern, example; legal tenure (*OED* Copy *sb* 4; 8c; 5b, a figurative use of 'copyhold'). See Supplementary Note, p. 258 below.

38 copy's copy is.

38 eterne eternal.

39–44 There's . . . note This speech and the next by Macbeth (45–56) are verbally complex, and precise meanings for many words and phrases would be especially elusive in performance. See pp. 54–5 above.

39 assailable attackable, vulnerable to assault. This line is *OED*'s earliest citation for the word (Schäfer).

40 jocund merry, cheerful.

41 cloistered The bat flies in and around buildings (which have cloisters, covered walks open to the outside) rather than in the open air (Hunter subst.).

41 Hecate See 2.1.52 n. Earlier, Shakespeare imagines Hecate as 'pale', appropriate for her other manifestations as Luna and Diana, but 'black' suits both night and Macbeth's invocation of evil to come.

42 shard-born born in dung (so *OED* Shard-born *a*), but another meaning of 'shard' and F's spelling 'borne' permit the popular gloss, 'borne [carried] aloft by its wing-cases' (Hunter), which *OED* rejects. Shakespeare elsewhere mentions 'the sharded beetle' in contrast with the 'full-winged eagle' (*Cym.* 3.3.20–1), and Enobarbus ironically describes Antony and Caesar as 'shards' to Lepidus's 'beetle' (*Ant.* 3.2.20); those contexts do not resolve the meaning here, which may be a quibble (Muir) on 'born' and 'borne'.

43 yawning This image may originate with a

                    A deed of dreadful note.
LADY MACBETH   What's to be done?
MACBETH   Be innocent of the knowledge, dearest chuck,   45
            Till thou applaud the deed. Come, seeling night,
            Scarf up the tender eye of pitiful day
            And with thy bloody and invisible hand
            Cancel and tear to pieces that great bond
            Which keeps me pale. Light thickens,   50
            And the crow makes wing to th'rooky wood;
            Good things of day begin to droop and drowse,
            Whiles night's black agents to their preys do rouse.
            Thou marvell'st at my words, but hold thee still;
            Things bad begun, make strong themselves by ill.   55
            So prithee, go with me.

                                                      Exeunt

bell's 'mouth', but also recalls 'drowsy' (42; see also 'droop and drowse' (52)). Macbeth imagines the beetle's soporific sound as the ringing of bells (= 'peal') that mark night's and sleep's arrival.

44 note notoriety. Another meaning ('musical sound') continues the imagery ('hums' and 'peal') of 42–3.

45–6 Be . . . deed Do not concern yourself in advance about an event (Banquo's murder) you will welcome when it has happened.

45 chuck Affectionate nickname derived from 'chick' (chicken); compare 'my dearest love' (1.5.56). See Supplementary Note, pp. 258–9 below.

46 seeling sewing; blinding. 'Seeling' is a technical term from falconry: the sewing together of a young bird's eyelids to condition it to accept the hood necessary for training. Compare 1.5.49–51. A metaphor from the validating of a written document by applying metal insignia to hot wax, 'sealing', is perhaps present; compare 49; 'Death's second self [sleep], that seals up all in rest' (Sonnet 73.8); Mahood, pp. 38–9, on the wordplay of 'deed', 'seeling'/'sealing', and 'pale' (both 'colourless' and 'a fence', something that constrains).

47 Scarf up Blindfold. This line is Shakespeare's only use of 'scarf' as a verb.

47 pitiful full of pity, compassionate.

49 bond contract, legal commitment; moral obligation. Banquo's 'bond of life' (*R3* 4.4.77), his very existence, keeps Macbeth 'pale' (50); to 'cancel' that

bond is to kill Banquo, but the phrase embraces all the moral, social, and political obligations (bonds) so far violated. See 4.1.83 and n.

50–1 These lines are metrically irregular.

50 pale Compare 2.2.61 and 68 and 'sickly' (3.1.106).

50 Light thickens It grows dark. The metaphor was probably moribund (see 'the Welkin thicks apace, / And stouping *Phebus* steepes his face' (Spenser, *The Shepheardes Calender* (1579), 'March', 115–16)), but the 'fog and filthy air' of 1.1 have made a viscous atmosphere a terrifying possibility.

51 makes wing flies.

51 rooky filled with rooks. The earliest citation under *OED* Rooky *a*[1] (Schäfer). The word has occasioned controversy because: (1) the line seems tautological; (2) 'crow' and 'rook' were common names for the same bird; (3) 'crow' could also distinguish the 'carrion crow' (*Corvus Corone*) from the 'rook' (*Corvus frugilegus*).

54 Thou marvell'st An implicit SD to Lady Macbeth.

54 hold thee still continue steadfast as you have been.

55 A Latin aphorism – 'per scelera semper sceleribus tutum est iter' ('through crime ever is the safe way for crime', Seneca, *Agamemnon* 115, trans. F. J. Miller) – and a proverb – 'Crimes are made secure by greater crimes' (Dent c826) – may have contributed to this line.

3.3 *Enter three* MURDERERS

FIRST MURDERER But who did bid thee join with us?

THIRD MURDERER   Macbeth.

SECOND MURDERER He needs not our mistrust, since he delivers
    Our offices and what we have to do
    To the direction just.

FIRST MURDERER [*To Third Murderer*] Then stand with us.
    The west yet glimmers with some streaks of day;   5
    Now spurs the lated traveller apace
    To gain the timely inn, and near approaches
    The subject of our watch.

THIRD MURDERER   Hark, I hear horses.

BANQUO (*Within*) Give us a light there, ho!

SECOND MURDERER   Then 'tis he; the rest
    That are within the note of expectation   10
    Already are i'th'court.

FIRST MURDERER   His horses go about.

Act 3, Scene 3   3.3] F (*Scena Tertia.*)   1 SH FIRST MURDERER] F (1.) *and throughout scene*   2 SH THIRD MURDERER] F (3.) *and throughout scene*   3 SH SECOND MURDERER] F (2.) *and throughout scene*   7 and] F2; end F   9 SH, SD BANQUO (*Within*)] F (*Banquo within.*)

Act 3, Scene 3

  The location is exterior and nocturnal, some distance (12–13) from the entrance to Macbeth's castle, now his 'palace' (13). As 3.4 will show more largely, this scene contains reminders of the social order and customs Macbeth is destroying: the hospitality of the 'timely inn' (7); the practice ('so all men do') of approaching the castle on foot (11–14; see n.); the homely mention of the weather (18).

  1 'But' indicates that the Murderers enter conversing; presumably First and Second have been questioning Third Murderer, whom they did not expect.

  1 SH THIRD MURDERER Critics have speculated on his identity: Ross, Macbeth (G. W. Williams, 'The Third Murderer in *Macbeth*', *SQ* 23 (1972), 261, raises strong theatrical arguments against this possibility, and Destiny have been proposed (see Muir), but NS reasonably suggests 'Macbeth, tyrant-like, feels he must spy even upon his own chosen instruments.' Third Murderer's presence also inserts tension into a necessary but predictable scene; see Martin Wiggins, *Journeymen in Murder: The Assassin in English Renaissance Drama*, 1991, pp. 77–8.

  2–4 He . . . just 'He' is momentarily ambiguous – Macbeth or Third Murderer? – and then is resolved when it becomes clear Third Murderer

has brought the 'direction' Macbeth promised on 'where to plant yourselves' (3.1.128). For a similarly significant confusion of pronouns, see 1.2.20–2 n.

  3 offices duties. A grim echo of 2.1.14: soon social duty will again turn to murder.

  4 just precisely, exactly.

  4 stand take position; hide.

  6 lated belated, overtaken by night (Hunter).

  7 timely opportune.

  8 I hear horses The sound of hoofbeats was common in the Tudor and Stuart theatre; NS cites W. J. Lawrence, *Pre-Restoration Stage Studies*, 1927, p. 217. For more hoofbeats, see 4.1.138–9; for other horses, see 1.3, headnote.

  9 SD Banquo calls to the grooms who will cool the horses while their riders walk to the castle (see 11–14).

  9–11 The other expected guests have already arrived. The Murderers serve as macabre butlers or doormen to Macbeth's feast.

  11–14 These lines explain the absence of horses on stage and make more plausible the Murderers' successful attack, since they assault two persons on foot rather than on horseback. See 1.3, headnote.

  11 go about walk an indirect route (to cool the horses).

THIRD MURDERER Almost a mile; but he does usually,
       So all men do, from hence to th'palace gate
       Make it their walk.

              Enter BANQUO *and* FLEANCE, *with a torch*

SECOND MURDERER A light, a light!   15
THIRD MURDERER 'Tis he.
FIRST MURDERER Stand to't.
BANQUO It will be rain tonight.
FIRST MURDERER   Let it come down.
       [*The Murderers attack. First Murderer strikes out the light*]
BANQUO O, treachery!
       Fly, good Fleance, fly, fly, fly!   20
       Thou mayst revenge – O slave!   [*Dies. Fleance escapes*]
THIRD MURDERER Who did strike out the light?
FIRST MURDERER   Was't not the way?
THIRD MURDERER There's but one down; the son is fled.
SECOND MURDERER We have lost best half of our affair.
FIRST MURDERER Well, let's away, and say how much is done.   25
                     Exeunt[, *with Banquo's body*]

---

14 SD FLEANCE . . . *torch*] F (*Fleans . . . Torch*)   18 SD *The Murderers attack*] This edn; *not in* F; *They fall upon Banquo and kill him; in the scuffle Fleance escapes*. / Rowe (*after* tonight); *They assault Banquo*. / Theobald   18 SD *First Murderer strikes out the light*] NS (*subst.*); *not in* F   21 SD *Dies. Fleance escapes*] Pope; *not in* F   25 SD *Exeunt, with Banquo's body*] Oxford; *Exeunt* F

13 from hence i.e. from where he dismounted.

14 SD *torch* The dialogue (22–3) makes clear that only Banquo and Fleance enter (i.e. there is no torch-bearer); Fleance probably carries the 'torch' here. Compare 2.1.0 SD and n.

15 A light, a light Second Murderer sees the targets first.

18 First Murderer makes the grim jest that Banquo, about to die, need not worry about the rain to come; simultaneously, First Murderer orders the attack.

18 come down rain; make a surprise attack (an absolute use (?) of *OED* Come *v* 56g, 'come down upon').

21 O slave! Banquo's dying execration, directed at his murderer.

22 way plan, method. First Murderer is an amateur. John C. McCloskey, 'Why not Fleance?', *Shakespeare Association Bulletin* 20 (1945), 118–20, argues that Fleance should extinguish the torch in self-defence.

23 the son is fled The son (Fleance, who flees) is also the *sun*, the light of day, which darkened Scotland will also lament. Compare 1.5.59, 2.4.5–10, and pp. 38–9 above.

24 best half i.e. Fleance's death. As Macbeth made clear (3.1.134–7), killing Fleance, Banquo's son and the source of further descendants, was more important (= 'best') than killing Banquo. Compare 5.8.18.

25 SD *Exeunt with Banquo's body* Actors were expected to remove their victims' bodies from the stage. Reminiscing about the actor Richard Fowler at the Fortune Theatre before 1642, a character recalls an occasion when Fowler neglected 'to bring off his dead men'; they 'crauld into the Tyreing house', but Fowler reappeared 'and told 'em, Dogs you should have laine there till you had been fetcht off (John Tatham (?), *Knavery in All Trades, or the Coffee-House* (1664), Act 3, sig. EIr).

3.4 *Banquet prepared.* [*Two thrones are placed on stage.*] *Enter* MACBETH [*as King*], LADY [MACBETH *as Queen*], ROSS, LENNOX, LORDS, *and Attendants.* [*Lady Macbeth sits*]

MACBETH You know your own degrees, sit down; at first and last, the hearty welcome.

[The Lords sit]

LORDS Thanks to your majesty.

MACBETH Our self will mingle with society and play the humble host; our hostess keeps her state, but in best time we will   5
require her welcome.

LADY MACBETH Pronounce it for me, sir, to all our friends, for my heart speaks they are welcome.

Enter FIRST MURDERER

Act 3, Scene 4   3.4] F (*Scaena Quarta.*)   0 SD.1 *Two thrones are placed on stage*] *This edn; not in* F   0 SD.2 MACBETH *as King*] *Oxford; Macbeth* F; *King Macbeth / Staunton*   0 SD.2 LADY MACBETH *as Queen*] *Oxford; Lady* F; *Queen / Staunton*   0 SD.3 *Lady Macbeth sits*] *This edn; not in* F   2 SD] *This edn; not in* F; *They sit. / Rowe*

Act 3, Scene 4
The audience must imagine a formal banqueting space, perhaps the 'hall' (2.3.127). The dialogue (especially 1, 4–5) seems to stipulate a throne (see 5 n.). See the description of King James in Parliament (*Parliamentary Diary of Robert Bowyer*, ed. D. H. Willson, 1931, p. 185) and Andrew Gurr, 'The "state" of Shakespeare's audiences', in Marvin and Ruth Thompson (eds.), *Shakespeare and the Sense of Performance*, 1989, esp. pp. 162–8, 174–7. Macbeth might first escort Lady Macbeth to the throne and then join the lords at 4. Speaking from the throne, or moving from it, Lady Macbeth recalls Macbeth to his duties as host at 32–7, and she certainly enters the main acting area at 53 when she intervenes to explain Macbeth's behaviour. The visual contrast between new royal status and old (?) companionability, followed by Lady Macbeth's urgent movement from throne to 'society' (4), emphasises the Macbeths' insecurity and the fragility of the order they seek to maintain or impose. See also 10 n. Jones, *Origins*, pp. 26–8 and 79–83, discusses the scene's possible sources in Suetonius's Life of Claudius and two plays from the Corpus Christi cycle known as *Ludus Coventriae*. This scene is the last in which Macbeth and Lady Macbeth appear together; see Appendix 1, pp. 281–2 below.

0 SD.1 *Banquet prepared* i.e. a 'banquet' placed on stage (presumably some conventional stage-representation). While a Jacobean 'banquet' might be a light collation of elaborate sweets, this one seems to be a state dinner (another available meaning): 'our great feast' (3.1.12); 'a solemn supper' (3.1.14); 'our feast' (3.1.29). See 1.4.56 n.

0 SD.1 *Two thrones . . . stage* See headnote.
0 SD.3 *Lady . . . sits* See headnote.
1–8 Metrically, 'F's arrangement is hopeless and editors' no improvement' here (Brooke, App. A, p. 223).
1 **You know your own degrees** You know the seating order appropriate to your respective ranks.
1 **degrees** social ranks. There is probably a quibble on 'degrees' = steps and = tiers of seats (see *MED* Degree *sb* 1a); 'degrees' was also a common term for temporary seating erected for courtly and other occasional theatrical performances.
1 **at first and last** to one and all (*OED* First *a* 5e).
3 SH, 49 SH, 92 SH LORDS F's 'Lords' presumably calls for intelligible hubbub, perhaps two or three lords (including those named at 0 SD.2–3) speaking in overlapping sequence rather than choric unison.
4 **society** companions; acquaintances.
4 **play** serve as, fill the capacity of. In some productions, Macbeth pours drinks for the guests.
5 **host** The word describes anyone who entertains another person, but especially pertains to an inn- or tavern-keeper (see Lady Macbeth's worries at 32–7).
5 **keeps her state** continues in her chair of state (Singer); 'state' = throne or formal chair, often with a canopy.
6 After this line, Rowe added *They sit*.
8 SD First Murderer is not noticed verbally by the other guests and perhaps not noticed by Macbeth until 12; see 10 n. Editors and producers have invented many stagings for this moment.

MACBETH   See, they encounter thee with their hearts' thanks.
Both sides are even; here I'll sit i'th'midst.   10
Be large in mirth, anon we'll drink a measure
The table round. [*To First Murderer*] There's blood upon thy
face.
FIRST MURDERER   'Tis Banquo's then.
MACBETH   'Tis better thee without, than he within.
Is he dispatched?   15
FIRST MURDERER   My lord, his throat is cut; that I did for him.
MACBETH   Thou art the best o'th'cut-throats,
Yet he's good that did the like for Fleance;
If thou didst it, thou art the nonpareil.
FIRST MURDERER   Most royal sir, Fleance is scaped.   20
MACBETH   Then comes my fit again: I had else been perfect;
Whole as the marble, founded as the rock,
As broad and general as the casing air:
But now I am cabined, cribbed, confined, bound in

---

13 SH FIRST MURDERER] F (*Mur.*) *and throughout scene*

9 An implicit SD to the lords and Lady Macbeth, who exchange some response (bows, or a toast?).

9 encounter go to meet (*OED* Encounter *v* 6, with citations only from Shakespeare), hence 'reciprocate' (?). Just as Lady Macbeth's 'heart speaks' (8), the nobles return 'hearts' thanks'.

10 Equal numbers of people sit on each side of the table; I'll sit half-way down one side (?). As contemporary paintings and accounts testify, the place of honour in the Elizabethan and Jacobean court varied: if the table was aligned with a room's width (as imagined here?) the honoured place was at the centre (the 'midst') of the side facing into the room; if the table was aligned with a room's length, the modern 'head of the table' became the honoured place. For a detailed account of royal protocol and King James's and Prince Henry's respective seatings at a banquet offered by the Merchant Taylors' company, July 1607, see *The Letters and Epigrams of Sir John Harington*, ed. N. E. McClure, 1930, p. 35.

11 large unrestrained.

11–12 drink . . . round share a toast or health with each person at the table (?); all share in a group toast (?); pass the cup from person to person (?). The first meaning is more likely if Macbeth continues his use (4–5) of the royal plural.

12 There's blood The audience may recall the bloody Captain of 1.2, especially if Macbeth 'is wearing the royal insignia first worn by Duncan' (D. J. Palmer in *Focus*, p. 55).

14 thee without . . . he within outside you than inside him. The line's callousness signals Macbeth's anxiety.

15 dispatched killed.

19 nonpareil one without equal.

20–1 F's lineation is puzzling, but one tentative explanation, 'justifying [the printed line] . . . or . . . indicating very long pauses' (Brooke, App. A, p. 223), is unconvincing, and Pope's and Collier's choices (adopted here) are not too prescriptive.

20 scaped escaped (an aphetic form).

21 fit It is proverbial 'To have an ague fit of fear' (Dent A82.1).

21 perfect Compare the two previous uses of the word, 3.1.107 and 3.1.129; see p. 52 above.

22–3 See 'As hard as marble' (Dent M638.1); 'As fixed (firm) as a rock' (Dent R151); 'As free as the air' (Dent A88).

22 founded based, firmly grounded. The earliest citation for *OED* Founded *ppl a*.

23 broad and general diffused and omnipresent.

23 casing encasing (aphetic form), encompassing. This line is *OED*'s earliest recorded use under Casing *ppl a* (Schäfer).

24 Alliteration of near-synonyms sounds like witch-language (e.g. 1.3.22); see p. 52 above, n. 1.

24 cabined cramped, confined (from 'cabin' = hut or cell).

24 cribbed shut up, hampered. This line is the earliest citation for *OED* Crib *v* 2a. A 'crib' is also an animal's stall, or a suspended, open-sided holder for animal fodder. The metaphorically appropriate 'crib' (= a child's lattice-sided bed) is not recorded before 1649, though *MED* Crib *sb* records the meaning 'manger' (e.g. as a bed for the infant Jesus) from very early.

24 bound in kept fast, chained.

> To saucy doubts and fears. But Banquo's safe?   25
>
> FIRST MURDERER   Ay, my good lord: safe in a ditch he bides,
> With twenty trenchèd gashes on his head,
> The least a death to nature.
>
> MACBETH   Thanks for that.
> There the grown serpent lies; the worm that's fled
> Hath nature that in time will venom breed,   30
> No teeth for th'present. Get thee gone; tomorrow
> We'll hear ourselves again.
>
> *Exit [First] Murderer*
>
> LADY MACBETH   My royal lord,
> You do not give the cheer; the feast is sold
> That is not often vouched while 'tis a-making,
> 'Tis given with welcome. To feed were best at home: 35
> From thence, the sauce to meat is ceremony,
> Meeting were bare without it.
>
> *Enter the Ghost of Banquo and sits in Macbeth's place*

---

32 hear ourselves] F (heare our selues); hear, ourselves *Steevens*   32 SD *Exit First Murderer*] F (*Exit Murderer.*)   34
a-making,] *Cam.*; a making: F   35 given with] F3; giuen, with F

---

25 safe i.e. dead. The euphemism reflects Macbeth's reaction, not Banquo's condition; see p. 49 above.

27–8 With . . . nature Compare Duncan's wounds (2.3.106–7).

27 trenchèd grooved, furrowed. This use antedates the earliest citation for a figurative use of the word at *OED* Trench *v* 2b.

28 The . . . nature First Murderer claims that any one of the 'gashes' would have been mortal, but the generalised expression recalls the apocalyptic language surrounding the discovery of Duncan's body in 2.3. As 3.2.16 partly anticipates, Nature is being killed.

29 worm Figuratively, a larva or grub (which will grow into a venomous snake).

32 hear ourselves i.e. speak together. *OED* Hear *v* does not include a reflexive form. Theobald emended to 'hear't our selves', and other grammatically 'correct' changes have been proposed. Compare 'known' for 'known each other' (*Ant.* 2.6.83) and 'see' for 'see each other' in Imogen's farewell to Posthumus, 'When shall we see again?' (*Cym.* 1.1.124).

32–7 My royal . . . without it Lady Macbeth forces Macbeth into his rôle as host. Earlier (1.7.30), she showed her concern for social form, however superficial or hypocritical.

32 royal lord The phrase emphasises Macbeth's new status and perhaps reminds him of his new duties.

33 give the cheer give a kindly welcome (*OED* Cheer *sb*[1] 5); give a toast to the company (?).

33–5 feast . . . welcome i.e. a hospitable dinner for guests is rather a commercial transaction ('is sold' (33)) if the host does not frequently affirm (= 'give the cheer' (33) and 'is . . . often vouched' (34)), while it happens, that the feast is freely, generously (= 'with welcome' (35)) given. Proverbially, 'Welcome is the best cheer' (Dent w258).

35 To feed were best at home i.e. one dines best in one's own dwelling.

36 From thence Away from home.

36 ceremony social rituals (of seating, serving, toasting, etc.).

37 SD Editors have moved the Ghost's entrance closer to the moment it is first recognised in the dialogue (before 48), but F's location is theatrically feasible, making 40–4 simply but effectively ironic and allowing the Ghost time to enter and to sit in a place that fills the table but is not in Macbeth's line of sight. Forman (11, 338) saw the actor playing Macbeth 'standing up to drincke a Carouse to' Banquo, 'And as he thus did . . . the ghoste of Banco came and sate down in his cheier behind him.' For the ways of enacting the Ghost's entrance, see Stanley Wells in Biggs, pp. 65–7.

37 SD *Ghost of Banquo* The same actor who played Banquo living, made up with stage-blood (see 51), usually animal's blood, and, possibly, flour. In other plays, a miller in his 'mealy miller's coate' is mistaken for a ghost (William Sampson, *The*

MACBETH   Sweet remembrancer!
        Now good digestion wait on appetite,
        And health on both.
LENNOX   May't please your highness, sit.
MACBETH Here had we now our country's honour roofed,   40
        Were the graced person of our Banquo present,
        Who may I rather challenge for unkindness
        Than pity for mischance.
ROSS   His absence, sir,
        Lays blame upon his promise. Please't your highness
        To grace us with your royal company?   45
MACBETH The table's full.
LENNOX   Here is a place reserved, sir.
MACBETH Where?
LENNOX Here, my good lord. What is't that moves your highness?
MACBETH Which of you have done this?
LORDS   What, my good lord?
MACBETH Thou canst not say I did it; never shake   50
        Thy gory locks at me!
ROSS Gentlemen, rise, his highness is not well.
        [*Lady Macbeth joins the Lords*]

52 SD] *This edn; not in* F

Vow-Breaker (1636), sig. 13v) and a character pretends to be his own ghost and enters, *his face mealed* (Francis Beaumont, *Knight of the Burning Pestle* (1613), sig. 13r). Henslowe (pp. 318, 321) inventories 'j [= 1] gostes sewt, and j gostes bodeyes [= bodice]' as well as 'j gostes crown'. On the Ghost's appearance, see also R. V. Holdsworth, '*Macbeth* and *The Puritan*', *N&Q* 235 (1990), 204–5. The co-presence of Death and (royal) festivity are frequent moral themes; skeleton-Death pours a king's wine in Hans Holbein the Younger's popular *The Dance of Death* (1538). See illustration 10, p. 53 above.

37 **remembrancer** one who reminds. The word was also the title of officials who collected debts owed to the crown. Macbeth speaks 'remembrancer' just as the Ghost enters as a reminder of another deed; compare the now-ironic 'remembrance' (3.2.30).

38 **wait on** attend, serve.

40 **honour** i.e. those professing and conferring honour, the nobility.

40 **roofed** i.e. beneath one roof, in one place.

41 **graced** favoured, endowed with special qualities.

42 **may I** I hope I may.

43 **mischance** accident. The false politeness recalls 1.6.

43–4 **His absence . . . his promise** Literally, Banquo's absence belies his promise to attend. There are two ironical meanings: Banquo's Ghost keeps his living vow ('promise'); Banquo's death ('absence') may be blamed upon 'his royalty of nature' (3.1.51), the qualities which boded so well for his future service to Scotland ('his promise'). On the second meaning, compare 'He hath borne himself beyond the promise of his age . . . He hath indeed better bettered expectation' (*Ado* 1.1.13–16).

46 **The table's full** Macbeth finds no empty place.

48 **moves** troubles (*OED* Move *v* 9). Macbeth has now reacted to the Ghost.

49 **Which . . . this** Macbeth may assume a practical joke (someone is pretending to be Banquo), or he may ask who has made Banquo a ghost.

50–1 The silent Ghost cannot accuse Macbeth of murdering Banquo.

51 **gory locks** bloody hair.

52 SD See headnote.

LADY MACBETH Sit, worthy friends. My lord is often thus,
            And hath been from his youth. Pray you, keep seat.
            The fit is momentary; upon a thought   55
            He will again be well. If much you note him
            You shall offend him and extend his passion.
            Feed, and regard him not. [*To Macbeth*] Are you a man?
MACBETH Ay, and a bold one, that dare look on that
            Which might appal the devil.
LADY MACBETH   O proper stuff!   60
            This is the very painting of your fear;
            This is the air-drawn dagger which you said
            Led you to Duncan. O, these flaws and starts,
            Impostors to true fear, would well become
            A woman's story at a winter's fire   65
            Authorised by her grandam. Shame itself!
            Why do you make such faces? When all's done
            You look but on a stool.
MACBETH Prithee, see there! Behold, look, lo! How say you?
            [*To Ghost*] Why, what care I? If thou canst nod, speak too. 70

---

62 air-drawn dagger] F (Ayre-drawne-Dagger)   70 Why, what . . . I? . . . too.] *Capell;* Why what . . . I, . . . too. F

54 keep seat remain seated.

55 fit paroxysm, seizure (*OED* Fit *sb²* 3). Compare 3.2.23 and n.

55 upon a thought Proverbial: 'As swift as thought' (Dent T240).

57 passion fit (*OED* Passion *sb* 6c).

58 Are you a man For similar questions, see 1.7.35–47 and 3.1.90.

60 proper stuff complete (or 'utter') nonsense.

61 painting image, illusion. Compare 1.3.95, 2.2.57, 2.3.23.

62–3 Lady Macbeth ridicules Macbeth's vision before he killed Duncan (2.1.33–43).

62 air-drawn imaged in the air; moved through the air.

63 flaws bursts of passion (*OED* Flaw *sb²* 2, quoting this line as its second example), a figurative use from 'squall of wind' (*OED* Flaw *sb²* 1).

63 starts sudden involuntary movements.

64 Impostors False imitations (because Macbeth has no true cause of fear); 'impostors when compared with true fear' (Mason, p. 145).

65–6 A woman's . . . grandam Shakespeare and others often associate the telling of a sad or frightening tale with women and winter; compare *R2* 5.1.40ff.; *WT* 2.1.22ff.; 'Now I remember those old womens words, / Who in my wealth [youth?] wud tell me winters tales, / And speake of spirits and ghosts' (Marlowe, *Jew of Malta* 2.1.24–6); Francisco's reaction to Isabella's ghost, 'So now 'tis ended, like an old wives' story' (Webster, *White Devil* 4.1.116); 'A winter('s) tale' (Dent W513.1).

66 Authorised Vouched for, confirmed. The word is stressed on the second syllable (Cercignani, p. 41).

66 grandam grandmother.

67 make such faces An implicit SD to the actor playing Macbeth.

67 When all's done Proverbial (Dent A211.1).

68 stool For Shakespeare's audience, chairs were rare and expensive, stools common, even in wealthy households (see *Tim.* 3.6.65); Lady Macbeth uses that social fact to express her contempt.

69 Behold, look, lo These synonyms urge the actor to gesture at the Ghost and its 'empty' place.

70 Why, what care I Presumably, Macbeth dares the Ghost to identify Banquo's murderer(s), but this phrase may be a question to Lady Macbeth (Halio) or the entire speech may be an aside (NS).

70 nod An implicit SD to the actor playing the Ghost, who must gesture significantly toward Macbeth (see 69 n.).

> If charnel-houses and our graves must send
> Those that we bury back, our monuments
> Shall be the maws of kites.

>   [*Exit Ghost of Banquo*]

LADY MACBETH   What, quite unmanned in folly?

MACBETH   If I stand here, I saw him.

LADY MACBETH   Fie, for shame.

MACBETH   Blood hath been shed ere now, i'th'olden time,   75
> Ere humane statute purged the gentle weal;
> Ay, and since too, murders have been performed
> Too terrible for the ear. The time has been
> That when the brains were out, the man would die,
> And there an end. But now they rise again   80
> With twenty mortal murders on their crowns
> And push us from our stools. This is more strange
> Than such a murder is.

LADY MACBETH   My worthy lord,
> Your noble friends do lack you.

MACBETH   I do forget –
> Do not muse at me, my most worthy friends.   85
> I have a strange infirmity which is nothing
> To those that know me. Come, love and health to all,

73 SD] F2–4 (*subst.*); *not in* F   73 What, . . . folly?] *Capell;* What? . . . folly. F   78 time has] *White;* times has F; times have F2–4

71 **charnel-houses** houses or vaults in which the bones of the dead are piled up (*OED* Charnel-house).

72–3 **our . . . kites** The unburied (or returned) dead will be consumed by carrion-eating birds ('kites') whose stomachs ('maws') will be the final resting-places ('monuments') of the dead.

73 **unmanned** made weak or timid (*OED* Unmanned *ppl a²*, citing only one example, from 1694). Lady Macbeth returns to the tactic that worked before (1.7.39–54), but murder, which she represented as manly, now unmans her husband. See 99.

74 **If I stand here** Compare the proverbial 'As true as you stand there' (Dent s818).

76 **humane statute** compassionate law. For F's 'humane', see 1.5.15 n.

76 **gentle weal** lawful (or 'non-violent') commonwealth. The line employs rhetorical prolepsis: the 'weal' is 'gentle' after it has been 'purged'.

80 **And there an end** Proverbially, 'And there's an end' (Dent E113.1).

81 **twenty** See 27.

81 **mortal** fatal.

81 **crowns** tops of (their) heads (as at 1.5.40), but 'crowns' recalls royal regalia, the 'golden round' (1.5.26): kingly crowns will adorn Banquo's children though his head wears 'twenty mortal murders' only.

82–3 **This . . . is** Responding to Lady Macbeth's scorn (73–4), Macbeth reviews the history of murder (75–80), and that review is meant to assert his manhood and bravery with its grim conclusion, 'And there an end.' The Ghost's uncanny appearance, however, is 'more strange', less explicable and therefore more terrifying, than murder because it overturns the rationalism of 75–80 and revives the doubts of 1.7.1–7; murder is not an 'end' and 'it' is not 'done' when ''tis done' (1.7.1).

83 Collier² added *Returning to her state* after 'My worthy lord'; Keightley marked the speech as an aside.

85 **muse** wonder, marvel. An implicit SD to the guests.

87 **Come . . . all** Macbeth proposes a toast to ease the tension.

Then I'll sit down. Give me some wine; fill full!

Enter Ghost [of Banquo]

I drink to th'general joy o'th'whole table,
And to our dear friend Banquo, whom we miss.   90
Would he were here! To all, and him we thirst,
And all to all.

LORDS   Our duties and the pledge.

MACBETH Avaunt and quit my sight! Let the earth hide thee!
Thy bones are marrowless, thy blood is cold;
Thou hast no speculation in those eyes   95
Which thou dost glare with.

LADY MACBETH   Think of this, good peers,
But as a thing of custom. 'Tis no other,
Only it spoils the pleasure of the time.

MACBETH What man dare, I dare;
Approach thou like the rugged Russian bear,   100
The armed rhinoceros, or th'Hyrcan tiger,
Take any shape but that, and my firm nerves

---

88 SD] F (*Enter Ghost*)   101 Hyrcan] F (Hircan)

88 SD For F's placing of this SD, see Textual Analysis, pp. 262–3 below.

89–92 The toast, divided into a prologue (89–91) where Macbeth identifies the ceremony's structure – he toasts the lords, then the absent Banquo – and the lines (91–2) during which the action of toasting – first Macbeth to the lords, then all to Banquo, then each lord to the others – takes place.

91 **Would he were here** Compare 1.3.80, where Macbeth wishes the witches had not departed; here, he gets his wish in an unwelcome way.

91 **him we thirst** the person (Banquo) for whom we long. The metaphor ('thirst' = desire) is appropriate to a drinking-ceremony.

92 **duties** respects.

92 **pledge** toast (*OED* Pledge *sb* 4, where the earliest citation dates from 1635). After this line, Oxford adds *They drink*.

93 Macbeth sees the Ghost again. Traditionally, Macbeth drops his toasting-cup here, or hurls it at the Ghost, who often sits in Macbeth's vacant throne, and the act recalls the 'poisoned chalice' (1.7.11); see D. J. Palmer in *Focus*, p. 60, and pp. 66–7 above.

94 **marrowless** lacking the vital or essential part (because Banquo is dead). This line is the earliest citation under *OED* Marrowless *a*¹ (Schäfer).

95 **speculation** power of seeing, sight (*OED*

Speculation 1, quoting this line).

96 **glare** look fixedly and fiercely (*OED* Glare *v* 2, first cited from 1609).

97 Lady Macbeth's understanding of 'custom' is different from Banquo's and from that of 'all men' (3.3.12–14), but her attempt to save the social moment has some precedent; see Warwick's defence of Henry IV, 'Be patient, Princes, you do know these fits / Are with his Highness very ordinary' (*2H4* 4.4.114–15).

99 See 73 and 1.7.46–7. Folger adds the SD *to the Ghost*.

100 **rugged Russian bear** Muir (Additional Notes) compares 'hearts more rugged / Then is the Russian Beare' (Dekker, *Whore of Babylon* 2.1.42–3), which may be an imitation or evidence of some proverbial analogy (see also Dekker [and Thomas Middleton], *The Roaring Girl* 3.3.50–1, where 'a russian Beare' is metaphorically 'wild'). Compare 'bear-like I must fight the course' (5.7.2).

101 **Hyrcan** Hyrcanian. Hyrcania was the classical name for the area on the south-east coast of the Caspian Sea (Sugden); following Virgil, *Aeneid* IV, 367, its tigers became proverbial for fierceness (Dent, *PLED* T287.02).

102 **any shape but that** any form but that of Banquo's ghost.

> Shall never tremble. Or be alive again,
> And dare me to the desert with thy sword;
> If trembling I inhabit then, protest me   105
> The baby of a girl. Hence horrible shadow,
> Unreal mock'ry hence.
>
> > > > > > > > > > > > > [*Exit Ghost of Banquo*]
> > > > > > > > Why so, being gone,
> I am a man again. – Pray you, sit still.

LADY MACBETH   You have displaced the mirth, broke the good
> > meeting
> With most admired disorder.

MACBETH   Can such things be,   110
> And overcome us like a summer's cloud,
> Without our special wonder? You make me strange
> Even to the disposition that I owe,
> When now I think you can behold such sights
> And keep the natural ruby of your cheeks,   115
> When mine is blanched with fear.

ROSS   What sights, my lord?

LADY MACBETH   I pray you speak not; he grows worse and worse.
> Question enrages him. At once, good night.
> Stand not upon the order of your going,

---

105 inhabit then,] F; inhabit, then F2–4   107 SD] *Cam. (subst.); not in* F; *Exit / after* shadow F2–4   107 being] F; be F3–4   108 again. – Pray] *Capell;* againe: pray F   117 and worse.] *This edn;* & worse F; and worse; *Theobald*

---

104 dare me to the desert challenge me (to fight you) in the desert. Muir compares 'I dare meet Surrey in a wilderness' (*R2* 4.1.74) and 'Hyrcanian deserts' (*MV* 2.7.41).

105 inhabit take as a habit (*Lexicon*, which adds that 'habit' may mean either 'costume' or 'custom', but without support at *OED* Inhabit). The verb ordinarily means 'dwell, occupy' and the phrase, often emended, could mean 'trembling I stay indoors' or, figuratively, 'I harbour a single tremor' (NS).

105 protest proclaim, denounce publicly. See 'yield thee coward' (5.8.23) and 'Do me right, or I will protest your cowardice' (*Ado* 5.1.147–8).

106 baby doll, puppet (*OED* Baby 2).

107 Unreal Shakespeare's neologism (Garner).

107 mock'ry The syncopation is common; see Cercignani, pp. 272–3.

108 Pray . . . still Macbeth addresses the company. Rowe added *The Lords rise.*

110 admired astonishing, surprising. Lady Macbeth uses 'admired' in its earliest sense, which did not include the element of pleasure or esteem the word now connotes.

111 overcome pass over (as a cloud does the sun); overwhelm, take by surprise (*OED* Overcome *v* 8b, citing only this line). More fully: 'The uncertain glory of an April day, / Which now shows all the beauty of the sun, / And by and by a cloud takes all away' (*TGV* 1.3.85–7).

112–13 make me strange . . . disposition regard (or represent) me as being unlike my usual self; 'self-alienated' (Muir). Compare 'strange and self-abuse' (142).

113 owe own.

115 ruby redness (indicating health and the absence of fear).

116 blanched whitened. Compare 5.3.11–12 and 5.3.14–17.

117–20 Lady Macbeth again tries to make the uncanny social (see 53–4). For 117–18, compare 4.1.88 n.

118 Question Questioning, interrogation.

119 Stand not upon Do not be meticulous about (*OED* Stand *v* 74 g, 'stand on', equivalent to *v* 78 g, 'stand upon', where this line is quoted).

119 order rank-determined precedence, protocol. Compare 'degrees' (1).

But go at once.

LENNOX   Good night, and better health   120
Attend his majesty.

LADY MACBETH   A kind good night to all.
                    [*Exeunt*] *Lords* [*and Attendants*]

MACBETH It will have blood they say: blood will have blood.
Stones have been known to move and trees to speak.
Augures, and understood relations, have
By maggot-pies, and choughs, and rooks brought forth   125
The secret'st man of blood. What is the night?

LADY MACBETH Almost at odds with morning, which is which.

MACBETH How sayst thou that Macduff denies his person
At our great bidding?

LADY MACBETH   Did you send to him, sir?

MACBETH I hear it by the way, but I will send.   130
There's not a one of them but in his house
I keep a servant feed. I will tomorrow –

121 SD Exeunt . . . Attendants] Malone; Exit Lords. F   125 maggot-pies] F (Maggot Pyes)   129 bidding?] F3; bidding. F
130 hear] F (heare); heard Keightley   132–3 tomorrow – / And . . . will –] Halliwell (subst.); to morrow / (And . . .
will) F

122 Proverbially, 'Blood will have blood' (Dent B458).

123 Earlier, Macbeth feared 'stones' would 'speak' and betray him (2.1.58). '[T]he idea of a speaking tree goes back to Virgil, *Aeneid* III, 22–68, but Shakespeare may have picked it up from Scot . . . XI.18, "Divine auguries were such, as . . . when trees spake, as before the death of Caesar"' (Foakes).

124 Augures Auguries, predictions. The obsolete disyllabic form is needed for the metre.

124 understood comprehended.

124 relations i.e. the links between cause and effect (or between the flight of certain birds and the facts being divined). 'Augury' is specifically divination through interpreting the flight of birds, although the word had a less exact meaning in this period (see Scot quoted in 123 n. above).

125 maggot-pies magpies. The birds mentioned here can imitate human speech, and there is probably some memory of 'Wishe the kyng no evil in thy thought, and speake no hurt of the riche in thy privie chamber: for a byrde of the ayre shall betray thy voyce, and with her fethers shall she bewray thy wordes' (Eccles. 10.20), in which case the 'relations' (124) would be stories revealing a hidden murderer. Schanzer (pp. 225–6) sees an allusion to a popular folktale, the 'Tell–Tale Bird', or to classical legend. Compare Dionyza's contemptuous remark to Cleon, 'Be one of those that thinks / The petty wrens of Tharsus will fly

hence / And open this [the supposed murder of Marina] to Pericles' (*Per.* 4.3.21–3) and Machevil's equally contemptuous 'Birds of the Aire will tell of murders past' (Marlowe, *Jew of Malta* Prologue 16).

125 choughs Common name for various species of crow. Magpies and choughs are birds of ill omen and recall other ominous fowl: see 1.5.36, 2.2.15, 2.3.51–2, 3.2.51–3.

126 secret'st man of blood most successfully concealed murderer (Brooke).

126 What is the night? An echo of Banquo's words (2.1.1), and phrased as ominously.

127 at odds with striving with (*OED* Odds *sb* 3). Compare 'this odd-even and dull watch o'th'night' (*Oth.* 1.1.123).

128 How sayst thou What do you think.

128 denies refuses. Macduff's absence 'is a studied insult . . . [an] act of feudal defiance' (Michael Hawkins in *Focus*, pp. 166, 176).

129 send i.e. send a message or messenger (*OED* Send *v.*[1] 8).

130 hear Keightley's emendation is possible because manuscript *heare* could be read as *heard*.

131 them the Scottish nobles.

132 feed bribed, paid a fee. Editors often print 'fee'd', but *OED* Feed *ppl a* does not recognise that form. This detail of spies everywhere appears in *Scotland*, p. 174b.

132 will 'go' is understood.

And betimes I will – to the weïrd sisters.
More shall they speak. For now I am bent to know
By the worst means, the worst; for mine own good,   135
All causes shall give way. I am in blood
Stepped in so far that should I wade no more,
Returning were as tedious as go o'er.
Strange things I have in head that will to hand,
Which must be acted ere they may be scanned.   140
LADY MACBETH   You lack the season of all natures, sleep.
MACBETH   Come, we'll to sleep. My strange and self-abuse
Is the initiate fear that wants hard use;
We are yet but young in deed.

Exeunt

3.5   *Thunder. Enter the three* WITCHES, *meeting* HECATE

FIRST WITCH   Why how now, Hecate, you look angerly?
HECATE   Have I not reason, beldams, as you are,

133 weird] *Theobald;* weyard F   135 worst; for] *Johnson* (*subst.*); worst, for F   144 in deed] *Theobald;* indeed F   Act 3, Scene 5   3.5] F (*Scena Quinta.*)   0 SD HECATE] F (*Hecat*)   2–3 are, / . . . over-bold? How] *Capell;* are? / . . . ouerbold, how F

133 betimes speedily, soon (*OED* Betimes 4), but perhaps also 'early in the morning' (*OED* Betimes 2).

134–5 For . . . good These lines combine two proverbial expressions: 'To know the worst is good' and 'It is good to fear the worst' (Dent w915 and w912, respectively).

136–7 I am . . . so far Proverbially, 'Having wet his foot he cares not how deep he wades' and 'Over shoes over boots' (Dent F565.1 and s379).

140 scanned looked at closely. The word does double duty: 'Strange things' (139) must be done quickly before others can see them and before Macbeth himself can see them. Compare 1.4.50–3 and 3.2.46–7.

141 season period during which something happens (*OED* Season *sb* 12a); perhaps also 'preservative' (as salt seasons meat), but *OED* offers no support.

142–3 My strange . . . fear My inexplicable violation of who and what I am arises from a novice's fear. 'My strange and self-abuse' is most plainly Macbeth's perception of Banquo's Ghost, which Macbeth now tries to dismiss as an hallucination. The grammar treats 'strange' and 'self' as adjectives modifying 'abuse'; 'strange' may therefore have the

resonances of uncanniness it had in 82 and of self-alienation it may have in 112. See *OED* Initiate *ppl a* and *sb* 1b, quoting only this phrase. Proverbially, 'Use makes mastery' and 'Custom makes sin no sin' (Dent U24 and C934). See p. 52 above, n. 2.

143 wants lacks.

144 young in deed just begun in action. So far the Macbeths lack 'hard use' (143) of evil. Spoken in the theatre, F's 'indeed' conveys both 'in truth' (= 'indeed') and 'in action' (= 'in deed'); compare the wordplay on indeed/in deed at *Ant.* 1.5.14–16.

Act 3, Scene 5
Like earlier witch-scenes, this one is unlocalised, perhaps at some place near wherever Macbeth now resides. This scene, evidently preparing the audience for 4.1 and establishing time and place (see 15–16 and 22), is probably not by Shakespeare. See 4 n., 33 SD–35 SD n., and Textual Analysis, pp. 272–3 below.

0 SD See Supplementary Note on 1.2.0 SD.2, p. 255 below.

1 angerly angry, angrily (*OED* Angerly 2).

2 beldams hags, witches (*OED* Beldam, -dame 3).

Saucy and over-bold? How did you dare
To trade and traffic with Macbeth
In riddles and affairs of death?   5
And I the mistress of your charms,
The close contriver of all harms,
Was never called to bear my part
Or show the glory of our art?
And which is worse, all you have done   10
Hath been but for a wayward son,
Spiteful and wrathful, who, as others do,
Loves for his own ends, not for you.
But make amends now. Get you gone,
And at the pit of Acheron   15
Meet me i'th'morning. Thither he
Will come to know his destiny.
Your vessels and your spells provide,
Your charms and every thing beside.
I am for th'air. This night I'll spend   20
Unto a dismal and a fatal end.
Great business must be wrought ere noon.
Upon the corner of the moon
There hangs a vap'rous drop profound;
I'll catch it ere it come to ground;   25

3 Saucy Impudent, ill-behaved.

4 Hecate's speech now becomes tetrameter couplets, returning to doggerel pentameters at 34. Hunter notes that unlike the earlier witch-language this speech uses iambic rather than trochaic rhythms and calls it 'poetically very accomplished'.

4 traffic have dealings, be concerned (*OED* Traffic *v* 2), but also synonymous with 'trade'.

7 close secret, hidden.

8 bear take, undertake.

10–13 NS notes that these lines have 'no relevance' to Macbeth but seem 'to echo jealous speeches by Hecate' in *Witch* 1.2.

11 wayward wilful, intractable. The 'wayward son' is presumably Macbeth (but see 10–13 n.). See Supplementary Note on 1.3.30, pp. 255–6 below.

13 Cares (about magic, prophecy, etc.) for his own purposes, not as an adept of, or believer in, the witches and their powers for themselves.

15 pit sunken place (especially associated with hell; see *OED* Pit *sb*[1] 4). Compare 'Conscience and grace, to the profoundest pit!' (*Ham.* 4.5.133) and next note.

15 Acheron A river in the classical Hades (hell) and only metaphorically in Scotland.

18 vessels implements (e.g. cauldrons) for magic rites.

18–19 spells . . . charms incantations . . . magical verses. The words are a 'synonym pair' (Schäfer, p. 195).

20 spend use, employ.

21 dismal malign, sinister.

21 fatal Both 'destined' and 'destructive' (Brooke subst.)

22 business work (*OED* Business *sb* 13).

24 vap'rous drop i.e. 'the *virus lunare* . . . a foam which the moon was supposed to shed on particular herbs, or other objects when strongly solicited by enchantment' (Steevens[3]). Compare 'O sovereign mistress of true melancholy [i.e. the moon, one of Hecate's manifestations], / The poisonous damp of night disponge upon me' (*Ant.* 4.9.12–13); 'night' is 'vaporous' and dangerous at *The Rape of Lucrece* 771 and *MM* 4.1.57. For the spelling 'vap'rous', see 3.4.107 n.

24 profound deep, with hidden qualities (Johnson subst.). The word is an obvious antonym for 'vap'rous' and, as Clarendon says, may be present mainly to rhyme with 'ground' (25).

And that distilled by magic sleights,
Shall raise such artificial sprites
As by the strength of their illusion
Shall draw him on to his confusion.
He shall spurn fate, scorn death, and bear   30
His hopes 'bove wisdom, grace, and fear.
And you all know, security
Is mortals' chiefest enemy.
    Music, and a song[, '*Come away, come away', within*]
Hark, I am called: my little spirit, see,
Sits in a foggy cloud, and stays for me.   [*Exit*]   35
FIRST WITCH   Come, let's make haste; she'll soon be back again.
                                    Exeunt

3.6 *Enter* LENNOX *and another* LORD

LENNOX   My former speeches have but hit your thoughts
Which can interpret further; only I say

---

26 sleights] F (slights)   33 mortals'] F (Mortals)   33 SD] *This edn; Musicke, and a Song.* F   35 SD *Exit*] *Capell; Sing within. Come away, come away, &c.* F   **Act 3, Scene 6**   3.6] F (*Scaena Sexta.*)   0 SD LENNOX] F (*Lenox,*)

26 sleights tricks, artifices (*Lexicon*).

27 artificial cunning, deceitful (*OED* Artificial *adj* 9), but perhaps also 'made up, factitious' (*OED* Artificial 3a). The word suggests that the witches produce the apparitions (they are not independent or 'natural' demonic forces), or that the witches know the apparitions will produce misleading information. In some productions (e.g. William Gaskill's, Royal Court Theatre, London, 1966), the witches visibly manipulate puppets or other 'artificial' representations of the apparitions.

28 illusion Either (1) deception, delusion (*OED* Illusion 2a), or (2) condition of being deceived (*OED* Illusion 2b).

30 spurn despise, reject contemptuously (*OED* Spurn *v¹* 6). The verb literally means 'kick' or 'trample'.

30–1 bear . . . 'bove sustain, cherish his hopes beyond. See the figurative meaning at *OED* Bear *v¹* 9. Hecate implies that Macbeth's hopes will put him beyond the influence of prudence, divine forgiveness, or terror.

31 grace fate, destiny (*OED* Grace *sb* 10); God's favour or blessing (*OED* Grace *sb* 11a).

32–3 security . . . enemy Proverbially, 'The way to be safe is never to be secure' (Dent W152).

32 security confidence (with the implication of 'over-confidence, complacency').

33 SD–35 SD These lines are the principal evidence for Thomas Middleton's authorship of this scene: see 0 SD n., 4n., and Textual Analysis, pp. 271–2 below. NS (p. 88), describing F's two SDs as 'obviously alternative', attributed one to the prompter; equally, the double SDs might arise from incomplete revision, or from a text prepared for use in both a public (amphitheatre) and a private (hall) theatre.

35 foggy cloud Possibly a theatrical 'machine' that lifted the actor from the stage. See Textual Analysis, pp. 256–7 below.

Act 3, Scene 6

This unlocalised scene implies that Macbeth knows of Macduff's flight to England (see 40–4), although that information apparently surprises and angers Macbeth in 4.1.140–1. See Textual Analysis, pp. 277–81 below. Like 2.4, this scene is choric commentary; its verse 'is serenely harmonious, and its tranquillity contrasts with the turbulence' (Knights, p. 30) of 3.4 and 4.1.

0 SD *another* LORD Compare the anonymous Old Man of 2.4.

1 hit coincided with, agreed with.

2 only I say i.e. I only say (Muir).

Things have been strangely borne. The gracious Duncan
Was pitied of Macbeth; marry, he was dead.
And the right-valiant Banquo walked too late,   5
Whom you may say, if't please you, Fleance killed,
For Fleance fled. Men must not walk too late.
Who cannot want the thought how monstrous
It was for Malcolm and for Donaldbain
To kill their gracious father? Damnèd fact,   10
How it did grieve Macbeth! Did he not straight
In pious rage the two delinquents tear,
That were the slaves of drink and thralls of sleep?
Was not that nobly done? Ay, and wisely too,
For 'twould have angered any heart alive   15
To hear the men deny't. So that I say,
He has borne all things well, and I do think
That had he Duncan's sons under his key –
As, an't please heaven, he shall not – they should find
What 'twere to kill a father. So should Fleance.   20
But peace, for from broad words, and 'cause he failed

4 dead.] F (dead:)   5 right-valiant] *Theobald;* right valiant F   6–7 Whom you may . . . not walk too late] F (walke); *not in* Q1673   7 fled.] F (fled:)   9 Donaldbain] F (*Donalbane*); *thus throughout remainder of play*   11 Macbeth!] *Capell;*
Macbeth? F   19 an't] *Theobald²;* and't F   21 'cause] F (cause)

3 borne endured, sustained. A transferred use of 'strangely' makes the line unclear: strange things have been suffered.

3 gracious Duncan Hunter suggests that Lennox echoes Macbeth's own phrases here and in 'right-valiant Banquo' (5): an opportunity for the actor.

4 pitied lamented.

4 marry See 2.3.23 n.

4 he was dead Duncan was dead. Macbeth 'pitied' Duncan after, not before, his death.

5 right-valiant very valiant.

7 Men . . . late All monosyllables, this under-statement initiates a satiric restatement (7–20) of Macbeth's version of recent events. As much as 4.3, this semi-choric scene marks a turning-point for Macbeth's fortunes: formerly frightened (and silent) Scots begin to speak, though 'broad words' (21) are still dangerous and will remain so (see 4.2.17–22). For omissions here in Q1673 and Davenant, see Supplementary Note, p. 259 below.

8 want lack. Technically, 'cannot' should read 'can', but the negative element in 'want' elicits denial ('cannot') which becomes intensification.

8 monstrous Pronounced trisyllabically ('monsterous') for the metre.

10 fact deed, action.

12 pious loyal, dutiful (*OED* Pious 2, where the earliest citation is from 1626, but the Latin *pius* means 'dutiful'). The phrase 'pious rage' is almost an oxymoron.

11–13 Did . . . sleep See 1.7.63–8.

13 thralls slaves (*OED* Thrall *sb*¹ 1b, quoting this line).

15–16 For . . . deny't The kind of double-talk needed if every listener may be a spy or a 'traitor': Lennox's remark means both that persons who believed Macbeth would be angered by the grooms' allegedly false denials and that the dead Duncan (who is not a 'heart alive') cannot confirm the grooms' innocence.

17 borne Compare 3 and 3.1.81.

18 under his key locked up, imprisoned.

19 an't if it. F's 'and' was a common early modern English synonym for 'if'.

20 So should Fleance i.e. were Macbeth to have Fleance 'under . . . key' (18), he would be condemned for murdering Banquo.

21 peace hush, be silent.

21 broad plain, unreserved: Compare 3.4.23 and n.

21 'cause because (aphetic form).

21 failed The word recalls Macbeth's injunction (3.1.29) to Banquo, who did 'attend'.

His presence at the tyrant's feast, I hear
Macduff lives in disgrace. Sir, can you tell
Where he bestows himself?
LORD   The son of Duncan,
From whom this tyrant holds the due of birth,   25
Lives in the English court and is received
Of the most pious Edward with such grace,
That the malevolence of fortune nothing
Takes from his high respect. Thither Macduff
Is gone to pray the holy king upon his aid   30
To wake Northumberland and warlike Siward,
That by the help of these, with him above
To ratify the work, we may again
Give to our tables meat, sleep to our nights,
Free from our feasts and banquets bloody knives,   35
Do faithful homage and receive free honours,
All which we pine for now. And this report
Hath so exasperate their king that he
Prepares for some attempt of war.
LENNOX Sent he to Macduff?   40

24 son] *Theobald;* Sonnes F   31 Siward] F (*Seyward*); *thus throughout play*   38 their] F; the *Hanmer*

24 **son** Malcolm. Compare other mentions of Donaldbain, 3.1.32 and 5.2.7. Compositor B may have remembered 'Duncan's sons' (18).

25 **holds** withholds.

25 **due** what is owed.

27 **Edward** Edward the Confessor (King of England, AD 1042–66).

28–9 **malevolence of fortune . . . high respect** i.e. exile from Scotland and deprivation of the kingship have not affected the great esteem shown Malcolm (see *OED* Respect *sb* 16b).

30 **Is gone** As 46–8 clarify, Macduff has departed for the English court, but has not yet (in 3.6) arrived.

31 **Northumberland . . . Siward** *Scotland*, p. 175b, makes clear in text and margin that 'Siward' is the family name of the historically appropriate earls of Northumberland. Apparently, father (who died, historically, two years before Macbeth) and son are referred to here, though the son is later described as having 'lived but till he was a man' (5.9.6), making 'warlike' an odd epithet; Blackfriars speculates that 'Northumberland' = 'the people of this northern English county'.

32 **him above** God.

33 **ratify** confirm, make valid.

34–5 Compare the homily, 'An Exhortacion con-

cernyng Good Ordre' (1547), regularly read aloud in church: 'Take awaye kynges, princes, rulers, magistrates, judges and such states of Gods ordre, no man shal ride or go by the high waie unrobbed, no man shall slepe in his awne house or bed unkilled, no man shall kepe his wife, children and possessions in quietnes' (R. B. Bond (ed.), *Certain Sermons or Homilies*, 1987, p. 161).

35 The syntax is unusual: Free our feasts and banquets from bloody knives; 'banquets' may recall 'Banquo'.

36 **Do . . . homage** Give faithful allegiance. The Lord implies that men render loyalty to Macbeth not out of faith and duty, but fear; see 5.2.19–20.

37 **pine** yearn, long (*OED* Pine *v* 6).

37 **this report** i.e. information about Malcolm's actions in England and Macduff's flight. The 'report' may be, however, Malcolm's account (to Edward) of events in Scotland.

38 **exasperate** exasperated (see Abbott 342).

38 **their king** King Edward, Northumberland's and Siward's ('their') king. This reading is controversial; see Textual Analysis, p. 277 below, and 'this report' (37 and n.).

39 **attempt** attack, assault (*OED* Attempt *sb* 3a, citing this line).

LORD   He did. And with an absolute, 'Sir, not I',
        The cloudy messenger turns me his back
        And hums, as who should say, 'You'll rue the time
        That clogs me with this answer.'
LENNOX   And that well might
        Advise him to a caution t'hold what distance   45
        His wisdom can provide. Some holy angel
        Fly to the court of England and unfold
        His message ere he come, that a swift blessing
        May soon return to this our suffering country
        Under a hand accursed.
LORD   I'll send my prayers with him.   50

                                                        Exeunt

4.1 *Thunder. Enter the three* WITCHES [*with a cauldron*]

FIRST WITCH   Thrice the brindled cat hath mewed.
SECOND WITCH   Thrice and once the hedge-pig whined.

---

41 'Sir . . . I',] *Pope* (subst.); Sir . . . I F   43–4 'You'll . . . answer.'] *Theobald* (subst.); you'l . . . Answer. F   45 t'hold]
F (t hold)   **Act 4, Scene 1**   **4.1**] F (*Actus Quartus. Scena Prima.*)   0 SD *with a cauldron*] *Padua, Rowe* (subst.)
1 brindled] F (brinded)   2 Thrice] F; Twice *Theobald*

41 absolute positive, decided (*OED* Absolute 11). Macduff is peremptory.

41 Sir, not I These are Macduff's words (Muir, Additional Notes).

42 cloudy sullen, frowning (*OED* Cloudy 6b, quoting *The Rape of Lucrece* 1084 and this line as the earliest examples).

42 turns me his back This phrase is slightly confusing for two reasons: the Lord continues to report an event he apparently did not witness directly, and he employs an 'ethical dative' ('me') to emphasise his astonishment at the messenger's discourtesy and to convey that reaction – 'Can you imagine? he turned his back.' See Peter J. Gillett in *Reader*, p. 119.

43 hums murmurs discontentedly (see *OED* Hum *v*[1] 2a).

43 rue the time regret the occasion. The line probably puns on the herbs thyme and rue; compare 'Rue and time grow both in one garden' (Dent R198, citing only *John* 3.1.323–5).

44 clogs burdens, hampers (*OED* Clog *v* 3).

45 caution taking heed, precaution (*OED* Caution *sb* 5)

49–50 suffering . . . accursed i.e. country suffering under an accursed hand. For the grammar, Muir cites 'As a long-parted mother with her child' (*R2* 3.2.8).

Act 4, Scene 1

The location of this scene is as doubtful as its narrative connection with 3.6 (see Textual Analysis, pp. 277–8 below). Hecate says it will be the 'pit of Acheron' (3.5.15), and it is an outdoor scene (horses gallop up at 139) and a place where the cauldron and apparitions may exist, but also an interior ('come in, without there' (134)), where a lock and knock may be imagined (46), a place where Lennox and presumably other courtiers are within earshot. The Padua promptbook stipulates the needed cauldron, and Rowe identifies the scene as 'A dark Cave, in the middle a great Cauldron burning'. The witches' 'cooking' inverts and contrasts with the banquet of 3.4 (see Knight, *Imperial*, p. 138, and Michael Hawkins, 'History, politics and *Macbeth*', in *Focus*, p. 166). Garrick, Macklin, and others developed elaborate sets for this scene. On various theatrical versions of Macbeth's behaviour here, see p. 79 above.

1 brindled Having fur marked by streaks of a darker colour. F's 'brinded' is archaic.

2 Thrice Theobald emended to 'Twice' (so that 'Twice and once' would = three times) because '*three* and *nine* are the Numbers us'd in all Inchantments, and magical operations'; Compositor B's eye might have caught 'Thrice' (1), but the repetition is also aurally effective.

2 hedge-pig hedgehog. This line is *OED*'s

THIRD WITCH   Harpier cries, ''Tis time, 'tis time.'

FIRST WITCH   Round about the cauldron go;
           In the poisoned entrails throw.   5
           Toad, that under cold stone
           Days and nights has thirty-one
           Sweltered venom sleeping got,
           Boil thou first i'th'charmèd pot.

ALL   Double, double toil and trouble;   10
           Fire burn, and cauldron bubble.

SECOND WITCH   Fillet of a fenny snake,
           In the cauldron boil and bake:
           Eye of newt, and toe of frog,
           Wool of bat, and tongue of dog,   15
           Adder's fork, and blind-worm's sting,
           Lizard's leg, and howlet's wing,
           For a charm of powerful trouble,
           Like a hell-broth, boil and bubble.

ALL   Double, double toil and trouble,   20
           Fire burn, and cauldron bubble.

THIRD WITCH   Scale of dragon, tooth of wolf,
           Witches' mummy, maw and gulf

---

3 ''Tis . . . time.'] *Cam.;* 'tis . . . time. F   5 throw.] *Rowe;* throw F   7 thirty-one] *Capell;* thirty one: F   8 Sweltered]
F (Sweltred)   10, 20, 35 double] *Steevens;* double, F   23 Witches'] *Theobald²;* Witches F

earliest citation for the word. Fairies sing a song
guarding the sleeping Titania from 'spotted snakes
with double tongue' and 'Thorny hedgehogs . . .
Newts and blind-worms' (*MND* 2.2.9–11); compare Timon's accusatory sequence 'toad . . . adder
. . . newt . . . eyeless venomed worm' (*Tim.* 4.3.181–
2) and 16.
   3 Harpier Presumably the name of a familiar
(see 1.1.9 n.); compare 'Graymalkin' and 'Paddock'
(1.1.9–10).
   7 thirty-one In Elizabethan pronunciation, a
true rhyme with 'stone' (6); see 5.9.41–2 and Cercignani, p. 136.
   8 Sweltered Exuded like sweat (as if) by heat
(*OED* Sweltered *ppl a* 1, treating this meaning as a
Shakespearean coinage and later used as quotations
from or allusions to it).
   8 venom poison. Toads were popularly supposed to be poisonous; compare *AYLI* 2.1.13.
Agnis Thompson, one of the witches James VI
interrogated, allegedly 'gathered the venome' of 'a
blacke Toade' to poison the Scottish king (*Newes*,
p. 16).
   10 toil severe labour (*OED* Toil *sb¹* 3a). Other

meanings are relevant: 'dispute, controversy' (*OED*
Toil *sb¹* 1) – witches were often accused of spread-
ing dissension among neighbours; 'net' or 'snare for
wild beasts' (*OED* Toil *sb²* 1–2). Compare 4.2.34.
   12 Lengthwise slice or section ('Fillet') of a snake
from marshlands (fens). See illustration 11, p. 56
above.
   14 newt A small, tailed amphibian similar to the
salamander.
   15 Wool Soft under-hair, down (*OED* Wool *sb*
1c, quoting 'The powder of the wooll of a Hare
burned . . . fasteneth the haire from falling off'
(Topsell, p. 274)).
   16 fork split tongue (supposed to carry venom).
See 2 and n.
   16 blind-worm slow-worm (a reptile with tiny
eyes); adder (*OED*).
   17 howlet owl, owlet (not archaic according to
OED).
   18 charm incantation, magical rhyme; compare
3.5.18–19.
   23 mummy mummia, 'a pitch used for embalm-
ing, and, hence, embalmed flesh' (Webster, *White
Devil* 1.1.16 n., and see *White Devil* 2.1.249:

Of the ravined salt-sea shark,
Root of hemlock, digged i'th'dark;   25
Liver of blaspheming Jew,
Gall of goat, and slips of yew,
Slivered in the moon's eclipse;
Nose of Turk, and Tartar's lips,
Finger of birth-strangled babe,   30
Ditch-delivered by a drab,
Make the gruel thick and slab.
Add thereto a tiger's chawdron
For th'ingredience of our cauldron.

24 salt-sea] *Capell;* salt Sea F   34 cauldron] F (Cawdron)

'Preserve her flesh like mummia'); preparation for magical purposes, made from dead bodies (*Lexicon*). The only witchcraft statute of James's reign, 1 Jac. I, c. 12 (1604), specified death for persons who exhumed bodies and their parts for use in witchcraft, as the Scottish witches James interrogated had allegedly done (*Newes*, pp. 16–17); compare James's description of how the Devil causes witches 'to ioynt dead corpses, & to make powders thereof' (*Daemonologie*, p. 43). The Jacobean statute is reprinted in Robbins, pp. 280–1, and compared with those of Henry VIII and Elizabeth I (Robbins, p. 166). The handkerchief Othello gave Desdemona 'was dy'd in mummy which the skilful / Conserved of maidens' hearts' (*Oth.* 3.4.74–5).

23 maw stomach.

23 gulf 'that which devours or swallows up anything' (*OED* Gulf *sb* 3); a bawdy meaning, 'vagina', was well established (Williams). The phrase 'maw and gulf' may be hendiadys for 'gulf-like maw', hence 'voracious appetite' (*OED* Gulf *sb* 3b) or 'ravenous appetite' (Muir).

24 ravined Compare 2.4.28 and n.

25 hemlock poisonous herb.

25 digged i'th'dark Lucianus will 'kill' the Player King with poison, a 'mixture rank, of midnight weeds collected, / With Hecat's ban thrice blasted, thrice infected' (*Ham.* 3.2.257–8). The apothecary was warned against 'superstitiouslie' selecting 'choyse days or houres . . . in gathering . . . herbes or other simples for the making of his drouges' (Andreas Gerardus (?), *The True Tryall and Examination of a mans owne selfe*, trans. Thomas Newton (1586), p. 39; in another witchcraft scene, several demonic ingredients 'must be taken in th'increasing of the Moone: / Before the rising of the Sun, or when the same is down' (*Fidele and Fortunio* lines 373–4). Compare 'moon's eclipse' (28) and n.

26 blaspheming i.e. denying that Jesus was

the Messiah. With Turks and Tartars (29), Jews and the 'birth-strangled babe' (30) would be especially vulnerable because unbaptised as Christians; see the Good Friday Collect: 'Have mercy upon all Jews, Turks, infidels, and heretics . . . And so fetch them home . . . that they may be saved' (*The Elizabethan Prayer Book*, ed. John E. Booty, 1976, p. 144). The Duke (or Doge) similarly associates Turks, Tartars, and Jews in *MV* 4.1.32–4.

27 goat Traditionally, a lecherous, irascible beast (compare 37 n.), hence its gall, or bile (see 1.5.46 n.), is appropriate for the witches' poisonous brew.

27 yew The yew tree was long associated with death (see Gerard, p. 1188, cited by H. T. Price. 'The yew-tree in *Titus Andronicus*', *N&Q* 208 (1963), 98–9), churchyards, and funerals. Compare 'My shroud of white, stuck all with yew' (*TN* 2.4.55) and 'Lay a garland on my hearse of the dismal yew' (*Maid's Tragedy* 2.1.72).

28 Slivered Cut off as a sliver or slip (from a tree).

28 moon's eclipse Traditionally, a lunar eclipse was the best time to collect magical and medicinal herbs. Compare 25 and n.

30 birth-strangled i.e. throttled by the umbilical cord during labour, or killed after birth by a mother who could not support her infant.

30 babe The word rhymed with the modern pronunciation of 'drab' (31) and 'slab' (32); see Cercignani, p. 178.

31 Ditch-delivered Born in a ditch (without the customary attendance of midwife and female friends or relatives).

31 drab prostitute; slattern.

32 slab semi-solid, viscid. This line is the sole use by Shakespeare and earliest citation at *OED* Slab *a*[1].

33 chawdron entrails. This line is the sole use by Shakespeare.

34 ingredience See 1.7.11 n.

ALL   Double, double toil and trouble,
          Fire burn, and cauldron bubble.   35
SECOND WITCH   Cool it with a baboon's blood,
          Then the charm is firm and good.

Enter HECATE, *and the other three Witches*

HECATE   O well done! I commend your pains,
          And every one shall share i'th'gains;   40
          And now about the cauldron sing
          Like elves and fairies in a ring,
          Enchanting all that you put in.
              Music, and a song, 'Black spirits, etc.'
                  [*Exeunt Hecate and the other three Witches*]
SECOND WITCH   By the pricking of my thumbs,
          Something wicked this way comes;   45
          Open locks, whoever knocks.

Enter MACBETH

MACBETH   How now, you secret, black, and midnight hags!
          What is't you do?
ALL THE WITCHES   A deed without a name.

---

38 SD HECATE] F (*Hecat*)   **43** SD.1] F (*Musicke and a Song. Blacke Spirits, &c.*)   **43** SD.2] *Muir; not in* F; *Hecate retires / Globe; Exit Hecate / Dyce*   **48** SH ALL THE WITCHES] *Oxford; All* F (*and for remainder of scene*)

37 SH, **44** SH In 1.1 and 1.3, the sisters speak in numerical sequence except when responding to First Witch's questions or commands; 4.1 has established a similar pattern, varied by the chorus (10–11, 20–1, 35–6). To preserve the earlier pattern, the speech at 37 certainly, and the one at 44 possibly, should therefore be assigned to First Witch, though it is odd to find the same witch speaking consecutively for her triad. Some Shakespearean dialogue was probably deleted when 38 SD–43 SD was inserted (see n.).

37 baboon Through demonic contraries, this animal's notoriously 'hot' blood appropriately cools the witches' brew: baboons 'are evill mannered and natured, wherefore also they are pictured to signifie wrath . . . they are as lustfull and venerous as goats, attempting to defile all sorts of women' (Topsell, p. 11). Compare the association of baboons and human lust at *TNK* 3.5.34–5 and 132, *Per.* 4.6.178–9, and Dekker (and Thomas Middleton), *The Roaring Girl* 4.2.129. The word is accented on the first syllable.

38 SD–**43** SD F's text and associated SDs are almost certainly not by Shakespeare, but belong to a pre-Folio revision-adaptation of *Macbeth* designed to increase the play's spectacle. See Textual Analysis, pp. 273–5 below, and Appendix 2, p. 286.

38 SD *the other three Witches* Many editors delete these figures as superfluous, but they appropriately dignify Hecate's entrance and seem to be singers (unlike the witches of 1.1 and 1.3), needed for the song of 43 SD. 1.

41 sing The cue for musicians (who may have been visible to the original audiences) to prepare to play. Compare 128 n.

42 ring Dancing fairies were supposed to create 'fairy rings', circles of darker grass in lawns or fields; compare *MND* 2.1.9, 86.

43 SD.2 Some editors direct Hecate (and presumably 'the other three Witches' who entered with her) to remain on stage, silent and inactive until the final demonic dance (see 131 SD n.), while other editors (Oxford, Brooke) and a few twentieth-century productions (e.g. Peter Hall and J. R. Brown's, National Theatre, London, 1978) incorporate here an extensive interlude from *Witch*.

44 pricking tingling.

45 Many editors add *Knocking* after 'comes', but Second Witch may speak metaphorically.

46 Scot records 'A charme to open locks' (XII, 14).

47 black baneful, malignant, deadly (*OED* Black *a* 8).

MACBETH I conjure you by that which you profess,
            Howe'er you come to know it, answer me.   50
            Though you untie the winds and let them fight
            Against the churches, though the yeasty waves
            Confound and swallow navigation up,
            Though bladed corn be lodged and trees blown down,
            Though castles topple on their warders' heads,   55
            Though palaces and pyramids do slope
            Their heads to their foundations, though the treasure
            Of nature's germen tumble altogether
            Even till destruction sicken: answer me
            To what I ask you.
FIRST WITCH   Speak.
SECOND WITCH   Demand.
THIRD WITCH   We'll answer.   60
FIRST WITCH Say, if thou'dst rather hear it from our mouths,
            Or from our masters'?
MACBETH   Call 'em, let me see 'em.
FIRST WITCH Pour in sow's blood, that hath eaten
            Her nine farrow; grease that's sweaten

---

55 warders] F (Warders)   **56** slope] F; stoop *conj. Capell* ('*Notes*', *sig.* 2c1v)   **58** germen] F (Germaine); germins
Theobald. See Commentary   **61** thou'dst] *Capell*; th'hadst F   **62** masters'?] *Capell*; masters. F; masters? *Pope*

---

49 conjure call on solemnly (*Lexicon*), entreat
in the name of something sacred.

49 profess claim to have knowledge of (*OED*
Profess *v* 5).

51 untie the winds undo the knot (release) the
winds. Mary Floyd-Wilson, 'English Epicures and
Scottish Witches', *SQ* 57 (2006), p. 149 quotes a
1616 witchcraft treatise which discusses witches'
granting sailors strings with three knots (each successive knot representing a wind of greater ferocity
than the previous one); hence this line seems a reference to 'the alleged practice of northern witches
selling winds in "knots".'

52 yeasty foamy, frothy (*OED* Yeasty 3, quoting
this line as its first example).

53 navigation shipping, or ships considered collectively (sole use in Shakespeare and earliest citation at *OED* Navigation 4).

54 bladed corn i.e. corn when the blade still
surrounds the ear. Staunton cited 'Some [affirm]
that they [witches] can transferre corne in the blade
from one place to another' (Scot, 1, 4).

54 lodged flattened, broken down (by wind and
rain).

55 warders guardians, persons in charge.

56 pyramids Shakespeare and other contemporary writers probably confused pyramids with
obelisks; see W. Watkiss Lloyd, *N&Q* 83 (1891),
283, and 'a *Pyramis* or piller' (Thomas Bell, *The
Anatomy of popish Tyranny* (1603), sig. H2v).

56 slope bend down. This line is the sole use in
Shakespeare and the earliest citation at *OED* Slope

*v*¹ 3.

58 F ends this line with a comma that makes all
the 'though'-clauses govern 'Even till destruction
sicken' (59); the punctuation adopted here treats
that phrase as a consequence of 58.

58 germen 'seeds or material essences of things'
(Hunter), the material (as opposed to divine or
spiritual) sources from which all creation springs.
W. C. Curry, *Shakespeare's Philosophical Patterns*,
1937, pp. 30–49, explains the patristic sources
for this idea. The word is apparently a collective
noun (not recorded in *OED* Germen before 1759),
but F elsewhere makes the word plural: 'Crack
nature's moulds, all germains spill at once' (*Lear*
3.2.8, where some editors read 'germens'). Compare 'seeds of time' (1.3.56) and 'make Nature
fight/Within herself' (*Queens* 135–6).

59 sicken i.e. become ill through consuming too
much. Destruction is personified as a glutton.

61 thou'dst thou hadst.

62 masters ministers, instruments (i.e., subor-
dinates). See Prospero's address to 'Ye elves . . . /
Weak masters thou ye be . . .' (*Temp.* 5.1.32, 41);
Stephen Orgel, ed. *Tempest*, Oxford Shakespeare
(1987) cites M. K. Flint and E. J. Dobson, 'Weak
Masters', *RES*, n.s. 10 (1959): 58–60.

63–4 Pour . . . farrow The natural history is
accurate: sows sometimes eat their young ('farrow').

64 sweaten exuded (Shakespeare invented the
-en form for the rhyme).

From the murderer's gibbet throw   65
Into the flame.
ALL THE WITCHES   Come high or low:
Thyself and office deftly show.

Thunder. [Enter] FIRST APPARITION, *an armed Head*

MACBETH Tell me, thou unknown power –
FIRST WITCH   He knows thy thought;
Hear his speech, but say thou nought.
FIRST APPARITION Macbeth, Macbeth, Macbeth: beware
        Macduff,   70
Beware the Thane of Fife. Dismiss me. Enough.   *Descends*
MACBETH Whate'er thou art, for thy good caution, thanks;
Thou hast harped my fear aright. But one word more –
FIRST WITCH He will not be commanded. Here's another,
More potent than the first.   75

Thunder. [Enter] SECOND APPARITION, *a bloody Child*

SECOND APPARITION Macbeth, Macbeth, Macbeth.
MACBETH Had I three ears, I'd hear thee.
SECOND APPARITION Be bloody, bold, and resolute; laugh to
        scorn

65 murderer's] F (Murderers)   67 SD *Thunder . . . Head*] F (*Thunder. / 1. Apparition . . . Head*)   68 power –] *Rowe;* power. F   70 SH] F (1 *Appar.*)   71 SD *Descends*] *Rowe; He Descends* F   73 more –] *Rowe;* more. F   75 SD *Thunder . . . Child*] F (*Thunder. / 2 Apparition . . . Bloody Childe*)   76 SH] F (2 *Appar.*)   77 I'd] F (Il'd)   78 SH] F (*Appar.*)

65 **gibbet** The gallows, a structure on which the condemned were hanged; structure from which hanged bodies were suspended and displayed (*OED* Gibbet *sb*[1] 1). On the latter meaning, see *Scotland*, p. 169a (quoted in 1.2.23 n.).

67 SD-93 For the contemporary context of this prophetic episode, see Jaech.

67 SD *armed Head* armoured, or helmeted, head. Critics, variously, have supposed the Apparition represents Macbeth's head (at the play's end), the mature Macduff, or Macdonald's head (at the play's beginning).

67 SD **office** duty; particular responsibility (*OED* Office *sb* 2a-b). Compare 'Do you your office, or give up your place' (*MM* 2.2.13) and 2.1.14 n.

71 **Thane of Fife** Macduff.

71 SD This SD (like 80 SD and 93 SD) suggests that the Apparition exits through a trap-door in the stage. Compare 105 and n.

72 **caution** word of warning (*OED* Caution *sb* 3).

73 **Thou hast** Probably elided ('Thou'st'); see

Cercignani, pp. 288–9.

73 **harped** guessed, hit upon (*OED* Harp *v* 7). This line is the sole use by Shakespeare in this sense and *OED*'s earliest citation.

73 **But one word more** Compare 99–104 and 1.3.68 ff.

75 SD *bloody Child* This Apparition may represent: baby Macduff, born by Caesarean section; Fleance, attacked by the Murderers; the phantasmagoric children of Banquo who will succeed Macbeth; any children who threaten tyrant Macbeth. It might thus prefigure (Halio) Macduff's murdered son (see 4.2); Halio cites various more elaborate possibilities.

77 The line may sound comical, but it stresses Macbeth's eagerness: even superhuman senses ('three ears') would await this information; alternatively, it may be bravado: no amount of supernatural speech or human hearing will frighten Macbeth.

78–9 Macbeth may 'scorn' 'The power of man' because all men are 'of woman born'. See Adelman, *passim*.

The power of man, for none of woman born
Shall harm Macbeth.   *Descends*   80
MACBETH   Then live, Macduff, what need I fear of thee?
But yet I'll make assurance double sure
And take a bond of fate: thou shalt not live,
That I may tell pale-hearted fear it lies,
And sleep in spite of thunder.

Thunder. [Enter] THIRD APPARITION, *a Child crowned, with a tree
in his hand*

                                    What is this,   85
That rises like the issue of a king
And wears upon his baby-brow the round
And top of sovereignty?
ALL THE WITCHES   Listen, but speak not to't.
THIRD APPARITION   Be lion-mettled, proud, and take no care
Who chafes, who frets, or where conspirers are.   90
Macbeth shall never vanquished be until
Great Birnam Wood to high Dunsinane hill
Shall come against him.   *Descends*
MACBETH   That will never be:
Who can impress the forest, bid the tree
Unfix his earthbound root? Sweet bodements, good.   95

---

82 assurance] *Pope;* assurance: F   85 SD *Thunder . . . hand*] F (*Thunder / 3 Apparition . . . Childe Crowned . . . Tree . . .
hand*)   89 SH] F (3 *Appar.*)   89 lion-mettled] Q*1673* (Lion-metled); Lyon metled F   93 SD] *Rowe; Descend* F   95
bodements, good.] F (boadments, good:); boadments! good! *Rowe*

79 of woman born all humankind. This and
similar biblical phrases (Job 14.1, 15.14, 25.4, Matt.
11.11, Luke 7.28) add solemnity and ambiguity
to the Apparition's supposed promise. Compare
5.7.12, 14, and 'one of woman born' (5.8.13).
   82 assurance The word has two main groups
of meanings: 'the action of assuring' (what the
Apparitions do to Macbeth); 'the state of being
assured' (Macbeth's response to the Apparitions).
See *OED* Assurance.
   83 bond contract, legal surety. By killing Macduff, Macbeth will make it impossible for Fate to
break the promise ('bond') given by the Second
Apparition. Compare the meanings of 'bond' at
3.2.49 and n.
   84 pale-hearted Compare 2.2.68, 3.4.116,
5.3.11, 5.3.15–17, and nn.
   84 it Fear (personified); the Second Apparition.
   85 SD The immediate *Thunder* makes Macbeth's
'in spite of thunder' ironic, or bravado.
   86 issue progeny, children.
   87 round royal crown, recalling 'golden round'
(1.5.26).

88 speak not to't Traditionally, witnesses to
conjured figures were warned not to interrogate
them; when Helen of Troy appears, Faustus advises
the Scholars, 'Be silent then, for danger is in words'
(Marlowe, *Dr Faustus* 5.1; line 1696), and Steevens[2]
cites 'be mute, / Or else our spell is marred' (*Temp.*
4.1.126–7). Compare 3.4.117–18.
   89 lion-mettled having a lion's qualities (here,
the lion's traditional courage).
   90 Who Whoever (Abbott 251).
   92 Dunsinane The word sometimes receives
primary stress on the first syllable (5.2.12), sometimes on the second, as here. Forman (11, 338)
spelled it 'Dunston Anyse'.
   93–100 Macbeth adopts the Apparitions' couplets.
   94 impress press-gang, force to join an army
(see *OED* Impress *v*[2] a, where this line is the second citation after *1H4* 1.1.21).
   95 Sweet bodements Attractive prophecies,
happy predictions. This line is the earliest citation
at *OED* Bodement.

Rebellious dead, rise never till the wood
Of Birnam rise, and our high-placed Macbeth
Shall live the lease of nature, pay his breath
To time and mortal custom. Yet my heart
Throbs to know one thing. Tell me, if your art   100
Can tell so much, shall Banquo's issue ever
Reign in this kingdom?

ALL THE WITCHES   Seek to know no more.

MACBETH I will be satisfied. Deny me this,
And an eternal curse fall on you. Let me know.
    [*Cauldron descends.*] *Hautboys*
Why sinks that cauldron? And what noise is this?   105

FIRST WITCH Show!

SECOND WITCH Show!

THIRD WITCH Show!

ALL THE WITCHES Show his eyes and grieve his heart,
Come like shadows, so depart.   110

[*Enter*] *a show of eight kings, and* [*the*] *last with a glass in his hand* [;
Banquo's Ghost following]

MACBETH Thou art too like the spirit of Banquo. Down!
Thy crown does sear mine eyeballs. And thy hair,

---

96 Rebellious dead] F; Rebellious Head *Theobald*; Rebellion's head *Hanmer*   **97 our high-placed**] *Rowe*; our high plac'd
F; on's high place *Oxford*   **104** SD] *Rowe* (*subst.*) *after 102*; *not in* F   **104** SD *Hautboys*] F (*Hoboyes*) *at right margin
opposite 104*   **110** SD] *Cam.* (*subst.*); *A shew of eight Kings, and Banquo last, with a glasse in his hand.* F   **112** hair] F
(*haire*); air *Johnson*; heir *conj. Jackson*

---

96 Rebellious dead i.e. Banquo and his ghost
(compare 3.4.75–83 and 3.4.93–6). Duncan faced
living rebels (see e.g. 1.2.9 ff.), Macbeth faces the
resurrected dead.

97 our high-placed our high-ranking. The
phrase is odd, Oxford's emendation ingenious.

98 lease of nature i.e. the limited time nature
grants one to live (Macbeth's natural life span).
Compare 3.2.38 and 40; 'if I might have a lease of
my life for a thousand years' (*2H6* 4.10.5–6); 'No
man has lease of his life' (Dent M327).

99 mortal custom i.e. the usual (customary)
length of human ('mortal') life.

103 I will be satisfied I must have an answer.

105 sinks An implicit SD suggesting that the
cauldron disappears through a trap-door in the
stage; the playing of hautboys (104 SD; see 1.6.0
SD and n.) conceals the sounds of the trap-door
and, perhaps, of the Apparitions' entry.

110 SD.1 *eight kings* When *Macbeth* was composed, eight Stuart kings and one Stuart queen
had ruled Scotland, but James IV and I's mother,

Mary Stuart, Queen of Scots, does not appear, perhaps because including her would recall her execution in 1587 (at Elizabeth's implicit order) and that
event was politically too sensitive to be acknowledged (see Brooke, pp. 73–4). These spectral beings
pass across the stage and exit by the time Macbeth
says 'What, is this so?' (123). For the entire SD, see
Supplementary Note, p. 259 below.

110 SD.1 *glass* magic crystal permitting visions
of the future (see 119–20); not a looking-glass or
mirror. See *OED* Glass *sb*[1] 8e and compare 'like a
prophet / Looks in a glass that shows . . . future
evils' (*MM* 2.2.94–5).

111 Thou . . . Banquo i.e. the first king too
closely resembles Banquo's 'spirit' or ghost (frightening Macbeth as the ghost had in 3.4 and confirming his fear that Banquo's sons will rule Scotland).

112 hair F's 'haire' was an available spelling
for 'hair' (the question of inheritance that so concerns Macbeth here), but the grammar of 'thy' and
'Thou' (113), both apparently addressed to the second king, make 'heir' less likely.

Thou other gold-bound brow, is like the first;
A third, is like the former.–Filthy hags,
Why do you show me this?–A fourth? Start, eyes!   115
What, will the line stretch out to th'crack of doom?
Another yet? A seventh? I'll see no more.
And yet the eighth appears, who bears a glass
Which shows me many more. And some I see,
That two-fold balls and treble sceptres carry.   120
Horrible sight! Now I see 'tis true,
For the blood-boltered Banquo smiles upon me,
And points at them for his.

        [*Exeunt show of kings and Banquo's Ghost*]

           What, is this so?

FIRST WITCH Ay, sir, all this is so. But why
     Stands Macbeth thus amazedly?   125
     Come, sisters, cheer we up his sprites,
     And show the best of our delights.
     I'll charm the air to give a sound,
     While you perform your antic round
     That this great king may kindly say,   130
     Our duties did his welcome pay.

---

113 gold-bound brow] F (Gold-bound-brow)   116 to th'crack] F3; to'th'crack F   118 eighth] F3–4; eight F, F2
122 blood-boltered] F (Blood-bolter'd); blood-baltered *Brooke*   123 SD] *Oxford (subst.); not in* F   123 What,] *Pope;*
What? F   124 SH FIRST WITCH] F (1); HECATE *Oxford (conj. Cam.)*

113 gold-bound brow i.e. head surrounded ('bound') by a crown ('gold').

115 Start Jump from your sockets (so Macbeth does not have to witness Banquo's succession); see 'I could a tale unfold whose lightest word / Would . . . / Make thy two eyes like stars start from their spheres' (*Ham.* 1.5.15–17).

116 crack of doom thunder ('crack') accompanying the Last Judgement ('doom'). Compare 2.3.72 and n.

118 eighth F3's 'eighth' is consistent with the other ordinal numbers in the passage, but F's 'eight' might refer to the number of Stuart males who had ruled Scotland (see 110 SD. 1 n.). Ordinals and cardinals were used interchangeably; see e.g. 'Harry the Eight' (Jonson, *Alchemist* 1.1.113).

120 two-fold balls and treble sceptres two balls and three sceptres. The line may refer to King James (see Supplementary Note, p. 259 below), but whatever the precise referent, Macbeth sees a long line of increasingly powerful kings. See illustration 12, p. 60 above.

122 blood-boltered matted, clogged with blood

(from the twenty wounds of 3.4.27 and 3.4.81). For 'blood-boltered', see *OED* Blood *sb* 21, where a link between 'bolter' and the archaic 'balter' is suggested but not substantiated; see also *OED* Balter *v* 4: 'clot or clog with anything sticky'.

123 his i.e. his sons. The *show* presents Banquo's royal descendants.

124–31 SD These lines explaining Hecate's and the witches' departure were probably written by Thomas Middleton; see Textual Analysis, pp. 273–5 below.

125 amazedly as in a maze (see 2.4.19 and 5.1.68 n.). The word rhymed with modern pronunciation of 'why' (124).

126–31 The witches offer a macabre version of a Jacobean courtly entertainment.

126 sprites spirits. See 2.3.73 n.

128 A cue for music (see 41 and n.).

129 antic round bizarre dance. See 1.3.33 n.

131 duties expressions of deference or respect.

131 did his welcome pay showed him the respect due to a monarch.

> *Music. The Witches dance, and vanish*

MACBETH Where are they? Gone? Let this pernicious hour,
Stand aye accursèd in the calendar.
Come in, without there!

> *Enter* LENNOX

LENNOX   What's your grace's will?
MACBETH Saw you the weïrd sisters?
LENNOX   No, my lord.   135
MACBETH Came they not by you?
LENNOX   No indeed, my lord.
MACBETH Infected be the air whereon they ride,
And damned all those that trust them. I did hear
The galloping of horse. Who was't came by?
LENNOX 'Tis two or three, my lord, that bring you word   140
Macduff is fled to England.
MACBETH   Fled to England?
LENNOX Ay, my good lord.
MACBETH [*Aside*] Time, thou anticipat'st my dread exploits;
The flighty purpose never is o'ertook
Unless the deed go with it. From this moment,   145
The very firstlings of my heart shall be

---

131 SD] F (*Musicke . . . Dance . . .*); *Globe adds* / *with Hecate*   135 weïrd] *Theobald;* Weyard F

131 SD Some editors treat this interlude as a dance of six witches and Hecate (see 43 SD. 2 and n.), but Shakespeare's original three witches earlier performed macabre dance routines and may again do so alone here.
132–3 On beliefs about propitious and unlucky days, see *John* 3.1.81–95 and Thomas, pp. 615–23.
133 aye ever.
135 Macbeth expects Lennox to recognise the witches; knowledge of them has apparently spread beyond Banquo and Macbeth.
137 air . . . ride A common belief about witches, but perhaps also a hint of early stage effects (see 3.5.34–5 and 3.5.35 n.).
138–9 I did hear / The galloping of horse See 3.3.8 n.
139 galloping Earliest citation under *OED* Galloping *vbl sb* (Schäfer).
141 Macbeth's ignorance here is inconsistent with speeches in 3.6; see Textual Analysis, pp. 277–8 below.
143–55 This speech may be an aside, with 154–5 addressed to Lennox, but Dessen, 'Problems', p. 143, cautions: 'To designate the speech as an aside . . . is to enforce . . . one choice at the expense

of other . . . options.' The question and command of 154–5 mark a substantial break, although they may indicate that Macbeth has become aware of Lennox, having delivered the preceding lines 'aloud' and not 'aside'.
143 thou anticipat'st you forestall, deal with beforehand (*OED* Anticipate *v* 3, where this line is the earliest citation); Blackfriars speculates that the word also means 'accelerates'.
143 dread terrible, fearsome.
143 exploits Stressed on the second syllable (Cercignani, p. 38).
144–5 The flighty . . . with it Trying to rationalise the metaphors, Capell (*Notes*, p. 23) found 'something like blunder' in these lines: 'if purpose and deed go together, *o'ertaking* can not be predicated of either'.
144 flighty swift, quick. Compare Lady Macbeth's description of Macbeth's attitude before the murder of Duncan (1.7.51–4).
146–7 The very firstlings . . . of my hand The division of motive and act into heart (or head) and hand is characteristically Shakespearean; various combinations (along with 'tongue') serve as images of sincerity, insincerity, determination, indecision,

The firstlings of my hand. And even now
To crown my thoughts with acts, be it thought and done.
The castle of Macduff I will surprise;
Seize upon Fife; give to th'edge o'th'sword   150
His wife, his babes, and all unfortunate souls
That trace him in his line. No boasting like a fool;
This deed I'll do before this purpose cool,
But no more sights. – Where are these gentlemen?
Come, bring me where they are.   155

                                    Exeunt

4.2 *Enter* [LADY MACDUFF], *her* SON, *and* ROSS

LADY MACDUFF What had he done, to make him fly the land?
ROSS You must have patience, madam.
LADY MACDUFF   He had none;
  His flight was madness. When our actions do not,
  Our fears do make us traitors.
ROSS   You know not
  Whether it was his wisdom or his fear.   5
LADY MACDUFF Wisdom? To leave his wife, to leave his babes,
  His mansion, and his titles in a place

---

154 sights. –] *Capell;* sights. F; flights. – *Collier²;* sprites. *White*   Act 4, Scene 2   4.2] F *(Scena Secunda.)*   0 SD LADY
MACDUFF] *Rowe; Macduffes Wife* F   1 SH LADY MACDUFF] *Rowe (subst.); Wife* F *(and throughout scene)*

and the like. Compare, among many examples, 'Yea
. . . didst let thy heart consent, / And consequently thy rude hand to act' (*John* 4.2.239–40)
and Claudius's praise of Polonius, 'The head is not
more native to the heart, / The hand more instru-
mental to the mouth' (*Ham.* 1.2.47–8).
  146 firstlings first things (here, impulses or
thoughts); firstborn. See *OED* Firstling a–b. Macbeth's figurative language invokes children – those
who will not succeed him, those (of Macduff) he
will kill, those (of Banquo's line) who will rule
Scotland. See p. 18 above.
  148 crown add the finishing touch to (*OED*
Crown *v*¹ 9). Echoes (1.3.142 and 1.5.40) link this
violent moment with Macbeth's earlier career.
  148 be it thought and done Proverbially, 'No
sooner said than done' (Dent S117).
  150 Fife See 1.2.48 n.
  152 trace him follow him, walk in his footsteps
(*OED* Trace *v*¹ 5).
  152 line descendants, collateral relatives; 'those
that may be traced up to one common stock from

which his line is descended' (Heath, p. 401).
  152 No boasting like a fool Compare 2.1.60–1.
  154 sights Macbeth apparently refers to the
'show' (110 SD. 1–2), but editors have been puzzled. The echo of 'sight' (1.3.89) can be emphasised vocally, as it was in Richard Eyre's production
(Royal National Theatre, London, 1993).

Act 4, Scene 2
  This scene takes place in some private room of
Macduff's castle in Fife (4.1.149–50). Macduff's
flight, his family's murder, and his testing by Malcolm are recorded in *Scotland*, pp. 174b–175b, but
there Macduff knows his loss *before* he flees to England, where he hopes Malcolm will help 'revenge
the slaughter'. Eighteenth- and nineteenth-century
productions omitted all or most of this scene; Davenant wrote a substitute.
  7 titles entitlements; assertions of right, claims
(*OED* Title *sb* 7c, not citing this line). Lady Macduff refers to more than her husband's titles of
nobility.

From whence himself does fly? He loves us not.
He wants the natural touch, for the poor wren,
The most diminutive of birds, will fight,   10
Her young ones in her nest, against the owl.
All is the fear, and nothing is the love;
As little is the wisdom, where the flight
So runs against all reason.

ROSS   My dearest coz,
I pray you school yourself. But for your husband,   15
He is noble, wise, judicious, and best knows
The fits o'th'season. I dare not speak much further,
But cruel are the times when we are traitors
And do not know ourselves, when we hold rumour
From what we fear, yet know not what we fear,   20
But float upon a wild and violent sea,
Each way and none. I take my leave of you;
Shall not be long but I'll be here again.
Things at the worst will cease, or else climb upward
To what they were before. My pretty cousin,   25

10 diminutive] F (diminitiue)   20 not . . . fear,] F (feare,); not . . . fear; *Theobald*   21 sea,] *Capell;* Sea F   22 way and none] *NS (conj. Clarendon);* way, and moue F

9 wants the natural touch i.e. lacks the sensibility or feeling that is the effect of being part of nature; perhaps a reference to Macduff's motherlessness.

9 wren The word begins a series of avian analogies and metaphors; compare 2.3.51 n., 32–6 below, and the appearances of birds real and metaphoric throughout the play.

11 Her . . . nest i.e. her young ones being in the nest (and therefore vulnerable to the owl); an absolute construction. Editors have noted that wrens do not behave this way.

14 coz cousin (a general, friendly appellation, not a specific term of kinship).

15 school discipline, bring under control (*OED* School *v*[1] 4b, quoting this line).

17 fits See 3.2.23 and n.; Steevens[3] cites Menenius's advice, 'The violent fit a'th'time craves . . . physic' *(Cor.* 3.2.33).

17–22 I dare. . . . and none Modern repunctuation hobbles F's complexity. F ends a major clause or sentence at 'ourselves' with a colon, but elsewhere uses only commas to separate clauses before the stop at 'none'; it therefore leaves uncertain whether the 'when'-clauses refer back to 'times' (18) or forward to 'what' (20).

19–22 For a similar rhetoric of indecision, compare Isabella's speech in *MM* quoted at 1.3.140–1 n.

19 do not know ourselves Like 2.2.76, this phrase may recall the proverbial 'Know thyself' (Dent K175).

19–20 when . . . From what we fear i.e. when we create rumours out of those things we fear. Compare 'Present fears / Are less than horrible imaginings' (1.3.136–7); here, the imaginings generate rumours of their own truth.

22 Each way and none i.e. (move) in many directions yet settle on no one direction. Circumstances ('the times' (18)) and fears ('what we fear' (20)) urge us to act, but we dart this way and that without finding a satisfactory course of action. In Elizabethan handwriting, 'none' and 'move' (written as 'moue'; see F) are differentiated by a single pen-stroke. The phrase has been much emended, but since it echoes the oracular 'nothing is, / But what is not' (1.3.140–1), a graphically plausible and Delphic emendation seems appropriate.

23 Shall It shall. Some versions (e.g. Roman Polanski's 1971 film) literalise Ross's promise and make him an accomplice of the murderers (76 SD).

24–5 Things . . . before A stoic counsel recalling Edgar's 'The lamentable change is from the best, / The worst returns to laughter' and his own rebuttal, 'The worst is not / So long as we can say, "This is the worst"' (*Lear* 4.1.5–6, 27–8). Compare the proverbial 'When things are at the worst they will mend' (Dent T216).

25 cousin i.e. Lady Macduff's son.

Blessing upon you.

LADY MACDUFF Fathered he is, and yet he's fatherless.

ROSS I am so much a fool, should I stay longer
It would be my disgrace and your discomfort.
I take my leave at once.   *Exit*

LADY MACDUFF   Sirrah, your father's dead,   30
And what will you do now? How will you live?

SON As birds do, mother.

LADY MACDUFF   What, with worms and flies?

SON With what I get I mean, and so do they.

LADY MACDUFF Poor bird, thou'dst never fear the net, nor lime,
the pitfall, nor the gin.   35

SON Why should I, mother? Poor birds they are not set for.
My father is not dead for all your saying.

LADY MACDUFF Yes, he is dead. How wilt thou do for a father?

SON Nay, how will you do for a husband?

LADY MACDUFF Why, I can buy me twenty at any market.   40

SON Then you'll buy 'em to sell again.

LADY MACDUFF Thou speak'st with all thy wit, and yet i'faith
with wit enough for thee.

SON Was my father a traitor, mother?

LADY MACDUFF Ay, that he was.   45

SON What is a traitor?

LADY MACDUFF Why, one that swears and lies.

SON And be all traitors, that do so?

LADY MACDUFF Every one that does so is a traitor and must be
hanged.   50

30 SD] F (*Exit Rosse*)   **48** so?] F3; so. F

27 He is 'Fathered' (= procreated), but he lacks a father (he is 'fatherless'). For the verbal inventiveness, see Kathleen Wales in *Reader*, pp. 186 and 189n. 33. See also pp. 22–3 above.

29 Ross apparently says he will 'disgrace' himself and 'discomfort' Lady Macduff through compassionate tears (compare 'fool' (28)), but the line could also refer to their joint danger from Macbeth's spies (see 3.4.132). Compare Macduff mourning his family's destruction (4.3.224 and 233).

30 Brooke understands (App. A, p. 224) F as employing prose from this line through 50, but while it may be true that there is 'a sharp contrast of tone after Ross's exit' the shift to prose need not occur instantly. The next lines may be half-verse, half-prose, though Capell felt 'a prose so near approaching to verse is not sufferable' (Capell,

Notes, p. 24).

30 Sirrah Here, a bantering form of abuse; compare 3.1.46 and n.

30 dead Macduff is metaphorically 'dead' because he is absent and cannot aid his family.

34 lime Lime placed on twigs and branches causes birds' feet to stick to the tree.

35 pitfall A trap for birds in which a cover falls over a hole.

35 gin snare, trap (for game).

36 Poor . . . for Inferior birds have no traps set for them.

41 Lady Macduff could have no use for twenty husbands unless she plans to resell (deceive) them, as in the proverbial 'To be bought and sold' (Dent B787) and in *R3* 5.3.305.

47 swears vows, takes an oath.

SON And must they all be hanged that swear and lie?

LADY MACDUFF Every one.

SON Who must hang them?

LADY MACDUFF Why, the honest men.

SON Then the liars and swearers are fools, for there are liars and   55
swearers enough to beat the honest men and hang up them.

LADY MACDUFF Now God help thee, poor monkey, but how wilt
thou do for a father?

SON If he were dead, you'd weep for him; if you would not, it were
a good sign that I should quickly have a new father.   60

LADY MACDUFF Poor prattler, how thou talk'st!

Enter a MESSENGER

MESSENGER Bless you, fair dame. I am not to you known,
Though in your state of honour I am perfect;
I doubt some danger does approach you nearly.
If you will take a homely man's advice,   65
Be not found here. Hence with your little ones.
To fright you thus, methinks I am too savage;
To do worse to you were fell cruelty,
Which is too nigh your person. Heaven preserve you,
I dare abide no longer.   *Exit*

LADY MACDUFF   Whither should I fly?   70
I have done no harm. But I remember now
I am in this earthly world where to do harm
Is often laudable, to do good sometime
Accounted dangerous folly. Why then, alas,
Do I put up that womanly defence,   75

59 you'd] F (youl'd)   66–7 ones. / . . . thus, methinks . . . savage;] F2–4 (subst.); ones / . . . thus. Me thinkes . . .
sauage: F   70 SD] F (*Exit Messenger*)   70 Whither] F (Whether)

57 **monkey** Term of playful contempt, especially for a child (*OED* Monkey 2b), based, presumably, on childish mimicry.
61 **prattler** chatterer.
63 Though I know very well your status and
reputation (Brooke subst.).
64 **doubt** fear, suspect.
65 **homely** simple, plain, unpolished (*OED*
Homely *a* 4b, quoting this line), but perhaps implying 'common' (not 'gentle' or aristocratic).
67 **methinks** it seems to me.

68 **fell** deadly.
69 **nigh** near, close to. The messenger refers to
the deadly danger already threatening Lady Macduff.
72–4 'She recognizes . . . that conventional moral
categories may be inadequate to actual human
dilemmas . . . Macduff's abandonment of his family and disloyalty to his king may be "to do good"'
(C. W. Slights, *The Casuistical Tradition*, 1981,
p. 122).

To say I have done no harm?

Enter MURDERERS

What are these faces?

A MURDERER Where is your husband?

LADY MACDUFF I hope in no place so unsanctified,
Where such as thou mayst find him.

A MURDERER   He's a traitor.

SON Thou liest, thou shag-haired villain.

A MURDERER   What, you egg!   80
Young fry of treachery!

[*Kills him*]

SON   He has killed me, mother,
Run away, I pray you!

Exit [*Lady Macduff*] *crying 'Murder'[, pursued by
Murderers with her Son*]

---

76 SD] *N.S; Enter Murtherers.* F (*after* faces)   77 SH, 79 SH, 80 SH] F (*Mur.*); 1. *M. / Capell; First Mur. / Cam.*
80 shaghaired] *Hudson* (*conj. Steevens* [2]); shagge-ear'd F   81 SD Kills him] *Brooke; not in* F   82 SD Exit . . . Son] *Brooke;
Exit crying Murther* F

76 **I have** The metre requires contraction ('I've').

76 SD MURDERERS Customarily, two in number and not always identifiable as being drawn from those in 3.1, 3.3, or 3.4; see 23 n.

76 **What are these faces?** Lady Macduff may rebuke her son, but the Murderers' entrance may be misplaced in F, in which case she addresses them and comments on their grim appearance. The staging adopted here assumes the latter.

77 SH, 79 SH, 80 SH F does not differentiate the Murderers, and its SH, *Mur.,* might indicate that they are to speak in unison (compare 3.1.76, 114, and 138), but the dialogue here seems better suited to a single speaker.

78 **unsanctified** unhallowed, not consecrated (to religious uses). Lady Macduff may regard the murderers as unbelievers, or as men excommunicated for previous crimes, or as hunted men who have temporarily left 'sanctuary' (hence 'unsanctified') to attack her; on the 'holy privilege / Of blessed sanctuary', see *R3* 3.1.40–56.

80 **shag-haired** with long, shaggy hair. Such hair was a villain's mark; compare 'a shag-hayr'd craftie Kerne' (*2H6* TLN 1673), 1.2.13 ('kerns'), and the nightmare vision of two Gunpowder plotters: 'Two Monsters skulles, which never plotted good, / Grim, gastly, pale, shag-hayre, sulphured eyes . . .' (Edward Hawes, *Trayterous Percyes and Catesbyes Prosopopeia* (1606), sig. A3r); the adjective is also used of villains in *King Leir* (1605), ed. W. W. Greg, MSR, 1907, line 2277, and *The Faire Maide of Bristow* (1605), sig. EIV. Two anecdotes originally told of Thomas Cromwell are conflated and applied to Thomas More when he condemns one Falkner, '*a ruffian*' with 'shag hair', to Newgate prison until he cuts his hair (V. Gabrieli and G. Melchiori (eds.), *STM*, 1990, 3.1.46 SD and 3.1.105). F's 'shagear'd' has been modernised as 'shag-eared' and explained as the result of judicial punishment: 'convicted villains frequently had their ears slit' (Brooke). Convicted individuals' noses were slit; ears, however, were bored or cropped and not, apparently, slit or slashed (so as to produce a grotesquely shaggy appearance). See, for instance, the punishment for vagabonds in the statute 27 Hen. VIII c. 25 (1535) and L. O. Pike, *A History of Crime in England*, 2 vols., 1873–6, 11, 73 and 97–8. Phonological evidence (Cercignani, pp. 233–5) cannot discriminate between 'shag-eared' and 'shag-haired' for F's reading.

80 **egg** Contemptuous epithet for a young person (*OED* Egg *sb* 2b, citing only this line and another from 1835); the Murderer agrees with the proverbial 'An evil bird lays an evil egg' (Dent B376). Once again, avian imagery links this moment with the Son's earlier conversation and with all the ominous and ironically positive birds of the play.

81 **fry** offspring, progeny.

4.3 *Enter* MALCOLM *and* MACDUFF

MALCOLM Let us seek out some desolate shade and there
        Weep our sad bosoms empty.
MACDUFF   Let us rather
        Hold fast the mortal sword and like good men
        Bestride our downfall birthdom; each new morn,
        New widows howl, new orphans cry, new sorrows   5
        Strike heaven on the face, that it resounds
        As if it felt with Scotland and yelled out
        Like syllable of dolour.
MALCOLM   What I believe, I'll wail;
        What know, believe; and what I can redress,
        As I shall find the time to friend, I will.   10
        What you have spoke, it may be so perchance.
        This tyrant, whose sole name blisters our tongues,
        Was once thought honest; you have loved him well –
        He hath not touched you yet. I am young, but something
        You may discern of him through me, and wisdom   15

Act 4, Scene 3   4.3] F (*Scaena Tertia.*)   4 downfall] F; down-fall'n *Johnson* (*conj. Warburton*)   15 discern] F (discerne); deserve *Theobald*

Act 4, Scene 3
    The setting is uncertain: near enough the out-of-doors to make seeking a 'desolate shade' (1) plausible, but close to a room of state where King Edward touches for the Evil (139 ff.). This scene often puzzles audiences and has an unsettling effect upon the play's treatment of its own representation; see pp. 88–93 above.
    3 fast firmly, tightly.
    3 mortal fatal, death-dealing.
    3–4 like good men . . . birthdom The image is of soldiers standing astride a fallen comrade to protect him from further injury; Capell (*Notes*, p. 24) cites Falstaff's request before the Battle of Shrewsbury: 'Hal, if thou see me down in the battle and bestride me, so; 'tis a point of friendship' (*1H4* 5.1.121–2).
    4 downfall downfallen, fallen from prosperity. The modern form is 'downfallen', but 'downfall' is needed metrically and also occurs in F at *1H4* 1.3.135 (where Q reads 'down-trod').
    4 birthdom inheritance, birthright; perhaps 'native kingdom'. This line is *OED*'s sole citation for the word.
    8 Like Similar, identical.

    8 dolour sadness.
    8 wail bewail, lament.
    10 to friend as a friend, on my side (*OED* Friend *sb* 6b).
    11 spoke See 1.4.3 n.
    12 sole alone, unaccompanied (*OED* Sole *a* 6). Macbeth's name alone is sufficient to blister 'our tongues'. The line may recall the proverbial 'Report has a blister on her tongue' (Dent R84).
    14 He hath not touched you yet Either (1) Macduff follows Macbeth loyally and is therefore safe, or (2) Macduff continues to love Macbeth only because Macduff has not yet been 'touched' (as Malcolm has).
    15 You may discern of him through me Macduff may see ('discern') a future Macbeth in Malcolm. Theobald's emendation is plausible ('discerne' and 'discerue' are easily confused in manuscript) and treats the line as Malcolm's fear that Macduff seeks advancement through betraying Malcolm to Macbeth, but the change devalues 'I am young' (14).
    15 and wisdom 'i.e. you may discern the wisdom' (Brooke), or 'and 'tis wisdom' (Upton, pp. 314–15).

            To offer up a weak, poor, innocent lamb
            T'appease an angry god.
MACDUFF I am not treacherous.
MALCOLM   But Macbeth is.
            A good and virtuous nature may recoil
            In an imperial charge. But I shall crave your pardon: 20
            That which you are, my thoughts cannot transpose;
            Angels are bright still, though the brightest fell.
            Though all things foul would wear the brows of grace,
            Yet grace must still look so.
MACDUFF   I have lost my hopes.
MALCOLM Perchance even there where I did find my doubts.   25
            Why in that rawness left you wife and child,
            Those precious motives, those strong knots of love,
            Without leave-taking? I pray you,
            Let not my jealousies be your dishonours,
            But mine own safeties; you may be rightly just,   30
            Whatever I shall think.
MACDUFF   Bleed, bleed, poor country.
            Great tyranny, lay thou thy basis sure,
            For goodness dare not check thee; wear thou thy wrongs,

---

17 god] F (God)

16 innocent lamb In the Christian tradition, the lamb emblematises innocence, and a proverbial expression, 'As innocent as a lamb' (Dent L34.1), appears about the time *Macbeth* was composed.

18–20 Malcolm seems to worry that Macduff's originally noble nature has decayed under Macbeth's royal command, but the lines may also reflect upon Macbeth's own degeneration and thus recall Holinshed's praise (*Scotland*, pp. 171b and 172b) for the historical Macbeth's first ten years on the throne.

19 recoil fall back, degenerate (*OED* Recoil v¹ 3b, quoting as its last example 'Be revenged, / Or she that bore you was no queen, and you / Recoil from your great stock' (*Cym.* 1.6.126–8)). Shakespeare uses the word only three times in this sense; it might have been suggested here by *Scotland*, p. 175b, where 'recoiled' describes Macbeth's withdrawal to Dunsinane.

20 charge burden.

20 crave beg, ask (*OED* Crave v 2b); not 'yearn for' (Crave v 5).

21 Compare 'your mistrust cannot make me a traitor' (*AYLI* 1.3.56).

22 the brightest Satan, one of whose names is 'Lucifer' (light-bearer). Brightness is no assurance of truth: 'for Satan himselfe is transfourmed into an angel of lyght. Therefore it is no great thyng though [if] his ministers also be transfourmed as the ministers of righteousnesse' (2 Cor. 11.14–15); compare Banquo's worry, 1.3.122–3.

23 brows face, or appearance (a figuratively extended meaning).

25 there i.e. Scotland, or under Macbeth's tyranny, or Macduff's leaving of his family (?).

26 rawness imperfection, incompleteness. This line is the only citation for a figurative meaning under *OED* Rawness 1. Clarendon compares Williams's challenge to the king concerning dead soldiers' 'children rawly left' (*H5* 4.1.141). Here, the 'rawness' is partly social: Macduff did not bid his family good-bye, but the aborted ceremony also stands for a failure of love and duty (compare Lady Macduff's anger, 4.2.1.ff.).

29 jealousies suspicions, mistrust (*OED* Jealousy 5).

32 basis foundation, base. This line is the first citation at *OED* Basis 8.

33 check limit, control.

> The title is affeered. Fare thee well, lord,
> I would not be the villain that thou think'st   35
> For the whole space that's in the tyrant's grasp,
> And the rich East to boot.
>
> MALCOLM   Be not offended.
> I speak not as in absolute fear of you:
> I think our country sinks beneath the yoke;
> It weeps, it bleeds, and each new day a gash   40
> Is added to her wounds. I think withal
> There would be hands uplifted in my right,
> And here from gracious England have I offer
> Of goodly thousands. But for all this,
> When I shall tread upon the tyrant's head,   45
> Or wear it on my sword, yet my poor country
> Shall have more vices than it had before,
> More suffer, and more sundry ways than ever,
> By him that shall succeed.
>
> MACDUFF   What should he be?
> MALCOLM It is myself I mean – in whom I know   50
>   All the particulars of vice so grafted
>   That when they shall be opened, black Macbeth

34 The] F; Thy *Malone*   34 affeered] *Hanmer;* affear'd F

34 The title is affeered Either (1) the epithet ('tyranny') is confirmed (= 'affeered'), or (2) the valid claim and claimant are frightened ('afeared': see *OED* Afear). These two possibilities, one referring to Macbeth, the other to Malcolm, depend upon a pun: affeered/afeared. Malone's emendation, 'Thy', is graphically possible, but F's sentence seems to alternate between clauses devoted to Macbeth ('Great tyranny . . . ' and 'wear thou . . . ') and clauses devoted to Malcolm ('For goodness . . .' and 'The title . . . ').

37 to boot in addition.

38 absolute perfect, entire (*OED* Absolute 4, 5, 6, especially 5).

39–100 The sequence of lament for Scotland, of vices recounted and elaborated, and of Macduff's responses, closely follows *Scotland*, pp. 174b–175b, but may also owe something to Samuel's attempt to dissuade the Israelites from adopting monarchical government (1 Sam. 8.9–20), a passage quoted and extensively discussed by James VI in *True Lawe*, pp. 62–7.

39–41 I think . . . wounds These lines may allude to Jesus's suffering on the way to crucifixion.

40 gash The word recalls the 'twenty trenchèd gashes' (3.4.27) inflicted upon Banquo.

43 England i.e. the King of England, Edward the Confessor.

44 thousands i.e. thousands of soldiers (to support Malcolm's claim).

48 sundry various, diverse.

49 What Who (Abbott 254, citing numerous examples of 'What is he' to mean 'Of what kind or quality is he'). Macduff is not dehumanising or treating as a monster Macbeth's hypothetical successor.

50–1 myself . . . so grafted Compare 'I will chide no breather in the world but myself, against whom I know most faults' (*AYLI* 3.2.280–1).

51 grafted 'made part of my being' (NS). The botanical metaphor describes the gardener's joining of one plant or species with another; compare the 'ingrafted love' Antony 'bears to Caesar' (*JC* 2.1.184) and 'an engraff'd madness' (*TNK* 4.3.48–9).

52–4 Many proverbial analogies and phrases – 'As white as snow' (Dent s591), 'To make black white' (Dent b440), 'As pure as snow' (Dent 11), 'As innocent as a lamb' (Dent l34.1) – may make Malcolm's speech plainly ironic.

52 opened i.e. born, made known. The metaphor is of a flower's bud (see 'grafted' (51

Will seem as pure as snow, and the poor state
Esteem him as a lamb, being compared
With my confineless harms.
MACDUFF   Not in the legions   55
Of horrid hell can come a devil more damned
In evils to top Macbeth.
MALCOLM   I grant him bloody,
Luxurious, avaricious, false, deceitful,
Sudden, malicious, smacking of every sin
That has a name. But there's no bottom, none,   60
In my voluptuousness: your wives, your daughters,
Your matrons, and your maids could not fill up
The cistern of my lust, and my desire
All continent impediments would o'erbear
That did oppose my will. Better Macbeth,   65
Than such an one to reign.
MACDUFF   Boundless intemperance
In nature is a tyranny; it hath been
Th'untimely emptying of the happy throne
And fall of many kings. But fear not yet
To take upon you what is yours: you may   70
Convey your pleasures in a spacious plenty
And yet seem cold. The time you may so hoodwink.
We have willing dames enough; there cannot be
That vulture in you to devour so many
As will to greatness dedicate themselves,   75

---

59 smacking] F; smoaking F2–4   72 cold.] F; cold, *Theobald*   72 hoodwink.] F (hoodwink:)   74 you] *Collier*; you, F

and n.)), but may also include 'dissection . . . Malcolm and Macbeth as moral cadavers' (Mackinnon,
p. 73).

55 confineless unconfined, limitless. This line is
the sole citation under *OED* Confineless (Schäfer).

55 legions multitudes, hordes. The word is used
biblically of angels (Matt. 26.53); compare 22.

58 Luxurious Lecherous, lascivious. See
'rumpfed' (1.3.5 and n.).

59 Sudden Rash, impetuous (*OED* Sudden 2b).

59 smacking having the flavour of. The later
Folios' reading is a variant spelling.

63 cistern (water) tank; large vessel (especially
for holding liquor). The Shakespearean connotations are always negative; see *Oth.* 4.2.61, *Ant.*
2.5.95, and *TNK* 5.1.46–7.

64 continent self-restraining (*OED* Continent *a*
1). The word has resonances – of 'containing' and

'land-mass' – which join with 'cistern' (63) to make
Malcolm's imagined lust a watery force of nature
overwhelming the land; compare the aftermath of
Duncan's murder (2.3.106–7 and n.).

66–7 Boundless intemperance . . . tyranny
Limitless uncontrol is a form of natural tyranny (?).
Macduff analogises 'voluptuousness' (61) or 'lust'
(63), private sins, with 'tyranny', a political sin. His
next words (67–9) suggest how the two cannot be
separated in the behaviour (and the fate) of a king.

71 Convey Carry on, manage (*OED* Convey *v*[1]
12).

72 hoodwink blindfold, deceive.

73–6 there cannot be . . . **inclined** i.e. you
cannot be so voracious as to consume the many
women who will volunteer to serve (sexually) your
high rank, once it is known you desire them.

Finding it so inclined.

MALCOLM   With this, there grows
In my most ill-composed affection such
A stanchless avarice that, were I king,
I should cut off the nobles for their lands,
Desire his jewels, and this other's house,   80
And my more-having would be as a sauce
To make me hunger more, that I should forge
Quarrels unjust against the good and loyal,
Destroying them for wealth.

MACDUFF   This avarice
Sticks deeper, grows with more pernicious root   85
Than summer-seeming lust, and it hath been
The sword of our slain kings; yet do not fear,
Scotland hath foisons to fill up your will
Of your mere own. All these are portable,
With other graces weighed.   90

MALCOLM   But I have none. The king-becoming graces –
As justice, verity, temp'rance, stableness,
Bounty, perseverance, mercy, lowliness,
Devotion, patience, courage, fortitude –
I have no relish of them, but abound   95
In the division of each several crime,

76 With this Along with this.

77 affection disposition, state of mind (*OED* Affection *sb* 4).

78 stanchless unstoppable. 'Stanch' refers particularly to stopping the flow of liquids (water, blood, and other bodily fluids especially); this line is *OED*'s earliest citation for the word (Schäfer). Compare 'continent' (64 and n.).

79 cut off put to death, kill.

81–2 my more-having . . . hunger more Proverbially, 'The more a man has the more he desires' (Dent M1144).

82 forge fabricate (Clarendon).

85 Sticks See 3.1.51n.

85 root The metaphor recalls 'For love of money, is the roote of all evyll' (1 Tim. 6.10), echoed in Holinshed, where Makduffe comments on Malcolm's claim of 'unquenchable avarice': 'avarice is the root of all mischiefe' (*Scotland*, p. 175a).

86 summer-seeming lust i.e. 'lust befits [= beseems] summer' (Vivian Salmon in *Reader*, p. 201); 'summer-seeming' evokes ideas of heat and brevity (so *Lexicon*, following Capell, *Notes*, p. 25).

87 sword of our slain kings i.e. the means by

which our kings died. Macduff may refer, anachronistically, to the numerous later Scottish kings who were murdered (see p. 13 above), or to kings who died in wars motivated by greed.

88 foisons harvests.

89 mere very.

89 portable bearable (*OED* Portable *a* 2, quoting 'How light and portable my pain seems now' (*Lear* 3.6.108), hence 'acceptable').

90 weighed balanced (*OED* Weigh v^1 11b); counterbalanced (*OED* Weigh v^1 16e).

92 verity truthfulness, sincerity.

92 temp'rance For the syncopation, see 3.4.107 n.

93 perseverance Accented on the second syllable.

93 lowliness humility, meekness.

95 relish trace (*OED* Relish sb^1 1c); slightest hint.

96 division partition(s), sub-division(s). This line is *OED*'s only evidence for a figurative meaning from musical vocabulary: 'variation, modulation' (*OED* Division 7b).

96 several individual, particular.

Acting it many ways. Nay, had I power, I should
Pour the sweet milk of concord into hell,
Uproar the universal peace, confound
All unity on earth.

MACDUFF   O Scotland, Scotland!   100
MALCOLM If such a one be fit to govern, speak.
I am as I have spoken.
MACDUFF   Fit to govern?
No, not to live. O nation miserable!
With an untitled tyrant, bloody-sceptred,
When shalt thou see thy wholesome days again,   105
Since that the truest issue of thy throne
By his own interdiction stands accursed
And does blaspheme his breed? Thy royal father
Was a most sainted king; the queen that bore thee,
Oft'ner upon her knees than on her feet,   110
Died every day she lived. Fare thee well,
These evils thou repeat'st upon thyself
Hath banished me from Scotland. O my breast,
Thy hope ends here.
MALCOLM   Macduff, this noble passion,
Child of integrity, hath from my soul   115

---

100 Scotland!] *Rowe;* Scotland. F   102 SH MACDUFF] *Rowe (subst.); Mac.* F   104 bloody-sceptred] *Pope;* bloody
Sceptred F   105 again,] *Theobald;* againe? F   107 accursed] F2–4 *(subst.);* accust F   109 sainted-king] F (Sainted-King)
113 Hath] F; Have *Rowe*

---

98 milk of concord Compare 1.5.15 and n.

99 Uproar Throw into confusion. Accent on
second syllable. This line is the first of two citations at *OED* Uproar *v* 1.

99 confound Accent on second syllable.

104 untitled without right to the title ('king').
The earliest citation at *OED* Untitled *ppl a*¹.

105 wholesome healthy, free from taint (*OED*
Wholesome 3b, quoting this line as its second
example and suggesting an element also of sense
1: 'salutary', 'beneficial').

106 issue child, offspring.

107 interdiction authoritative prohibition
(*OED* Interdiction 1). The word has a specialised
meaning in Scottish law (various forms of restraint
placed upon people incapable of managing their
own affairs) inapplicable here, but the Scottish
association has attracted editors.

107 accursed Some editors print 'accus'd', but
OED offers no evidence for F's 'accust' as a past

tense of 'accuse', or a form of 'cuss' (which developed from 'curse' in the nineteenth century). See
Cercignani, p. 358.

108 blaspheme his breed slander or calumniate
his heritage, his family line (= 'breed').

111 Died . . . lived i.e. she lived each day as
virtuously as if she were to die that day (and face
divine judgement). Compare St Paul's claim, 'I dye
dayly' (1 Cor. 15.31).

112–13 These evils . . . Scotland The very evils
Malcolm has recited are those which, in Macbeth,
made Macduff flee Scotland. By implication, these
evils will prevent Macduff from helping Malcolm
return to Scotland.

113 Hath Singular verb in -*th* with plural subject (Abbott 334).

115 Child Macduff's honesty is metaphorically
joined with the new generations that will defeat
Macbeth (see Knight, *Imperial*, pp. 149–50).

Wiped the black scruples, reconciled my thoughts
To thy good truth and honour. Devilish Macbeth
By many of these trains hath sought to win me
Into his power, and modest wisdom plucks me
From over-credulous haste; but God above   120
Deal between thee and me, for even now
I put myself to thy direction and
Unspeak mine own detraction, here abjure
The taints and blames I laid upon myself,
For strangers to my nature. I am yet   125
Unknown to woman, never was forsworn,
Scarcely have coveted what was mine own,
At no time broke my faith, would not betray
The devil to his fellow, and delight
No less in truth than life. My first false speaking   130
Was this upon myself. What I am truly
Is thine, and my poor country's, to command:
Whither indeed, before thy here-approach,
Old Siward with ten thousand warlike men
Already at a point was setting forth.   135
Now we'll together, and the chance of goodness
Be like our warranted quarrel. Why are you silent?
MACDUFF Such welcome and unwelcome things at once,
'Tis hard to reconcile.

---

133 thy] F2; they F   133 here-approach] *Pope;* heere approach F

116 scruples doubts, troubling thoughts (*OED* Scruple *sb²* 1). They are 'black' because they concern Malcolm's suspicions that Macduff is evil.

118 trains stratagem, trick. Malcolm feared that Macduff was an *agent provocateur* pretending disloyalty to Macbeth in order to trick Malcolm into returning to Scotland.

119 plucks restrains forcibly.

120 over-credulous too quick to believe. The adjective is transferred from Malcolm to his 'haste'; 'over-credulous' is a neologism (Garner).

122 put myself to thy direction submit myself to your guidance.

123 abjure disavow.

125 For As being (Abbott 148).

126 Unknown to woman i.e. not having had sexual intercourse with a woman, but perhaps recalling 'none of woman born' (4.1.79).

126 forsworn perjured, (one who) betrayed an oath.

133 thy here-approach your coming here. See 'my here-remain' (150).

135 at a point prepared, in readiness. Compare Goneril's ironic remark about her father, 'to let him keep / At point a hundred knights' (*Lear* 1.4.323–4).

136 Now we'll together i.e. now we'll journey together.

136–7 chance . . . quarrel i.e. may the result be as fortunate as our grievances are justified.

136 chance of goodness good fortune or outcome. Etymologically, 'chance' derives from Latin *cadere,* to fall, hence its meanings 'to befall', 'to happen'. See p. 40 above.

138–9 Such . . . reconcile Macduff's puzzlement at Malcolm's trickery is never resolved; see pp. 92–3 above.

Enter a DOCTOR

MALCOLM   Well, more anon. –
              Comes the king forth, I pray you?   140
DOCTOR   Ay, sir: there are a crew of wretched souls
              That stay his cure; their malady convinces
              The great assay of art, but at his touch,
              Such sanctity hath heaven given his hand,
              They presently amend.   *Exit*   145
MALCOLM   I thank you, doctor.
MACDUFF   What's the disease he means?
MALCOLM   'Tis called the Evil.
              A most miraculous work in this good king,
              Which often since my here-remain in England   150
              I have seen him do. How he solicits heaven
              Himself best knows, but strangely visited people
              All swoll'n and ulcerous, pitiful to the eye,
              The mere despair of surgery, he cures,
              Hanging a golden stamp about their necks   155
              Put on with holy prayers, and 'tis spoken
              To the succeeding royalty he leaves
              The healing benediction. With this strange virtue,
              He hath a heavenly gift of prophecy,

---

139 anon. –] *Capell;* anon.F   145 SD *Exit*] F; *Exit Doctor / Capell (after 146)*   150 here-remain] *Pope;* heere remaine F
153 swoll'n] F (swolne)   156 on with] F *corr.;* on my with F *uncorr.*

---

139 SD For the location of this SD, see Textual
Analysis, pp. 262–3 below.
    139–61 Well . . . grace These lines have been
regarded as interpolation or revision; see Textual
Analysis, pp. 278–9 below.
    141 crew company, group.
    142 stay his cure await his healing touch
(Clarendon).
    142 convinces overcomes. See 1.7.64.
    143 assay best effort (*OED* Assay *sb* 14, quoting
this line).
    145 SD The Doctor's exit might follow Mal-
colm's thanks, but thanks (or dismissal?) and departure are probably simultaneous.
    148 Evil The King's Evil, scrofula (an inflamma-
tion of the lymph nodes, often in the neck, causing swelling and suppuration). An early account
(*c.* 1066) describes Edward the Confessor's cure of
what may be this ailment (Barlow, pp. 8–9), and
Scot (XII, 14) offers a remedy. For the belief that
monarchs of France and of England could cure this
affliction, see Bloch, pp. 11–91, Barlow, pp. 14–

15, and, on the ceremony in the Tudor and Stuart period, Bloch, pp. 181–92, and Supplementary
Note, p. 259 below.
    151 solicits entreats, petitions.
    154 mere very, entire.
    155 stamp coin, medal (*OED* Stamp *sb*3 15).
Elizabeth and James gave a gold coin, an 'angel'
depicting the Archangel Michael, to those they
touched. See Bloch, pp. 65–7, 210–12.
    156 holy prayers The English ceremony for
'touching' involved a special prayer said by the
monarch.
    157 succeeding royalty following monarchs.
The power to cure the Evil supposedly descends
in the royal line and was popularly associated with
the monarch's anointing at his or her coronation.
    158 benediction kindly favour, grace (*OED*
Benediction 2).
    158 strange unusual, inexplicable.
    158 virtue ability, merit (*OED* Virtue *sb* 5a);
power, efficacy (*Lexicon*).

And sundry blessings hang about his throne   160
That speak him full of grace.

Enter ROSS

MACDUFF   See who comes here.
MALCOLM   My countryman, but yet I know him not.
MACDUFF   My ever gentle cousin, welcome hither.
MALCOLM   I know him now. Good God betimes remove
          The means that makes us strangers.
ROSS   Sir, amen.   165
MACDUFF   Stands Scotland where it did?
ROSS   Alas, poor country,
          Almost afraid to know itself. It cannot
          Be called our mother, but our grave, where nothing,
          But who knows nothing, is once seen to smile;
          Where sighs, and groans, and shrieks that rend the air   170
          Are made, not marked; where violent sorrow seems
          A modern ecstasy. The deadman's knell
          Is there scarce asked for who, and good men's lives
          Expire before the flowers in their caps,

---

162 not] F (nor)   170 rend] F (rent)

161 **speak** bespeak, proclaim.

161 SD For the placing of this SD, see Textual Analysis, pp. 262–3 below.

162 **My . . . not** Malcolm recognises Ross as a Scot through his costume. See Supplementary Note, pp. 259–60 below.

164 **betimes** in due time, before it is too late; compare 3.4.133 and n.

165 **means** interposed (or intervening) conditions (*OED* Mean *sb²* 6, quoting 'So do I wish the crown, being so far off, / And so I chide the means that keeps me from it' (*3H6* 3.2.140–1)).

166 **Stands Scotland where it did** Is Scotland in its former condition.

167–75 **It cannot . . . sicken** This passage has been held to describe exactly 'the lamentable condition of London in this terrible summer [1603]' of plague; see F. P. Wilson, *The Plague in Shakespeare's London*, 1927, p. 98.

167 **Almost afraid to know itself** Ross so described the Scots (4.2.17ff.).

168 **mother . . . grave** On the simultaneity of birth and death in nature, see 'The earth that's nature's mother is her tomb; / What is her bury-

ing grave, that is her womb' (*Rom.* 2.3.9–10) and 'Time's the king of men / He's both their parent, and he is their grave' (*Per.* 2.3.45–6).

168–9 **nothing . . . nothing** no one – no 'thing' – except those who know nothing; 'i.e. children or idiots' (Brooke).

169 **once** ever.

170 **rend** tear. F's 'rent' is an obsolete form.

171 **marked** noticed.

172 **modern** present; common, everyday.

172 **ecstasy** See 3.2.22 n.

172–3 **The deadman's . . . who** Death is so common in Scotland no one asks for whom the bell tolls. The church bell was rung 'when anye Christian bodye is in passing . . . and after the time of his passing . . . one shorte peale: and one before the burial, and another shorte peale after the buriall' (*Advertisements . . . for due order in . . . common prayers* (?1565), sig. B1r). See 2.1.63, 3.2.43–4, 5.9.17, and p. 55 above.

172 **deadman's** F's 'Deadmans' represents an earlier form and metrical stress (see *OED* Deadman), different from most modern editors' reading, 'dead man's'.

         Dying or ere they sicken.

MACDUFF   O relation   175
         Too nice, and yet too true.

MALCOLM   What's the newest grief?

ROSS   That of an hour's age doth hiss the speaker;
         Each minute teems a new one.

MACDUFF   How does my wife?

ROSS   Why, well.

MACDUFF   And all my children?

ROSS   Well, too.

MACDUFF   The tyrant has not battered at their peace?   180

ROSS   No, they were well at peace when I did leave 'em.

MACDUFF   Be not a niggard of your speech: how goes't?

ROSS   When I came hither to transport the tidings
         Which I have heavily borne, there ran a rumour
         Of many worthy fellows that were out,   185
         Which was to my belief witnessed the rather
         For that I saw the tyrant's power afoot.
         Now is the time of help. [*To Malcolm*] Your eye in
            Scotland
         Would create soldiers, make our women fight
         To doff their dire distresses.

MALCOLM   Be't their comfort   190

182 goes't] F (gos't)

175 **or ere they sicken** before the flowers show signs of illness. The comparison (173–5) expresses both the brevity of 'good men's lives' and the suddenness of their deaths.

175 **relation** account, statement. See 3.4.124 n.

176 **nice** carefully accurate, precise. See *OED* Nice *a* 7–9 for the connotative range of this complex word. Ross's account is terrible because it accurately conveys the horror of life in Scotland.

176 **newest** most recent, most worthy of being told as news. See 5.9.20 and n.

177 **hiss** mock, accuse sarcastically (*OED* Hiss *v* 3).

178 **teems** breeds, gives birth to.

179 **well . . . Well, too** Proverbially, 'He is well since he is in Heaven' (Dent H347); Steevens³ compares 'we use / To say the dead are well' (*Ant.* 2.5.32–3).

179 **children** Trisyllabic ('childeren').

181 **at peace** in harmony; dead. Legalistically, Ross tells the truth; he left Macduff's family before their slaughter. Ross, hesitating to deliver bad news

(or fearing the consequences of telling what he knows), becomes another Scot who knows but cannot speak a truth, or act upon it: compare 1.7.77, 3.6.7 n., 5.1.32–3, and p. 92 above.

182 **niggard** miser, withholder.

183–90 Ross dodges Macduff's direct question about his family.

185 **out** abroad, in the field (preparing for battle). This line is the earliest citation at *OED* Out *adv* 15c.

186–7 **witnessed . . . afoot** Macbeth's forces on the march confirm that their opponents are also mobilising.

187 **power** army, military forces.

188 **help** aid, assistance (*OED* Help *sb* 1a), but probably also 'relief, cure, remedy' (*OED* Help *sb* 5a).

188 **eye** i.e. person. An example of synecdoche, where 'eye' stands for Malcolm's body; compare 1.7.24 and n.

190 **doff** put off (another image of clothing).

We are coming thither. Gracious England hath
Lent us good Siward and ten thousand men –
An older and a better soldier none
That Christendom gives out.

ROSS   Would I could answer
This comfort with the like. But I have words   195
That would be howled out in the desert air,
Where hearing should not latch them.

MACDUFF   What concern they?
The general cause, or is it a fee-grief
Due to some single breast?

ROSS   No mind that's honest
But in it shares some woe, though the main part   200
Pertains to you alone.

MACDUFF   If it be mine,
Keep it not from me; quickly let me have it.

ROSS Let not your ears despise my tongue forever
Which shall possess them with the heaviest sound
That ever yet they heard.

MACDUFF   H'm – I guess at it.   205

ROSS Your castle is surprised; your wife and babes
Savagely slaughtered. To relate the manner
Were on the quarry of these murdered deer
To add the death of you.

MALCOLM   Merciful heaven –
What, man, ne'er pull your hat upon your brows: 210
Give sorrow words; the grief that does not speak,
Whispers the o'erfraught heart and bids it break.

197 they?] *Theobald;* they, F   205 H'm –] *Brooke;* Humh: F

197 **latch** receive (*OED* Latch *v*¹ 4a).
198 **general cause** everyone's (= all Scotland's) interest.
198–9 **fee-grief . . . single breast** grief owned entirely by one person ('some single breast'); a grief concerning one individual. The metaphor may derive from legal terminology: 'An estate in fee simple is the most nearly absolute and perpetual estate in land known to the law' (Clarkson and Warren, p. 50; for this line, see p. 51 n. 22).
204 **possess them with** inform them.
204 **heaviest** saddest.
208 **quarry** Heap made of the deer killed at a hunting (*OED* Quarry *sb*¹ 2a; 2b is a transferred meaning, 'pile of dead [human] bodies').

208 **deer** animals; beloved ones (= 'dear').
210 **pull your hat upon your brows** A conventional gesture of sorrow or melancholy. Elizabethan actors usually wore hats, while modern ones do not, making this moment difficult to stage realistically.
211–12 **the grief . . . bids it break** The contrast is between 'speak' (say aloud) and 'whisper' (speak softly). Compare the proverbial 'Grief pent up will break the heart' (Dent G449) and the Senecan tag, 'curae leves loquuntur, ingentes stupent' (*Hippolytus* [*Phaedra*] 607: supportable griefs speak, unbearable ones stupefy), often echoed in early modern plays (e.g. 'Dear woes cannot speak', *Dutch Courtesan* 4.4.56). In this period, 'break' was pronounced to rhyme with modern 'speak' (Cercignani, p. 161).

MACDUFF My children too?
ROSS   Wife, children, servants, all
        That could be found.
MACDUFF   And I must be from thence?
        My wife killed too?
ROSS   I have said.
MALCOLM   Be comforted.   215
        Let's make us med'cines of our great revenge
        To cure this deadly grief.
MACDUFF He has no children. All my pretty ones?
        Did you say all? O hell-kite! All?
        What, all my pretty chickens and their dam   220
        At one fell swoop?
MALCOLM Dispute it like a man.
MACDUFF I shall do so;
        But I must also feel it as a man;
        I cannot but remember such things were   225
        That were most precious to me. Did heaven look on,
        And would not take their part? Sinful Macduff,
        They were all struck for thee. Naught that I am,
        Not for their own demerits but for mine,
        Fell slaughter on their souls. Heaven rest them now. 230
MALCOLM Be this the whetstone of your sword, let grief
        Convert to anger. Blunt not the heart, enrage it.
MACDUFF O, I could play the woman with mine eyes

215 SH ROSS] F *corr*: (*Roffe*); *Roffe* F *uncorr*.   219 say] F, F2–4; see Q*1673*   228 struck] F (strooke)

214 from thence i.e. away from home.
215 I have said A proverbial phrase (Dent S118.1).
216–17 Proverbially, 'To lament the dead avails not and revenge vents hatred' (Dent D125) and 'A desperate disease must have a desperate cure' (Dent D357). Compare the metaphors of 5.2.3–5, 27–9.
218 He has no children The phrase has several possible meanings depending upon the referent for 'He'. Malcolm ('He') has no children and cannot therefore understand Macduff's pain; see the proverbial 'He that has no children knows not what love is' (Dent C341). Macbeth ('He') has no children and (1) cannot therefore know what their loss means or (2) therefore has no one upon whom Macduff may exact a fitting revenge for the loss of his children. On the last, see 'You have no children, butchers; if you had, / The thought of them would have stirred up remorse, / But if you ever chance to have a child, / Look in his youth to have him so cut off / As, deathsmen, you have rid this sweet

young prince!' (*3H6* 5.5.63–7).
219 hell-kite hellish bird of prey; hence, figuratively, a human predator.
220 dam female parent. Like 'chickens' (compare 'chuck' (3.2.45)), the metaphor treats humans as animals; 'dam' is usually contemptuous when applied to humans: 'This brat is none of mine, / . . . Hence with it, and together with the dam / Commit them to the fire!' (*WT* 2.3.93, 95–6).
221 At one fell swoop Shakespeare seems to have invented this now-proverbial phrase (Dent S1046.1), echoed in 'at one swoop' (Webster, *White Devil* 1.1.6).
221 fell fierce, savage, cruel.
222–6 Macduff's conception of 'manliness' joins those of Macbeth (1.7.46–7, 2.3.101–4, 3.4.99–108) and of Ross (4.2.28–30).
227 part side, cause.
228 Naught Wicked (*OED* Naught *adj* 2).
233 play the woman with mine eyes weep. The phrase was becoming proverbial (Dent

And braggart with my tongue. But gentle heavens,
Cut short all intermission. Front to front   235
Bring thou this fiend of Scotland and myself;
Within my sword's length set him. If he scape,
Heaven forgive him too.

MALCOLM   This tune goes manly.
Come, go we to the king; our power is ready;
Our lack is nothing but our leave. Macbeth   240
Is ripe for shaking, and the powers above
Put on their instruments. Receive what cheer you may:
The night is long that never finds the day.

Exeunt

5.1 *Enter a* DOCTOR OF PHYSIC, *and a* WAITING-GENTLEWOMAN

DOCTOR   I have two nights watched with you, but can perceive no
    truth in your report. When was it she last walked?

---

236 myself,] *Capell;* my selfe F   238 tune] *Rowe²;* time F   Act 5, Scene 1   5.1] F (*Actus Quintus. Scena Prima.*)
1 two] F (too)

W637.2; earliest citation from 1598); see 'I was
forced to turn woman, and bear a part with her.
Humanity broke loose from my heart, and streamed
through mine eyes' (*Widow's Tears* 4.1.45–7).

234 braggart with my tongue Compare Macbeth's boasting followed by self-correction at
2.1.60–1 and 4.1.152.

235 intermission pause, interval in action.
Compare Macbeth's decision (4.1.145–8), to which
this one directly answers.

235 Front to front Face to face (or forehead to
forehead).

237–8 If . . . too In Roman Polanski's film *Macbeth*, Macduff (Terence Bayler) strongly emphasises 'too', suggesting that if Macbeth escapes Macduff's vengeance, he might possibly earn God's forgiveness, but not Macduff's.

237 scape escape (an aphetic form, as *OED*
Scape notes).

238 tune style, manner; temper, mood (*OED*
Tune *sb* 4a, 5). F's 'time' and 'tune' look very similar in Secretary hand, but 'F might be defended
as "rhythm" (*OED* [Time *sb*], 12a)' (Oxford) and
hence as a reference to some martial music for
which there is no SD. The proverbial 'Times change
and we with them' (Dent T343) may support F.

239 power army, force.

240 leave official permission (to depart).

241 ripe for shaking i.e. ready to fall (from the
fruit tree, from the throne).

241 powers above heavenly influences (recalling
King Edward and his holiness: see 143–5, 158–61).

242 Put on Don, clothe themselves in.

242 instruments agents, tools; here, probably
'weapons' (*OED* Instrument *sb* 2a).

243 Proverbially, 'After night comes the day'
(Dent N164); compare 1.3.146.

Act 5, Scene 1

This scene occurs in Lady Macbeth's private
rooms, probably in the castle at Dunsinane (5.2.12).
Like Macduff, who lost 'His wife, his babes, and
all unfortunate souls / That trace him in his line'
(4.1.151–2), Macbeth here loses his closest relation
and dearest confidant. Shakespeare often employs
prose when a character who ordinarily speaks verse
becomes deranged; see *Oth.* 4.1.35–43. For a similar scene in which a doctor observes a disturbed
person, see *TNK* 4.3.

0 SD DOCTOR OF PHYSIC Physician. The specificity implies costume or props and distinguishes
this actor from the common Elizabethan and
Jacobean use of 'Doctor' as a title for a cleric. Lady
Macbeth's condition is represented as a medical
rather than a spiritual one; she needs physical ther-
apy, not the exorcism a Roman Catholic (but not a
Protestant) clergyman might claim to offer. See 64
n., and Textual Analysis, pp. 278–9 below.

0 SD WAITING-GENTLEWOMAN Personal attendant who is 'gentle', not 'common'. In the
Jacobean court, the queen's personal attendants
were aristocrats; in Shakespeare's imagined courts,
the attendants' ranks are often unclear.

1 watched observed; perhaps 'stayed awake
observing' (*OED* Watch *v* 2).

GENTLEWOMAN Since his majesty went into the field, I have seen
  her rise from her bed, throw her night-gown upon her, unlock
  her closet, take forth paper, fold it, write upon't, read it, after-   5
  wards seal it, and again return to bed, yet all this while in a
  most fast sleep.

DOCTOR A great perturbation in nature, to receive at once the
  benefit of sleep and do the effects of watching. In this slumbery
  agitation, besides her walking and other actual performances,   10
  what at any time have you heard her say?

GENTLEWOMAN That, sir, which I will not report after her.

DOCTOR You may to me, and 'tis most meet you should.

GENTLEWOMAN Neither to you, nor anyone, having no witness to
  confirm my speech.   15

Enter LADY [MACBETH], *with a taper*

Lo you, here she comes. This is her very guise and, upon my
life, fast asleep. Observe her, stand close.

DOCTOR How came she by that light?

GENTLEWOMAN Why, it stood by her. She has light by her continually, 'tis her command.

---

9 watching.] F; watching! *Dyce*   15 SD LADY MACBETH] *Rowe: Lady* F

---

3 **his majesty** Macbeth.

3 **went into the field** mobilised an army for battle.

4 **night-gown** See 2.2.73 n., where it was 'a
means of deceit'; here, however, it is an 'icon of
human mortality' (Houston Diehl, 'Horrid image,
sorry sight, fatal vision: the visual rhetoric of *Macbeth*', *S.St.* 16 (1983), 196).

5 **closet** cabinet; lockable chest or box for valu-
ables. 'Closet' often means small private chamber,
but the usage here is supported by *JC* 3.2.129 and
Lear 3.3.11.

5 **fold** In early modern practice, a letter-writer
usually folded or creased a sheet of paper to form
the left- and right-hand margins of the text-area
before writing the letter itself; once the letter had
been completed, the sheet was folded several more
times to create its own 'envelope', a blank outside
upon which directions for its delivery were written.
See next note.

6 **seal** Place a personal mark in hot wax upon a
document as a sign of authenticity. Shakespeare's
contemporaries ensured the privacy of letters by
folding them and sealing over the fold. Seals were
also used to validate legal documents.

9 **effects** appearances, outward manifestations
(*OED* Effect *sb* 3a).

9 **watching** waking (*OED* Watch *v* 1).

9 **slumbery** sleepy, slumberous (*OED*).

10 **actual** active (*OED* Actual *a* 1, quoting this
line).

13 **meet** fitting, appropriate.

14–15 The Waiting-Gentlewoman fears to repeat
what she has heard without a witness because it
would be treasonable; the same issue appears when
Cymbeline asks the queen's ladies to confirm Cor-
nelius's account of her confession (*Cym.* 5.5.61–2).

15 SD *taper* candle.

16 **Lo** See 3.4.69 n.

16 **very guise** exact manner, custom, or habit.

16–17 **upon my life** An oath.

17 **close** concealed, hidden, out of sight. The
word expresses the speaker's anxiety at being a
witness; she ignores the fact that the sleepwalking Lady Macbeth sees nothing (22) even though,
uncannily, 'her eyes are open' (21).

18 The Doctor's realistic question (why does a
sleepwalker need light?) leads to an eerie inference:
awake or asleep, Lady Macbeth evidently fears
the dark. Unlike her famous predecessor, Hannah
Pritchard, who emblematically indicated the 'spot'
(30) by looking at her palm (see the illustration
reproduced in 'Macbeth in the twentieth century',
TQ 1, 3 (1971), 21), Sarah Siddons set down the
taper so that she could mime hand-washing at lines
23, 27, 30; see Sprague, p. 271.

DOCTOR You see her eyes are open. 20

GENTLEWOMAN Ay, but their sense are shut.

DOCTOR What is it she does now? Look how she rubs her hands.

GENTLEWOMAN It is an accustomed action with her, to seem thus
washing her hands; I have known her continue in this a quarter 25
of an hour.

LADY MACBETH Yet here's a spot.

DOCTOR Hark, she speaks; I will set down what comes from her to
satisfy my remembrance the more strongly.

LADY MACBETH Out, damned spot! Out, I say! One, two. Why
then 'tis time to do't. Hell is murky. Fie, my lord, fie, a soldier,
and afeard? What need we fear? Who knows it, when none can
call our power to account? Yet who would have thought the old
man to have had so much blood in him?

DOCTOR Do you mark that? 35

LADY MACBETH The Thane of Fife had a wife. Where is she
now? What, will these hands ne'er be clean? No more o'that,

---

22 are] F, F2–4; is Q1673   30 spot!] *Steevens;* spot: F   30 say!] *Steevens;* say. F   32 afeard] F (affear'd)   32 fear? Who knows] F (feare? who knowes); fear who knows *Rowe²*   33 account] F (accompt)   34 him?] *Rowe;* him. F

---

22 are The plural verb may have been influenced by 'their', as Muir suggests, but compare 'Their wives have sense like them' (*Oth.* 4.3.94), where 'sense' is plural, and Sonnet 112.10–11, where the word seems a collective noun.

25–6 a quarter of an hour The Waiting-Gentlewoman can still tell time and relies upon its stability. See pp. 19–20 above.

28 set down write down, note. An implicit SD: the Doctor uses a pocket notebook (compare 1.3.150–1 and n.).

29 satisfy meet the needs of, content (*OED* Satisfy *v* 4b).

30 One, two Presumably, the striking of a bell (e.g. that mentioned at 2.1.62) or a clock (e.g. the Porter's 'second cock' (2.3.20)).

31 murky gloomy, dark. Sleepwalking, Lady Macbeth relives her experiences and (unheard) dialogue with Macbeth in 2.3; here, the audience may imagine she repeats words that the audience supposes Macbeth said.

32 afeard afraid.

32–3 Who knows . . . account The murder of Duncan cannot be said to be 'known' because no one has the power or authority to hold the Macbeths responsible; compare her assurance before the murder: 'Who dares receive it other' (1.7.77). Rowe² and most later editors change F's punctuation to create a more straightforward question: 'what need we fear who knows it, when none can

call our Power to account –'; Rowe apparently assumed that the question mark after 'fear' was superfluous, although Q1673 retains F's punctuation and Davenant compromises with 'what need we fear? who knows it? There's none dares call our Power to account.' F often includes more question marks than modern conventions demand (see e.g. the collation for 1.3.130, 133), yet these lines make a difficult but appropriate sense, and I have retained F's punctuation.

33–4 Yet . . . him Lady Macbeth's surprise depends upon the conventional assumption that ageing dries the blood and diminishes its movement; see 'Time hath not yet so dried this blood of mine' (*Ado* 4.1.193) and 1.5.41–2 n. The flat, almost disinterested, phrasing – 'who would have thought' – and the neutral reference to Duncan, who earlier reminded her of her father (2.2.12–13), as 'the old man' suggest Lady Macbeth's despair, a guilty helplessness represented as sleepwalking and very different from her energetic action in 1.7, 2.2, and 3.4.

36 Thane of Fife Macduff.

37 What . . . clean Lady Macbeth may speak of her own hands (see 23–6 and (42–3), or she may be repeating something Macbeth said. Steevens³ compares 'here's a white hand: / Can blood so soon be wash'd out?' (Webster, *White Devil* 5.4.82–3). See 2.2.63–4 and n.

my lord, no more o'that. You mar all with this starting.

DOCTOR Go to, go to; you have known what you should not.

GENTLEWOMAN She has spoke what she should not, I am sure of   40
that. Heaven knows what she has known.

LADY MACBETH Here's the smell of the blood still; all the perfumes of Arabia will not sweeten this little hand. O, O, O.

DOCTOR What a sigh is there! The heart is sorely charged.

GENTLEWOMAN I would not have such a heart in my bosom for   45
the dignity of the whole body.

DOCTOR Well, well, well –

GENTLEWOMAN Pray God it be, sir.

DOCTOR This disease is beyond my practice; yet I have known
those which have walked in their sleep who have died holily in   50
their beds.

LADY MACBETH Wash your hands, put on your night-gown, look
not so pale. I tell you yet again, Banquo's buried; he cannot
come out on's grave.

DOCTOR Even so?   55

LADY MACBETH To bed, to bed; there's knocking at the gate.
Come, come, come, come, give me your hand; what's done
cannot be undone. To bed, to bed, to bed.   *Exit*

DOCTOR Will she go now to bed?

GENTLEWOMAN Directly.   60

DOCTOR Foul whisp'rings are abroad; unnatural deeds
Do breed unnatural troubles; infected minds

---

38 this] F; *not in* F2–4   42 the blood] F; of blood F3–4   47 well –] *Rowe;* well. F   58 SD] F (*Exit Lady.*)

38 starting flinching, recoiling nervously (as Macbeth did upon meeting the witches; see 1.3.49).

39 Go to Come, come (a remonstrance).

40 spoke spoken (see 1.4.3 n.). This obsolete usage may arise from Compositor B's desire to justify the line of type.

42–3 perfumes of Arabia Spices (from which perfumes that 'sweeten' (43) are made) and the legendary phoenix (which died and was reborn in aromatic flames) are the commonest early modern literary associations with (Saudi) Arabia; see Sugden under Arabia; 'your daughter's womb . . . that nest of spicery' (*R3* 4.4.423–4); the 'innocent cradle, where, phoenix-like, / They [flowers] died in perfume' (*TNK* 1.3.70–1). Lady Macbeth's phrase allusively links crime (the smell of blood, the hand that cannot be sweetened) with scent and reproduction (the phoenix) and the failure of Macbeth's line (see 'unlineal' (3.1.64)).

44 sorely charged grievously burdened, heavily loaded.

46 dignity rank, status (as queen).

49 practice professional skill, art (Brooke).

53 pale Compare 2.2.61 and n.

54 on's of his.

57–8 what's done cannot be undone The dialogue's third use (see 1.7.1 and 3.2.12) of the proverbial 'Things done cannot be undone' (Dent T200).

57 give me your hand This gesture has a profound history in the play; see 1.2.21 and 2.2.63–4 and nn., 37.

60 Directly At once, straightaway.

61 whisp'rings For the syncopation (which also saves space in a very full line of type in F), see 3.4.107 n., and contractions in Macbeth's letter (1.5.2) and the Porter's prose (2.3.3–6).

To their deaf pillows will discharge their secrets.
More needs she the divine than the physician.
God, God forgive us all. Look after her;   65
Remove from her the means of all annoyance,
And still keep eyes upon her. So, good night,
My mind she has mated, and amazed my sight.
I think, but dare not speak.

GENTLEWOMAN   Good night, good doctor.

Exeunt

5.2 *Drum and colours. Enter* MENTEITH, CAITHNESS, ANGUS, LENNOX, *Soldiers*

MENTEITH The English power is near, led on by Malcolm,
His uncle Siward, and the good Macduff.
Revenges burn in them, for their dear causes

Act 5, Scene 2   **5.2**] F (*Scena Secunda.*)   **3** them,] *Oxford;* them: F*;* them*; Collier*

64 More needs she . . . physician i.e. she is beyond medical help and requires spiritual counsel. The line rests upon proverbial comparisons: 'Where the Philosopher ends, the Physician begins; and he ends . . . where the Divine begins' (Samuel Purchas, *Purchas his Pilgrimes* (1619), sig. 2SIV as quoted in Dent, *PLED* P252.11, 'Where the Philosopher ends the physition begins'). When Bardolph reports that Falstaff is 'In bodily health', Poins replies, 'Marry, the immortal part needs a physician, but that moves not him: though that be sick, it dies not' (*2H4* 2.2.103–5).

66 The Doctor anticipates that Lady Macbeth might commit suicide (a conventional literary consequence of the Christian sin of despair, or loss of belief in God's grace), as Malcolm later suggests she did (5.9.37–8).

66 annoyance injuring, troubling (*OED* Annoyance 1, quoting this line).

67 still always.

68 she has The phrase is probably elided in performance ('she's'); see Cercignani, pp. 288–9.

68 mated daunted, stupefied (*OED* Mate *v¹* 4).

68 amazed astonished. The word derives from 'maze'; the Doctor is in a mental labyrinth. Compare 2.4.19, 4.1.125, and 'like a labyrinth to amaze his foes' (*Venus and Adonis* 684).

69 I think . . . speak Like the Waiting-Gentlewoman (14–15), the Doctor is afraid to acknowledge the evidence of regicide he now possesses. This line is the earliest known evidence for the proverbial 'One may think that dares not speak' (Dent T220).

Act 5, Scene 2
This scene is located in Scotland, where the native nobles await the arrival of the joint Scottish and English army, and represents the first action against Macbeth's tyranny, although 3.6 and the end of 4.3 anticipate it. For analysis of the final battles, see Brennan, pp. 156–63, who notes 'how much Shakespeare emphasizes the role of Macbeth and his isolation' (p. 162).

0 SD *Drum and colours* Drummer and flag-bearer(s). Like F's *Hautboys* (players of hautboys) and *Torch* (torch-bearer) at 1.6.0 SD, these two words indicate actors performing a function; the SD calls for a military presence and martial sounds.

1 power military force. Elision ('pow'r') helps the metre.

2 His uncle Siward According to *Scotland*, p. 171a, Siward was Malcolm's maternal grandfather, but (as NS notes) F's 'Vnkle' is metrically more convenient.

3–5 Revenges . . . man The clearest meaning of this complex clause is that Malcolm and Macduff's motives for revenge are powerful enough to make a dead, or near-dead, man answer the call to arms. Mahood (pp. 136–7) notes the hint of resurrection in these lines and links them with 4.1.96; see, more appositely, 2.3.69–74.

3 Revenges Desires to repay injuries by inflicting hurt in return (*OED* Revenge *sb* 1b, citing 'my revenges were high bent upon him' (*AWW* 5.3.10)).

3 dear honourable; precious. 'Dire, grievous' (*OED* Dear *a²* 2) is another possible meaning, as in 'dear peril' (*Tim.* 5.1.228).

Would to the bleeding and the grim alarm
Excite the mortified man.
ANGUS   Near Birnam Wood   5
Shall we well meet them; that way are they coming.
CAITHNESS Who knows if Donaldbain be with his brother?
LENNOX For certain, sir, he is not. I have a file
Of all the gentry; there is Siward's son
And many unrough youths that even now   10
Protest their first of manhood.
MENTEITH   What does the tyrant?
CAITHNESS Great Dunsinane he strongly fortifies.
Some say he's mad; others that lesser hate him
Do call it valiant fury, but for certain
He cannot buckle his distempered cause   15
Within the belt of rule.
ANGUS   Now does he feel
His secret murders sticking on his hands.
Now minutely revolts upbraid his faith-breach;
Those he commands, move only in command,
Nothing in love. Now does he feel his title   20
Hang loose about him, like a giant's robe
Upon a dwarfish thief.
MENTEITH   Who then shall blame

10 unrough] F (vnruffe)   11 tyrant?] F4; Tyrant. F

4 bleeding running with blood (*OED* Bleeding *ppl a* 1b); the flowing of blood (*OED* Bleeding *vbl sb* 1a); the letting of blood (*OED* Bleeding *vbl sb* 2).
5 mortified dead; insensible.
7 The first mention of Donaldbain since 3.6.9, and the last in the play.
8 file list. Compare 3.1.94 and n.
10 unrough i.e. unbearded, young.
11 Protest Affirm, proclaim.
11 first beginning, first part (*OED* First quasi-*sb* 5c).
12 Dunsinane See 4.1.92 n.
15–16 buckle . . . belt of rule i.e. contain his sick government through control.
17 sticking on adhering to (a figurative meaning of *OED* Stick *v*¹ 8c, where this line is quoted). The words recall the blood on Macbeth and Lady Macbeth's hands (2.2.62–70) and Macbeth's fears of Banquo's 'royalty of nature' (3.1.50–2). For clothing that does not 'stick' on Macbeth, see 20–2 below.
18 minutely happening every minute. This line is the first citation under *OED* Minutely *a*

(Schäfer).
18 upbraid reproach, reprove (*OED* Upbraid *v* 2).
18 faith-breach broken loyalty; treason. A noun has been made from the common phrase 'breach of faith'; this line is the only citation at *OED* Faith *sb* 14.
19–20 only . . . love Compare 'He knows that you embrace not Antony / As you did love, but as you feared him' (*Ant.* 3.13.56–7).
20 Nothing Not at all (*OED* Nothing *adv* 1a). 'Nothing', like 'only' (19), modifies 'move' (19): only 'command' (19), not 'love', motivates Macbeth's followers to obey him.
20–2 Now . . . thief The conclusion of the metaphors linking titles, clothing, and ambition; compare 1.3.106–7, 1.3.143–5, 2.4.38, and Sebastian's exchange with Antonio: 'I remember / You did supplant your brother Prospero. / True. / And look how well my garments sit upon me, / Much feater than before' (*Temp.* 2.1.270–3, cited by Slater, p. 168).

His pestered senses to recoil and start,
When all that is within him does condemn
Itself for being there?   25
CAITHNESS   Well, march we on
To give obedience where 'tis truly owed;
Meet we the med'cine of the sickly weal,
And with him pour we in our country's purge,
Each drop of us.
LENNOX   Or so much as it needs
To dew the sovereign flower and drown the weeds.   30
Make we our march towards Birnam.

Exeunt, marching

5.3 *Enter* MACBETH, DOCTOR, *and Attendants*

MACBETH Bring me no more reports, let them fly all;
Till Birnam Wood remove to Dunsinane,
I cannot taint with fear. What's the boy Malcolm?
Was he not born of woman? The spirits that know
All mortal consequences have pronounced me thus: 5

---

25 there?] *Pope;* there. F   **Act 5, Scene 3**   5.3] F (*Scaena Tertia.*)   5 consequences] F; consequents, *Steevens³ omitting here;* consequence, *Singer*

23 pestered vexed, plagued. Compare the description of Macdonald (1.2.11–12).

23 recoil See 4.3.19 n.

23 start See 1.3.49, 5.1.38, and nn.

24–5 When . . . there i.e. Macbeth is in rebellion against himself. Compare 2.2.76.

27 med'cine physician (*OED* Medicine *sb²*), i.e. Malcolm (the 'him' of 28). Compare 'I have seen a medicine / That's able to breathe life into a stone' (*AWW* 2.1.72–3) and the medical language of 5.3.40–8, 51–7.

27 weal state; community; common weal (*OED* Weal *sb¹* 3b). Other available meanings include 'well-being, happiness' (*OED* Weal *sb¹* 2).

28 purge cleansing; purgative, a medicine causing the bowels to empty.

30 dew moisten (*OED* Dew *v* 2). The liquid Caithness (28–9) and Lennox have in mind is blood, not water. Compare Lennox on the 'due of birth' (3.6.25).

30 sovereign royal; supreme; efficacious. Mahood (p. 135) notes that this last meaning (by extension, 'healing') 'recalls the curative powers of the holy [King] Edward' described at 4.3.149–58.

30 weeds Metaphorically, the moral and political chaos of Scotland; compare Hamlet's description of 'this world' as 'an unweeded garden / That grows to seed' (*Ham.* 1.2.134–6) and the analogy between government and gardening in *R2* 3.4. There may be wordplay on 'weeds' = clothing.

31 SD *marching* This SD indicates drumming as well as a martial, ordered departure.

Act 5, Scene 3
The imaginary location is Macbeth's castle, Dunsinane.

0 SD Macbeth's first appearance since 4.1; for the play's complex patterns of characters' presence and absence, see Appendix 1, pp. 281–2 below.

1 them The 'false thanes' (7) who desert Macbeth.

3 taint lose courage, become weak (*OED* Taint *v* c.3b, where this citation is the first of only two, the second from 1639).

5 mortal human.

5 consequences outcomes, eventualities. 'Sequence, succession, course' (*OED* Consequence *sb* 2b) is not quite apposite. Adopting Singer's

'Fear not, Macbeth, no man that's born of woman
Shall e'er have power upon thee.' Then fly false thanes
And mingle with the English epicures;
The mind I sway by and the heart I bear
Shall never sag with doubt nor shake with fear.   10

Enter SERVANT

The devil damn thee black, thou cream-faced loon.
Where got'st thou that goose-look?
SERVANT There is ten thousand –
MACBETH   Geese, villain?
SERVANT   Soldiers, sir.
MACBETH Go prick thy face and over-red thy fear,
Thou lily-livered boy. What soldiers, patch?   15
Death of thy soul, those linen cheeks of thine
Are counsellors to fear. What soldiers, whey-face?
SERVANT The English force, so please you.
MACBETH Take thy face hence!

                                             [*Exit Servant*]
Seyton! – I am sick at heart,

6–7 'Fear . . . thee.'] *Singer* (*subst.*); Feare . . . thee. F   **12** goose-look?] F4; Goose-looke. F   **13** thousand –] *Rowe*; thousand. F   **19** SD] *Collier*²; *not in* F   **19** Seyton! –] *Rowe*; *Seyton*, F

emendation, 'consequence', NS says 'Both style and metre support the change', and Shakespeare elsewhere uses only the singular, which would here give the line a universal, timeless application. Further, compositors seem prone to add or drop *s*, but since F's line is perfectly intelligible, emendation here is really editorial 'improvement'.

8 epicures gluttons, sybarites.

9 The mind I sway by The mind that rules me; the mind by which I rule (Chambers).

11 On stage, Macbeth sometimes (e.g. Laurence Olivier, Old Vic, London, 1937; Alan Howard, Royal National Theatre, London, 1993) assaults the Servant here; see 5.5.34 n.

11 cream-faced having a face the colour of cream (i.e. pale). Compare 'blanched with fear' (3.4.116).

11 loon rogue. The word is a Scotticism; for his English audience, Patten explains (sig. 18v, margin), 'A lound is a name of reproch as a villain or suche lyke.' See also *OED* Loon *sb*¹ 1 and F4's spelling, Lown.

12 goose-look foolish or witless appearance. Proverbially, geese were 'giddy' and only ironically 'wise' (Dent G347.1 and G348).

14 over-red redden over, cover with red (*OED* Over-red, quoting only this line and an allusion from 1826). Macbeth urges the Servant to replace pale fear with ruddy courage.

15 lily-livered having a liver (traditionally the organ of courage) the colour of a lily, white, hence cowardly. Compare 'the liver white and pale, which is the badge of pusillanimity and cowardice' (*2H4* 4.3.104–6, cited by Steevens²) and 'A white-livered fellow' (Dent F180).

16 Death of thy soul May your soul die (a curse).

16 linen white (i.e. cowardly). 'As white as linen' is an ancient analogy (Dent L306.1).

17 counsellors advisers (*OED* Counsellor 1a *fig*), confidants (*Lexicon*). The word seems both active and passive: the effect (white cheeks) is an associate of the cause (fear) as well as the stimulus to others' fear (including Macbeth's?).

17 whey-face face the colour of whey (i.e. milky pale with fear).

19 Seyton This proper name may have been pronounced as 'Satan'; if so, Macbeth summons an attending officer who also represents demonic power. See Supplementary Note, p. 260 below.

When I behold – Seyton, I say! – this push   20
Will cheer me ever or disseat me now.
I have lived long enough. My way of life
Is fall'n into the sere, the yellow leaf,
And that which should accompany old age,
As honour, love, obedience, troops of friends,   25
I must not look to have; but in their stead,
Curses, not loud but deep, mouth-honour, breath
Which the poor heart would fain deny, and dare not.
Seyton!

Enter SEYTON

SEYTON What's your gracious pleasure?
MACBETH   What news more?   30
SEYTON All is confirmed, my lord, which was reported.
MACBETH I'll fight till from my bones my flesh be hacked.
         Give me my armour.
SEYTON 'Tis not needed yet.
MACBETH I'll put it on;   35
         Send out more horses; skirr the country round.
         Hang those that talk of fear. Give me mine armour.
         How does your patient, doctor?
DOCTOR   Not so sick, my lord,

---

20 behold – . . . say!–] *Rowe*; behold: . . . say, F   21 disseat] F (dis-eate); disease F2–4   36 more] F (mo)

20 **push** attack; thrust (of a weapon).
21 **cheer** comfort, console; gladden (*OED* Cheer *v* 2; 4). There is probably a pun on 'chair' (= throne).
21 **disseat** unseat. *OED* Disseat doubts this reading; if the word is correctly printed (it also appears at *TNK* 5.4.72), it is Shakespeare's neologism.
22 **way** course, manner (*OED* Way *sb*¹ 14). The word also has overtones of 'freedom of action' (*OED* Way *sb*¹ 6) and 'pilgrimage, journey' (*OED* Way *sb*¹ 7e).
23 **sere** dry, withered. The word hovers between being an adjective modifying 'leaf' and a noun ('the sere') meaning something like 'the withered state' (see C. T. Onions, *TLS* 24 October 1935, p. 671).
23 **yellow leaf** i.e. the season when leaves of deciduous trees lose their green colour and winter approaches; metaphorically, period shortly before death. Compare 'That time of year thou mayst in me behold / When yellow leaves, or none, or few, do hang / Upon those boughs . . . where late the sweet birds sang' (Sonnet 73.1–4) and 4.3.173–5.
25 **troops** flocks, swarms (*OED* Troop *sb* 1d, quoting *Err.* 5.1.81 as the earliest example).

25 **friends** followers, retainers, supporters.
26 **stead** place. F's 'steed' probably represents a contemporary pronunciation with a lengthened vowel (Cercignani, p. 83).
27 **mouth-honour** i.e. respect and duty merely verbal (hence insincere, not from the heart). Compare 4.1.146–7 n., and Timon's curse for those who deceived him, 'You knot of mouth-friends' (*Tim.* 3.6.89). H. B. Sprague (ed.), *Macbeth*, 1889 (quoted in Furness), cites 'Therfore thus hath the Lorde sayd: Forsomuche as this people when they be in trouble, do honour me with their mouth and with their lippes, but their heart is farre fro[m] me, and the feare whiche they have unto me proceedeth of a commaundement that is taught of men' (Isa. 29.13).
28 **fain** gladly; gladly under the circumstances (*OED* Fain *adv*).
36 **horses** i.e. warriors mounted on horses.
36 **skirr** pass rapidly over, scour (*OED* Skirr *v* 3, where this line is the earliest citation). Compare 'scour' (57).
38 **sick** i.e. physically (as opposed to mentally) ill.

As she is troubled with thick-coming fancies
That keep her from her rest.   40

MACBETH   Cure her of that.
Canst thou not minister to a mind diseased,
Pluck from the memory a rooted sorrow,
Raze out the written troubles of the brain,
And with some sweet oblivious antidote
Cleanse the stuffed bosom of that perilous stuff   45
Which weighs upon the heart?

DOCTOR   Therein the patient
Must minister to himself.

MACBETH Throw physic to the dogs, I'll none of it.
Come, put mine armour on; give me my staff. –
Seyton, send out. – Doctor, the thanes fly from me. –   50
[*To Attendant*] Come sir, dispatch. – If thou couldst,
    doctor, cast
The water of my land, find her disease,
And purge it to a sound and pristine health,
I would applaud thee to the very echo
That should applaud again. – Pull't off, I say! –   55
What rhubarb, cynne, or what purgative drug
Would scour these English hence? Hear'st thou of them?

DOCTOR Ay, my good lord; your royal preparation

---

40 Cure her] F2–4; Cure F   **49–51** staff. – / . . . out. – . . . me. – / . . . dispatch. –] *Capell* (*subst.*); Staffe. / . . . out: . . . me: / . . . dispatch. F   **53** pristine] F (pristiue)   **55** again. – Pull't . . . say! –] *Singer* (*subst.*); againe. Pull't . . . say, F   **56** cynne] *This edn;* Cyme F; Cæny F2–3; senna F4

39 thick-coming crowding (*Lexicon*). Compare the tales and posts of 1.3.95–6.

40 Cure her F2–4 add the pronoun which may therefore be the result of vulgarisation, overscrupulous metrics, or false modernisation; *OED* Cure v^1 1a–b cites absolute uses that support F, or the compositor's error.

41 Compare 'she has a perturbèd mind, which I cannot minister to' (*TNK* 4.3.59–60).

43 Raze Eradicate, uproot.

44 oblivious causing forgetfulness or oblivion.

45 The repetition of 'stuffed . . . stuff' has been considered an error (compare 3.2.20 n.), but no emendation (NS provides a comic list) is persuasive. In the theatre, the actor (e.g. Roger Allam, Stratford, 1996) may pause before 'stuff', indicating a tired inability to find another word.

48 physic medicine (*OED* Physic *sb* 4).

51 dispatch make haste.

51–2 cast / The water analyse ('cast') the urine ('water'). Inspection of urine and other bodily secretions (especially of female patients) was common practice in early modern medicine. Compare 'To look to one's water' (Dent W109).

52–7 This passage recalls the commonplace analogies of human body and political state, microcosm and macrocosm; see 'single state' (1.3.139 and n.).

53 pristine former, ancient. F's 'pristiue' may contain a 'turned' *n* or result from Compositor B's (easy) misreading of manuscript *n* for *u*.

56 rhubarb A medicinal plant, the so-called Chinese rhubarb, and not the common or garden European and New World variety (*OED* Rhubarb *sb*). See next note.

56 cynne senna (medicinal plant prescribed as both emetic and purgative). Gerard (p. 1115) recommends mixing senna and rhubarb as a purge. F's 'cyme' may be a misreading of 'cyne' or 'cynne', spellings of 'cæny' (F2–3) or 'sene', the word Gerard and others use for 'senna' (F4's spelling, adopted by many editors though it creates a hypermetric line).

Makes us hear something.

MACBETH   Bring it after me. –
I will not be afraid of death and bane,   60
Till Birnam Forest come to Dunsinane.

                                    [*Exeunt all but Doctor*]

DOCTOR   Were I from Dunsinane away and clear,
Profit again should hardly draw me here.   *Exit*

5.4 *Drum and colours. Enter* MALCOLM, SIWARD, MACDUFF, *Siward's
son,* MENTEITH, CAITHNESS, ANGUS, *and* SOLDIERS, *marching*

MALCOLM   Cousins, I hope the days are near at hand
That chambers will be safe.

MENTEITH   We doubt it nothing.

SIWARD   What wood is this before us?

MENTEITH   The Wood of Birnam.

MALCOLM   Let every soldier hew him down a bough,
And bear't before him; thereby shall we shadow   5
The numbers of our host and make discovery

---

59 me. –] *Capell;* me: F   **61** SD] *This edn (after Steevens³); not in* F. *See Commentary*   **63** SD] *Steevens³;
Exeunt* F   Act 5, Scene 4   **5.4**] F (*Scena Quarta.*)   **0** SD.1 SIWARD] F (*Seyward); old* SIWARD *Capell*   **0** SD.2 *Siward's
son*] F (*Seywards Sonne*)   **3** SH SIWARD] F (*Syew.*)

59 it Either the piece of armour or other equipment referred to at 49, 51, 55, or 'something' (59), news or reports of the enemy.

60 bane murder, death, destruction (*OED* Bane *sb¹* 3, quoting this line).

61 SD–63 SD F offers only a general *Exeunt* at the scene's very end; the Doctor's lines must therefore be marked as an aside (Hanmer) or Macbeth and others must be directed off after 61, with the Doctor's couplet spoken directly to the audience (Steevens). I select the latter because: (1) Macbeth's abruptness (59) and couplet (60–1) are more effective if he immediately leaves the stage; (2) the Doctor's satirical couplet makes a better contrast with Macbeth's couplet if it stands alone; (3) comic scene-ending closers seem often to have been directed to the audience (see e.g. *John* 1.1.276 and *Lear* 1.5.51–2).

63 A joke about physicians' greed, already an ancient satiric target.

Act 5, Scene 4
This scene occurs wherever and before whatever

the audience imagines as Birnam Wood (3). *Scotland*, p. 176a, records the ruse by which Malcolm and his army conceal themselves from Macbeth's scouts. It appears earlier in British history as a legend concerning the county of Kent's defiance of William the Conqueror through a similar trick; see Raphael Holinshed, *The Third Volume of Chronicles* (1587), p. 2a, and John Selden's discussion of Drayton's *Poly-Olbion*, song 18 (Michael Drayton, *Works*, ed. J. W. Hebel *et al.*, corr. edn, 5 vols., 1961, IV, 385–6).

0 SD *Drum and colours* See 5.2.0 SD n.

0 SD.1 SIWARD Editors rename this character 'Old Siward' in SDs and SHs to distinguish him from his son, called *young Seyward* at 5.7.4 SD and *Y.Sey* in the SHs for his few speeches in 5.7, but F's distinction of son from father is sufficient without intruding a distinction of father from son.

2 chambers rooms (but with the extended sense of 'private dwellings').

6 discovery military reconnaissance, reconnoitring (*OED* Discovery 3b, where *Lear* 5.1.53 is the first citation).

                 Err in report of us.
A SOLDIER   It shall be done.
SIWARD   We learn no other, but the confident tyrant
         Keeps still in Dunsinane and will endure
         Our setting down before't.
MALCOLM   'Tis his main hope,   10
         For where there is advantage to be given,
         Both more and less have given him the revolt,
         And none serve with him but constrainèd things
         Whose hearts are absent too.
MACDUFF   Let our just censures
         Attend the true event and put we on   15
         Industrious soldiership.
SIWARD   The time approaches
         That will with due decision make us know
         What we shall say we have and what we owe;
         Thoughts speculative their unsure hopes relate,
         But certain issue strokes must arbitrate.   20
         Towards which, advance the war.

                                    Exeunt, marching

5.5 *Enter* MACBETH, SEYTON, *and Soldiers, with drum and colours*

MACBETH Hang out our banners on the outward walls;

7 SH] F (*Sold.*)   8 SH] F (*Sym.*)   11 given] F (giuen); taken *Keightley*   16 SH] F (*Sey.*)   20 arbitrate.] *Pope*; arbitrate;
F; arbitrate: *Theobald*   **Act 5, Scene 5**   5.5] F (*Scena Quinta.*)

7 Err Mistake, make an error.

8 no other i.e. no other news, no other reports, of Macbeth's plans.

8 but except.

10 setting down laying siege, encamping.

11 given yielded (? an impersonal use of *OED* Give *v* 40). If the line has been accurately set, its obscurity presumably results from wordplay on 'given' (12).

12 more and less i.e. aristocrats and common- ers.

12 given him the revolt have revolted from his service.

14–15 Let . . . event Let a true evaluation ('just censures') of military matters await the bat- tle's outcome ('event'). Macduff advises patience and prudence; Siward expands the point (16–21). Compare Lucius's pre-battle remark to Cloten: 'the event / Is yet to name the winner' (*Cym.* 3.5.14– 15), and 'Let th'event, / That never-erring arbitra- tor, tell us / When we know all ourselves' (*TNK*

1.2.113-15).

19 unsure Accented on the first syllable (Cer- cignani, p. 33).

20 issue result, outcome (*OED* Issue *sb* 10). For the word here and earlier, see p. 52 above.

21 After the couplet (19–20) closing his elabora- tion of Macduff's speech, Siward presumably turns from the group of leaders to address the army at large.

21 war soldiers in fighting array (*OED* War *sb*¹ 6b, with earliest citation from 1667), war-party.

Act 5, Scene 5

This scene occurs outside, or in a courtyard of, Dunsinane ('our castle' (2)), where a gathering of soldiers is possible (o SD), but close enough to Lady Macbeth's rooms for the 'cry of women' (8) to be heard.

o SD *drum and colours* See 5.2.0 SD n.

The cry is still, 'They come.' Our castle's strength
Will laugh a siege to scorn; here let them lie
Till famine and the ague eat them up.
Were they not forced with those that should be ours,   5
We might have met them dareful, beard to beard,
And beat them backward home.

A cry within of women

What is that noise?

SEYTON It is the cry of women, my good lord.

MACBETH I have almost forgot the taste of fears;
The time has been, my senses would have cooled   10
To hear a night-shriek and my fell of hair
Would at a dismal treatise rouse and stir
As life were in't. I have supped full with horrors;
Direness familiar to my slaughterous thoughts
Cannot once start me. Wherefore was that cry?   15

SEYTON The queen, my lord, is dead.

MACBETH   She should have died hereafter;
There would have been a time for such a word.
Tomorrow, and tomorrow, and tomorrow

---

2 'They come.'] *Pope (subst.); they come:* F   7 SD] F *(after* noise)   8 lord.] F; lord. *Exit. / Collier*²   15 me.] F; me.
Reenter SEYTON *Collier*²

4 **ague** violent fever, shaking fit.

5 **forced** strengthened, reinforced (*OED* Force *v*¹ 13a).

6 **dareful** full of defiance. This line is *OED*'s first citation for the word, with only one other (from 1614).

6 **beard to beard** i.e. face to face. Compare the ancient proverb 'To meet in the beard' (Dent B143.1).

8–16 Clarendon conjectures a servant who enters and tells Seyton what the 'cry' (8) signifies, while Dyce and other editors add SDs for Seyton's exit and re-entrance (so as to learn off-stage what 'the cry of women' means), but Dessen (pp. 5–7) argues that such additions may be over-realistic and reduce F's eeriness.

9–13 These lines initiate a series of echoes of, or allusions to, earlier moments when Macbeth's mind, body, and conscience responded differently to horrifying sounds and images. Compare 1.3.134 ff.

11 **fell** head, shock.

13 **As** As if (Abbott 107); see 1.4.11 n.

13 **supped full with horrors** Figuratively, 'filled up with, dined full of, horrors', but literally 'had supper with Banquo's Ghost' at Macbeth's banquet in 3.4.

14–15 **Direness . . . me** i.e. my murderous thoughts have made me familiar with fearsome things that no longer have the power to frighten me. Compare Macbeth's terror at the knocking that follows Duncan's murder (2.2.60–1).

14 **Direness.** Horror *OED*'s earliest citation for the word (Schäfer).

14 **slaughterous** murderous, destructive (*OED* SV).

16–17 **She . . . word** Two meanings seem possible: (1) Lady Macbeth would have died sooner or later, a time would inevitably come for her death; (2) it would have been more suitable had Lady Macbeth died at some future time, when word of her death might receive proper mourning. On the former, see 3.2.38; on the latter, see 4.3.232–8, when war interrupts and displaces Macduff's mourning. Booth (p. 95) notes that 'hereafter' (Macbeth's last reference to his wife) 'echoes Lady Macbeth's first words to Macbeth' (1.5.53); see also 'hereafter' at 1.3.48 and 1.4.38.

Creeps in this petty pace from day to day
To the last syllable of recorded time;   20
And all our yesterdays have lighted fools
The way to dusty death. Out, out, brief candle,
Life's but a walking shadow, a poor player
That struts and frets his hour upon the stage
And then is heard no more. It is a tale   25
Told by an idiot, full of sound and fury
Signifying nothing.

Enter a MESSENGER

Thou com'st to use thy tongue: thy story quickly.
MESSENGER Gracious my lord,
I should report that which I say I saw,   30
But know not how to do't.
MACBETH   Well, say, sir.

30 I say] F; I'd say *Hanmer; omitted by Keightley*

19 petty small; hence, 'trivial, insignificant'. The word (like the speech) moves from physical to figurative, from tiny steps to the journey's pointlessness.

20 syllable smallest portion, merest trace. Compare 4.3.8.

20 recorded written; told, narrated; recollected, remembered (*OED* Record v^1 9a, 8a, 4, respectively). Given the atemporal mood of the speech, its sense of being out of or beyond time, Mason's gloss (p. 151) seems right: 'not only the time that *has been*, but that also which *shall be* recorded'.

22 Out, out, brief candle Compare Lady Macbeth's 'Out . . . Out' (5.1.30) and her taper (5.1.15 SD).

23–5 Jones (*Origins*, p. 280) compares Seneca's description of 'this drama of human life, wherein we are assigned the parts which we are to play so badly'; Seneca then contrasts the actor's humble circumstances and the royal parts he plays: 'Yonder is the man who stalks upon the stage with swelling port and head thrown back . . .' (Seneca, Epistle 80.7, trans. R. M. Gummere).

23 walking shadow Grey (II, 154) cites biblical passages where the brevity and insubstantiality of human life are compared with a shadow: 1 Chron. 29.15, Job 14.2, Ps. 102.11, and Eccles. 8.13, for example. Compare also 'Life is a shadow' (Dent L249.1) and the lines Chapman derived from Pindar via Plutarch and Erasmus, 'Man is a Torch borne in the winde; a Dreame / But of a shadow,

summ'd with all his substance' (Chapman, *Bussy D'Ambois* 1.1.18–19).

23 poor player bad actor. For similar contempt, see the 'strutting player, whose conceit / Lies in his hamstring' (*Tro.* 1.3.153-4).

24 frets chafes, worries. The underlying theatrical metaphor suggests that the player's willingness to adopt a feigned passion makes him lose his individuality. Clarendon compares the taunting 'Stamp, rave, and fret' (*3H6* 1.4.91) addressed to the captive Richard of York, and Dent (F672.1, SS19, SS21) records combinations of 'fret', 'fume', 'stamp', 'stare', and 'rave' as common satirical responses to boasting, 'raging', bravado, and the like treated as theatrically overdone.

24 stage i.e. life. Proverbially, 'This world is a stage and every man plays his part' (Dent W882); see Jaques's speech beginning 'All the world's a stage . . .' (*AYLI* 2.7.139–66).

25–6 It is a tale / Told Compare 'For when thou art angry, al our dayes are gonne; we bring our yeeres to an ende, as it were a tale that is tolde' (Ps. 90.9), prescribed for the burial service by the Book of Common Prayer; the same psalm is the source for 2.4.1. There may be a pun on 'told'/'tolled' (a bell rung): compare 3.2.40–4 and 4.3.172–3.

30 report . . . saw i.e. relate that which I have already claimed to see (?). The sentence seems to have a surplus verb, 'I say', which Compositor B's eye may have caught from 31.

MESSENGER As I did stand my watch upon the hill
   I looked toward Birnam and anon methought
   The wood began to move.
MACBETH   Liar and slave!
MESSENGER Let me endure your wrath if't be not so;   35
   Within this three mile may you see it coming.
   I say, a moving grove.
MACBETH   If thou speak'st false,
   Upon the next tree shall thou hang alive
   Till famine cling thee; if thy speech be sooth,
   I care not if thou dost for me as much.   40
   I pull in resolution and begin
   To doubt th'equivocation of the fiend
   That lies like truth. 'Fear not, till Birnam Wood
   Do come to Dunsinane', and now a wood
   Comes toward Dunsinane. Arm, arm, and out! 45
   If this which he avouches does appear,
   There is nor flying hence nor tarrying here.
   I 'gin to be aweary of the sun
   And wish th'estate o'th'world were now undone.
   Ring the alarum bell! Blow wind, come wrack; 50
   At least we'll die with harness on our back.

               Exeunt

---

37 false] F (fhlse) 38 shall] F; shalt F2 43–4 'Fear . . . Dunsinane'] *Pope;* Feare . . . Dunsinane F

34 Rowe added *Striking him* after 'slave', which may represent Restoration theatre-practice; the SD persisted until Singer's edition, where it was omitted in response to the objections of a celebrated actor, J. P. Kemble, in *Macbeth and King Richard the Third,* enlarged edn, 1817, pp. 109–11, though stage Macbeths have continued 'ignobly' to strike the Messenger.

36 mile i.e. miles. This use of the singular 'mile' with a plural number was common into the nineteenth century (*OED* Mile *sb*[1]); Travers regards 'Within this three mile' as a Scotticism.

39 cling shrivel, parch (*OED* Cling *v*[1] 3c, quoting this line). The Messenger's hanging body will shrink and contract without food.

39 sooth truth, true.

41 pull in rein in, arrest, withdraw. This line is the earliest citation for *OED* Pull *v* 26d, which does not offer a satisfactory definition.

42 equivocation See 2.3.26 n.

42 fiend i.e. the Third Apparition, whose 'lies like truth' (43) Macbeth now recalls (43–4); see 4.1.89–93.

45 out i.e. sally forth, attack the enemy.

46 avouches claims, states.

47 nor . . . nor neither . . . nor.

47 tarrying staying, remaining (*OED* Tarry *v* 4).

48 'gin begin (an aphetic form).

49 estate o'th'world the world's settled order (Clarendon).

50 Ring the alarum bell The command may be a sound-cue. Macbeth repeats Macduff's cry when he discovers Duncan's body (2.3.68); words (and sound?) link crime and approaching punishment.

50 wrack See 1.3.113 n.

51 harness armour.

5.6 *Drum and colours. Enter* MALCOLM, SIWARD, MACDUFF, *and their army, with boughs*

MALCOLM Now near enough; your leafy screens throw down
        And show like those you are. You, worthy uncle,
        Shall with my cousin your right noble son
        Lead our first battle. Worthy Macduff and we
        Shall take upon's what else remains to do,   5
        According to our order.
SIWARD   Fare you well.
        Do we but find the tyrant's power tonight,
        Let us be beaten if we cannot fight.
MACDUFF Make all our trumpets speak; give them all breath,
        Those clamorous harbingers of blood and death.   10

                                    Exeunt
        Alarums continued

5.7 *Enter* MACBETH

MACBETH They have tied me to a stake; I cannot fly,

Act 5, Scene 6   5.6] F (*Scena Sexta.*)   0 SD SIWARD] F (*Seyward*); old SIWARD *Capell*   Act 5, Scene 7   5.7] F (*Scena Septima.*): scene continues, *Rowe* (*with no further divisions*)

Act 5, Scene 6

Malcolm's army and that represented in 5.2 have apparently joined and approach Dunsinane, screened with boughs hewn from Birnam Wood. Dessen, 'Problems', p. 149, outlines the producer's difficulties created by F's absence of SDs at this scene's start. If the soldiers enter with boughs (realistic or otherwise), are the boughs thrown down at 2 and later picked up and carried off? Are they thrown down at the end of the scene? Do they remain in view for the rest of the play? Or (a possibility Dessen omits) does 'throw down' (1) mean 'lower', with each soldier revealing himself but not releasing the 'bough' he holds and then later carries off-stage? This last possibility seems practicable and is consistent with F (although any proposal might be construed as consistent with silence), but Dessen makes a case for the symbolic values, some positive, some negative, of leaving the stage strewn with greenery from this moment forward.

0 SD *Drum and colours* See 5.2.0 SD n.

2 show . . . are Like Malcolm testing Macduff (4.3.44ff.), the anti-Macbeth forces do not first appear 'as [they] are' any more than Macbeth himself initially appears as he is (see e.g. 1.5.61–4).

2 uncle See 5.2.2 n.

4 battle An army, or one of its main divisions. See 1.1.4 n. and *OED* Battle *sb* 8.

4 we Malcolm uses the royal plural prematurely.

7 power military forces.

10 harbingers See 1.4.45 n.

10 SD.2 *Alarums continued* Battle sounds minimise the change of time or place between 5.6 and 5.7; the audience's imagination is transferred to another part of the battlefield.

Act 5, Scene 7

This scene takes place before or within the castle of Dunsinane.

1–2 Compare 'Their valiant temper / Men lose when they incline to treachery, / And then they fight like compelled bears, would fly / Were they not tied' (*TNK* 3.1.66–9).

1 tied me to a stake Macbeth finds himself a bear, chained ('tied') to a post ('stake') and attacked by dogs for spectators' entertainment, an event that often occurred in some of early modern London's public theatres, at the Tower of London (for the pleasure of King James and his guests), and in other places of amusement. Compare Octavius's

But bear-like I must fight the course. What's he
That was not born of woman? Such a one
Am I to fear, or none.

Enter YOUNG SIWARD

YOUNG SIWARD What is thy name?   5
MACBETH Thou'lt be afraid to hear it.
YOUNG SIWARD No, though thou call'st thyself a hotter name
    Than any is in hell.
MACBETH   My name's Macbeth.
YOUNG SIWARD The devil himself could not pronounce a title
    More hateful to mine ear.
MACBETH   No, nor more fearful.   10
YOUNG SIWARD Thou liest, abhorrèd tyrant; with my sword
    I'll prove the lie thou speak'st.
          Fight, and young Siward slain
MACBETH   Thou wast born of woman.
    But swords I smile at, weapons laugh to scorn,
    Brandished by man that's of a woman born.
              Exit [with young Siward's body]

Alarums. Enter MACDUFF

MACDUFF That way the noise is. Tyrant, show thy face!   15
    If thou be'st slain, and with no stroke of mine,
    My wife and children's ghosts will haunt me still.
    I cannot strike at wretched kerns whose arms

4 SD YOUNG SIWARD] F (*young Seyward*)   14 SD.1 *Exit . . . body*] *This edn (after Oxford); Exit* F   16 be'st] F (beest)

desperate remark, 'for we are at the stake, / And bayed about with many enemies' (*JC* 4.1.48–9), and 'To be bound to a stake' (Dent s813.1).

2 course attack (by dogs baiting a bear); see *OED* Course *sb* 27b, where this line is the earliest citation. More generally, the word means 'continuous process of time, succession of events' (*OED* Course *sb* 17a).

2–3 What's . . . born of woman Adelman (p. 131) points out that this question 'mean[s] both itself and its opposite': only one not of woman born can conquer Macbeth; there is no one not of woman born.

8 Than any is Than any which is.

12 Thou wast born of woman A chilling sardonicism, recalling the Bible (see 4.1.79 n.) and Macbeth's remark to First Murderer (3.4.14).

14 SD.1 *with young Siward's body* E. K. Cham-

bers (*William Shakespeare: A Study of Facts and Problems*, 2 vols., 1930, 1, 472) thought the absence of an SD for removing this corpse indicated textual corruption, and Swander speculates that this body should remain on stage, as it does in some productions, but F may here assume a conventional act (see 3.3.25 SD n.), and Ross says the body was 'brought off the field' (5.9.10). See Textual Analysis, p. 265 below, n. 4.

14 SD.2 The stage has been cleared of actors, and a new scene might be marked here and, for the same reason, at 24 SD; Oxford does so. The continued sound effects, however, and the sense that the Malcolm–Siward dialogue (25–30) concludes the mass battle justify letting F stand. See headnotes to 5.8 and 5.9 and, more generally, Textual Analysis, pp. 265–6 below.

18 kerns See 1.2.13 n.

Are hired to bear their staves; either thou, Macbeth,
Or else my sword with an unbattered edge   20
I sheath again undeeded. There thou shouldst be;
By this great clatter, one of greatest note
Seems bruited. Let me find him, Fortune,
And more I beg not.   *Exit*

      Alarums. Enter MALCOLM *and* SIWARD

SIWARD This way, my lord; the castle's gently rendered.   25
The tyrant's people on both sides do fight;
The noble thanes do bravely in the war.
The day almost itself professes yours,
And little is to do.
MALCOLM   We have met with foes
That strike beside us.
SIWARD   Enter, sir, the castle.   30
                                Exeunt
      Alarum

5.8 *Enter* MACBETH

MACBETH Why should I play the Roman fool and die
On mine own sword? Whiles I see lives, the gashes

24 SD.2 *Alarums*] F (*at right margin opposite 24*)   24 SD.2 SIWARD] F (*Seyward*); *old Seyward / Capell*   25 SH SIWARD] F
(*Sey.*); *thus throughout remainder of play*   30 SD.1–2] F (*as one line following* castle)   **Act 5, Scene 8**   **5.8**] *Dyce; scene*
continues F

19 staves lances (*Lexicon* under Staff).
19 either thou, Macbeth i.e. either I strike at you, Macbeth.
20 unbattered undamaged (by use in battle).
21 undeeded having done nothing (*Lexicon*), without accomplishment or 'deed'. This line is *OED*'s sole citation for the word.
21 There i.e. where I hear the most noise ('this great clatter' (22)).
22 The line puns on 'note' as musical sound ('clatter') and as 'reputation' or 'fame'; compare the imagery of 3.2.43–4 and nn.
23 bruited noised, reported.
23–4 Let . . . not A prayer to the goddess who momentarily favoured Macdonald (1.2.9–15).
25 gently rendered calmly (i.e. without further loss of life) or 'nobly' surrendered.
29–30 foes / That strike beside us Either 'enemies who deliberately miss when they attack', or

'enemies who fight on our side'.

Act 5, Scene 8
F does not mark a scene division here, and the action might be continuous with 5.7, but the stage has been cleared (a customary sign of a scene's conclusion), and it is not evident that this scene takes place within 'the castle' Malcolm and Siward entered at 5.7.30. More likely, it takes place on the battlefield before that castle. Edelman (pp. 160–2) compares this scene with the duel ending *R3*.
1–2 play . . . sword Roman honour required a defeated warrior to commit suicide rather than be captured; see *Ant.* 4.14 and *JC* 5.3, 5.5.
2 Whiles While.
2 lives living creatures (*Lexicon* Life *sb* 1, though *OED* Life *sb* 6c cites this line for 'Vitality as embodied in an individual person').

Do better upon them.

Enter MACDUFF

MACDUFF   Turn, hell-hound, turn.
MACBETH Of all men else I have avoided thee,
But get thee back, my soul is too much charged   5
With blood of thine already.
MACDUFF   I have no words;
My voice is in my sword, thou bloodier villain
Than terms can give thee out.

Fight. Alarum

MACBETH   Thou losest labour.
As easy mayst thou the intrenchant air
With thy keen sword impress as make me bleed.   10
Let fall thy blade on vulnerable crests;
I bear a charmèd life which must not yield
To one of woman born.
MACDUFF   Despair thy charm,
And let the angel whom thou still hast served
Tell thee, Macduff was from his mother's womb   15
Untimely ripped.
MACBETH Accursèd be that tongue that tells me so,
For it hath cowed my better part of man;

---

8 *labour.*] *Collier;* labour F

---

5 charged weighted, burdened. The Doctor uses the same word of Lady Macbeth (5.1.44).

8 terms words, expressions (*OED* Term *sb* 14a).

8 SD *Alarum* Battle continues elsewhere.

8 Thou losest labour You waste effort. The remark is proverbial (Dent L9).

9 easy easily. See 2.3.130 n.

9 intrenchant incapable of being cut. This line is the only citation at *OED* Intrenchant *a¹* (Schäfer) and Shakespeare's sole use of the word. The context of sword and flesh parallels 'Let not the virgin's cheek / Make soft thy trenchant sword' (*Tim.* 4.3.115–16).

10 keen sharp; eager, ardent (*OED* Keen *a* 3a and 6a). This 'keen sword' answers Lady Macbeth's 'keen knife' (1.5.50).

10 impress mark, press (*OED* Impress *v¹* 5a, quoting *LLL* 2.1.236 and this line as its earliest examples). The word 'impress' appears here when Macbeth's supposed invulnerability fails, just as it appeared when he was first assured of it (4.1.94–5).

11 vulnerable The earliest citation for the word in *OED* (Schäfer).

13 one of woman born See 4.1.79 n.

13 charm magical incantation; amulet (?). The latter meaning might be supported theatrically with some prop. See 3.5.19 and 4.1.18 and nn.

14 angel i.e. 'genius', tutelary deity. See 3.1.57–8 and n.

16 Untimely ripped i.e. born by Caesarean section. Having to choose, early modern medical practitioners sought to save the baby rather than the mother; Caesarean section always killed the mother. See the popular guide for physicians and midwives, Eucharius Roesslin, *The Birth of Mankynde*, trans. and enlarged by Thomas Raynald (1565), sig. P2r, and p. 22 above.

18 cowed intimidated, dispirited. This line is the first citation at *OED* Cow *v¹* a.

18 my better part of man larger proportion ('more than half') of my courage. Compare Falstaff's maxim, 'The better part of valour is discretion' (*1H4* 5.4.119–20) and *OED* Better *adj* 3b, where 'better half' is first cited from *c.* 1580 and 'better part' from 1586. *OED* Better *adj* 3c partly defines 'better part' as 'soul', an appropriate

And be these juggling fiends no more believed
That palter with us in a double sense,   20
That keep the word of promise to our ear
And break it to our hope. I'll not fight with thee.
MACDUFF Then yield thee coward,
And live to be the show and gaze o'th'time.
We'll have thee, as our rarer monsters are,   25
Painted upon a pole and underwrit,
'Here may you see the tyrant.'
MACBETH   I will not yield
To kiss the ground before young Malcolm's feet
And to be baited with the rabble's curse.
Though Birnam Wood be come to Dunsinane   30
And thou opposed being of no woman born,
Yet I will try the last. Before my body,
I throw my warlike shield. Lay on, Macduff,

23 thee coward,] F (Coward); thee, coward, *Rowe*   27 'Here . . . tyrant.'] *Pope;* Heere . . . Tyrant. F

meaning here (see 'fiends' (19)); a passage not cited in *OED* makes this second meaning evident: 'Let comme that fatall howre . . . Yit Shall the better part of mee assured bee too clyme / Aloft above the starry skye' (Ovid, *Metamorphoses*, trans. Arthur Golding (1567), ed. W. H. D. Rouse, 1904, xv, 986, 989–90).

19 juggling deceitful, cheating (*OED* Juggling *ppl a*). Early audiences might have associated the word with the (Roman Catholic) exorcists who claimed to heal possessed individuals (see 5.1.0 SD n.).

20 palter equivocate, deal evasively, trick (*OED* Palter *v* 3, quoting 'what other bond / Than secret Romans, that have spoke the word / And will not palter' (*JC* 2.1.124–6) as the earliest instance).

20 double sense equivocal meaning.

21–2 keep . . . hope fulfil the prophecy (of kingship) in a (merely) verbal way, the way we hear (= 'to our ear'), or wish to hear, 'the word of promise' (21), and fail to fulfil 'it' (the promise) as we expected (= 'our hope'). Macbeth now recognises the effective difference between the sisters' ambiguous prophetic speech and his own ambitious hope. See 5.3.27 n.

23 yield thee coward surrender yourself as a coward; state (or concede) you are a coward. On the second meaning compare 'to yield myself / His wife who wins me' (*MV* 2.1.18–19) and 'Antonio's dead! If thou say so, villain, / Thou kill'st thy mistress; but well and free, / If thou so yield him, there is gold' (*Ant.* 2.5.26–8, quoted as sole citation

for *OED* Yield *v* 12b). See also *OED* Yield *v* 18, and Celia Millward in *Reader*, pp. 302–4. Rowe and most other editors regard the noun as a vocative: 'yield thee, coward, . . .'

25–7 An accurate, and humorous, description of the circuslike or carnival atmosphere and sights available at a local fair or tavern. Compare Benedick's ultimately futile boast: 'if ever the sensible Benedick bear it [the "yoke" of marriage] . . . let me be vividly painted, and . . . let them signify under my sign, "Here may you see Benedick the married man"' (*Ado* 1.1.262–8); Lovewit's question: 'What should my knave advance, / To draw this company? He hung out no banners / Of a strange calf, with five legs, to be seen? / Or a huge lobster, with six claws?' (Jonson, *Alchemist* 5.1.6–9); Trinculo's first impulse when he encounters Caliban: 'Were I in England now . . . and had but this fish painted [in a sign], not a holiday fool there but would give a piece of silver' (*Temp.* 2.2.27–30); Richard D. Altick, *The Shows of London*, 1978, chapters 1 and 3. See p. 7 above.

28 To kiss the ground A proverbial phrase (Dent D651) for surrender or abnegation.

29 baited taunted.

29 rabble crowd, common people, multitude.

32 try the last experience (or undergo) the conclusion (or extremity). See *OED* Last *a, adv*, and *sb⁶* 9c and 9g; 'I will run the hazard to the end' (*Lexicon* Last *a*).

33 shield Probably a 'target' or 'targe', 'held . . . by straps around the forearm' (Edelman, p. 34,

And damned be him that first cries, 'Hold, enough!'
                              Exeunt[,] *fighting. Alarums*

Enter [*Macbeth and Macduff,*] *fighting*[,] *and Macbeth slain*
                        [*Exit Macduff, with Macbeth's body*]

5.9 *Retreat, and flourish. Enter with drum and colours,* MALCOLM,
SIWARD, ROSS, *Thanes, and Soldiers*

MALCOLM I would the friends we miss were safe arrived.
SIWARD Some must go off. And yet by these I see,
          So great a day as this is cheaply bought.
MALCOLM Macduff is missing and your noble son.
ROSS Your son, my lord, has paid a soldier's debt;   5
          He only lived but till he was a man,
          The which no sooner had his prowess confirmed
          In the unshrinking station where he fought,

---

34 'Hold, enough!'] *Johnson* (*subst.*); hold, enough. F   34 SD.2 *fighting*] F (*Fighting*)   34 SD.3 *Exit . . body*] *Oxford; not
in* F   **Act 5, Scene 9   5.9**] *NS; scene continues* F; SCENE VIII *Pope*   0 SD.2 SIWARD] F (*Seyward*); *old Seyward* / *Capell*

contradicting *OED* Target *sb*[1] 1). One contemporary theatre company had numerous targets made of iron, of copper, and of wood; see Henslowe, p. 320.
34 Hold, enough Stop, I surrender. Compare 1.5.48–52.
34 SD.1–2 Many editors have doubted F's SDs here, suggesting that they are confused, or imprecise, or represent two different stagings (one for the outdoor, one for the indoor theatre?). However inadequate, the SDs convey a shifting duel, moving from place to place on stage. See Textual Analysis, p. 263 below.
34 SD.3 Malcolm's comment (5.9.1) seems to stipulate a stage empty of dead bodies, and Macduff needs to remove Macbeth's body in order to 'behead' it. On customary dramatic practice, see 3.3.25 SD n.

Act 5, Scene 9
   F does not mark a new scene here, although many editors since Pope have done so with at least two good reasons: the stage has emptied of actors, and the audience needs some conventional encouragement to imagine a change of place from wherever Macbeth and Macduff fight to wherever Malcolm

and his company are when they receive the news and evidence of Macbeth's defeat and death. See Textual Analysis, pp. 265–6 below.
   0 SD.1 *Retreat* '[A] signal on the trumpet to recall a pursuing force' (NS). The SD presumably indicates that Macbeth's remaining supporters withdraw (or surrender) off-stage.
   0 SD.1 *drum and colours* See 5.2.0 SD n.
   0 SD.2 *Thanes* F treats the supporting noblemen collectively. Malone lists Lennox, Angus, Caithness, and Menteith.
   2 go off die (Clarendon). Compare 'goes hence' (1.5.57).
   5–9 Once again, Ross tells a father of his child's death; compare 4.3.194 ff.
   5 soldier's debt what a soldier owes (i.e. his death). See 1.4.10 n. Compare the proverbial 'Death pays all debts' (Dent D148) and 'To pay one's debt to nature' (Dent D168), and Hal's remark to Falstaff before the Battle of Shrewsbury: 'Why, thou owest God a death' (*1 H4* 5.1.126).
   8 unshrinking station i.e. brave act of standing. 'Station' is the martial posture (*OED* Station *sb* 1) young Siward adopted when he would not retreat (shrink) from Macbeth's attack.

But like a man he died.

SIWARD   Then he is dead?

ROSS Ay, and brought off the field. Your cause of sorrow   10
    Must not be measured by his worth, for then
    It hath no end.

SIWARD   Had he his hurts before?

ROSS Ay, on the front.

SIWARD Why then, God's soldier be he;
    Had I as many sons as I have hairs,   15
    I would not wish them to a fairer death.
    And so his knell is knolled.

MALCOLM   He's worth more sorrow,
    And that I'll spend for him.

SIWARD   He's worth no more;
    They say he parted well and paid his score,
    And so God be with him. Here comes newer comfort.   20

Enter MACDUFF, *with Macbeth's head*

MACDUFF Hail, king, for so thou art. Behold where stands
    Th'usurper's cursèd head. The time is free.

9–20 Siward's reaction – 'heartiness . . . phlegmatic grief' (Ernst Honigmann, *Shakespeare: Seven Tragedies*, 1976, p. 144) – has bothered critics, but it is the play's final response to a loved one's death (compare Malcolm and Donaldbain in 2.3, Macduff in 4.3, Macbeth in 5.5), with the difference that this loss directly serves the cause of freeing Scotland, as Siward's pun on 'hairs' (see 15 n.) suggests. Raphael Holinshed, *The First . . . Volumes of Chronicles* (1587), p. 192a, briefly and confusingly reports this incident, but William Camden may provide a more convincing 'source' (see p. 15 above, n. 2). Compare 'Friends, I owe mo[r]e tears / To this dead man than you shall see me pay' (*JC* 5.3.101–2).

10 brought off the field i.e. the body recovered (for burial).

12 hurts before wounds on the front (of his body), i.e. wounds gained while he fought the enemy, rather than wounds 'behind', on his back, which would indicate he died running away. The idea that only 'hurts before' were honourable has classical origins; see 'Life of Pelopidas' in Plutarch, *The Lives of the Noble Grecians and Romans, Compared*, trans. Thomas North (1595), p. 315.

15 hairs Siward echoes the biblical use of 'the hairs of my head' as a periphrasis for 'a very large number' (see e.g. Ps. 40.13 and 69.4). Mahood (p.

141) finds a homophonic pun on 'heirs' and 'hairs' (see 4.1.112 n.): 'Young Siward's death represents the last blind attempt of Macbeth to render his enemies childless', without heirs (or 'hairs'); Cercignani (p. 335) doubts the pun.

17 knell (church) bell rung to mark the death of a member of the congregation. See 2.1.63 and 4.3.172–3 and n.

19 score bill, amount owing. The word could mean something as mundane as a tavern debt, but here alludes to the soul one owes God. See 5 n.

20 newer more recent, fresher. Compare *OED* New *adj* 6a and 4.3.176.

20 SD *Macbeth's head* Malone added *on a pole*, following *Scotland*, p. 176a, and other bloodthirsty SDs (e.g. Collier²'s *Sticking the pike in the ground*) may record stage-practice; compare 1.2.23 n., and see illustration 4, p. 31 above. Modern productions rarely follow F's SDs; for both early and later, see William W. French, 'What "may become a man": image and structure in *Macbeth*', *College Literature* 12 (1985), 191–201.

21 Hail The word, repeated twice here (26) and common in Act 1, has not been used since 'all-hail' (1.5.53) and 'hailed' (3.1.61); it now links Macbeth with Malcolm, the sisters with the victorious Scots.

21 so thou art i.e. evidence of Macbeth's death (the head) confirms Malcolm's kingship.

I see thee compassed with thy kingdom's pearl,
That speak my salutation in their minds;
Whose voices I desire aloud with mine.   25
Hail, King of Scotland.

ALL   Hail, King of Scotland.
                                Flourish

MALCOLM We shall not spend a large expense of time
Before we reckon with your several loves
And make us even with you. My thanes and kinsmen,
Henceforth be earls, the first that ever Scotland   30
In such an honour named. What's more to do
Which would be planted newly with the time, –
As calling home our exiled friends abroad
That fled the snares of watchful tyranny,
Producing forth the cruel ministers   35
Of this dead butcher and his fiend-like queen,
Who, as 'tis thought, by self and violent hands
Took off her life, – this and what needful else
That calls upon us, by the grace of Grace
We will perform in measure, time, and place.   40
So, thanks to all at once and to each one,
Whom we invite to see us crowned at Scone.
                                Flourish
                                        Exeunt

                    FINIS

26 SH] F (*All.*); ALL BUT MALCOLM *Oxford*   32 time, –] *Capell*; time, F   38 life, –] *Capell (subst.)*; life. F   42] SD.1–2]
F (*Flourish. Exeunt Omnes.*), as one line

23 pearl finest members or parts, noble examples (*OED* Pearl *sb*¹ 3a).

28 reckon settle accounts with (*OED* Reckon *v* 11, quoting this line). See 19, 29, and nn.

28 several separate, distinct.

29 make us even square our accounts, make us quits. The phrase is the last of several commercial or financial metaphors: 'spend . . . expense . . . reckon' (27–8).

29–31 My thanes . . . named Among the thanes made earls, *Scotland*, p. 176a, specifies Fife (i.e. the play's Macduff), Menteith, Caithness, Ross, and Angus.

31–2 What's . . . time As Booth (p. 91) notes, Malcolm's metaphor echoes Duncan's, addressed to Macbeth (1.4.28–9); the cycle of trust and betrayal renews itself, as it does more plainly in Polanski's

filmed *Macbeth* (see p. 87 above).

33 exiled friends abroad i.e. friends exiled abroad. Compare 5.2.7 n.

37–8 by self . . . life Malcolm's guess that Lady Macbeth committed suicide (see 5.1.66 and n.) is not supported by the text, and *Scotland* is silent, though it reports (p. 169a) that Macdonald killed 'his wife and children, and lastlie himselfe' to escape captivity. See above, p. 34.

39 calls upon invokes (*Lexicon*); demands, summons.

39 grace of Grace 'the grace of God, apostrophized as the essence of graciousness' (Brooke).

40 measure due proportion (*OED* Measure *sb* 11a).

42 Scone Compare 2.4.31, 4.1.7, and nn.

SUPPLEMENTARY NOTES

1.1.0 SD WITCHES A hint of the witches' early costuming appears in a Jacobean satire: 'my *Lady* . . . holdeth on her way, perhaps to the *Tyre makers Shoppe*, where she shaketh out her Crownes ['coins', but punning on the 'crown' of the head] to bestowe upon some new fashioned *Atire*, that if we may say, there be deformitie in Art, upon such artificall deformed *Periwigs*, that they were fitter to furnish a *Theater*, or for her that in a *Stageplay*, should represent some Hagge of Hell, then to bee used by a Christian woman . . .' (Barnaby Rich, *The Honestie of this Age* (1614), sigs. B3v–4r). Wardrobe records from 1602 mention 'a wi[t]ches gowne' (see Henslowe, p. 218) as if it were a conventional garment, and by 1634, a witch's – even, perhaps, a Scottish 'weird' sister's – costuming may have become a theatrical convention. In *The Late Lancashire Witches*, a mother panders to her daughter's social aspirations: 'Ile . . . weare as fine clothes, and as delicate dressings as thou wilt have me', and the daughter scornfully describes the mother's present garb: 'Is this a fit habite for a handsome young Gentlewomans mother . . . you look like one o'the Scottish wayward sisters' (*Lancashire*, sig. C2v).

Productions have represented the witches as comic and ridiculous (see p. 68 above), as young and beautiful women (see e.g. one of Goethe's Weimar productions, discussed in Simon Williams, *Shakespeare on the German Stage: 1586–1914*, 1990, p. 95, and Bryan Forbes's production (Old Vic, London, 1980)), as hideously masked figures, and in many other ways. The 'weïrd sisters' derive from the three classical Fates (see Supplementary Note to 1.3.30), who were often represented in early modern graphic art as an old, a middle-aged, and a young woman; see David Acton's catalogue entry for Pierre Milan's 'The Three Masked Fates' (after Rosso Fiorentino) in Cynthia Burlingham, Marianne Grivel, and Henri Zerner (comp.), *The French Renaissance in Prints*, 1994, pp. 298–300. Roman Polanski's film, *Macbeth* (1971), and Trevor Nunn's 1976–8 RSC production and the Thames Television production based on it (directed by Philip Casson, 1978; broadcast 1979), partly follow this pattern in representing the sisters.

1.2.0 SD.2 This direction seems to mean either that actors enter separately (e.g. from doors at the back of the stage) to indicate joint arrival at a new location, or that one group (mentioned first) enters to find another already present. This latter type of direction is common in Thomas Middleton's plays, uncommon elsewhere (Brooke, p. 58, citing unpublished work by R. V. Holdsworth).

In addition to this example, *meeting* occurs in five other SDs in Shakespeare's works:

Thunder. Enter the three Witches, meeting Hecate. (*Macbeth* TLN 1429–30/3.5.0 SD)
Enter Bast. and Curan meeting. (*Lear* Q (1608), sig. D3v.1/2.1.0 SD)
Enter Varro's man, meeting others. (*Timon* TLN 1117/3.4.0 SD)
Enter three Senators at one doore, Alcibiades meeting them, with attendants. (*Timon* TLN 1255–6/3.5.0 SD)
Enter two Gentlemen, meeting one another. (*H8* TLN 2377/4.1.0 SD)

Remarkably, of these examples only the one from *Lear* has not been challenged as non-Shakespearean: the Hecate passages in *Macbeth* may be Middleton's (see Textual Analysis, pp. 271–5 below); the first six scenes of Act 3 of *Timon* are now generally considered to be by Middleton (see e.g. *Textual Companion*, p. 501); Act 4, Scene 1 of *H8* is thought to be by John Fletcher, Shakespeare's collaborator on that play (see Cyrus Hoy, 'The shares of Fletcher and his collaborators in the Beaumont and Fletcher canon', *SB* 15 (1962), 71–90, especially 80–1, and *Textual Companion*, p. 618).

Whether *Macbeth* Act 1, Scene 2 is partly or entirely by Thomas Middleton, then, it seems likely that the opening direction is, or imitates, his. With *meeting*, Middleton always places an actor or actors on stage before the entrance of one or more other actors; thus, early stagings of *Macbeth* probably placed the wounded messenger on stage and directed the king's company to enter *to* him.

1.3.30 weïrd This word does not appear in F. The characters called 'witches' in the SDs name themselves 'sisters' (see 1.1.0 SD n.), and Macbeth so names them (3.1.58). They are thrice called 'weyward' (Compositor A: TLN 130, 355, and 596) and thrice 'weyard' (Compositor B: TLN 983, 1416, 1686). *OED* (Weird *a*) says 'weyward' 'was no doubt due to association with *wayward*', an appropriate, if less colourful, adjective. 'Weird' in various forms does occur, however, in texts Shakespeare and his audiences either knew or could have known. From at least 1400, Scottish texts apply 'weird sister' to the three classical Fates, the Parcae (see *OED* Weird *a* 1); by about 1420, Andrew of Wyntoun begins to domesticate these figures – making '*the* weird sisters' (emphasis added) into 'weird sisters' – when he writes that Macbeth 'saw thre women by gangand' in a dream: 'And thai three women than thocht he / Thre werd sisteris like to be' (*The Original Chronicle*, ed. F. J. Amours, 6 vols., 1903–14, IV, 274–5). The fanciful *Scotorum historiae* (1526 and 1575) of Hector Boethius (or Boece) calls these beings 'the fates' and 'prophesying nymphs': 'Verum ex eventu postea parcas aut nymphas aliquas fatidicas diabolico astu preditas fuisse interpretatum est vulgo' (Book 12, f. 258r; sig. K2r) and later on the same page, 'the sisters' ('sorores'). And John Bellenden's Scots translation-adaptation of Boece, *The Hystory and Croniklis of Scotland* (?1540), reports that Macbeth and Banquo 'met be ye gait thre wemen clothit in elrage [eldritch] & uncouth weid [weed = clothing]. They were Jugit to be the pepill to be weird sisteris' (f. 173r) and uses 'weird sisteris' three further times on the same page. The 1531 manuscript of Bellenden's translation here reads 'thre weird sisteris or wiches'; see *The Chronicles of Scotland*, ed. R. W. Chambers and E. C. Batho, 2 vols., 1938–41, II, 150. Aware of both Boece and Bellenden, Holinshed (*Scotland*, pp. 170b–171a) says these beings resembled 'creatures of elder world' and were thought to be 'the weird sisters, that is (as ye would say) the goddesses of destinie, or else some nymphs or feiries'.

While no one of these antecedent texts needs dictate the language of *Macbeth*, they are united in calling the beings who prophesy to Macbeth 'weird' rather than 'wayward'. Beside spellings unique in F – neither 'weyward' nor 'weyard' is a recorded form of *wayward* – other evidence suggests that the compositors of *Macbeth* would not have hesitated to set some more recognisable form of 'wayward' if that were the word they thought they saw in the play's manuscript. Compositor B, for instance, uncomplicatedly set 'wayward' (3.5.11), and he and Compositor A had no difficulties elsewhere in F: Compositor A set both 'way-ward' (sig. B5r/*TGV* TLN 211) and 'waiward' (sig. 14v/ *Ado* TLN 472), and Compositor B set 'wayward' four times (sig. H6r/*Err.* TLN 1284; sig. c3r/*R2* TLN 786; sig. r1r/*R3* TLN 494; sig. tt5r/*Oth.* TLN 1927). Compositor B's consistent 'wayward' elsewhere in F makes his equally consistent 'weyard' in *Macbeth* seem a deliberately composed unusual word rather than an accidental and unique form of *wayward*, or (*pace* Cercignani, p. 365) an historical pronunciation of it. Moreover, when Compositor B met this word in the first column of Folio *Macbeth* that he composed, he would have had few preconceptions about the play and little familiarity with his copy's handwriting and is therefore likely to have set what he thought was before him. Compositor A also met the word he set as 'weyward' in his first stint on *Macbeth*; it first occurs three lines after 'Wrackt, as homeward he did come' (TLN 127), and a kind of 'compositor's antonymy' – 'homeward'/'awayward' – may have influenced him toward 'weyward'. Such errors may be much rarer than the substitution of synonyms, but they do apparently occur (see *Textual Companion*, pp. 519 and 526, on *Lear* Q (1608) 16.10 and 24.166, respectively). Later Folios leave Compositor A's spelling unchanged, but modify Compositor B's: TLN 983 is normalised to A's spelling ('weyward'), while TLN 1416 and 1686 become 'wizard' and 'Wizard' (or, in F4, 'Wizards'), respectively. Although 'weyard' and 'wizard' might be confused in Secretary handwriting, 'wizard' may be a 'correction' from Holinshed where the phrase 'certeine wizzards' (*Scotland*, p. 174b; 'haruspicibus' in Boece, f. 261r) occurs in the text paralleling *Macbeth* TLN 1416 and 1686.

The question of what F's compositors saw and therefore what modern word or words F's 'weyward' and 'weyard' might represent cannot be decided. Adopting 'wayard', as A. P. Riemer does (The Challis Shakespeare, 1980), is unsatisfactory not least because it is a nonce-word, but 'wayard' also contradicts F and almost 200 years of earlier Scots and English Macbeth-narratives. In the Everyman edition of *Macbeth* (1993), John Andrews retains F's two spellings, believing them to be the same word with double meaning, modern 'wayward' and archaic 'wyrd' (see his 1.3.30 n.), but that decision substitutes commentary for modernisation. Post-*Macbeth* uses of 'wayward', as in 'the Scottish wayward sisters' (*Lancashire*, sig. C2v; compare Hunter, *New*, II, 162), or of 'weird', as in Peter Heylyn's equation of 'Witches' with '*Weirds*' (*Microcosmos*, 2nd edn (1625), p. 509), have no evidentiary value. Thus, there are reasons to doubt that Compositor A mis-set manuscript 'wayward' as 'weyward' and reasons to believe that Compositor B's 'weyard' is an honest effort at what modern English represents as 'weird'. In sum, and especially in view of Compositor B's practice in *Macbeth* and elsewhere in F, Theobald's emendation of 'weyward' and 'weyard' to 'weïrd' seems a plausible and metrically justifiable change.

1.3.89 sight F reads 'fight', but Compositor A could have easily confused 'fight' and 'sight' in Secretary handwriting; moreover, the ligatured types *fi* and *ſi*, each cast on a single body, are also easily confused since they were side-by-side in the compositor's case. The traditional reading is 'fight', printed in Cam. and Furness without comment; Oxford and Brooke print 'sight', also without comment or collation.

2.2.8 SD Dorothea Tieck's German translation of *Macbeth* has Macbeth enter *oben* (*above*) to deliver this line, exit, and enter again to speak 14; Oxford and Brooke attribute this staging to E. K. Chambers's 'Red Letter Shakespeare' (1904) where it does not appear, although Chambers does adopt it in his 'Warwick Shakespeare' edition of *Macbeth* (1893). Other editors have instructed Macbeth to speak 8 *within* (i.e. offstage). All seek to explain Lady Macbeth's apparent ignorance that it is her husband who speaks line 8 (see 9–10 n.). One effective staging (accepted here and compatible with F's directions) construes her puzzlement as the consequence of the stage's (imaginary) darkness: two anguished actors, uncertain of each other's identity but in full view of the audience, deepen the scene's terror. Dessen, 'Problems', pp. 154–6, usefully discusses F's staging here, although it is also possible that F prints the SD too early.

2.3.0 SD *a* PORTER   The apocryphal gospel of Nicodemus recounts Jesus's release of Adam, Eve, Moses, and others from limbo; this episode (the 'Harrowing of Hell') appears widely in medieval art and verse, and in all four of the surviving Corpus Christi dramatic cycles which often represent hell as a castle-like location, occasionally with Porter-like speakers. Several Middle English poems on the subject specify a devil-porter (compare 14: 'I'll devil-porter it no further'), as do, apparently, several graphic works (see e.g. British Library MS. Additional 47682, f. 34, upper image – the horn used there by one devil atop the battlemented limbo identifies him as a porter (W. O. Hassall, *The Holkham Bible Picture Book*, 1954, p. 139) – and illustration 9, p. 51 above). Although none of the Corpus Christi cycle plays clearly identifies a devil as a porter, John Heywood's interlude, *The Four PP* (first printed about 1545), includes a lying contest in which the Pardoner describes a visit to hell where he encounters a 'deuyll that kept the gate' [i.e. a devil-porter], and the Pardoner 'at laste / Remembred hym [this devil] . . . For oft in the play of Corpus Christi [i.e one of the cycle plays?] / He hath played the deuyll at Couentry' (Adams, p. 378). See further, Jones, *Origins*, p. 32, Wickham, 'Castle', and, for a summary of previous interpretations, Anne Lancashire in *Mirror*, pp. 223–41, especially pp. 224–7.

2.3.74   In the Folio, this and the following line appear as:

> To countenance this horror. Ring the Bell.
> 　　　　*Bell rings. Enter Lady.*
> *Lady.* What's the Businesse?

'Ring the Bell' repeats Macduff's earlier order, 'Ring the Alarum Bell' (68), and F's TLN 835 is immediately followed by *Bell rings. Enter Lady.* Brooke, echoing Keightley, says, 'since Macduff's order in . . . [68] has not yet been obeyed, his impatience is intelligible'. A widely accepted, if over-realistic, objection was offered by Lewis Theobald, who omitted the phrase 'Ring the Bell': 'if the Bell had rung out immediately, not a Word of What he [Macduff] says could have been distinguish'd. *Ring the Bell*, I say, was a Marginal Direction in the *Prompter's* Book for him to order the Bell to be rung, the Minute that *Macduff* ceases speaking.' Theobald continues with a metrical argument: 'we may observe, that the Hemistich ending *Macduff*'s Speech ['To countenance this horror'], and that beginning Lady *Macbeth*'s ['What's the business?'], make up a compleat Verse'. Theobald's realistic argument and Shakespeare's largely unrealistic practice coincide: sound effects frequently follow a character's speech no matter when they have been commanded. I agree, therefore, with Theobald's view and have deleted the phrase.

2.3.83 SD   Capell removed Ross from F's SD (*Enter Macbeth, Lenox, and Rosse*) and explained (*Notes*, 11, 13), 'he is no speaker [in 2.3], went not out with them [i.e. Macbeth and Lennox at 67 SD], [and] enters too immediately [at the start of 2.4] in another place after what should be his exit in this'. In fact, F's 2.3 provides no exit for Ross by name; he could leave in the final *Exeunt* (139 SD) or, as several editors have suggested, he could help Lady Macbeth off-stage at 112 or 118, though even that action is debatable. If Ross does exit at the scene's end, it would be most unShakespearean for him to begin the next scene; even an exit with Lady Macbeth would allow him an unusually short time off-stage to help the audience understand the gap of time and change of place between 2.3 and 2.4. Ross is a mysterious character; he has, for instance, been proposed as Third Murderer (see 3.3.1 SH n.), and his political allegiances are particularly unclear (in 4.2, for instance, he might be played as sympathetic to Lady Macduff or as Macbeth's agent ensuring that she and her children remain unalarmed long enough for their murderers to arrive – a directorial choice Roman Polanski seems to have adopted in his film (1971) of the play). Although Oxford retains Ross here because 'a "ghost" [i.e. a mute character once intended to enter and perhaps to speak but forgotten by the playwright] seems unlikely in a prompt-book', much, if not all, of his 'mystery' is probably the result of a script that theatrical professionals tidied up as a matter of course without influencing the written copy for F. Editors do not have such latitude, and it seems best to delete him here, especially since no actor will lose lines.

3.1.91–107   Although this speech at first seems a distended analogy (dogs and men are alike in their variety, some good, some bad), Macbeth's rhetorical tactics contradict his criminal purposes. The varied plenitude of dogs and men to which Macbeth appeals represents a universal and social order he has violated and now seeks to violate further; the premise of varied quality leads as easily to negative valuations of the men as to positive; 'bounteous nature' has given each a different 'gift', but Macbeth's analogy holds that nature has given his hearers the 'gift' of destroying nature. Some of the inherent moral contradictions appear in 'Not i'th'worst rank' (102), which for Macbeth means 'capable of murder' and recalls such self-contradictory phrases as 'Worthy to be a rebel' (1.2.10). This speech appeals to the men's pride in their manhood and is, therefore, Macbeth's version of Lady Macbeth's earlier speech (1.7.35 ff.); her appeal and her threatened contempt pivot on a comparison between herself and Macbeth ('had I so sworn / As you have done . . .'), but her husband's speech weakly and self-defeatingly turns on the man/dog comparison and promises the love of a man, Macbeth, self-described as 'sickly' (106).

John D. Rea proposed that this passage 'is probably taken from Erasmus' colloquy *Philodoxus*' ('Notes on Shakespeare', *MLN* 35 (1920), 378), where a few general, moralised analogies between human and canine behaviour are mentioned. It seems more likely that Shakespeare here transformed matter from Dr John Caius, *Of Englishe Dogges, the diversities, the names, the natures, and the properties*, trans. Abraham Fleming (1576). Fleming's delightful translation of Caius's Latin text (1570) is incorporated whole in Topsell, pp. 164–81, and matches *Macbeth* 3.1 in taxonomic rigour ('A gentle kind . . . A homely kind . . . A currishe [kind] . . .'). John Caius, who gave his name to the Cambridge University college Gonville and Caius, as well as (perhaps) to the French doctor in *Wiv.* (see Lord McNair, 'Why is the French doctor in *The Merry Wives of Windsor* called Caius?', *Medical History* 13 (October 1969), 311–39), devoted a section of his book to 'other Dogges . . . wonderfully ingendered . . . The first bred of a bytch and a wolfe' (sig. F2r), that is, a 'demi-wolf', the offspring of a dog and a wolf specified at 3.1.93 (see n.). Of this cross-breed Caius observes: 'we have none naturally bred within the borders of England. The reason is for the want of wolfes, without whom no such kinde of Dogge can be engendred.' Note, as a measure of its popularity, that Caius's book on dogs attracted the attention of the king, as recounted in a famous anecdote: 'When King James passed through this college [Gonville and Caius], the master thereof presented him a [book by] Caius "De Antiquitate Cambridgiae", fairly bound; to whom the king said, "What shall I do with this book? give me rather Caius "De Canibus" [i.e. *Of Englishe Dogges*], a work of the same author, very highly praised, but hardly procured' (Thomas Fuller, *The History of the Worthies of England*, new edn, P. Austin Nuttall, 3 vols., 1840, II, 490).

3.2.38 in them Nature's copy's not eterne Lady Macbeth asserts that Banquo and Fleance are not immortal. So much is unquestioned, but the meaning of individual words has been disputed. The line may mean that Banquo and Fleance are 'copies' of a natural pattern for the human body, or that they are patterned after nature's model. More controversial is an interpretation most succinctly represented by Joseph Ritson's note in Steevens[3]: 'an *estate for lives* held by *copy of court roll*'; this explanation refers 'copy' to a form of common law possession of land called 'copyhold', one way in which a tenant occupied and could bequeath land technically owned by his lord. Since some copyholds could be terminated by the death of the tenant, critics were attracted to the legal interpretation of the line. An article by P. S. Clarkson and C. T. Warren, 'Copyhold tenure and *Macbeth*, III, ii, 38', *MLN* 55 (1940), 483–93, has led Muir and Brooke to reject this interpretation. Clarkson and Warren, however, depend upon a legalistic understanding of Shakespeare, of Ritson, and of other editors, and ignore the fact that dramatists often used legal terms loosely, as Clarkson and Warren themselves amply document in their magisterial *The Law of Property in Shakespeare and the Elizabethan drama*, 1942. As in most legal arguments, the pros and cons of 'copy' = 'copyhold' are complex, but they turn on (1) who is the lord and who the tenant and (2) how Macbeth understands his wife's remark. I suggest that Lady Macbeth's intervention forwards her husband's thoughts: if Banquo and Fleance are tenants 'for life', their deaths (which her line prompts Macbeth to consider directly) will terminate their tenure in 'Lord' Nature's land (i.e. in existence); they will die. Clarkson and Warren consider this interpretation – 'Banquo and Fleance would be the tenants and *Nature would be the lord*') – but reject it because 'Macbeth then would have no right to terminate the tenure, and it would be no comfort to him that Nature might at some time do so' (*MLN* 55 (1940), p. 493). The objection is not pertinent. Macbeth's 'right' cannot be an issue; his wife invites him to consider murder, not some action at the common law. Lady Macbeth's line, whatever interpretation we adopt, is no more than a commonplace: people die. Reminded so starkly of this fact – indeed, virtually told that killing Banquo and Fleance will relieve his scorpion-filled mind – Macbeth takes heart: 'There's comfort yet, they are assailable.' Clarkson and Warren are probably right (Shakespeare gets his law wrong); yet they forget that Shakespeare invokes legal language not before a court, the King's Bench, but for an audience that might (must?) have had as vague, or as figurative, an understanding of legal terminology as he did. The main point is that the law is to be broken – the common law, the law of land-tenure, the law of the Ten Commandments, 'Thou shalt not kill.'

3.2.45 chuck An aristocratic couple's use of such an endearment is quite unusual, at least in the drama. Shakespeare elsewhere uses 'chuck' variously: four times (*LLL* 5.1.111 and 5.2.661, *TN* 3.4.113, *H5* 3.2.25) humorously by a male character to males; three times (*Oth.* 3.4.49 and 4.2.24, *Ant.* 4.4.2) between husband and wife or lover and lover. In a scene that may be John Fletcher's work, Theseus calls Hippolyta 'sweet heart' (*TNK* 3.5.148). Realistic and unromantic Crispinella rebukes her sister Beatrice who has called her fiancé 'love': 'Prithee, call him not love: 'tis the drab's phrase; nor sweet honey, nor my cony, nor dear duckling: 'tis the citizen terms' (*Dutch Courtesan* 3.1.129–31). For the contemporary English use of, and controversy over, endearments, see Houlbrooke, p. 101, and William Gouge's pastoral rebuke to his congregation over couples' public use of affectionate nicknames, including 'chick' [= 'chuck'] (A. C. Carter, 'Marriage counselling in the early seventeenth century: England and the Netherlands compared', in J. Van Dorsten (ed.), *Ten Studies in Anglo-Dutch Relations*, 1974, p. 117), and compare 'You jig and amble . . . you nickname God's creatures and make your wantonness your ignorance' (*Ham.* 3.1.144–6).

3.6.6–7 Q1673 lacks 'Whom you may . . . walk too late'; at the same point Davenant prints only 'Men must not walk so late'. These omissions may have some particular topical origin, but the Restoration evolution of 'night-walker' as 'prostitute' and 'ruffian' (see *OED* Night-walker) has a long history: 'night-walking' had been a misdemeanour since 1331 (see 'Nightwalkers' in *Jowitt's Dictionary of English Law*, 2nd edn, ed. John Burke, 2 vols., 1977). See also 'night-walking heralds' (i.e. sexual go-betweens, *R3* 1.1.72) and 'This is enough to be the decay of lust and late-walking through the realm' (*MWW* 5.5.143–5). Shakespeare's lines may have become unacceptably comic by 1673, or the omission may arise from a desire to avoid even a hint of wrong-doing among the legendary ancestors (Banquo, Fleance) of James's grandson, Charles II, king when Q1673 and Davenant were printed.

4.1.110 SD F's dialogue contradicts its SD by giving Banquo, rather than the eighth king (118), the *glass*; in F's text, Banquo (or his ghost, or 'shadow') comes last (122–3), following the 'show' of eight kings, the last of whom 'bears a glass' (118). Early revision and theatrical changes probably made the copy for F's SD inconsistent with its dialogue, and Cam.'s SD (following Hanmer) resolves the contradiction with the fewest changes to F.

4.1.120 two-fold balls and treble sceptres Upon being crowned and on other formal occasions, the monarch carries symbolic accoutrements (orb, sceptre); editors and critics have tried to link this line with the historical circumstances of King James, monarch of both Scotland and England. NS quotes E. K. Chambers: '[This phrase] can have nothing to do . . . with the triple style of King of Great Britain, France, and Ireland, adopted . . . [by James I on] 20 Oct. 1604. The earlier English style was triple, and there were no sceptres for France and Ireland. The "two-fold balls" must be the "mounds" borne on the English and Scottish crowns, and the "treble sceptres" the two used for investment in the English coronation and the one used in the Scottish coronation.' (A 'mound' is an orb of gold, often topped by a cross; mounds surmount the Scottish and English royal crowns.) For 'balls', 'sceptres', and 'mounds', see illustration 12, p. 60 above. The 'treble sceptres' may, however inaccurately, refer to England, Scotland, and Wales; in a letter to James VI, Henry Percy, ninth Earl of Northumberland, foresees James's accession to the English throne as 'the anexing of theas thrie kingdomms' and describes how James will integrate his Scottish subjects, 'to wnite [unite] the tuo nations . . . to make them one, as nowe england and walles are' (John Bruce (ed.), *Correspondence of King James VI. of Scotland*, Camden Society 78 (1861), 53 and 56). In 1541–2, the Irish Parliament and Henry VIII himself declared the English king, 'King of Ireland' (J. J. Scarisbrick, *Henry VIII*, 1968, pp. 424–5), and E. B. Lyle, 'The "twofold balls and treble scepters" in *Macbeth*', *SQ* 28 (1977), 516–19, persuasively concludes that the spectral kings 'bear triple scepters in token of rule over Great Britain, France, and Ireland, and double orbs signifying that Great Britain was formed by the union of Scotland and England' (p. 519).

4.3.148 John Ernest, Duke of Saxe-Weimar, witnessed James touching for the King's Evil after divine service on 19 September 1613:

> When it [the service] was concluded, his Majesty stood up . . . immediately the Royal Physician brought [the sufferers] who were afflicted . . . and bade them kneel down . . . and as the Physician had already examined the disease (which he is always obliged to do, in order that no deception may be practised), he then pointed out the affected part . . . to his Majesty, who thereupon touched it, pronouncing these words: *Le Roy vous touche, Dieu vous guery* (The King touches, may God heal thee!) and then hung a rose-noble round the neck [of the sufferer] . . . with a white silk ribbon . . . The ceremony of healing is understood to be very distasteful to the King, and it is said he would willingly abolish it . . .
> (W. B. Rye, *England as seen by Foreigners*, 1865, p. 151).

Arthur Wilson's hostile account (*History of Great Britain*, 1653, p. 289) claims James's ceremonies were a politic fraud: 'he [King James] knew a *Device*, to aggrandize the *Virtue* of Kings, when *Miracles* were in fashion . . . though he smiled at it, finding . . . the strength of the *Imagination* a more powerful *Agent* in the *Cure*, than the *Plasters* his *Chirurgions* prescribed for the *Sore*'. For evidence of James's early (?September–October 1603) ambivalence about the ceremony, see F. David Hoeniger, *Medicine and Shakespeare in the English Renaissance*, 1992, pp. 281 and 371 n. 14.

4.3.162 While the invention of the clan tartan lay two centuries in the future, Highland males (that is, most of the cast of *Macbeth*) already had for Jacobean audiences a well-known and distinctive regional costume:

> Their habite is shooes with but one sole apiece; stockings . . . made of a warme stuffe of divers colours, which they call Tartane: as for breeches, many of them, nor their forefathers never wore any, but a jerkin of the same stuffe that their hose is of, their garters being bands or wreathes of hay or strawe, with a plead about their shoulders, which is a mantle of divers colours, much finer and lighter stuffe than their hose, with blue flat caps on their heads, a handkerchiefe knit with two knots about their necke . . .

Nor, the English observer continues, is this costume restricted to the poor:

> any man of what degree soever that comes amongst them, must not disdaine to weare it . . . if men be kind unto them, and be in their habite; then are they conquered with kindnesse . . .
> (John Taylor, *The Pennyles Pilgrimage* (1618), in Taylor, *Works*, 1630, p. 135)

Contemporary English dramatic representations of Scots almost always included the blue flat cap and a short sword called a 'whinyard'.

5.3.19 Seyton Critics have frequently suggested that the name would have been pronounced and heard as 'Satan'. Patten's explanation of why the Scots called the 1547 Battle of Pinkie, or Musselburgh, by a different name supports the claim: 'Sum of them cal it Seton felde (a toune thear nie too) by means of a blynd prophecie of theirs, whiche is this or sum suche toy, Betwene Seton & the sey [sea], many a man shall dye that daye' (Patten, sigs. a7r–v), where 'sea', 'day', and the first syllable of 'Seton' apparently rhyme. The 'prophecy' is very old: a version appeared in the fourteenth century (see *The Romance and Prophecies of Thomas of Erceldoune*, ed. James Murray, 1875, pp. 34 ff.), and another is current in *Prophesie* (sig. A4r), a volume originally published to mark the fulfilment of one of Merlin's most celebrated prophecies, the union of Scotland and England. See also Nosworthy in *Mirror*, pp. 216–7, where he argues that Seyton = Satan on internal evidence and notes the oddity of stressing 'Seyton', given the extreme rarity of proper names in the play's dialogue.

TEXTUAL ANALYSIS

General editorial procedures

The First Folio (F) divides *Macbeth* into acts and scenes; editors have changed that division in Acts 2 and 5 (see below). F's divisions are recorded in the collation, along with plausible editorial versions. In the dialogue, personal names (e.g. Fleans, Lenox) and place names (e.g. Envernes, Fiffe) and their derivatives (e.g. Norweyan) have been silently modernised (Fleance, Lennox, Inverness, Fife, Norwegian, respectively) unless the change affects the metre. Many uncontroversial modernisations have not been included in the collation; for example, changes of F's 'I' (for 'ay'), 'Ile' (for 'I'll'), and 'then' (for 'than') have not been recorded, and F's 'Oh' and 'enow' become 'O' and 'enough' without note. Among the less obvious silent modernisations, F's 'bad' (the past tense of 'to bid') appears here as 'bade'; so, too, F's 'ha's', 'do's', and 'Prey's', for example, appear as 'has', 'does', and 'preys'. On the same principle, F's various spellings for the 'hautboy', a musical instrument which is not the modern oboe, have been silently normalised. Fairly consistently, the Folio represents the syncopated *-ed* in past tenses and past participles as *-'d*, the stressed as *-ed*; in this edition, these suffixes are represented as *-ed* and *-èd*, respectively, and the collation silently treats earlier editions as observing the same conventions.[1] Similarly, other merely conventional differences (archaic spelling, punctuation, etc.) between earlier editions and this one are not noted in the collation. In this text, F's italics for proper nouns have been silently omitted, along with its archaic and merely conventional capitalisation; its obsolete abbreviations (e.g. y^u for 'thou' at 4.3.33/TLN 1852 and 5.3.57/TLN 2279) are silently expanded. (Quotations from F in the collation are treated differently; see below.) Folio *Macbeth* only once uses the apostrophe to mark a singular possessive ('Life's Feast', 2.2.43/TLN 696); elsewhere it does not distinguish among plural nouns and singular and plural possessives. All such distinctions are editorial and for a reader's convenience, since the differences would often be hard to hear in the theatre; these editorial distinctions are not noted in the collation but doubtful instances appear in the Commentary. Other uncontroversial, normalising, and modernising editorial punctuation (of contractions, marks of exclamation, and vocatives, for instance) has not been collated, but any changes of or additions to punctuation (e.g. quotation marks and changes of address marked by dashes) that affect sense or theatrical delivery as I understand them have been collated and usually are discussed in the Commentary. Directions for a character to speak *to*

---

[1] Thus, at 4.3.34 the collation records Hanmer's edition as the first to replace F's 'affear'd' with the different word 'affeered', though Hanmer's conventions led him to print 'affeer'd', and the conventions used in this edition did not appear until S. W. Singer's first edition (1826), where he prints 'affeered'; in my collation, Hanmer is credited with the change, and Singer is unmentioned. Albrecht Wagner, *Shakespeares Macbeth . . . mit den Varianten der anderen Folios*, 1890, meticulously collates F *Macbeth* with the later seventeenth-century folios.

another or *aside* are all editorial, and most derive from eighteenth-century editions; such directions are placed within square brackets and should be regarded with caution. Substantive changes and additions to F's stage directions appear in square brackets, and all are collated, but uncontroversial modernisations like that made in the dialogue proper and the imposition of New Cambridge Shakespeare series conventions (e.g. no final punctuation in entry- and exit-directions, capitals for the names of speakers in entry-directions) are not collated.

Most speech headings are silently expanded and normalised unless F's ascription might seem confusing (e.g. *Mac.* for Macduff, not Macbeth, at 4.3.102/TLN 1930), or where there is a wide, local variation (as in the three different speech headings for Siward in the short Act 5, Scene 4) or where the assignment of a speech has been changed or plausibly conjectured; in such cases, the collation records F's reading and any change or conjecture. Where F indicates a member of a category (witch, murderer, apparition) by a number, the speech heading has been expanded (e.g. FIRST WITCH, THIRD MURDERER, SECOND APPARITION) and the change collated. It has often been suggested that as Shakespeare composed he sometimes thought (and wrote) of the speakers not by name but by social status or familial relation. F's speech headings always refer to Duncan as *King.*, to Malcolm as *Mal.* (or *Malc.* or *Malc,*), to Lady Macbeth as *Lady.* (or *La., La:* or *Lad.*), to Lady Macduff as *Wife.*, to her male child as *Son.*, and to Macbeth as *Mac.* (or *Macb.*); some or all of the implied patterns and distinctions may be Shakespeare's.[1] These speech headings have been normalised: 'Duncan', 'Malcolm', 'Lady Macbeth', 'Lady Macduff ', 'Son', and 'Macbeth', respectively.

Like the speech headings, the Folio's stage directions also reflect a professionally abbreviated nomenclature: Lady Macbeth is once *Macbeths Wife* (1.5.0 SD/TLN 348), once *Macbeths Lady* (3.2.0 SD/TLN 1151), at all other times, *Lady*; Lady Macduff is *Macduffes Wife* (4.2.0 SD/TLN 1711); Duncan is always *King*. Such usages are normalised here (e.g. as 'Lady Macbeth' and 'Lady Macduff ', respectively); the collation records their first occurrence and, where appropriate, notes that they appear '*throughout*', as do similar collation entries for speech headings. At 3.1.10 SD/TLN 992, F reads *Enter Macbeth as King*, and this theatrical direction (which indicates or implies costume, props, blocking, and the like) authorises the insertion of similar directions for Macbeth and Lady Macbeth in Act 3, Scene 4. On several occasions (see the SDs at 1.2.44/TLN 66, 2.3.34/TLN 784, 2.4.20/TLN 949, 3.4.37/TLN 1299, 3.4.88/TLN 1363, and 4.3.139/TLN 1968), the Folio contains so-called 'anticipatory' stage directions signalling the moment an actor stepped on to the Globe's capacious stage or when the book-holder alerted an actor to prepare to enter rather than the moment the actor 'entered' the dialogue or was

---

[1] Speech headings in *Macbeth* and their variants are listed in Marvin Spevack, *A Complete and Systematic Concordance to the Works of Shakespeare*, 9 vols., 1968–80, VII (1975), pp. 753–5. The claim that type-names or social or familial designations for characters derive from the author (rather than the theatre or printing-house) appears in R. B. McKerrow, 'A suggestion regarding Shakespeare's manuscripts', *Review of English Studies* 11 (1935), 459–65; it has been roundly trounced in Paul Werstine, 'McKerrow's "Suggestion" and twentieth-century Shakespeare textual criticism', *RenD*, n.s. 19 (1988), 149–73, but in part at least supported by Random Cloud, ' "The very names of the Persons": editing and the invention of dramatick character', in David Scott Kastan and Peter Stallybrass (eds.), *Staging the Renaissance: Reinterpretations of Elizabethan and Jacobean Drama*, 1991, pp. 88–96.

noticed verbally by other speakers. Since many entrances, especially those of Banquo's Ghost in Act 3, Scene 4, have great theatrical potential – a potential the reader may at least partly share with the spectator – I have not moved F's directions to their more 'regular' places according to modern stage conventions.

Quotations from F in the collation retain original orthography (except for 'long' s) and italicisation, with various forms of the ampersand represented as '&' and abbreviations silently expanded. Unless original orthography is relevant to the argument, quotations from F elsewhere and from other sources follow modern conventions for u and v, i and j, and 'long' s even if, for example, the modern editions I cite preserve original spelling. In these quotations, abbreviations are silently expanded, ampersand forms appear as '&', and texts originally using black letter with roman or italic type for emphasis appear as roman with italic for emphasis.

Copy for the Folio

The manuscript from which Folio *Macbeth* was printed probably originated in the theatre, either having served as the promptbook for contemporary productions or being a specially prepared transcript of such a promptbook. Regarding the former view as 'beyond reasonable doubt', W. W. Greg noted particularly that 'the record of entrances and exits is almost complete' and 'there is practically no inconsistency, much less ambiguity, in the designation of the characters'.[1] More minor features of F's text also support this view: for example, a theatrical instruction 'Ring the bell' has apparently been incorporated in the text of Act 2, Scene 3 (see Supplementary Note on 2.3.74, p. 257 above), and numerous stage directions for sound and lighting, *Oboes. Torches.* (1.7.0 SD), and supernumeraries, *Drum(me) and Colours* (5.2.0 SD, 5.4.0 SD, 5.5.0 SD, 5.6.0 SD, 5.9.0 SD), for instance, are professionally terse. The Folio is not, however, flawless as a theatre script. Greg complains that two different stagings of Macbeth's death seem to be conflated in F's stage directions,[2] and on at least one other occasion (the end of Act 3, Scene 5, discussed below as an example of adaptation) two inconsistent stagings seem to appear in the directions.

Whatever processes prepared F's manuscript copy for performance or printing, or the normalisation imposed by that printing itself, have removed most traces of any putative Shakespearean spelling habits, and it seems most unlikely that his holograph went to Jaggard's printing-house. Greg did, however, accept Richard Flatter's contention that the unique '*Banquoh*' (1.2.34/TLN 54) represented Shakespeare's own version of

[1] Greg, p. 395; 'F's copy may itself have been the prompt-book, or a transcript of it' (*Textual Companion*, p. 147; see also p. 543). See also Gary Taylor and John Jowett, *Shakespeare Reshaped 1606–1623*, 1993, pp. 46, 85, 87, and 240, where it is claimed that *Macbeth* is a scribal transcript that 'derives from a late theatrical text' (p. 87). Some of the evidence for F's copy is far from unassailable; early theatrical professionals probably tolerated, or had to tolerate, more inconsistency (in SHS and SDS, for example) than modern scholars imagine they did.
[2] Greg, p. 394. NS strongly defends F's staging of this moment; see Edelman (pp. 165–7) for a summary of editorial and critical comment and theatrical practice.

Holinshed's spelling, 'Banquho'.[1] Further, 2.2.15/TLN 667 and 2.3.48/TLN 805 contain two unusual spellings, 'schreame' and 'Schreemes', respectively. *OED* records these forms only here and comments (*OED* Scream *v*): 'In Shakespeare's [spellings] . . . *sch* probably stands for (sk) after the spelling of words of classical derivation.'[2] Whatever the merit of *OED*'s speculation – I suppose it refers to such classical names as 'Moschus' – it has long been recognised that Shakespeare probably wrote some other words beginning with *s* in an unusual way. For instance, the spelling *scilens* (silence) occurs, so far as is known, only in the portion of the manuscript of *The Booke of Sir Thomas More* supposed to be in Shakespeare's handwriting and eighteen times (text and didascalia) in the quarto of *2H4* (1600), believed to have been set from autograph copy or from copy that retained authorial spellings.[3] Elsewhere, there occur numerous unusually spelled proper names (which compositors might hesitate to normalise): 'Sceneca' (*Hamlet* Q2 (1604), sig. F3, line 1, for 'Seneca'); 'Scicion' (*Ant.* 1.2.113, 114, 119, for 'Sicyon'); 'Scicinius' (*Cor.* 2.1.204 SD and *Scicin.* or *Scici.* in some SHs, for 'Sicinius').[4] Given this admittedly patchy evidence, it seems possible that 'schreame' and 'Schreemes' in Folio *Macbeth* represent Shakespeare's own autograph spellings.[5]

Scene division in the Folio

Shakespeare and other early modern English playwrights apparently composed their plays in scenic units defined by location and time.[6] A new scene begins when the stage empties of actors, and the audience is asked to imagine that the following action takes place at a later time or in a new location, or both.[7] Printed designations of scene

---

[1] Richard Flatter, '"The true original copies" of Shakespeare's plays: outline of a new conception', *Proceedings of the Leeds Philosophical and Literary Society* 7, part 1 (July 1952), 31–42; p. 36.

[2] Although other parts of the words were gradually modernised, the unusual *h* disappears from 'schreame' and 'Schreemes' only in F4 (1685); the compositors of Q1673 and F2 and F3 evidently felt the spelling unusual enough to forbear changing it. The same may have been true of the F compositor when he read his manuscript copy.

[3] See Vittorio Gabrieli and Giorgio Melchiori (eds.), *STM*, 1990, 2.3.55 and n.; Matthias A. Shaaber (ed.), *2H4*, 1940, pp. 488–94; Giorgio Melchiori (ed.), *2H4*, 1989, p. 189. A. C. Partridge, *Orthography in Shakespeare and Elizabethan Drama*, 1964, p. 62, has, however, found very similar early printed and manuscript spellings: 'scylens' and 'scilence'.

[4] Hinman, 1, 380–1 and 383–4, treats the last spelling as characteristic of Compositor A, who set both 'schreame' and 'Schreemes', and the *sc*-forms of the proper names mentioned here are not unknown in other contemporary works.

[5] This argument naturally makes one suspect other words beginning *sch*- in *Macbeth*, particularly the famous crux 'Banke and Schoole of time' (1.7.6/TLN 480), and might in that instance seem to support modernising the crucial word as 'school' rather than 'shoal', the reading I adopt. The oddity of 'schreame' and 'Schreemes', however, lies in those spellings (like 'scilens') not having been found thus far outside Shakespearean texts, though there are some near approaches; the spelling 'Schoole' for 'shoal' is well documented elsewhere and represents a plausible scribal or compositorial choice. For other proper and common nouns in *sc*- where contemporary orthography preferred *s*-, see n. 4 above and Lee Bliss, 'Scribes, compositors, and annotators: the nature of the copy for the First Folio text of *Coriolanus*', *SB* 50 (1997), 224–61, esp. n. 14.

[6] The few surviving early modern English manuscript plays by professional playwrights exhibit all the possible variations: no divisions marked, acts only marked, complete or partial act and scene division. For comment and a tabular summary, see Anthony Munday, *Fedele and Fortunio*, ed. Richard Hosley, 1981, pp. 68–73.

[7] See James Hirsh, *The Structure of Shakespearean Scenes*, 1981.

changes appear only sporadically in vernacular plays between Thomas Sackville and Thomas Norton's *Gorboduc* (1565), divided into acts, and John Lyly's *Mother Bombie* (1594), divided into acts and scenes; the practice becomes common in the first decade of the seventeenth century.[1] It is important to stress, however, that scene divisions are a printed, not a theatrical, phenomenon. Where a printed text marks a new scene, the stage will exhibit a blank, an absence of actors. The marking of scenes and of acts (the grouping of scenes) is thus mainly a convenience for readers, for devotees of print culture, and for those who require a succinct reference-system.[2] What the reader experiences as marks on the page the spectator experiences as a shifting of bodies and voices on the stage. Thus, and significantly for *Macbeth*, editorial scene division affects readers very differently from the way the stage action affects spectators.

Even though Elizabethan and Jacobean conventions for scene division seem relatively clear, ambiguous cases do arise. Aside from Alexander Pope and a few others who sought to impose a neo-classical system on the Folio's plays, editors have plausibly altered *Macbeth*'s Folio scene divisions only in Acts 2 and 5. Nicholas Rowe, the first named editor of the play, and others have found F's division of Act 2, Scene 2, from Act 2, Scene 3, unnecessary, in part because the location does not change from some vaguely imagined 'Macbeth's Castle'.[3] Puzzlement over the setting is understandable, because it is here unusually fluid, but the stage has emptied of speakers, the customary indication of a scene-break, and F's division makes readerly sense.

The series of conflicts ending Act 5 has proved more controversial. As a coda to an unconvincing argument that young Siward's body should remain on stage after his death, Homer Swander claims that F's *Scena Septima* (the last it marks in Act 5) is 'a clear, straightforward, efficiently theatrical unit', but that modern editors '[u]nanimously . . . deform it, either enlarging it by joining it with Scene Six or (more often) cutting it up into whatever small units the editor finds attractive'.[4] Linking F's Scenes 6 and 7, G. K. Hunter notes that the play's ending is

[u]sually printed as four separate scenes, but logic would demand either more divisions . . . or none at all. The battle is a series of spotlights but the action must be continuous. The alternation between sides that has marked Act V so far now speeds up, till the two blur into one victory and one defeat.[5]

[1] See Trevor Howard-Hill, 'The evolution of the form of plays in English during the Renaissance', *Renaissance Quarterly* 43 (1990), 112–45, p. 142, and W. T. Jewkes, *Act Division in Elizabethan and Jacobean Plays, 1583–1616*, 1958.
[2] Scene and especially act divisions have some theatrical uses, of course, particularly once pauses between sections of action become conventional.
[3] Bevington, pp. 130–1, argues against dividing 2.2 from 2.3; Mark Rose, *Shakespearean Design*, 1972, argues (pp. 39–43) that the first three scenes of Act 2 'should be considered a single scene' (p. 39), and Rowe, Theobald, and White, among others (see Furness), do so.
[4] Homer Swander, 'No exit for a dead body: what to do with a scripted corpse?', *Journal of Dramatic Theory and Criticism* 5 (1991), 139–52; quotation from p. 149. On reasons to think Swander wrong about young Siward's corpse, see 5.7.14 SD.1 n., 3.3.25 SD n., and Edelman, p. 163; Roy Walker, *The Time Is Free*, 1949, p. 220, seems the first to suppose that young Siward remains, dead, on stage; for productions that keep the corpse on stage, see Rosenberg, pp. 632 and 650, and Richard Eyre's 1993 Royal National Theatre (London) production, which also cut the part of (Old) Siward.
[5] Hunter, p. 186.

While I have chosen Hunter's alternative of 'more divisions' rather than 'none at all', his view seems to me unassailable and theatrically neutral, since printed scene divisions – any one, all, or none – need have no theatrical consequence whatsoever, and the Folio's divisions are quite probably not Shakespeare's at all.[1] The headnotes to Scenes 7, 8, and 9 and the Commentary on 5.7.14 SD.2 discuss specific local issues of scene division in Act 5.

Compositors and the printing of the Folio

It is generally agreed that two compositors, customarily called 'A' and 'B', converted manuscript *Macbeth* into printed *Macbeth*. Exigencies of early modern printing required the two compositors to set the text in an order different from the one we read. This is the sequence: 1.1.0–1.3.103/TLN 1–210 (Compositor A); 2.3.66–2.4.19/TLN 827–947 (A); 2.4.19–3.1.21/TLN 948–1006 (Compositor B); 3.1.22–77/TLN 1007–70 (A); 2.2.50–2.3.65/TLN 704–826, 3.1.78–3.2.37/TLN 1071–1195, 2.1.6–2.2.49/TLN 579–703, and 3.2.38–3.3.25/TLN 1196–1252 (A); 3.4.0 SD–3.4.45/TLN 1253–1310 (B); 1.6.21–2.1.5/TLN 457–578 (A and B); 3.4.46–3.5.5/TLN 1311–1435 (B); 1.4.50–1.6.21/TLN 338–456 (A); 3.5.6–4.1.28/TLN 1436–1555 (B); 1.3.104–1.4.49/TLN 211–337 (A); 4.1.29–134/TLN 1556–1685, 5.4.15 – *Finis*/TLN 2311–2530, 5.2.15–5.4.15/TLN 2192–2310, 4.3.224–5.2.14/TLN 2071–2191, 4.3.112–223/TLN 1939–2070, 4.3.0 – 111/TLN 1812–1938, and 4.1.135–4.2.82 SD/TLN 1686–1811 (B).[2] After collating over fifty copies of the Folio, Charlton Hinman (1, 300–1) found only six press-corrections (changes made after some surviving pages were printed) in *Macbeth*; only two (both on sig. nn2) are substantive. The collation records those two (at 4.3.156 and 4.3.215 SH).

Compositors made characteristic changes (or errors) in setting their copy.[3] In plays where the Folio was set from an earlier, surviving printed text, for example, it can be shown that compositors sometimes omitted small or substantial amounts of text if they had underestimated how much space would be required to convert their copy into print. If they miscalculated in the opposite direction and allowed too much space for transferring manuscript copy to print, compositors employed detectable techniques for stretching their copy to fill the available space. And there are other typical flaws in compositors' work. Each compositor mistakes characters' names in the first batch of text he set. Not yet aware that the play's king is named Duncan, Compositor A did not set a comma in the entry SD for Act 1, Scene 2, and amalgamated the king and his elder son: *Enter King Malcome*. Compositor B, similarly unaware that Lennox is a thane and that Macbeth's wife is consistently referred to as *Lady*, treated two characters,

---

[1] Swander maintains (p. 150) that questioning the 'Shakespearean authority' of F leaves us 'as readers, in the chaotic world of editorial disagreement'; indeed it does, but such questioning and the editorial redivision that follows in no way restrict equally chaotic theatrical reshapings of the play's conclusion, and 'Shakespearean authority' is nebulous.

[2] See Hinman, 11, 182–219 and 516, T. H. Howard-Hill, *'Macbeth': Oxford Shakespeare Concordances*, 1971, pp. xi–xii, and *Textual Companion*, p. 154.

[3] On Compositors A and B in particular, see Werstine and, for a summary of studies of all the Folio compositors, *Textual Companion*, pp. 148–9.

Macbeth's Queen (or *Lady*) and the Thane of Lennox, as one – *Enter Macbeth as King, Lady Lenox* . . . (TLN 992) – in the first column of text he composed.[1]

In Folio *Macbeth*, however, the main difficulty partly created by A and B is the play's lineation, its setting out of verse and prose and the regularity of its verse. Compositor A 'had a regrettable tendency to rearrange normal blank verse into a succession of irregular lines', while B 'had a tendency to set up prose as though it were verse'.[2]

Lineation in the Folio

Protesting against the rearrangement and rewriting of short and/or unmetrical lines, especially by George Steevens, Charles Knight complained:

> We admit that it will not do servilely to follow the original in every instance where the commencement and close of a line are so arranged that it becomes prosaic; but on the other hand we contend that the desire to get rid of hemistichs, without regard to the nature of the dialogue, and so to alter the metrical arrangement of a series of lines, is a barbarism which ought to be corrected as swiftly as possible. But when this barbarism is carried a degree farther, and the text is daubed over after the fashion of a sign-painter mending a Claude, we hold that the offence of republishing such abominations is a grave one . . . we proceed on our work of restoration.[3]

Since Knight wrote, the 'work of restoration' has come to seem less clear cut; critics now admit a greater flexibility (or 'looseness') in Shakespeare's metrics, especially in the latter half of his career, and recognise the influence of those (including Shakespeare) who prepared the plays' manuscripts for performance and the compositors who set those manuscripts in type.[4] Most critics agree that the Folio obscures one Shakespearean metrical practice, the sharing between two or more speakers of a single iambic pentameter line. In the clearest cases, these shared lines represent a syntactical or thematic unit. Since the late eighteenth century, editors have reproduced such units typographically by indenting the words that complete the line.[5] Question and answer are obvious examples:

> MACBETH How now, you secret, black, and midnight hags!
>   What is't you do?
> ALL THE WITCHES   A deed without a name.

---

[1] As Werstine observes in 'McKerrow's "Suggestion"', p. 160, what may be a contemporary promptbook of Anthony Munday's *John a Kent and John a Cumber* omits commas in SDs in such a way as to amalgamate characters. Unfamiliarity with the word modernised here as 'weïrd' may also explain the compositors' choice of 'weyward' and 'weyard', respectively; see the Supplementary Note to 1.3.30, pp. 255–6 above.

[2] *Textual Companion*, p. 637, summarising Werstine. For relineation in this edition, see Appendix 3, p. 291 below.

[3] Knight (ed.), *Tragedies*, 11, 9 note c.

[4] Note, too, that F does not always mark the contractions (especially of pronouns before verbs) and other forms of syncopation and slurring (e.g. "em' for 'them', 'th" for 'the') required to manifest a moderately regular blank verse.

[5] Although Steevens[3] established this convention for later editions of verse drama, Ben Jonson had employed a similar convention in the Jacobean period, and it is fully and elegantly established in Robert Gomersall's possibly unacted *Tragedy of Lodovick Sforza* (1628) (see W. W. Greg, *A Bibliography of English Printed Drama*, 4 vols., 1939–59, IV, clx); *Gorboduc* (1565) occasionally indents the second part-line (see Howard-Hill, 'Evolution', p. 142 n. 82) and, as Werstine (pp. 117–18) shows, so does the manuscript of the medieval Towneley plays.

Here F prints 'A deed . . .' immediately following the speech heading. Moments later, the typographic convention helps actors and readers perceive a choric response to Macbeth's question:

> though the treasure
> Of nature's germen tumble altogether
> Even till destruction sicken: answer me
> To what I ask you.
> FIRST WITCH   Speak.
> SECOND WITCH   Demand.
> THIRD WITCH   We'll answer.

The Folio prints each of the witches' speeches as a separate line, flush left after the speech heading, whereas modern conventions dictate that 'To what . . . We'll answer' be regarded as a single line. Current convention also underscores visually such ironic moments as the instant of Banquo's murder:

> BANQUO It will be rain tonight.
> FIRST MURDERER   Let it come down.

and reinforces dramatic tension metrically in such moments as

> MACDUFF I am not treacherous.
> MALCOLM   But Macbeth is.

or

> ATTENDANT The king comes here tonight.
> LADY MACBETH   Thou'rt mad to say it.

In these cases, again, the Folio aligns successive speeches immediately after the respective speech headings. These examples and scores more demonstrate that Shakespeare, like his contemporaries, used metrically shared lines for dramatic effect.[1]

So metrically complex a play as *Macbeth* provides instances where adopting or relining the Folio approaches arbitrary choice. As illustrations, here are two examples – in one, this edition follows the Folio; in the other, its lines have been rearranged. G. K. Hunter appropriately draws attention to the moment Macbeth returns to his wife after murdering Duncan.[2] The Folio supplies:

> *Lady.* I heard the Owle schreame, and the Crickets cry.
> Did not you speake?
> *Macb.* When?
> *Lady.* Now.
> *Macb.* As I descended?
> *Lady.* I.

---

[1] For an ample discussion of Shakespeare's use of short and shared lines, see George T. Wright, *Shakespeare's Metrical Art*, 1988, pp. 116–42.
[2] Hunter, p. 196.

Like many modern editors, Hunter prints:

> LADY   I heard the owl scream and the cricket's cry.
>   Did not you speak?
> MACBETH   When?
> LADY   Now.
> MACBETH   As I descended?
> LADY   Ay.

This layout does not represent graphically a plausible enactment: while the sharing of a pentameter (but which words should make up the line?)[1] might indicate the Macbeths' joint fear and collective guiltiness, few audiences will be able to hear, and fewer actors will be eager to convey, the line's metrical integrity. Such integrity, of course, is not the only sort dramatic speech may have: Mozart's or (sometimes) Verdi's quartets and quintets, for example, blend multiple voices into an enveloping unity-of-difference, but musical or sonic unity (also available in the theatre) is not necessarily metrical, as Shaw's effort to orchestrate the voices speaking his *prose* demonstrates: 'Opera taught me to shape my plays into recitatives, arias, duets, trios, ensemble finales, and bravura pieces.'[2] Imposing a hypermetrical but nominally single line on the reader's eyes violates my sense of the theatrical moment in *Macbeth* Act 2, Scene 2.[3] For whatever reasons of typographical convenience or printer's convention, the Folio's layout stipulates less, leaves the text more open to both reader and actors, than the conventional modern one, and I have therefore followed the Folio:

> LADY MACBETH I heard the owl scream and the crickets cry.
>   Did not you speak?
> MACBETH When?
> LADY MACBETH Now.
> MACBETH As I descended?
> LADY MACBETH Ay.

By contrast, a reader or speaker of a passage in Act 4, Scene 3, of the Folio benefits from having the underlying metrical shape revealed typographically:

>   . . . and good mens liues
> Expire before the Flowers in their Caps,
> Dying, or ere they sicken.
>   *Macd.* Oh Relation; too nice, and yet too true.

---

[1] As many editors note in discussing these matters, vocatives (usually proper names) and interjections (here, 'Ay') seem to have been excluded from the metrics of shared pentameters. Marlowe's far more regular practice almost always excludes vocatives from the line's metre; see C. F. Tucker Brooke, 'Marlowe's versification and style', *SP* 19 (1922), 186–205.

[2] Quoted in Michael Holroyd, *Bernard Shaw*, 5 vols., III (1991), 357. I owe the operatic objection to Brian Gibbons; the Shavian rebuttal is my own.

[3] The editorial or typographical choice (single pentameter or metrically unrelated and disjointed reactions) is truly a theatrical choice: Lisa Harrow, a distinguished Shakespearean actor, has forcefully claimed to me that the exchange echoes the 'heartbeat' of Lord and Lady Macbeth and should, therefore, be treated as a shared pentameter. The editorial choice here probably indicates a hesitant, stunned Macbeth rather than an eagerly conspiratorial one.

> *Malc.* What's the newest griefe?
> *Rosse.* That of an houres age, doth hisse the speaker,
> Each minute teemes a new one.
> *Macd.* How do's my Wife?
> *Rosse.* Why well.
> *Macd.* And all my Children?
> *Rosse.* Well too.
> *Macd.* The Tyrant ha's not batter'd at their peace?   (TLN 2007–18)

In this edition, the passage appears as:

>   and good men's lives
> Expire before the flowers in their caps,
> Dying or ere they sicken.
> MACDUFF   O relation
>   Too nice, and yet too true.
> MALCOLM   What's the newest grief?
> ROSS That of an hour's age doth hiss the speaker;
>   Each minute teems a new one.
> MACDUFF   How does my wife?
> ROSS Why, well.
> MACDUFF   And all my children?
> ROSS   Well, too.
> MACDUFF The tyrant has not battered at their peace?   (4.3.173–80)

If 'children' is trisyllabic (as it is elsewhere in Shakespeare's verse), this rearrangement produces regular pentameters that graphically represent the dialogue's association of ideas and emotions. Whether this second example is clearly or sufficiently different from the first, only the reader or actor can say.

Macbeth includes sequences of three separate lines which might form two different combinations of one and one-half pentameter lines. Consider this exchange between Macbeth and Seyton in the Folio:

> *Macb.* Ile fight, till from my bones, my flesh be hackt.
> Giue me my Armor.
> *Seyt.* 'Tis not needed yet.
> *Macb.* Ile put it on: (TLN 2251–4)

''Tis not needed yet' might be joined metrically with either the preceding or following part-line; it is an 'amphibious' line. Recent editorial practice has been to follow the Folio's lineation on these occasions and not to force the amphibious line into metrical marriage with one or the other of its possible partners, and I have been content to imitate this irenic practice. And nowhere have I rearranged the Folio's lines on the assumption that some stage action can be – or was by Shakespeare in planning his verse lines – substituted for one or more metrical feet.[1]

---

[1] Compare Fredson Bowers, 'Establishing Shakespeare's text: notes on short lines and the problem of verse division', *SB* 33 (1980), 74–130, pp. 91–2, and 'the completion of a line may patently depend on a dramatic pause, or even an action; but it must be clearly realized that there is no consistency about this: many pauses,

One further common occurrence is a part-line at the beginning or, more often, at the end of a regularly lined speech which is itself framed by regularly lined speeches.[1] When Duncan names Malcolm Prince of Cumberland, his speech ends with a part-line and is immediately followed by a thoroughly plausible pentameter:

> But signs of nobleness like stars shall shine
> On all deservers. From hence to Inverness
> And bind us further to you.
> MACBETH The rest is labour which is not used for you . . .   (1.4.41–4)

Unless compositorial malfeasance can be suspected, these part-lines have been allowed to stand. At certain places, especially in the work of Compositor A, no rearrangement seems to restore a regular metre and no obvious principle seems to govern the Folio's lineation. Thus, to choose an early example:

> For brave Macbeth – well he deserves that name –
> Disdaining Fortune, with his brandished steel
> Which smoked with bloody execution,
> Like Valour's minion carved out his passage
> Till he faced the slave,
> Which ne'er shook hands, nor bade farewell to him,
> Till he unseamed him from the nave to th'chaps . . .   (1.2.16–22)

These moments may, of course, indicate cutting, revision, printing catastrophe, or any combination of these or other events, but whatever intervention has occurred cannot now be guessed at or rectified. Part-lines must therefore be accepted, perhaps as theatrically motivated, perhaps as accidental.

Thomas Middleton's contribution to the Folio

Collaborative writing was common in Tudor and Stuart theatre: 'as many as half of the plays by professional dramatists in this period incorporated the writing at some date of more than one man'.[2] Folio *Macbeth* is probably no exception and may print passages not written by Shakespeare but (most probably) by Thomas Middleton; Act 1, Scene 2, has been especially controversial. On two occasions, the Folio may allude to, but does not print fully, texts that are also probably not by Shakespeare. Ever since Isaac Reed privately published *A Tragi-coomodie* [*sic*], *called The Witch* (1778) from a manuscript with a dedicatory epistle signed 'Tho: Middleton' (though not in his autograph), scholars have known that Middleton's play contains two songs verbally

---

moves, etc., are certainly required which have, as it were, to be extra-metrical – the verse continues without regard to them' (Brooke, App. A, p. 215).

[1] Bowers, 'Establishing Shakespeare's text', pp. 78–9, demonstrates that part-lines more frequently end than begin speeches.

[2] G. E. Bentley, *The Profession of Dramatist in Shakespeare's Time 1590–1642*, 1971, pp. 199 and 205–6, and Carol Chillington Rutter (ed.), *Documents of the Rose Playhouse*, 1984, pp. 26–8.

similar to fragmentary references in F's stage directions.[1] Neither song is especially well integrated into Folio *Macbeth* and each fits smoothly into Middleton's tragicomedy; so, while the date (composition or performance) of Middleton's play is unknown, these coincidences seem more than chance. They may thus be: the result of Middleton, and/or Shakespeare, and/or a third party sharing a source or sources; borrowings (in any direction) among the known plays, other printed texts, and hypothetical unknown texts; the result of deliberate adaptation of one or the other surviving play. The two instances are not identical and require separate discussion.

After TLN 1466, F reads '*Sing within. Come away, come away, & c.*', and Thomas Middleton's *The Witch* has a passage of song and action including '*Come away: Come away: / Heccat: Heccat, Come away*' (*Witch* lines 1331–2). William Davenant's adaptation of *Macbeth* (1674) incorporates a version of this song and the action that seems to accompany it, particularly Hecate's 'flying' departure, which also seems to be called for in *The Witch*:

> *Hec* [*ate*]. hye thee home with 'em
> Looke well to the House to night; I am for aloft.
> *Fire* [*stone*]. Aloft (quoth you?) I would you would breake yo[r] necke once,
> that I might haue all quickly: hark: hark Mother.
> they are aboue the Steeple alredy, flying
> over your head with a noyse of *Musitians*
> *Hec.* they are they indeed: help: help me: I'm too late els.
> Song: *Come away: Come away:* }
> } *in y[e] aire.*
> *Heccat: Heccat, Come away*}
> *Hec. I come, I come, I come, I come,*
> *with all the speed I may*
> *with all the speed I may.*
> *wher's Stadlin?*
> *Heere* } *in y[e] aire.*
>
> . . . .
>
> *Hec. going vp*}. *Now I goe, now I flie,*
> *Malkin my sweete Spirit, and I.*
> *oh what a daintie pleasure 'tis*
> *to ride in the Aire*
> *when the Moone shines faire*
> *and sing, and daunce, and toy, and kiss . . .*
>   (*Witch* lines 1324–37, 1358–62)[2]

If Folio *Macbeth* refers to this song and to some or all of its accompanying action, it may therefore represent a performance in which Hecate leaves the stage through the use of a 'machine', a theatrical effect evidently possible in the Blackfriars theatre (the King's Men's city location after the winter of 1609), but not so certainly available at the Globe

---

[1] The manuscript is now MS. Malone 12 in the Bodleian Library, Oxford. Epistle and text were probably transcribed by Ralph Crane *c.* 1618–27; the 1778 'edition' is by George Steevens (see Edward J. Esche (ed.), *A Critical Edition of Thomas Middleton's 'The Witch'*, 1993, pp. 12 and 15).

[2] Appendix 2, p. 285 below, reprints Q1673's version of part of this text and action, which also appears in Davenant's adaptation.

(which they continued to use – as a summer venue – after acquiring the Blackfriars).[1] Simon Forman, who says he saw *Macbeth* at the Globe in 1611, does not record any such spectacular moment, although F may also call for the witches to make a flying exit in Act 1, Scenes 1 and 3.[2] One explanation for the added song (and action?) in Act 3, Scene 5, is that the machinery that 'flew' Hecate off-stage (a human-powered winch seems likely) was both slow and noisy, and realistic illusion (if it were desired) therefore required extensive covering sound and action; that is, Middleton and/or the adapter(s) of *Macbeth* exploited necessity to add theatrical spectacle. This theoretical possibility does not explain, however, why no text 'covers' the two earlier moments when the witches have been thought to depart 'flying', incidents that similarly require – on the posited assumptions – dialogue and action to conceal noisy and/or slow machinery.

In sum, if a Jacobean Hecate departed Act 3, Scene 5, via some primitive flying machine, the time and noise of that operation may have demanded dialogue (and/or song and action), and Middleton's *Witch*, or some adapted form thereof, may have provided the requisite words and action. As G. K. Hunter sagaciously remarks, however, 'Shakespeare's *Macbeth*, indeed, needs no more than the first two lines of the song [in Middleton's play], to be followed by Hecate's flying exit.'[3] And one is justified in asking why the witches' putative flying exits in the first act lack analogous textual cover. Rather than insert text into *Macbeth* Act 3, Scene 5, especially since Act 1, Scenes 1 and 3, arguably require similar but unavailable text, I reprint lines from Middleton's *The Witch* in Appendix 2 and suggest readers and producers make their own choices.

After TLN 1571, F reads '*Musicke and a Song. Blacke Spirits, &c.*' and Thomas Middleton's *The Witch* contains two seemingly relevant passages:

---

[1] Simple ascents and descents were apparently used in medieval French and English religious drama (see e.g. Alan Nelson's remarks in Jerome Taylor and Alan H. Nelson (eds.), *Medieval English Drama*, 1972, pp. 134–5, and David William Young, 'Devices and Feintes of Medieval Religious Theatre in England and France', unpublished Ph.D. thesis, Stanford University, 1960) and were widely used in Italian religious and secular drama in the sixteenth century (see e.g. Edward Carrick, 'Theatre machines in Italy, 1400–1800', *Architectural Review* 70 (1931), 9–36). Henslowe, p. 7, offers unquestionable evidence for a flying 'throne' at the Rose in 1595, but John H. Astington strongly argues that public theatres had, or could have had, at least simple 'flying' machinery as much as two decades before; see Astington, 'Descent machinery in the playhouses', *Medieval & Renaissance Drama in England* 2 (1985), 119–33. Shakespeare's later plays, in particular *Cymbeline* and perhaps *The Tempest*, seem to call for 'flying' entrances or exits, but the textual evidence suggests that different stagings may have been employed at the Globe and the Blackfriars – that is, the texts are composite or hybrid and represent plural (and mutually incompatible) stagings. Reviewing the textual evidence concerning apparatus for flying actors at the Globe, T. J. King concludes: 'such machinery was not *required* in the vast majority of plays, which suggests that it was also not available in the vast majority of playhouses'; see *Shakespearean Staging, 1599–1642*, 1971, pp. 36–7 and 148 n. 2. The Blackfriars theatre, however, apparently had effective and not noisy apparatus for flights; see Irwin Smith, *Shakespeare's Blackfriars Playhouse*, 1964, pp. 414–18.

[2] For Forman, see pp. 57–8 above; for the witches' exits, see 1.1.13 SD n. and Wickham, 'Fly'. On the possibility that F conflates alternative stagings, see above, p. 263 and n. 2.

[3] See Hunter, 3.5.36 n., although Hunter's proposal may envisage more modern theatrical equipment than that available to the King's Men. See also Peter Thomson, *Shakespeare's Theatre*, 1983, where he describes 3.5 as 'a "reminder scene" – "meanwhile the Witches . . ."' (p. 152), and later remarks, 'there are excuses for cutting it in performance. All that happens, after all, is that an overbearing, and presumably gorgeously costumed, Hecate scolds her inferiors and promises to stir up trouble for Macbeth, before heading off (and up) to a foggy cloud' (pp. 152–3).

> *Titty, and Tiffin, Suckin*
> *and Pidgen, Liard, and Robin*
> *white Spirits, black Spiritts: gray Spiritts: redd Speritts:*
> *Deuill-Toad: Deuill-Ram: Deuill-Catt: and Deuill Dam*   (lines 183–6)

and *A Charme Song: about a Vessell* that begins, '*Black Spiritts, and white: Red Spiritts, and Gray,* / *Mingle, Mingle, Mingle, you that mingle may.*' (lines 1999–2000).[1]

Middleton knew Reginald Scot's influential work, *The Discoverie of Witchcraft* (1584), which contains an appended 'Discourse upon divels and spirits'. Scot's 'Discourse' paraphrases *A true and just Recorde of the Information, Examination and Confessions of all the Witches . . . at S. Oses . . . Essex* (1582) by one 'W. W.' recounting an investigation by Brian Darcy, JP.[2] Echoing the pamphlet, or perhaps a ballad made from it, Scot writes of

he spirits and shee spirits, Tittie and Tiffin, Suckin and Pidgin, Liard and Robin, &c: his white spirits and blacke spirits, graie spirits and red spirits, divell tode and divell lambe, divels cat and divels dam . . .   (Scot, p. 542)[3]

Scot's account, and W. W.'s, beg to be commercialised, and Middleton's play virtually quotes Scot.

In early modern England, no less than in many societies today, sensational events – accusations of witchcraft, gruesome murders, and the like – were fodder for every available medium (at that time, drama, pamphlet, and ballad), or, as one later contemporary wrote, such events were 'Staged, Book'd, and Balleted'; one witch pamphlet was published specifically to discredit 'the most base and false Ballets, which were sung at the time of our returning from the *Witches* execution'.[4] The similarities among the texts by W. W., Scot, Middleton and the Folio are striking, but they do not indicate any clear sequence of borrowing and indebtedness. Middleton certainly, and Shakespeare very probably, knew Scot's *Discoverie;* each may have known W. W.'s pamphlet; each may have known lost ballads, pamphlets, plays, letters, gossip, or other written or oral sources concerning contemporary witchcraft practices.[5] Moreover, the most

---

[1] For the complete *Witch* text, see Appendix 2, p. 286 below.

[2] Many have speculated that Darcy himself was in some way responsible for the pamphlet; it is reprinted in Rosen, pp. 104–57.

[3] I cite the original (1584) edition's page numbers, as given in Nicholson's 1886 reprint. The similarity among W. W.'s pamphlet, Scot, and Middleton was noted by Malone (IV, 386) and discussed by Nicholson, pp. 544–5. See *Witch*, pp. xi–xii, where W. W. Greg oddly claims that Middleton is unlikely to have known W. W.'s pamphlet because only two copies survive: for popular, ephemeral texts of this sort, the fewer the survivals the more likely it is that copies were read to destruction.

[4] See Thomas Taylor, *The Second Part of the Theatre of Gods Judgments* (title page dated 1642, but bibliographically integrated into the 1648 edition of Thomas Beard's earlier *Theatre of Gods Judgments*), sig. 3K2v, p. 94, and Henry Goodcole, *The wonderfull discoverie of Elizabeth Sawyer* (1621), sig. A3v, respectively. Goodcole later remarks that certain sensational events were 'shamelessly printed and openly sung in a ballad' (sig. D1r, margin), though no ballad of this episode survives. Compare the speed with which similar modern events reach print, film, television, popular songs, and other public representations.

[5] Hyder E. Rollins, *An Analytical Index to the Ballad-entries (1557–1709) in the Stationers' Register, SP* 21 (1924), 1–324, lists two witchcraft episodes which generated both books and ballads: the Chelmsford witches (1589) and the witches of Warboys (1593); see Rollins, pp. 131 and 124, and Rosen, pp. 182–9 and 239–97. For Shakespeare's likely knowledge of Scot, see Bullough, 1, 371–3 (on *A Midsummer's Night's Dream*).

distinctive verbal features linking the surviving documents (the coloured spirits, devilish animals, spirit names) hardly appear in the Folio, particularly since associating
witches' spirits with various colours was a commonplace recalled, for example, by Mistress Quickly's invocation as Queen of Fairies, 'Fairies, black, grey, green, and white, /
You moonshine revellers, and shades of night' (*Wiv.* 5.5.37–8).[1] Furthermore, in
what seems indisputably to be Shakespearean text, the witches complete their brew –
'Cool it with a baboon's blood, / Then the charm is firm and good' (4.1.37–8) –
but the action that follows Middleton's song in *The Witch*, action that Oxford and
Brooke incorporate into *Macbeth*, includes further additions to the cauldron, accompanied by obscene analogies between sexual intercourse and putting in those ingredients. Adding Middleton's witches to Shakespeare's text confuses the audience
and confounds the recipe.[2] These (Middletonian?) witches 'are less successful than
Shakespeare's own arresting presentation because they speak not to Macbeth's fears
but to the audience's . . .'[3]

Thus, while the Folio's laconic '*Blacke Spirits, &c.*' may point to the '*Charme Song*'
of Middleton's *The Witch*, it may equally point to another passage in the same play
(*Witch* lines 185–6) or to an entirely different and so far unknown song made from
similar or identical materials. These possibilities, it seems to me, confound an editor
who seeks a 'snapshot' of a pre-Folio Shakespeare – Middleton *Macbeth*. Rather than
adding suspect text to Folio *Macbeth*, as editors have done or been tempted to do
ever since *The Witch* was rediscovered, I have preferred to reprint Middleton's text in
Appendix 2, p. 286 below, where readers and producers may make what use of it they
choose.

Revision in the Folio

Given the almost inarguable presence of one other author's writing in Folio *Macbeth*,
it is not surprising that passages and even entire scenes have been regarded as non-
Shakespearean. What E. K. Chambers famously called the 'disintegration of Shakespeare' was a peculiarly nineteenth-century phenomenon, and a less intuitive variant
has reappeared in recent claims for revision or adaptation (by Shakespeare or others)
during the early theatrical life of plays subsequently printed in F. Many arguments for
non-Shakespearean writing (e.g. of the Porter's speeches beginning Act 2, Scene 3)
have been rejected as the product of a critic's (or an age's) assumptions or prejudice.[4]

---

[1] The witchcraft pamphlets reprinted by Rosen generally identify familiars by species and colour, e.g. two
toads called Great and Little Browning, p. 70 (Dorset, 1566); two cows called Crow (black and white) and
Donne (red and white), p. 152 (Essex, 1582); two black frogs, Jack and Jill, p. 184 (Chelmsford, 1589);
a thing called Blue, p. 283 (Huntingdon, 1593); Ball, a brown dog, p. 365 (Lancashire, 1613). W. W.'s
pamphlet shows how colour and spirit may be combined casually: '*Tyffen* is like a white lambe' (sig. A3v)
and '*Tyffyn* her white spirit' (sig. c8).

[2] Inga-Stina Ewbank, 'The middle of Middleton' (in Biggs, pp. 158–60), succinctly shows the difference
between Shakespeare's and Middleton's witches.

[3] Mackinnon, p. 69.

[4] In Appendixes E–G of his Warwick Shakespeare edition, E. K. Chambers judiciously reviews the
nineteenth-century debate over various passages and scenes.

Here, I propose one example of possible revision (presumably by Shakespeare, but not necessarily so) and consider two other examples that have the most sustainable claims.

A section of Act 2, Scene 3 (TLN 885–94), begins and ends with identical lines: Macduff says, 'Look to the lady', and so does Banquo; the intervening five lines are Malcolm's and Donaldbain's *sotto voce* worries about who murdered their father and about their own futures.[1] Identical lines in close proximity often mark 'repetition brackets', signs of a copyist's or compositor's inaccurate treatment of added or deleted text. The mechanical details of how such repeated lines might have been included in a printed text are amply documented,[2] and they suggest that someone interrupted the scene's original development to add text (irregularly lined in F) 'covering' Lady Macbeth's business and motivating Malcolm's and Donaldbain's flight.[3] At some point before F's copy arrived at the form the compositors saw, the text might have read (modernised) something like this:

> LADY MACBETH Help me hence, ho!
> MACDUFF   Look to the lady.
> And when we have our naked frailties hid,
> That suffer in exposure, let us meet . . .

Repetition brackets usually occur within the speech of a single character, and F's attribution of the first 'Look to the lady' to Macduff and the second to Banquo is slightly puzzling. If someone thought about Banquo's earlier status as one who had 'no less deserved' (1.4.18)[4] than Macbeth, however, that person might have decided to make Banquo the leading respondent to Duncan's murder. At some point, perhaps when Malcolm's and Donaldbain's speeches were written and their insertion marked (with the link, 'Look to the lady', or some similar phrase), the marking of (new) speech headings went slightly wrong.[5]

---

[1] In the following discussion, I have supposed that the dramatist would avoid repeating the same line in close succession. Another, more theatrical (?), argument would hold that the repeated lines appropriately draw attention to Lady Macbeth's behaviour, a claim similar to the one defending an earlier repetition at TLN 829 and 835/2.3.68, 74 (see Supplementary Note on 2.3.74, p. 257 above). In contrast, my argument assumes a common Shakespearean technique: several things are happening on stage at once, or nearly so (precisely when, for example, does Lady Macbeth exit?), and the printed text inescapably records those simultaneous stage-events as a temporal reading-sequence. Print cannot easily represent simultaneous events on stage: Lady Macbeth does whatever she does when she says 'Help me hence, ho'; some character says, 'Look to the lady'; Malcolm and Donaldbain speak; some character says, 'Look to the lady.'

[2] Robert Kean Turner, 'Revisions and repetition brackets in Fletcher's *A Wife for a Month*', *SB* 36 (1983), 178–90, summarises and develops the work of Wilson (who coined the term 'repetition bracket') and Greg (who showed how 'the brackets may theoretically indicate either addition or omission'). See John Dover Wilson, 'The copy for "Hamlet", 1603', *The Library*, 3rd ser., 9 (1918), 153–85, pp. 173–4, and Greg, pp. 165–6.

[3] See e.g. Halio 2.1.138 n., and Brooke speculates: 'It is possible that these lines were an afterthought, since they first articulate the suspicions that are previously only implicit in the dialogue, and F has similar problems with Malcolm and Donalbain' in the scene's final dialogue (Brooke, App. A, p. 220).

[4] See also 2.1.15–16 n.

[5] Added speeches of the length of Malcolm's and Donaldbain's might be written in the manuscript's margin or more probably on slips pasted to the manuscript (thus producing the lineation oddities of F?). The manuscript (British Library Lansdowne MS. 807) of the so-called *Second Maiden's Tragedy* elaborately illustrates such amendments and additions and is notable for the way the 'link lines' (the cross-references

I propose that if (and when) the speeches by Malcolm and Donaldbain were inserted, 2.3.118–25 was transferred from Macduff, who came from outside the castle, to Banquo, the royal confidant important enough to spend the night inside the castle and the character who now takes charge of the crisis. This hypothetical change supports Banquo's status as near co-equal with Macbeth in the first part of the play and reserves Macduff for the prominence his flight, his family's murder, and his alliance with the English give him in the second part of the play. When the amended text was recopied and/or when it was set in type, none of the changes of speakers and all of the additions of speeches were made, producing the Folio text.

At the end of Act 3, Scene 4 (TLN 1410 ff.), Macbeth worries about Macduff's absence from the banquet and asserts he 'will send' to learn the reason. In Act 3, Scene 6, an anonymous Lord tells Lennox that Macduff 'Is gone' to 'the English court' (3.6.30, 26) seeking military assistance, Lennox and the Lord acknowledge that Macbeth 'sent . . . to Macduff', the Lord relates how Macduff insulted Macbeth's messenger (41–4), and Lennox hopes that an angel will speed Macduff's message to Edward (46–8).'[1]

All these matters are treated as past and known, but in Act 4, Scene 1, the 'galloping of horse' (4.1.139) Macbeth hears is the horses of messengers come to tell him that Macduff 'is fled to England' (141), news he greets perhaps with incredulity, perhaps with anger, certainly with surprise: 'Fled to England?' Macbeth determines upon more sudden and violent responses henceforth: 'From this moment, / The very firstlings of my heart shall be / The firstlings of my hand' (145–7). Act 3, Scene 6, also includes smaller puzzles: one popular emendation not accepted here makes F's apparent reference to the English King Edward, 'their king' (3.6.38), into a reference to King Macbeth (Hanmer and most other editors: 'the king'),[2] but nothing can be done to mitigate the abruptness with which Lennox introduces Macbeth and the anecdote of the 'cloudy messenger' whom Macduff rejects: 'Sent he to Macduff?' (40), where 'he' must be King Macbeth, not King Edward.

In the unlikely event of an audience paying minute attention to problems of this sort, the matter might just be resolved by a timetable:

1. Macbeth 'sends' to Macduff to demand a reason for his absence in Act 3, Scene 4.
2. The messenger is rebuffed.
3. Macduff starts for England; some Scottish courtiers, but not Macbeth, know that fact.
4. Reassured by the prophecies of Act 4, Scene 1, Macbeth first decides he has nothing to fear from Macduff (4.1.81) and then determines to kill him (83).

telling a reader, copyist, or compositor where to add material) do not exactly duplicate the main text. See Anne Lancashire (ed.), *The Second Maiden's Tragedy*, 1978, and Eric Rasmussen, 'Shakespeare's hand in *The Second Maiden's Tragedy*', *SQ* 40 (1989), 1–26.

[1] The main modern treatments of the apparent confusions at the end of Act 3 and the beginning of Act 4 are Muir, p. xxxiv (compare Muir's revised 9th Arden edition, 1962, pp. xxxiv–xxxv) and Brooke, pp. 51–3. The earliest comment I have found on the narrative and temporal problem here appears in 'Christopher North' [i.e. John Wilson], 'Dies Boreales. No. V', *Blackwood's Edinburgh Magazine* 66 (November 1849), 649–53. See also, and more generally, Brian Richardson, '"Hours dreadful and things strange": inversions of chronology and causality in *Macbeth*', *PQ* 68 (1989), 283–94.

[2] The confusion of abbreviated 'the' and 'their' would have been easy in contemporary (Secretary) hand, since each might consist of *y* followed by a single suspended symbol.

5. Lennox (who knew of Macduff's flight in Act 3, Scene 6) reports that messengers have arrived to say that Macduff 'is fled to England' (4.1.141).
6. Macbeth decides to attack Macduff's castle, family, and retainers (4.1.149–52).

A partial solution to these narrative inconsistencies would be to reverse the order of Act 3, Scene 6, and Act 4, Scene 1, but whatever further revision has taken place makes that switch unsatisfactory, since Lennox's speeches (3.6.40–50 and 4.1.140–1) in the two scenes would remain realistically inconsistent.[1] A reversal of F's order redistributes, but does not solve, the inconsistencies, and has the further liability of juxtaposing the play's final witch-scenes (3.5 and 4.1 in F).[2]

The original sequence, if it was different, may have attributed one or the other of Lennox's speeches to a different character, as Muir suggests (p. xxxiv). The speeches assigned to 'Lennox' throughout *Macbeth* are puzzling: in Act 3, Scene 4, the character appears a courteous, if confused, guest at his new king's banquet; in Act 3, Scene 6, he seems an opponent of Macbeth, as he does in Act 5, Scene 2; in Act 2, Scene 3, and Act 4, Scene 1, he seems to support, or at least to accept, King Macbeth. There are various possible explanations: consistent characterisation was not important to the dramatist(s); Lennox's speeches may have been incorrectly identified; a revision may not have been carried through completely; 'Lennox' may have been chosen as chorus in Act 3, Scene 6; 'Lennox' is a vague type-designation meant to be clarified and rationalised in performance.[3]

Even granting that the time references of Act 3's final three scenes and of Act 4, Scene 1, may be neither precise nor clear, and granting that the timetable above makes 'Lennox' markedly inconsistent (or the victim of incomplete revision), an audience of narrative and dramatic accountants is hard to imagine. And in fact such an audience has not been imagined by producers who, since before Davenant (see p. 61 above), have regularly cut, trimmed, or adapted the Folio's otherwise excellent Act 3, Scene 6. The reason is obvious: rationalised or not, Act 3, Scene 6, destroys the theatrical effect of time (and Macduff) overtaking Macbeth's schemes and of Macbeth's appallingly violent reaction in Act 4, Scenes 1 and 2.

Act 4, Scene 3, lines 139–61 (TLN 1968–91), Malcolm's dialogue with the doctor and his explanation of the King's Evil, have been regarded as an interpolation by Shakespeare or another author into a pre-existing text,[4] and it is true that Macduff's ''Tis hard to reconcile' (4.3.139) makes a pentameter line with his 'See who comes here' (161). Linked or 'linkable' part-lines of this sort have been claimed as signs

---

[1] According to Muir (p. xxxiv), the reversal was first suggested by G. Crosse, 'Spurious passages in *Macbeth*', *N&Q* 90 (1898), 321–2, but Ludvig Josephson's 1880 Stockholm production apparently used (with cuts?) the Folio's scenes in the sequence 4.1, 3.5, 3.6; see Ann Fridén, '*Macbeth*' *in the Swedish Theatre 1838–1986*, 1986, p. 53.

[2] The banquet scene (3.4) and the cauldron scene (4.1) would, however, not adjoin as Muir (p. xxxiv) claims.

[3] Further, at some point in *Macbeth*'s composition or revision the sequence of events may have been contaminated by memories of Holinshed's account, where Macduff's flight occurs after his family's slaughter (*Scotland*, pp. 174b–175a).

[4] See Clarendon, pp. x–xi; NS, pp. xxxii–xxxiii; and the vigorous objections of Nevill Coghill, '*Macbeth* at the Globe, 1606–1616 (?): three questions', in Joseph G. Price (ed.), *The Triple Bond*, 1975, p. 231. The passage is frequently cut in performance.

of revision,[1] and it is certainly arguable that F does not resolve Macduff's justified puzzlement at Malcolm's earlier words and behaviour. A further objection to this passage, and one not hitherto considered, is the description of the entering character as a *Doctor* (4.3.139 SD) evidently of medicine, whereas his Scottish counterpart in Act 5, Scene 1, is more specifically identified as *a Doctor of Physicke* (TLN 2093). The distinction may be fortuitous,[2] but the slacker terminology of Act 4, Scene 3, might point to a revising author's haste or inattention. There are, however, strong dramatic arguments for the passage's value as a development of the contrast between good and bad kingship represented in Malcolm's and Macduff's earlier conversation: Edward the saintly physician–doctor of his kingdom versus Macbeth the demonic murderer of his, a monarch haplessly asking his doctor-figure to 'cast / The water of my land' (5.3.51–2).[3]

---

[1] See e.g. W. A. Wright (ed.), *King John*, 1866, 3.4.68n., where lines 21–67 are considered an interpolation because the preceding and following half-lines make a pentameter. Note also that what may be 'repetition brackets' appear in this passage: 'Bind up those tresses' and 'Bind up your hairs.'

[2] See 5.1.0 SD n. on the distinction between a medical and a clerical 'doctor'. The distinction affects costuming and is significant in the demonic context of Act 5, Scene 1.

[3] Muir appropriately cites L. C. Knights, *Explorations*, 1946, p. 31, and G. W. Knight, *Wheel of Fire*, 1949, p. 148, in defence of the passage.

APPENDIX 1: CASTING *MACBETH*

Modern accounts of acting styles and production practices in Shakespeare's theatre are largely guesswork. Contemporary evidence states that Richard Burbage first played Shakespeare's Richard III, Hamlet, Othello, and Lear for the Lord Chamberlain's and later the King's Men as well as many other important rôles (see Edwin Nungezer, *A Dictionary of Actors*, 1929). It seems likely that Burbage also originated Macbeth. Jacobeans extolled Burbage for his naturalism and pathos in tragic rôles, but all such accounts employ unknowable standards and relative conventions. As acting styles and conventions in the silent and talking cinema show, one period's performance of genius becomes for another audience (in ten, or twenty, or fifty years) an overblown or under-played failure.

We may guess that the King's Men's principal comic played the Porter (today often a nearly unperformable part), and that actor was probably Robert Armin, whose known rôles and writings suggest he was an actor who did 'not talk *with* but [was] heard *by* his audience . . . [an actor who] talks to his own alter ego rather than to the audience' (David Wiles, *Shakespeare's Clown: Actor and Text in the Elizabethan Playhouse*, 1987, pp. 151, 161), just as the Porter invents conversation-partners and stipulates the audience's reaction in Act 2, Scene 3, and just as the actor playing Falstaff might in his honour-catechism (*1H4* 5.1.129 ff.3). For similar casting reasons, 'the Murderers were [in the eighteenth century] the proscriptive property of the low comedians' (William Archer and Robert W. Lowe, ' "Macbeth" on the stage', *English Illustrated Magazine* (December 1888), 239).

Bartholomeusz (pp. 10–12) guesses that John Rice, a young actor of genius according to contemporary reports, played Lady Macbeth, but the early casts and how they filled their rôles cannot be convincingly recovered. Like several other Shakespearean heroines (Cleopatra and Volumnia in particular), Lady Macbeth proves a controversial case, and scholars have claimed that an adult male, not a pre-pubescent boy, played such rôles; for contrasting views, see G. E. Bentley, *The Profession of Player in Shakespeare's Time, 1590–1642*, 1984, pp. 113–14, and Carol Chillington Rutter (ed.), *Documents of the Rose Playhouse*, 1984, pp. 224–5.

While the list of speaking and silent characters is long, *Macbeth* was probably per-formed in Shakespeare's theatre with a relatively small number of actors, several of whom 'doubled' or even 'tripled' parts – that is, one actor played two or three speaking or silent rôles. Believing that the King's Men usually cast sixteen adult men and a variable number of boy-actors, David Bradley finds that the company had run out of available adult men in early productions of Act 5, Scene 3: 'the servant with the goose-look in *Macbeth* [5.3.12] must certainly be a boy, as Macbeth calls him, for although the term is sometimes used to mean "coward", all sixteen men in the cast, apart from the two attendants who enter with Macbeth, are fully occupied elsewhere, preparing to enter as Malcolm's soldiers' (*From Text to Performance in the Elizabethan Theatre*, 1992, p. 39). A fine ensemble production of *Macbeth*, Trevor Nunn's Royal Shakespeare Company version with Judi Dench and Ian McKellen in 1976–8, employed only some fourteen actors (see p. 82 above), doubling Ian McDiarmid as Ross and the Porter and Tim Brierley as Donaldbain and Seyton (who also appeared in numerous Folio 'Messenger' rôles, as the actor of 'Seyton' had since Davenant's and Garrick's texts), for instance. 'Political' interpretations often double Ross: Roman Polanski's film (1971) made Ross both the Third Murderer of Act 3, Scene 3, and at least an accomplice of the murderers of Lady Macduff in Act 4, Scene 2. Lennox is also susceptible to such thematic, 'Machiavellian' doublings. Productions using a larger company will none the less often double a few rôles: Peter Hall's 1967 RSC production doubled Jeffery Dench as the Old Man of Act 2, Scene 4, and the Scottish Doctor of Act 5, Scene 1, and Daniel Moynihan as the Captain (or 'Sergeant') of Act 1, Scene 2, and the Lord of Act 3, Scene 6. Twentieth-century productions – for example, Glen Byam Shaw's (Stratford, 1955) – doubled Duncan and the Scottish Doctor very effectively; the 5 November 1928 London revival of Barry Jackson's modern-dress production (originally Birmingham Repertory) doubled Duncan with First Murderer, Banquo with the Scottish Doctor, and the latter doubling was repeated in Andrew Leigh's Old Vic (London) production the next year. The play's two principal female rôles, Lady Macbeth and Lady Macduff, are very rarely doubled. Nunn's production doubled Lady Macduff and one of the witches, and Braham Murray's Royal Exchange (Manchester) production set in a Nazi death camp more provocatively doubled Lady Macbeth (Frances Barber) and one of the witches 'in white shifts' (see *North West Times*, 4 November 1988, and Jeremy Kingston, *The Times*, 5 November 1988); Andy Hines's Bristol Theatre Royal production included what are probably Thomas Middleton's lines for Hecate and doubled the part with that of Lady Macduff (see B. A. Young, *Financial Times*, 10 November 1987). Lavish casts have one main advantage in Act 5: the series of short scenes documenting the Anglo-Scottish attack on Macbeth may demonstrate – through an ever-fuller stage – the volume of right's recoil upon wrong.

How old are Lord and Lady Macbeth? The Folio text gives little explicit help with this important decision for the producer. In his film, Polanski cast young actors as the couple and thereby emphasised both their naïveté and their sensuality, but middle-aged sensuality also has a powerful appeal (compare *Antony and Cleopatra*), and one Hungarian production, at least, made Lady Macbeth distinctly older than her husband and Macbeth consequently 'pliable' (Leiter, p. 386). Less obviously, the represented age of a relatively minor character, Lennox (who claims a 'young remembrance' (2.3.54)), can strongly influence the audience's experience.

When a character appears or does not appear on stage subtly affects the audience's responses: Macduff, for instance, first appears in Act 2, Scene 3, very late for so important a figure; Lady Macbeth appears often and crucially in the first three acts (1.5, 1.6, 1.7, 2.2, 2.3, 3.1, 3.2, 3.4) and then not again and finally until Act 5, Scene 1. Her continued presence and then her long absence measure a changing private as well as a changing public relation, both that of wife and husband and that of Lord/ King

Macbeth with Scotland and his heart. This gap poses serious problems for the actor, and many productions prepare for the sleepwalking scene (Act 5, Scene 1) by having Lady Macbeth show incipient signs of mental or physical weakness at the end of the banquet scene (Act 3, Scene 4); in many productions, too, Macbeth explicitly dismisses her – with the possibly neutral line, 'While then, God be with you' (3.1.45) – before he meets the Murderers, thus indicating her diminished part in Macbeth's plans. Macbeth disappears after Act 4, Scene 1, when about two-thirds of the play's lines have been spoken, and returns in Act 5, Scene 3, when the audience has witnessed a further fifth of the play's dialogue. While Macbeth is absent, the Anglo-Scottish political and military alliance gathers against him. (This absence is also a customary Shakespearean 'rest' for the principal tragic actor, who needs to gather energy for the play's conclusion.)

Anthony Brennan's statistics in *Onstage and Offstage Worlds in Shakespeare's Plays* (1989) confirm many common impressions about the relative importance of Macbeth and Lady Macbeth compared with major rôles in some of Shakespeare's other tragedies. Macbeth takes up a great deal of his eponymous play: he speaks more than 30 per cent of the play's lines and is on stage for more than half the dialogue (Brennan, p. 97). Macbeth's rôle accounts for a higher percentage of his play's lines than the rôle of any other Shakespearean tragic character except (by tiny margins) the Prince in *Hamlet* and Iago in *Othello*. Only Hamlet, Titus, Romeo and Juliet, Richard II and Bolingbroke, Othello and Iago slightly outpoint Macbeth in the second category, presence on stage. These same statistics, however, do not confirm what might be another common impression. Measured in lines of dialogue, Lady Macbeth has a small part, only about 10 per cent of the play's spoken lines (hers is the second-largest part in *Macbeth*, but smaller than Juliet's in *Romeo and Juliet*, or Claudius's in *Hamlet*, and about the size of Desdemona's in *Othello*), though she is on stage for more than a quarter of the play's spoken lines (Brennan, p. 97). She last appears with her husband (Act 3, Scene 4) after only slightly more than half the play's lines have been spoken (Brennan, p. 17). Banquo, as a living figure and as a ghost, appears in nearly a third of the play's scenes, almost the equal of the seemingly ubiquitous Ross, who speaks more lines.

Treating part-lines as full lines and using this edition's lineation and attribution of speeches, here are some line-counts (compiled by Michael Cohen) for various rôles:

First Witch: 61 lines
Duncan: 69 lines
Malcolm: 206 lines
Lennox: 64 lines
Ross: 134 lines
Macbeth: 700 lines
Banquo: 112 lines
Lady Macbeth: 254 lines
Porter: 29 lines
Macduff: 174 lines
Lady Macduff: 42 lines
Siward: 30 lines

A modern, hypothetical Jacobean casting of *Macbeth* in T. J. King, *Casting Shakespeare's Plays*, 1992, finds that 'Nine men can play twelve principal male rôles, and eight boys play seven principal female rôles and Macduff's Son' (p. 91), and Bradley, *From Text to Performance*, p. 237, finds a cast of sixteen adults and four to eight boys 'probable'.

APPENDIX 2: ADDITIONAL TEXT AND MUSIC

As the Textual Analysis argues (pp. 271–9 above), *Macbeth* has been revised, adapted, and otherwise changed from very early in the play's theatrical existence. Spectacle – especially the weïrd sisters and their appearance, and the action, songs and dances associated with them – has been the primary focus of change (see '*Macbeth* in performance', pp. 57–84 above). Whatever changes we may guess the Folio records, the first documented evidence of adaptation or revision appears in Q1673, where the text mainly, though not exclusively, follows the Folio but has certain substantial additions, all connected with the sisters.

At the end of *Macbeth* Act 2, Scene 2, after 'Wake *Duncan* with thy knocking:/I would thou could'st. *Exeunt.*' (TLN 739–40), which Q1673 treats as a single line, the quarto prints (sig. D2):

> *Enter Witches, and Sing.*
> 1. *Speak, Sister, is the Deed done?*
> 2. *Long ago, long ago.*
> *Above twelve Glasses since are run.*
> 1. *Ill Deeds are seldome slow.*
> *Nor single following Crimes on former wait*
> *The worst of Creatures fastest propagate.*
> *Many more murders must this one ensue,*
> *As if in Death were propagation too.*
> *He will, he shall, he must spill much more blood,*
> *And become worse to make his Title good.*
> *Now let's Dance. Agreed, agreed, agreed.*
> Chorus. *We should rejoyce when good Kings bleed.*
> *When Cattle dye, about we go,*
> *What then, when Monarchs perish, should we do?*
> *We should, &c.*

At the end of *Macbeth* Act 2, Scene 3, after '*Exeunt.*' (TLN 922), the quarto prints (sig. D4v):

> *Enter Witches, Dance and Sing.*
> *Let's have a Dance upon the Heath,*
> *We gain more Life by* Duncan's *Death.*
> *Sometimes like brinded Cats we shew,*
> *Having no musick but our mew.*
> *Sometimes we Dance in some Old Mill,*
> *Upon the Hopper, Stones, and Wheel,*
> *To some Old Saw, or bardish Rhime,*
> *Where still the Mill-Clack does keep time.*
> *Sometime about a hollow Tree*

A Round, a Round, a Round Dance we:
Thither the chirping Critick comes,
And Beetles singing drowsie hums.
Sometimes we Dance o're Fens and Furrs,
To howls of Wolves, and barks of Currs.
And when with none of these we meet,
We Dance to the Ecchoes of our Feet.

                                                                                    [*Exeunt.*]

At the conclusion of *Macbeth* Act 3, Scene 5, after 'Sits in a Foggy cloud, and stayes
for me.' (TLN 1466), Q1673 (sigs. F3v–F4r) replaces '*Sing within. Come away, come away,*
&c.' (TLN 1467) with song and action apparently derived from Thomas Middleton's
The Witch (see Textual Analysis, pp. 272–3 above):

Sing within. 1 *Come away* Heccat, Heccat, *Oh, come away;*
              2 *I come, I come, with all the speed I may,*
                I come, I come, with all the speed I may.
              1 *Where's* Stadling?
              3 *Here.*
              1 *Where's* Puckle?
              4 *Here*; and *Hopper* too, *and* Helway *too;*
              1 *We want but you, we want but you.*
                Come away, make up the 'count
                I will but noint, and then I mount
                I will, &c.
              1 *Here comes one, it is*
                To fetch his due, a kiss,
                I [Ay] *A Cull, sip of blood;*
                And why thou stayst so long, I muse,
                Since the Aire's so sweet and good;
                O art thou come! What News?
[sig. F4r]   2 *All goes fair for our delight,*
                Either come, or else refuse,
                Now I am furnish'd for the flight,
                Now I go, now I flie.
                Malkin *my sweet spirit and I.*
              3. *Oh what a dainty Pleasure's this,*
                To sail i'th' Air,
                While the Moon shines fair,
                To sing, to toy and kiss,
                Over Woods, high Rocks and Mountains,
                Over misty Hills and Fountains,
                Over Steeples, Towres and Turrets,
                We flie by night 'mongst Troops of spirits.
              Cho. *No Ring of Bells to our ears sounds,*
                No Howls of Wolves, nor Yelps of Hounds,
                No, nor the Noise of Waters breach,
                Nor Cannons Throats our height can reach.

Q1673 then ends the action, as the Folio does (TLN 1468–9), with

1 Come let's make hast, shee'l soone be
Backe againe.   *Exeunt*

The quarto of 1673, that is, places non-Folio text and action (some of it derived from *Witch*) at, respectively, the conclusions of Folio *Macbeth* Act 2, Scene 2, Act 2, Scene 3, and Act 3, Scene 5.

After the murder of Duncan, Davenant's adaptation, which exists in an incomplete early manuscript (see Christopher Spencer, *Davenant's 'Macbeth' from the Yale Manuscript*, 1961) and a quarto (1674), brings Macduff and Lady Macduff together on 'An Heath' to witness (quarto, pp. 26–7), abruptly, versions of 'Speak, Sister. . . ' (headed '*First Song by Witches*') and then 'Let's have a dance' (headed '*Second Song*'), where there is an added quatrain:

> At the night-Raven's dismal voice,
> Whilst others tremble, we rejoyce;
> And nimbly, nimbly dance we still
> To th'ecchoes from an hollow Hill.

Davenant's scene ends with dialogue in which Macduff questions the sisters about his future as Macbeth and Banquo had earlier about theirs. Davenant then reverses *Macbeth* Act 3, Scenes 5 and 6, and extends (pp. 44–5) with minor variants the Folio's Act 3, Scene 5, as Q1673 had done, returning to the Folio text at the end of the scene, adding:

> 2. But whilst she moves through the foggy Air,
>   Let's to the Cave and our dire Charms prepare.

Unlike Q1673, which repeats the Folio's laconic SD at 4.1.43 (TLN 1571: '*Musicke and a Song. Blacke Spirits, &c.*'), Davenant's text expands 'Black spirits' with a version of lines apparently from Middleton's *The Witch*, where there are two possible 'sources' (see Textual Analysis, pp. 273–4 above). The shorter is reprinted in the Textual Analysis (p. 274); the longer, headed '*A Charme Song: about a Vessell.*', follows:

> *Black Spiritts, and white: Red Spiritts, and Gray,*
> *Mingle, Mingle, Mingle, you that mingle may.*
> *Titty, Tiffin: keepe it stiff in*
> *Fire-Drake, Puckey, Make it Luckey.*
> *Liand, Robin, you must bob in*
> *Round, a-round, a-round, about, about*
> *All ill come running-in, all Good keepe-out.*
> *1. witch heeres the Blood of a Bat.*
> *Hec [ate]. Put in that: oh put in that.*
> *2. heer's Libbards Bane*
> *Hec [ate]. Put-in againe*
> *1. the Iuice of Toad: the Oile of Adder*
> *2. those will make the yonker madder.*
> *Hec [ate]. Put in: ther's all, and rid the Stench.*
> *Fire [stone]. nay heeres three ounces of the red-haired wench.*
> *all Round: around: around &c:/.*
>
> (*Witch* lines 1999–2014; compare Davenant, 1674, p. 47)

Along with *The Witch* and Davenant's slight reworking of its lines, several musical scores with slightly variant texts of 'Come away, come away' have survived; they are elaborately collated in Brooke, as are the available versions – *The Witch*, Davenant's manuscript, and the quarto of 1674 – of 'Black spirits and white'.

Just how and by whom the songs of the revised *Macbeth* may have been set to music before the famous Matthew Locke settings for Davenant's version is unclear. The best concise treatment of the seventeenth-century musical settings appears in Bryan N. S. Gooch *et al.*, *A Shakespeare Music Catalogue*, 5 vols., 1991, 11, 705–803; as the authors advise (11, 739), 'the chronology of this tradition can best be followed if [the relevant *Macbeth*] entries are read in the following order: 6925, 7013, 6971, 7101, and 6705'. For musical scores, John H. Long, *Shakespeare's Use of Music: The Histories and Tragedies*, 1971, pp. 193–5 and 199, offers the following possibilities:

'Come away, come away', probably by Robert Johnson, in John H. Long's transcription from New York Public Library Drexel MS. 4175

'First Witches Dance', possibly by Robert Johnson, in John H. Long's transcription from Robert Dowland, *Varietie of Lute-Lessons* (1610)

APPENDIX 3: RELINEATION OF THE FOLIO

With a few exceptions noted below, this appendix records places where F's lineation has been changed; using the customary short titles (see the List of Abbreviations, pp. xi–xii above), each entry lists the source or sources (if more than one editor's relineation has been adopted in a single, continuous passage) of the relineation, F's line-division (represented by the terminal word of each line and an oblique bar to mark the line end), and any other plausible relineation. (For clarity, some notes cite more than a line's last word.) Since neither spelling nor punctuation is at stake here, quotations from F are modernised, readings from other editions are silently normalised as they are in the collation, and punctuation is omitted unless required for clarity. Centred SDs which form a separate line in F are omitted. On a few occasions, the notes record places where F has been retained, followed by a rejected change. Not recorded here are uncontroversial impositions of the modern typographical convention that when two or more speakers share a pentameter line, text should be indented to show that fact (see Textual Analysis, pp. 267–8 above). Also not recorded are the places where a metrically regular line was too long to fit into the space available in the Folio's rather narrow two-column format and where, therefore, the compositors had to 'turn over' one or more words and (as they quite often did) happened to capitalise the first word of the turned-over text, making it appear to be a new verse line; the note to 3.1.48–52 records what may be an exception to this practice. The few relineations involving changes in SHs are recorded in the collation.

[1.2]
35 *Oxford; as two lines* eagles / . . . lion F
41–2 *Oxford;* Golgotha / . . . faint F
46–7 *Hanmer; as three lines* eyes / . . . strange./ . . . king. F
58–9 *Brooke; as three lines* happiness / . . . king/ . . . composition F
[1.3]
4 *Pope; as two lines* munched / Give . . . I F
76 *Pope; as two lines* greeting / . . . you. F
80 *Capell; as two lines* wind. / . . . stayed. F
106–7 *Capell; as three lines* lives / . . . robes / . . . yet F
130–1 *Rowe;* good. / . . . success F
139–41 *Pope; as four lines* man / . . . surmise / . . . not / . . . rapt F
142 *Rowe; as two lines* king / . . . me F
148–55 *Pope;* favour / . . . forgotten / . . . registered / . . . leaf / . . . them / . . . upon / . . . time / . . . speak / . . . other / . . . gladly / . . . enough / . . . friends F

[1.4]

1–8 *Capell (lines 1–2); Pope (lines 2–8);* Cawdor / . . . returned / . . . back / . . . die / . . . he / . . . pardon / . . . repentance / . . . him / . . . died F

23–7 *Pope;* itself / . . . duties / . . . state / . . . should / . . . love / . . . honour / . . . hither F

[1.5]

20–1 *Pope; as three lines* win / . . . cries / . . . it F

[1.6]

1–2 *Rowe;* seat / . . . itself F

11–12 *Brooke;* hostess / . . . trouble F

18–21 *Pope;* broad / . . . house / . . . dignities / . . . hermits F

[2.1]

4 *Rowe; as two lines* sword: / . . . heaven F

7–9 *Rowe; as three lines* sleep / . . . thoughts / . . . repose F

9–11 *Hanmer;* there / . . . friend F

13–14 F; *divided* pleasure and / Sent *Cam.*

16–17 *Pope; as three lines* hostess / . . . content / . . . unprepared F

25–6 *Rowe;* consent / . . . you F

[2.2]

2–6 *Rowe;* fire / . . . shrieked / . . . good-night / . . . open / . . . charge / . . . possets F

13–14 *Rowe;* done't / . . . husband? / . . . deed / . . . noise F

19–20 F; *as one line Brooke; as two lines* . . . descended? / Ay. *Cam. See Textual Analysis,* pp. 252–3 *above*

21–2 F; *as two lines* Hark / . . . Donaldbain *Steevens³*

25–8 *Rowe;* sleep / . . . other / . . . prayers / . . . sleep / . . . together F

36 *Pope;* throat / . . . thought F

68–9 *Pope;* white. *Knock* / . . . entry / . . . chamber F

72 *Pope;* unattended. *Knock* / . . . knocking F

75–7 *Pope;* thoughts / . . . deed, *Knock* / . . . self / . . . knocking / . . . could'st. *Exeunt* F

[2.3]

20–1 *As prose Johnson; as verse* cock / . . . things. F

40 *Steevens³; as two lines* hour / . . . to him F

41–3 *As prose Brooke;* you / . . . one / . . . pain / . . . door / . . . service F; *as verse* you / . . . one / . . . call / . . . service *Cam. See Commentary*

44–5 F; *as one line Steevens³*

46–8 *Rowe;* unruly / . . . down, / . . . air / . . . death F

51–3 *Hanmer; as four lines* time / . . . night / . . . feverous / . . . shake F

55–7 F; it / . . . heart / . . . thee *Rowe;* it / . . . heart / . . . matter *Steevens³*

62–4 F; *as two lines* life / . . . majesty? *Cam. See Commentary*

74–6 *Theobald;* horror. Ring the bell. / . . . business / . . . parley / . . . Speak, speak / . . . lady F; trumpet / . . . house / . . . lady *Brooke*

79–80 *Theobald; as three lines* fell / . . . murdered / . . . alas F

97–8 F; *as three lines* pillows / . . . life / . . . them *Steevens³*

113–17 *Brooke;* tongues / . . . ours / . . . here / . . . hole / . . . away / . . . brewed
/ . . . sorrow / . . . motion F
128–34 *Rowe;* do / . . . them / . . . office / . . . easy / . . . England / . . . I / . . . safer
/ . . . smiles / . . . bloody F
[2.4]
14 *Pope; as two lines* horses / . . . certain F
19–20 *Pope; as three lines* so / . . . upon't / . . . Macduff F
32–3 *Brooke; as three lines* invested / . . . body / . . . Colmkill F
[3.1]
36–7 *Pope; as three lines* horse / . . . night / . . . you F
44–5 *Theobald; as three lines* welcome / . . . alone / . . . you F
48–52 *Capell;* palace /Gate / . . . us / . . . thus / . . . deep / . . . that F
73 *Pope; as two lines* utterance / . . . there F
77–90 *As prose Brooke; as verse* then / . . . speeches / . . . past / . . . fortune / . . . self
/ . . . conference / . . . you / . . . crossed / . . . them / . . . might / . . . crazed / . . .
Banquo / . . . us / . . . so / . . . now / . . . meeting / . . . predominant / . . . go / . . .
man / . . . hand / . . . beggared / . . . forever / . . . liege F*; as verse* now / . . . Know
/ . . . you / . . . been / . . . you / . . . you / . . . instruments / . . . might / . . . crazed
/ . . . us / . . . now / . . . find / . . . nature / . . . gospelled / . . . issue / . . . grave / . . .
liege *Rowe. See Commentary*
109–10 *Steevens³; as three lines* do / . . . world / . . . another F
113–14 *Rowe;* on't / . . . enemy / . . . lord F
127 *Pope; as two lines* you / . . . most F
[3.2]
16 *Pope; as two lines* disjoint / . . . suffer F
22 *Rowe; as two lines* ecstasy / . . . grave F
27–33 *Singer;* on / . . . looks / . . . tonight / . . . you / . . . Banquo / . . . tongue / . . .
lave / . . . streams F
43–4 *Pope; as three lines* peal / . . . note / . . . done F
50–1 F*; crow / . . .* wood *Rowe. See Commentary*
[3.3]
9–10 *Pope; as two lines* he / . . . expectation F
19–21 F*; as two lines* fly, fly fly / . . . slave *Hanmer*
22 *Steevens³; as two lines* light / . . . way F
24 *Pope; as two lines* lost / . . . affair F
[3.4]
1–6 *As prose Brooke; as verse* down / . . . welcome / . . . majesty / . . . society / . . .
host / . . . time / . . . welcome F*;* last / . . . majesty (*remainder as* F) *Capell*
16–17 F*; as two lines* cut / . . . cut-throats *Brooke*
20 *Collier; as two lines* sir / . . . scaped F
21 *Pope; as two lines* again / . . . perfect F
48 *Capell; as two lines* lord / . . . highness F
69 *Capell; as two lines* there / . . . you F
109–10 *Capell; as three lines* mirth / . . . disorder / . . . be F

122 *Rowe; as two lines* say / . . . blood F

[3.5]

36 *Pope; as two lines* be / . . . again F

[3.6]

1 *Rowe; as two lines* speeches / . . . thoughts F

[4.1]

70 *Rowe; as two lines* Macbeth /Beware Macduff F

78 *Rowe; as two lines* resolute / . . . scorn F

85–6 *Rowe; as two lines* thunder / . . . king F

132 *Rowe; as two lines* Gone / . . . hour F

[4.2]

27 *Oxford; as two lines* is / . . . fatherless F

34–50 *As prose Brooke; as verse* bird / . . . lime / . . . gin / . . . mother / . . . for / . . . saying / . . . dead / . . . father / . . . husband / . . . market / . . . again / . . . wit / . . . thee / . . . mother / . . . was / . . . traitor / . . . lies / . . . so / . . . traitor / . . . hanged F

57–8 *As prose Pope; as verse* monkey / . . . father F

76–7 *Oxford; as four lines* harm / . . . faces / . . . *Murderers* / . . . husband F

[4.3]

17–18 *Steevens*³; . . . God / . . . treacherous / . . . is F

25 *Rowe;* there / . . . doubts F

102–3 *Pope; as one line* F

114 *Steevens*³*; as two lines* here / . . . passion F

139–40 *Muir; as three lines* reconcile / . . . forth / . . . you F

175–6 *Theobald; as three lines* sicken / . . . true / . . . grief F

213–15 *Capell; as five lines* children too / . . . found / . . . killed too / . . . said / . . . comforted F

[5.1]

23 *Pope; as two lines* now / . . . hands F

39 *Pope; as two lines* go to / . . . not F

43 *Pope; as two lines* hand /O, O, O. F

[5.6]

1 *Rowe; as two lines* enough / . . . down F

[5.9]

21 *Rowe; as two lines* art / . . . stands F

READING LIST

This list includes details of certain books and articles which may serve as a guide to those who wish to undertake a further study of the play.

Adam, R. J. 'The real Macbeth: King of Scots, 1040–54', *History Today* 7 (1957), 381–7

Adelman, Janet. *Suffocating Mothers: Fantasies of Maternal Origin in Shakespeare's Plays, 'Hamlet' to 'The Tempest'*, 1992

Anglo, Sydney (ed.). *The Damned Art: Essays in the Literature of Witchcraft*, 1977

Bartholomeusz, Dennis. *'Macbeth' and the Players*, 1969

Beale, Simon Russell. 'Macbeth' in Michael Dobson (ed.), *Performing Shakespeare's Tragedies Today: The Actor's Perspective*, 2006, pp. 107–18

Booth, Stephen. *'King Lear', 'Macbeth', Indefinition, and Tragedy*, 1983

Bradley, A. C. *Shakespearean Tragedy*, 1904

Brooks, Cleanth. *The Well Wrought Urn*, 1947

Brown, John Russell (ed.). *Focus on 'Macbeth'*, 1982

Bushnell, Rebecca W. *'King Lear' and 'Macbeth', 1674–1995: An Annotated Bibliography of Shakespeare Studies*, Pegasus Shakespeare Bibliographies, 1996

Calderwood, James L. *If It Were Done: 'Macbeth' and Tragic Action*, 1986

Campbell, L. B. *Shakespeare's Tragic Heroes: Slaves of Passion*, 1930

Campbell, O. J. 'Shakespeare and the "New Critics" ', in *Adams Memorial Studies*, ed. James G. McManaway *et al.*, 1948, pp. 81–96

Carroll, William C. (ed.). *'Macbeth': Texts and Contexts*, 1999

Charlton, H. B. *Shakespearian Tragedy*, 1948

Clark, Stuart. 'Inversion, misrule and the meaning of witchcraft', *Past and Present* 87 (May 1980), 98–127

Crosse, Gordon. *Shakespearean Playgoing 1890–1952*, 1953

De Grazia, Margreta and Stanley Wells (eds.). *The Cambridge Companion to Shakespeare*, 2001

De Quincey, Thomas. 'On the knocking at the gate in *Macbeth*', in *The Collected Writings of Thomas De Quincey*, ed. David Masson, 14 vols., 1889–90, x, 389–95

Dollimore, Jonathan. *Radical Tragedy: Religion, Ideology and Power in the Drama of Shakespeare and his Contemporaries* (1984), 2nd edn, 1989

Eagleton, Terry. *William Shakespeare*, 1986

Edwards, Philip, *et al.* (eds.). *Shakespeare's Styles: Essays in Honour of Kenneth Muir*, 1980

Empson, William. *Seven Types of Ambiguity* (1930), 3rd edn, 1953

Farnham, Willard. *Shakespeare's Tragic Frontier* (1950), rpt. 1963

Fergusson, Francis. ' "Macbeth" as the imitation of an action', in *English Institute Essays 1951*, ed. Alan S. Downer, 1951, pp. 31–43

Floyd-Wilson, Mary. 'English Epicures and Scottish Witches', *SQ* 57 (2006), 131–61

Freud, Sigmund. 'Some character-types met with in psychoanalytic work', in *The Standard Edition of the Complete Psychological Works*, trans. James Strachey *et al.*, 24 vols., 1953–74, XIV (1957), pp. 311–30

Gardner, Helen. 'Milton's "Satan" and the theme of damnation in Elizabethan tragedy', in F. P. Wilson (ed.), *English Studies 1948*, 1948, pp. 46–66

Greenblatt, Stephen. 'Shakespeare bewitched', in Tetsuo Kishi *et al.* (eds.), *Shakespeare and Cultural Traditions*, 1994, pp. 17–42

Honigmann, Ernst. *Shakespeare: Seven Tragedies*, 1976

Howard-Hill, T. H. (ed.). *'Macbeth': A Concordance to the Text of the First Folio*, 1971

Jorgensen, Paul A. *Our Naked Frailties: Sensational Art and Meaning in 'Macbeth'*, 1971

Kliman, Bernice W. (ed.). *Shakespeare in Performance*: *'Macbeth'*, 2nd edn, 2004

Knight, George Wilson. *The Imperial Theme*, 1931
    The Wheel of Fire, 1930

Knights, Lionel C. 'How many children had Lady Macbeth?' (1933), rpt. in Knights, *Explorations*, 1946, pp. 1–39

Leggatt, Alexander (comp.). *William Shakespeare's 'Macbeth': A Sourcebook*, 2006

Leiter, Samuel L., *et al.* (comp.). *Shakespeare Around the Globe*, 1986

Lemon, Rebecca. *Treason by Words: Literature, Law, and Rebellion in Shakespeare's England*, 2006

Mahood, M. M. *Shakespeare's Wordplay*, 1957

Maley, Willy and Andrew Murphy (eds.). *Shakespeare and Scotland*, 2004

Masefield, John. *A 'Macbeth' Production*, 1946

McDonald, Russ. *Look to the Lady: Sarah Siddons, Ellen Terry, and Judi Dench on the Shakespearean Stage*, 2005

Miola, Robert S. (ed.). *'Macbeth': Authoritative Text, Sources and Contexts, Criticism*, 2004

Morse, Ruth. 'Monsieur Macbeth: from Jarry to Ionesco', *S.Sur. 57* (2004), 112–25

Moschovakis, Nicholas (ed.). *'Macbeth': New Critical Essays*, 2008

Muir, Kenneth, and Philip Edwards (eds.). *Aspects of 'Macbeth'*, 1977

Norbrook, David. '*Macbeth* and the politics of historiography', in Kevin Sharpe and Steven N. Zwicker (eds.), *Politics of Discourse*, 1987, pp. 78–116

Nosworthy, J. M. *Shakespeare's Occasional Plays: Their Origin and Transmission*, 1965

Paul, Henry N. *The Royal Play of Macbeth*, 1950

Rosenberg, Marvin. *The Masks of 'Macbeth'*, 1978

Shakespeare, William. *Macbeth*, ed. Horace Howard Furness, rev. edn Horace Howard Furness, Jr, 1915

Sinfield, Alan (ed.). *'Macbeth': New Casebooks*, 1992

Spencer, Theodore. *Shakespeare and the Nature of Man*, 1942

Spender, Stephen. 'Time, violence, and Macbeth', in *Penguin New Writing*, ed. John Lehmann, 1941, pp. 115–26

Sprague, Arthur Colby. *Shakespeare and the Actors: The Stage Business in his Plays 1660–1905*, 1944

Tredell, Nicolas. *Shakespeare, 'Macbeth': A Reader's Guide to Essential Criticism*, 2006

Trewin, J. C. *Shakespeare on the English Stage, 1900–1964*, 1964

Wain, John (comp.). *Shakespeare: 'Macbeth': A Casebook*, 1968

Waith, Eugene M. 'Manhood and valor in two Shakespearean tragedies', *ELH* 17 (1950), 262–73

Walker, Roy. *The Time is Free: A Study of 'Macbeth'*, 1949

Walter, Harriet. *Macbeth*, 2002

Watson, Robert N. *Shakespeare and the Hazards of Ambition*, 1984

Wells, Stanley (ed.). *The Cambridge Companion to Shakespeare Studies*, 1986

Wells, Stanley, and Gary Taylor with John Jowett and William Montgomery (eds.). *William Shakespeare: A Textual Companion*, 1987

Wheeler, Thomas. *'Macbeth': An Annotated Bibliography*, 1990

Wilders, John. *'Macbeth': Shakespeare in Production*, 2004

Williams, George Walton. *'Macbeth*: King James's Play', *South Atlantic Review* 47.2 (1982), 12–21

Williams, William Proctor (ed.). *Macbeth*, The Sourcebooks Shakespeare, 2006

Willson, Robert F., Jr. 'Macbeth the player king: the banquet scene as frustrated play within the play', *Shakespeare Jahrbuch* (Weimar), 114 (1978), 107–14